Romantic Medicine and John Keats

Romantic Medicine and John Keats

HERMIONE DE ALMEIDA

New York   Oxford
OXFORD UNIVERSITY PRESS
1991

Oxford University Press

Oxford   New York   Toronto
Delhi   Bombay   Calcutta   Madras   Karachi
Petaling Jaya   Singapore   Hong Kong   Tokyo
Nairobi   Dar es Salaam   Cape Town
Melbourne   Auckland

and associated companies in
Berlin   Ibadan

Copyright © 1991 by Oxford University Press, Inc.

Published by Oxford University Press, Inc.
200 Madison Avenue, New York, New York 10016

Oxford is a registered trademark of Oxford University Press

Library of Congress Cataloging-in-Publication Data
De Almeida, Hermione, 1950–
Romantic medicine and John Keats / Hermione de Almeida.
p. cm. Includes bibliographical references. ISBN 0-19-506307-4
1. Keats, John, 1795–1821—Knowledge—Medicine.
2. Medicine in literature. 3. Romanticism—England.
4. Medicine—England—History—19th century. I. Title.
PR4838.M4D4 1991 821'.7—dc20 89-72153

9 8 7 6 5 4 3 2 1

Printed in the United States of America
on acid-free paper

For George H. Gilpin

Acknowledgments

I wish to thank the American Council of Learned Societies, the National Humanities Center, the National Endowment for the Humanities, the Woodrow Wilson International Center for Scholars, and the University of Miami Research Council for both fellowship support generously granted and continuing confidence in a long project. In particular I am grateful for the assistance I received from the director of the National Humanities Center and the Wilson Center, Charles Blitzer, and the assistant director and resident Greek scholar of the Wilson Center, Ann Sheffield; from the inter-library loan staff of the National Humanities Center, Alan Tuttle and Rebecca Vargha, of the Wilson Center, Zed David and Georgann Juneau, and of the University of Miami's Richter Library, Patricia Pardo and Rosemary Rowland; also, from Eloise Doane of the Wilson Center typing services, and Dave Liston, the director of Smithsonian Security, who worked overtime one cold and drear-nighted December in Washington to extract the manuscript from a stubborn word processor. My gratitude is also due the staff of the British Library, the Columbia University Medical Library, the Wellcome Library for the History of Medicine, the Hunterian Library of the Royal College of Surgeons, especially Ian Lyle, Susan Palmer of the Greater London Record Office, the head gardener of the Chelsea Physic Garden, and, in particular, Andrew Baster, the history of medicine librarian of Wills Library, Guy's Hospital. Harvard University Press has my thanks for permission to quote from *The Letters of John Keats*, 1814–1821, edited by Hyder E. Rollins (1958), and *The Poems of John Keats*, edited by Jack Stillinger (1978).

In his last letter to Fanny Brawne, in a bitter mood "sickened at the brute world," Keats wrote: "I wish you could infuse a little confidence in human nature into my heart." This book has occupied more than ten years of my life, and some of those years were long enough to bring echoes of Keats's dark words. Throughout that time, however, I have been blessed by a company of friends who did put "confidence in human nature into my heart" and who gave kindness and support immeasurable and without stint: this company includes Mike Abrams, Arthur and Dorothy Brown, John Clubbe, Larry Donovan, George Gilpin Sr. and Billie Gilpin, Tassie Gwilliam, Phil Herring, Gene Man, Jerry McGann, Leslie Marchand, Don Reiman, Frank Palmeri, Manny Papper, Priscilla Perry, Bonnie Robinson, Norman Sherry, Stuart and Sophie Sperry, Jack Stillinger (who read my manuscript without clenching his teeth too often and gave advice at once cheerful and astute), Frank Stringfellow, and Mihoko Suzuki. To my friends, especially to Carl and San Woodring, my sister Diana de Almeida Rutkus, and George Gilpin Jr., I echo a happier line by Keats, written to his friends: "I wish, at one view, you could see my heart towards you." Two others also belong in my catalogue of beneficence and love freely given: Hecate, our Keatsian "silken-furr'd Angora cat" who was born proximate to the time when first I conceived of this book and slept through its various stages, and our unborn daughter, another Hermione but a Texan version, who seems to have timed her arrival to coincide with the appearance in print of this book.

Coral Lake, Florida   H. de A.
April 1990

Contents

PART IV ORGANIC PERFECTION, 217

Romantic Medicine and John Keats

A *lovely tale of human life we'll read*

"Sleep and Poetry," 110

hieroglyphics old,
Which sages and keen-eyed astrologers
Then living on the earth, with labouring thought
Won from the gaze of many centuries:

Hyperion, I, 277–80

The poetry of earth is never dead

"On the Grasshopper and Cricket," 1

Introduction: Reading Life

The period of Romantic medicine has existed as a hiatus in the history of science. Unified in its intellectual concerns yet conceptually distinct, and spanning the three decades of a recognized era, Romantic medicine has been ignored at once by historians of medicine whose studies end around 1794 with the triumph of French mechanism and semiotics in the newly established clinics of the late eighteenth century and by the chroniclers of modern medicine who begin their studies with the invention of the high-resolution doublet lens microscope in 1829 that permitted Robert Brown's discovery of cell nuclei, Theodor Schwann's cell theory, and Rudolf Virchow's description of cellular pathology.[1] Also, theorists of Romantic art, secured perhaps by the common but otherwise insupportable twentieth-century assumption of the alienation of Romanticism from science, have chosen largely to exclude the issues of early-nineteenth-century medicine from their consideration. As a fertile period of transition between the birth of the clinic and the discovery of the cell, as an era of speculative insight between the imaginative reading of life signs and the visual knowledge of bacterial life, Romantic medicine engendered biology, zoology, immunology, clinical diagnoses, and evolution theory.

The anatomical chart of life and death drawn by Bichât, the surgical insights of the heirs of John Hunter, the zoonomic speculations of Erasmus Darwin, the evolutionary studies of Cuvier and Lamarck, the chemical research of Lavoisier, Davy, and Saussure, the analysis of specific poisons by Orfila, Vauquelin, and Berzelius, the homeopathy and minute dosage prescribed by Hahnemann, the fraught implications for pathology and subspecial diversity of Alexander von Humboldt's South American journeys, the experiments with induced "suspended animation" during surgery of Hickman, the stethoscope of Laënnec and microscope lenses of Brewster and Wollaston, the revelation of electromagnetic principles by Oersted and Faraday, the linkage of psychology and biology by Cabanis, the study of brain anatomy by Charles Bell, and the attempt to map the geography of the nervous system and the personality by Gall and Spurzheim—all these belong to Romantic medicine and its high concern with the issues of life. They mark the recognized change in the prevailing scientific paradigm from theoretical physics to practical biology that occurred at the turn of the century,[2] but they also express a more comprehensive participation in the Romantic movement and its fundamental aspiration to know life and read its meaning with all the radical specificity possible to human thought and discourse—and sight.

To balance the grand imaginings of life as a unified and harmonious, albeit invisible, entity by the German *Naturphilosophen* (a Romanticism for which the period is perhaps best known), the early nineteenth century fostered an extensive renewal of microscopical studies of plant and animal life, perhaps as another expression of its need to see and comprehend the minute particulars of life.[3] British Romantic artists joined concern with their scientific counterparts in England and Europe in testifying to the era's commitment to the specifics of empirical, existential truth: they eschewed the metaphors of infinity once borrowed from physics for the metaphors of finitude born of contemporary life science and medicine. Blake proposed that infinity occurs in the space between heartbeats; Coleridge found ample stock of poetic metaphors in Davy's chemical pursuits and creative truth in their conversance with "the minute form of things"; Wordsworth resolved that his verse would "deal boldly with substantial things."[4] And Keats, the youngest of these Romantic artists and most direct poetic heir to the concepts of contemporary life science, whose very lifetime (1795–1821) spans the period of Romantic medicine, declared that "axioms in philosophy are not axioms until they are proved upon our pulses." "Nothing," he said, in echo of the method he had learned in medical school, "ever becomes real till it is experienced—Even a Proverb is no proverb to you till your Life has illustrated it."[5]

Romantic Medicine and John Keats addresses the fundamental intellectual issues of Romantic medicine—the physician's task of life, the meaning of life, the constituents of health and prescriptions of disease, and the evolution of matter and mind—as these find focus and exemplary conceptual expression in the poetry and aesthetic theory of Keats, the British Romantic poet who was a licensed apothecary and general practitioner of medicine. The book traces the geneses of these issues and marks the occasion and reason for their immediate relevance to the Romantic period as a whole. It identifies these issues as the primary philosophic counters of the artistic and scientific debates of the revolutionary period and discusses them and their ideologies in the context of the era's belief in the art of healing as the foremost humanistic discipline and its conceit of the artist—or poet—as a physician of the soul. Finally, through the detailed invocation of these four subjects in close and sustained readings of major poems by Keats, my study illustrates their essential place in the comprehension of his particular genius and the aesthetic verities of his generation.

Keats's access to the intellectual ferment of the London medical circle, both during his apprenticeship to the surgeon Thomas Hammond and at Guy's Hospital, from 1810 through 1816, provides a unique opportunity to scrutinize from within the philosophic issues of a complex intellectual period. The conceptual evolution of Keats's poetry, itself born of these broadly based and diffused intellectual concerns of the era, provides a means to focus and ground the discussion and to reanimate those living links between scientific and aesthetic theory that were once assumed by all Romantic thinkers. The poet's clinical residency at Guy's Hospital during 1815–1816 occurred at the height of the interdisciplinary debate on life sparked by the doctors Abernethy and Lawrence and coincided with the publication of the first volume of Lamarck's *Histoire naturelle des animaux sans vertèbres* and the ensuing controversy over the notion of radical evolution. Working backward through the years of Keats's medical education, we find other events contributing to the intellectual tumult of London scientific circles: inventions such as Davy's miner's lamp, Laënnec's stethoscope, and Brewster's kaleidoscope (all in 1815); publications such as Orfila's full-scale and systematic study of poisons (1814), Cuvier's study of quadruped fossils (1812), Charles Bell's novel perspective of the anatomy of the brain (1811), Gall and Spurzheim's diagram of the nervous system and Hahnemann's manifesto of homeopathic therapy (1810); and practical research and surgical insight on regeneration and tissue decay of the military physicians after the Battle of Waterloo in 1815.

Keats's awareness of these advances was enhanced by the enactment in Parliament of the Apothecaries Act, also in 1815, which required at least six months of course work and clinical training at a major teaching hospital for all apothecaries or general practitioners of medicine. Contrary to the assertions of Foucault and Ackerknecht, the advent of the clinic as teaching and research institution took place not in France in 1794, with the reorganization of the Paris medical school, but in England in the 1770s, with the establishment of the major London hospitals as the primary medical institutions for teaching and experimental study. Othmar Keel has documented conclusively that clinical teaching existed in British hospitals long before the emergence of academic schools in Europe and that clinical instruction in the London hospitals—especially at Guy's, St. Thomas's, St. Bartholomew's, and the London Hospital—attained a rare level of achievement in the early nineteenth century that far surpassed the European schools and, in fact, served as an example to the French clinics.[6]

By the time that Keats enrolled, Guy's Hospital, with 438 beds, was reputed to be the best of the five hospitals that had been founded in London in the eighteenth century. Its eight wards were all used for instruction, including a lunatic ward and two designated "clinical" wards for incurables (from terminal cancer patients to consumptives and monstrous births) where experimental medicine and semiotic prognosis were practiced. Keats had daily instruction in the wards during his year of residency, and as a surgeon's dresser during his second semester he would have served actively in these wards, occasionally as the only practitioner on duty.[7] Instructing physicians and surgeons at Guy's Hospital like Astley Cooper, Alexander Marcet, Henry Cline, Jr., and James Curry (all of whom were Keats's teachers) not only collaborated but also shared information with the best medical researchers in Britain and Europe.

Indeed, their interpersonal connections mirrored their close association in laboratory and ward: in the Guy's circle, Cooper, the Clines, Joseph Henry Green, and the Hammond brothers were all related by marriage; beyond Guy's, Cooper was married to the sister of Everard Home, John Hunter's nephew; Cooper and Cline, Sr., were connected through John Thelwall to the radicals in the Paris medical circle; and Cooper and Marcet, close friends, worked together with the French toxicologist, M.J.B. Orfila. Moreover, the burgeoning number of scientific journals and societies, along with the annual lectures instituted at places like the Royal College of Surgeons and the Hunterian Museum, ensured the rapid exchange of new ideas between the medical circles of London and Edinburgh and those of the major research cities of Europe.

Romantic Medicine and John Keats uses the poetic and philosophic constructs of Keats to focus discussion of the primary concepts of Romantic medicine, even as it uses the research and learning of the medical circle at Guy's during Keats's apprenticeship to organize a vast and interrelated field of knowledge with inextricable ties to the social and political movements of the age. My inquiry has been helped, and rendered more credible, by access to the 1840 Charity Commission Report on British hospitals in the Greater London Record Office; to the archives of the Society of Apothecaries (including the historical planting maps of its Chelsea Physic Garden, where Keats studied medical botany with William Salisbury, its head botanist); and to the shelflists and catalogues from 1807 to 1823 of the Physical Society Library of Guy's Hospital. The first source made possible a comparative evaluation of the advanced level and currency of Keats's medical training. The second source verified that a knowledge of contemporary theories of health and both specific poisons and the nonspecificity of the *pharmakon* lay behind Keats's euphonic and supposedly romantic evocation of herbs, flowers, and "sweet health" in his poetry. The last and most important set of sources (a fascinating admixture of manuscript and printed lists) established the range and comprehension of the scientific texts and philosophic treatises that were available to the teaching physicians of Guy's Hospital during Keats's residence there; these included not just the primary medical research of contemporary Britain and Europe but current philosophy and psychology from Herder and Stewart to Spurzheim and Mme. de Staël.

Keats happened to attend Guy's Hospital in the decade when its medical library was being formally established and organized as a research institution, with a charter from the Physical Society to acquire all books of historical and contemporary research significant to the practice of medicine.[8] We cannot know if the poet read any of the books in the Physical Society Library; indeed, given the schedule of students and dressers at Guy's during this period, it would be most unlikely that he did. However, to assume that his teachers, who were members of the Physical Society and who paid for the library books with personal contributions and lending fines,[9] were equally ignorant of the books they ordered and purchased would stretch credulity. My book reads Romantic medicine to establish that Keats's teachers were knowledgeable of the most advanced scientific and philosophical lines of inquiry; it reads Keats's poetry and philosophy to show what he learned from them. It proposes, further, that he used his education to exemplary artistic effect, the perceptual advances of Romantic medicine reflected in his poetry rendering his achievement fully representative of the integration of medicine and literature in his time.

Contemporary treatises on the ethics and duties of the medical profession— and we can credit Romantic medicine for being the first era in the history of European medicine to foster the subject of medical ethics—stress personal responsibility and comprehensive knowledge. One proposes that "no profession requires so comprehensive a mind as medicine"; another declares that there are "few departments of either physical or moral science with which [medicine] is not, in a greater or lesser degree, connected";[10] and all, from Gregory and Percival to Brodie, insist on the practitioner's need to know everything from the physical sciences and related disciplines that might assist in the healing of life and on the physician's responsibility to keep current with research in these fields. Keats's medical education was substantial and wide-ranging of necessity; it extended well beyond the specifics of practical, professional training, was fully conversant with the major intellectual issues of its time, and was more contemporary with early-nineteenth-century philosophic and political contexts and forms of knowing than a traditional university education of the time. All this bears vital implications for his poetry and his place among his generation of Romantic poets.

This view has not been universally accepted. Alfred North Whitehead in 1925 called Keats's poetry an example of literature untouched by science. Arthur Henry Hallam in 1831 characterized Keats as a poet of sensation rather than reflection, giving voice to the Victorian misconception of Keats as a poet of suspect sensuousness whose occasional thought was largely derived from Wordsworth and whose verse reconstructing the rainbow recently demolished by Newton was to be taken with delicious caution lest its excesses endanger health. This view is expressed at its prurient best in an anonymous review of 1850:

> In the poetry of Keats, as all must feel, there is an excess of greenth and vegetable imagery; in reading his descriptions, we seem either to breath the air of a hothouse, heavy with the moist odours of great-leaved exotics, or to live full-stretched out at noon in some shady nook in a wood, rank underneath with the pipy hemlock, and kindred plants of strange overgrowth. In Wordsworth, as we have seen, there is no such unhealthy lusciousness. . . .[11]

Consumptive poets who know too much of medicine for the good of their underdeveloped brains and overdeveloped senses, this view held, can engender unhealthy verse on subjects at once addictive and claustrophobic; their pleasures are of the senses, morbidly aroused, self-generated, and without redeeming thought. Such a Victorian vision of Keats as a very sickly "pet lamb" given to effusions of "natural" poetry prevailed through the early twentieth century. Two full generations of Keats scholars (at least, from Thorpe to Bate to Sperry, from Murry to Ricks to Barnard) and critics since have done much to neutralize this view of the poet among Romanticists; Ward, Gittings, and Goellnicht in particular, have marked the importance of Keats's medical training to his early development,[12] and Ryan and Stillinger have reminded us of the skeptical tradition underlying the poet's assumptions. Nevertheless, a certain view of Keats persists: he was, if not ill-educated but for a few trade skills in bloodletting and tooth pulling, then self-educated on a few books lent to him by his friends. It subsumes the very stance of those contemporary critics who would see him as a lower-class poet without experience writing a poetry without a context, who would read his poems as one long exercise in self-engendering aesthetic creation; it underlies the related ideology of those readers who view the major poetry as a verbal continuum that begins with a poetics of creation but that thereafter functions independent of thought.[13]

The absence of abstruse speculation and esoteric symbolism in Keats's poetry does not imply the lack of a sophisticated intellectual life any more than the scant records of his library prove the limited "self-education" of a Cockney poet. Keats's formal education within the London medical circle of the early nineteenth century was at least as good as the brief university educations of Coleridge, Byron, and Shelley, and it exceeded theirs in its philosophical and practical intensity. Indeed, when one realizes that Wordsworth was trained for three years at a purportedly "scientific" Cambridge University in late-seventeenth-century- and early-eighteenth-century thought and learning,[14] Keats's medical education suddenly takes on a unique contemporaneity among British artists: it was fully of its time in the early nineteenth century in that it embodied the forms and subjects of the new way of knowing and studying life even as it encompassed the philosophies of the prior century through their influence on the new disciplines. It has been customary to connect the philosophic side of Keats to Wordsworth and the concepts of British empiricism and German idealism usually associated with the first generation of English Lake poets.[15] In fact, Keats belongs first with a late generation of Romantic poets, with Byron and Shelley, who wrote *after* the European theories of mechanistic life (a far more voracious mode of perceiving existence than the local empiricism it replaced) had invaded, enrolled, and then taken possession of most of the new as well as the traditional disciplines of human discourse. Keats was indeed a poet of sensation in that he eschewed, finally, what could not be proved upon the pulses: the disciplines of medicine had trained him to avoid speculation and theoretical diagnosis; as a medical insider and one of a generation of late Romantic artists who bore the limiting conceptual brunt of the theories of the French physiologists, he could not fail to be truthful to his training, to what he knew, and to the limits of what he could know. More than the other Romantics of his skeptical late generation, because of the very comprehensiveness of his medical education, Keats wrote truly under the shadow of Waterloo and beneath the dark conscripts of European mechanism. His poetic achievement looms very large in the new history of his scientific age precisely because he adhered to the genuine inspiration of that small portion of truth that could be gleaned from a disciplined and verifiable reading of life.

I have divided this work into four parts that serially address the issues of the physician's task, the meaning of life, disease and its prescriptives, and the evolution of physical and perceptual life. Each subdivided part expands, first, to the Romantic medical milieu and its intellectual precedents; isolates for discussion certain philosophic concepts or ideologies pertinent to the subject of the part; contracts to the experiential knowledge of Keats and its representative use in discrete poems; focuses the subject at hand with a sustained reading of a particularly illustrative major poem or passage; and finally advances out again to consider the consequent exemplary conceptual expansion of scientific ideas under the imaginative impetus of art. "Apollo's Poet," the first part, seeks to describe the Romantic physician and identify his primary concern. It invokes the tradition of Apollo as god of poetry, pestilence, and medicine as it finds contemporary interpretation (by way of *Naturphilosophie* and Wordsworth) in Keats's notion of the "fore-seeing" god embodied in the Romantic poet as "sage, . . . humanist, physician to all men."[16] Subjects discussed include medical ethics and the new humanitarianism of the age; the era's acute consciousness of the physician's prescriptive power (as fueled by its doctrines of minute dosage and *similia similibus curantur*); interdisciplinary concepts of medical sight from Landré-Beauvais on the clinical reading of signs beyond the visible surface of symptoms to Friedrich Schlegel's notion of the physician's "penetrating glance" and Hazlitt's concept of the artist who is born with an anatomist's eye; the capsulated perspective of the artist's pocket camera lucida (an 1811 by-product of microscope lens research); the connection between poetic prophecy and semiotic prognosis; and the real and imaginary nature of insight in poet and in physician, in their dual, related comprehension of suffering. Part I comments on the ethical and visionary issues underlying the portrayal of false physicians in *Endymion* and other poems before proceeding to a sustained reading of the verse-epistle to Reynolds and Keats's sense there of having seen "Too far . . . [and] too distinct into the core / Of an eternal fierce destruction" of all natural forms ("Dear Reynolds," 94–98). Part I concludes with the late Romantic poet's resolve in *The Fall of Hyperion* to be a true physician and "seek no wonder but the human face" (I, 163) and attempts to determine what the mortal poet of that dream-vision sees of "immortal life" as it is graven upon the suffering goddess Moneta's blanched face and hollow skull; this last discussion integrates those medical, poetic, and philosophic interests that are involved in the Romantic envisioning of pain.

Because life is the primary concern of the physician, it is the overriding philosophic crux and subject of study for the Romantic physician. The theories of life prevalent in scientific and literary circles during the early nineteenth century and their uses by Keats are the chief subjects of Part II. Dominant concepts of life from German *Naturphilosophie* (Schiller's notion of life as nerve spirit, Alexander von Humboldt's genius of opposition that resists putrefaction), British medicine (John Brown's principle of excitability or life as a forced state, Erasmus Darwin's notion of "sensorial power," the widespread tendency to equate sensitivity with living power), and French physiology (Bichât's concept of life as the sum of all functions) are presented first. I then discuss those ideas from contemporary chemistry as taught at Guy's Hospital on the multiplicity of life and its elemental origins and composition (Marcet's research on the chemistry of the Dead Sea, medical experiments with electricity in the wards of St. Thomas's and Guy's, current research on natural irridescence or "living light" and putrescent phosphorescence), and Keats's informed use of these ideas in poems like *Endymion* and *Lamia*. I focus on Hunter's real concept of the life of blood—and Keats's compounding invocation of it in his fraught image of living blood in poems like *Isabella; or, The Pot of Basil* and *The Fall of Hyperion*. After reviewing the Abernethy–Lawrence controversy on the vitalistic and mechanistic consequences of John Hunter's "vital principle," I summarize the ideas underlying Coleridge's concept of polarity as the energy or sensitive principle of life. The concluding section of Part II is a multileveled close reading of Keats's "Ode on a Grecian Urn" as that poem encapsulates the era's concerns with the principle of life and uses its very subject, the perfection of art, to delineate and defiantly choose the process of life. Keats's "Urn," I propose, finds rightful place within the intellectual tumult of the ongoing debate on vitality because it is a profound meditation not on art, as is usually supposed, but on life.

Part III addresses the interlocking concepts of health and disease in the Romantic period and that era's necessary assumption of every ambiguity borne by the concept of the *pharmakon*. The treatment of disease as a presupposition of health was peculiar to Romantic medicine; it generated such theories as Schelling's proposal that disease was disingenuous life or the precondition of organic life, Schiller's description of health as the tendency to permanency, Bichât's notion of disease as the revolt of otherwise silent or healthy organs, and John Brown's concept of sthenic and asthenic disease. All these theories find place in Keats's poetic treatment of disease and the varieties of febrile energy. Subsequent sections of Part III treat Romantic prescriptives and the ambiguity of the *pharmakon* for Keats and his generation of physicians.

The metaphorical and pharmacological traditions of the *pharmakon* as a healing drug, corrosive poison, beguiling perfume, and tincturing essence find real and immediate verity in Romantic toxicology; speculations on the connection of the potencies of plants or minerals with the power of animal venom and the influence of morbid poisons also find conceptual place in Keats's evocation of specific *pharmaka* in his poetry. "Even bees, the little almsmen of spring-bowers, / Know there is richest juice in poison-flowers," Keats says in *Isabella*, and the variety of potions real and metaphysical in his poetry—from the power of "a domineering potion" to induce transcendent vision to the notion of sudden perceptual knowledge as "a fierce potion, drunk by chance" (*The Fall of Hyp.*, I, 54, *Isabella*, 103–4, 267)—find focus in a close reading of the "Ode on Melancholy" and the philosophic consequence of its technical knowledge of specific poisons. Part III concludes with an evocation of the bewitching potions in three narrative poems, "La Belle Dame sans Merci," *The Eve of St. Agnes*, and *Lamia*, as these presume psychosomatic influence and express the fully Romantic construct of the *pharmakon* as love-philtre. Lamia's "bewildering cup," Porphyro's magical and tinctured feast in *The Eve*, and la belle dame's fragrant "honey wild, and manna dew" become paradigms of the philtre/pharmakon as a consumptive and consuming formula—a Romantic potion for the induction of dreams that are both healthy and diseased.

Part IV, "Organic Perfection," enunciates the centrality of the idea of evolution, as conceived during an age of revolution, to the specific content and overall aesthetic of Keats's poetic achievement. Notions from Romantic evolutionary theory form the subject of Keats's two epic poems, *Endymion* and the Hyperion fragments; these ideas serve as substratum for the poet's statements on perceptual evolution during his formative year (1817–1818) and inform his description of Apollo's genius as emblematic of Romantic artistic creation and its distinct perceptual advance over the understanding of earlier centuries. Part IV focuses on the complex theories that are born of the new and verifiable certainty of the extinction of species as these theories underlie Keats's concepts of "living death" and "fresh perfection" in *Hyperion* and inform his vision of simultaneous supersession and deathless pain in *The Fall of Hyperion*. Subjects that I address include the change in evolutionary constructs from preformation to transformation, from the repetitious continuation of primordially complete forms to the perfection in time of both matter and mind; the fully Romantic aspect of the Lamarckian notion of radical and periodic upheaval within a complacency of nature; the new notion of perfection as temporary, renewable, and multiple; the place of Blumenbach's *Bildungstrieb* in changing the focus of evolutionary thought from pigmentation to structure and conceptual form; Astley Cooper's teaching of the creatural instinct for development and the medical consequence of comparative anatomy; Erasmus Darwin's proposal of evolution as self-directed and self-originating in primeval waters; Keats's reading of Buffon and contemporary evolutionists while he composed his well-known statements on the nature and distinctions between Miltonic, Wordsworthian, and late Romantic (Keatsian) genius; the parallels between Lamarck's "appetence" (the impulse to evolve) and Romantic "aspiration"; the Janus-faced character and retrospective meaning presumed by the theories on the escalation of being and perception advanced by Schelling, Oken, and Herder; the research on fetal abnormalities by John Haighton (a

Guy's physician); and Joseph Henry Green's public address on how such malformations could reveal in retrospection the secret, vital dynamics of matter
and mind. "So on our heels a fresh perfection treads, / A power more strong in
Beauty," the suddenly mortal Titan, Oceanus, says in *Hyperion* (II, 212–13) of
what will be the poet's retrospective and healing vision of "immortal sickness"
in the late fragment, *The Fall of Hyperion*.

Part IV concludes with a sustained discussion of the predicaments of the
newly extinct Titans and their replacements, the breed of Apollo who bear
"signs of purer life," as these are portrayed in the Hyperion fragments. Aesthetic creation and the perceptual motions of poetic endeavor may be the
subjects of these fragments as Keats came, finally, to know and articulate
them, but the language and philosophic impetus of these subjects is contemporary evolutionary thought as it involved the Romantic physician. Saturn's
discovery that brute power is not evolutionary might but a sign of malformation and potential extinction that masks a limited perceptual power; Apollo's
new beauty, which reveals itself as intense sensitivity or sympathy or the
poetic ability to perceive beauty; the connection of physical beauty with
evolutionary progress by W. C. Wells of St. Thomas's Hospital in 1813; and the
connection of the perception of beauty with an advanced conceptual power
to heal the psyche by Keats (Apollo's "negative capability" in *The Fall of
Hyperion*)—these issues introduce the poet's final resolution on life in his last
great poem, "To Autumn." My book concludes that Keats's somber and most
perfect ode, in illustration of his life's work as a whole, reads life through the
poetry of an earth never dead.

In 1951 Lionel Trilling marked Keats's "massive" and "historical importance" to European thought when he declared that the poet "stands as the
last image of health at the very moment when the sickness of Europe began
to be apparent. . . ." The poet's concern with health is something consistent
with the general outlook of Romantic art: Trilling reminded us of the belief
Keats shared with Wordsworth and Coleridge that "poetry depended upon a
condition of positive health in the poet" and proposed further that "the
spiritual and moral health of which [Keats] seems the image" has been
unattainable since and, as such, is exemplary of its age's accomplishments.[17]
Historians of ideas and literary critics of our time continue, nevertheless, to
assume a Romantic ignorance of the concerns of health and an innocence in
English Romanticism—despite the facts of Keats's training—of the components of disease.[18] Spiritual and moral health in Romantic artists hardly
precludes full knowledge of the imaginative implications of physical and
psychic disease, or full awareness of the artist's duty in the face of these. The
image of health that Keats presents to us through his poems and letters
cannot be seen apart from the sickness, present and future, that he apprehends as a Romantic physician of the soul. More than his peers, because of
his unique historical circumstance, because also of his perceptual ability to
integrate medical and literary concerns, Keats points the way through sick-

ness, sorrow, and pain—through the medium of a poetry of life—to spiritual wholeness and imaginative health.

This book uses the medical milieu, philosophic stance, and poetic achievement of Keats to illustrate the unity of inquiry during the revolutionary period of the two arts traditionally linked in the healing of life: poetry and medicine. It is, as such, a broad description of Romantic medicine as an integrant of the larger artistic and political movement called Romanticism. Romantic medicine was indeed a specific period in the history of science, but it is best understood as a distinct and definably Romantic way of interpreting and thinking about the central issues of medicine. Keats's unique and profound poetic evocation of these concerns is particularly revealing of the psychologies of his age and their unusual scientific and philosophic ways of perceiving. The "and" in my title is an important word, and I request patience alike from the Keatsian who would read more of the poetry and know less of its intellectual framework and from the historian of science who would know *what* precisely Keats and his generation of poets knew of medical truths and read nothing of the conceptual advances of these medical and literary concerns expressed as poetry. Readers of this book must suspend their knowledge of the facts of twentieth-century science, and approach its subjects with the same spirit of wonder as did those revolutionary scientists and poets of the Romantic period; only then will they know both the prescience of these thinkers in the face of so little scientific fact and the imaginative potency of their misconceptions. The history of science has always favored the discovery of scientific truth and neglected the conceptual leaps inherent in scientific error; Romantic medicine has, therefore, suffered for its transcendental blunders and for its enlightened misconceptions. In a critical tradition of Romantic literary scholarship that has theorized on aesthetics only and the self-generating impetus of "readings," Keats has suffered for the facts of his medical training and for his purported lack of speculation.

Romantic medicine and the poetic practice of Keats, facts and fancies together, illuminate one another. Our knowledge of Keats's scientific currency and philosophic genealogy changes the ways in which we read his poems, conceive of his place among Romantic artists, and understand these artists' location within the intellectual ferment of their age. Our comprehension of the perceptual advances possible through art (and Keats's art in particular) on the familiar issues of medical discourse changes our ways of comprehending both the disciplines of Romantic science and the ideologies of their forms of Romanticism. *Romantic Medicine and John Keats* addresses the parallel subjects of early-nineteenth-century medicine and literature, identifies those areas where the two fields overlap in concept and construct, and charts the conceptual passage of these subjects between the disciplines. Its real and ultimate interest may well lie in that living region of "hieroglyphics old" where the boundaries between these two ways of knowing are difficult to discern and preemptive of all attempts to ascribe error or truth.

PART I

APOLLO'S POET

I am ambitious of doing the world some good....

Keats, *Letters*, 1:387

In February 1815, while still apprenticed at Hammond's surgery and seven months before beginning formal medical training at Guy's Hospital, Keats wrote an "Ode to Apollo," that was to be the first of numerous invocations declaring fealty to the "God of Bards." The "God of the meridian," Keats knew from the start, was also the "God of the golden bow, / And of the golden lyre, / And of the golden hair, / And of the golden fire" (1–4), and his powers included both the ability to impregnate "the free winds" with "music's kiss" "And with a sympathetic touch" unbind "Eolian magic from their lucid wombs," and the ability to afflict with "misty pestilence" and thereafter purify with therapeutic fire (End., I, 784–86; Fall of Hyp., I, 205). The legendary energy of Apollo has always extended broad and tutelary sway over the parallel domains of poetry and medicine, music and disease, prophecy and prognosis; any declared and lifelong commitment like that of Keats to the myth would therefore have to encompass the manifold associations of Apollo's power.

Lemprière's *Classical Dictionary*, Tooke's *Pantheon*, and Spence's *Polymetis* were Keats's primary sources for mythological lore concerning Apollo and the related deities of poetry and healing.[1] Lemprière describes Apollo as "the god of all the fine arts, of medicine, music, poetry, and eloquence, of all which he was deemed the inventor," and he notes further that Apollo "received from Jupiter the power of knowing futurity." Tooke, also, declares that Apollo "advanced to the highest degree of honor and worship" through the parallel "invention of physic, music, poetry, and rhetoric," and that the god presided over the nine Muses and "taught the arts of foretelling events." Spence, meanwhile, describes the symbolic implications of the laurel tree, the bow and arrow, and the lyre in artistic representation of Apollo and discusses the portent of these symbols for the "fine arts" that Apollo is reported to have invented, taught, and patronized.[2] Through the figure of Apollo, Western mythology has connected poetry and the making of music with the creation of medicine and that power of life and death inherent in the practice of physic; in Apollo's legendary foresight amid his arts it has allied, furthermore, the physician's tasks of diagnosis and prognostication with the basic powers of divination and prophecy. We know from Charles Cowden Clarke that Keats virtually memorized Lemprière while still a schoolboy in Enfield and can presume that knowledge of the mythic connections of medicine and poetry came to Keats early. Certainly, it preceded his conscious decision to become, first, a physician, and then, a poet.

The Hippocratic oath familiar to all generations of physicians including those of the Romantic period swears fealty to duties in the restoration of life "by Apollo the physician, and Asclepius, and Hygeia, and Panacea, and all of the gods and goddesses" connected with the discipline of health. Asclepius, as Keats would have learned from his mythologies, was the son of Apollo by Coronis, the brother of Artemis or Diana, and the father of Hygeia and Panacea; as the most commonly invoked deity of healing of the ancient world, Asclepius was known to have studied herbal knowledge and the art of medicine from the centaur Chiron, Prometheus's teacher; the god's usual attributes in representation were a laurel wreath signifying the potency of his physic, a knotted staff signifying the complexity of his discipline, and a serpent coiled about his staff and wrist, which signified herbal wisdom and foresight; Asclepius's specific reputation, derived from the legend of Glaucus's resuscitation, focused not simply in the ability to restore health but in a power to resurrect from the dead.[3] In Greek and Latin mythology, moreover, Asclepius or Aesculapius stands at the vortex of a tradition of true or sacred medicine whose life-giving power is derived directly from Apollo and whose followers as *paeonii* (physicians) belong to the race of Paeon;[4] this tradition of altruistic healing precedes and is quite distinct from a later but otherwise parallel tradition of false or profane medicine, a self-interested and often deadly magic practiced by chthonian deities like Circe, Pluto, and Hermes. Many of the names and emblems from this medical mythology recur, as we know, in Keats's poetry from *Endymion* to *Lamia*. The connection between poetry and medicine in Keats's mind, far from being distant and incidental to the poetic homage to Apollo, was thoroughgoing, obvious, traditional, and ever present in his consciousness.

Although students of Keats have noticed the importance of Apollo in the poet's self-fashioning, only a few scholars among them have marked Apollo's "dual nature" as the god of medicine and poetry and its place behind Keats's individual sense of the poet as healer and declared resolve to be a physician of the soul of suffering humanity.[5] But Apollo's powers are multiple, not dual, and none of Keats's critics has noticed that the poet's presiding deity is also and simultaneously the author of pestilence, the god of disease, and, as the teacher of prophecy and foresight, the patron of a special kind of perception or interpretive sight that is common to the physician and the poet as conceived by the early nineteenth century. It is through these less familiar natures of Apollo that we must comprehend the traditional ties between Keats's chosen disciplines, the inextricability of these associations in the poet's understanding, and their consequence for his evolving sense of his duties and concerns as a Romantic physician.

In Lemprière, Apollo is described as "surrounded with beams of light" when active as the patron of healing and future sight, and when he is "the deity who . . . inflicted plagues . . . in that moment he appear[s] surrounded with clouds"; in support of the latter representation, we are given the stories of Apollo inflicting the Trojan subjects of Laomedon with pestilence and striking the Greek soldiers of Agamemnon with plague-arrows. Tooke says Apollo "is called *Paeon*, either from allaying sorrows, or from his exact skill in hunting" and striking down with arrows, darts, or rays; thus, spectators at the god's combat with the Python encouraged him with the cry "Strike him, Paeon, with thy darts," even as the diseased invoked Apollo with a cry for aid, "Heal us, Paeon." Spence, describing the plague-arrows or fiery darts employed by the Apollo-Phoebus of the ancient artist, proposes the Apollonian afflictions to be actual and imaginary:

> The wounds, the arrows, and the deities themselves, were sometimes supposed to be all visible; and sometimes, to be invisible. But even in the latter case, the effect was plain: the dead body lay before them; and their credulity helped out all the rest. The artist therefore . . . did very well in generally omitting the wounds too; which they [Apollo and Diana] were supposed to make sometimes in the vitals, without leaving any mark on the outside of the body; as it often happens in the strokes given by lightning.[6]

Apollo's power of pestilence is invariably represented as a purging or cauterizing influence,[7] a swift penetration beneath the skin and entrance into the body, an intent to possess or know first and then force out and dispel from within.

At the center of the god of healing's physic resides an intimate knowledge and power of affliction, and his power to treat any disease presumes an internal comprehension or illumination of that disease. The two characteristics common to all representations of Apollo, according to Spence, are an intense physical perfection that makes him the standard of beauty and a "certain brightness beaming from his eyes"; Tooke connects the characteristic "penetrating gaze" of Apollo with the healing attributes of the sun in "darting" its rays to dispel disease and cauterize wounds so that "by its light it dispels darkness and makes manifest" hidden disease and concealed truth.[8] The Apollonian gaze of futurity and divination conflates thus into the physician's vision into the darkness of disease and, beyond that, of the future course of invisible pestilence. Those who would swear allegiance to Apollo must read the signs of the disease they would treat from within with an illumination or interpretive vision that combines diagnosis with prognosis, and prior knowledge of present disease with impending prophecy of the end of future disease. All this bears distinct relevance to the Romantic physician schooled by the clinical semiotics of the late eighteenth century to read the invisible signs of specific disease lurking beneath the visible symptoms of general ill health. It is more germane yet to the Romantic poet who would know the truth of life by reading the faces of human suffering.

The story of Apollo's lyre, the symbol of his sway over the domains of music and poetry, compounds yet further the art of his physic. When Aesculapius was killed by Jupiter for having used his physic to revive the dead, Apollo, according to Tooke, took revenge for the death of his son by killing the Cyclopes with his plague-arrows; banished to earth because of this, Apollo played shepherd to Admetus's cattle for many years, "where, tired with pleasure, to pass away his time, it is said, that he first invented and formed a harp."[9] This seven-stringed instrument formed of a tortoise's shell was the means wherewith Apollo made music to soothe the creatures in his care and ease the anxieties of banishment in his own diseased soul. Hermes, who witnessed Apollo's dependency upon harmony and who had long coveted the wand that Apollo used to drive the animals, stole the lyre and so engineered an exchange that forced Apollo to give up the caduceus—and thereby a measure of his creative power—in return for the lyre and its music. Although later tradition has credited Hermes-Mercury with the invention of the lyre (in a moment of boredom, from the shell of a creature he had just eaten alive), it is certain that there was no fair exchange between Apollo and Hermes, and that the occasion of Hermes's receipt of the caduceus represented a dilution of the god's power to heal and a perversion of the god's curative knowledge of pestilence. At the center of the humanitarian tradition of medicine was established, thus, a tradition of false medicine, of magic or sorcery, represented by the likes of Hermes-Mercury and Circe. Where Asclepius bore a knotted staff with a single wise serpent coiled about it in symbol of the wisdom and altruism of his healing art, Hermes wielded a caduceus with wings and mirrored double snakes as symbol of the doubling and self-interested trickery of his fantastic art.[10]

A concern about the function of medicine and the duties of the physician in his practice was thus inherent in the very origins of the idea of medicine. The creation of music and poetry, as aspects of the same power of Apollo, also carried the same concern about the function of those arts and the aspirations of their creators. In all of his poetry, and especially when he used the myths of Hermes and Circe in tandem with recurring homage to the god of poetry and medicine, Keats revealed full knowledge of the complexities in the tradition underlying his mission as physician and poet. It is, as he said in "God of the meridian," "an awful mission, / A terrible division, / And leaves a gulf austere / To be fill'd with worldly fear" both of one's task and of the duties of one's task (5–8). Always, as the poet grieved to his brother, George, there was the danger that the vocation might prove false and the vision evanescent:

> That I should never hear Apollo's song,
> Though feathery clouds were floating all along
> The purple west, and, two bright streaks between,
> The golden lyre itself were dimly seen.
>   ("To My Brother George," 9–12)

The poet's re-creation of Apollo's song once heard and his physician's vision of life and of the lyre that was to soothe the suffering read therein might be wrong. Worse, it might not occur at all. Apollo was a hard taskmaster, and Keats knew this all too well. "Apollo's Poet," the first part of *Romantic Medicine and John Keats*, will therefore address the qualifications, duties, ethics, concerns, and vision of him who would show fealty to Apollo in a Romantic age.

Chapter 1

The London Medical Circle

Contrary to the Victorian fantasy of Keats as a sensitive juvenile artist forcibly apprenticed to a craft of medicine, the poet was not only a willing and able student of Romantic medicine but a committed and enduring one. His decision to study medicine, made in 1810 in the months following his mother's death and within the context of his recent experience nursing her through the last stages of consumption, formalized what had already become a compelling concern for the suffering and distress of those around him. The choice of medicine, and it was indeed a choice, expressed the young Keats's conscious resolve to eschew the kind of mercantile occupation logical for one in his situation (and taken by his two brothers when they apprenticed at Richard Abbey's countinghouse in London) and to commit, instead, to a profession that was not merely practical but intellectually creative, socially responsible, and altruistic. Charles Cowden Clarke, a boyhood friend of Keats's, described the "arrangement" of Keats's apprenticeship to Thomas Hammond, the Edmonton surgeon and apothecary who had treated the poet's mother, as one that "evidently gave him satisfaction," that the medical duties of it were "by no means . . . onerous," and that the entire five-year period of the apprenticeship was, as even the poet agreed in retrospect, "the most placid period of his painful life."[1]

Keats's commitment to the humanity of medicine endured through the years when he was active as a poet; he kept his textbooks, remained current in his medical reading, and never quite gave up the idea of practicing medicine in tandem with or as an alternative to writing poetry. In March 1819, well after the mixed receptions of his first book of poems and *Endymion* and just after his engagement to Fanny Brawne and successful composition of *The Eve of St. Agnes*, we find the poet considering whether he should study for a degree from the Edinburgh College of Physicians:

> I have been at different times turning it in my head whether I should go to Edin-
> burgh & study for a physician; I am afraid I should not take kindly to it, I am sure I

could not take fees—and yet I should like to do so; it is not worse than writing poems, & hanging them up to be flyblown on the Reviewshambles—[2]

The thought of studying medicine in Edinburgh and then practicing as a full-fledged physician and surgeon appealed to Keats, and he saw no difference in the commitment—and vulnerability of the psyche—necessitated by the practices of poetry and medicine. Late May of 1819 shows the poet speculating again on the two professions and whether he should become a ship's surgeon and travel to South America and India or continue in his lonely quest for recognition as a poet:

> I have the choice as it were of two Poisons (yet I ought not to call this a Poison) the one is voyaging to and from India for a few years; the other is leading a feverous life alone with Poetry—This latter will suit me best—for I cannot resolve to give up my Studies. . . .[3]

Anxiety over the potential for error in performing surgery, along with a profound repugnance to the prospect of charging fees to alleviate human pain, made Keats question his aptitude for the profession of medicine to the same degree that he doubted, recurringly, his fitness for the isolated life of a poet. Certainly, it was not just monetary need and the hostility of reviewers but a much larger awareness of the ramifications of the tasks involved that led Keats to categorize medicine and poetry as equal poisons and equally appealing professions; his ambivalence and his commitment to the two disciplines that he had chosen thus continued through his lifetime. As late as June 1820, at the end of his *annus mirabilis* in poetry and just before the publication of *Lamia, Isabella, The Eve of St. Agnes, and Other Poems*, we find the poet firmly resolved toward medicine in the future: "This shall be my last trial; not succeeding, I shall try what I can do in the Apothecary line."[4]

What appealed to Keats in the discipline of medicine, always and finally, were both the tangible satisfaction of healing the sick and the intellectual promise—inherent in its practice and common to the writing of poetry—for strengthening the mind and advancing its perceptual sympathy for the invisible connections between the forms of life. When a friend advised Keats against becoming a ship's surgeon lest the isolation and horror of his duties affect his poetic sensibilities, he responded:

> Your advice about the Indiaman is a very wise advice . . . though you are a little in the wrong concerning its destroying the energies of Mind: on the contrary it would be the finest thing in the world to strengthen them—To be thrown among people who care not for you, with whom you have no sympathies forces the Mind upon its own resourses, and leaves it free to make its speculations of the differences of human character and to class them with the calmness of a Botanist.[5]

The contemplation of pain in those with whom one would seem to have no immediate sympathy, and the treatment of perceived sickness in patients too ill to have feeling or care for him who would heal them, challenge the imaginative sympathy and speculative foresight of the physician in his diagnoses no less than these do the comprehending imagination and negative capability of the poet who would experience the sensibilities of every creature. For Keats, the intellectual challenge and the potential for good work were parallel in medicine and in poetry. As he said in 1818: "Were I to study physic or rather Medicine again,—I feel it would not make the least difference in my Poetry; when the Mind is in its infancy a Bias is in reality a Bias, but when we have acquired more strength, a Bias becomes no Bias. Every department of knowledge we see excellent and calculated towards a great whole."[6] The energies of mind displayed in the best practice of each discipline were not only fully related but, assuredly, equally fine manifestations of Apollo's patronage and power.

The facts of Keats's medical training are easily catalogued: we know of his five-year apprenticeship in the flourishing Edmonton practice of the surgeon-apothecary Thomas Hammond (midsummer 1810 through mid-1815), his two-semester attendance of lectures at the Borough Medical School of the United Hospitals of Guy's and St. Thomas's in London (1815 to 1816), his eight-month clinical attendance in the wards of the two hospitals (October 1815 to May 1816) in fulfillment of the 1815 Apothecaries Act requirement that all licentiates "walk the wards" of a major teaching hospital (a kind of clinical residency) for at least six months, and his early appointment as a surgeon's dresser or assistant to the Guy's surgeon William Lucas, Jr., in October 1815, and actual service in the dressership for twelve months (March 1816 to March 1817).[7] The medical courses Keats took at "The Guy's School," as it was known, and the teachers of these courses can also be tracked through the Apothecaries Hall register and the syllabi advertisements for the two hospitals:[8] the poet took two courses in chemistry from William Babington, Alexander Marcet, and William Allen; a course in the practice of medicine from Babington and James Curry; a course in the theory of medicine and materia medica taught by Curry and James Cholmeley; a course in medical botany from William Salisbury, which included excursions outside London and instruction at the Society of Apothecaries' working laboratory, the Chelsea Physic Garden; a course in anatomy and the operations of surgery taught by Astley Cooper and Henry Cline, Jr.; and another course in the principles and practice of surgery taught by Astley Cooper alone. In addition, Keats studied morbid anatomy and dissection with Joseph Henry Green.

The full extent of Keats's practical and theoretical medical knowledge, which ranges well beyond the facts listed above, can be known only through a comparative study of textbooks and lecture notes of his instructors (and the common sources on which these were based), records of clinical instruction at Guy's and the other London teaching hospitals, and the parallel requirements of medical practice in the major cities of England. For example, we know for certain only that Keats took and passed on 21 July 1816 the certifying examination in therapeutics and practical medicine given by the Society of Apothecaries that licensed him as an apothecary and general practitioner anywhere in England. But we can deduce the range of his knowledge of contemporary pharmaceutical chemistry and materia medica alone when we discover that the examination required practical and theoretical familiarity with all the items likely to occur in physicians' prescriptions (the catalogue of materia medica currently in use runs over 113 pages in the Encyclopaedia Britannica of 1810), a knowledge of the botanical origins and relationships and the medical histories of these pharmaceuticals, and an accurate ability to translate entries and symbols of the Pharmacopoeia Londinensis.[9] Furthermore, we can infer the quality and range of the knowledge in medicine and pathology required by the examination Keats took when we review textbooks on the subject by Babington, Curry, and Cholmeley, and know that they included both current theoretical medicine (along with the history of these ideas) and practical instruction in diagnosis and semiotics as developed and advanced in the London clinics of the time. Again, although we have no records describing Keats's apprenticeship to Thomas Hammond, we do know that Hammond had a flourishing practice in Edmonton that necessitated two assistants, that he was a respected surgeon-apothecary who trained at Guy's Hospital with teachers like Henry Cline, Sr., who had studied with John Hunter, and that he had served as an apprentice to the well-known Guy's surgeon William Lucas, Sr. Hence, at the end of his five years with Hammond and before he went up to London to study at Guy's, Keats would have already had the requisite training in surgery, diagnosis, and prescription deemed necessary for a provincial doctor, and his familiarity with the full complement of common diseases, injuries, and the complications of childbirth would have far exceeded the range of the specialized London physicians or surgeons. Thomas Percival's 1803 description of the knowledge and duties of contemporary apothecaries preempts any suggestion that these practitioners, even before the 1815 act requiring additional course work and clinical training, were simple dispensers of pills and plasters: "The skill of an apothecary is a much nicer and more delicate matter than that of any artificer whatever; and the trust which is reposed in him is of much greater importance. He is the physician of the poor in all cases, and of the rich when the distress or danger is not very great." The apothecary invariably had more diagnostic knowledge than the physician of rank called in to consult on a given case: "Being acquainted with the rise and progress of the disease, with the hereditary constitution, habits, and disposition of the patient, he may furnish very important information" that the consulting physician had to acknowledge. In social terms, only those who graduated in theoretical medicine from Oxford, Cambridge, and Edinburgh possessed the official title of "Physician," and, from 1800, only those licensed by the Royal College of Surgeons carried the title of "Surgeon," but according to Percival, few could deny "the education, skill, and persevering attention, as well as the sacrifice of ease, health, and sometimes even of life, which this profession [the apothecary's] requires...."[10] Apothecaries like Keats, especially those with the additional training in physiology and clinical practice required of them by the Apothecaries act of 1815 (and the poet was a member of the first class affected by the act's passage), were in fact the physicians who doctored England.

From Astley Cooper, whose pirated lectures on surgery became a textbook in the British teaching hospitals well before they were published in authorized form, the physician Keats learned not only the specifics of surgery but the importance of diseased physiology and the need to observe comprehensively "the finest and most perfect organization we know of," so as to locate disease anatomically in the living human body.

> You should know the nature of the human machine well, or how can you pretend to repair it? If you have a watch injured, you will not give it to a tinker to repair—you will get the best watchmaker you can to set it right. How then can it be supposed, that the finest and most perfect organization we know of, when out of order, should be consigned to the hands of unlearned persons?[11]

The high consciousness of the body in all of Keats's poetry belies the poet's scattered note taking of Cooper's lectures, and the fragmented notes themselves reveal a breadth of subjects learned: anatomy, physiology, pathology, the blood, arteries, diseases of the veins, absorbents, reticular membranes, nerves, physiology of the nervous system, muscles, glands, osteology, vertebrae, facial and skull formations, structure of the heart, lymphatic system, absorbent vessels, the absorption of poisons and medicines, morbid anatomy of the brain and spine, and so on.[12] In Joseph Henry Green's dissecting theatre at St. Thomas's Hospital, Keats learned morbid anatomy or the physiology of the diseased human body in death. In the wards of Guy's and St. Thomas's hospitals, among seven hundred or more patients admitted by his teachers and other resident physicians and surgeons, Keats learned of the manifold experiences of the diseased but still living human body. Not from textbooks or lectures but in the clinic of suffering comprising the wards of the hospitals, Keats learned to recognize disease and read the course of pain in the living human organism. From this last aspect of the poet's medical training we learn most about his knowledge as a physician and of the experiences whereby his poetry derives its first and final energy.

"In England," the Italian medical historian A. Flajani wrote in 1807 in his comparative study of British and European instruction, "the hospitals have attained a degree of perfection rarely attained in other countries."[13] Modern clinical teaching, or the practical instruction in surgery, medicine, and prognostication of disease at the patient's bedside, began in the city hospitals and infirmaries of mid-eighteenth-century England.[14] The actual existence of clinics in the major hospitals of England thus preceded by several decades the 1794 chartered birth of the clinic in France claimed by Foucault and Ackerknect. The concept of the hospital as a teaching institution and laboratory of medicine found root in the very practice of British medicine; it flourished during the eighteenth century in the infirmaries for the poor and the charity hospitals for the critically ill in metropolises like London and Edinburgh until these became advanced models for the clinics and medical schools that were to be established in France and Europe during the Revolutionary period. When Felix Vicq d'Azyr wrote his *Plan de constitution pour la médicine en France*, which became the charter for the Paris School, he described the English teaching hospitals as specific models for future French institutions of medicine and surgery: "The teaching project exposed herein can only be carried out within the hospitals for it is with the eyes rather than the ears that students must learn in this area of study."[15] Amid the desperate illnesses of their country's poor, the would-be physicians of England's general populace learned, first, to know disease by sight; they counted, without the benefits of bacteriology, the multiplicity of disease through the panorama of its suffering; they witnessed the visible treatments and failures of medicine and surgery; and they learned to read the prognosis of disease and life itself through the visual comparison of symptoms known by experience and signs intuited through foresight. The "eyes" and "hands-on" approach of British medicine as taught in the teaching hospitals was what gave it that exemplary edge or "degree of perfection" in the new and revolutionary century that was to be, among other things, a century of medicine.

In his comparison of "all the great hospitals" of Britain, Flajani found the "most interesting" practical lessons in medicine and surgery to be those taught in the wards of "St. Bartholomew's, St. Thomas's, Guy's, and the London [Hospital]," and he marveled that bedside instruction was given not only in the designated "clinical" wards of these hospitals but in all the wards, that physicians other than the registered professors gave clinical instruction, and that even ordinary and consulting physicians to the hospitals kept a daily journal of their visits so that students admitted to view the patients could read and compare case histories. Because clinical lessons depended upon the diseases represented in the wards, Flajani singled out the Guy's School with its seven hundred or more patients (represented by the total bed count of the two hospitals) for the breadth of its instruction and the quality of its instructors: "So it is that at Guy's Hospital, which is one of the best, the three physicians that direct it, Drs. Babington, Curry, and Marcet, alternately give *excellent clinical lessons.* . . ."[16] Marcet, Curry, and Babington were, as we know, Keats's teachers.

During the period 1768 to 1805, Guy's Hospital was the only London medical school that had organized courses in the medical, chemical, and physical branches of medicine.[17] Because these courses were taught by the hospital's clinical physicians and surgeons who also practiced experimental medicine in its wards, the Guy's School came close by the early nineteenth century to fulfilling its charter as the foremost *teaching* research institution in London. Thomas Guy's will of 1732 had described his hospital's purpose as a place for the treatment of incurable disease with desperate remedies: it was to admit

> four hundred poor persons or upwards, labouring under any distempers, infirmities or disorders *thought capable of relief by physic or surgery*; but who, by reason of the small hope of their cure or the length of time which for the purpose may be required or thought necessary are or may be adjudged or called incurables, and as such, not proper objects to be received into or continued in the present hospital of St. Thomas, or other hospitals in and by which no provision has been made for distempers deemed or called incurable.[18]

The experimental surgery and chemical therapy practiced upon these "incurable" patients by men like Astley Cooper and Alexander Marcet during the early nineteenth century were well known among the medical communities of England and Europe; the diseases that they treated with new and desperate "physic" included terminal cancers and consumptions, multiple psychosomoses, unremitting insanity, and progressive congenital malformations.[19] Here, it is important to recall that Keats was not simply one of the ordinary pupils who observed clinical practice in the wards of Guy's and St. Thomas's hospitals but that he served as a surgeon's dresser in the Guy's wards for an entire year and was, hence, responsible for the care—and sometimes the treatment—of these desperately ill patients. Guy's Hospital retained a total of twelve dressers picked by merit from its approximately seven hundred pupils per year for its three surgeons; these dressers paid an additional fee for the privilege of what they would learn: they assisted in regular surgery and made daily rounds of the wards with their surgeons; they provided subsidiary care after drastic surgery and unusual experimental therapy; they substituted for their surgeons on "taking-in day" each week and could admit emergency patients on their own judgment during the rest of the week; in addition, they were expected to reside at the hospital and serve as dresser-in-charge for one week each semester, and on the weekends of this week the dresser-in-charge would be the only practitioner on duty at a given ward.[20] Keats's year-long dressership to the "neat-handed, but rash in the extreme" William Lucas, Jr.,[21] presumes not only unusual ability (and a strong stomach) in the apprentice surgeon but also, given the kinds of incurably diseased patients that Guy's routinely admitted and the kinds of extreme remedies employed for these patients by the Guy's staff, an extraordinary commitment and responsibility in the would-be poet. At Guy's between October 1815 and March 1817, amid the ten thousand or more patients admitted each year by the hospital staff, Keats had ample opportunity to observe, study, and sometimes treat the full complement of dreaded diseases, physical and mental, known to human life in early-nineteenth-century England. If we are accustomed to acknowledging the concern and commitment for a suffering humanity of Keats the poet, we cannot possibly make light of what Keats first learned first hand of unremitting human pain in the experimental wards of Guy's Hospital.

Keats's education at Guy's was neither simple nor simply practical. The existence of a full-fledged scientific society at Guy's Hospital during the early nineteenth century, which served as a primary forum for the exchange of ideas, medical news, and cases among the Guy's staff, and for the formal reading of papers on research in progress within the Guy's circle, insured that the instruction Keats received from his teachers was theoretically comprehensive and current with contemporary practice. Membership in the Physical Society at Guy's was open to teaching and practicing staff of the borough hospitals and related institutions; all of Keats's professors were members during this period, as were two of the examiners from Apothecaries Hall, Everard Brande and Gregory Johnson, and the radical thinker John Thelwall; meetings of the society and the reading room of its library were open to all at the hospital, including students.[22]

The Physical Society Library bears particular notice. It was the first medical school library in London to organize at the turn of the century, and the years immediately preceding Keats's tenure at the hospital saw formal effort to catalogue and safeguard holdings and to increase acquisitions: printed catalogues of the books in the Physical Society Library began to appear in 1804; the society resolved in 1811 to have a salaried librarian responsible for the lending and preserving of the books; and, from 1816, the books were insured for one thousand pounds per annum. William Babington, Keats's chemistry teacher, was librarian and treasurer of the Physical Society for thirteen years (1782–1795), followed by Richard Stocker, the translator of the *Pharmacopoeia Officinalis Britannica* (1810), and Richard Cox, the publisher of medical books in London, who became the first hired librarian in 1811.[23] James Curry, the president of the Physical Society until 1811 and also one of Keats's teachers, was largely responsible for the early catalogues and, because of his "extensive reading" and vast personal library of medical and philosophical books, was the primary advisor on the acquisition of books for the library. Indeed, when there was an unexplained loss of books in 1811, Curry was brought in from retirement to assist in acquiring book collections at auctions, and the executive membership was dunned fifty pounds apiece to fund Curry's book purchases for the library; a committee of twelve executive members (which included three of Keats's teachers: Babington, Marcet, and Curry himself) was then established and charged to supplement and greatly increase the existing library.[24] The fruits of their labor, a vastly expanded list, can be observed in the extant shelflist or *Numerical Catalogue of Books in the Library* compiled by the new librarian, Mr. Simmonds, in 1817.

It is unlikely that Keats saw more than a few basic books in the Physical Society Library, and, without lending records for students, we cannot guarantee that the poet read any of the library books. We do know that the books in the 1817 list served as a working medical library for his teachers. A review of the kinds of books and periodicals that these professors deemed necessary to their teaching, practice, and research—and that they had voted to purchase with personal funds and dues by 1816—will tell us much about the quality of their instruction and the intellectual tenor of the Guy's community during Keats's time at the hospital. Davy, Priestley, John Brown, Erasmus Darwin, James Gregory, Brodie, Prichard, William Lawrence, William Brande, Abernethy, John Murray, Monro, John Barclay, Hutton, Duncan, Elliotson, Fowler, Fordyce, Ferriar, Baillie, Pearson, Playfair, Saumarez, Heberden, Young, John and Charles Bell, Percival, Adams, Home, and Walker, were some of the contemporary authors in medicine and science represented in the cabinets of the library, often in duplicate, along with the collected works of major medical figures like Hunter, Haller, and Cullen, and a full complement of textbooks published by current and recent members of Guy's Hospital. Nor were the books confined to recent English studies, for one could also find editions (usually in translation) of European physicians and scientists like Orfila, Broussais, Landré-Beauvais, Blumenbach, Bichât, Laënnec, Alexander von Humboldt, Bayle, Gall, Spurzheim, Lavater, Bischoff, Sauvages, Cuvier, and Lamarck. Seminal medical texts from previous centuries were also available, not just of Sydenham, Morton, Mead, and Beddoes but also of Morgagni, Leewenhoek, Boerhaave, Fontana, Hoffmann, and Van Helmont, along with the complete works of naturalists like Linnaeus and Buffon. Pharmacopoeias of the major hospitals and infirmaries, dictionaries like *Quincy's Lexicon-Medicum*, and encyclopedias (including the first five editions of the *Encyclopaedia Britannica*) provided a range of general knowledge for library users, and these were further supplemented by philosophical works by authors as diverse as Paley, Newton, Thomas Brown, and Herder.[25] In addition, the Guy's Physical Society Library by 1816 held subscriptions to an unusual variety of periodicals: there were specialized journals like the *Medical Quarterly Review*, the *London Medical and Physical Journal*, the *Medical Transactions* of the College of Physicians, the *Dublin Hospital Reports*, *Medical Essays and Observations*, *Medico-Chirurgical Transactions*, *London Medical Review*, *Medical Commentaries*, *Edinburgh Medical and Surgical Journal*, the *Memoirs of the Medical Society of London*, and the *Quarterly Journal of Foreign Medicine*; there were also more broadly based scientific and cultural journals on the reading counters, items like Nicolson's *Journal of Natural Philosophy, Chemistry, and the Arts*, Tilloch's *Philosophical Magazine*, the *Memoirs of the Philosophical Society of Manchester*, the *London Magazine of Natural History*, and the *Philosophical Transactions of the Royal Society*.

"If a surgeon or apothecary has had the education, and acquired the knowledge of a physician, he is a physician to all intents and purposes, whether he has a degree or not, and ought to be respected and treated accordingly."[26] By the early nineteenth century in England—and certainly by 1820, as Ivan Waddington has documented—the apothecaries were recognized as general practitioners of medicine, and the respect accorded them as physicians in practice and in education was fully justified.[27] We can neither doubt the range of theoretical and technical knowledge owned by Keats's professors nor question the comprehensiveness of their instruction of the poet's generation of medical practitioners. The Romantic era may have witnessed the division of the medical profession into three purported classes of descending social order—physicians, surgeons, apothecaries—but the need to keep abreast of the ever-expanding body of medical knowledge during the period insured intellectual parity among them. In 1817 we have surgeons like Astley Cooper and physicians like Alexander Marcet (both teachers of Keats) calling for educational and disciplinary unity within the profession: Cooper declares that "every Surgeon should I think be a Physician," and Marcet proposes that "a physician . . . conversant with surgery" will perform "with greater certainty and success" just as "a surgeon will derive incalculable advantage . . . from the knowledge he may have acquired of pathological principles."[28] Of course, in training and practice, if not in economic reward, the general practitioners of medicine of the period did meet the proposed criteria for interdisciplinary knowledge. Economic forces had encouraged the divisions within the medical profession of the early nineteenth century, but intellectual dependency upon one another and the need to train an underclass of general practitioners who could perform the functions of all three groups kept the circles of medical knowledge open.

The immediate group of Keats's teachers at Guy's provides an example of intellectual ties common in the Romantic period both within the London medical circle and with the larger European scientific community. Astley Cooper, for instance, who was a student of John Hunter and brother-in-law to Everard Home (Hunter's nephew and heir), worked in the private dissecting room of Henry Cline, Sr., a surgeon at St. Thomas's and one of Hunter's associates. Cooper also attended surgical sessions in 1787 in Edinburgh, where he studied with James Gregory and students of William Hunter (John's older brother) and met scientists like Charles and John Bell, Andrew Fyfe, and Dugald Stewart.[29] Cline, Sr., was a close friend of the radical speaker John Thelwall, who had trained at Guy's (and who, after his trial and imprisonment for treason, did important work on stuttering, idiocy, retardation, and "intellectual capability"). Cooper met Thelwall through Cline, Sr., and when he visited Paris in 1792 to study surgery with Desault and Chopart, he also attended debates at the National Assembly with Thelwall's Jacobin associates. Cooper kept his ties to the French intellectuals—he visited Cuvier at the Jardin des Plantes in 1802—and, in later years, collaborated with the famous toxicologist M.J.B. Orfila. William Babington not only had connections to Romantic physicians and scientists like Joseph Priestley, Humphry Davy, and Robert John Thornton (the second was a close friend who dedicated his book on fly-fishing to Babington; the third was a well-known botanist from Guy's with links to Erasmus Darwin and the Lunar Society) but was also the founder and first president of the London Geological Society and so associated with geologists like James Hutton and John Playfair. James Curry was a friend of Royal Society President Joseph Banks and had ties, through him, not only to the German naturalist explorers in South America but also to the Anglo-Indian surgeons and tropical nosologists (Curry did eight months of research in Bengal in 1789).[30] Alexander Marcet, an experimental chemist of considerable renown in England and Europe, was cofounder of the Medico-Chirurigical Society and along with John Abernethy, Mathew Baillie (the son of Dorothea Hunter, John's sister), and Astley Cooper, an influential trustee of the society. Joseph Henry Green, whom we might know best for his friendship with Coleridge, had vital and continuing associations with the medical and artistic circles of England and Germany: Green, married to a daughter of the Hammond family of surgeons, was the nephew of Henry Cline, Sr., and the brother-in-law of Henry Cline, Jr.; he studied medicine as well as "modern philosophy" (with Professor Solger, by way of Ludwig Tieck's introduction) in Germany, and read the *Naturphilosophen* with Coleridge; his appointment as professor of anatomy to the Royal Academy and the six lectures on the relationship between anatomy and the fine arts that he gave each year insured his intellectual influence and currency during the period.[31]

"We are unanimously of [the] opinion that the tumour on His Majesty's head should be removed." This document from Carlton Palace providing a joint diagnosis and treatment for George IV's illness is signed by Henry Cline, Jr., Astley Cooper, Everard Home, and Benjamin Collins Brodie.[32] The presence at the new king's bedside of two of Keats's teachers, and the fact that they were joined there by two significant medical figures of the age—the former, Home, was the overseer of Hunter's massive empire; the latter, Brodie, was to become the foremost British physiologist of the mid-nineteenth century— attest to their general reputation within the circles of British medicine. Nor was the general knowledge of teachers like Cooper and Cline, Jr., confined to the sphere of British medicine as recently practiced by the likes of T. L. Beddoes and Erasmus Darwin or as taught by the disciples of John Hunter and John Brown. (And, in fact, the influence of Hunter and Brown was not confined to practitioners of British medicine—Hunter's genius loomed very large over the clinical medicine of England and France during the Romantic period, and Brown's theory erupted upon Romantic Europe, and Germany, in particular, with what Virchow described as "the effect of an earthquake.")[33] Because of the proliferation of scientific societies during the early nineteenth century in England (and *all* of Keats's professors were fellows of the prestigious and broadly based Royal Society from which these societies took their example); because of the wide distribution of scientific journals and the multiple availability of all the key textbooks used in the instruction of medicine in Europe and England made possible by inexpensive printing presses of the period; and because the medical circles in England and on the Continent, inspired, no doubt, by the general intellectual ferment of the age, actively exchanged information through lecture tour and translation and prosyletized their discipline, the medical education of general practitioners like Keats was fully cognizant of the best of British medicine and fully current with contemporary European medical research and philosophy.

In the Romantic era, the individual schools of medicine in England and on the Continent remained distinct or at least recognizable through the kinds of treatments they favored, but the variety of medical and scientific ideas fostered by these schools formed a vast network of interlocking circles without final boundary. Joseph Henry Green is just one example of the way in which German medicine and natural philosophy, as well as the suspect concepts of Spurzheim and Hahnemann, could infiltrate the bastion of Hunterian clinical medicine in London, where Hunter's disciples, like William Lawrence, believed they practiced real medicine based on the mechanistic physiology of radical France.[34] Indeed, not even the French clinics of the Romantic period, however much they claimed foundation in the new and national experimental physiology of physicians like Bichât, were free of foreign influence—of British Brunonian theory, which came to them by way of the practice of Broussais, of the more expansive theories of *Naturphilosophie* that came to them by way of the evolutionary teachings of Cuvier, Geoffroy St. Hilaire, and Lamarck.[35] When Schelling declared in 1802 that medicine "should become the comprehensive science of organic nature, so that the parts now separated from it would be merely branches of it," when William Lawrence insisted in 1817 that "the science of medicine" raise itself above narrow empirics and blind dogma to become established "on a foundation no less extensive than the whole empire of living nature," and when Green proposed in 1832 that contemporary medicine was an interdisciplinary and unifying sphere of knowledge—"I assert that, not only our profession lives in the science, but that the science lives and grows in our profession"[36]—all three spoke as Romantic physicians from within an extraordinarily diverse, revolutionary ferment of knowledge. They were not exaggerating the potential and real depth of Romantic medicine.

Chapter 2

Physicians True and False

In its emphasis on visual knowledge and practical treatment, early-nineteenth-century medicine reveals its inspiration to be Hippocratic, not Galenic; with its emphasis on diagnostic insight and ethical duty in the individual practitioner, early-nineteenth-century medicine declared itself, consciously, to be Hippocratic *and* Romantic. When Andrew Duncan defined medicine for his age in 1810 as a "human invention" and "social art," he spurned the theoretical medicine and superstitious practices of earlier centuries and instructed his age to look to Hippocrates as the true forebear of "modern medicine."[1] The practice of medicine as a Greek art for Hippocrates was tied inextricably to the physician's social duty to humanity: "Love of the art," the *Precepts* say, "and love of mankind go together. . . . For where the love of man is there is also the love of the art"; furthermore, there was no final difference between the practice of medicine and philosophy because "all the qualities of the good philosopher should also be found in the physician."[2] This perception of medicine as at once humanitarian philosophy and practical art for knowing life was assumed—and espoused repeatedly—by Romantic physicians and poets.

Schiller, who studied medicine and practiced as a regimental doctor prior to becoming a dramatist, poet, and *Naturphilosophe*, inscribed his dissertation to his patron in 1799 as follows: "*Your Grace* has raised the Hippocratic art from the narrow sphere of a mechanical, bread-winning science to the higher rank of a philosophical discipline. Philosophy and medicine are most harmoniously related: medicine lends philosophy some of its riches and splendour, philosophy endows medicine with interest, dignity and charm." Novalis, another German Romantic poet who studied medicine and came to believe, like Goethe before him, that life was the primary inquiry and metaphor for each discipline, declared in 1798 that physicians or "researchers into nature, and poets, have always shown themselves to be one race of men through their one language."[3] William Lawrence spoke for his generation of English physicians and surgeons in 1817 when he proposed that poetry or letters and medical

34

science "supply common objects of interest, in which the selfish unsocial feelings are not called into action." John Hunter's teachings on the "sympathy" between organs and parts commonly observed by clinicians in the hospitals of England led him in 1794 to address a parallel "sympathy of the mind" vital to the study of life by the creative artist or physician: "One of its chief uses is to excite an active interest in favour of the distressed, the mind of the spectators taking on nearly the same action with that of the sufferers, and disposing them to give relief or consolation: it is therefore one of the first of the social feelings. . . ." Joseph Henry Green was to credit Hunter with having established medicine as a "philosophy and science of life and living being" and as a practical art appropriate for a new century. And B. C. Brodie expressed the humanitarian foundations of this art when he told his students in 1843 that the "knowledge of human nature" possible in medicine was "the most difficult, the most interesting, the most useful science in which the mind of man can be engaged," and one that was, finally, no different from that known "by instinct" and sympathy of mind by the great poets.[4] Romantic principles like these found their way into the classrooms of hospitals like Guy's, often in the opening lectures of the teaching surgeons and physicians: in Cooper's warning that the first rule of surgery was "never to perform on another any operation which we ourselves, under the like circumstances, would not immediately submit to," and that "gentleness" was an "essential character" for every practitioner; in Marcet's caution that in the clinical reading of life at Guy's Hospital "the comfort and well-doing of our patients" came first, and students and teachers alike were "never [to] lose sight of the primary object of this, and all other hospitals, which is—the relief of suffering humanity."[5]

If, as Foucault has proposed, the early nineteenth century was to see life redefined through the bedside perception of its clinicians, and if the doctors of the postrevolutionary years did indeed see themselves "as the natural heirs of the Church's two most visible missions—the consolation of souls and the alleviation of pain,"[6] then the conduct of the practitioner—the very meaning of his vocation as physician—had to be of primary issue to the age now defined as Romantic: F.N.L. Poynter has reminded us that the word *humanitarianism* was first used in its modern sense of compassion for the weak, sick, and deprived in the era following Waterloo, and that it was the young practitioners who saw the pathos of war firsthand (like Frederick Tyrrell, Keats's roommate at Guy's) who returned home and brought about the real, radical reform of the profession.[7] Economic and social forces at the turn of the century in England may have led to the division of the medical profession into the three categories corresponding to the specific practices of surgery, internal medicine, and prescription. But the actualities of practice, the need for informational exchange among the three kinds of doctors in the early decades of the century, along with the attempt to formulate a larger professional identity through published codes of conduct, underscored the age's evolving and profound concern with the humanitarian purpose of the physician. The sudden currency and variety of texts on medical ethics during this period, not just Percival's *Ethics* and Gregory's revised *Duties* (which appeared in multiple editions and were made required reading in the major hospitals) but conduct treatises by famous researchers like Brodie and regimental surgeons like James Wallace, and handbooks by renowned general practitioners like Anthony Carlisle and Abraham Banks, as well as the pamphlets on staff manners and perspective in the clinics drawn up by the individual teaching hospitals, were all testament to the Romantic age's growing preoccupation with defining who knew most of life and pain and so deserved best the accolade of physician.[8]

In their role as Romantic physicians, the practitioners of medicine in Keats's time were expected to have both comprehensive knowledge of the disciplines connected with medicine (not only of the physical or life sciences but of mathematics, optics, mechanics, and natural history) and comprehending minds able to use this knowledge in the practice of their art. Cautioned that "no profession requires so comprehensive a mind as medicine," that the practitioner of "first rank" must know "more than Medicine," and that there was no excuse for the professional who did not keep current with research and devote some time "to the general cultivation of his mind," practitioners were also advised on the kind of mind requisite for clinical practice.[9] Wallace said the medical student of the period must have "a natural quickness of parts—a ready perception—a sound judgement—a good memory" but also "that degree of solidity . . . characteristic of a mind given to thought" and a "degree of acuteness . . . characteristic of the mind that can turn its thoughts to account"; Brodie told the students of St. George's that practitioners often functioned in isolation, and since "no two cases exactly, and in all respects, resemble each other," they had to cultivate the talent of observing for themselves and perceiving accurately the meaning of the signs of disease before them; Gregory, most significantly, declared that the "proper education" of a practicing physician necessitated something beyond education—namely, the mental "concurrence of a penetrating genius" and an interpretive "quickness of apprehension."[10]

Ethical advice for the Romantic physician focused on his conduct at the patient's bedside. Compassion for the peculiar conditions of the sick, humility at his limited knowledge of cures, and, most of all, the sympathetic ability to recognize physical and mental pain were the marks that distinguished the true physician from the mere practitioner. Gregory and Carlisle chose "humanity" or the ability to feel "for the misfortune of his fellow creatures" as chief among "the moral qualities peculiarly required in the character of the physician." Abernethy and Brodie focus on the commitment to serve humanity: the latter told his students that there is "nothing in this world so good as usefulness," the former informed the august body of surgeons at the Royal College that their only value was "the enviable power of being extensively useful to your fellow-creatures." Brodie and Banks, in particular, marked humility as "the highest distinction" in the practitioner, vital both to the patient's trust and improvement and to the physician's "self-improvement."[11] Special cautions were given to practitioners who would be called upon to perform surgery or minister to the mentally ill. Every ethical text of the period echoed Percival's urging of *"tenderness with steadiness"* in the clinic. Astley Cooper's opening lecture at Guy's on the ethics of the surgeon specifically echoed Gregory's injunction that a "good physician" does not necessarily make "a good operator," that surgery required "self-possession" as well as "gentleness of manner," and that no experimental surgery should be performed in general practice. (If Cooper's words lead us to recall Keats's decision that he had neither the temperament nor the hand for surgery, the recollection becomes poignant when we read in ethics tracts like Wallace's that children should not be apprenticed to medicine before the age of sixteen—Keats was fourteen—lest the "responsibility" weigh too heavily upon the health and sanity of the child.)[12] "Disorders of the imagination," whether these took the form of psychosomatic illness or real insanity, were "properly the object of a physician's attention" in the Romantic era because "of all distresses [they are] the greatest" and "their sufferings are real." The absence of real cures for psychic diseases, moreover, reiterated the necessity for the ethical treatment of them: handbooks were unanimous in suggesting sympathy, gentleness, tolerance, and other "moral treatments" to the Romantic physician who found himself treating diseases of the soul that were beyond the practical knowledge and strictly medical intuitions of his discipline.[13]

The "great end / Of poesy," Keats wrote in one of his earliest poems, was "that it should be a friend / To sooth the cares, and lift the thoughts of man" ("Sleep and Poetry," 245–47). Throughout the poetry written thereafter, up to and including the final stanza on "This living hand"—which is, conceivably, about the palpable hand of comfort and power of a living albeit dying physician and poet—Keats reveals an absolute preoccupation with defining the role of the poet through the concerns and characteristics of the true physician. This preoccupation includes his anxieties about the usefulness of his early verse, his declared wish to do "some good" in the world, his resolve to serve humanity as a poet, his fears of unfulfillment, and his conviction that an artist's negative capability of imagination could be selfless. It finds its apotheosis, certainly, in the scene in The Fall of Hyperion where the poet as narrator meets the goddess of mythic memory and asks two questions on the nature of physic and vision. The first question, "Are there not thousands in the world, . . . / Who feel the giant agony of the world; / And more, like slaves to poor humanity, / Labour for mortal good?" receives the following reply: "They whom thou spak'st of are no visionaries, / . . . They are no dreamers weak, / They seek no wonder but the human face. . . ." The second question, "sure[ly] not all / Those melodies sung into the world's ear / Are useless: sure[ly] a poet is a sage; / A humanist, physician to all men," elicits an even more direct equation of true poet and true physician and their parallel, real vision into human suffering:

>The poet and the dreamer are distinct,
>Diverse, sheer opposite, antipodes.
>The one pours out a balm upon the world,
>The other vexes it.
>   (I, 154–63, 187–202)

Moneta's words confirm what the poet had intuited from the start: "Poesy alone," the real poetry of life written as tonic for pain by "those to whom the miseries of the world / Are misery, and will not let them rest," "can tell her dreams . . . can save / Imagination from the sable charm / And dumb enchantment" (I, 8–11, 148–49).

Readers of Keats usually assume that he derived his belief in the poet as physician from Wordsworth's concept, derived in turn from *Naturphilosophie*, that poetry medicines the mind. But concepts of service to humanity, usefulness, commitment to the alleviation of distress, and the ability to function practically in the presence of extreme pain and intuitively in the face of incomprehensible disease are all subjects that find place—perhaps first for Keats—in the ethical teachings and practice of Romantic medicine. Phrases from common medical ethics texts of the period, that physicians must look with steadfast eyes "upon the sufferings of humanity," that they must not dream beyond their limited knowledge of eradicating pain and misery because "the universe would be disturbed,"[14] read like strange echoes of Moneta's challenge to the poet of *The Fall of Hyperion* that he bear witness to the unremitting pain reflected upon her face (I, 247-64) and her warning that self-centered dreaming vexes the miseries of the world to further pain. Whatever Keats learned of the physician's ethical duty during his experiences in the wards of Guy's would preempt these coincidences of word; they link, in fact, the concerns and the functions of physician and poet in Keats's mind years before he made his conscious choice between two equal, and equally responsible, vocations. The early verse and unfinished fragments of his opus show us a physician trying to convince himself—with increasing success— that if he could read the faces of human suffering much as the true physician did in diagnosis in the clinic, and if he could sympathize with and translate the unremitting pain of human life, he would be a poet in fact.

Real poetry, in Keats's terms, was supposed to save imagination from the spell of dumb enchantment and the fancies of foolish dreamers. The real and modern medicine of the Romantic period, according to its physicians, was supposed to rescue itself from both the fanciful superstitions of traditional medicine and the "servile submission" to closed dogmas and sects, or established doctrines and parties, of eighteenth-century theoretical practice.[15] Romantic medicine defined itself in contradistinction to the magic practices and secretive closed-mindedness of prior centuries of medicine: it was a "human invention" and a secular art whose primary concern was life; its knowledge was empirical and accessible to all; its various practitioners functioned to-

gether and shared information for the common good; it spurned the quick
theoretical resolution for patient observation of sign and symptom; its treatments, hardly the secret *nostrum* of prior medical magic or the blind dogmas of
schools, were practical and wide open to public scrutiny.[16] More than any
earlier medical generation, Romantic physicians felt compelled to protect the
reputation of their profession from the quackery and false medicine of prior
ages; they defined the "true" physician, the better not to be mistaken for
practicing an art that was not real. Figures of physicians, both true and false,
can be found everywhere in Keats's poetry, and the real healers are invariably
distinguished from those who pretend to medicine or play dissembling magician. The poet's differentiation between these figures is in keeping with the
ethos of Romantic medicine and its commitment to defining the practice of
true medicine; it also forms part of his need to keep clear the distinction
between the creative vision of the poet and the fanciful but vexing magic of
the dreamer. True Romantic poets—at least for Keats—must practice real
medicine.

The dark underside of the myth of Apollo has always carried an association
of magic with medicine through the story of Hermes' caduceus, and the way in
which it came to represent a perversion or dilution of the power borne by
Apollo's musical lyre and medicinal arrows. Because Keats addresses Hermes
in poems like *Endymion* and *Lamia*, it is useful to notice in the myth of Hermes-
Mercury the compounding associations with false practice. The god's facile
passage to and from the underworld—and Keats hails him, appropriately, as
"star of Lethe" in *Lamia* (I, 81)—reiterates the ambiguity of his power and
patronage over travelers, merchants, rhetoricians, thieves, pickpockets, and
magicians. Given the power to conduct the souls of men to their proper place
by Jupiter, as Lemprière and Spence note, Hermes was most feared for the
mistakes he could make. Pictured in Greek art, according to Tooke, "with chains
of gold flowing from his mouth, with which he linked together the minds of
those that heard him," the untrustworthy god's ability to charm with words and
rhymes paralleled his ability to inflict grievous torment with curses and recipes.[17] The suspect variety of Hermes' magical spells, wrought by the caduceus
he bargained away from Apollo, extended thus from the most playful or fanciful
to the most dangerous. Keats, of course, was fully aware of the multiple range
of Hermes' false medicine: in *Endymion* Mercury is described as "Foot-feather'd"
and operating "by stealth," and "Hermes pipe" is invoked for "ravishments more
keen"; his power to induce "visions in the air" and dangerous fancies, meanwhile, receives special mention in a sonnet on Dante's benighted lovers where
Hermes is described as having "lulled," "baffled, swoon'd and slept" the hapless Argus until his "whirlwind" of "idle sprite" "So play'd, so charm'd, so
conquer'd, so bereft / The dragon-world of all its hundred eyes" (*End.*, I, 562; II,
875–76; IV, 331, 827–30; "As Hermes once took," 1–10).

More significant and direct yet is Keats's use of the figure of Hermes in
Lamia and, through the god's dealings with the snake-siren of that poem, his

connection of Hermes back to the figure of patently false medicine in *Endymion*, Circe. Hermes arrives on the isle of Crete in *Lamia* "bent on warm amorous theft," having first "stolen light ... to escape the sight" of Jove; the "ever-smitten" and derelict god leaves behind an empty throne to satisfy a selfish passion of "celestial heat," and he uses his considerable powers of invisibility, transformation, and smooth passage to find the "secret bed" of a nymph who has no need of his medicine and would prefer not to be known (I, 7–34). Hermes' jealous and fully self-centered passion for the nymph who does not know him reads as a parody of Apollo's love for Daphne and as a perversion of Apollo's power of healing and prophecy represented in the laurel; the quasi-infernal god's ministries find appropriate object in Lamia, that ambiguous and magical creature of many forms. Keats has Hermes and Lamia swear out, in the most eloquent rhetoric available, a pact of mutual aid; both swear by the tools of their trade of magic—Hermes by his "serpent rod" and Lamia by her "starry crown." The former "put[s] to proof" the transformational power of his "lythe Caducean charm," and the latter breaks her promise of "compassion" to keep the nymph invisible (I, 87–90, 106–10, 133–35). The "blandishments" of Hermes and Lamia succeed beyond all mortal expectations, and we know that the recipe of their passion, whether for the nymph or Lycius, will be no cure.[18]

Lamia would have derived her power of rendering living creatures invisible from Hermes, much as Circe, in mythic tradition, derived her ability to vex creation into degeneracy from her fellow chthonian deity. The power to transform living creatures into forms not their own—flowers into human shape, men into beasts, youths into elders, snakes into women (*End.*, IV, 67; III, 514, 590–92; *Lamia*, I, 120)—would certainly have seemed to Keats to be examples not of benign magic but of sinister and cruel influence. After all, transformations like these would be a Romantic naturalist's worst nightmare of the living world and a Romantic physician's worst sight of the energy of life turned monstrous birth or deformed, freak creation. Mythic tradition and medical consciousness thus combine in Keats's portrayal of Circe as a "cruel enchantress," a physician patently false and potently bad. The "Potent goddess" does not relieve but inflicts "pains resistless:" she brings "piercing trial" to "pitiable bones" and turns her ward of visitors into the "Shrieks, yells, and groans of [a] torture-pilgrimage; / Until their grieved bodies 'gan to bloat / And puff from tail's end to stifled throat"; then, once the physical symptoms of the disease appear full-blown, she banishes "These phantoms with a rod" into a hell of eternal psychic affliction (III, 513–40). When the lovesick Glaucus seeks her out as a physician who might have "some relief" for him, she curses him with "such a love" that he withers immediately into aged infirmity (III, 412, 590–99). Circe represents the prototypal false physician of Keats's verse; she is one who owes her powers not to patiently acquired medicine but to the god of quick fixes. She is the worst pattern for other more subtle agents of harmful quick medicines in the poetry: la belle dame sans merci, who spirits young knights to her "elfin grot" and afflicts them with deathly dreams (29, 35–40); Porphyro, in *The Eve of St. Agnes*, who "hold|s| water in a witch's sieve" and would use trickery and haste to save his bride from an unmarried state worse than death (120–21); Hum, the magician who presides in boredom over all the unhappinesses of *The Jealousies*, who finds the cost of potions and plasters too dear (289–99); Lamia, who uses the potion of freedom she has purchased from Hermes to weave dreams of speedy imprisonment and white affliction for a healthy and unsuspecting young Lycius.

"I am ambitious of doing the world some good: if I should be spared that may be the work of maturer years—in the interval I will assay to reach as high a summit in Poetry as the nerve bestowed upon me will suffer," Keats said in 1818 in his letter describing the "poetical Character"; elsewhere in the letters he talks of the "glory of dying for a great human purpose," declares he would "jump down Aetna for any great Public good," and proposes "doing some good for the world" to be the only "worthy purpose" of existence.[19] Comments like these, along with the recurring images of healing and true medicine in the poetry bring "a feeling / Of all that's high, and great, and good"—from Sir Clerimond's "hand heaven made to succour the distress'd" to the acknowledgment that the fledgling poet also has his "blisses . . . to bless and sooth" to the potent balms of the Hyperion poems ("To George Felton Mathew," 9–10; "Calidore," 106; "On Receiving a Curious Shell," 43–44)—are all expressions of Keats's growing conviction that the commitment to study life and alleviate its suffering was the very same in poet and in physician. They form part of his early resolve to shun the kind of poetry written by those indolents who would "Fly from all sorrowing" and could "see |nought| / In water, earth, or air, but poesy," and to write instead a verse that would bring "sweet dreams, and health, and quiet breathing" to an always suffering humankind ("To My Brother George," 19–22, *End.*, I, 5). The multiple figures of true physic in *Endymion*, the "venerable priest . . . with ministring looks" of Book I, the fountain-nymph who "bubble|s| up / To fainting creatures in a desert wild" of Book II, the Nereids of Book III who "usher back |Endymion's| spirit into life," Glaucus, who tends the bodies of the lovelorn, Peona, the "midnight spirit nurse" of the epic who tends to her brother with "busy hand," "upon her Knees" and with the medicine of "a sister's sorrow," and Endymion himself, the epic's hero, who learns through the life-giving consequence of a book of prophecy the meaning of his vocation as a poet (I, 149–50; II, 118–19; III, 1014–5; II, 410, 413, 444; III, 781–84), are all verse embodiments of the poet's resolution to study life as a physician and do "some good" through the poetry of "maturer years."[20]

According to the peculiar book of prophecy found on the ocean floor in *Endymion*, the scientist who "*utterly / Scans all the depths of magic, and expounds / The meanings of all motions, shapes, and sounds*" in life and the physician who accepts responsibility for the bodies of dying youth and assumes "*the savage overwhelming loss*" of his "*task of joy and grief*" "*shall not die*" (III, 695–704). According to the

terrifying Moneta of *The Fall of Hyperion*, "None can usurp this height" of knowledge of life and pain except those "to whom the miseries of the world / Are
misery, and will not let them rest," and who, like the poet in the poem, have
"felt / What 'tis to die and live again before / Thy fated hour" (I, 141–49). To
these prophecies that combine the knowledge of the scientist with the commitment of the physician and the experience of the poet, and to Keats's sense
of the parallel duties of these vocations, we must add the specific advice
against indolence and the shrinking from difficulty and pain given to practicing physicians of the Romantic era:

> To be prepared for difficulties; to meet them in a proper spirit; to make the neces-
> sary exertion when they occur; all this is absolutely necessary for your success,
> whatever your profession or your pursuit of life may be. . . . *The natural tendency of
> mankind is indolence; to shrink from difficulties; to try to evade them, rather than to overcome them.
> Never yield to this disposition on small occasions;* and thus you will acquire a habit which
> will enable you to do what is wanted on great occasions, without any violent or
> painful effort. It is by neglecting their conduct in the smaller concerns of life, that so
> large a portion of mankind become unequal to the performance of their higher and
> more important duties.[21]

The "pursuit of life" and life's meaning by the Romantic physician and Keats's
kind of poet was a practical and profound commitment to humankind. We
understand better what Keats meant when he said in 1818, just after the
publication of *Endymion*, that he had chosen the study of life over "an exquisite
sense of the luxurious:" "I mean to follow Solomon's direction of 'get
Wisdom—get understanding'—I find cavalier days are gone by. I find that I
can have no enjoyment in the World but continual drinking of Knowledge —I
find there is no worthy pursuit but the idea of doing some good for the
world—some do it with their society—some with their wit—some with their
benevolence— . . . there is but one way for me—the road lies through application study and thought."[22]

Chapter 3

Medical and Artistic Vision

In the *Anatomy of Melancholy* when speaking of the need for the patient's trust in his physician and the physician's confidence in his cure, Burton proposes that "the form of health is contained in the Physician's mind."[1] Romantic physicians also speculated similarly, but they did so without confidence in any theoretical system of medicine and without firm belief in any ideal of health. Their concern that the form of health (such as it was) might be contained in the individual physician's mind and be subject to his mood became, hence, an alarmingly real prospect. For example, the verse-epistle that Keats wrote in 1818 to his friend John Hamilton Reynolds is usually treated by readers as an example of the poet's sudden maturity of talent and vision, but it is also an occasion where one can follow the poet's attempt to use his imagination to soothe and comfort a sick friend and to counteract actual disease with images of health.

Reynolds lies "sick and ill" in bed at the start of the verse-letter, and Keats writes not just to wish that his friend "get health" but to dispel the dark moods occasioned by the illness. The poet would distract Reynolds with "Titian colours touch'd into real life," "flowers bursting out with lusty pride," "young Aeolian harps," and other images of joy and vigor from the creative and living world (17–19); a recent visit to see Claude's painting, "Enchanted Castle," based on the story of Psyche and Eros inspires a resolve "To shew this castle, in fair dreaming wise / Unto my friend, while sick and ill he lies" (31–32). The castle, as remembered from the painting, was a "mossy place, a Merlin's hall, a dream," picturesque with "clear lake," "little isles," and "mountains blue" (34–36). But, in the process of re-creating Claude's fantasy in paint to solace his friend's real melancholy, the poet finds that he sees through and beyond the surface of the painting: the trees about the castle "seem to shake / From some old magic," the environs appear "alive to love and hate," the building seems animated by an unnerving "giant, pulsing underground" behind and beyond its created surface (28–40).[2] The hysteria, real or imagined, that appears to energize Claude's artwork stimulates the poet's intuition to larger images of unease and disruption—"a Lapland witch turn'd maudlin nun," "a beauteous woman's large blue eyes / Gone mad," "a mason-devil's groan," an eerie "sweet music" that creates "fear in the poor herdsman" (46–64).

Clearly, Keats's reimagination of Claude's "Enchanted Castle" will neither soothe nor comfort his sick friend. If anything, the verse-picture will vex the dark moods occasioned by Reynolds's physical illness to further mental disease. The poet realizes as much, hence his lament, "O that our dreamings all of sleep or wake / Would all their colours from the sunset take . . . / Rather than shadow our own soul's daytime / In the dark void of night" (67–71). We realize, moreover, that Keats's dark re-creation "Of shapes, and shadows, and remembrances" from Claude is, in fact, an extension of his own frame of mind when he began his letter of comfort and found his imagination teeming with "Things all disjointed"—"Two witch's eyes above a cherub's mouth," hellish noses, wild boars' tusks, and mermaids with toes (3–16). Visitings such as these can preempt any projected wish or idea of health contained in the physician's mind; neither physician nor poet can "take away the pain of existence" with a mind in such a state:

> I am now so depressed that I have not an Idea to put to paper—my hand feels like lead—and yet it is and |an| unpleasant numbness it does not take away the pain of existence—I don't know what to write—Monday—You see how I have delayed—and even now I have but a confusing idea of what I should be about my intellect must be in a degen|er|ating state—it must be for when I should be writing about god knows what I am troubling you with Moods of my own Mind. . . .[3]

It would be easy to dismiss the verse-epistle to Reynolds as one more example of a Romantic poet habitually reading "passion, life and physiognomy into the landscape,"[4] as an unimportant occasion where Keats exercises his mind to fanciful end. But Claude's "Castle" for Keats, we need to remember, was not a natural landscape but a finished work of art about a mythic story of unearthly beauty and actual abandonment. Moreover, when Keats turns away from the painting to an actual scene in nature—the seashore at twilight—in search of positive images for his letter of healing, the consequences are far more serious, both for the poet's mood and for the kind of positive containing vision that he seeks as a physician for his friend:

> Dear Reynolds, I have a mysterious tale
> And cannot speak it. The first page I read
> Upon a lampit rock of green sea weed
> Among the breakers.—'Twas a quiet eve;
> The rocks were silent—the wide sea did weave
> An untumultuous fringe of silver foam

> Along the flat brown sand. I was at home,
> And should have been most happy—but I saw
> Too far into the sea; where every maw
> The greater on the less feeds evermore:—
> But I saw too distinct into the core
> Of an eternal fierce destruction,
> And so from happiness I far was gone.
>   (86–98)

At home and viewing the beauty of a seascape at dusk, the poet should have been "most happy" and most able to comfort a sick friend. Instead, Keats sees with the horrific but real vision of a Romantic physician and naturalist, and his letter of healing becomes a poem of despair about the kinds of things that poets and doctors of his time must envision, intuit, and comprehend, even as they would heal. With a vision that recalls the "penetrating genius" of Gregory's ideal physician and the illuminative sight or "brightness beaming from his eyes" of Apollo as god of medicine, Keats sees beneath the skin of the sea and through its fringe of silver foam "into the core / Of an eternal fierce destruction," of life consuming life "the greater on the less . . . evermore." The poet sees "too distinct" and with the vision of an anatomist of what is hidden and multiple beneath the unified surface of the sea's body. He sees "Too far into the sea" with the same horrific but intuitive vision used in the clinic by Romantic physician and medical semiotician when confronted, simultaneously, with the physical signs of serious disease, prior knowledge of the destructiveness of diseased energy, and prognostic awareness of the future consequence of as yet invisible disease. Keats's untumultuous but living sea writhes below its surface with a "most fierce destruction" and feeding frenzy of death. This time, unlike the earlier attempted vision of Claude's enchantment, the sight is real and true of "The shark at savage prey—the hawk at pounce, / The gentle robin, like a pard or ounce, / Ravening a worm" (99–105); it is an unfantastic but terrifying insight that remains to haunt the daytime of the poet—"Still am I sick of it." Thus, the "first page" of the poet's sensed vision of a real nature endures as a "mysterious tale" of horror to corrupt and to undermine a prior and simple idea of health for his sick friend.

As Keats well knew, there was a negative and disturbing as well as a positive and healing element to the Romantic physician's clinical vision. The physician had to know the worst before he could attempt to contain or cure it. The verse-epistle to Reynolds did not serve as a potion of healing and comfort for his friend's disease nor did it serve as solace for the poet himself; it was, at best, an attempted cure. We must appreciate both his physician's humility in realizing this and the extent of his sense of unfulfillment as poet: "but my flag is not unfurl'd / On the admiral staff—and to philosophize / I dare not yet!" (72–74). The process of writing the epistle, nevertheless, taught Keats the enormousness of the task of medicining humanity as a philosophical poet; it also told him of the debilitating effects of the insightful "healing" vision that was necessary to take away "the pain[s] of existence."

"God of Song, / Thou bearest me along / Through sights I scarce can bear," Keats says in "God of the meridian" (17–19); it is certain that Apollo requires much in the way of insightful and interpretive vision from his mortal physician or poet. When Matthew Arnold commented on Keats's remarkable "clear-sightedness" and "lucidity," he pointed, in particular, to the poet's practical and palpable gaze, "with the eye on the object, a radiancy and light clearness being added," with which the major poems were composed.[5] The kind of "clear-sightedness" that Arnold identifies as typical of Keats could also be the medical sight of the Romantic physician described in philosophical and ana-tomical texts of the period. Doctors saw first into the life of things for Frie-drich Schlegel, and the seeds of a philosophy of life had lain hidden for centuries "in embryo, in the womb of medical art and lore." Schlegel, who studied clinical medicine and anatomy, credited Hippocrates' practical medi-cine with having instigated "the rapid and searching glance of genius into the secret laboratories of life"; he proposed that the various disciplines that composed medical study in his time were "merely the materials . . . of medical practice . . . [whereas] the essential qualification . . . [was] this penetrating glance which searches out the inmost secrets of the bodily temperament." Thus, in the "complete understanding of life" that Schlegel projected for his Romantic century, "the searching glance of the true physician arrives the nearest to such a point, penetrating, as it does, deep into the manifold fluctuation and struggle between the two [states of life and death], and into the secrets of their conflict. . . ."[6]

Romantic physicians were to read the living human bodies in the hospital much as the anatomists of the decades just preceding had read the diseased corpse. "Open up a few corpses," Bichât told his experimental clinicians in 1801, "you will dissipate at once the darkness that observation [of external symptoms] alone could not dissipate." And Foucault has demonstrated how the postrevolutionary clinics rediscovered Morgagni's dissecting lessons so that "knowledge of the living, ambiguous disease could be aligned upon the white visibility of the dead," and "the whole dark underside of disease came to light . . . in the deep, visible, solid, enclosed, but accessible space of the human body."[7] Just how what was "fundamentally invisible" within the living body was offered up to the "illuminating gaze" of the Romantic physician and the extent to which morbid anatomy taught living medicine to read disease in Keats's time can be seen in most of the textbooks and lectures of the period. Andrew Bell's summary essay "Anatomy" in 1810 described anatomy as a "branch of natural knowledge" vital to medicine and a "civilized art" inherited from the Greeks; Astley Cooper's lectures repeatedly cited the Greeks' exam-ple in dissection, urged his students that "no opinion or theories can interfere with the information acquired from dissection," and warned them that "opera-tions [on the living] cannot be *safely* undertaken" without prior knowledge and

vision of morbid anatomy; even Joseph Henry Green in his practical demonstration of anatomy at Guy's and St. Thomas's would caution students like
Keats that the Romantic physician's knowledge "should be particular and
even minute" and of a kind "acquired by actual dissection alone," and that the
philosophical insight that could be derived thereby depended on "the degree
of observation and activity of mind."[8] Because of the way in which things
could come to life under "the illuminating gaze" of the first clinicians and
through the semiotics they practiced in clinics, Romantic medicine declared
its territory to be "the domain of the careful gaze" described by Foucault and
by Friedrich Schlegel before him; its particular insightful and visionary way of
knowing was based neither on its well-known rejection of theoretical systems
nor yet on a simple rediscovery of the visible and palpable but on an intuitive
and informed reading of "that manifest and secret space" that "opened up
when a millennial gaze paused over men's sufferings."[9]

Anatomy, always a subject of some import to artists since the Greeks, was of
particular significance to Romantic artists both as a discipline and as a metaphor for their way of knowing. We have the words of Keats's painter friend,
Benjamin Robert Haydon, who took a course in dissection and brain anatomy
from Charles Bell in 1806, to tell us of the importance of the subject to the
artist's technique and vision: his students were to learn sketching by first
"drawing and dissecting" human and animal bodies for two to four years, eight
hours a day; the best of his own work could be credited to his knowledge of
anatomy, for "Northcote said that my anatomical studies would make me a
good surgeon" and "Fuseli swore that he learnt by looking at them"; and he
ascribed his fascination with the Elgin Marbles, "so evident with their life and
circulation," and his recognition of "their superiority to all other sculptures" to
his comprehension of the human frame acquired through dissection.[10]

Hazlitt in 1816 had distinguished the particular excellence of the Marbles as
something born of an unusual and revolutionary dissector's awareness of
what lay beneath the surface of living forms:

> In these majestic colossal figures, nothing is omitted, nothing is made out by
> negation. The veins, the wrinkles in the skin, the indications of the muscles under
> the skin (*which appear as plainly to the anatomist as the expert angler knows from an undulation
> on the surface of the water what fish is playing with his bait beneath it*), the finger-joints, the
> nails, every the smallest part cognisable to the naked eye, is given here with the
> same ease and exactness. . . .

In a subsequent essay of 1817, "On Imitation," Hazlitt described the parallel
perspective and satisfaction of anatomy student and artist:

> The learned amateur is struck with the beauty of the coats of the stomach laid bare,
> or contemplates with eager curiosity the transverse section of the brain, divided on
> the new Spurzheim principles. It is here, then, the number of the parts, their

distinctions, connections, structures, uses; in short, an entire new set of ideas, which occupies the mind of the student, and overcomes the sense of pain and repugnance, which is the only feeling that the sight of a dead and mangled body presents to ordinary men. It is the same in art as in science.

Because "truth, nature, beauty, are almost different names for the same thing" to Hazlitt and his generation, the attempt to recreate a prior vision of natural form, whether by the artist, anatomist, or scientist, functions "by exciting a more intense perception of truth, and calling out the powers of observation and comparison.... The gardener [or natural philosopher] delights in the streaks of a tulip, or 'pansy freak'd with jet'; the minerologist in the varieties of certain strata, because he understands them. Knowledge is pleasure as well as power."[11]

The excellence or intensity of every art, Keats said (in the letter describing "negative capability" that was inspired by Hazlitt's comments on West's painting "Death on a Pale Horse"), is its capability for "making all disagreeables evaporate, from their being in close relationship with Beauty & Truth."[12] When the poet remarked that he looked forward to isolation on an Indiaman because it would allow him to speculate on human diseases and character alike "and to class them with the calmness of a Botanist," and when he has Oceanus in *Hyperion* declare that "the pain of truth" or "top of sovereignty" is "to bear all naked truths, / And to envisage circumstance, all calm" (II, 203–5), he echoes Hazlitt on the related perspective of anatomist and artist. Each discipline or art invoked the powers of observation to intuit living action beneath the surface of natural form; each excited a more intense perception of truth through penetrating glance and comparative vision; each achieved through comprehension of the pain of truth a parallel satisfaction and calm wonder. Wordsworth, of course, partly anticipated these ideas of Hazlitt and Keats in 1802 when he related the visualization of nature, pleasure of knowledge, and consequent sympathy with pain of poet, scientist, chemist, and anatomist.[13]

The landscape painter Constable spoke for a generation of Romantic artists *and* scientists when he declared that the art of "seeing Nature is a thing almost as much to be acquired as the art of reading the Egyptian hieroglyphics."[14] To read life and comprehend its existence through its pains, as Romantic thinkers in clinic and studio alike believed they must, required a two-planed vision that was simultaneously close range and panoramic. William Hyde Wollaston, in 1807, believed he had invented just such an instrument for viewing—or reading—both the human body and the natural landscape. He called his patented invention a camera lucida and recommended it to professional medical artists in operating theatres as well as to landscapists in nature. Wollaston was a physician, chemist, natural philosopher, microscopist, astronomer, and geologist, and he was best known for his work on refining prismatic reflection and the microscope's doublet lens.[15] His camera lucida, quite distinct in use and construction from Robert Hooke's 1668 invention of the same name (which projected large-scale inverted reflections and was commonly called a "magic lantern"), was an offspring of his research on high resolution lenses for microscopes. It was a small, pocket-size instrument that used a prism and a convex lens to connect two planes of vision, a perpendicular one where the object stood and a horizontal one that was the drafting surface, so that the viewer saw both simultaneously and could draw in perspective and make accurate copies that were in scale regardless of the size of the object or paper.[16]

Camera lucidas were popular both as gimmicks and as real optical tools during the early nineteenth century: they were used by landscape artists who appreciated their ability to translate distant panoramic vistas into sharply detailed graphic miniatures that could be traced on paper or canvas without any distorting movement of the head or eye; they were even more widely employed by medical researchers and textbook illustrators because they allowed for accurate, proportioned and seemingly three-dimensional reproductions of what was seen in dissections and surgery. When Hazlitt described art as "the microscope of the mind, which sharpens the wit as the other does the sight; and converts every object into a little universe in itself," he undoubtedly had the function of the camera lucida in mind; Lord Lister used the camera lucida to recreate his investigations of cases of pyaemia; and we know that Keats and Charles Brown viewed the Keswick "mountain scenery in miniature" through a camera lucida during their 1818 tour of the North.[17] The significance of the camera lucida, whether employed in physiology and dissection or landscape art and reproduction, lay in the unique perspective it provided of two perpendicular planes of sight—one distant, the other immediately at hand—as one continuous experience of vision. Wollaston's pocket glass brought the comprehensive picture of the object up close as a whole "magnitude" of full dimension even as it preserved the flat, single-dimensional accuracy of what was immediately at hand under the microscope's lens.

Semioticians in the clinics and hospitals of the early nineteenth century were supposed to read the signs of disease in the living body with a dual-planed vision similar to that made possible by the camera lucida. Until late in the eighteenth century, medicine was largely symptom oriented, and all symptoms in an illness were treated with equal weight; the new and clinical sense of a living pathology owned by Romantic medicine changed this to stress, instead, the symptoms of diagnostic significance or the physical signs that could be read and interpreted in the context of both the living body and the generating disease. August-Jacques Landré-Beauvais, whose doctrine of signs informed the practice of medical semiotics in the Paris School, said in 1813 that signs were the means whereby the Romantic clinician attained "knowledge of hidden effects:" a "sign, essentially, is a conclusion that the mind draws from the symptoms apparent to the senses [observés par les sens] while a symptom is only a matter of sense perception [n'est qu'une perception des sens]."[18] Signs involved the judgment and perception of the physician, whereas symptoms derived first meaning from the patient's subjective report; thus, what the early-nineteenth-century clinicians tried to do in the hospital wards of England and France was to locate and analyze the original and generative signs of disease behind and beneath the multiple and often dissembling symptoms of the body. This constituted no less than an attempt to visualize pathology,[19] to see the immediate disease and the long-range progress of the disease simultaneously as one living existence housed temporarily in an existing human body. The growing awareness among early-nineteenth-century naturalists and medical men that diseases were distinct natural and historical entities gave the nosologies inherited from eighteenth-century medicine a tangible and palpable reality that they now sought to visualize further through their own clinical sense perceptions; hence, as Foucault reminds us, "the clinical eye discovers a kinship with a new sense" in its diagnoses, and Romantic physicians, using palpation and aescultation to sound the depths of the body, evoke the "metaphor of 'touch' (*le tact*)" to synaesthetically "define their glances."[20]

Romantic physicians saw and touched individual disease in all its varieties in the immediacy of the clinic even as they comprehended broad living pathology in all its multiplicity through this immediacy and the retrospection of the postmortem. Diagnosis and prognosis thus become one action in the medical semiotics practiced by clinicians of the early nineteenth century in France as well as England. If a "combination of the natural historical and the postmortem approach to disease was central to the medicine of the Paris School of the early nineteenth century," this was no less true of the medicine taught in the London hospitals of Keats's time: Astley Cooper, in 1816, proposed the principles of surgery to be "founded upon observation of diseased beings, and the examination of diseased dead Animals, and on experiments made on the living"; he told his students that "by observing the diseases of the living Body, we learn to read their symptoms and their causes, and the effects produced by the remedies applied, [and] by examining Dead Bodies, we become acquainted with the changes produced by Disease, and its nature, whether curable, or incurable. . . ."[21]

Likewise, if a semiotic reading of living disease and a practical doctrine of signs was essential to the practice of the postrevolutionary French clinics, London hospitals of the period, like Guy's, also taught and practiced the semiotics of living pathology: Babington and Curry's course on the practice of medicine taught that because there were "many different *forms* and *degrees* of disease" there existed "the necessity of accurately distinguishing them from each other by certain *signs* or *characters*," and that an accurate reading and comparative knowledge of these formed the real "science of Nosology"; Curry's course on pathology and therapeutics also emphasized a living pathology that was at once individual and general so that the student needed to study "the *nature* of those *Morbid Conditions* that most frequently occur in the human body;—the *Causes*, whether *predisposing* or *exciting*, which gave rise to them;—the *Signs* or

Symptoms by which they are known; and the *functions* or parts in which they more especially take place . . . ."[22] Keats's self-diagnosis of his consumptive disease and parallel prognostication of its future is fully contemporary with the medical semiotics taught and practiced at that time—he reads the signs of his deadly but individual disease even as he reveals a comprehension of their general and ineradicable living pathology: "The day on which I was getting ill I felt this fever to a great height, and therefore almost entirely abstained from food the whole day . . ."; "Not that I have any great hopes of that, for, I think, there is a core of disease in me not easy to pull out."[23]

Through the practical medical semiotics of their clinics, Romantic physicians came to read the hieroglyphics of the natural body with immediacy and comprehension. Their palpable practice of signs and simultaneous dual vision of disease as individualized and independent took Romantic medicine full circle and back to the forebear it claimed. Hippocrates, first, proposed by "the visible" to get "knowledge of the invisible, by the invisible knowledge of the visible, by the present knowledge of the future, by the dead knowledge of the living," and he declared practical medicine to be the new and only true form of "seercraft"; Andrew Duncan, the spokesman for early-nineteenth-century British medicine, credited Hippocrates with having set the example for their reading of the signs and "minute circumstances of diseases" and parallel "*writing [of] the history of disease:*" "Thus he not only distinguished one disease from another by the signs which properly belong to each; but by comparing the same sort of distemper which happened to several persons, and the accidents which usually appear before and after, he could often fortel a disease before it began, and afterwards give a right judgement of the event of it."[24] So, also, did the Romantic physicians of Keats's time, through their comprehensive and comprehending vision of the hieroglyphics of living disease, acquire the simultaneous ability to foretell as yet invisible specific disease and know its immediate treatment, and to read in the fading white traces of past illness the illuminating prognoses of future dark malady.

The faculty for seeing, visualizing, and interpreting the signs of the living body and mind, whether in disease or health, was finally no different for Romantic physicians and Romantic poets. Humphry Davy saw the creative process in art and science to be an identical "rapidity of combination, a power of perceiving analogies, and of comparing them by facts," and he pointedly refuted the idea that the imagination could "be passive in physical research."[25] Wordsworth, meanwhile, believed that the poet's imagination could accommodate itself to the sense perceptions and ways of knowing of any discipline—"he will follow wheresoever he can find an atmosphere of sensation in which to move his wings"—and he hypothesized about a future generation of comfortably scientific poets:

If the labours of Men of science should ever create any material revolution, direct or indirect, in our condition, and in the impressions which we habitually receive, the

Poet will sleep then no more than at present; he will be ready to follow the steps of the Man of science, not only in those general indirect effects, but he will be at his side, carrying sensation into the midst of the objects of science itself. The remotest discoveries of the Chemist, the Botanist, or Mineralogist, will be as proper objects of the Poet's art as any upon which it can be employed, if the time should ever come when these things shall be familiar to us, and the relations under which they are contemplated by the followers of these respective sciences shall be manifestly and palpably material to us as enjoying and suffering beings.[26]

Certainly, Wordsworth's speculation here achieves reality in the naturalistic imagination and interdisciplinary ease of the best poetry written by Keats. The young poet could not and would not separate the healing visions of the medicine he knew and the poetry he practiced: he, too, and in a very real sense, had "an eye / That hath kept watch o'er man's mortality" and had looked "through death" with faith,[27] and his prayer in Burns's country that he might "keep his vision clear from speck, his inward sight unblind" ("There is a joy," 48) owes its formulation as much to the simultaneous duality of vision and the penetrating "glance" of Romantic clinicians as to that speculative and visionary power of imagination evoked by poets like Wordsworth, Blake, and Burns. An early and simple lyric by Keats evokes the child's ability to stare at a flame in order to describe the poet's unflinching vision of "the lyre, / In a flame of fire . . . / Past the eyesight's bearing—" of disease and its progress, of poetry and its end:

> It stares, it stares, it stares;
> It dares what no one dares;
> It lifts its little hand into the flame
> Unharm'd, and on the strings
> Paddles a little tune and sings
>   (" 'Tis the 'witching time of night,' " 31–46)

The poet's fearless and steady vision of pain and his transformation of pain into music, as implied in this simple poem, become in the dream-vision of *The Fall of Hyperion* part of a complex resolve to see through the film of death and past the flame of healing fire. The poet asks Moneta to let him see "What in thy brain so ferments to and fro," and his request, born of his own pain of dying and living, is answered with a vision of unremitting pain that responds to no physic:

> Whereon there grew
> A power within me of enormous ken,
> To see as a God sees, and take the depth
> Of things as nimbly as the outward eye
> Can size and shape pervade.
>   (I, 289–90; 302–6)

The poet's diagnosis will also be his prognosis. Permitted to see the goddess's face and read its message, what the poet of *The Fall of Hyperion* sees finally is a white and brilliant "immortal sickness" (I, 258) that resides beyond the face and beneath its skull as a horrific and painful ferment of knowledge and sorrow. After such vision, the form of health must indeed be contained in the physician-poet's mind.

Chapter 4

Reading the Faces of Pain

Faces, expressions bearing the full ranges from joy to sorrow, from innocence to knowledge, of human, natural, and mythic forms, dot the landscape of Keats's poetry. Early lyrics invoke the "open face of heaven" and "the half-veil'd face of heaven" ("To one who has been long in city pent," 3, "To Hope," 45); Spenser is invoked as a "clear sun-rise" because his brows "are arched, open, kind," and George Felton Mathew's goodness mirrors "The placid features of a human face" ("Specimen," 49, "To George F. Mathew," 88-89); "I stood tip-toe" describes Dian's face to be as "clear as infant's eyes," "Sleep and Poetry" sees nothing "More serene than Cordelia's countenance" and "The face of Poesy" shines forth from between the figures of Petrarch and Laura (199, 9, 394); in *Endymion*, Peona reads "Something more high perplexing" in her brother's face, Endymion declares that he has just seen "The same bright face I tasted in my sleep," and Glaucus describes how he found Scylla when "Upon a dead thing's face my hand I laid" (I, 515, 895; III, 618); the sonnet "When I have fears that I might cease to be" broods upon "the night's starr'd face," and a poem written while traversing Burns's country transfixes itself with the thought "O horrible! to lose the sight of well remember'd face" (33); Otho the Great chooses "a jailor, whose swart monstrous face / Shall be a hell to look upon" for Ludolph (II, i, 91–92); Angela dies with "meagre face deform" in *The Eve of St. Agnes* (396), and the grim brothers of *Isabella* know "Lorenzo's face" even though "The thing was vile with green and livid spot" (475–78); in *Hyperion*, that poem filled with Titanic faces, visages can be read for their message of power and energy: Oceanus asks the Titans, "Have ye beheld . . . / My dispossessor? Have ye seen his face?" and Enceladus sees "a gleam of light" reflected in each Titan's face at mention of Hyperion's as-yet-unfallen power (II, 232–33, 352).

The late-eighteenth-century pseudoscience of physiognomy achieved some respectability in the early nineteenth century by wedding itself to the medical semiotics of the clinics; its practitioners during the Romantic period preferred to call their art a "Semiology of the Countenance." Keats, of course, was quite familiar with the basic ideas of physiognomy, not only in its original form but in its adaptations by the craniologists, who read the bumps on the skull instead of the face; by the phrenologists, who mapped the contents of the skull according to a diagram of faculties and emotions; and by the landscapists, who read the natural terrain for human emotions. A letter of 1818 from George Keats to John Taylor declares that Taylor "must see Mrs. Keats since you are a physiognomist and discover if the lines of her face answer to her spirit." In a letter to Tom Keats in 1818, the poet himself speaks of the physiognomy of the landscape at Winander: "What astonishes me more than any thing is the tone, the coloring, the slate, the stone, the moss, the rock-weed; or, if I may so say, the intellect, the countenance of such places." A letter of 1819 addresses the social consequences of physiognomy and speculates on the medical diagnosis of handwriting: "We judge of peoples hearts by their Countenances; may we not judge of Letters in the same way? if so, the Letter [from George] does not contain unpleasant news—Good or bad spirits have an effect on the handwriting. This direction is at least unnervous and healthy."[1] The 1818 poem written by Keats and Brown, "On Some Skulls in Beauley Abbey, near Inverness," meanwhile, reveals knowledge of the basic phrenology of Gall and Spurzheim even as it borrows Hamlet's sardonic manner to read the life-styles of the brethren through the "psychological" evidence of their skulls.

During the eighteenth and early nineteenth centuries, physiognomy and its offshoots were a popular and diffuse subject, and one that was easily invoked to support diverse theories and interests from physiology to religion to aesthetics. The naturalist Buffon, for example, whom Keats read in the spring of 1818, made physiognomy a branch of evolutionary physiology so as to form a theory of the passions: "When the mind is at rest, all the features of the visage are in a state of profound tranquillity . . . . *When the soul, however, is agitated, the human visage becomes a living picture,* where the passions are expressed with as much delicacy as energy; where every motion is expressed by some correspondent feature." Buffon focused, moreover, on the eyes: "It is particularly in the eyes that the passions are painted, and most readily discovered. The eye seems to belong to the soul more than any other organ; it seems to participate of all the emotions . . . it not only receives, but transmits by sympathy into the soul of the observer all the secret fire with which its mind is agitated. . . ."[2] Lavater, who is usually credited with the invention of the "science of reading faces" and whose *Physionomische Fragmente* (1775) was widely read in England by Romantic artists and thinkers like Fuseli and Mary Wollstonecraft, saw his discipline as a theology of the face wherein the practitioner sought for evidence of the regenerative potential of the spirit. The English brain anatomist Charles Bell, meanwhile, sought to rescue physiognomy from Lavater's excesses with his *Essays on the Anatomy of Expression* (1806), which was an attempt to establish a medical physiognomical science for reading the exterior facade of patients for diagnostic signs to their inner bodily states.[3]

Naturphilosophen, like Schiller, used physiognomic ideas to support their interest in defining beauty and their speculations on the nature of psychosomosis and spiritual health: "neural connection" formed "the basis for the communication of feelings" and the revelation of emotional disease, and facial expression and eyes revealed the relative goodness or beauty of the individual—"Thus the mild expression of the philanthropist is inviting to the needy, while the defiant look of the angry man repels."[4] If some of these concepts remind us of several of the ideas behind Keats's portrayal of the sculptured Titans in the Hyperion fragments—and, in particular, of Moneta's "planetary eyes" that hold "with a benignant light" and beam a humanitarian vision to the poet's waiting mind in The Fall of Hyperion (I, 281, 265, 244-54)— then we must remember that it was another German Romantic, August Wilhelm Schlegel, who rescued a "philosophical" version of physiognomy or "science of physiognomics" from what he called the "spook visions" of Lavater and the "crass materialism" of Gall and located it "in works of art, particularly in the ancient sculptured figures of the gods."[5]

Thea's face, "large as that of Memphian sphinx . . . / When sages look'd to Egypt for their lore. / But oh! how unlike marble was that face: / How beautiful, if sorrow had not made / Sorrow more beautiful than Beauty's self," Oceanus's thoughtful face of "severe content," Caf's "dusky face" that bears "More thought than woe," the nameless Titans with their "thousand eyes / Wide glaring for revenge," Ops's "pale cheeks," with "hollow eyes" and "all her forehead wan," Saturn's face, agitated by "all the frailty of grief / Of rage, of fear, anxiety, revenge, / Remorse, spleen, hope, but most of all despair," Mnemosyne's "silent face" in which Apollo reads "a wondrous lesson" (Hyp., I, 31–34; II, 165, 56, 323–24, 114–15, 92–96; III, 112)—all these anticipate and foreshadow Moneta's "bright blanch'd" "wan face" whose surface and inner substance the poet is forced to read in The Fall of Hyperion (I, 256–63). Moreover, the goddess's very instruction to the poet, that he must "seek no wonder but the human face," is a medical and philosophical charge born of the message of "high tragedy" and "ferment" that he reads within and beyond this face "In the dark secret chambers of her skull" (I, 163, 277–90). Ever increasingly for Keats, as we can see, the "face of Poesy" was a face of illness, and the faces that he was required to read as the poet of an era following Waterloo were the faces of "agitation," injury, "severe content," and general distress both physical and psychic. Nor were these faces simply the horrific images of decay revealed by lessons in morbid anatomy, or even the chilling "Hippocratic face"—a euphemism for the face of imminent death—defined by the medical textbooks of the Romantic period.[6] The faces of Keats's poetry, which he would imagine, read, and translate as a physician, are all faces of pain—physical and mental, real and imagined, occasionally passing but, usually, unrelenting.

Elaine Scarry, in her study The Body in Pain: The Making and Unmaking of the World (1985), has spoken of the essential "unsharability" of pain, of the difficulties of articulating one's own pain or imagining another's pain, and of the resistance to language inherent in pain: "Physical pain does not simply resist language but actively destroys it, bringing about an immediate reversion to a state anterior to language, to the sounds and cries a human being makes before language is ever learned." Precisely because those in intense distress often cannot speak and verbalize their pain, there is a need for spokespersons who can articulate the pain of others and avenues whereby the immensely private experience can enter into the world of public discourse; Scarry identifies medicine as the most obvious of the avenues and the physician as the most potentially effective speaker and translating medium of pain: "for the success of the physician's work will often depend on the acuity with which he or she can hear the fragmentary language of pain, coax it into clarity, and interpret it."[7] Keats assumed the reality of these ideas when he sought to define the physician's (and poet's) task, tied real knowledge to the palpable and subjective experience of suffering, and described the world in which the poet had to acquit himself as "The vale of Soul-making:"

> I will call the *world* a School instituted for the purpose of teaching little children to read—I will call the *human heart* the *horn Book* used in that School—and I will call the *Child able to read, the* Soul made from that *school* and its *hornbook*. Do you not see how necessary a World of Pains and troubles is to school an Intelligence and make it a soul? A Place where the heart must feel and suffer in a thousand diverse ways! Not merely is the Heart a Hornbook, It is the Minds Bible, it is the Minds experience, it is the teat from which the Mind or intelligence sucks its identity.[8]

Romantic physicians like Keats were taught that pain could "arise from every vehement sensation," including sympathy, and that the analytical reading of the signs of disease by the physician required both sentience of the individual affliction and imaginative insight into the pain of disease.[9] Hence, the Romantic physician and Keats's poet were expected to have a dual consciousness of pain—as a patient and as a physician—and healing knowledge, and the comprehending imagination of disease was tied to the actuality and actual experience of pain. As Keats said to his friend Reynolds in May 1818, "Until we are sick, we understand not. . . ."

When Paul de Man traced what he describes as Keats's recurringly real "humanitarian dream" of poetry as a healing and redeeming force in a world of sorrows, he noted the negative implications inherent in this dream: "If poetry is to redeem, it must be that there is a need for redemption, that humanity is indeed 'languid sick' and 'with temples bursting.' The redemption is the happier future of a painful present. One of the lines of development that Keats's poetry will follow reaches a deeper understanding of this pain which, in earlier texts, is merely a feverous restlessness. . . ."[10] The Hyperion fragments, connected as they are to an occasion of great personal loss and pain (the death of Tom Keats), mark the point at which Keats reached this deeper understanding of present pain. The pattern of sympathy by which this occurred was apparent

to the poet, for he described in Hyperion itself how "the laden heart / Is perse-
cuted more, and fever'd more, / When it is nighing to the mournful house /
Where other hearts are sick of the same bruise" (II, 101–4). Thus, when the
goddess Moneta volunteers as part of her humanitarian instruction of the poet
of The Fall of Hyperion to show him "the scenes / Still swooning vivid through
[her] globed brain, / With an electral changing misery . . . , / Free from all pain,
if wonder pain thee not" (I, 244–48), we are to understand that the wonders of
the goddess's face will be a mortal, feeling comprehension of her immortal
pain. Moneta's "curse," her negative and inarticulate experience of pain, becomes the poet's positive humanitarian vision. Her promise of a knowledge of
pain is like a "grain of gold" found "upon a mountain's side," and the "view of
sad Moneta's brow" makes the poet ache to see more: he strains out his eyes
and sets himself "Upon an eagle's watch" that he "might see, / And seeing ne'er
forget" (I, 271–76, 308–10). This felt and fully imagined vision of pain is, finally,
what Keats seeks to know and articulate when he resolves to be a physician-
poet and seek no wonder but the human faces of pain. This is the invisible lyre
in a flame of fire that he would see, touch, articulate, and make visible. Able to
think "till thought is blind" amid the pathos and melancholy of Burns's country
("This mortal body of a thousand days," 12), Keats was also resolved to feel
until he saw. As James Russell Lowell said in 1854 in recalling a line from
Donne, Keats was a poet "in whom the moral seems to have so perfectly
interfused the physical man, that you might almost say he could feel sorrow
with his hands, so truly did his body, like that of Donne's mistress, think and
remember and forebode."[11] Those "hieroglyphics old, / Which sages and keen-
eyed astrologers . . . / Won from the gaze of many centuries" (Hyp., I, 277–80),
become, in the clear vision of Keats's maturity, the furrows and creases in the
many faces of pain that he will read and know with feeling as a poet serving
humanity.

PART II

LIFE

Life is all a variorum.

Robert Burns

In 1795, four months before the birth of Keats and twenty-four years before the composition of the "Ode on a Grecian Urn," Alexander von Humboldt, the renowned naturalist and chemical physiologist, published a fable on the nature of organic life in Friedrich Schiller's journal, Die Hören.[1] Humboldt (1769–1859) was a close friend of Goethe and brother to the Naturphilosophe and philologist Wilhelm von Humboldt.[2] His fable of life, "Die Lebenskraft oder der Rhodische Genius," told of a mysterious painting owned by the people of ancient Syracuse called "The Genius of Rhodes." The painting depicted a multitude of young women and men who stretched out their arms toward one another in desperate yearning; between them, seeming to represent what prevented these lovers from consummating their desires, stood a tense, poised figure. This bright spirit held a burning torch aloft, and a golden butterfly with parted wings rested on its shoulder. The citizens of Syracuse puzzled over the meaning of this picture until, finally, a pendant to the painting was found in Rhodes. In the counterpart the young people were shown joined in the consummation of their love; they lay sated with their fevered passions spent and their ecstasy was captured in the final moment before dissolution. The genius lay crushed beneath their senseless and motionless prone bodies; the torch was extinguished and cast aside, and the butterfly was gone. A philosopher who examined both paintings, Humboldt concluded, found the correct interpretation. The young lovers represented the elements in an organism; their urge to submit to the laws of their chemical or elective affinities was restrained by the vital force represented by the genius, and as soon as the spirit or power lost control over them they united in what is called putrefaction.

Unlike the naive people of ancient Syracuse and Rhodes, the sentimental philosophers and physiologists of Keats's time would have had no trouble deciphering the myth of "The Genius of Rhodes." The butterfly has always been a symbol of life, from the earliest notions of the anima to contemporary notions of psyche and will. "Psyche," in Greek, means both "soul" and "butterfly." Lemprière notes that in Greek art Psyche is represented with the wings of a butterfly "to intimate the lightness of the soul," and that among the ancients, when a person expires, a

61

butterfly appears to flutter above the mouth of the deceased.[3] The phrenologists and neurophysiologists of the early nineteenth century did
not fail to see the symbolic shadow of the human skull in the pattern on
the wings of the death's-head moth—nor did philosophers and poets
like Schelling and Coleridge neglect to see in the evolving chrysalis of
the butterfly the pattern of the unfolding of human consciousness and
universal will. The genius of Rhodes's flaming torch, moreover, is a
common symbol of the life force, from earliest vitalistic notions of life as
light and energy to nineteenth-century mechanistic notions of life as
electricity and galvanic motion. Humboldt's portrayal of life as those
forces that resist putrefaction through the tension of their combined
opposition was a familiar concept during Keats's time; indeed, it found
unexpected support in the old belief in spontaneous generation from
putrescent matter, and in contemporary observations of the connection
between the phosphorescence of decaying bodies and living creatures
like electric eels and fireflies. It was evoked alike by the vitalistic theorists of life who believed in a fine essence or ethereal will, by the electrochemical theorists of life who saw this essence as no more than an
electromagnetic spark or chemical catalyst, and by the mechanistic
theorists of life who saw both essence and electricity as nothing more
than the products of motion, countermotion, and organization.

The poets of the early nineteenth century, also, would have easily
read in Humboldt's myth and its mysterious works of art the meaning
of organic life. In the nervous energy represented by Humboldt's vital
spirit, we recognize Schiller's definition of life as "nerve spirit," a subtle, mobile force of unknown origin that resides in live nerves and, as a
perceiving or transmutative force, was the animating link between matter and mind, world and soul.[4] In the stationed, controlling figure of
the genius of Rhodes we recognize elements of Coleridge's comprehensive theory of life as "*the principle of individuation*" without unity; as "the
manifestation of one power by opposing forces"; as a tendency to
individuate existing in parallel to a tendency to connect, which operates according to a general law of polarity and rests only in equilibrium; as a power that subsists in the union of opposing forces and
consists (or manifests itself) in their strife.[5] In the attitude of the
restrained and satiated young lovers in Humboldt's myth of life, we
recognize the stilled, pent-up figures of the Grecian urn, their mortal
antitheses, and the genius of the urn's vital supremacy and fraught
emptiness of form.

All of the sciences that the Romantics inherited, including mathemat-

ics, astronomy, and the most abstracted extensions of Newtonian physics, were studied and invoked as possible life sciences, so as to gauge
their usefulness to the new age's preoccupation: the foundation of a
science of life. Indeed, the Romantic era was the last historical occasion
to view the various disciplines of science as related and united. The new
science of biology—Romantic biology—was to be a cumulative discipline that symbolized this union and facilitated the common inquiry
into life; it first surfaced as a concept in the speculation of German
Naturphilosophie. Evolving between 1790 and 1800 as a term to designate
the *whole* of the theory of the living, the first recorded use of *biology*
occurred in 1802 in the work of the natural philosopher G. R. Treviranus.
Biologie, oder Philosophie der lebenden Natur appeared in six volumes between 1802 and 1822, and in the first volume Treviranus said that his
subject was "the different forms and phenomena of life, the conditions
and laws under which they occur and the causes whereby they are
brought into being. The science which concerns itself with these objects
we shall designate Biology or the Science of Life."[6] Biology, or living
physiology, as the natural knowledge of life in all its manifestations and
perfections, was a discipline that could have arisen and flourished only
in Romantic thought. Foucault has remarked that we cannot speak of
biology in the eighteenth century—not just because the word was not
(and could not be) coined before the end of the century but because the
very concept of "life" could not exist in the restrictive, classifying, and
mechanistic philosophy prevailing at that time.[7]

Life, both as a broad concept and as a complex issue for debate, subsumed all the more specific subjects of the early-nineteenth-century
disciplines from medicine to metaphysics. The Romantic thinkers' fascination with the phenomena of life in its broadest sense finds no
better—and no more ironic—example than that of comparative physiologist William Lawrence's exhortation that the eighteenth-century
naturalists' wealth of classifying descriptions be exploited to explore
the "active state" of living structures so as to expand "our knowledge of
life"; and that comparative anatomy or "the history of living beings"
was the branch of knowledge "most interesting to mankind in general"
because it fostered the very proper study of the "life and essence" of
man.[8] Yet, William Lawrence was the arch-mechanist among English
men of letters during Keats's years in medical school.

The debate between William Lawrence and John Abernethy over
John Hunter's purported theory of life was perhaps the most public and
specific manifestation in England of the age's preoccupation with the

phenomena of life. The years during which the debate flourished, between 1814, when Abernethy published his *Enquiry into the Probability and Rationality of Mr. Hunter's Theory of Life*, and 1819, when Lawrence published his final salvo in the form of the article "Life" in Abraham Rees's *Cyclopaedia* (a time during which accounts of Humboldt's scientific expeditions in South America were also appearing in England), were a period that roughly coincided with Keats's medical apprenticeship in London and his study of physiology and surgery with John Hunter's most famous pupil, Astley Cooper. Discrete examples of the intense interest in life among those of Keats's circle in London would include Alexander Marcet's research at Guy's Hospital on salinity and the viability of life in the Dead Sea, Mary Shelley's *Frankenstein* (conceived, she said, after reading in Davy's chemistry and a long discussion with Byron and Shelley about the nature of the life principle), and Benjamin Bailey's essays "What Is Power?" and "The Unity of Nature" (two subjects, he said, that were his "greatest speculations").[9] Coleridge's 1798–1799 *Wanderjahre* through Germany had an incalculable influence upon English science and poetry; the questions he raised in his *Theory of Life*, meanwhile, invoked his English and German influences on the subject, even as they shaped his scientific and religious (and poetic) musings thereafter.[10] When we mark the probability that the *Theory of Life* was conceived toward the end of 1816 and completed sometime between 1817 and 1819, after Coleridge had read the writings of Schelling and Steffans on comprehensive life, and after he was thoroughly informed of the issues in the debate between Abernethy and Lawrence,[11] *Theory of Life* and its ties to Joseph Henry Green become immeasurably significant.

Green, Coleridge's amanuensis, returned from medical study in Germany to be apprenticed to Henry Cline, Jr., his uncle; he was chief demonstrator or dissector at Guy's Hospital from 1816. Green's intellectual collaborations with Coleridge were most intense between 1817 and 1824, when he became professor of anatomy at the Royal College of Surgeons; his opening lectures to the college on the idea of life and the ascent of life, moreover, showed clear knowledge of Coleridge's arguments in *Theory of Life*.[12] We will never know the specific subjects of discussion during the legendary walk Keats took with Green and Coleridge in April 1819,[13] but we can be certain that Green served Keats not just as an instructor in the anatomy of corpses but as a primary intellectual conduit for prevailing European and English theories of life.

"Then, what is Life?"—the question that ends Shelley's *Triumph of Life*

becomes the enduring question for the early nineteenth century's discrete disciplines. It is the real question that allies the apparent diversities of poetry, philosophy, and science. "We are born," Shelley says in
his 1819 essay on life,

> and our birth is unremembered and our infancy remembered but in frag-
> ments. We live on, and in living we lose the apprehension of life. How vain it is
> to think that words can penetrate the mystery of our being. Rightly used they
> may make evident our ignorance to ourselves, and this is much. For what are
> we? Whence do we come, and whither do we go? Is birth the commencement,
> is death the conclusion of our being? What is birth and death?[14]

Life remains, unanswered, a question of endlessly fruitful debate for
Romantic intellectuals; speculations upon it served the important function for the early nineteenth century of restoring to some degree what
they perceived to be an original apprehension of life.

The newest science of the Romantic age, biology, joined with the
oldest scientific art, healing, upon the threshold of the mystery of life,
for, if the subject of life was primary for all the disciplines of the early
nineteenth century, then, as even mechanistic scientists like William
Heberden could note, medicine was the one science whose very existence depended upon it: "The art of healing, therefore, has scarcely
hitherto had any guide but the slow one of experience," nor could it
until "some superior genius" among its ranks appeared to discover
"that great principle of life, upon which its existence depends. . . ."[15]
Medicine depended upon discovery of the meaning of life, and, according to Romantic philosopher Friedrich Schlegel, all the other disciplines depended upon medicine to uncover those first clues to life. The
prevailing sciences and philosophies provided "a rich treasury of valuable materials" for use in any proposed comprehensive science of
nature, "but they do not give us that profound knowledge, of which
alone the physician's penetrating glance into life and its constitution
furnishes the first commencement and essay," Schlegel said.[16] In the
reinstatement of an original apprehension of life Romantic medicine
held the vantage point. The Romantic physician bore witness to life;
his penetrating glance saw the first clues to the answer for the profound question of his age; his reading of life, born of experience and
tentative in its assays, was nevertheless more profound than the age's
other disciplines, for it made human knowledge possible. Only the first
steps of Romantic medicine could put in motion the formation of an
inclusive philosophy of life.

Chapter 5

Naturphilosophie and John Brown

The Life of Man is like a great Mountain—his breath is like a Shrewsbury Cake—he comes into the world like a Shoeblack and goes out of it like a Cobler—he eats like a Chimneysweep, drinks like a Gingerbread Baker and breathes like Achilles—So it being that we are such sublunary creatures let us endeavour to correct all our bad Spelling. . . .

Letters, 1:151

Human knowledge, Friedrich Schlegel said, must commence with the study of the life of man; his statements on the philosophy of life summarized for Keats's generation of scientists and poets those formulations on life of German *Naturphilosophie.* Schlegel said that his philosophy of life set out from a single assumption, that of life or "a consciousness to a certain degree awakened and manifoldly developed by experience"; he identified the element that some *Naturphilosophen* called "the aether of the nerves," an invisible and insubstantial entity existing within "the whole nervous tissue," as "the spirit of life in the organic body"—not life itself but merely one symbol or unfolding of a comprehensive life that is ultimately "the source from which both the external object of material existence and the inner thought, life, or consciousness, alike take their rise." Schlegel's notion of life as a "true living harmony" between the external world of nature and the inner conceptional world of the consciousness, in which "that which exists and that which is conscious" are fused,[1] was perhaps *Naturphilosophie*'s most inclusive conceptualization on the nature of life. It took as its preface the basic presupposition of mind for all living systems of German metaphysics, of Schiller, Schelling, and of Kant— each of whom, as we know, began his philosophical studies in medicine.

Kant defined life as the power of a substance to determine an activity by an inner principle—the only recognized principle of change of any substance was desire, and the only known inner activity was thought. Organic nature was simply "an analogon of life" for Kant, and inert matter was necessarily lifeless,[2] with its always divisible molecules activated by either of two antithetical forces termed variously as the positive and negative, the attractive and repellent, or the active and passive forces.[3] Natural philosopher Treviranus easily adopted Kant's theory of matter in his formulations on *Biologie*: for him life was something "entirely extraneous" to matter, it consisted in the faculty of giving "relative uniformity to the absolute irregularity of external agents"; organization was the consequence of life; and (as volume 2 of *Biologie* proved) vital forces and matter are "determined reciprocally the one by the other."[4]

For Schelling, nature was "the idea in its otherness," and natural organisms were solidified manifestations of the idea of life; an 1802 essay, "On the Study of Medicine and Organic Nature," described how the organism was

> the expression of the entire act by which the subject became object, because in it matter (which at a lower stage was opposed to light and manifested itself as substance) combines with light (thus combined, the two can only be *attributes* of one substance) to become a mere accident or inessential characteristic of the organism and, hence, pure form. In the eternal transformation of subjectivity into objectivity, objectivity or matter can only be an accident, the opposite of which is subjectivity as the essence or substance. Substance, however, loses its absolute character in this opposition and manifests itself as the relatively ideal (i.e., as light). Hence, it is the *organism* that shows substance and accident in perfect unity, integrated, as they are in the absolute act by which the subject becomes the object.[5]

Natural life, as Coleridge correctly understood Schelling, was a continuous flux of polar forces in a dynamic tension whose very opposition and ultimate identity (or synthesis) constituted matter with its powers; in the inter-relation of polar forces and the dynamism of every department of nature, scientists and natural philosophers alike could realize the unity of life.[6] Because of Schelling's lead, Oersted could demonstrate in his *Soul in Nature* how the "world and the human mind were created according to the same laws,"[7] and Oken could set forth in 1802 his "Physio-philosophy" of the laws whereby the elements and heavenly bodies mysteriously took their origin from apparent nothingness until "by self-evolution into higher and manifold forms, they separated into minerals, became finally organic, and in Man attained self-consciousness."[8]

Conceptual echoes from *Naturophilosophie* can be heard in Keats's description of life in *Hyperion* as "symbols divine, / . . . Diffus'd unseen throughout eternal space" (I, 318–20), which, in turn, recalls that "Plastic and vast" "intellectual breeze" that sweeps through created nature in Coleridge's "Eolian Harp" and that "*active* Principle" assigned "To every Form of being" in Wordsworth's *Excursion* that "subsists / In all things, in all natures; in the stars / Of azure heaven, the unenduring clouds, / In flower and tree" and rock, in "moving waters, and the invisible air. . . ."[9] If German metaphysics (and perhaps an older Neoplatonic tradition) is the source for all three of these evocations of life as an indwelling and invisible consciousness in creation, then it was Schiller who, as a medical student, first attempted to give visible place to what Keats describes in *Endymion* as "the leaven" "spreading in this dull and clodded earth," "An element filling the space between; / An unknown" (I, 296–302). A force exists between matter and mind, Schiller wrote in 1779, which "is quite distinct from the world and the mind. If I remove it, the world can have no effect on the mind. And yet the mind still exists, and the object still exists. Its disappearance has created a rift between world and mind. Its presence illuminates, awakens, animates everything about it—I shall call it the transmutative force." This transmutative force could reside "in an infinitely subtle, simple and mobile substance, which flows through the nerve, [which serves as] its channel"; Schiller therefore identifies it as "not elemental fire, not light or ether, not electrical or magnetic matter, but nerve spirit." As a perceiving but also receptive force, this nerve spirit resided as much in the nerves identified by the anatomists in physical creation as it did in the psychical links of the world soul—albeit there "portion'd to a giant nerve" (*Hyp.*, I, 176). Nerve spirit caused animation, connection, and consciousness; it polarized even as it nurtured fragile (and receptive) perception: remove or "damage the nerve, [and] the link between world and soul is destroyed."[10]

Possible sources for Keats's knowledge of German metaphysical theories of life are numerous, and they pervade both his medical and literary circles. They cannot be countered simply by our knowledge of the dominance in England during the years of Keats's maturity of French mechanistic notions of life. If the poet's literary circle did not provide a conduit for the ideas of philosophers like Schiller, his medical mentors almost certainly could have proved source for the ideas on life of the more physiological and "scientific" *Naturphilosophen* like Alexander von Humboldt. J. H. Green's medical study in Germany, for example, resulted in a lifelong interest in German literature and philosophy; he returned there in 1817 to study with the philosopher Solger, who was a friend of Tieck and a pupil of Schelling and Fichte. Indeed, the Scottish physician John Barclay, in his entry for the 1810 edition of the *Encyclopaedia Britannica*, identified physiology as the physical science that "makes the nearest approach to the region of metaphysics"; in clear testimony to the acknowledged and pervasive influence of German metaphysics on English science, the entry marks that "whenever the economy of living bodies indicates design, and cannot result from any combination or structure of organs, it must be supposed the effect of something different from matter, and whose explanation belongs to that science which is called *metaphysics*, or which we might term the *philosophy of the mind*." Mechanistic organization necessarily presupposed mind and a philosophy of mind and physiology: to Schiller and those "metaphysical physiologists" who contend "that every living system of organs supposes mind," the 1810 *Encyclopaedia Britannica* responds, "This truth we partly acknowledge."[11] Girtanner, Hufeland, and the younger Humboldt, significantly, find prominent place among Barclay's German sources for his summary of prevailing English knowledge of physiology and life.

Christoph Wilhelm Hufeland's *Art of Prolonging Life* defined the vital power as "the most subtle, the most penetrating, and the most invisible agent of nature"; the most general and powerful of all the powers of nature, it exceeded even those agents like "light, electricity, and magnetism, with which . . . it seem[ed] to have the closest affinity."[12] Christoph Girtanner, a friend of Humboldt's, attempted to show in his "Memoirs on Irritability, Considered as the Principle of Life in Organized Nature" (1790) that the newly discovered oxygen was the principle of irritability, which, in turn, was the principle of life and the "genius of organization."[13] Alexander von Humboldt's accounts of his experiments to discern the vital force in creatures such as electric eels were being published in England during Keats's lifetime;[14] the "electric" force and the galvanic or magnetic force were identical to Humboldt and he insisted, as early as 1793, that life, as an "internal fire which breaks the bonds of chemical affinity and prevents the elements from being joined to one another at random," was an active polarizing energy that exceeded these forces.[15] The younger Humboldt may have been the most "scientific" and specifically materialistic physiologist among the German Naturphilosophen, but he nevertheless asserted that he owed the inspiration of his experiments on life to poetry: an 1807 frontispiece for his work, which was dedicated to Goethe, portrayed the spirit of poetry unveiling the mystery of nature above the manuscript of Goethe's 1790 poem, The Metamorphosis of Plants. Coming full circle and closer to home, we must now recall that Humboldt, Girtanner, and Hufeland were self-acknowledged, avid Brownists: each owed the inspiration for much of his thinking and his experiments on life to the Scots physician John Brown; furthermore, each had been referred to Brunonian theory by the Naturphilosophie of Schelling, who had declared,

If the only merits of Brown's theory were its freedom from empirical explanations and hypotheses, its recognition and thorough application of the great principle of purely quantitative difference, and its consistent adherence to a single basic principle and the scientific method, its originator would still be unique in the history of medicine, the creator of a new world in this field of knowledge.[16]

John Brown argued in Elementa Medicinae (Edinburgh, 1780; revised translation, 1795) that a principle of excitability that manifested itself in a cycle of exhaustion and animation was the vital property of all organized or animated existence. Healthy life depended upon the principle of excitability being maintained in even supply in the animated body; too little excitement presaged loss of energy and debility (the asthenic diseases); excessive excitability or stimulation worked the body at too high a pitch and allowed for no renewal during sleep, thereby producing a state of overwrought intensity (the false energy of all sthenic diseases) that masked imminent, terminal depletion. Death resulted from "a perfect extinction of the excitement, either from a complete exhaustion or extreme abundance of excitement."[17]

Brunonian excitability accounted for the various categories or manifestations of life, even as it provided the basis for the classification and treatment of disease and the maintenance of health. Its wide applicability found quick currency among contemporary physicians, French physiologists, Romantic poets, and German natural philosophers. French mechanists like Broussais and De La Mettrie used Brunonian theory to describe natural irritation as nothing more than mechanical response to chemical stimuli, and German *Naturphilosophen* like Girtanner and the Humboldts invoked Brown's excitability to show the identity of electric or nervous power in animals and in the universe. Indeed, Brownist elements can be found, as we shall see later, in the otherwise various theories of life of Englishmen like Astley Cooper, William Lawrence, John Hunter, Coleridge, and Erasmus Darwin. Significantly, all Brownists (whether they were German metaphysical vitalists or French and English physiological mechanists) saw this principle of excitability as consisting of "a peculiar attractive and repulsive force," an "animal electricity" formed of the tension between polarities: it subsisted between the particles of animal matter and was maintained by the concurrent operation of various physical and chemical agents, but, like the phenomena of electricity, it was susceptible to augmentation, diminution, and temporary modification because it existed as "a vital combination of attractive and repulsive motion."[18]

John Brown saw his system as a distinct advance over the teachings of William Cullen and Albrecht von Haller. Life was a function of nervous energy for Cullen, and he proposed the existence of a "nervous fluid" that could exist in varying degrees of "excitement:" "It is in the *excited* state of this fluid that I suppose Life to consist," he wrote, "and when it is no longer *excitable* in any degree, we call this a state of Death."[19] Brown owed the term *excitability* as characteristic of life to Cullen; he owed the concept of life as a state made manifest through appropriate stimulation to Haller. Irritability or the power to contract upon touch was an essential property of all bodies possessing muscular fibers, Haller had said; the greater and quicker the response to stimuli, the higher the level of irritability in the given animal. The animal bodies that possessed nervous tissue owned an additional power to communicate such stimuli to the soul (or brain) called sensibility. Haller's 1752 distinction between the irritability of muscles and the sensibility of nerves, and his further distinction between these characteristics of animal bodies and the elemental and unresponsive productivity of the plant kingdom were basic to all subsequent natural history.[20] Naturalists and physiologists could use Haller's system to distinguish between plant and animal forms, and to assign living entities to gradations of life power according to the quantities of irritability and sensibility they possessed. Botanical physiologists like Johann Friedrich Gemlin were soon able to isolate the vital point where plant productivity became animal responsiveness in those "sensitive" plants that reacted with irritability to certain physical stimuli and manifested excitability to degrees of heat and touch.[21] Common English medicinal plants like burdock, bastard saffron, and globe thistle, which Keats encountered on the walks through the

English countryside with botanist William Salisbury and at the Chelsea Physic Garden, were all known sensitive plants; Benjamin Stillingfleet's popular 1811 treatise, "Irritability of Some Flowers," invoked these very plants to describe a particularly Brunonian sense of plant sensitivity: "Once touching is sufficient to debilitate the floscules [of these plants or flowers], and render them unable to move themselves again, touch as much as you please. This languor lasts three minutes at most, till the floscule in this short repose is refreshed, and regains its first vigour."[22] Irritability and sensibility—or sensitivity—were qualities responsive to stimulation and capable of depletion. With a peculiarly Romantic penchant for integration, and with the help of the sensitivity of certain flowers, Brunonian excitability could undo Hallerian distinctions (and eighteenth-century classifications) between plant substance, muscle, and nerve. Irritability and sensibility were reintegrated as the same sensitivity to diverse stimuli; both were expressions of a capacity for excitation that could be alternately evoked and exhausted. Brunonian excitability partook of the fibrous and expressive diversity of organs and organisms,[23] but it remained singular as the principle of life.

The popularity of John Brown's theory in Europe and England was due in large part to its ability to absorb other concurrent systems into its own. Galvanism and mesmerism were systems popular in their own right, with direct conduits to the German Romantics and other European intellectuals; seen from the perspective of Brown (whose revisions of the *Elements* were in fact inspired by their ideas), these systems were nevertheless merely partial formulations of the principle of excitability. Animal electricity, according to Galvani's *De Viribus Electricitatis* (1791), resided in a nervous fluid secreted by the brain and conducted by the nerves to the muscles; it was stored as passive energy in the muscles, as in a Leyden jar, until redundancy stimulated its release in muscular contractions; it could be temporarily depleted and renewed during the animal's lifetime; and its complete exhaustion was synonymous with death.[24] "I saw the hideous phantasm of a man stretched out, and then, on the working of some powerful engine, show signs of life, and stir with an uneasy, half vital motion."[25] Mary Shelley's waking vision of Frankenstein's creature in 1818 points to the particular speculative focus of the galvanic experiments during Keats's time: their fascination with the partial or "imperfect animation" present in newly dead matter and the means whereby the latent electric or vital power of animals could be stimulated or elicited *after* voluntary motion had ceased. Vital power or animal electricity, for the galvanists, was passive until provoked (or galvanized) into muscular action by internal redundancy or external stimuli. Vital power for the mesmerists, which they called animal magnetism, was an overt power that could be actively transmitted from one animal body to another through the exertion of will. Anton Mesmer's notions (published in his memoirs in 1799) were widely practiced and popularly ridiculed in Europe in the 1770s.[26] His *fluid universale* was believed to be an invisible, miraculous *vis vitae* that was at once the principle of animation and a power that could be transmitted from one organic body to another less vital body as a healing and vitalizing agent.

Speculations on mesmerism's contributions to psychosomosis and the mind-body issue were a recurring subject for *Naturphilosophen* like Schiller and Hoffmann—many of whom, like Hufeland, were themselves mesmerists. Poets like Coleridge could identify in 1817 the particular fascination mesmerism had for Romantic philosophy in that it provided tangible example (and symbol) for the intangible and influencing operations of will or mind:

> The will or (if you prefer it as even less theoric) the *vis vitae* of Man is not confined in its operations to the Organic Body, in which it appears to be seated; but under certain previously defined Conditions of distance and position, and above all of the relation of the Patient to the Agent and of the Agent to the Patient, is capable of acting and producing certain pre-defined Effects on the living human bodies external to it. —Thus the *Gymnotus Electricus*, and Two other Fishes, possess a power of acting on bodies at a distance.[27]

Physiologists like Alexander von Humboldt (who, like Coleridge, believed that animal magnetism and electricity were expressions of the same "nervous" power) performed practical experiments to reveal the nature and medium of this power. Humboldt's experiments between 1795 and 1810 focused on the galvanic or electric force as it interacts with chemicals, metals, and gases;[28] his subsequent experiments and observations, published in England between 1810 and 1820, centered on the electric or nervous force of South American gymnoti.

Humboldt was fascinated, like John Hunter before him, who had dissected gymnoti (and of whose dissections Keats's notes make specific mention), by the abundance of nerves possessed by the gymnoti. The Indians of Cano de Bera, Humboldt said, caught electric eels by driving wild horses into the river so that the eels' electric force could act on the vital power of the horses, until the vital energies of both horses and eels were exhausted and the depleted gymnoti could be safely handled. These gymnoti Humboldt described as of "a fine olive-green colour. The under part of the head is yellow, mingled with red. Two rows of small yellow spots are placed symmetrically along the back, from the head to the end of the tail." Dressed in Lamia's skin of many colors, these brilliant electric snakes of Humboldt used their superior vital power to influence and possess from a distance bodies of lesser vital power: "Gymnoti are neither charged conductors, nor batteries, nor electromotive apparatuses. . . . The electric action of the fish depends entirely on its will," for it is "capable of directing the actions of its organs to an external object."[29] Although the "electrical organ" of the gymnoti acted under the immediate influence of its heart and brain, the electric action of animals was nevertheless "*a vital action*" and as such strictly "subject to their will." Humboldt saw in the higher motivation of hungry gymnoti to strike small prey from great distances proof that the electric eel possessed the higher vital faculty "of darting and directing its stroke according to its will. . . ."[30] Organic life shared all the polarizing characteristics of the phenomena of electricity; its powers extended beyond the physical boundaries of the organism; most of all, and hardly an unconscious reaction to diverse stimuli, life was propelled and interconnected with conscious will.

Life was a *forced state* for John Brown. The initial popularity of the Brunonian theory of life, and the reason that it was ultimately found wanting by so many of its diverse followers in Germany, France, and England can be traced to this central and centrally flawed perception of life in Brown's system: "It is a certain and demonstrated fact, that life is a forced state; that the tendency of animals, every moment, is to dissolution; that they are kept from it by foreign powers, and even by these with difficulty, and only for a little; and then, from the necessity of their fate, give way to death."[31] Animal existence tends to dissolution or putrifying union (as in Humboldt's myth or the mechanists' paradise of inert but vulnerable matter), and this dissolution is forcibly—albeit temporarily—prevented by foreign stimuli or external agents. In life, force is received (as the galvanists would see it) or force is given (as the mesmerists would see it). If the Industrial Revolution was a revolution operating upon inert Kantian matter, which took place "at the very sources of dynamics, at the origins of force,"[32] then Brown's notion of the forced state of finite organic life belongs with the mechanical revolution even as his notion of life energy as elemental force declares itself to be vitalistically Romantic. To perceive life as forced was limiting and ultimately unacceptable to a Romantic age. Against the manifest tendency to dissolution in life the poets and philosophers of Keats's time offered the indestructibility of matter and the inexhaustibility of elemental (and conscious) force in earth, water, air, fire—and mind.

Chapter 6

The Four Elements

"Shed no tear," urges the 1819 jingle for Charles Brown's fairy tale, "The flower will bloom another year," for "Young buds sleep in the root's white core" (1–4). The prospect of endless natural renewal vindicated the metaphysicians' belief in life's infinity; it also supported the mechanists' chemical experiments proving life's finitude and imminent dissolution. The prospect was an old one, and it was faced with new urgency by the thinkers of Keats's time.

Lucretius first sang "how SEED / Proceeds to MAKE, and to DISSOLVE Things made":

> And yet the Mass of Things feels no Decay:
> For when those BODIES part, the Things grow less,
> And old: but they do flourish, and increase,
> To which they join; thence too they fly away;
> So Things by Turns increase, by Turns decay:
> Like Racers, bear the Lamp of Life, and live,
> And their Race done, their Lamp to others give.
> And so the Mass renews: few Years deface
> One Kind, and strait another takes the Place.[1]

Keats had certainly read Creech's translation of Lucretius by 1816; he also knew of Erasmus Darwin's important experiments and forgettable verses on "Immortal matter:" "Organic forms with chemic changes strive, / Live but to die, and die but to revive! / Immortal matter braves the transient storm, / Mounts from the wreck, unchanging but in form."[2] Although the mature Keats was to conclude that matter and genius alike were finite and limited, living experiments conducted by scientists during the years of his childhood seemed to prove everywhere in nature the infinity of life. Humoral theory from Galenic medicine and in Burton's *Anatomy of Melancholy*, and courses in basic chemistry at Guy's, moreover, gave initial support to the idea of an enduring existence of elemental matter: Salamander, Zephyr, Dusketha, and Breama

74

could well exist in an eternal bower of the earth ("Song of Four Fairies"), and the "haunted forest boughs . . . the air, the water, and the fire" might well teem with "holy" life ("Ode to Psyche," 38–39).

The Romantic scientists found "In desolate places, where dank moisture breeds / The pipy hemlock to strange overgrowth," not just the sweetly poisonous melody to which the melancholy Pan listens in *Endymion* (I, 238–41) but the teeming motion and multiplicity of life itself. In earthly substance they saw—or believed they saw—the paradox of life beginning with spontaneous energy amid the lifeless conditions of stagnant morbidity. The "maggots of putrefaction," generated without apparent cause in decaying organic matter, were "one of the clearest possible proofs that all nature is animated" for Friedrich Schlegel: "So much so, and so eminently is this the case, that even in death and corruption, in foulness and disease, it still livingly operates and produces life—the lowest grade, undoubtedly, of life—or, if any so prefer to call it, a false life—but still a life. . . . Nought are they but the dissolving and crumbling matter of life, which even in dissolution is still living."[3] Life lives in its own dissolution; false life proved to be life evolving from its own decomposition. Experiments by the likes of Erasmus Darwin provided the very spectacle of microscopic animals engendered spontaneously in apparently lifeless animal and vegetable matter, in dunghills and graveyards, in compost heaps, in putrid hay, even in damp black pepper: hence "when a Monarch or a mushroom dies / Awhile extinct the organic matter lies" until "Alchemical powers the changing mass dissolve"; thus "without parent by spontaneous birth / Rise the first specks of animated earth." Linnaeus's hydra, which grew best in stagnant waters and manifested miraculous powers "to revive after it has been dried, to be restored after being mutilated, to multiply by being divided, to be propagated from small portions, to live after being inverted,"[4] was composite proof of the truths of spontaneous generation and the essential inextinguishability of life for this Romantic age. In slimy corruption resided the very source of human life. It was indeed possible "To breathe away as 'twere all scummy slime / From off a crystal pool, to see its deep, / And one's own image from the bottom peep" (*End.*, III, 330–32). Leeuwenhoek's microscope had made visible those spontaneously generated minute "Bodies, which no Eye can see" that Lucretius had first proposed; the refinements on his microscope made possible the gradual disproving of this doctrine by Swammerdam, Malpighi, Spallanzani, and others.[5] Belief in the doctrine of spontaneous generation of life in decomposed matter nevertheless persisted among Romantic philosophers and scientists through the early nineteenth century; even among the English scientists like John Hunter and Astley Cooper, where it did not present the fact of inextinguishable animation in nature, the teeming compost provided symbol for the way in which the life force could manifest itself in dissolving earthly matter. Truly, "Where soil is men grow, / Whether to weeds or flowers. . . ." (*End.*, II, 159–60).

But the life of man, like those microscopic animals generated in soil, requires moisture, the element of water—and even the deity of love, Venus, is an "ooze-born Goddess" for the young Keats (End., III, 893). Oken formulated the doctrine of life's origin from primordial ooze for natural philosophy between 1802 and 1805. Man, Oken said, is the offspring of some warm and gentle seashore, and was first produced through a certain mingling of water, earth, blood-warmth, and atmosphere somewhere in India; more specifically, every organic thing has arisen out of primitive ocean slime created during planetary evolution and is nothing but slime in different forms. Oken's doctrine of Ur-Schleim assumed an infinity of microscopic spherical bladders whose form was nature's unit; each bladder had an outer dense and an inner fluid content or infusorium that together created the three life processes of feeding, digestion and respiration. The whole organic world consisted of such infusoria, or "cells" as they would be called by Theodor Schwann, modified according to class.[6] In Endymion "ethereal things" "poise about in cloudy thunder-tents / To watch the abysm-birth of elements"; the poor folk of the sea-country "strew sweet flowers on a sterile beach" and are rewarded "With daily boon of fish"; and Glaucus, before the "slime" or "thin pervading scum" of his "long captivity," beheld each summer's day's "birth upon the brine" (III, 25–28, 368–71, 334–35, 361–62). Keats may have known of Oken's theory only through J. H. Green and Coleridge, but he did know of Darwin's formulation in The Temple of Nature on life as beginning spontaneously in the sea, and he had read Taylor's translation of Plato's Timaeus, where Proclus proposes that ocean "is the cause of all secondary natures, of all motion, whether intellectual, animistic . . . or natural."[7]

Alexander Marcet's contribution to the contemporary debate on the origins and nature of life was his research at Guy's Hospital on the composition of the waters of the Dead Sea and the Jordan River. Marcet began his research in 1806 with the blessings of the Royal Society, whose president, Sir Joseph Banks, had provided him with samples of the waters from the society's own repository; his findings (read to the society and published the following year) triggered considerable discussion on the nature of life among the fellows. Marcet's research focused on the conditions necessary for the maintenance and generation of life. The Dead Sea, "from time immemorial celebrated on account of the intense saltness of its waters, which is such as to prevent either animals or vegetables from living in it," was of particular fascination for Marcet and his audience; life had never existed there, according to legend, and contemporary science suspected that the sea was a sterile black void in otherwise teeming nature. Marcet's analysis found the Dead Sea highly dense yet perfectly transparent, with a saline quality distinct from common salt; it was as bitter and pungent as any mythical Styx, and its waters contained lime, sulphuric acid, and marine acid.[8] Its chemical composition proved it to be fully insupportable of and contrary to life and the generation of life.

Parallel analysis of the water of the River Jordan, known in legend for its power to heal and regenerate all life, produced startling results. "From the perfect pellucidity of this water, its softness, and the absence of any obvious saline taste, I was led to suppose that it was uncommonly pure, and could in no degree partake of the peculiar saline qualities of the Dead Sea"—but the living river, Marcet found, had the same salinity, lime, and muriats as the Dead Sea. From this, and knowing that the Jordan's only outlet was the Dead Sea, Marcet inferred that the river was the *source* for those "saline ingredients of the Dead Sea" that were hostile to life, or that they at least shared "the same source of impregnation."[9] The paradoxical conclusions of these analyses provoked more puzzling inferences from Marcet's audience and students, testaments to the way in which limited scientific experiments on life could spawn far-reaching philosophical speculations in this Romantic age. The sacred and baptismal Jordan appeared to be the source of the Dead Sea's deadness; the river's moving waters at their "priestlike task / Of pure ablution" provided also a saline hostility to life and healing; the fertile river began its life in a country of petrified stone, pestilential winds, and poisonous volcanoes.[10] The Dead Sea, meanwhile, appeared to possess the malevolent powers of Glaucus's Circe to "stagnate all [the] fountains" of River Jordan (*End.*, II, 954), to fossilize its creatures and dissolve its teeming life. Both bodies of water, moreover, seemed to find their literal, scientific, and symbolic source in a singular element responsible at once for life and life's absence, its impregnation and its termination, its fruitfulness and its sterility. Or, as Keats asked of the same mysterious element in his fifteen-minute sonnet on the Nile, "Art thou so fruitful?"—"We call thee fruitful, and, that very while, / A desert fills our seeing's inward span" ("To the Nile," 3–6).

Elemental air, once synonymous with *anima* or the breath of life itself, presented a like paradoxical crux of science and symbolism for the Romantic age. Airs (like water and poetry) could be good and bad, fertile and stagnant, supportive of life and noxious to life, according to the chemistry course taught by Marcet, Allen, and Babington at Guy's Hospital. "*Oxygen Gas*," the 1816 syllabus of this course reads, "called formerly *Dephilogisticated*, *Pure*, *Empyreal*, or *Vital Air*," formed "a constituent part of the *Atmosphere*," was "heavier than common air," had "a powerful affinity with a great variety of substances, particularly inflammable bodies," combined to form new compounds such as "*Caloric* and *Light*," and served "the purposes of *Respiration* and *Combustion* in an eminent degree."[11] We can therefore be certain that Keats knew of oxygen, its properties, and the prior names and theories connected with the unidentified atmospheric substance that Newton had once identified as "Aether" and made identical with the breath of life in animate nature. In *The Eve of St. Agnes*, Porphyro "listen'd to [Madeline's] breathing," "And breath'd himself" (246–49). The close connection between life and respiration has been noticed by ordinary observers since antiquity, and certainly since Greek artists pictured butterflies issuing from the mouths of dying humans as their symbols of the breath of life. Robert Boyle (1627–1691) demonstrated for the seventeenth century that air was necessary for life and combustion, and the late eighteenth and early nineteenth centuries produced the atmospheric experiments of Lavoisier, Priestley, Scheele, and Davy. Lavoisier found that only one-sixth of the air, which he called "pure air," was capable of supporting respiration and combustion; Priestley, who called this portion of the atmosphere "dephilogisticated" or "vital air," demonstrated that respiration or combustion converted this mobile gas into *acid crayeux aeriform* or "fixed air" containing "philogiston";[12] Scheele labeled this vital atmospheric substance "oxygen"; and Davy marked how knowledge of this "elastic fluid," empyreal gas, "fire-air," or "oxygen" was of priceless significance to the philosophy of chemistry and electromagnetism.[13] Knowledge of the atmosphere's vital gas, as mobile and fiery as life itself, increased scientific perception immeasurably—and intensified the paradoxes of air itself.

Keats prescribes "clear ether" "To one who has been long in city pent" (13–14), but a long prescriptive harangue both echoes Burton's "Digression on Air" on the connection between temperaments and airs, and notes the poet's conviction that "there is as harmful Air to be breath'd in the country as in Town," for healthy breathing depends as much upon the natural environment as upon individual occupation and constitution:

> See the difference between a Peasant and a Butcher. I am convinced a great cause of it is the difference of the air they breathe—The one takes his mingled with the fume of slaughter the other with the damp exhalement from the glebe—The teeming damp that comes from the plough furrow is of great effect in taming the fierceness of a strong Man more than his labour—. . . . Agriculture is the tamer of men; the steam from the earth . . . enervates their natures. . . . And if this sort of atmosphere is a mitigation to the energies of a strong man; how much more must it injure a weak one—unoccupied—unexercised—For what is the cause of so many men maintaining a good state in Cities but occupation—An idle man; a man who is not sensitively alive to self interest in a city cannot continue long in good Health— . . . . If you were to walk leisurely though an unwholesome path in the fens, with a little horror of them you would be sure to have your ague.[14]

So also Darwin warns of the "suffocative breath" and "tainted air" in the atmospheric energy of tornadoes and siroccos, and of the debilitative "Contagious vapours" and "dank steam" that "the reeking marsh exhales" from its indifferentiated reproduction of life and disease.[15] So also Coleridge warns of the dangers malaria presents if a man of unhealthy constitution and weakened will should travel through the Pontine Marshes, permit "his animal energies to flag," and surrender himself to the drowsiness that the "teeming damp" of the marshes usually evokes: "then blast upon blast strikes upon the cutaneous system, and passes through it to the musculo-arterial, and so completely overpowers the latter that it cannot re-act, and the man dies at once, instead of only catching an ague."[16] These contributions to early-nineteenth-century pathology belong, first, with the age's concern with life and its frequently inexplicable and insubstantial connections with atmospheric substance.

The 1816 chemistry course at Guy's would have provided Keats with a partial explanation of the nature of those airs that "on inspiration prove noxious to *Animal life*," of their artificial and natural sources in "*carburetted hydrogen*," distilled "*animal, vegetable* and *bituminous* matter," "*Ammoniacal Gas*," "the decomposition of *Water* by *Metals*," and of their frequent presence "in *Coal Mines*, on the surface of *Stagnant Waters*, and rising through the waters of certain *Springs*."[17] Pneumatic medicine, as administered and taught by Robert Thornton at Guy's, prescribed superoxygenated or vital air for everything from fevers to festering sores. Atmospheric compounds formed vital air necessary for the generation and maintenance of healthy, respiring life, but as the "fume of slaughter" or "the damp exhalement from the glebe" they could also be fixed air, the noxious exhaust of dissolving nature.

For Keats, fixed air becomes the active agent and symbol working against life's energized motions and electric polarities: it fills the petrified abode of the fallen Titans in *Hyperion*, and it creeps into the radiant palace of Hyperion as a dull philogiston—releasing a glow to replace the ebbing life of his domain, to dissolve the weakened light, or will, of the god himself.

> From Chaos and parental Darkness came
> Light, the first fruits of that intestinal broil,
> That sullen ferment, which for wondrous ends
> Was ripening in itself. The ripe hour came,
> And with it Light, and Light, engendering
> Upon its own producer, forthwith touch'd
> The whole enormous matter into life.
> (*Hyp.*, II, 191–97)

Ripeness is all, and according to Oceanus's vision of creation, the sullen and undifferentiated ferment of earth, water, and air united in one ripe and passing hour to produce the substance and symbol of life: dissolving light—first fruit of that intestinal broil, and able, alone among the four elements, to work remarkable change and engender upon its own producers.

"Is not Fire a Body heated so hot as to emit Light copiously?" "Is not Flame a Vapour, Fume or Exhalation heated red hot, that is, so hot as to shine?" Newton asked in his *Opticks* (1704). Light was particulate like any other substance for Newton, and fire was the light emitted by heated bodies; all bodies, when their particles were sufficiently agitated by heat, friction or chemical activity, emitted light.[18] Newton provided the most articulate source for the late-eighteenth and early-nineteenth-century mechanists' notion of light as the substance produced during the composition or decomposition of material bodies. Vitalists of this time, meanwhile, found Jean Baptiste Van Helmont's earlier theory of vital luminosity to be exemplary of their sense of life as that which was manifestly superadded to inert matter and random motion, of light as that which "touch'd / The whole enormous matter into life." Light (sometimes manifest as heat), according to Van Helmont, accounted for the specificity and commonality of living substances, be these metals, microbes, or man; luminescent *Archeus* (which subsumed earlier concepts of seed and soul, ferment and form), the multiformed living entity in animate nature that preserved and imparted existence to things, "contained brilliance or brightness" that acted as a directing force to conduct the particular form of living matter to the end appropriate to its kind; this splendor or luminosity, unlike the "formal light" of God, existed only in relation to nature, was present in rising degrees of intensity according to the gradations of life, and came to an end *in the process of shining*.[19] Life's motions and intensities were expressed in light; whether visible or undetectable, light was the cause of existential change, the fleeting manifestation of living chemistry. Indeed, life betrayed itself through light.

Consider the light and life of Keats's Lamia:

> Left to herself, the serpent now began
> To change; her elfin blood in madness ran,
> Her mouth foam'd, and the grass, therewith besprent,
> Wither'd at dew so sweet and virulent;
> Her eyes in torture fix'd, and anguish drear,
> Hot, glaz'd, and wide, with lid-lashes all sear,
> Flash'd phosphor and sharp sparks, without one cooling tear.
> The colours all inflam'd throughout her train,
> She writh'd about, convuls'd with scarlet pain:
> A deep volcanian yellow took the place
> Of all her milder-mooned body's grace;
> And, as the lava ravishes the mead,
> Spoilt all her silver mail, and golden brede;
> Made gloom of all her frecklings, streaks and bars,
> Eclips'd her crescents, and lick'd up her stars:
> So that, in moments few, she was undrest
> Of all her sapphires, greens, and amethyst,
> And rubious-argent: of all these bereft,
> Nothing but pain and ugliness were left.
> Still shone her crown; that vanish'd, also she
> Melted and disappear'd as suddenly.
>   (*Lamia*, I, 146–66)

Alone, and agitated by invisible stimuli, Lamia froths, burns, and changes: phosphor and sharp sparks inflame her train, and a deep volcanian yellow replaces the milder-mooned light and color of her body. This deep yellow light, more intense than the colorful brilliance it replaces, spoils silver mail and golden brede, and paradoxically makes "gloom" of all frecklings, streaks, bars, crescents, and stars until the shining splendor of rubious-argent, "sapphires, greens, and amethyst" lies fully "Eclips'd" by a greater and more integrated but also darker and more destructive light. The transformation of Lamia, an evolutionary change of creatural form and purpose, necessitates the dissolution of Lamia. What Trilling once described to his students as the too bright and flashy burlesque of Lamia's form is in fact, as Sperry correctly notes, the realistic content of a chemical experiment[20]—Romantic chemistry's macabre equivalent of nature red in tooth and claw, of life's "Eternal fierce destruction." Lamia burns in response to agitation as Newton would say she must, and she reveals the intensity of her life best, as Van Helmont would say, in the splendor of her shining. "Wherein lies [Lamia's] happiness?" Endymion's question (I, 777–80), long identified in the critical tradition with Romantic chemistry, can well be asked of Lamia, albeit with far fewer prospects for an unambiguous response: "Full alchemiz'd" from immortal snake to mortal woman, Lamia is hardly "free of space"; her "fellowship with essence" involves the searing intensity of fire as well as the loss of light and color; we cannot say whether she releases more warmth as a cold-blooded but brilliant snake, or as a warm-blooded but sober-tinted woman; nor is it clear whether she is transformed into a "lady bright" high on the evolutionary scale, or to a reductive dark-humored mortal of pain and ugliness.

The chemistry course that Keats took at Guy's Hospital taught the "Nature of Light," its connection with caloric and oxygen, its " *reflexion* and *refraction*," its "*decomposition* into seven coloured rays" that "differ in their power of producing light" and heat. The course also discussed the power of living bodies like glowworms, lantern flies, and luminescent fish to generate their own light, the power of minerals like the Bolognian stone to absorb and reflect light from living sources, and the tendency for decaying matter like rotten wood and putrifying animal bodies to release a phosphorescent glow as they dissolved.[21] At dusk in *Endymion* "Glow-worms beg[i]n to trim their starry lamps," and the fountain-naiad who bubbles life "To fainting creatures in a desert wild" offers "All the bright riches" of her "crystal coffer" to heal the "bitterness of love"—

> all my clear-eyed fish,
> Golden, or rainbow-sided, or purplish,
> Vermillion-tail'd, or finn'd with silvery gauze;
> Yea, or my veined pebble-floor, that draws
> A virgin light to the deep;
> (End., II, 141, 118–19, 105–13)

The Indian Maid sings prettily of Sorrow's borrowing "The lustrous passion from a falcon-eye" "To give the glow-worm light" or "tinge, on syren shores, the salt sea-spry" (IV, 152–57). Picturesque and sentimental as are these references to shining bugs and iridescent fish, as signs of life manifest as imminently dissoluble light, they partake of an age's general interest in natural or "spontaneous light" and its place in the science of life and healing. Spontaneous light promised to prove the existence of motion-generated animal electricity for the mechanistic scientists—even as it seemed manifest symbol of the "white radiance" of life's eternity for metaphysicians from Van Helmont to Shelley.

Newton, Priestley, Davy, Hunter, Beccari, Linnaeus, and numerous other scientists investigated the nature of incandescence in living creatures and phosphoric matter. The "radiant Worm," the burning "tropic Beetle," the "insect-sparks" of luminescent protozoa in tropical seas, the radiant glow of herring from northern shores, the electric "ethereal fire" of the "dread Gymnotus" eel, even presumably the shiny creatures in the Ancient Mariner's psychedelic sea,[22] shared a common light—and life—for Erasmus Darwin. He expressed common scientific assumptions of his time when he noted that the "phosphoric light" or "animal sulphur" of living creatures functioned within them like slow combustion and, as such, was connected with respiration and the supply of oxygen; its lucidity could be increased by motion and an excess of blood, and could be transferred or reflected in solid bodies brought in contact with them.[23] Papers by Nathaniel Hulme in the *Philosophical Transactions* of the Royal Society published between 1800 and 1802 moreover sought to prove by experiment that light was the constituent principle of animation in all glowing marine and animal life, and that it was the first principle to escape after the death of fish and insects. Experiments with glowworms found the creatures shone more intensely—as if respiring—in moving air and in response to warmth and lost light when exposed to cold; experiments with dead herring showed that those exposed to oxygenated air became very luminous and that this luminosity gradually faded as the air became fixed and as putrefaction continued.[24]

Research in the 1820s brought a clear sense of distinction between the spontaneous light of living creatures and the phosphoric incandescence of putrid matter. The former was "dependent on the will of the animal" and produced by some "mechanical cause" in the process of living—a sui generis feature of animal physiology that ended with life; the latter began in putrefaction and was dependent on the generation of phosphoric chemicals through decomposition.[25] But the first two decades of the nineteenth century puzzled endlessly over the apparent and paradoxical connections between oxygen, fire, living fluid, putrefaction, respiration, combustion, the living light emitted willfully and with great force by animate creatures, and the ghostly vapors of phosphorescence rising spontaneously from decomposing organisms.[26] The Ancient Mariner, we recall, hallucinated over an ocean that was both dead and alive, a stagnant, rotting sea with bright albeit slimy creatures in it. His nightmare vision saw no distinction between the light of the living and the dead, much as in real life the thinkers of Keats's time fretted with fascination over the seeming alliance of luminosity between fire-air, romantic glowworms, electric eels, rainbow-sided fish, and the "virgin light" of oceans, and will-o'-the-wisps, marsh fires, floating marine "corpusance," and other such lamias of swamp and graveyard. Natural light dissolved in the process of shining and seemingly dissolved the distinctions between life and death.

Dissolve is an important word in the language of Keats's poetry. The Shakespearean poet of the verse-epistle to John Hamilton Reynolds and the "Ode on Melancholy" has the sacred task of seeing beyond pleasure and beyond pain: he dissolves those horrid "Moods of [one's] mind" and sees meltingly through both Newtonian white light and the Titian colors of the world's sunset. Dissolution is also an important concept for early-nineteenth-century chemistry, physiology, and medicine. The figurative senses of the verb—to melt or soften the heart or feelings, to relax or enervate with pleasure or luxury, to immerse oneself in some engrossing occupation, to loosen, release or set free, to vanish gradually—were invoked frequently by Romantic poets and especially by Keats. To these senses must be added the more literal and specific notions of the verb to dissolve from nineteenth-century science: the chemical sense—to reduce to a liquid condition so as to part into formative elements or destroy physical integrities, as in Priestley's "vegetable and animal substances dissolved by putrefaction . . . emit philogiston"; the medical sense—to "disperse (morbid humours), reduce (swellings), remove or assuage (pains or ailments)"; and the physiological sense—to release from life or cause to disappear from existence, to destroy, consume, or cause death.[27] The figurative and largely passive connotations of dissolution combine easily in Keats's poetry with the active and fraught scientific meanings: in Isabella Lorenzo's catalytic spirit "mourn'd 'Adieu!'—dissolv'd and left / The atom darkness in a slow turmoil" (321–22); the poet of the "Ode to a Nightingale" would "Fade far away, dissolve, and quite forget," thereby achieving mental withdrawal from his world; formal "illuminings" from the constellation Aquarius "Dissolve the frozen purity of air" in Endymion (IV, 586); "Why does your tender palm dissolve in dew?" Lycius queries of the eminently dissoluble Lamia, whose very "words dissolv'd" earlier, and earlier still, during her passing life as a snake, Lamia bears silver moons that "as she breathed, / Dissolv'd, or brighter shone" (I, 370, 170, 52) in a manner no different from those experimental glowworms warmed by heat or those dying fish exposed to oxygen.

We cannot tell for certain whether Lamia's "spontaneous" light is the bioluminescence of a living creature or the biolysis of a dissolving former organism.

> She was a gordion shape of dazzling hue,
> Vermillion-spotted, golden, green, and blue;
> Striped like a zebra, freckled like a pard,
> Eyed like a peacock, and all crimson barr'd;
> And full of silver moons, that, as she breathed,

Dissolv'd, or brighter shone, or interwreathed
Their lustres with the gloomier tapestries—
(I, 47–54)

"So rainbow-sided" is the nameless and undifferentiated creature, she can bear affinities at once with the fountain-nymph's "Vermillion-tail'd" "rainbow-sided" fish (in Endymion) and with Nathaniel Hulme's newly dead herring. She is as ridiculous and magical as those neutral creatures that simultaneously live and die in the Ancient Mariner's sea. Thermometers and prisms exist in her poem to remind us of the changes wrought in life's light by heat and cold, of the refraction and decomposition of this light into colors, and of the dissolution of all color in the intensity of white light. Change is rapid, and the distinction between transformation and dissolution is often too quick and subtle to notice. Abruptly "melting into one colour," the multicolored Lamia changes light and form very quickly: "Still shone her crown; that vanish'd, also she / Melted and disappear'd as suddenly" (I, 165–66). We presume that Lamia's life as a colorful snake represented the staining of an original, purer being; that her transformation to a less colorful but warmly vibrant woman is an evolutionary ascent or return, a purer expression of life's light splendor. Yet we know that in her condition as a cold-blooded snake Lamia glows more brightly than in her life as a warm-blooded mammal, and that her final whiteness emits neither warmth nor light, vibrancy, passion, or intensity. Apollonius's vision without "passion to illume" and color unweaves all form (II, 274–76); Lamia's final transformation is a devolution from color to blight, a disintegration from transitory form to no form; she changes not to the "white radiance of Eternity" but to "a deadly white" of nothingness. Her lucid snakeskin and "dazzling frame" turn transparent vacuum. The consummate irony or paradox is that Lycius's deformed and passion-clouded imagination sees this dissolution of his nameless bride to be a separation instead of a melting union of distinctions marked by the satiation of love.

Life was exempt from corruption the scientists preceding the Romantic age had asserted. But as Humboldt's myth of the Genius of Rhodes pictured indelibly for his century, life was merely that which temporarily prevented putrefaction and dissolution—or what chemistry called the free combination and decomposition of elements. As the researchers into life's energy and the possibility of anaesthesia saw, the high intensity of the South American hummingbird masked its fragile heart, and surgery under "suspended animation" (as practiced by Henry Hickman) neutralized the differing sensations of life and death. Where the early eighteenth century saw in the concept of dissolution the very distinction between life and death,[28] the early nineteenth century looked too far and saw into the core of an eternal, fierce destruction; it sought proof of life's preservation from corruption in the cyclic indestructibility of nature only to find that nature's continuity masked decomposition and dissolution everywhere, a random chemistry of affinities that presaged finitude and eventual exhaustion. Nothing was exempted from corruption, and the distinction between life and death, far from being clear, proved only their reciprocity.

"For me, I sometimes think that Life is Death, / Rather than Life a mere affair of breath," Byron said in ironic echo of his age's primary anxiety.[29] The Romantic inquiry into the nature of life revealed everywhere the reversing truth of Thomas Mann's statement that "all interest in disease and death is only another expression of an interest in life."[30] Inquiry into what Keats called "this being's lease" revealed the essential dependence of life upon what John Hunter called the "stimulus of death."[31] At once "absolute fact and the most relative of phenomena" in the medical thought of this time, death was "the end of life" and disease; as Foucault says, "With death, the limit had been reached and truth fulfilled, and by the same breach"—in death the very signs of life and disease "intersected in indecipherable disorder" for "Death was that absolute beyond which there was neither life nor disease...."[32] Keats's own "But death's intenser—death is life's high mead" sums up the speculative potential of death's place as the culmination and consummation of life, as an active albeit finally unknown phenomenon of living, which was at once the mead, recompense, or just desert, and the terminal mystery of life itself.

When the brothers in *Isabella* disinterred the living basil plant from their sister's pot of memories, they found "The thing was vile with green and livid spot, / And yet they knew it was Lorenzo's face" (473–76). Lorenzo's passionate face, the lush basil, the molding brain-filled skull, and Isabella's green memory are inextricably one. Just as we cannot ignore the interconnection of cold weather and passion's heat in *The Eve of St. Agnes*,[33] so also can we never forget the inalienable interdependence of living and dead, cold memory and living desire, in Keats's version of Boccaccio's old tale.

> "I am a shadow now, alas! alas!
>   Upon the skirts of human-nature dwelling
> Alone: I chant alone the holy mass,
>   While little sounds of life are round me knelling,
> And glossy bees at noon do fieldward pass,
>   And many a chapel bell the hour is telling,
> Paining me through: those sounds grow strange to me,
> And thou art distant in Humanity.
>
> "I know what was, I feel full well what is,
>   And I should rage, if spirits could go mad;
> Though I forget the taste of earthly bliss,
>   That paleness warms my grave, as though I had
> A Seraph chosen from the bright abyss
>   To be my spouse: thy paleness makes me glad;
> Thy beauty grows upon me, and I feel
> A greater love through all my essence steal."
>   (*Isabella*, 305–20)

Dwelling alone upon the outskirts of human nature, the shadow that was once Lorenzo finds that the "little sounds of life" (of glossy bees, the traditional symbol of life's activity) knell his advancing deathliness, even as the passage of living hours and humans marked by the chapel bells brings enlivening pain to his dead state. The spirit of Lorenzo feels "full well what is" as the absence of "what was," and the cold paleness of Isabella's impending death warms his grave and gladdens his heart. Indeed, in concert with a central idea of Romantic psychological pathology, the apparition of Lorenzo is sufficient medical sign that Isabella labors under terminal consumptive disease.[34] Like those hungry spirits of Homer's and Virgil's underworlds, Lorenzo's deathliness feeds upon life and reverses life's signs: Isabella's beauty grows upon him even as she fades, disease ridden, into a seraph from the bright abyss (where life, as light, is fully indistinguishable from death), and a greater love steals through all his deathly essence bearing stolen life and earthly bliss. Truly, "when a soul doth thus its freedom win" from "this being's lease," "It aches in loneliness—is ill at peace" (219–20). Lorenzo feels loss, distinction, and reversal, and we are reminded thus by Keats of the interconnection or reciprocity of life and death, and of the ambiguities that pervade all scientific and poetic attempts to mark their individual signs and define their distinctions.

The deathly immortality of the fallen Titans in the two Hyperion poems provides no answer and defies all such distinction. Neither in "that old spirit-leaved book" of Uranus, "nor in sign, symbol, or portent / Of element, earth, water, air, and fire,— / At war, at peace, or inter-quarreling / One against one, or two, or three, or all / Each several one against the other three," not even "in that strife, / Wherefrom I take strange lore, and read it deep, / Can I find reason why ye should be thus:" Saturn tells his fellow divinities (Hyp., II, 133, 139–43, 146–49). The mortalized god can find no explanation for the Titans' fate in the lore of earth, water, air, and fire, but the Romantic poet finds in the dissolution of elements singly and together, and in the paradox of ripeness and love, keys to the recurring indistinctions of life and death.

Chapter 7

Hunter and the Life of Blood

Coagulation I conceive to be an operation of life; and I imagine it to proceed exactly upon the same principle as the union by the first intention; it is particle uniting with particle, by the attraction of cohesion, which, in the blood, forms a solid; and it is this coagulum, uniting with the surrounding parts, which forms the union by the first intention; for union by the first intention is no more than the living parts when separated, whether naturally or by art, forming a reciprocal attraction of cohesion with the intermediate coagulum, which immediately admits of mutual intercourse, and, as it were, one interest.

. . . .

In many modes of destroying life the blood is deprived of its power of coagulation, as happens in sudden death produced by many kinds of fits, by anger, electricity, or lightning; or by a blow on the stomach, etc. (Hunter, *Treatise on the Blood, Works*, 3:34)

Mr. Hunter who thought the Blood possessed Vitality thought it underwent a change like the contraction of Muscular Fibres at the time of death. The Muscles do not relax and the Blood does not coagulate in an Animal killed by lightning. Mr. C's opinion is the Blood is prevented from coagulating by nervous energy. (Keats, *Anatomical and Physiological Note Book*, Fourth Page, p. 5)

Cooper's and Cline's lecture "On the Blood" in their anatomy class was verbatim Hunter, and Keats's marginal notations here on Hunter's research on coagulation show full familiarity with those essentials that gave rise to Hunter's first declarations on the nature of life: life resided in the blood, which served as the place and medium for vitality; coagulation, an operation of life that proceeded upon the same principle as the union by the first intention, was the contractive response of living blood to the stimulus of injury or death; and polarizing energy, the materia vitae of living creatures or the electricity of inanimate nature, normally prevented coagulation within the body and promoted coagulation outside the body.[1] The life of blood was undeniable, Hunter said in his culminative work, *Treatise on the Blood, Inflamma-*

tion, and Gun-Shot Wounds (1794). (The Guy's Hospital Physical Society Library owned this work in its 1794 and its 1812 editions.) His research had showed conclusively the unique powers of the blood to unite living parts, to become vascular like other living parts, to maintain its uniform temperature even in the body's limbs and despite extreme environmental changes of heat and cold, to respond to stimuli as in the act of coagulation, to be "alive itself" while supporting life "in every part of the body," and to preserve life and prevent mortification in the paralytic parts of the body that lacked both motion and sensation.[2]

Blood released from the body formed discrete globules of fluid no different from those spherical units of life that Oken called *infusoria* and declared to be the living forms of all nature. Hunter declared that the blood "coagulates from an impression" in answer to "the necessary purpose of solidity"; it had, thus, a will or "the power of action within itself, according to the stimulus of necessity, which necessity arises out of its situation."[3] During the process of coagulation the fibres in the blood necessarily performed a distinctly vital act that was akin to muscular contraction: the more alive and in health the blood was, the more quickly it coagulated; in cases of ill health and specifically inflammation, the blood was less alive, less sensible to the stimulus of exposure, and less quick to coagulate. Coagulation thus revealed itself to Hunter as a living response that nurtured and promoted healing in healthy bodies, and, finally, in a contractive but living response to the stimulus of death, rendered forth its living principle.[4] "Accordingly," J. C. Prichard explains,

> when a quantity of blood flows into a basin, it is for a time, in the language of Mr. Hunter, truly alive. It soon dies, however, or is abandoned by the vital principle, and the last act of life is, like the convulsion which often takes place in the entire body at the moment of dissolution, a sort of stiffening and contraction, which produces the condensation of substance.[5]

The blood, therefore, was always alive; it manifested its living power in the maintenance and renewal of parts during the life of the animal, and its ability to clot during injury or in death revealed a unique and self-sufficient life power to respond to stimuli by increasing its degree of organization *outside the body*. Hunter believed that a quality of life, beyond the verities of chemical and mechanical research, was a precondition for living bodies' resistance to heat, cold, and putrefaction: "Mere organization can do nothing even in mechanics; it must still have something corresponding to a living principle. . . ."[6] In the life of blood, its manifest vital powers, its continual "unsettled state," its ceaseless motion, its independent power of action to coagulate in response to necessity, its pervasive presence in the body that yet maintained an integrity and independence from other secretions and all parts including the nerves and brain, Hunter found such a living principle.[7]

Other scientists before Hunter, not just vitalists like Hoffmann and Willis but numerous medical thinkers between Harvey and Galen, had noted the preeminence of the blood.[8] Even before these men, the ancient Greeks had understood *haema* to be the living substance that the child inherited from its parents, and Hebrew medicine had treated the blood as the vital principle in accordance with the saying in Genesis (9:4) that the soul of the flesh is the blood. But Hunter brought to his theory of the life of blood, and to his subsequent utterances on a vital principle that derived from this theory, a trusted reputation, the evidence of the operating room, and the weight of years of anatomical research. As a good physiologist of the new age he had sought for the source of life in the tangible materials of his discipline, and his empirical method had found it conclusively present in the blood of the physical body. So certain, verifiable, and recognizable did Hunter's theory on the life of blood seem (and so effective was its dissemination by Hunter's own printing press) that it gained quick and wide currency in the teachings, textbooks, and encyclopedias of the early nineteenth century. *Quincy's . . . Medical Dictionary* (1817) reminded medical students of the singularly vital place of blood as stimulant, respondent to stimuli (or injury), generator of warmth, regenerator of tissue, omnipresent nourisher of diverse parts, and living entity distinct from all other secretions and organs. John and Charles Bell's textbook on the anatomy of the human body noted that all "living properties are continued and propagated through the influence of the circulating blood," that although "nerves, muscles, and bones" have "all that is necessary to the mechanism of the frame," it is the blood with its "arteries, veins, and lymphatics, which are necessary to their constitution as living parts."[9] The fourth edition of the *Encyclopaedia Britannica* specifically supported Hunter's theory of the blood as the location and source of the vital principle over and against those who would "consider the brain and nervous system as the fountain of life":

> [It is] plain, even to demonstration, that the fluid secreted in the brain is *invisible* in its nature; and as we know the nervous fluid hath its residence in the brain, it is very probable, to use no stronger expression, that it is the peculiar province of the brain to secrete this fluid from the blood, and consequently that the blood originally contains the vital principle.

Far from deriving its vitality from an invisible and possibly nervous fluid, the blood provided the brain and other organs with a vitality appropriate to their organization; it was the specific source and conveyor of the invisible vital fluid (purportedly) present in the nervous system and secreted by the brain.[10]

The life ascribed to blood by Hunter became for the mechanistic thinkers a reiteration of their belief in the essential mechanism of the heart and circulatory system; its suggestion of an implicit rationality in the blood[11] became for the vitalistic philosophers of mind clear support for their belief in a conscious first cause; its pervasive integrity within the body, meanwhile, became manifest symbol for the Neoplatonists of a plastic force pervading the universe.

These theoretical interpretations of Hunter's vital principle, exemplified in the Abernethy-Lawrence debate of 1814–1819, lost sight of where this principle found its tangible source and of the method of practical observation that had revealed it to Hunter. Keats, nevertheless and by way of Hunter's clinical students, learned to appreciate the direct vitality of the blood, those "ruddy drops of life" (End., III, 546) and of its sufficiency "without / Any more subtle fluid" (Lamia, I, 305–7) for mortal existence. This knowledge endured in its factual simplicity to solace and haunt the years of his maturity as a poet.

Images of the blood in Keats's work—there are sixty-two of these in the poetry alone—are always true to Hunter's original doctrine of the life of blood; they neither draw speculative conclusions from this doctrine nor show preference for any one of Hunter's redactors. The tangible immediacy of these images endures even within the most abstract contexts. Endymion chooses mortal love over dreaming at the end of his poem, and his choice declares both a clinical knowledge and a poet's faith in "living blood," even as it reveals a renunciation of lifeless permanence born of an awareness true and terrible of the mortal contingencies of this blood and its expiring serum of life:[12]

> one human kiss!
> One sigh of real breath—one gentle squeeze,
> Warm as a dove's nest among summer trees,
> And warm with dew at ooze from living blood!
> Whither didst melt?
> (IV, 664–68)

Lamia finds it necessary to assure Lycius "that she was a woman, and without / Any more subtle fluid in her veins / Than throbbing blood" (I, 306–8)—which flows, forms discrete globules, oozes pale serum, melts, and dissipates with an even greater animate consistency, as Lycius (and Endymion before him) discovers, than inanimate dreams. Blood gels, congeals, and coagulates in "beaded dew drops" to provide one more archetypal image for the familiar Keatsian concept of arrested motion. Despite its characteristic "unsettled state," as volatile, moving fluid or coagulating mass of suspended globules, this living blood is nevertheless more pervasive and reliable in its responses than the ideals and insubstantialities that Keats would have it counter, often alarmingly so as the poet of The Fall of Hyperion discovers when faced with "the tyranny / Of that fierce threat" to live more intensely:

> suddenly a palsied chill
> Struck from paved level up my limbs,
> And was ascending quick to put cold grasp
> Upon those streams that pulse beside the throat:
> I shrieked; and the sharp anguish of my shriek
> Stung my own ears—I strove hard to escape

> The numbness; strove to gain the lowest step.
> Slow, heavy, deadly was my pace: the cold
> Grew stifling, suffocating, at the heart;
> And when I clasp'd my hands I felt them not.
> One minute before death, my iced foot touch'd
> The lowest stair. . . .
> > (I, 119–20, 122–33)

The response of the poet's living blood and inflamed senses to the forces of cold and fear and to the impending stimulus of injury or death, and the congealing chill that elicits a parallel response of polarized and coagulating stillness, are all anatomically correct and more fruitful as threats because they are factually true. The very life of blood and its living response threatens life. Exposure, Hunter said, triggers the living response of coagulation; too much exposure or external threat, here, elicits from blood that is always alive and feeling a consummate response to the stimulus of death: shocking stillness, torpidity, and senselessness—a suspension of life that is not essentially different from the stationing of autumn or the petrified movement of marbled artifacts. Hypostasis, the medical disorder characterized by an excess of blood in the organ, finds common ground with metaphysical hypostasis as the underlying substance or unchanging attitude of an entity.

The living action of blood can promote healing or presage death; it can also be summoned by the poet's memory for his last poem to invoke the terrifying power and immediacy of warm and volatile "red life" yearned for and remembered:

> This living hand, now warm and capable
> Of earnest grasping, would, if it were cold
> And in the icy silence of the tomb,
> So haunt thy days and chill thy dreaming nights
> That thou would wish thine own heart dry of blood,
> So in my veins red life might stream again,
> And thou be conscience-calm'd. See, here it is—
> I hold it towards you.

This macabre conceit of life luridly remembered and longed for long after its purported consummation (or final living response to the most intense "high mead," the stimulus of death) has as its central image an unnatural transfusion of blood between living and dead. Cold terror in *The Fall of Hyperion* made the poet's "heart too small to hold its blood" (I, 254); a ghoulish stimulus (of life remembered after death) in this poem would cause its listener to render forth an excess of blood from a heart suddenly too small to contain its allotted quantity of blood. In the earlier passage from *The Fall of Hyperion*, the poet is saved when, at the moment of cold death, his foot touches the marble stair and warm "life seem'd / To pour in at the toes" (I, 133–34); he responded correctly as a poet to "the tyranny / Of that fierce threat" (119–20) and was thereby rewarded with an infusion of life that is both physical and spiritual, mortal and transcendent. There, life's warmth exceeded the tyrannical and inescapable challenge of deadly coldness, and the distinction between life and death was made, miraculously, absolute. Here, the tyranny is born not of a need to exceed the intensity of death with a greater intensity for life but of a deathly intensity that requires the nutriment of "red life" and indeed preys upon life's blood precisely because the stimulus of death has been so strong that it attracts life too intensely and must therefore be transfused with living blood to nourish its very deathliness. The blood of "This living hand" (itself an incubus of the numerous hands of healing and succor in the poetry that precedes it) chills and dries the blood of those it would address. Death's heat here becomes life's cold; the transfusion, no longer strange, is the result of the natural law of affinity between seemingly opposing elements. Nature, even in its most macabre manifestations, seeks the merging of distinctions and an equilibrium between polarities.

We are reminded of Lorenzo's vampirish incubus in *Isabella* and the life it derives from her expiring love, of the reciprocity of life and death as a medical and poetic complex in all of Keats's poetry, and of the sense of shifting measures implied by the laws of affinity between intensities that was common to early-nineteenth-century scientific conceptualizations. Lamia succeeds in convincing the dreaming Lycius that she has no "more subtle fluid in her veins / Than throbbing blood." The poem of their union, meanwhile, takes pains to reveal that this "blood" is more subtle, more volatile, more capable of strange organizations outside the body (and therefore of a different order), and hints of the inevitable, unnatural consequences of these distinctions to their union. Lamia's life intensity, greater or lesser than Lycius's at all times, undermines the mask of human life that she wears and reveals the necessary distinction between species. Worse, it discovers her inconstant place between species—as a "palpitating snake" whose veins bear a cold and toxic serum and as a "lady bright" whose "elfin blood in madness ran" (I, 147). Hunter's formulations on living blood's unique power to maintain a constant temperature and resist the laws of equilibrium with regard to environmental cold gave impetus to contemporary research on the varying blood heat of reptiles, birds, and lemurs[13] and what this meant for the overall knowledge of life. Keats's whimsical composition of a creature like Lamia who requires no constancy of blood, and whose heart (such as it is) can alternately burn, seduce with "warm and tremulous" tones, and transfix with an "icy" chill, is an ironic contribution to the scientific inquiry of his age.

More direct and physiologically accurate evocations of the temperature, color, and action of the blood as the substance and emotional mirror of mortal life occur everywhere in Keats's poetry. "Yet at that moment, temperate was my blood," the poet says, on seeing a lock of Milton's hair (40), and the sonnet "On Fame" chides "the man who cannot look / Upon his mortal days with temperate blood"; young maiden's cheeks "flush wi' timid blood," in the early lyrics, and Endymion's story is punctuated with descriptions of "how the blood / Left his young cheek," or moments when he feels "suddenly a warm / Of his heart's blood" ("Ah, ken ye what," 27; *End.*, I, 727, III, 106–7). Blushing can be a characteristic of young love and joy ("Blush joyous blood through every lineament," Conrad says in *Otho*, I, i, 28), but also of things in a psycho-logically potent environment: Hyperion's palace "Glar'd a blood-red through all its thousand courts" (I, 179), and "A fan-shaped burst of blood- red, arrowy fire" volcanizes the atmosphere of *The Jealousies* (663). Slaves "melt / In blood from stinging whip," and a Ceylon diver's "ears gush'd blood" (as Astley Coo-per's paper on the tympanum showed they would) for Isabella's mercenary brothers, and at the end of the poem the brothers seek banishment with "blood upon their heads" that is both tangible and metaphorical (109–10, 115, 480). Blood-tinged guilt finds substantial and more complex place in *The Eve of St. Agnes* when "A shielded scutcheon blush'd with blood of queens and kings," depicted among the "carven imag'ries" of her bedroom casement, casts "blood red gules" upon "Madeline's fair breast," to stain her pale purity with the characteristic color of her "hot-blooded," "blood-thirsty race" (*Eve*, 209, 216, 218; ms. 207/208; 86, 99). The pulsating release action of the blood finds a graphic, stationed image when Endymion's horses "dully drop / Their full-veined ears, nostrils blood wide, and stop" (IV, 399–400), and when the poem "To Fanny" invokes the active form of the verb "to blood" to station its moment—"Physician Nature! let my spirit blood!"; specific images of the pulse as bearer of the action of the heart and blood, meanwhile, extend from tangible picture of the indolent subject whose "pulse grew less and less" in the "Ode on Indolence" (17) to a metaphorical expression of kindred intoxica-tion with Burns—"My pulse is warm with thine old barley-bree" in "This mortal body of a thousand days" (5).[14]

> A young man's heart, by heaven's blessing, is
> A wide world, where a thousand new-born hopes
> Empurple fresh the melancholy blood:
> But an old man's is narrow, tenantless
> Of hopes, and stuff'd with many memories,
> Which, being pleasant, ease the heavy pulse,
> Painful, clogg'd up and stagnant.
>   (*Otho*, III, ii, 180–86)

These lines from Keats's late and ever-sinking drama, although only marginally successful as poetry, are nevertheless physiologically true. Like the verse deal-ing with similar subjects in the early apprentice poetry—for example, Glaucus's declaration to Endymion: "I saw thee, and my blood no longer cold / Gave mighty pulses: in this tottering case / Grew a new heart" (III, 304–6)—they re-mind us that Keats's knowledge of contemporary research on the blood and its circulatory system was thorough, that his interest in it as a tangible symbol was enduring, and that his sense of the nature of mortal life (at least in its physical aspects) was very close to John Hunter's original theory of the life of blood.

Hunter had emphasized the extraordinary power of the blood to promote healing and the regeneration of organs, to the extent of even organizing itself outside the body in a polarized act of coagulation, and of its ability to accomplish these things independent of the nerves and brain.[15] While he had not specifically suggested that the blood could grow "a new heart," Hunter's research did place first emphasis on the blood and heart as the origin of life and source of all animal motion, warmth, and nutriment.[16] Hunter's theory of living blood, given its wide currency among the scientists of Keats's time, helped temporarily derail the growing tendency among theorists of life to see the brain and nervous system as the center of life in favor of a more basic (perhaps even traditionally Greek and Aristotelian) integrated physiology. Hunter's focus on the performance of living blood in the body as the key to mortal life emphasized the physiological connection between the actions of the blood and the manifestation of emotions like hope, fear, melancholy, and love; he thereby renewed interest in what was soon to become a Romantic concern, psychosomatic medicine, which was itself part of the Romantic search for an integrated philosophy of life.

In Book I of *Endymion* the young protagonist falls from the "dangerous sky" into a more dangerous cavern of seeming waste and sterility similar to the Titans' abode in the Hyperion poems; "hollow sounds" awaken him and he resolves to faint again,

> I was distracted; madly did I kiss
> The wooing arms which held me, and did give
> My eyes at once to death: but 'twas to live,
> To take in draughts of life from the golden fount
> Of kind and passionate looks:
>   (I, 653–57)

Love, even the adolescent variety, nurtures life; lovers can "take in draughts of life from the golden fount / Of kind and passionate looks." Love may very well be the manifestation of life, the moment when an intangible principle of life bodies (or bloods) forth—as some more successful lines later in the same poem suggest:

> but who, of men, can tell
> That flowers would bloom, or that green fruit would swell
> To melting pulp, that fish would have bright mail,
> The earth its dower of river, wood, and vale,
> The meadows runnels, runnels pebble-stones,
> The seed its harvest, or the lute its tones,

Tones ravishment, or ravishment its sweet,
If human souls did never kiss and greet?
(I, 835–42)

A truly unoriginal exclamation of Endymion from Book II—"O my love, / My breath of life, where art thou" (686–87)—makes the secular connection between love and life even more directly. Tiresome as is Endymion's emotionalism, and however difficult it may be to tell whether he suffers from the trials of life or merely the turmoil of lovesickness, or whether he feels most intensely when awake or in a faint, his verse-story nevertheless has its purpose. In the course of writing *Endymion*, Keats learned to write poetry. The young doctor and apprentice poet in him also came to see clearly—pertinent to our subject—in the blood's manifestation of its life in the bloom of health and the blush of emotion, the inextricable connection between the physiology of living blood and the psychology of human love. Keats's belief in the physicality of life and the truth of the passions—embodied in his comment of March 1819 to the George Keatses, "Though a quarrel in the street is a thing to be hated, the energies displayed in it are fine"—never let him forget this connection, and it informs (sometimes at several removes) even the most abstract subjects of his poetry. Sympathy was indeed, as Astley Cooper taught, the characteristic response of living tissue. Love and life, with the tangible substance of living blood in common between them, and sharing (in elective affinity and in instinctive coagulation) the symbol of a nurturing act of polarized unity, were interchangeable complexes; they could be invoked equally in moments of lovelorn emotion (in early verses like *Endymion*) or moments of intense verity (in poems like *Isabella* or *The Fall of Hyperion*).

The pattern for seeing a bloodlike nurturing (or life-giving) aspect in the power of emotional attachments or friendship is set in *Endymion*. There, at the top of "the chief intensity" (and Keatsian intensity itself is a complex derived from his medical readings on the nature of evolving life, as we shall see in Part IV) sits "a crown" made up of love and friendship. Friendship is the "ponderous and bulky worth" of this crown,

> but at the tip-top,
> There hangs by unseen film, an orbed drop
> Of light, and that is love: its influence,
> Thrown in our eyes, genders a novel sense,
> At which we start and fret; till in the end,
> Melting into its radiance, we blend,
> Mingle, and so become a part of it,—
> Nor with aught else can our souls interknit
> So wingedly: when we combine therewith,
> Life's self is nourish'd by its proper pith,
> And we are nurtured like a pelican brood.
> (I, 805–15)

Life, friendship, love, and the selfless act of nourishment combine, mingle, and melt here. However "winged" the concepts of this much-glossed passage, the final image of "Life's self . . . nourish'd by its proper pith" is a physical one; and lest we forget the primary source for both concepts and image, the fable to which the last line refers tells us that the pelican's blood nourishes her brood.

The pediment surmounting the central part of the broken architrave in the façade to Guy's Hospital depicts a female figure, perhaps Hygeia, holding a tightly swaddled infant and supported at the elbow by a sculpted composition of a pelican feeding her brood with her own blood. The bird crouches over her young, her neck extended downward in a semicircle to bite at a breastbone artery, and the mouths of the chicks gape hungrily toward the wound. The image is identical to that found in one of the carved wooden roof bosses at nearby Southwark Cathedral, and we are reminded of how Renaissance iconography made Christian a pagan tale of self-sacrifice and nourishment in the animal kingdom. John Hunter had treated of the life of blood without overt reference to Christian mythology, and Keats's generation of medical students inherited the myth as at once secular, sacred, and biologically true.[17] We are nurtured like a pelican brood; mortal life is nurtured by its own blood, its own emotional vitality.

> "Love! thou art leading me from wintry cold,
> Lady! thou leadest me to summer clime,
> And I must taste the blossoms that unfold
> In its ripe warmth this gracious morning time."

Lorenzo's courtly speech to Isabella at the start of their friendship is notable for its images of growth, warmth, and imminent blooming ripeness. Their love, we are told shortly thereafter, "Grew, like a lusty flower in June's caress" (65–72). The lovers themselves bloom and blush in manifest sign of a healthy love; they nurture one another to a greater vitality that is also a more intense love. Lorenzo's murder, which prevents their future natural union, is also an unnatural and macabre substitute for the consummation of love. With Lorenzo's death the polarizing energy of their love begins to dissipate, and Isabella, "soon to be / Among the dead," begins to die: "She withers, like a palm / Cut by an Indian for its juicy balm" (446–48). Whatever remains of the energy of their emotion now begins to congeal around the memory of their love; whatever remains vital in Isabella goes to nurture the tangible symbol of this remembered love, the basil plant. The "continual shower / From her dead eyes" (452–53), be this shower tears, balm, or the serum of her ebbing life, provides nutriment for the green memory of an intense emotion, a center for a vitality that was once so great that even Lorenzo's fading spirit can draw temporary strength from it: "I feel," the apparition of Lorenzo says of Isabella's bloodless face, "A greater love through all my essence steal" (319–20). Life energy is finite (as Keats well knew from medicine and from the wisdom of maturity), even the vitality of such a pair of lovers; energy consumes energy to exhaustion. Once the basil plant is removed from its enlivening place between the pair, the polarizing counter of what remains of the union is lost, Lorenzo's spirit dissipates, and we hardly notice the actual death of Isabella (497–98).

When Isabella grows pale, "That paleness warms [Lorenzo's] grave" (316). This exchange of blood warmth or vitality between lovers is a familiar pattern in Keats's poetry; energy is given and taken (or stolen) between lovers according to their relative life intensities; they burn, blush, turn pale, or chill alternately, and an equilibrium of vitality is maintained for the duration of the relationship or union. When Hermes "burns" for the nymph in *Lamia* and "towards her stept: she, like a moon in wane, / Faded before him ... self-folding like a flower / That faints into itself at evening hour: / But the God fostering her chilled hand, / She felt the warmth ... And ... Bloom'd" (I, 136–43). Unlike the great but nevertheless mortal love of Isabella and Lorenzo, or even that fine passion of Madeline and Porphyro in *The Eve of St. Agnes* that waxes and wanes in parallel motion to St. Agnes's moon, the love intensity of Hermes and the nymph does not fade: "Into the green-recessed woods they flew; / Nor grew they pale, as mortal lovers do" (144–45). Immortality guarantees inexhaustion of passion as of life energy. Only two other sets of lovers in Keats's poetry are permitted such luxury: Psyche and Eros and the young lovers on the Grecian urn. Both sets burn without burning out, and they can maintain a polarized union that is not followed, according to Humboldt's law of life and love, by satiety, exhaustion, and dissolving corruption. Psyche and Eros lie with "Their arms embraced, and their pinions too; / Their lips touch'd not, but had not bade adieu"; they endure "ready still past kisses to outnumber" (16–19), and their sublime excuse is that they are immortal. The "more happy love" of the callow lovers on the Grecian urn is of a different order from the immortal love of Eros and Psyche (or Hermes and the nymph), and of a different degree from mortal love. It is, as we will discuss in a later chapter of this part, an excess without excuse, and a luxury most dearly bought: wrought by mortality, the Grecian lovers marbled love manifests itself finally as an overwrought life substitute without substance.

Chapter 8

The Quarrel over Hunter's Principle

John Hunter said in 1786 that the living principle was distinct from elemental matter. It was "something superadded" to animate parts that was manifest in their irritability; as such, life could be recognized by its "power of resisting the operations of external chemical agency" so as to prevent decomposition in the bodies where it resided.[1] Keats's notes on anatomy and physiology (of the course he took from Astley Cooper and Henry Cline, Jr.) are marked by elements from Hunter's theory and experiments on life:

> It is supposed that Ganglia are giving power to Nerves which give involuntary Action. The opinion of late years entertained concerning the Cause of nervous energy was stated by Mr. J. Hunter. He examined [the] Body of a Gymnotus Electricus [and] he found it provided with [an] abundance of Nerves sufficient to account for its electric properties. From this he inferred that the Nerves were conductor[s] of electric fluid. Galvani found that a[n] action of [the] Nerves was produced by applying Metal thereto. The present opinion therefore is that a fluid, like that of the electric is secreted in [the] brain which is thence communicated along the Nerves.[2]

Nerves stimulated by irritation to involuntary motion, the purported connection between nerves, nervous power and electrical properties, the notion of a vital fluid secreted by the brain and communicated through the body by the nerves—all these concepts belong with Hunter's premises on animation and with the theories on life of Galvani, Haller, and the electromagnetists of Hunter's time. In his lectures Astley Cooper translated the teachings on life of his mentor into a theory of life and motion based on nervous irritability and sympathy, as Keats's notes of these lectures show:

> Mr. C. believes that the power of parts are supported neither by [the] Brain nor the M.S. [muscular system?] but by their particular Nerves. *Sympathy.* By this the Vital

Principle is chiefly supported. The function of breathing is a sympathetic action—from irritation produced on the beginning of [the] Air Tube [that] affects [the] Abdominal Muscles and produces coughing. Sneezing is an instance of complicated sympathy. We need not say any thing about the sympathy between the Breast and [the] uterus.[3]

Sympathy, elicited directly or indirectly by the vital principle, supported the vital principle and was the characteristic response of living tissue. In an assumption of Hunter's thinking on the vital principle, the Brunonian doctrine of excitability, and contemporary notions of muscular and nervous responsiveness to stimuli, Cooper took irritability to be the measure and mark of animated life:

In infancy the irritability is excessive, and the system is easily excited to destruction: after the period of two years, the irritability is considerable, but the powers of restoration are great. In middle age, the irritability is less, and the restorative power is still considerable: in old age the irritability is much diminished, but the powers of restoration are less also.[4]

Although the entry "Irritability" in the 1810 edition of the Encyclopaedia Britannica defines it as quite distinct from sensibility in that it is a characteristic of muscles and not nerves, the more general entry "Physiology" in the same edition proposes that "irritability partakes of and is a (lower) form of sensibility." For Cooper, irritability was the measurable and latent mark of life in both muscular and nervous tissue; sympathy or the response of living creation to the stimulation of this irritability, likewise, was characteristic of muscles and nerves, senses and will. Cooper's formulation on irritability as the single property of all living tissue is not a passing confusion of Haller's seventeenth-century distinctions between irritability and sensibility but rather a deliberate albeit mechanistic attempt (influenced by Brunonian excitability) to establish relation and teach by inclusion. The speculative implications of the concepts of irritability and sympathy as they are evoked in Astley Cooper's teachings on the nature of life, moreover, allow them to be seen as first seed for the Keatsian concepts of intensity, negative capability, and the unpoetical poetic character.

Astley Cooper was not Keats's only source for formulations on what came to be called "the Hunterian principle" of life during the 1814–1819 quarrel between John Abernethy and William Lawrence. Teachers at Guy's Hospital like Babington and Curry, for example, began their lectures on the practice of medicine by noting that the difference between an inanimate machine and the living body was owed "to the latter being endowed with PRESERVING PRINCIPLE, or Vis Medicatrix Naturae." An older perception from English medicine on natural cure and living tissue's propensity for health combined with Hunter's oft-defined "principle" to describe life for Babington and Curry's students as "a principle of activity and of preservation, most remarkable in the nervous and muscular substance. . . ."[5] Babington and Curry cautioned students on the "Ambiguity of the term Vis Vitae," and of the impossibility of defining a principle that was "diffused throughout both solids and fluids of the body, and apparently existing in these in different degrees in different persons, and under different circumstances." John Haighton, a lecturer on physiology and midwifery at Guy's during Keats's tenure there, warned more specifically in his first lecture on "Life": "Attempts have been made to give an idea of life by analogy: as to the Spring of a Clock which gives movement to its different parts, others have compared it to Electricity which likewise gives motion to light bodies; and others again have compared it to Magnetism as communicated to Iron. But none of these analogies give us an adequate idea of Life."[6] Qualifications such as these testify to the overall impossibility of defining life; they also testify specifically—and most notably in Haighton's attempt to give equal weight to individual theories of life even as he declares them cumulatively inadequate—to the wide currency in London during Keats's student years of those controversial ideas on life that were fueling the Lawrence-Abernethy debate over what Hunter thought and taught about life.

Life could not exist independent of the animal body according to William Lawrence; it was immediately dependent upon organization, and nothing more than "the assemblage of all the functions."[7] Lawrence was a former student of John Abernethy and, from 1815, a junior lecturer of anatomy and physiology at the Royal College of Surgeons; his formulations on life to the college between 1816 and 1818 were ostensibly in response to what he declared were Abernethy's vitalistic misinterpretations of John Hunter's mechanistic theory of life. Experience and observation, not metaphysical subtlety or immaterial abstractions, had convinced him, he said, that life was "merely the active state of the animal structure" that included all notions of sensation, motion, and volition; he found the analogy between electricity and vitality to be foolish and ridiculed Abernethy's attempt to make the properties of a substance extraneous to the substance:

> The powers, properties, or qualities of a substance, are not to be regarded, then, as any thing superadded to the substance, or distinct from it. They are only the substance itself, considered in relation to various changes that take place, when it exists in peculiar circumstances. . . . To call life a property of organization would be unmeaning:—it would be nonsense. The primary or elemental animal structures are endued with vital properties; their combinations compose the animal organs, in which, by means of the vital properties of the component elementary structures, the animal functions are carried on. The state of the animal, in which the continuance of these processes is evidenced by obvious eternal signs, is called life.[8]

Ample proof of all this could be found in the research of John Hunter. Lawrence allowed that living bodies exhibited a striking distinction from inanimate matter—an apparent exception from the laws of chemistry—"composed of matters extremely prone to decomposition, and surrounded by all the influences of heat, air, and moisture," they are nevertheless free from dissolution. But Lawrence could explain even this phenomenon as the product of constant internal motion, "an uninterrupted admission and assimilation of new, and a corresponding separation and expulsion of old particles. . . . While this motion lasts, the body is said to be alive;—when it has irrecoverably ceased, to be dead. The organic structure then yields to the chemical affinities of the surrounding agents, and is speedily destroyed." Thus, "Life presupposes organization [or the composition and arrangement of constituent parts], as the movements of a watch presuppose the wheels, levers, and other mechanism of the instrument."[9]

Lawrence assailed religious teachings: he questioned the biblical account of creation and queried whether Noah's ark could have held all the species. He doubted the immateriality of the soul and wondered whether the commonly observed connection between life and respiration, coupled with a misinterpretation of the Greek and Latin terms for "breath" and "spirit," had produced "all the abstractions and fancies, all the verbal sophistry and metaphysical puzzles about spirit."

> If the intellectual phenomena of man require an immaterial principle superadded to the brain, we must equally concede it to have more rational animals which exhibit manifestations differing from some of the human only in degree. If we grant it to these, we cannot refuse it to the next in order, and so on in succession to the whole series—to the oyster, the sea-anemone, the polype, the microscopic animalcules. Is any one prepared to admit the existence of immaterial principles in all these cases? If not, he must equally reject it in man.[10]

Oysters could not think. Only the woolly-headed metaphysicians and poets of earlier ages would so ascribe an immaterial principle of life and intellect to mollusks, polyps, and sea anemones; clear-thinking scientists of the early nineteenth century knew from observation that immaterial principles were as uncertifiable in man as in animals and machines. Indeed, "Each animal may be considered as a partial machine, co-operating with all the other machines, the whole of which form the universe." For Lawrence and the French physiologists from whom he derived his inspiration, the human body was a complex machine of tightly synchronized action, and consciousness was nothing more than a ghost in the machine.[11] No wonder then that Lawrence was an object of peculiar (and occasionally repellent) fascination for the London medical students (like Keats) and poets (like Shelley and Byron) of his time.

A difference in degree—manifest by a certain radical attitude of mind—distinguished the mechanistic physiology of the late Romantic era in England, exemplified by Lawrence's formulations, from the more complacent and limited mechanism of earlier periods and philosophies. William Lawrence's particular brand of mechanism, cast first in the skeptical tradition of British empiricism, belongs to the extreme, pervasive, and determined mechanism of the mid-to-late-eighteenth-century European physiologists. In Bichât's declaration that "life consists in the sum of the functions, by which death is resisted," and in his description of how living organisms resist their chemical environment (which tends to their destruction) through a principle of reaction that is tailored to the tissue of the individual organs, and in Cuvier's declaration that life was but "the totality of the phenomena" that occasioned its formation,[12] we easily recognize the first sources for Lawrence's definition of life. When Lawrence directly acknowledges the inspiration of Bichât's "account of the division of the animal functions" and Cuvier's "luminous and philosophical" but also thoroughly materialistic "view of life" upon what he summarizes as the early nineteenth-century's conception of life for Rees's *Cyclopaedia* (1819), we are forced to note that Lawrence believes his narrowly mechanical perception of life to have preemptive precedence and scientific right over earlier more inclusive vitalistic formulations; we are also forced to acknowledge that Lawrence speaks not just for himself but for his generation of late Romantic thinkers in declaring allegiance to the French mechanists.

The specifically radical nature of Lawrence's formulations, furthermore, are to be traced beyond Bichât and Cuvier to the spare and minimal ideas concerning life of d'Holbach, La Mettrie, and the early Cabanis. D'Holbach's *Système de la nature* (1770) explained evolution as the response of natural forces to the necessities of climate; La Mettrie's L'*Homme machine* (1748) purported to prove that matter was self-determinate, and animated bodies like the swamp polyp had "all that is necessary to them in order to move, feel, think, have remorse, and to conduct themselves";[13] Cabanis proposed that all morality was chemistry, for just as the stomach, liver, and other glandular organs produced their typical secretions, so also did the healthy brain produce moral thought.[14] In Romantic England, eighteenth-century French mechanism combined with a vengeance with the skeptical empiricism of Locke, Hume, and Hartley. Scientists like John Hunter could absorb such ideas into their empirical research and subsume them within a more comprehensive and implicitly vitalistic science of life. But the generation that followed Hunter, witnessing the rapid specialization of the sciences and the seeming omnipotence of empirical method as assumed by the mechanists, could not rest so easy. To these radical and yet minimalistic ideas on the nature of life as they found larger expression in Lawrence and his fellow skeptical physiologists, and to the wider and negating implication of these ideas for Romantic biology and *Naturphilosophie*'s comprehensive metaphysics, Romantic thinkers of the second and third decade of the nineteenth century were, suddenly and alarmingly, fully vested heirs.

Coleridge in 1816 looked back and blamed not the eighteenth-century French or contemporary English physiologists but Newton himself for having given the primary impetus to a "Corpuscular and mechanical Philosophy," a stark worldview of a universe made up of machines whose ultimate elements were indivisible particles of matter capable of being set in motion, and for having perpetrated the monstrous fiction of a creator of reality who accorded with his creation, a mindless but omnipresent mover and mechanic of all the particles.[15] The attitude of mind revealed in the radical mechanistic philosophy voiced by Lawrence was, as Coleridge and Abernethy correctly saw, dangerous to the quest for knowledge and injurious to human society: it espoused a discipline of voracious territorialism, even as it encouraged the separation and breakdown of the disciplines of human knowledge. Early Romanticism, especially in its German inspiration, had defended a qualitative and comprehensive knowledge against Newtonian physics; it had placed physiology and the science of life at the center of this transcendent knowledge, as the ultimate inextinguishable bulwarks against physics' conquest by rule and number. The vigorous and territorial mechanism of English physiologists like Lawrence, which proudly evoked the atheistic inspiration of the French who had succeeded Newton, began with a physiological study of life that quickly transformed itself into a comprehensive mode of skeptical inquiry directed at life itself; life was not just material, it was mechanical. And the very physiology of life was used to undermine life as a whole and those theories on soul, creation, and the indestructibility of life forms that supported it.

An earlier and somewhat benign materialism was thus replaced during Keats's lifetime by a "mechanical" way of thinking that was both philosophy and method. Animal energies were the product of chemical agitation and physical function, and the physiologist fascinated by the new science of biology found he had to be a chemist and physicist first before he could be a biologist.[16] Biology was thus divorced forever from theology and metaphysics and allied necessarily with chemistry and the newer physics of spatial and thermal dynamics. The rules applied equally to processes in the organic and nonorganic world. Moreover, the parts were equal to the whole; there was need for neither Newton's watchmaker nor *Naturphilosophie*'s transcendent force. Indeed, the very terms *force* and *energy*, once exclusively used by the *Naturphilosophen* and vitalists to evoke the mysterious and subtle nature of life, were now possessed by the mechanists to justify and codify their thinking— the manifestations, modifications, and interactions of forces and energies, whether in chemical dynamics, electrodynamics, or thermodynamics, were *the* subject of mechanistic science;[17] a material or immaterial substratum in which these forces might inhere was unnecessary to explain either life or the laws of the living universe. It was manifestly against the laws of physics, chemistry, and even biology for Noah's ark to have contained all those species of life. Thus, with their spare and narrow definition of evolving life, Lawrence and his fellow skeptics aimed, grandly, to replace the science of life, by way of a reductive and dissolving electrochemistry, with an abstracted and eminently verifiable science of space, dimension, and motion. The irony is that the radical and voracious mechanism which so horrified Romantic philosophers like Coleridge and Friedrich Schlegel, and Romantic physicians like Abernethy and J. H. Green, as the very thing anathema to all Romantic values of vital integration grew out of the ranging and fearless inquiry into life that Romanticism inaugurated. Lawrence dedicated his lectures to J. F. Blumenbach, one of Coleridge's heroes, and displayed considerable knowledge of German scientific literature. Schlegel and the *Naturphilosophen* who preceded him sought a comprehensive philosophy of organicism at whose center resided a science of life and the Romantic physician's primal vision of it; mechanists of the first half of the nineteenth century, like Lawrence, believed they had inaugurated such a revolutionary and encompassing science in a mechanical philosophy of organic textures and functions whose methods and terms could absorb biology into the very center of its machinery and embrace not just the new sciences of chemistry and atomic physics but even natural history, anthropology, and sociopolitical theory. Life depended upon organization, the mechanists said, and in William Lawrence's later theories of natural history and anthropology the biological and social senses of the term *organization* coincided. A philosophy that denied the age-old notion that organs possessed a special and individualized vital power which was responsible for their diverse functions and asserted instead and conclusively that organic function was accounted for by the mechanical construction of the organ, that the whole operated according to the physical configuration of the parts, and that the only substratum of life was an all-too-scrutable diversity of texture, made organization a key activity of inner and outer life; it was thus eminently accessible and inclusively hospitable to the revolutionary theorists of its polity who proposed that Carnot had "organized victory" and declared Napoleon to be "*un génie organisateur.*"[18]

We cannot underestimate the influence of such radical mechanistic philosophy upon the intellectual makeup of late Romantics like Shelley, Byron, and Keats. George Felton Mathew considered Keats to be "of the skeptical and republican school. An advocate for the innovations which were making progress in his time. A faultfinder with everything established."[19] In London during the critical period between 1814 and 1817, Keats would have known of the new ideas in physiology being debated in the London medical community and, though he was not a student of Lawrence, would certainly have been familiar with the key aspects of the Abernethy-Lawrence controversy.[20] Keats's physiological notebook shows a familiarity with Abernethy, and he would have known the substance of the controversy from his teachers and student friends. His teachers at Guy's and St. Thomas's were heavily influenced by the contemporary mechanistic physiology: Astley Cooper, for example, expressed Jacobin ideas in his lectures (he had visited Paris in 1792 to see the revolution and was a close associate of the radical atheist Thelwall)[21] and was largely mechanistic in his teachings.

In 1822 Lawrence, tired of the public outcry over his "atheistic views," and faced with the very real threat of losing his appointment as surgeon to the royal hospitals of Bridewell and Bethlem, withdrew his *Lectures* from circulation and promised to refrain from future publications "on similar subjects."[22] The quarrel with Abernethy over the nature of life, at its height between 1816 and 1818, had fostered a much larger controversy on the subject that continued after Lawrence left the fray and through the next two decades, with leading spokesmen like Thomas Charles Morgan, Thomas Rennell, Charles Bell, and J. C. Prichard. In what was essentially his last salvo, the summary article "Life" for Rees's *Cyclopaedia*, Lawrence articulated the nature of the insoluble problem that was to haunt thinkers on both sides of the philosophical debate:

> So narrow are the limits of the human understanding, that the knowledge of first causes seems placed forever beyond our reach. The thick veil which covers them, envelops in its innumerable folds whoever attempts to break through it. In the study of nature, principles are certain general results of first causes, from which innumerable secondary results proceed; the art of discovering the connection between these primary and secondary results is the object of every judicious mind. To seek the connection between first causes and their general effects, is like walking blindfold through a road from which we may stray by a thousand parts.[23]

The metaphor, Janus-faced, points both ways. Shelley, Lawrence's friend, in 1821 referred to those vital principles or "general results of first causes from which innumerable secondary results proceed," which the mechanists themselves considered to be life and the object of their inquiry, as "the painted veil which / We call life."

The grave attempts by the mechanists to undermine what lay beneath and beyond the apparent vital properties and functions, to mistake the painted veil for the thing itself and so use life's refractions to obliterate life, alarmed the English vitalists of Keats's time to such a degree that they rushed to denounce the "band of modern skeptics," thereby themselves risking envelopment by the "innumerable folds" of the "thick veil" that (as one of these skeptics had maintained) human understanding could not break. Consciousness, they insisted, could transcend the empirical reasoning of mechanism and penetrate the mystery of life. Abernethy, Lawrence's most energized opponent, declared, "We should not . . . suffer crude speculations to go forth, bearing the seeming stamp of medical authority, when they are contrary to the sentiments of the bulk of the profession, derogatory to its character, and injurious to society."[24] The mechanists with their deductive reasoning were the crude speculators on an unknown territory of life; young medical minds of the profession of healing, and life itself, were to be protected from such limiting presumptiveness. The imaginative intensity of the counterrevolution launched during the years of Keats's intellectual maturity by Romantic physicians and philosophers like Coleridge, Green, and Abernethy himself, especially in the fractured but ultimately vital options it provided poets who were schooled too well in the methodic irrefutabilities of mechanistic science, requires equal time.

John Hunter's "vitalism" was a simple concept—which he tendered cautiously on those occasions when the findings of his anatomical research necessarily fell short. "Animal and vegetable substances differ from common matter in having a power superadded totally different from any other known property of matter," he said. Life in plants is "a power of action within the vegetable itself, independent of any mechanical power"; in plants and animals alike it regulates heat, causes action, and is "something that prevents the chemical decomposition" to which dead matter is prone. Because principle could not succeed modification, the living principle had to exist as "something superadded to this peculiar modification of matter."[25] But Abernethy proposed that if "these opinions should become so established as to be generally admitted by philosophers," and if thinking persons

> once saw reason to believe that life was something of an invisible and active nature superadded to organization; they would then see equal reason to believe that mind might be superadded to life, as life is to structure. They would then indeed still further perceive how mind and matter might reciprocally operate on each other by means of an intervening substance. Thus even would physiological researches enforce the belief which I may say is natural to man; that in addition to his bodily frame, he possesses a sensitive, intelligent and independent mind. . . .[26]

This visionary and moral—but as he believed logical—elaboration of John Hunter's theory of life was Abernethy's answer to those skeptical mechanists who would make the life of matter their exclusive domain and the only subject of scientific inquiry, even as they sundered life from all concepts of mind. Abernethy conceded that "the brain is as much an organ of sensation and thought, as the liver and stomach are organs for the secretion of bile and gastric fluid," but he read in Hunter's denial that life was the result of organization proof that "life actually constructed the very means by which it carried on its various processes." Far be it that Milton should have "from the glands of his brain / Secreted his Paradise Lost." From Hunter's suggestion that the functions of life were "the result of subtle principles commixed with the visible fabric of living beings," Abernethy deduced that the brain did not merely and mechanically produce sensations and thoughts but rather was an organ of mind or intellect which, in the form of consciousness, was superimposed upon certain living matter.[27]

Abernethy assumed the task of finding analogies of Hunter's purported theory in past medical thought and in contemporary research. He found the symbol for the Hunterian principle of life, a "subtile, mobile, invisible substance" that Hunter might have located in his dissection of electric gymnoti, in contemporary research on electricity:

The phaenomena of electricity and of life correspond. Electricity may be attached to, or inhere, in a wire; it may be suddenly dissipated, or have its powers annulled, or it may be removed by degrees or in portions, and the wire may remain less and less strongly electrified, in proportion as it is abstracted. So life inheres in vegetables and animals; it may sometimes be suddenly dissipated, or have its powers abolished, though in general it is lost by degrees, without any apparent change taking place in the structure; and in either case putrefaction begins when life terminates.

For Abernethy, Humphry Davy had proved that chemistry was really electricity—he had "solved the great and long hidden mystery of chemical attraction, by shewing that it depends upon the electrical properties which the atoms of different species of matter possess." Abernethy would prove that electricity was the analogue, if not the actuality, of life. Hunter's theory of a vital principle was fully verifiable by demonstration and deduction, for "by showing that a subtile substance of a quickly and powerfully mobile nature, seems to pervade every thing, and appears to be the life of the world," the phenomena of electricity made "probable that a similar substance pervades organized bodies, and produces similar effects in them."[28] Davy's electrical experiments had realized the speculations of ancient philosophers concerning the Anima Mundi. It was possible to be a scientist and a vitalist, and the way was prepared for replacing Newton's watchmaker and the ghost of machines past with a universal electrochemist[29] resident in all living bodies and manifest as an imminent and overweening original consciousness.

The vitalism of Abernethy, and the vitalism of those (like Coleridge, Bell, and Green) who joined the debate on his side, is to be distinguished from the vitalism of earlier periods and the century preceding him by its deliberate and urgent attempt to place consciousness at the center of the theory of life. Hunter's formulations on life largely avoided utterance on the subject of mind and consciousness and preferred instead the more tangible symbols of coagulation and blood. Abernethy invoked Hunter's principle of life and placed it in uneasy alliance with insubstantial and metaphysical declarations on life from Thales to Van Helmont and Stahl, not just in order to incorporate matter and mind and bind physiology and psychology together inextricably but to posit the manifest existence of a knowledgeable and creative consciousness. To preempt criticism, Abernethy called upon contemporary theories of electrochemistry and atomic physics and used the current terminologies of mechanical function and organization to support his formulations. The probability of Abernethy's success in formulating a visionary, comprehensive, and convincing theory of life can be gauged from the fragmented, limited, and ultimately uneasy utterances on life of the very scientists whose work he had invoked, like Davy, Priestley, and Saumarez.

Erasmus Darwin, also a vitalist well learned in French mechanism (and seeking to be *the* Baconian physician of the Romantic age) had made a less sophisticated but no less ambitious attempt at a comprehensive theory of life in *Zoonomia* (1796). A single subtle fluid rather like Abernethy's Hunterian electricity, the "sensorial power," was responsible for the organization of life and all its irritative, sensitive, voluntary, and associative phenomena; external stimulants worked through this "sensorial power" or "spirit of animation" which was invisible except by its effects and "too subtle to be long confined in any part of the system" but nevertheless declared its presence as the "single living filament" essential to living organization and existing in every gland and organ of the body. However, Darwin took care to delineate the limits of his subject: "By the words spirit of animation or sensorial power, I mean only that animal life which mankind possess in common with brutes, and in some degree even with vegetables, and leave the consideration of the immortal part of us, which is the object of religion, to those who treat of revelation."[30] With such circumscriptions Darwin sought to remain true to his trust in the physiological even as he avoided charges of vitalistic speculation and heretical materialism. But by proposing two kinds of life of which only the first or material kind was the domain of medicine, Darwin advocated a necessary division between matter and spirit for the proper inquiry into life. He also drew attention to the common problem of nineteenth-century physiologists, namely, that the distinction between material and spiritual life was hardly clear and could shift according to the physiological research of the scientists, much as it did with the speculative vitalism of the philosophers.

Darwin's spirit of animation, for all his disclaimers, was conceptually no different from Humboldt's more vitalistic conception of the genius of Rhodes; each had produced, out of his physiological research, comparably speculative conceptions of life that nevertheless expressed their respective materialistic and vitalistic philosophies. Their definitions of life are representative of the Romantic physician's "first glimpse" into the nature of life at the start of the nineteenth century, and of the limitations inherent in all such attempts to prescribe the nature of life—witnessed by the controversy over life in England during the second decade of the nineteenth century. Indeed, when Prichard sought to summarize what his century knew and thought about life in 1829, he found little progress beyond the unifying Romantic vision of certain vitalistic physicians; other mechanistic and electrochemical theories had made fragmentary contributions to the truths of life but these were limited by a specificity that undermined the larger concept of life. For example, he acknowledged that the state of vitality in living bodies like seeds, in which vital action had yet to commence, could be explained by the laws of chemical organization and mechanical structure but declared unacceptable the mechanists' insouciance before the mysterious "tendency in the internal actions of the living machine to the preservation of its existence, and to the renewal of its organs and inward structure," and before the overall "development of forms, according to their generic, specific, and individual diversities. . . ." Life for Prichard, despite the overwhelming materialistic evidence to the contrary, remained an

unresolved and mysterious force that could "only be accounted for by ascribing it to the universal energy and wisdom" of an intelligent Creator.[31]

"The poetry of earth is never dead," Keats asserted in 1816 ("On the Grasshopper and Cricket," 1) in an attempt, among other things, to affirm a vitalistic
sense of the world as living matter while yet remaining true to the fundamental empiricism of his education. From Buffon, even before he began his formal
study of medicine, Keats had learned that nature was composed of living
matter and inanimate substance, and his early verse abounds with the com-
forting discovery of the former: sightings of "the leap / Of buds into ripe
flowers" and Nature's other "gentle doings," the sounds of "little noiseless
noise among the leaves," "low rumblings [of] earth's regions under," and the
"gentle whispering / Of all the secrets of some wond'rous thing / That breathes
about us in the vacant air," and invocations to the "congregated majesty" of
animistic spirits "whose charge / It is to hover round our pleasant hills" and
the larger transcendent force made manifest when "The winds of heaven blew,
[or] the ocean roll'd / Its gathering waves" ("I stood tip-toe," 110–11, 63–64,
11; "Sleep and Poetry," 28–31, 207–8, 188–89). These examples may be directly reminiscent of the "active universe" of the early Romantics, which in
turn expressed their common attempt to refute Buffon's distinction between
animate and inanimate matter with the revelation that inanimate objects in
nature like rocks and stones were living, generative, and vital.[32] But unlike
Wordsworth and his generation, the young Keats makes these vitalistic assertions with nostalgic urgency and failing conviction in spite of the materialistic
knowledge and persuasively mechanistic method of his discipline. His assertions are confined to the early verse and do not recur after his "strawberry-
eating" phase of poetic apprenticeship.

The feeling poet of Keats's maturity knows and acknowledges fully that
Buffon and those who followed Buffon were more than right: no animate force
can enliven the fact of stone. The marble of the Grecian urn and Lord Elgin's
statuary and the stones of the sacrificial altar in *The Fall of Hyperion* do not feel;
they exist without living. He is also forced to recognize that deathly sensitivity
or "The feel of not to feel" in drear-nighted December, or to exist without
feeling life as the fallen Titans do, is worse than simple deadness and the
condition of inert matter. Keats's response to the controversy over the nature
of life and the apparent victory of the mechanists during his time was neither
to denounce both materialism and trancendentalism in favor of a Platonic
theory of life, as Shelley did,[33] nor yet to find solace, as Coleridge (and
Wordsworth) did, in a theory of consciousness encompassing matter and
mind that gave meaning and pattern to life. Keats refuses to speculate: wary
by training of the more fanciful theorizing of the philosophers of mind, he is
also repelled by the invasive and no less abstract or speculative theories of
mechanistic science. With its recurring evocations of sensation, emotion, and
pain as the varying intensities of life, and with its refusal to speculate and
theorize beyond the verifiable confines of mortal understanding, Keats's ma-

ture poetry is both a balanced and honest contribution to the debate on life and a direct reflection of the narrow verities and restricting methodology learned from the empirical discipline of contemporary science. Unable to ignore the burgeoning evidence of his age's scientific research, Keats makes the best of his poetic subjects given what he knows to be true of them from his study of medicine. As we shall see, he writes of life, but of life only as it can be proved upon the pulses.

Chapter 9

Polarity and Coleridge

The concept of polarity, of a powerful but restrained force made manifest in the tension between opposites of all orders, subsumes John Hunter's declarations on the performance of living blood. The life of the blood resisted the external chemical agencies of decomposition; it coagulated in a polarized healing response to the forces of injury; and it contracted in a final living response to the more intense stimulus of death. In much of the research preceding his culminative work on the vitality of blood, from his dissections of torpedoes, gymnotus eels, and other "electric" animals to his experiments on animals to discern their manner of producing heat, Hunter had found energy or living action manifest through the interplay of opposing principles. Well before he wrote his treatise on the polarized and polarizing energy of living blood, Hunter had noted the importance of a basic principle of opposition to the science of life: "Animal matter has a principle of action in every part," he said, and whenever the action of one part causes action in another it is through "stimulating the living principle of that other part."[1] This living principle of action, which Hunter found most visible in the power to generate heat of live animals, and which he was finally to locate in the blood, was "a power only of opposition and resistance" that was not found to exert itself spontaneously and "unprovoked but must always be excited by the energy of some external frigorific agent or disease" that existed in opposition to it. The principle of life arose out of "a peculiar arrangement of the most simple particles," which in turn gave rise to "a principle of preservation"; this singular principle of life was best apprehended through its analogy with magnetism:

This simple principle of life can with difficulty be conceived; but to show that matter may take on new properties without being altered in itself as to the species of matter, it may be not improper to illustrate this idea by such acquirements in other matter. Perhaps magnetism affords us the best illustration we can give of this. Iron appears at all times the same, whether endued with this property or not:

111

magnetism does not seem to depend on the formation of any of its parts. A bar of iron without magnetism may be considered like animal matter without life; set it upright and it acquires a new property, of attraction and repulsion, at its different ends.[2]

Life was superadded to matter and discernible through laws of polarity kindred to those operating in electromagnetism.

Organic and mineral life evolved, according to Erasmus Darwin, through the operation of basic laws of attraction and repulsion: "First HEAT . . . / With strong REPULSION parts the exploding mass . . . / ATTRACTION next, as earth or air subsides, / The ponderous atoms from the light divides,"

> Last, as fine goads the gluten-threads excite,
> Cords grapple cords, and webs with webs unite;
> And quick CONTRACTION with ethereal flame
> Lights into life the fibre-woven frame.[3]

In *Zoonomia*, Darwin called the essential living element of the universe the "spirit of animation" or "sensorial power"; he saw this power as a polarizing "intermediate agent" responsible for the action, motion, and growth of all phenomena from muscular contraction to electromagnetism. His spirit of animation was distinct from prior notions of subtle fluids or electric ethers, Darwin insisted, because it was a power of attraction *and* opposition; uncertain of its origin or final nature, he was nevertheless certain that it was the energy that occasioned the attractions of organic particles, the agent of contraction of animal muscles, and the power that stimulated the "opposition of new parts" to form the embryo in the more perfect (complex) forms of life.[4] The "hieroglyphic figure of Adonis," which in tradition signified life "perpetually wooed or courted by organic matter, and which perished and revived alternately," Darwin took to be the emblem and anticipation of his own concept of life as the spirit of animation manifested everywhere in forms alternately passive and polarized.[5]

We recall here the crucial place of Adonis in Book II of *Endymion*—of whom "it was decreed he should be rear'd / Each summer time to life," and to whom Venus brings "A tumult to his heart, and a new life / Into his eyes" (II, 477–78, 528–29)—of the important relationship Endymion bears to Adonis as the intermediate agent of "sweet life" who alternately awakens and soothes nature, even as he is himself alternately energized or cast into a dreaming swoon. We are reminded, also, that the overruling subject of *Endymion* (written, significantly, in 1817) is life, as it is variously portrayed in the youth of Endymion, the age of Glaucus, the metamorphosis of Scylla by Circe, and in the transmutative power of Cynthia, who, "with silver lip" kisses "dead things to life" (III, 56–57). Late eighteenth and early-nineteenth-century science commonly explained life and natural phenomena in terms of polarity, the contrariety of stimuli, the diversity of excitability, and law of opposition operating within all complexities of organ or entity.

If John Hunter and Erasmus Darwin were the best-known sources among Romantic physicians for Keats's awareness of the concept of polarity as it concerned life, then Coleridge (at least by way of Joseph Henry Green) would have to be Keats's most obvious literary source for the concept. The two great "*causae effectivae*" laws of nature, Coleridge said, are "Identity—or the Law of the Ground: and Identity in the difference, or Polarity—the Manifestation of unity by opposites."[6] If one were to abstract one principle common to prevailing scientific suppositions concerning the nature of life and organic phenomena, one would have neither "fluids, nor chemical compounds, nor elementary matter,—but the idea of *two--opposite--forces*, tending to rest by equilibrium. These are the sole factors of the calculus, alike in all the theories," Coleridge found, and implicit in them is a universal "*system* of electricity. . . ." He hailed those philosophers who "in the true spirit of experimental dynamics" had rejected "the imagination of any material substrate, simple or compound" instead to "contemplate in the phaenomena of electricity the operation of a law which reigns through all nature, the law of POLARITY, or the manifestation of one power by opposite forces"; and who could "trace in these appearances, as the most obvious and striking of its innumerable forms, the agency of the positive and negative poles of a power essential to all material construction. . . ."[7]

Coleridge came to his notion of experimental dynamics in the universe through his vast reading in English and European scientific and philosophical thought;[8] he learned from electrochemists like Humphry Davy of the universal pattern that could be inferred from the manifest operations of electricity; he also learned from chemical physiologists like Alexander von Humboldt of physical powers in the animal body that could act like electricity to prevent the putrefaction and decomposing union necessitated by the laws of chemical affinity. When Coleridge entered the fray of the Abernethy-Lawrence debate with his "Hints Towards the Formation of a More Comprehensive Theory of Life,"[9] he sought systematically to expand those ideas on life engendered by Hunter and championed by Abernethy so as to carry them "further back, even to their ultimate principle," and to use the very principle of polarity to reveal the unity that prevailed beyond the multiplicity of disciplines and behind their common search for the meaning of life.

Bichât's definition of life as the sum of all the functions substituted paraphrase for definition, and a term for the thing itself, Coleridge said; it meant nothing more than "life consists in being able to live." Other definitions, like those that mistook a function of life for the sign of life itself, or those that presumed a characteristic property of living nature (for example, antiputrescence) to be the common vital principle, were no less limiting, for they confined "the idea of Life to those degrees or concentrations of it, which manifest themselves in organized beings, or rather in those the organization of which is apparent to us." The only comprehensive formula to which life could be reduced without limiting the idea, for Coleridge, "would be the internal copula of bodies" or "the *power* which discloses itself from within as a principle of *unity* within the *many.*"

> I define life as *the principle of individuation*, or the power which unites a given *all* into a *whole* that is presupposed by all its parts. The link that combines the two, and acts throughout both, will, of course, be defined by the *tendency to individuation.* . . . I have shown, moreover, that this tendency to individuate can not be conceived without the opposite tendency to connect, even as the centrifugal power supposes the centripetal, or as the two opposite poles constitute each other, and are the constituent acts of one and the same power in the magnet. We might say that the life of the magnet subsists in their union, but that it lives (acts or manifests itself) in their strife. . . .
>
> . . . individuality is most intense where the greatest dependence of the parts on the whole is combined with the greatest dependence of the whole on its parts. . . . Finally, of individuals, the living power will be most intense in that individual which, as a whole, has the greatest number of integral parts presupposed in it; when, moreover, these integral parts, together with a proportional increase of their interdependence, as *parts*, have themselves most of the character of wholes in the sphere occupied by them.[10]

In the Coleridgean concept of life as the principle of unity within multeity, the tendency to individuation coexists with the equally irremissive tendency to connect, polar forces manifest but one power that passively subsists in their union and actively manifests itself in their strife, and the degree of living power (or the intensity of individuality) is directly proportionate to the number of interdependent but integral parts. Coleridge called this, in the manner of Schelling, a vital, dynamic, constructive philosophy of life. With it he could account for all life—conscious and material, perfected and potential—as generated by the interplay of the same elemental powers operating according to the universal "Law of Polarity." These inherent energies or powers, as the generative and sustaining elements of the universe, could exist only in relation to one another and could operate only in contradistinction to one another. Neither physical nor phenomenal but metascientific and prephenomenal, these elements can only be imagined, and it is only in what Coleridge called their synthetic "living and generative interpenetration" that they "achieve the condition of matter, and so move into the phenomenal realm available to the senses."

> This "universal life" of ever-renewing strife and reconciliation pulses through all individual forms and all the orders of being, beginning with "the life of metals"— where it is in its "utmost *latency*" . . .—up through the progressive levels of "individuation" to the human consciousness, which in its living reciprocity with its specific contrary, nature, is capable of achieving the awareness that there is only one Life within us and abroad.[11]

Coleridge made clear for the nineteenth century the important distinction between organic interaction and mechanical organization. Earlier decades had seen "organic" and "mechanical" as synonymous terms,[12] and the mechanists had defined organic life as organization, dependent upon the construction of the organ and operating according to the physical configuration of parts and the diversity of texture. The evolution of biology during the century as the science of living process established this distinction, but it was Coleridge who first saw the error of physiology in not distinguishing between "what may be called the general or fundamental life—the *principium vitae*, and the functional life—the life in the functions." Inoculation affected the fundamental life without any change in the functions; gout and hydrophobia "leave the life untouched" but disorder the functions to dreadful degree.

> Organisation must presuppose life as anterior to it: without life, there could not be or remain any organisation; but there is also *a* life in the organs, or functions, distinct from the other. Thus, a flute presupposes,—demands the existence of a musician as anterior to it, without whom no flute could ever have existed; and yet again, without the instrument there can be no music.[13]

Heard melodies are sweet, but those unheard are sweeter; soft pipes forever piping ditties of no tone presuppose and indeed demand the existence of an (albeit unseen) unwearied melodist forever piping songs forever new. We are suddenly in the still and silent world of quietude of the Grecian urn and its immortal organized art that presupposes mortal organic life.

Chapter 10

The Grecian Urn

Life was wrought, according to a majority of thinkers of the early nineteenth century, in the interplay of opposing forces. In the captured motion of the frenzied figures on its surface, and in the intense, stressed quietude of its form (and in direct defiance of the old distinction between *natura naturans* and *natura naturata*), Keats's Grecian urn presents an image of life contained, with its contraries reconciled and energized process held at bay, and of infinite power gathered up and concentrated within a finite, hollowed space. Humboldt's myth of "The Genius of Rhodes" and the "Ode on a Grecian Urn" find common center in their portrayal of poised young lovers bound by the implicit energy of their potential union. Beyond this image, the myth and the ode appear to diverge. The former declares itself to be a myth of life, with traditional symbols of butterfly and torch;[1] the latter is usually taken to be a measured ode to art, one that would seem to disregard all natural and supernatural machinery.

Humboldt's myth is an easily understood fable of the fact of organic life as proven by scientific research; it is intended as a simplified representation of life for scientific novices, complete with pendant for the slow-witted people of ancient Rhodes, and supplementary interpretation by a dull-brained philosopher. Keats's ode, with its silent urn and unheard melodies tells a flowery tale of a fictive city with simple folk and mysterious priest but no town historian; the attic form of the urn, silent like a tongueless Philomela or stonefaced Sphinx, "dost tease us out of thought / As doth eternity" (44–45). The condition of the lovers in Humboldt's two paintings is at best equivocal: they face either the deprivation of love unconsummated, or the putrefying dissolution of chemical (albeit loving) union. The lovers on Keats's Grecian urn know a simple and pure devotion that is "All breathing human passion far above" (28); without knowledge of the tangible and painful contrast of mortal love, theirs is a "More happy love" because of the implicit contrast with the very knowledge of "a heart high-sorrowful and cloy'd" from which they are saved.

Between Humboldt's lovers in the first painting stands the primary figure of the genius of Rhodes, symbol of the controlling spirit of vitality operating everywhere in the organic world. In Keats's ode there is no bright spirit of life to detract from the depiction of happy lovers, joyous sacrifice, and empty town; the marble urn, possessed by the artist's energizing and unifying genius of imagination, is the primary and only figure of the ode.

Perfect power is power contained and able to contain itself. The genius of vital force, natural philosophers of the early nineteenth century would agree, is the restraint of this force's natural expression. The "Ode on a Grecian Urn," singing "A song of love, too sweet for earthly lyres" (*Lamia*, I, 299), is first and foremost a celebration of the stasis and stationing of life and love made possible by art in spite of the irremissible power and necessarily changing currents of life. The urn's stasis is its perfection; its depiction of stasis, meanwhile, is a symbol of the perfection of art. The sonnet "Bright star," which may have been drafted just before the ode,[2] invokes those very virtues of art that we have come to see embodied in the Grecian urn: steadfastness, self-sufficient splendor within teeming nature, unchangeability of form and brightness within a natural flux of light and motion. The term "Fair attitude" conjoins these virtues by suggesting (according to the *Oxford English Dictionary*) both the "disposition of a figure in statuary or painting; *hence* the posture given to it" and a "posture of the body proper to, or implying, some action or mental state." The urn's stationing of life and containment of energies peculiar to life involve, hence, a conceptual or figurative act, an imaginative component not necessarily represented in material life.

When speaking of the perceiving or transmutative force as the power responsible for universal life, Schiller allowed that such a force "may be inconceivable" since if one does not "perceive the transmutative force itself on the occasion of each perceptual act but only alterations in it that register external changes, it is excluded *per se* from our field of perception." We perceive signs or alterations in the life force but we cannot conceive of it. But just because one cannot "experience the transmutative force," Schiller goes on to argue in his essay on the philosophy of physiology, "should this then make it an impossibility? I am unable to perceive change without motion, and yet I am still convinced that thought is not motion. Who would be so unjust that he would not accept this as true of the transmutative force also? This force is not a total philosophical impossibility, and does not need to be probable provided that it really exists."[3] The inability to conceive of or experience the life force, to know only the alterations of it manifest in external changes, does not refute its existence. Something along the order of this reasoning governs our first perception of the Grecian urn's achievement (and art) in the first two stanzas of the ode. The static and lifeless art of the urn purportedly captures life and the motions of life. It does so by invoking the poised figures of young lovers common to so many figurative representations of the life force. Blackstone has said that the hollow urn "is a center of *power*," that elemental earth, water, fire, and air "are powers, energies, which concentrate themselves in the *silence* of the sacred form. . . . The potter builds the same energies into the urn, on his scale, as the Demiurge built into the universal urn-form at its creating."[4] The urn holds still the turning, ebbing universe of its creator. By capturing the moving figures of tree, lover, townsfolk, priest, and heifer, the Grecian urn implicitly captures the inconceivable and elusive but nevertheless existing life. Mortal life becomes, through the urn, immortal. The Grecian urn, thus, does much more than its outward form would suggest. Its art transcends its own lifelessness to portray life. Its hollow form implies both the potential and the perfection of creation.

But, lest we forget, this is an ode built on paradox. It could well be that the urn does far less than what first it promises.

> Fair youth, beneath the trees, thou canst not leave
> Thy song, nor ever can those trees be bare;
> Bold lover, never, never canst thou kiss,
> Though winning near the goal—yet, do not grieve;
> She cannot fade, though thou hast not thy bliss,
> For ever wilt thou love, and she be fair!
>
> Ah, happy, happy boughs! that cannot shed
> Your leaves, nor ever bid the spring adieu;
> And, happy melodist, unwearied,
> For ever piping songs for ever new;
> More happy love! more happy, happy love!
> For ever warm and still to be enjoy'd
> For ever panting, and for ever young;
> (15–27)

The stasis of the urn's art, given image and form in the lines above, suggests a curious suspended state, a foster life born of endless recurrence, an unnatural condition that combines quietude and agitation. The "Ode on Indolence," where the three sleepwalking figures—"like figures on a marble urn" (5)—directly recall those on the Grecian urn, also presents a disturbing picture of a static, recurring condition marked by alternating excitation and lassitude. The poet of "Indolence" begins and ends in the same mood, and the fleeting agitation that the figures' repeated appearances elicit from him is finally overcome by indolence. Furthermore, the "masque-like figures on the dreamy urn" of indolence (56) manifest within their lassitudinal forms an implicit interior agitation: Ambition shows fatigue and is pale of cheek from some prior exertion, and the serene figure of Poesy bears a visage "most unmeek" (26–30). The silent attitude of the urn, we now recall, bears a curious "brede / Of marble men and maidens overwrought" upon its surface (41–42). "Over-wrought" means fashioned upon the exterior of the urn, but it could also mean at this period "exhausted by overwork," "worked up to too high a pitch;

over-excited."[5] Brunonian physicians of this time claimed that life depended upon an even maintenance of the principle of excitability: an excess of agitation or stimuli worked the body at too high a pitch to produce a state of overwrought intensity, a condition that masked but directly presaged imminent, deathly exhaustion. The condition of the overwrought lovers (and the hyperactive townsfolk at the sacrifice) could well be diagnosed as a diseased state of excessive excitement or stimulation; theirs is an artful but nevertheless realistic expression of the false energy that precedes debility, a hollow manifestation of life and love. Their connection with the disturbed figures of the "Ode on Indolence"—invoked variously by Keats as "shades," "Ghosts," and "Phantoms"—certainly grows closer when they are viewed as the ghostly and overwrought victims of *sthenic* excitation, the unnatural stilled agitation preceding death.

The diagnosis grows more true yet when cast with Spence's description of Eros-Anteros in Greek mythological art: the pair of cupids at the feet of the Venus de Medici represented, for example, Eros and Anteros. The former was considered "the cause of love; and the other, as the cause of its ceasing"; and "a Cupid fondling or burning a butterfly, is just the same with them as a Cupid caressing or tormenting the goddess Psyche, or the soul."[6] Lovers are alternately caressed and tormented. In Keats's poetry, if we may take the examples of *Endymion* and the "Ode on a Grecian Urn," they can be caressed to life and their wings nurtured to new flights of fancy, or they can be frenzied to death—tormented at fever pitch and without completion until, wingless, they become sods to their own high requiem. The scene of "wild ecstasy" depicted on the cold surface of the urn becomes, in this contest, a frenzied scene willfully evoking the familiar medical signs of dis-ease and exhausted life at the end of its tether. The scene is reminiscent of the cultivated fear and anxiety of the discarded first stanza to the "Ode on Melancholy." The unremitting, high-pitched unfulfillment of the lovers depicted in the scene, meanwhile, finds parallel with the "forced state" of excitability we witness in the crazed knight of "La Belle Dame sans Merci," whose pale brow, "anguish moist and fever dew" (9–10) are symbolic testament and medical sign to his condition of unconsummated and therefore self-consumptive love.

The urn's lifeless but immortal lovers would appear to represent neither the warm love of mortal passion nor the genial nurturing of living blood-friendship; theirs, rather, is the torment of relentless unconsummation, of love imagined intensely but not felt that medical thinkers of the early nineteenth century recognized as the particular terminal symptom of the exhausted but unnaturally excited consumptive patient. Dying tubercular patients loved too much, not wisely, and without relief. Mortal love's consummation produces "a heart high-sorrowful and cloy'd" (or putrefying union according to Humboldt); immortal love, like that represented on the urn or witnessed by the besotted knight of "La Belle Dame" provokes the petrifying condition of stilled action and unanswerable need preceding death: "A burning forehead, and a parching tongue," and "starv'd lips" "With horrid warning gaped wide" ("Urn," 29–30, "La Belle Dame," 41, 42).

> "When from this wreathed tomb shall I awake!
> When move in a sweet body fit for life,
> And love, and pleasure, and the ruddy strife
> Of heart and lips!"
>   (Lamia, I, 38–41)

Lamia's wreathed tomb is composed of a cold and hollow snakeskin that is shed and replaced each spring, and a torpid body that subsists in icy stillness all winter long. Her sepulchred condition as a snake in a "serpent prison-house" is nevertheless better than that of Shelley's Beatrice Cenci, who, once she has been tainted by the violence of forced union and unnatural affinity with her father, can see herself only as dead and imprisoned in a medium of putrefying flesh:

> No, I am dead! These putrefying limbs
> Shut round and sepulchre the panting soul
> Which would burst forth into the wandering air!
>   (III, i, 26–28)

The choice between immortal snakehood and mortal indeterminacy is clear for Lamia: she chooses what some scientists of the time had defined as the endless strife and attraction between chemical elements, and what some philosophers had described as the polarized energy manifest in the meeting of opposing forces within an organic wholeness: "a sweet body fit for life, / And love, and pleasure and the ruddy strife / Of heart and lips!" Lamia's love as a mortal woman is far removed from the static happiness of the urn's lovers. Her passing mortal life, kindred to the experiential flux of Endymion's Indian Maid—"With all her limbs on tremble, and her eyes / Shut sofly up alive" (IV, 103–4)—bears no conceivable relation to the enduring lovers, trees, and townsfolk molded upon the urn's enduring form.

The urn's figures are conceived through what they cannot experience. Certainly from the experiential perspective of breathing passion's "burning forehead," "heart high-sorrowful" and "the ruddy strife / Of heart and lips," more is deprived of them than is bestowed.[7] The Greek artist's happy youth are, in fact, "Chilly lovers," "aguish fairies" with "frozen breath, / Colder than the mortal death" ("Song of Four Fairies," 64–67). Above "All breathing human passion," the urn's bloodless lovers are also beyond the "stimulus of death." It is in this, their undisturbed condition of suspended, artful excitation, that the urn's lovers reveal their disturbing connection with those "Poor lovers" preserved in eternal sleep in Book III of Endymion.

> So in that crystal place, in silent rows,
> Poor lovers lay at rest from joys and woes.—
> The stranger from the mountains, breathless, trac'd
> Such thousands of shut eyes in order plac'd;
> Such ranges of white feet, and patient lips
> All ruddy,—for here death no blossom nips.
> (735–40)

Keats, as yet unable to mix his metaphors like Milton, arranges his anesthetized lovers "line by line" like "warriors thousands on the field supine" (733–34): dead like the gunshot-wounded, stiffened corpses found scattered upon a battlefield (which John Hunter had once made the focus of his research on the life of blood), they nevertheless masquerade the ruddy life of live soldiers in the orderly action of battle. The metaphor continues, depicting them as angelic embryos in a briny womb with shut eyes, patient lips, smooth brows, and wrists crossed at the heart (738–44), immune at once to the ripening of life and death. The lovers' crypt is a place of immaturity. And in this unreal "crystal place" of their resting, as upon the pale surface of the Grecian urn, death has no dominion—the ravages of putrefaction are held at bay because the stimulus of death that triggers it (and presupposes life) is missing.

The dead lovers of Book III of *Endymion*, an orderly arrangement of once-living forms suspended in the saline embalming solution of their magical underwater cell, are thus preserved like specimens in a Hunterian medical museum. The analogy grows stronger when we note that the "bright portal" of this tomb-museum beneath "unfathom'd brine" is wrought of "a fabric crystalline, / Ribb'd and inlaid with coral, pebble, and pearl," which leads to a cavern "vast, and desolate, and icy" (627–29, 632). This is a place distinctly reminiscent of the Dead Sea and its volcanic environs as described by Alexander Marcet (see discussion above) in his analysis of the sea's saline inability to support life while yet preserving life's shells and skeletal forms. It is also a place reminiscent of Buffon's underwater caverns of preserved fossils described in the opening pages of *Histoire Naturelle*. Glaucus leaves the dead Scylla in a niche of this vault, but as he flees his "scathing dread / Met palsy half way," and his limbs become "Gaunt, wither'd, sapless, feeble, cramp'd, and lame" (635–38); his accelerated aging in this place is similar to the fate of titanic Saturn in *The Fall of Hyperion*, whose face, resembling that of Blake's Urizen, wrinkles as he falls to his final resting place (I, 225). This last abode, moreover, is no less cold, desolate and lifeless than the lover's saline crypt in *Endymion*, and Saturn lies there preserved, along with his withered and superannuated race, as a nerveless shell of his former self (I, 310–24).

Regions such as these can be dissolved in the dream-world of *Endymion*; their pictures of desolate emptiness can be dispelled for life-filled visions of decrepit lovers regaining their youth, or dead lovers revitalized in their watery tombs like those seed-embryos given life by Shelley's West Wind. Blood can be made to flow through the cold bodies of the lovers in Endymion, but neither art nor vision can send it coursing through the icy veins of the Titans in The Fall of Hyperion—or through the marbled features of the lovers graven upon the Grecian urn. Where the dream world of Endymion is composed of ethereal substances that ascend, slip, slide, and vaporize, the worlds of the urn and The Fall of Hyperion, also dream-structures but cast as visions of perfection and Druidic endurance, are formed of more ponderous substance: petrified stone. Circumstance or event in both latter poems, moreover, remind us of the stories of petrification connected with the stone rings in the English country-side, and in particular of the legend associated with the Stanton Drew stone circles, located just above Glastonbury near Bath, which Keats may well have visited on his way to Bath to see Bailey during his tour of Devon and Cornwall. The Stanton Drew legend, born of a most "dismal cirque / Of druid stones, upon a forlorn moor" (Hyp., II, 34–35), tells, according to the eighteenth-century antiquarian William Stukeley, of a wedding party during which the couple and guests are led to dance through the night, endlessly and with ever-increasing frenzy, by the hypnotic music of an evil and mad musician; the music ceases at dawn when the piper disappears, and the young celebrants are left petrified forever in the marbled postures of frenzied joy and despair upon the silent moor.

The cold kinship of marble between the "Ode on a Grecian Urn" and The Fall of Hyperion presents itself at once. When the poet of The Fall of Hyperion drinks from "a cool vessel of transparent juice," a "cloudy swoon" comes upon him and he sinks "Like a Silenus on an antique vase" (I, 42, 56). "When sense of life return'd," the poet sees before him "the carved sides"

> Of an old sanctuary with roof august,
> Builded so high, it seem'd that filmed clouds
> Might spread beneath, as o'er the stars of heaven;
> So old the place was, I remembered none
> The likes upon the earth; what I had seen
> Of grey cathedrals, buttress'd walls, rent towers,
> The superannuations of sunk realms,
> Or nature's rocks toil'd hard in waves and winds,
> Seem'd but the faulture of decrepit things
> To that eternal domed monument.
>   (I, 62–71)

The superannuations of nature and civilization alike are but poor patterns, the faulture of decrepit things in comparison to this marbled monument to the passage of time and life. This monumental old sanctuary confines and en-closes: a "silent massy range" of columns "ending in mist / Of nothing" delin-eate its spaces to the north and south; to the east "black gates / Were shut against the sunrise evermore"; a massive effigy and an altar, meanwhile, guard the western entrance to this vault and mark the place where all journeys of *Nekyia* end. Two sets of stairs lead to the altar at this western entrance (I, 83–92). Altar, stairs, and balustrade, like the sanctuary itself, are all formed of marble.

Like the faults in ancient ruins and the geological fissures of prehistoric rock formations, the old sanctuary is a monument to time *without life*, to an endurance that is possible once the signs of life have been stilled or removed. The hollow vault of this monument contains the stilled forms of the once-powerful Titans within its marble confines, much as that other marble vessel of containment, the Grecian urn, holds the forms of life apart from the process of living. Flesh and common dust are no match to the cold endurance of marble, the poet of *The Fall of Hyperion* is told:

> "If thou canst not ascend
> These steps, die on that marble where thou art.
> Thy flesh, near cousin to the common dust,
> Will parch for lack of nutriment—thy bones
> Will wither in few years, and vanish so
> That not the quickest eye could find a grain
> Of what thou now art on that pavement cold."
> (I, 107–13)

The poet's living response to the stimulus of cold marble is graphic and physiologically correct: his blood congeals, as John Hunter said it must. Feeling "the tyranny / Of that fierce threat" (119–20), and striving "hard to escape / The numbness" wrought upon his senses by the tyranny of marble, the poet diagnoses his own condition: "the cold / Grew stifling, suffocating, at the heart; / And when I clasp'd my hands I felt them not. / [Until] One minute before death, my iced foot touch'd / The lowest stair" (127–33). Living blood, according to the anatomical observations of John Hunter, responded to the challenge of injury or exposure to its living power by coagulating so as to promote healing and regeneration. The blood's living response to the insurmountable stimulus of death was a final coagulating stillness and stiffening, wherein the blood's warm energy cohered with the cold power of death so as to nullify life-giving opposition and produce instead a life form that was no longer alive. We are to recognize the kind of stimulus that the poet's senses feel emanating from the monumental tyranny of marble before him:

> when suddenly a palsied chill
> Struck from the paved level up my limbs,
> And was ascending quick to put cold grasp
> Upon those streams that pulse beside the throat
> (I, 122–25)

This is the stimulus of death, an overweening coldness that elicits not continuing opposition but one single terminal response that manifests itself in kindred coldness and quietude. In *The Fall of Hyperion* the poet is able at the last moment to counter the deadly stimulus that strikes from the marble pavement. His mortal effort to attain the stairs proves sufficient creative energy to counter the implacable stillness of immortal marble; because of the continued opposition, "life seem'd / To pour in at the toes" (133–34). The poet's living creative energy is mortal, a power "to die and live again" before the fated hour (142) that the original sculptor of the Grecian urn also owned once. Because this is a mortal power, it is one denied alike to the energyless but immortal Titans and to the everlasting figures carved upon the Grecian urn. Far from responding with creative opposition, the lovers carved upon the urn and the Titans postured within their monument express terminal kinship with their marble medium; they endure because of it, not in spite of it. They provide only the semblance of a continuing opposition between medium and living form, the creative tension of life belongs to their mortal artists alone.

> We can compare these Marbles to nothing but human figures petrified: they have every appearance of absolute *fac-similes* or casts taken from nature [Hazlitt says]....
> The utter absence of all setness of appearance proves that they were done as studies from actual models. The separate parts of the human body may be given from scientific knowledge:—their modifications or inflections can only be learnt by seeing them in action .... The veins, the wrinkles in the skin, the indications of the muscles under the skin (which appears as plainly to the anatomist as the expert angler knows from an undulation on the surface of the water what fish is playing with his bait beneath it), the finger-joints, the nails, every the smallest part cognisable to the naked eye, is given here with the same ease and exactness, with the same prominence, and in the same subordination, that it would be in a cast from nature, *i.e.* in nature itself.[8]

We see the beauty of the Elgin Marbles, according to Hazlitt, through the expert eyes of the anatomist whose art can station and reveal the processes of life. The Marbles are stilled forms of life that fulfill their art through being preserved or removed from life. They are human figures petrified, like fossils or glacial tides, in the postures of living motion, "*fac-similes* or casts taken from nature" complete with every physiological detail available through keen scientific observation. Veins, muscles, finger joints, and nails of these postures are rendered so visually true by the artist-anatomist that we would sense the motions of life processes beneath the skin. The signs of life appear present, to be recognized and read by passing observer and diagnosing physician alike, even as the symptoms of life are missing and the fluidity of life process is frozen. Hazlitt's characterization of the enduring beauty of the Elgin Marbles reiterates for us the chilling connections between the congealing blood within once-living flesh witnessed by the anatomist, the petrification of once-living forms and moving waters witnessed by geologists, the Druidic rock formations of the Titans to whose former existence Moneta bears witness as "sole priest-ess" of their present desolation, and the marbled figures (of lovers, musician, priest, and townsfolk) borne upon the Grecian urn in mute testimony to its mortal sculptor's wholesome vision of a living festival incorporating the many contraries of love and sacrifice. All are monuments, or victims, of "slow time." The Elgin Marbles mingle "Grecian grandeur with the rude / Wasting of old time" (sonnet, 12–13) necessarily, and to no less degree of intensity than does the poet's vision of the wasted Titans petrified in their faultured sanctuary, or the poet's picture of the Grecian urn as a "foster-child of silence and slow time" (2).

The poet of The Fall of Hyperion looks past the marble altar and through the veils covering Moneta's face into the "hollow brain" and "dark secret chambers of her skull" (276–77) that contain the crumbling vault of memory and time wherein the Titans must endure in pain. He looks with "the quickest eye" of the anatomist alert to every detail and symptom, and with the interpretive power of the physician-poet to the meaning of every sign thus seen. He sees the Titans changed past change. The "two shapes" of Thea and Saturn, once "postured motionless, / Like natural sculpture in cathedral cavern" over one long "moon, with alteration slow" in Hyperion (I, 83–86), are now "fixed shapes" enwombed forever beyond the passage of cyclic time, at the farthest remove from the processes of life.

> Long, long, these two were postured motionless,
> Like sculpture builded upon the grave
> Of their own power. A long awful time
> I look'd upon them; still they were the same;
> The frozen God still bending to the earth,
> And the sad Goddess weeping at his feet;
> Moneta silent. Without stay or prop
> But my own weak mortality, I bore
> The load of this eternal quietude,
> The unchanging gloom, and the three fixed shapes
> Ponderous upon my senses. . . .
>   (Fall of Hyp., I, 382–92)

The Titans are past change, past "The lily and the snow," because they are the full and completed victims of the laws of change and process common to all evolutionary life. No longer compared to "natural sculpture in cathedral cav-ern," the Titans are now "sculpture builded up upon the grave / Of their own power." They are like those described in Endymion as "not yet dead, / But in old marbles ever beautiful" (I, 318–19), and their power is one less strong and less feeling than the poet's "own weak mortality." Like the Elgin Marbles (which were themselves builded upon the cold remnant of a once-living igneous rock to commemorate the wonders of a passing civilization), the Titans are bleak shadows of a former magnitude ("On Seeing the Elgin Marbles," 14). Without the power "to live and die," and except for the skilled intensity of their pictured pain, the Titans are without sense. At one with the rocks and stones of their abode, they know only "the feel of not to feel it" in drear-nighted December (21). The "eternal quietude" of their dis-eased condition bodes ill for the immortal achievements of other petrified forms.

Saved by art from the natural law of process as perfection espoused in *Hyperion*, the Grecian urn and its fabled figures nevertheless show their kinship with those perfected figures in *The Fall of Hyperion* who have experienced this law in full measure. The undying happiness of the urn's young lovers bears curious resemblance to the aged Titans' immortal inability to feel anything fully; the lovers' finely honed excitation wrought to excess parallels the numbing senselessness of the fallen gods' excessive pain. Humboldt's fable of the Genius of Rhodes was a myth of life, of that which resists putrefaction; its figures of vibrant and exhausted lovers would stand thus as ironic patterns for the flowery tale of the Grecian urn whose statuary figures, far from resisting, welcome petrifaction on an attic shape. "How get from lifeless marble life and pain?" the poet Chamisso asks of his lifeless statue;[9] his lament on nature's ultimate ability to evade all artistic media is one common to all artists, including those ancients of the Elgin Marbles. In reverse, in spite of and perhaps because of its beauty, the urn's marble art is the art of *médusée*, the transfixing of action and the turning into stone. Life's energetic polarities are stopped up, and its fluidities are drained; all action is stilled, stationed, made stone. Early-nineteenth-century mechanists and vitalists alike proposed that motion was necessary to life, but the urn renounces motion in favor of the cessation of action; it chooses the symptoms of death that it might endure in a manner artful of life. Indeed, if the fate of the lovers who can never kiss and of the musician who may never leave his song carries overtones of necessity and coercion,[10] then the fault lies as much in the medium as in the art. As evocations of life matter, these lamentations of fading beauty, fevered love, and wrinkling despair reiterate, by contrast, the coercions of the marble medium.

The urn's white figures transfixed in their happiness, even as they triumphantly resist the natural law espoused in *Hyperion*, necessarily bear a deathly connection to those frozen statues with "carved features" marbled by pain that frame the poet's aching vision of *The Fall of Hyperion* (I, 225). Postured motionless upon the grave of their own power, the three "fixed shapes" fulfill the laws of natural reciprocity—or the exchange of powers between opposing energies in nature—in relation to their mortal witness. The poet's "own weak mortality" must bear the load of their "eternal quietude" without stay or prop; and, in turn, the unchanging gloom and quietude of these fixed shapes feed reciprocal and ponderous upon the poet's life senses (I, 382–93). No wonder, then, that the domineering sight of the Titans leaves the poet with a heart too small to hold its blood (I, 254). We are forced to ask whether the "leaf-fring'd legend[s]" that haunt about the shape of the urn (5) do not also draw life and sustenance from their mortal counterparts in a manner similar not only to the deathly albeit "not yet dead" Titans but also to the chilling and hungry presence from beyond the grave in the poem "This living hand." Surely, the "marble men and maidens overwrought" graven upon the urn, and the haunting "silent form" of that brooding "bride of quietness" itself (42–44), bear a relationship of reciprocal exchange with their mortal contacts and seek "fulfillment" in their immortal stasis from the finite sense energies and blood of living motion.

The "Fair attitude" of the Grecian urn invoked by Keats in the last stanza of the ode is that marble object's accomplished fulfillment as a postured attitude of life. "Taken from nature," to borrow Hazlitt's phrase, the Grecian urn *takes* from nature. It is an artifact framed against natural patterns, with its figures sustained by the very living actions that they cannot perform. It is a cold pastoral that draws out the signs of life and empties to desolation a little town that it might "with garlands" dress its hollow form.

> What little town by river or sea shore,
>   Or mountain-built with peaceful citadel,
>   Is emptied of this folk, this pious morn?
> And, little town, thy streets for evermore
>   Will silent be; and not a soul to tell
>   Why thou art desolate, can e'er return.
>   (35–40)

It is a flaw in happiness to see beyond our bourne. The poet in Keats must set against the purported festival of gods, men, and beasts artfully represented upon the urn his own imaginings of a ghostly town deprived of all the signs of life—its streets empty and silent, its desolation unaccounted for, and, since none "can e'er return," without promise of change or reinstitution of the life cycle to its "peaceful citadel." What the poet sees by seeing too far beyond the surface festival of the urn reveals a habit of perceptual vision learned from his earlier profession of medicine.

Medical semiotics of the time sought to look beneath the manifest symptoms of a body to those more interpretable, universal signs of healthy or diseased life. The Romantic physician was charged to invoke his trained eye and penetrating vision to read beneath the smooth surfaces of an otherwise healthy body the yet-to-be-manifest signs of corroding disease, and to see beyond the specific symptoms of a ruptured organ or part to the larger signs of universal disturbance in the organism. Poet and physician look thus at elusive mortal life as it is stilled and made accessible within the confines of an immortal Grecian urn. Keats sees not just a town emptied of life by sacrifice (be this human festival or natural epidemic), nor just a demented musician playing songs that he alone can hear, but trees unable to shed their leaves or "ever bid the spring adieu"—condemned thereby to a permanent embryonic state that by avoiding death permits no ripeness. He sees, further-more, beyond the happy picture of lovers who can neither fade nor have their bliss, the disturbing vision of unconsummated love and the deprived passion of phthisis. The urn's lovers are forever panting but nevertheless above all breathing, in clear sign of the wasting disease of the consumptive patient whose chest (or heart) is always too small to hold his breath (or blood). Below the trees' eternal springtime lurk the specific symptoms of retarded growth. Beneath the lovers' wild ecstasy and the musician's obsessive and unending melody resides a chronic condition of ill health that precedes the terminal exhaustion of tuberculosis and madness.

If these visions be occasions of seeing too far, at once too clinical and too close to the dark moods and corrosive vision described in the verse-epistle to Reynolds, and they are indeed forms of those shadowed visitings to the "soul's daytime / In the dark void of night" (70–71), we must nevertheless face the first verity of the Grecian urn: it is hollow. The marbled figures of joy and pious ritual that garland the smooth surface of the urn mask a vacuous space. The urn's quietude partakes of this echoing vacuity and to it belong the toneless ditties of the too-spiritual musician and the desolate silence of the abandoned town. If the urn has a mysterious tale to tell, it cannot tell it lest it undermine the fraught indeterminacy of its artistic content.

The ashes of the dead, the wine for sacred libations, the perfumed oil for ritual initiation or embalmment, the *katharmata* or herbal potpourri of ancient medicine, grain offerings to the gods of the autumnal harvest—these are some of the possible substances for which the Grecian urn was once made. The ode itself steers us away from speculations as to the specifics of content by focusing on the surface of the urn and the quietude of its form. Its inner space thus becomes full of potential significance, a region of promise illimit-able by the specifics of known entities. Blackstone has seen in the urn's very hollowness the ultimate example of resonant receptacles in Keats's poetry. "His verse moves among resonant hollows, foci of speechful silence. The winds breathe 'Eolian magic from their lucid wombs'; sea-noises in caves are therapeutic; Moneta displays 'In the dark secret chambers of her skull' the agonies of a fallen dynasty. Power dwells in these spaces. And power is gathered up, constantly, into 'the supreme shape' of the urn."[11] But what if power is not contained within the urn but, rather, haunts about the figures upon its surface who themselves draw power from mortal life? To what extent is the hollow urn the obverse of Moneta's skull, a false pregnancy, a gravid container that is merely filled with the ashes of life where the other teems with living memory and pain? Nothing in our experience of Keats's mature poetry would favor the highly affirmative interpretation: nightingale flights escape us, the gods' picnics prove to be the abandoned refuse of a meal, and the celebrations of autumn can be of its most minimal offerings. What if the echoing space contained within the urn be nothing but a reminder of life resonant with unfulfillment like the old shells of mollusks, or the husks and stalks of summer fruits left behind by angels for the poet to taste as best he can, or the sedimentary deposits forming desolate natural sanctuaries, or the marble remnants sculpted for a civilization long dead?

"And, silent as a consecrated urn" (*Endymion*, III, 32). The very lines that critics have invoked in justifying the interpretation of the Grecian urn as a receptacle of sacred power also suggest for Blackstone that it is a funerary vessel. But if the phrase "silent as a consecrated urn" promises sacred presence therein, the original draft of this line reads not as a promise but as a threat of eternal meaninglessness: "And silent, as a corpse upon a pyre." The urn of Keats's ode contains emptiness as easily as it does sacred significance; its purported sacred signification could be as easily of good as of ill. We are reminded of Hesiod's story of Pandora and the jar full of evils. In it, the concept common to many mythologies of a receptacle whose magic contents are either an asset or a liability depending upon their treatment combines with the ritual of the "Opening of the Jars" of new wine in the Dionysiac festival of the *Anthesteria*.[12] The wines of the Dionysiac festival were magical substances or *pharmaka* whose portent could be positive and healthful or sinister, but Pandora's jar bore specifically evil elements; more portentous and implicitly sinister than an urn bearing the remains of the dead, the jar restrained active powers of negation within its confines. It undermined both the benevolence of immortal beings and the artistic claims of order of mortal civilizations.

The urn of Keats's ode encloses an ambiguous space. While we may see this vacancy as without portent and merely part of the Grecian urn's ductile art, it is expressive nevertheless of the object's infinite ability to define its existence through the absence and negation of mortal life. The urn, we recall, is bloodless. It proposes a most singular love without passion, to renounce both parthenogenesis and what Erasmus Darwin called "the chef d'oeuvre" or "masterpiece of nature,"[13] that it might better protect itself from the consequences of consummation. Its marble medium lacks the characteristic sympathy of living tissue, energy is drawn from mortal existence and consumed into its vacant shape without reciprocity, and the urn's only mortal kinship is with the motionless and already dead petrified forms in nature. As a unravished bride of quietness, the urn shares harmful symptoms with the victims of hysteria familiar to early-nineteenth-century medicine, for it can neither speak nor tell why it is desolate.[14] As a "friend to man," it is a distracting enigma that, without thought itself, teases us out of thought. The extent of the urn's achievement as a wrought work of art is undermined finally, as also are the Elgin Marbles in Keats's sonnet, by the pathos of what is absent. Without consciousness, or even the ability to know what it lacks, the urn is also without life.

In the first three stanzas of the ode Keats at once visualizes the urn's consummate accomplishment as art and consummates his own ability to celebrate such achievement. The lines of the third stanza celebrating the fair attitude of a love that is "For ever warm and still to be enjoyed" mark a moment of intensity wherein the artistic vision of fulfillment—as much for the artifact and its sculptor as for the ode and its poet—becomes achieved perfection. We are accustomed to seeing such moments in Keats's poetry turn "to poison while the bee-mouth sips." The poet-physician sees too far into the signs of passing fulfillment; occasions of integration are undermined by the sudden awareness of the dissolution and reversal that must follow; and the stationed perfections of art coincide abruptly with the dislocated truths of reality. For example, in the odes to autumn and to a nightingale, the celebration of autumn becomes a wailful choir to autumn's most minimal signs of life ("last oozings," chafe, and stubbled plains), and the poet's flight of fancy with the nightingale reveals at the very moment of purported identification (stanza 5) his blind distinctions from the bird. So also does the achieved vision of a love forever warm in the third stanza of the "Ode on a Grecian Urn" turn abruptly upon this love's mortal contraries:

> For ever warm and still to be enjoy'd
> For ever panting, and for ever young;
> All breathing human passion far above,
> That leaves a heart high-sorrowful and cloy'd,
> A burning forehead, and a parching tongue.

The cloying counters of mortal love, a heart high-sorrowful, a burning forehead, a parching tongue, heighten by contrast the perfection of immortal love pictured upon the urn. We are informed of the vast distance that separates this picture of fulfillment from the world of consummated love, represented in the "Ode to a Nightingale" as a place "Where youth grows pale, and spectre-thin, and dies" and "Where Beauty cannot keep her lustrous eyes, / Or new Love pine at them beyond to-morrow" (26, 29–30). The leavings and remainders of mortal love follow too close and cast too dark a retrospective shadow upon the portrait of everlasting love. Awareness ensues, necessarily, that this is but an attitude of warm love maintained by artistic fiat upon the cold and stilled surface of a Grecian urn.

The last two stanzas of the ode cannot continue to celebrate this mockery of love. There must be an alternate or other side of what has been represented so far of love and life upon a funerary jar. Indeed, much as Humboldt's fable of the Genius of Rhodes provided a pendant to the painting of anticipatory but restrained young lovers, which served as the means of fulfilling and explaining what had been promised of life in the original portrait, so also do the last two stanzas of Keats's ode serve as a pendant picture or ironic coda to what has been pictured of immortal love and life on one side of the urn. Keats's alternate vision of a reality composed of mysterious ritual and lifeless town is a sacrificial summary, born of mortal and perceptual necessity, of an earlier unreal vision of poised perfection.

> Who are these coming to the sacrifice?
> To what green altar, O mysterious priest,
> Lead'st thou that heifer lowing at the skies,
>   And all her silken flanks with garlands drest?
> What little town by river or sea shore,
>   Or mountain-built with peaceful citadel,
>   Is emptied of this folk, this pious morn?
>   (31–37)

Questions distance us, as they did in the opening stanza of the ode, from the recently achieved integration of the third stanza. We are presented with the ambiguous image of a priest, cast suspiciously like a Grecian version of the Pied Piper of German folklore, leading a multitude of eager and anticipatory townsfolk to a green altar where they can watch the sacrificial goring of their favorite ox.

We are led to wonder to what extent this sacrifice, performed presumably for the sacred fulfillment of the mesmerized attendants, is a violent substitute for the restrained passion and lack of consummation represented on the other side of the urn. The "unravished bride of quietness," with the help of a charming priest, has plundered a quiet and retiring little town. The town "emptied of this folk, this pious morn" by the artist's too-vivid imagination of the ritual's consequences, resides in insular security or pious indifference "by river or sea shore," or atop a mountain as a "peaceful citadel." "Pious" is a suspect word in the Keats lexicon, and the "peaceful citadel" provides peace at the expense of the high walls of its fortress, which are designed as much to keep its inhabitants within and in subjection as to protect them from external threat and knowledge. The "little" town's empty fate to forever "silent be," which is graven upon the dark inside of an equally empty urn, is perhaps bathetic, the more so when we speculate that its silent streets might parody the heavy and sacred silence of the urn's "silent form." Too many flanks, meanwhile, endow that sacrificial heifer that imposes herself upon our sight with "*all* her silken flanks with garlands drest." Lest we have failed to hear the unexpected dissonances of the stanza, or note the willful near-rhymes of "priest" and "drest," "sacrifice" and "skies," even "morn" and "return," we are jarred alert by the heifer's lowing—loud, long, and discordant. This is the only heard melody of the entire ode. Not soft pipes or joyful timbrels but a cacaphonic bovine cry from a virginal animal that breaks the ponderous silence and protests (with good reason) the impending sacrifice. Life asserts itself with brute energy over ritual and art. On this pious morn the sacred has overflown its container.

A hellish nose peeps through the curtains of transcendent vision, the mermaids grow toes, witch's eyes sport above a cherub's mouth, wild boars show their tushes, and a cow's frightened cry can disrupt the artistry of man and nature, and signal the disjunctions beneath the smooth surface of marbled men and maidens. The nightmare vision of the verse-epistle to Reynolds shadows with a vengeance the wrong side of the Grecian urn. The triumphant manifesto uttered in high tone, "Beauty is truth," is followed by a dark echo, "truth beauty" uttered in low monotone.

The poet has seen behind the images of the ancient sculptor and too far forward to an eternal fierce destruction. Hence, the Grecian urn of Keats's ode tells no story. Its depictions have no recognizable connection to mythology or ancient rite, and none of the connections to specific mysteries that, say, Darwin's Portland Vase has to the Eleusinian stories. Nor do its pictures bear any knowable significance to the personal history of the ancient artist. Keats willfully withholds legend, myth, and history; he provides selective images instead and addresses specific but nevertheless ambiguous figures of make-believe passion and violence. What the urn represents on its surface is deliberately not represented in full to us. The complete ode is more a minimal than a measured ode to art; it celebrates art through the least that art can accomplish. At its least, to the ironic vision of the last stanzas, the Grecian urn is an "Attic shape," a quaint nonsensical fragment of the magnitude that was the Elgin Marbles. At its best, to the same excoriating vision, the urn is a "Fair attitude" of life, a cold and unheard sylvan paean that fails its subject and neglects to speak of love.

> A thing of beauty is a joy forever:
> Its loveliness increases; it will never
> Pass into nothingness; but still will keep
> A bower quiet for us, and a sleep
> Full of sweet dreams, and health, and quiet breathing.
>   (*End.*, I, 1–5)

The Grecian urn's achievement as a thing of beauty, estimated by Keats's ode, is a tempered version of the claim above. Its loveliness is constant; it has the potential to be "ravished" by "slow time" and crumble to nothingness; its quiet bower echoes with the possibility of violence and sacrifice; and its sleep of quietude may well mask unquiet breathing, breathless exhaustion induced by unconsummated excitation, and unhealthy deprivation. By the end of the ode, the Grecian urn's attempt to transcend the disorders and unpleasantries of life is shown to be doubly imperfect: its art ultimately has proceeded to transcend life itself, and its artistic perfection is undermined by the very processes of life. Drawing energy and image from reality, the urn is delineated by reality.

John Bayley spoke to the origins of this dilemma when he marked that among the English Romantics it was Keats (and Byron) who first revealed "the kind of anxiety and guilt about the relation of art to reality" that is now common to contemporary poetry. "To be so much aware of the division between life and literature is to see life, involuntarily, as a literary concept: 'life for life's sake' is no more and no less meaningful than 'art for art's sake,' because it expresses the same attitude to both." If "poetry was both the whole of life and a dream that must be rejected in favor of life,"[15] then the ambiguous invocations of art and life of the "Ode on a Grecian Urn" are microcosmic formulations of a larger poetic debate.

Unlike Yeats's "Sailing to Byzantium," the ode does not make clear the distinctions between art and life the better to gather itself "Into the artifice of eternity." In it, the Grecian urn does not succeed in celebrating art to the exclusion of life because, to Keats's perspective, the celebration of art must be hobbled by mortal life since it is dependent for its very terms and patterns upon this mortal life. An "indescribable feud" and "most dizzy pain" accompanies the poet's viewing of the Elgin Marbles (sonnet, 10–16) precisely because these marbles mingle permanent Grecian grandeur with the rude wastings of old time, the pains of human life with the immortal aspirations of the artist, mortal shadows with marble magnitudes. Slow time will erode the urn's beauty much as it has weathered the Elgin sculptures and the old sanctuary of the fallen Titans. All three share the same reality because their species of beauty, however formal, permanent, or transcendent, is derived from organic beauty and finds meaning only through the passing phases and sacrificial process of this beauty.

By default and by intention the "Ode on a Grecian Urn" reveals much of life and organic sacrifice; it does so despite the purported message on the supremacy of art of the Grecian urn—and perhaps because of it. Order and the pleasing images of art are maintained by the urn and its sculptor through willful ignorance and the refusal to verbalize what lies beyond or beneath these images. What the poet imagines in stanza four of the ode of the heifer's impending sacrifice and the little town's renunciation speaks specifically of the fear, abandonment, and recurring destruction common to the scenes of mortal life but missing from the surface of the urn. We recall a parallel scene pictured directly through painting, instead of by implication as the absent underside of a marble urn, in the verse-epistle to John Hamilton Reynolds:

> The sacrifice goes on; the pontif knife
> Gleams in the sun, the milk-white heifer lows,
> The pipes go shrilly, the libation flows:
> A white sail shews above the green-head cliff,
> Moves round the point, and throws her anchor stiff.
>   (20–24)

The "Titian colours touch'd into real life" of the line preceding these become the true colors of this sacrifice. Keats's eye probes beneath the smooth surface of Claude's painting "Enchanted Castle" to discern signs of fear and underlying disorder; he senses thereby sacrifice more real than that represented as ritual in another of Claude's paintings, "Sacrifice to Apollo."[16] The teeming life of the ocean reveals itself to his perception—at once that of poet, naturalist, anatomist and physician—as "the sacrifice of generations," an un-ending sacrifice without ritual, a universal and unrelenting rapacity, an "eter-nal fierce destruction." The sacrifice to Apollo continues, after art as before, and the white sail that shows above the green-headed cliff recalls for us another myth of everlasting love born of real sacrifice and misinterpreted ritual. In the story of Tristan and Isolde the sign of healing, the white sails, is deliberately misinterpreted. Isolde arrives too late and lives; Tristan dies, poisoned and deceived; and the sacrifice of life and death goes on. The fate of these eternal lovers, no less than of those lovers in Alexander von Humboldt's myth of life, must shadow the lovers graven upon the Grecian urn and the exclusive art that transfixes them in their happiness.

The "Ode on a Grecian Urn" is all about life, mortal life that can draw even the immortality of Grecian art into its processes. The sculptor's attempt to use life to exalt art by contrast, and to show what art can accomplish with the forms of life even upon the simple surface of marble, becomes in the ode not so much a celebration as a profound reiteration of life and the "muddy lees" of reality. The urn's icy beauty of perfection (Beauty is Truth) finds more than its equal in life's cruel beauty of process. Its status as a "still unravish'd bride of quietness" includes an implicit vulnerability to ravishment in the future by an intensity greater than the quietude of its art. Its role as "foster-child of silence and slow time," meanwhile, is precarious and hardly privileged when the true progeny of these ponderous counters are the mortal generations of life.

The Grecian urn's achievement when cast in the sober light of Keats's ode must read as a consummate artistry that mimics but cannot capture life. The urn's very resolve to speak of art and say the least of life is suspect, a brave declaration of intention that must fail despite the achieved artistic perfection. The tragedy of the urn's perfection is that its static art presupposes life, defines itself in terms of life, masquerades the forms of life, feeds its false excitation upon the energy of life, and tells through its "flowery tale" a fable of chemical life no less true than that one of electric polarity and chemical affinity told by Alexander von Humboldt in 1795. The "Ode on a Grecian Urn" is Keats's informed contribution to the contemporary debate on the meaning of life. It is a masterful ellipsis of the philosophies of life of his time from a poet who could not deny for the sake of art what he had been trained to believe was the Romantic physician's first concern. The poem's argument constitutes a conscious and intense debate on the nature of vitality.

Its focus is the moment of animation—the very subject that inevitably preoccupied all participants in the debate on life—a stationless quickening of vitality that science had yet to apprehend, and that artifacts like the Grecian urn or the Elgin Marbles appeared to station, albeit fruitlessly. Through the process of Keats's subdued ode to life we are taught to read life as Romantic physicians, with the same questions and with the same eye to recognize for what they are the signs of the absence of life. Art is not life, and its perfection is not process. The question of life persists.

PART III

THE PHARMACY OF DISEASE

Here's his health in water.

Robert Burns

Apollo! faded, far flown Apollo!
Where is thy misty pestilence. . .?

Keats, *The Fall of Hyperion*, I, 204–5

"Banish money—Banish sofas—Banish Wine—Banish Music—But right Jack Health—honest Jack Health—true Jack Health—banish health and banish all the world,"[1] Keats writes to Reynolds in 1817. But what is health? This is a question as much for the "chamelion Poet," consumptive lover, and fatally self-potioned dreamer as for the physician of the early nineteenth century. If Keats "stands as the last image of health at the very moment when the sickness of Europe began to be apparent,"[2] and if the poet's immediate experience as mortally ill tubercular patient is incidental to his poetic achievement, sickness and the treatment of sickness are nevertheless crucial to the "image of spiritual and moral health" that his poetry presents. No definition of health existed apart from the concept of illness for the scientists of the Romantic period. Medical aetiology revealed to them as much about the morbific causes of disease as it did about the physiology of health; diagnosis or the interpretation of illness and revelation of that which poisons health disclosed agents, extrinsic and intrinsic, tangible and intangible, that disrupted, altered, and destroyed—but also invigorated, transformed, and renewed—health.[3]

The ideal of perfect health has always been a scientific and philosophical hypothesis, an early presupposition of knowledge posited only for its potential use in the understanding of sickness. Novalis spoke for several of his generation (and for *all* of the generation of decadence that followed him) when he observed in 1798 that perfect health was a scientific ideal, less interesting by far to thinkers— artists as well as the scientists themselves—than the "electrifying" notion of sickness that brought both meaning and "individualizing" to the subject. For a Romantic age that had yet to discover bacteria and yet to comprehend a pathology of germs, disease revealed all the questions that lay hidden in a hypothetical and impossible health. In Keats's poetry metaphors of health are outnumbered only

137

by metaphors of disease. But the distinction between health and sickness, the point at which health becomes disease, no less than the point at which the treatment becomes malignant and the potion turns poison, or the moment at which the energizing emotion of the lover turns consumptive and debilitative so as to flesh and magnify the neuroses of which it would be cured, are distinctions not easily made. Conrad, in Keats's "sinking" tragedy, *Otho the Great*, invokes this ambiguity at just one level when he speaks of the sparkle of "healthy fevers" (I, i, 84–86). When in 1830 Coleridge declared that "all remedies without exception are in their effects Diseases,"[4] he restated the law of similars of Romantic homeopathy, *similia similibus curantur*: every disease is curable by such medicines as would produce in a healthy person symptoms similar to those that characterize the given disease;[5] that medicines produce diseases in healthy people; and that a naturally occasioned disease can be cured by a medicinally induced disease. But he also articulated what was for his age a fundamental interconnection of meaning and perhaps dependency of any concept of health upon prevailing concepts of sickness. Romantic medicine functioned upon the very energizing ambiguity that underlay all treatments, whether physiological or mental, specifically medical or largely philosophical.

Early-nineteenth-century anatomy learned its very patterns of inquiry from disease; as Foucault says, the pathological spontaneously anatomizes, and "disease is an autopsy in the darkness of the body, dissection [while] alive." The Romantic era's declared unification of medicine, surgery, and pharmacy as disciplines sharing a single interest in human life, and its anatomists' and clinicians' revelation through their work on the human body of "what for centuries had remained below the threshold of the visible and the expressible,"[6] produced two distinguishing characteristics in the *modus operandi* of its physicians: a dependence on the clinical observation of the physical symptoms of illness, and a fascination with the revealing varieties of pathological evolution. Two minor manifestations of these in Keats would be his advice to his brother Tom—"send him [Dr. Solomon Sawrey] a correct accou[n]t of all your sensations and symptoms concerning the Palpitation and the spitting and the Cough"—and his later accurate reading of the deathly sign of his own symptoms: "I know the colour of that blood;—it is arterial blood;—I cannot be deceived in that colour;— that drop of blood is my death-warrant;—I must die."[7] The Romantic physician's duty to heal and apprehend life correctly led, inevitably, to a preoccupation with disease: to its morbid patterns of signs and to its debilitating but lively evolution.

"I intend to cut all sick people if they do not make up their minds to cut sickness—a fellow to whom I have a complete aversion, and who strange to say is harboured and countenanced in several houses where I visit—he is sitting now quite impudent between me and Tom—He insults me at poor Jem Rice's—and you have seated him before now between us at the Theatre—where I thought he look'd with a longing eye at poor Kean."[8] In this sardonic paragraph of March 1818, Keats delivers, with the observant eye of a practical physician, a summary of what illness meant to early-nineteenth-century medicine before the discovery of bacterial pathology. Disease could be a divisive external agent, a ravenous or cancerous internal agent, or a neutral agent of disequilibrium that preyed upon a presumed but unprovable complacent harmony. Following close upon the advances of eighteenth-century medicine, which had established semiotics and the reading of the signs of diseased life as basic clinical practice, but without the insights of cellular structure that were to make possible Virchow's pathology, the Romantic era in medicine had to be one of unbounded speculation on the character and progress of disease. In this period between the birth of the clinic and the discovery of the living cell, rivaling theories of disease and its treatment could and did flourish, and the Romantic fascination with the "energizing" ambiguity of illness found ample domain.

Schelling, Schiller, and Friedrich Schlegel provide the perspective on disease conceived by German Romantic medicine. For Schelling in 1802, disease is a precondition of organic life that reveals the potential limitations of the organism's physiology: "The individual is confined within certain limits which cannot be transgressed without making its [his] existence impossible; hence, he is subject to disease." Linnaeus, in *Genera morborum* (1763), had applied his botanical classifications of orders, classes, genera, and species to diseases; in Schelling's *Naturphilosophie*, the laws of evolution of organic life could prevail over the species as well as over the diseases of the species because disease belonged to the perfections of creation:

Laws that govern the metamorphoses of disease also govern the universal transformations that nature effects in producing the different species. . . . Clearly medicine will not be integrated in the universal organic theory of nature until it construes the species of disease—which are, so to speak, "ideal organisms"—as unmistakably as natural history construes the species of real organisms.[9]

To this interrelation between the "real organisms" of the species and the "ideal organisms" of their diseases belongs the young Schiller's notion that health is merely "a tendency to *permanency*" that disease, as "ideal organism," counterbalances and vitiates.[10] "That the air and atmosphere of our globe is in the highest degree full of life, I may, I think, take here for granted and generally admitted," Schlegel says in his *Philosophy of Life*; noting the "chaotic struggle" between the "balsamic breath of spring" and "the most deadly vapours" in the earth's atmosphere, he asks, "What else, in general, is the wide spread and spreading pestilence, but a living propagation of foulness, corruption, and death? Are not many poisons, especially animal poisons, in a true sense, living forces?"[11] The notion of disease as living energy can be found even in the French mechanists of the period; Bichât defines disease in terms of living tension between opposites: life is "the totality of functions which resist death," and disease, which "opposes" life, is the "revolt" of those organs whose "silence" constitutes health.[12]

In England, prevailing theories of disease largely owed their origins to the teachings of William Cullen and his pupil John Brown. Cullen's *Nosology, or A Systematic Arrangement of Diseases by Classes, Orders, Genera, and Species* (1772) evoked Linnean evolutionary classification to treat disease as varying nervous disorder: diseases originated in the nervous system from an excess or deficiency of living nervous fluid. John Brown carried the Cullen theory of disease further and described all diseases as the result of an excess or a deficiency of nervous "excitability" or the principle of life. Brunonian theory of disease implied that the task of the physician was never done because the body was always in a state of disease requiring medicines that either stimulated or debilitated it;[13] the practical implementation of this theory in the London clinics during Keats's apprenticeship could be viewed in the electrical department at St. Thomas's Hospital, where shocks and sparks were administered as stimulants, and point discharges as sedatives.[14] John Hunter had also subscribed to the notion of a vital principle in physiology that was active in producing disease, and he treated disease as integral to life, "the solution of which is to be sought in the great laws of life, as perturbations indeed of the order, which these laws maintain";[15] Hunter also believed in a natural constitutional tendency to certain diseases, and so introduced into medical perception the concept "disposition" to denote the subjective state of the potentially diseased individual.[16] When John Abernethy summarized the nature of disease as conceived by contemporary English medicine in

1815, he remained within the models set by Cullen, Brown, and Hunter: "Disorder, which is the effect of faulty actions of nerves, induces disease. . . . Disorder excites to disease. . . ." By 1819 Abernethy's statements on disease included the larger theorizing on the life of disease of the German *Naturphilosophen*.[17] General sources of the period defined disease with even less specificity. *Quincy's . . . Medical Dictionary* (1817), a standard reference for students of the London hospitals, carries the definition "Any alteration from a perfect state of health is a disease"; Duncan in the *Encyclopaedia Britannica* (1810) is no more explicit: "A *disease* takes place, when the body has so far declined from a sound state, that its functions are either quite impeded, or performed with difficulty. A disease therefore may happen to any part of the body either solid or fluid, or to any one of the functions."[18] Even Babington and Curry's "practical definition of disease" for the students of Guy's Hospital was pointedly inexplicit: "*An uneasiness,—excess,—or defect, in one or more of the functions of the body or mind,—recurring so often, or continuing so long, as to demand medical assistance.*"[19]

No longer able to believe in the old concept of an ideal state of health, nor able to hypothesize prior health because of new knowledge of the potential "disposition" for disease in any given individual, Romantic medicine found disease to be a cipher fully without resolution. Hence the absence of a single, independent, and functioning theory of disease during the early century. Hence also the enlightened and perceptive speculation in the theories of disease catalogued above. If disease was that which was opposed to the mechanism of life according to Bichât, it was also, as the Brunonians believed, dependent on a vitalistic principle of life; if disease represented a tangible deviation within organic life to French pathologists, it was also an "ideal organism" to the German natural philosophers; if disease threatened or attacked life with disorder, it also imitated life—species of diseases existed in a natural order, and each morbid group was organized according to the model of living organisms. Thus, the rationality and ordering of life was identical with the rationality and ordering of that which threatened life. Indeed, with the comprehension of multiple pathological life, a knowledge that there was a life of tubercles and a life of cancers, came also, as something made possible by Bichât's revelation of a common texture to the tissues and F.J.V. Broussais's revelation (*Examen des doctrines médicales*, 1816) that certain diseases were nothing more than complex movements of tissues in reaction to irritation, a sense not just of the kinships between diseases but that these resemblances were no different from the living interconnections in healthy life.

In 1813 Coleridge remarked that "no Disease was ever yet cured, but merely suspended."[20] In 1817 Keats wrote to Bailey along similar lines: "The little Mercury I have taken has corrected the Poison and improved my Health—though I feel from my employment that I shall never be again secure in Robustness—."[21] Both poets express a belief common (and commonly feared by Romantic physicians) that disease might not be multiple, discernible, and specific but idiopathic, that it was an irreducible sign, a cipher inseparable from the cipher of life, a process of recurrence like life, and, therefore, a mystery that defied common notions of external cause and cure. Two illnesses that gave great validity to this notion of disease were tuberculosis and cancer, afflictions we know to be of specific concern to Keats. These two paradigms of disease were incomprehensible in their workings to every prevailing system of medicine: they were recurrent, they responded to no items in the materia medica, they could attack any and all organs of the body, they were influenced alike by mental state and external environment, they masqueraded as other diseases, and terms like *excitation* and *intensity* could be used to describe the symptoms of both. The only medical sign of both diseases as read in the clinics of the early nineteenth century saw them as the manifestation of the energy (albeit a deformed energy) of life itself.

In the special research wards at Guy's Hospital the incurable patients were predominantly tubercular and cancer victims. Because of the nature of cancer, and because of the general medical hope that an understanding of the "poison" that produced cancers would be the clue to the understanding of all other morbid poisons and the "growth" of consumptive disease, cancer patients became a focus for experimental research in surgery, drugs, and nosology itself. Astley Cooper and Alexander Marcet were among those physicians and surgeons who practiced radical surgery and chemical therapy in the two wards designated for clinical research at Guy's; they used and witnessed the use of desperate remedies, of poisons like hemlock poultices to shrink visible tumors, and deadly stramonium to reduce the intense pain of invisible tumors.[22] Cooper's *Notes on Cases* (1818) devotes a long last section to the variety of tumors he treated, and he wrote an important treatise on breast cancer. His brother-in-law, Everard Home, whose primary practical research was of breast tumors, wrote what was considered to be the definitive study of cancer. Home's *Observations on Cancer* (1805) tells us of the prevailing suppositions about cancer: it is a poison whose origin is in the body, it occurs in a part previously altered in tissue structure by some *other* agent, certain constitutions are more vulnerable to its occurrence, it operates invisibly, its symptoms can mask those of other diseases and often mimic other diseases, it reveals no comprehensible medical signs, and it tends to purge other afflictions even as it consumes or debilitates health.[23] To Home and his generation of Romantic physicians, cancer was a paradigm of disease and of life as disease.

Novalis (in 1798) had also defined cancer as an inexplicable energy kindred to life itself when he discussed cancer and gangrene as "full-fledged *parasites*—they grow, are engendered, engender, have their structure, secrete, eat."[24] Schelling's description of disease as disingenuous life supports the paradigm of cancer:

> There thus arises a life which is indeed a life, but is false, a life of lies, a growth of disquiet and corruption. . . . Disease of the whole organism can never exist without the hidden forces of the depths being unloosed; it occurs when the irritable principle which ought to rule as the innermost tie of forces in the quiet deep, activates itself, . . . and steps forth into the surroundings. . . . Disease is indeed nothing essential and is actually only an illusion of life and the mere meteoric appearance of it—a swaying between being and non-being—but nonetheless announces itself in feeling as something very real.[25]

Thus, cancer became for the early nineteenth century a monstrous energy born of life, modeled on and feeding upon the energy of life. It was, as such, a sign of enduring life that manifests itself through its passing deformities. More pertinent yet to the Romantic sense of disease as a cipher to life is Home's opening statement in the *Observations*:

> Cancer is a disease which must engage the attention of every practitioner in surgery, in a greater or lesser degree; for even those who have no particular turn for investigation, must be led, by feelings of humanity, to employ their minds upon the consideration of a complaint, which so frequently baffles all their skill, and destroys such numbers of both sexes, but more particularly females.[26]

Keats was speaking of the unaccountability of pain, the illogic of disease, and the overwhelming power of illness to undermine human achievement when he said that he would "reject a petrarchal coronation—on accou[n]t of my dying day, and because women have Cancers."[27] His thinking nevertheless finds one source in his experience in the clinical wards for incurables at Guy's and in his immedi-

ate awareness as a Romantic physician of the real unaccountability
of disease upon which all treatments were based.

The energy that Keats as mortal poet of *The Fall of Hyperion* invokes
against selfish dreamers, mock poets, and false physicians requires
scrutiny through the Romantic physician's perspective on disease:

> Then shouted I
> Spite of myself, and with a Pythia's spleen,
> "Apollo! faded, far flown Apollo!
> Where is thy misty pestilence to creep
> Into the dwellings, through the door crannies,
> Of all mock lyrists, large self worshippers,
> And careless hectorers in proud bad verse.
> Though I breathe death with them it will be life
> To see them sprawl before me into graves.
>   (I, 202–10)

Apollo's "misty pestilence," an energy born of his infinite power of
life, will bring death and life, disease and health, once it has insinu-
ated its power into all "dwellings." The plague-arrows of the "God of
the golden bow," we recall from Part I, can inflict pestilence or cure
with fiery power; the ambiguity of their action when they kill in the
Odyssey (III, 280) endures even in translation, in Lattimore's "painless
arrows," in Cook's "soothing shafts," in Fitzgerald's "unseen arrows."
But is Apollo's power one that brings pestilence or one that brings
forth a pestilence? And how does a pestilence that cures pestilence
function? Does the god's power (pestilence) excite a fever that expels
an internal disease? Or does it incite an incipient tumor, a poison
within the body to raven and erupt? Does its fire consume, or nurture
to health internal consumption? Most of all, whether Apollo's power
excites or incites, how can the Romantic physician tell whether what
it brings is health or disease?

The poet of *The Fall of Hyperion* calls on Apollo with "a Pythia's
spleen." Pythias were the women mouthpieces of Apollo in his temple
at Delos; they raged, foamed at the mouth, and uttered prophecy. As a
Pythia, the poet in the poem speaks with inspired frenzy, but he also
manifests spleen that is at once mythical dementia, righteous passion,
and the tangible (black) effluvia of disease; as a Pythia foaming forth
like a snake, he further recalls the Python that Apollo once destroyed
to save his mother's life. The "misty pestilence" invoked manifests
itself, moreover, as both a fire-breathing snake that would "creep / Into
the dwellings" and strike all "careless hectorers" and as a murky and

polluting effusion that would seep "through the door crannies." As a plague, the pestilence will cause disease, exposure, and death to all false physicians and prophets, as a fiery or pharmaceutical purge, the pestilence will bring healing, health, and life to all true physician-poets. If we are to trust the faith of the poet of *The Fall of Hyperion*, who is himself afflicted by Apollo, disease brings health, its purging affliction makes whole, its debilitation brings life, its suffering brings the exposure of knowledge, and its meaning can ever be transformed into the signs and paradigms that govern health and art. All diseases, to reverse Coleridge's remark, can be in their effects the remedies of health; the cipher of disease is a conduit to life and the knowledge of life. The task of the Romantic physician and poet is to follow the conduit and pursue its meaning.

Chapter 11

The Pharmakon

Apollo's arrows, or snakes, or mists warrant further pursuit. When Apollo discharged his arrows into the Greek host besieging Troy, pestilence followed. But this pestilence, we are told by Homer, was occasioned by Agamemnon's crime. The source of the pestilence remains uncertain. We are left to speculate whether Apollo's arrows are poisoned, and come as an affliction to punish Agamemnon's men for his sin; or whether the god's arrows are dangerous simply because they are his, expressions of divine power that automatically reveal the internal corruption of the mortal Greeks (or their leader). If the divinity manifest in Apollo's arrows was not poisonous, the reverse association prevails nevertheless and the mystery and inexplicability of the *quid divinum* thus attaches itself to the earliest conceptions of pestilential poison.[1]

A similar, larger ambiguity prevails with Apollo's other symbol, the evergreen laurel. The god's legendary pursuit of Daphne made the laurel sacred to his followers: his male initiates wore it in wreath form for its intoxicating perfume, and the Pythian priestesses at Delphi chewed laurel leaves to induce the frenzy of oracular inspiration. Apollo's laurel wreath, as *the* symbol of poetic achievement ever since, finds repeated mention in Keats, in the "laurel chaplets," proud laurel wreaths and flowering sprigs that the aspiring poet invokes ("To Charles Cowden Clarke," 45, "God of the golden bow," 9, "I stood tip-toe," 134), and in the "incense pillow'd," "pure freshness of [Apollo's] laurels green" that "Breathless the laurel'd peers" inhale in this young poet's imaginary world (*End.*, II, 999, "Specimen of an Induction," 54, "Ode to Apollo," 20). But laurel, as the poet certainly knew, was a potent narcotic poison. A source for prussic or hydrocyanic acid, laurel was recognized in all its plant manifestations and chemical compounds by a strong and distinctive odor of bitter almond. Robert Burton had described laurel as "hot and dry in the fourth degree," and the strongest purger of melancholy. The drug was certainly well known in the early nineteenth century for its poisonous subtlety and for its rapidity of action;[2] it acted on the brain and the nervous and respiratory systems, and its mythical intoxicating power and ability to induce breathless poetic frenzy were but the first and least of symptoms that included convulsion, paralysis, and coma. Even the smallest dose of laurel extract, "the most active poison known to the human as well as all other animal existence" according to William Salisbury, could produce these symptoms and a telltale aroma about the patient; the epileptic fit induced by prussic acid ingestion was brief and invariably followed by a rapid and agonized death.[3] If one may rudely excise from their context the words of Conrad (*Otho the Great*, I, i, 3) and transplant them to the mouth of the god of pestilence and poetry, Apollo would say, correctly, to Agamemnon, sinners, physicians, and poets since, "For every crime I have a laurel-wreath."

From its inception the Greek *pharmakon* has expressed the duality of its first legendary employer to mean both "healing drug" and "corrosive poison."[4] The Latin derivation of the word *poison*, *potio* or *potionem*, means simply and ambiguously "a drink," a potion that can be wholesome or unwholesome.[5] The word *toxicology* derives from the Greek words *toxon*, which means "bow," and *toxikon*, which means "pertaining to a bow"; *toxicon pharmakon* was the substance with which one smeared arrows to make them more dangerous and true to their object. The effect of using *toxikon* (or the Latin *toxicum*) as short for the Greek phrase for "poisoned arrows" gradually led to the interchange of meanings between *pharmakon* and *toxikon*. *Poison* thus became a general term for dangerous substances, whether pharamaceutical or pestilential.

Furthermore, the Greek *ios* means both "arrow" and "venom,"[6] and the Latin *venenum*, meaning "poison, potion, drug, dye," is by way of *venin*, the potion of Venus, the source for the word *virus*, which was used to denote both the poisonous secretion of snakes and the pestilential effluvia of marshes and carrion grounds. The Latin derivations of the word *infection* (like the Greek derivations of its equivalent, *miasma*), meanwhile, return to the most ambiguous connotation of the term *pharmakon* or *venenum*: a "dye," an ink, a substance that in small quantity colors, tinctures, changes, subverts, and transforms—for good or ill. *Infectio* means staining or dyeing; the verb *inficere*, like its Greek counterpart *miaino*, means principally to put or dip into something, where that something may be a dye; or to mix with something, especially a poison or drug; or to stain something in the sense that it becomes tainted, polluted, corrupted, or spoiled.[7] The visible tincture that the druggist or alchemist (or barber) used in small quantities to color and influence large amounts of fluid or substance became the analogy for the invisible tincture of pestilence in its ability to infect through the most minute agents and quantities, singly or in epidemics, large bodies of living things. Both the tincture and its analogy harked back to the first *pharmakeus* in each of his roles as god of medicine, disease, music, prophecy, and poetry.

The interwoven ambiguities of pharmacy were traditional and contemporary for Keats's generation of physicians. Guy's Hospital maintained its own botanic garden to supply its pharmacy during the early nineteenth century, but the established teaching and research institution for clinical students was the Society of Apothecaries' Chelsea Physic Garden.[8] There, Keats and his fellows would have seen growing side by side and categorized by function all the plant sources for the botanical potions known to Romantic medicine; the head botanist, William Salisbury, would have lectured to the students on the uses and origins of these herbs. The Chelsea Physic Garden remains a functioning botanical laboratory to this day; the original teaching area and herb garden in the north corner have been preserved largely as they would have been when used for instruction by the society and the medical botanists of the Royal and Borough hospitals, and in the north quarter one can see the herbs grouped in the traditional categories. One finds soothing and regenerative medicinal plants, highly poisonous homeopathic plants, dyeing plants known for their tincturing powers, perfumery plants, and culinary herbs—these categories grow in adjacent beds to form distinct yet related sections, and plants like the peony, poppy, and hemlock that bear more than one use are carefully duplicated in the beds. The hypothetical multiplicity of the *pharmakon* in medical tradition thus finds startling, contemporary, palpable truth in the oldest of England's physic gardens that Keats visited regularly during the spring of 1816.[9] Nightshade, wolfsbane, henbane, green, white, and black hellebore, foxglove, ruby madder, adder's tongue, yellow chamomile, woodbine, mandrake, hyssop, and buttercup narcissus all find their place by specific pharmaceutical use in the Chelsea Physic Garden—as they do in the physic of Keats's poetry.

"The fertile earth," Homer says, produces many subtle drugs, "many good in mixture, [and] many malignant"; Friar Lawrence, in *Romeo and Juliet*, also invokes the interdependence of poison and potion when he observes that the same flower may provide both succor and weapon: "For this, being smelt, with that part cheers each part, / Being tasted, stays all senses with the heart."[10] Linnaeus's classification of plants (1735–1737) provided for the century that followed not only the pattern for the life of the species and their diseases but also proof of the tangible pattern and genealogy whereby plants revealed themselves to be agents for health or of death. Over the years, in tandem with the evolution of medical thinking and literary tradition, and always reflecting back to the original *pharmakeus* (Apollo), the concept of the *pharmakon* or potion for beneficence or maleficence has compounded its connotations: as "the powerful grace that lies / In plants, herbs, stones,"[11] *theriaca*, panacea, *nostrum*, the bewitching charm of the Greek sorcerer, the jeweled talisman of the medieval magician, the witch's amulet, the philosopher's elixir, the sacred oil, the dark brew, the blistering plaster, the soothing ointment, the curse, the *logos* spoken or sung, the honeyed pill, the secret recipe, the perfumed philtre. What the early nineteenth century discovered, as witnessed by Coleridge's homeopathic remark that all remedies are in their effects diseases, was the literal and pharmacological verity of the "richest juice in poison-flowers" (*Isabella*, 104). As the *pharmakon* had implied in its earliest connotations,[12] no remedy can be harmless or fully wholesome; beneficence is not a simple good, pestilence could be a *pharmakon* or remedy, the beneficial virtue of a substance does not prevent it from causing pain, and pain and disease themselves could be the agents for health and the absence of pain.

The rampant practice of professional poisoning in Italy, France, and (to a lesser extent) England in the sixteenth and seventeenth centuries gave place by the early nineteenth century to a widespread professional interest in poisons and their function. This interest was crucial in the absence of germ theory to the concept and treatment of disease. In 1813 and 1829 respectively, M.J.B. Orfila and Robert Christison, building upon the more specialized poison research of physiologists like Felice Fontana (*Ricerche fisiche sopra il veleno della vipera*, 1767), Joseph Adams (*Observations on Morbid Poisons, Phaegedaena, and Cancer*, 1795), and William Heberden (*Commentaire de historia et curatione*, 1802), published the first comprehensive, systematized studies of toxicology. Orfila's *Traité de toxicologie générale* drew on the botanical, minerological, and pestilential research of England, Italy, Germany, and France that had preceded it, and included a special section on animal venoms. It was translated into English in 1815, and widely reviewed in the scientific journals of the time.[13] Christison's *Treatise on Poisons* summarized and advanced Orfila's work to include the new research in England that had been inspired by Orfila's work. Christison was a student of John Abernethy and William Lawrence before he went to study under Orfila in Paris; by 1842 he was the recognized authority on poisons.[14] These two studies marked both the significant relation of toxicology to medicine and the natural sciences, as well as the popular fascination with the subject of poisons—not just the garden varieties but the mineral and animal poisons; not just the European poisons but the strange and curious poisons of South America and the Far East.

Travelers to South America like Alexander von Humboldt and August de St. Hilaire brought back stories of peculiar and powerful plant poisons like curare that could infect living creatures as well as poison the air and water.[15] Travelers to the Far East like N. P. Foersch brought back accounts of the U*pas-antiar* or poison-tree of Java that could destroy through its effluvia all living things within a twelve-to-fourteen-mile radius so that it grew in a splendid and barren wasteland with no other living company except two younger trees of its own species.[16] The story of this tree found imaginative credibility with Blake ("The Human Abstract," *Songs of Experience*), Byron, who told of Fez where "many a poison-tree has root" (*Don Juan*, IV, 40), and Coleridge, who wanted to write a poem describing "a Tartarean Forest all of Upas trees"[17]; Francis Danby painted the tree amid a barren landscape in 1820; the legendary tree also found believers in scientists like Erasmus Darwin, who wrote a bad stanza on the "HYDRA-TREE of death" in his *Botanic Garden*, and in Orfila himself, who thought the tree might be related to the strychnos vine, which bore the nux vomica poison fruit.[18] If Keats did not encounter Orfila's work directly, current ideas on the subject were nevertheless available to him because English physicians like Astley Cooper, Everard Home, Benjamin C. Brodie, and Alexander Marcet corresponded and occasionally worked with Orfila.[19] Cooper's lectures on surgery and physiology at Guy's Hospital while Keats was there included a substantial lecture on the subject of poisons;[20] Brodie is cited repeatedly by Orfila and by James Curry, Keats's teacher on the practice of medicine who purchased copies of Orfila in 1815 for the Guy's Physical Society Library; furthermore, while Brodie assisted Everard Home and Astley Cooper in cancer research, he also completed his own work on vegetable poisons that was to win him the Copley Medal of the Royal Society in 1811.[21]

All the definitions of poison by the physicians of the early nineteenth century are inherently ambiguous and marked by a careful nonspecificity. Orfila begins his treatise with the recognition that *toxicology* derives from the Greek words for healing drug, poison, dye, and discourse; "the name of poison is given to any substance, which, taken inwardly, in a very small dose, or in any kind of manner applied to a living body, impairs health, or destroys life." The 1817 edition of *Quincy's . . . Medical Dictionary*, noting that "it is extremely difficult . . . to give a definition of a poison," marks the inaccuracy of its own statement that poison is "that substance which, when applied externally, or taken into the human body, uniformly effects such a derangement in the animal economy as to produce disease. . . ." Christison denotes a poison to be "any substance which, acting on living bodies in small quantities, occasions serious disturbance of their functions. . . ." Astley Cooper's definition, "Poisons are those substances which, in small quantities, produce deleterious effects on the human body," is tied to a homeopathic recognition that "there is no substance considered as poisonous which in very small doses is not capable of producing a beneficial effect."[22] All substances that act vigorously on the human body are poisonous for Orfila and Christison; all poisonous substances in small doses can be beneficial medicines for Astley Cooper; the most active poisons for *Quincy's . . . Medical Dictionary*, "in small doses, form the most valuable medicines."[23] Homeopathy had always maintained that dosage alone distinguishes the point where materia medica become toxic poisons; and, worse, that medicines compound and collect in the body to return later as ghostly poisonous agents. As Coleridge says, "Mercury strongly illustrates the theory *de vi minimorum*. Divide five grains into fifty doses, and they may poison you irretrievably."[24] William Babington's first lecture on materia medica at Guy's instructed that "on a familiar and intimate knowledge of the properties of the Materia Medica alone, can the doctrine of prescription be founded. This is a test by which all medical information may be examined"; the prescription of poisonous substance had to be born of a thorough clinical knowledge of the remedy's effects.[25] Substances in the *Guy's Hospital Pharmacopoeia* like arsenic, mercury, corrosive sublimate, antimony, opium, foxglove, camphor, nux vomica, hellebore—which Keats would have known and prescribed—were poisonous in even the smallest of doses. "The little sweet doth kill much bitterness" (*Isabella*, 97), Keats says, highlighting a common medical and poetic crux on the frequent indistinguishability between sweet sustenance, physic, and poison.

For Coleridge, "that which is digested wholly, and part of which is assimilated, and part rejected, is—Food"; that "which is digested wholly, and the whole of which is partly assimilated, and partly not, is—Medicine"; and that "which is digested, but not assimilated, is—Poison." Food, medicine, and poison are all fully digested by the human body, but only food is fully consumed.[26] Medicines are partly assimilated by the human body, like food; poisons are not. Coleridge's sense that assimilation is what distinguishes the remedy from the poison is fundamental to early-nineteenth-century drug therapy. Undermined by Coleridge's remark that all remedies are diseases, it is also undermined by the source of Coleridge's remark: the homeopathic law of similars, which said that the poisons that incited and mimicked the symptoms of disease in health, like Hahnemann's quinine or Peruvian bark, were the best medicines in disease. Whether medicines are active, inciting agents or inert substances that the human system incorporated, unassimilable foreign agents, or natural assimilable substances becomes the primary issue behind all definitions of medicine in Keats's time.

Andrew Duncan's *Edinburgh New Dispensatory* (1803) affirmed generally that "every substance employed in the cure of diseases, whether in its natural state, or after having undergone various preparations, belongs to the materia medica, in the extended acceptation of the words."[27] Thomas Percival, noting that "no branch of the healing art" has undergone "so many doctrinal vicissitudes" nor been "in itself more intricate and obscure" than pharmacology, defines medicines simply and generally as "the instruments, employed for the preservation of health, or the cure of diseases. . . ."[28] The *Encyclopaedia Britannica* of 1810 notes that all prevailing drug theories follow the counters in the mechanism-vitalism debate: "Medicines can act on the human system only in two general modes; either as it [i.e., the system] is composed of inert matter, or as it forms a living organized system. In the first mode, medicines may act either mechanically or chemically; in the second, they act entirely through the medium of the vital principle."[29] Definitions of medicine such as these invariably mimic current definitions of poison; they are no more specific and no less ambiguous. It is not simply that a "very close connection subsists between medicinal and poisonous action" but, as Christison speculates, "the two properties, medicinal virtue and poisonous influence, are plainly nothing else than manifestations of the same action, differing merely somewhat in degree . . . the activity of the substances as drugs being proportioned to their energy as poisons," with the best medicines being the most active and influential poisons.[30] The energy of poisons and medicines, like the energy of disease and health, has a common source; the actions of all are similar, assimilated, and often indistinguishable.

"Even bees, the little almsmen of spring-bowers, / Know there is richest juice in poison-flowers" (103–4), Keats says in *Isabella; or, The Pot of Basil* of Isabella's immortal love for what will soon be Lorenzo's putrefying (and therefore morbidly poisonous) corpse. He embraces by this complex, at once, every metaphorical and pharmacological implication of the *pharmakon*. His lines invoke the question addressed by contemporary physicians like Thomas Percival—"Is there in the grateful taste of *saccharum saturni* any indication of a deadly poison?"[31]—and point to the early-nineteenth-century physiologists' preoccupation with the mystery of how substances in the pharmacopoeia functioned. The sense that a common energy activated healing and poisonous drugs focused attention on these substances' apparent mode of action; hence, poisons and medicines were classified by the symptoms they produced. Orfila lists six classes of poisons, each of which finds representation, as we shall see, in Keats's poetry: corrosive poisons, like copper, brass, tin, and zinc, that irritate, inflame, and corrode the organs; astringent poisons, like lead, that constrict and inflame the organs and nervous system; acrid poisons, like nitrous acid, convolvulus, hellebore, castor, and wolfsbane, that taste caustic and produce both dry corrosion and suppuration of the organs; stupifying or narcotic poisons, like nightshade, datura stramonium, henbane, yew, and laurel, that cause stupor, paralysis, convulsions, and apoplexy; narcotico-acrid poisons, like belladonna, hemlock, mercury, mushrooms, carbonic acid, that act at the same time as narcotics and rubefacients; and the septic or putrefying poisons, which include all contagious miasmata, poisonous chemical gases, and animal venom, and that produce general dissolution of the body and syncope without affecting the intellectual faculties.[32] Astley Cooper's classification of poisons echoes Orfila's and further divides the poisons by immediate source: those derived "from the *animal* and *vegetable* kingdom," those from "*mineral* and *chemical* sources,—and another furnished by man himself"—*morbid poison*.[33]

The classifications of medicines in the early nineteenth century also follow the same general distinction by function of the poisons. Cullen's *Materia Medica* had established two primary divisions for English medicines: the stimulants, which are "powers capable of increasing the mobility, and of exciting the motion of the nervous power"; and the sedatives, which are "medicines which diminish the sensibility and irritability of the system, and thereby the motions and powers of motion in it."[34] Sedatives and stimulants popularly employed by physicians of the time in England could be substances from the *Pharmacopoeia Officinalis Britannica*, elements not yet catalogued but in common use, as well as medical practices like baths and electric shocks. Erasmus Darwin classed among the "incitantia" substances like opium, laurel, alcohol, cherry pits, tobacco, belladonna, thorn apple, hart's tongue bark, hemlock, and delphinium, as well as heat, ether, labor, and the poetically potent passions of love, joy, and anger; his "torpentia" included mineral acids, oils, vegetable mucilages, and antacids, but also antifermentation poultices, cold water, warm baths, venesection, arteriotomy, and the sublime influences of silence and darkness.[35] John Brown's theory of excitability led to an emphasis on the stimulating power of medicines in most contemporary pharmacologies: John

Murray's *Elements of Materia Medica and Pharmacy* (1804), for example, saw medicines as operating exclusively "by stimulating the living fibre, or exciting it to
motion . . . however diversified their effects may appear to be, such diversities
are to be referred merely to the different degrees of force in which they exert
the general stimulant power they possess."[36] As in the case of bark that could
be both a bitter and a tonic, all medicines were stimulants in Romantic
therapy; even the so-called sedatives or torpentia were stimulants in fact,
differing merely in the effects or symptoms they elicited from different parts of
the body at different times or under different conditions of disease. To this
sense belongs Keats's entry in his *Physiological Note Book* on the *soothing* actions
of certain stimulants: "Stimulus when applied where there is great debility is a
Tonic. In Typhus Stimulants will reduce the pulse. Digitalis considerably dimin-
ishes the frequency and force of the Pulse."[37] The 1810 version of Murray's
Materia Medica, significantly, declared all medicines to be stimulants, with the
difference in their stimulating action being the only foundation for their
division into classes: cathartics, diuretics, emmenagogues, and diaphoretics
were "local" stimulants; tonics, astringents, antispasmodics, and narcotics
were "general" stimulants.[38]

Categorizing poisons and materia medica by action did little to explain
their true mode of action. Speculation abounded on how the influence of
substances in the pharmacopoeia was transferred from outer to vital organs,
or from vital organs to the cerebronervous system; how some poisonous or
medical substances could initially affect the physical but not the mental
functions, and others the mind and sense but not the body. B. C. Brodie said
that the principal object of his experiments with vegetable and mineral poisons was to determine on which of the vital organs the particular poison
employed exercised "its primary influence, and through what medium that
organ becomes affected"; his research proved what Astley Cooper taught, that
poisons could operate on either the vascular-arterial system, or on the
cerebronervous system, or on both systems at once, and that the medium
whereby this affect took place was not always distinguishable.[39] Orfila, Erasmus Darwin, and Christison subscribed to the notion that poisons could act
not only by absorption into the glandular-circulatory system but by *sympathy*
and *without absorption*—by making a peculiar impression "on the sentient extremities of the nerves," which is "conveyed thence along their filaments to
the brain," so that "death takes place through the sympathetic irritation of the
nervous system, without the poison being absorbed."[40] (Darwin's example of a
poison that worked through sympathetic action without being absorbed was
arsenic, the young Chatterton's chosen death potion.)

Thomas Percival, meanwhile, applied this notion of sympathetic influence
of nervous action to the operation of medicines:

> The minutest agent, therefore, may excite a movement capable of being propagated
> to any part of the system, or even through the whole of it, by a sympathetic energy,

independent and far beyond the power of the primary instrument of motion. ... A medicine is only the *cause of a cause*, ... its proper action is confined to the nerves or fibres to which it is immediately applied.[41]

The *Encyclopaedia Britannica*, in 1810, reiterated Percival's theory that medicines may act on the human body either by direct absorption into the circulatory systems, or through an *"immediate and peculiar impression"* on the nerves of the organs to which they come into contact.[42] Keats's notes on drugs for stimulating absorption, like mercury, digitalis, antimony, and aloe, and on distant "sympathetic secretions" in response to these drugs,[43] clearly belong to teachings based on theories such as these, as do Cooper's teachings on organic sympathy discussed in Part IV. Both, necessarily, find their influential place behind Keats's concept of poetic sympathy or negative capability. To the early nineteenth century not only did specific medicines operate on different parts and systems of the body at different times, they could promote nervous reaction without absorption, and the "sensible qualities" of any substance had no direct relation to its medicinal action: Peruvian bark (Hahnemann's inspirational cinchona) did not owe its efficacy to bitterness, and insipid-tasting antimony was violent in its operations on the stomach.[44] The common texture of tissues and the "discovery" of sympathy thus verified the essentially mysterious operation of medicines and poisons.

Popular fascination with the pharmacopoeia combined with the experiments and chemical analyses of Romantic scientists to intensify the ambiguities of pharmacy and disease. Astley Cooper liked to end his lecture on poisons with an experiment illustrating the essentially mysterious nature of potent substances. "I shall conclude this lecture by shewing you the effect of a powerful poison called ticunas, with which the Indians, in the back settlements of Demerara, arm their arrows," Cooper would say to his students at Guy's. "There is a very minute portion of the poison on a stick in this little box, which is sufficient, however, to poison every one of you. I shall insert a small particle, I know not what fraction of a grain, into the cellular tissue of a rabbit, and you will see that, in the space of three or four minutes, the animal will die, without appearing to suffer the least pain. It will probably continue to eat the parsley on the table till it dies."[45] In their action for good or ill, poisonous elements in the materia medica could act swiftly or with agonizing slowness (as in Coleridge's story of slow poisoning by arsenic);[46] their "sensible" qualities were no clue to their potency; they could have immediate and local effects, or they could influence remote organs or textures without any sign of direct local action or absorption; this influence on remote organs could be of various modes depending on the substance and the subject. The quantity or chemical form of the substance, the texture of the organ acted upon, the habit and constitution of the subject, and the stage of disease were all variables that could neutralize or enhance the action of the pharmacological substance, for "substances which induced disease in one person or animal, do not induce diseases in others."⁴⁷ Even national character had its place in the action of poisons, for we find Keats marked the following passage on "Medicinal Physic" in his copy of Burton's *Anatomy of Melancholy*: "*Opium* in *Turkey* doth scarce offend, with us in a small quantity it stupifies; *circuta* (or hemlock) is a strong poison in *Greece*, but with us it has no such violent effects."⁴⁸ Vauquelin's 1812 analysis of deadly nightshade in Nicolson's *Journal* concludes "But neither these salts, nor these acids, impart to the matter its poisonous qualities. These unquestionably reside in the vegetable substance itself." The chemical analysis of the *pharmakon*, the attempt to reduce it to its primary components, thus produced irreducible mystery of substance and action. Romantic medicine had no answer to the question posed by Vauquelin's conclusion, "What then is the order of composition, that makes thus, with the same principles, both our food [or medicine] and such deadly poisons?"⁴⁹

Keats was richly aware of the potency of the *pharmakon*'s composite associations and irreducible properties in both the Western tradition and the medical research of his time. Potions, benign or malignant, tangible or intangible, ministered to body as to soul, are a recurring image in all his poetry. When Cupid the "Bright-winged Child" of *Endymion* is hailed as a "delicious poisoner" bearing a "venom'd goblet" (III, 978–89), we are reminded, at once, of the *saccharum saturni* and animal venom of early-nineteenth-century poison research, of the medieval alchemical and Romantic chemical fascination with the transmutation wrought by unchanging catalytic *pharmaka*, and of the old Greek tradition of the love-philtre (*philtron*) as an ambiguous potion given beneficent or sinister meaning according to the intention of the giver. Hence Circe, "arbitrary queen of sense," malevolent temptress, and "Potent goddess" of "pains resistless," bears a truly venomous "black dull-gurgling phial" in *Endymion* (III, 459; 539–40, 515); her phial is, in turn, the "receipt" (or recipe) for the "love philtres" with which Auranthe bewitches Ludolph in *Otho the Great* (III, ii, 14–15), and the prototype of the malignant "roots of relish sweet" that la belle dame sans merci feeds the hapless knight at arms (25).

Porphyro in *The Eve of St. Agnes* provides the most interesting summary of the connotative potion when he brings forth from the closet "with glowing hand"

> a heap
> Of candied apple, quince, and plum, and gourd;
> With jellies soother than the creamy curd,
> And lucent syrops, tinct with cinnamon;
> Manna and dates, in argosy transferr'd
> From Fez; and spiced dainties, every one,
> From silken Samarcand to cedar'd Lebanon.
> (262–70)

This feast that Porphyro lays out for the fasting, sleeping Madeline represents the most-worked-over lines (according to Stillinger) of all of Keats's manuscripts; it is a rich evocation, as Ricks notes, not so much of eating as of edibility.[50] We must ponder whether this feast is wholesome, fully assimilable food according to Coleridge's definition, a simple and harmless love potion given with the best intentions of a lover, or something of tempting edibility far more intricate and ambiguously true to its multiplicity of source.

To the luxury of "candied apple, quince, and plum," the sensuous smoothness of "jellies soother than the creamy curd," the exotic and magical "spiced dainties," "manna and dates," Porphyro adds "lucent syrops, tinct with cinnamon." With this last item, syrups colored and perfumed with cinnamon, Porphyro's feast of wholesomeness takes on all the ambiguous characteristics of the *pharmakon* as a drug, a poison, a dye, and a perfume. "Drowsy syrup," lest we forget, is a medical term; and dyeing was a secret art and subspecialty of the pharmacist that exploited, as Salisbury taught his students in medical botany at Guy's, basic chemical principles of an intermediate agent or mordant to effect its secret or magical results.[51] We are led to ask, is Porphyro's magical colored and perfumed syrup designed to make wholesome and elicit a harmony of love? Or is it a potion to divide and corrupt an innocence of health? Is it a potion to induce a unifying dream? Or a potion to terminate an alienating nightmare? Is it a substance to ensure that Porphyro's "bride" passes smoothly and unfeelingly into "a long immortal dream" (*Lamia*, I, 128)? Or an erotic agent to induce feverous overwrought excitation like that known by the lovers on the Grecian urn? Perhaps, like its protoypes the Apollonian laurel and the *pharmakon*, the love-philtre of the *Eve* is all these at once. The "drowsy Morphean amulet" (257) that Porphyro subsequently calls for in his role as demonic tempter, hoodwinking seducer, and false physician becomes thus a highly tangible if dubious "Solution sweet" for the patient dreamer Madeline. Her remedy is her disease.

The same interleaving complexity of meaning from literary and medical sources is present in Keats's evocations of less tangible potions. Vision can be potion in Keats. Indeed the *pharmakon* as love-philtre in Keats is no less ambiguous and fraught with significance than is the *pharmakon* as knowledge or vision. In *Hyperion* "Knowledge enormous" like "some blithe wine / Or bright elixir peerless" makes a god of Apollo even as Fate pours "A disanointing poison" of "mortal oil" upon the heads of the Titans (III, 113, 117–19, II, 96–98). Apollo's vision as an elixir of knowledge combines notions of the invigorating and stimulating intoxicant with alchemical associations of gold and immortality; his vision as the soothing balm of the god of medicine and poetry stands in opposition to the "mortal oil" that poisons and disanoints the Titans, to accomplish metaphorically for the Titans what the mortician's balm would accomplish literally. Moreover, the potion of knowledge or truth elsewhere in Keats is both a soothing sedative and a painful stimulant: if the Titans in *Hyperion* are urged by Oceanus to "Receive the truth, and let it be your balm" (II, 243), Endymion nevertheless feels truth like "a death-dart," "come / Naked and sabre-like against my heart," and knowledge of "That curst magician's name" stings and numbs at once (III, 555–58) like a potent poison. Isabella's situation in *Isabella; or, The Pot of Basil* is kindred and more complex, for knowledge of her brothers' crime comes to her in the form of a vision "like a fierce potion, drunk by chance:"

> And she had died in drowsy ignorance,
>   But for a thing more deadly dark than all;
> It came like a fierce potion, drunk by chance,
>   Which saves a sick man from the feather'd pall
> For some few gasping moments; like a lance,
>   Waking an Indian from his cloudy hall
> With cruel pierce, and bringing him again
> Sense of the gnawing fire at heart and brain.
>
> It was a vision.—
>   (265–73)

Isabella's "fierce potion" awakens her from a death in "drowsy ignorance"; it is a powerful stimulant more poisonous and "deadly dark than all." But, like the spear that awakens with pain the Indian drowsed by the fumes of burning herbs or, more pertinently, like a drug that briefly resuscitates a dying person, "bringing sense of gnawing fire at heart and brain," or perhaps like the surgeon's sacrificial lance that brings sensation and relief at the cost of pain, Isabella's "fierce potion" hastens death through ensuing debilitation. This *pharmakon*, lest we forget, is knowledge in the form of a vision: it hastens the onset of death, but it also excites and enlightens like Apollo's "bright elixir peerless" of immortality.

All connotations of the intangible potion combine in the parallel "domineering potion" that the poet of *The Fall of Hyperion* drinks from a "vessel of transparent juice" (I, 42–54). We are reminded first of the ceremonial opening of the wine in the Dionysiac festival of the Anthesteria where the new wine is referred to as a *pharmakon*, a magical substance of favorable or unfavorable effect. Plutarch, in *Moralia*, explains the new wine ritual: "In olden times they poured a libation from it before drinking it, and prayed that the use of the *pharmakon* might be without hurt to themselves, and a source of salvation."[52] More potent than the Anthesteria's new wine, this potion exceeds the power of any "elixir fine" to invigorate and enlighten, of any "poison gender'd in close monkish cell" to debilitate and destroy, or of any "Asian poppy" or *pharmakon* made of "fragrant husks and berries crush'd" to intoxicate and sedate simultaneously before bringing death; an "ethereal balm" like "Sweet Hope" ("To Hope," 5), it is nevertheless without hope and full of mortal urgency. It applies itself to body and to soul and brings, at once, sensation and cessation, pain and its relief, sorrow and knowledge, life and death, bound together in the conscious intensity of a waking dream. "That full draught," says the poet of *The Fall of Hyperion*, "is parent of my theme." As it is, of course, also that of Keats.

> For as Physicians use,
> In giving Children Draughts of bitter Juice,
> To make them take it, tinge the Cup with Sweet,
> To cheat the Lip; this first they eager meet,
> And then drink on, and take the bitter Draught,
> And so are harmlessly deceiv'd, not caught:
> For by this Means they get their Health, their Ease,
> Their Vigour, Strength, and baffle the Disease.
> So since our Methods of Philosophy
> Seem harsh to some; since most our Maxims sly,
> I thought it was the fittest way to dress
> In pleasing Verse these rigid Principles,
> With Fancy sweet'ning them; to bribe the Mind
> To read my Books. . . .[53]

From Lucretius, the young Keats learned of the physician's occasional need to "harmlessly deceive" both patient and disease, to "cheat the Lip" and "baffle the Disease"; and of the connection between this medical end and the philosopher's intent to dress "rigid Principles" and "Maxims sly" in "pleasing Verse" sweetened with Fancy so as to "bribe the Mind." To cheat with fancy was the task of the ancient Greek *pharmakos* or sorcerer, and it points up the original connection between medicine and magic discussed in Part I, the magical nature of diseases and their modes of treatment, and most of all, the nature of drugs as "pharmaceutical enchantments."[54] But students of medicine in the London and Edinburgh hospitals of the late eighteenth and early nineteenth centuries were enjoined by Thomas Percival's ethics to practice no magic and dispense no secret potions: "No physician or surgeon should dispense a secret *nostrum*, whether it be his invention, or exclusive property. For if it be of real efficacy, the concealment of it is inconsistent with beneficence and professional liberality. And if mystery alone gives it value and importance, such craft implies either disgraceful ignorance, or fraudulent avarice." Medical etiquette of the early nineteenth century further cautioned against "cloathing medicinal preparations in false colours, such as mixing rose pink with linseed meal, vermillion with epsom salts, burnt sugar with goulard water," and other such medical chicanery.[55]

The physician Keats was forbidden from prescribing secret recipes and doctoring common substances; the poet in Keats nevertheless saw the potent implications of the potion's indeterminate substance. Jacques Derrida in his attempt to chart a connection between *bibla* and *pharmaka* through an assay of Plato's *Phaedrus* evokes the standard magical connotations of the *pharmakon*: "*Pharmakon* in Greek means healing drug, poison, and dye, but all, for better or worse, are magical."[56] Writing and the pharmaceutical art, for this critic, share a transmutational power; they are beguiling, subversive, and suspect. But as we shall see from the multiplicity of Keats's potions, which can be ingested, rubbed, sprinkled or chanted over a person, seen, heard or smelled, or all these at once, the traditional connection between pharmacy and poetry is more complex and much older than Derrida suspects.

The fragrant ashes or *katharmata* of a sacrifice, especially those ashes of herbs or perfumed woods of cinnamon and laurel from the rituals to Apollo, formed a kind of sacred pharmacopoeia for the ancient Greeks.[57] "Through almond blossoms and rich cinnamon" the aspiring poet of "Sleep and Poetry" is enticed, until he is taught to sacrifice his strawberry-eating ease to the "strife / Of human hearts" (118, 124–25); and the old shepherds in *Endymion* hope to pass "through almond vales" "by divine converse, / Into Elysium" (I, 380, 371–72). Bitter almond and laurel, lest we forget, are recognized by their scent and share a common chemical base in prussic acid or cyanide. At the old sanctuary, where the poet of *The Fall of Hyperion* finds himself after his potion of "fragrant husks and berries crush'd," the "Maian incense" from Moneta's "lofty sacrificial fire," like the sudden mid-May release of "frozen incense from all flowers . . . fills the air with so much pleasant health" and brings "Forgetfulness of every thing but bliss." Then, from the altar's "white fragrant curtains" of "soft smoke," the poet hears "Language pronounc'd" (I, 52; 95–107). As in the sacred tradition of Apollo, his almond-scented laurel, his perfumed *pharmakon* of health, pestilence, and inspiration—all embodied in the ambiguous complex of early Greek pharmacy and religious ritual— perfume, music, words, and sacred signification form a pharmacological complex that compounds Keats's poetic potions.

Ointment and perfume "*rejoice the heart*, and, as some say, nourish," Burton said; and Keats, in his personal copy of *The Anatomy of Melancholy*, underlined all the "Odoraments to smell" that composed Burton's cures for head-melancholy: "Rose-water, Violet flowers, Balm . . . do much recreate the brains and spirits. . . ."[58] Perfume embodies the masking, ductile and manipulative qualities of the *pharmakon*. Thomas Lovell Beddoes hailed perfume as an "Exquisite masquer,"[59] and we recall that Porphyro's feast or love potion in *The Eve of St. Agnes* fills Madeline's room with a "perfume light" that combines with the music of a "hollow lute" to make, much "as the rose / Blendeth its odour with the violet," a "Solution sweet," indistinct, mixed, and dubious (*Eve*, 275; 289, 320–22).

The *Eve*'s metaphorical roses and violets evoke for us the more literal but also more ominous "Fast-fading violets" and "coming musk-rose, full of dewy wine" that the "Ode to a Nightingale" (46–48) summons forth to escape and mask an incurable melancholy. Porphyro's feast, which includes "manna" "in argosy transferr'd / From Fez" (268–69), meanwhile, reminds us that Endymion, amid his melancholy and lovelorn pains, "seem'd to taste a drop of manna-dew, / Full palatable; and a colour grew / Upon his cheek . . ." (I, 765–68). Endymion's "manna-dew" could be the mysterious nourishment of the

Israelites, or the cathartic, sweet, pale yellow juice of the manna ash or Persian manna tree, or the granular form of frankincense that was also called "manna."[60] Since it is a potion ministered to him by Peona, out of and for love, and therein at once nourishing and cathartic, sedating and invigorating, it is probably a composite of all three and a positive anticipation of la belle dame's deadly and disarming "manna-dew." The "glowing banquet-room" at Lamia's wedding feast is filled with perfumed wreaths of smoke "From fifty censers," each "fed with myrrh and spiced wood," and "by a sacred tripod held aloft"; these fumes are "still mimick'd" as they rise by "the mirror'd walls" of the palace, and the "sole perhaps and lone / Supportress of the faery-roof" with its multiplying "twin-clouds odorous" is "A haunting music" (*Lamia*, II, 173–82, 121–24). Images of feasting, perfume, sacred ritual, sacrifice, merging reflections, and bewitchment thus join together to form "the whole charm" that is Lamia's palace of sweet sin—her potion for Lycius, and through him for the doctoring of his guests.

Perfume and music share the quality of ductility, they are conveyances of the power (or the magic) of the potion: Porphyro's is a "hollow lute," the "cold serpent-pipe" in *Isabella* brings forth "odorous ooze" "Of precious flowers pluck'd in Araby" (410–12), serpentine Lamia breathing perfume and music at once is the medium of her own enchantment, and in *Endymion* "fair Syrinx" turns pipy reed and grows "where dank moisture breeds / The pipy hemlock" (I, 239–44) so that Pan may make enchanting transforming music of his love turned poison. Finally, in *Hyperion*, the presence of Apollo's power is signaled first by perfume, "a sweet clime was breathed from a land / Of fragrance, quietness, and trees, and flowers," and then by music, "new blissful golden melody" and families "of rapturous hurried notes." Healing becomes hymn (or paeon, from Paeon, Apollo's other name as the deity of healing). Apollo's power comes as "enchantment with the shifting wind," a perfumed, sounding balm that is "Full of calm joy" "and soft delicious warmth," even as it brings "A living death" borne with "each gush of sounds." (II, 262–66, 276–82). These are, "in truth," "Strange thunders from the potency of song; / Mingled indeed with what is sweet and strong, / From majesty" ("Sleep and Poetry," 230–32). Lest we forget what Keats never did, Apollo, whose *pharmakon* brought healing or death, was also the god of music and poetry; the charm of the first *pharmakeus* has found potion for good or ill in rhyming words ever since.

> Soft went the music the soft air along,
> While fluent Greek a vowel'd undersong
> Kept up among the guests, discoursing low
> At first, for scarcely was the wine at flow;
> But when the happy vintage touch'd their brains,
> Louder they talk, and louder come the strains
> Of powerful instruments:
> (*Lamia*, II, 199–205)

Music and the "vowel'd undersong" keep rhythmic pace with the flow of new and heady wine at Lamia's wedding banquet. Before Lamia's potion has time to work its effect, as one might expect, both the music and the guests' Greek remain "discoursing low," but once "the happy vintage touch'd their brains" the strains from guests and instruments grow loud and powerful. The high mead of their madness flows. In Book II of *De Rerum Natura* Lucretius speaks of the power of music to cure or incite mental disease: of the power of certain strong instruments "to swell the Soul to Rage and Fury," and of the power of gentle pipe-music to soothe through an "Enthusiastick Harmony." In a note to his text, Lucretius cites from tradition on the power of music to cure physical as well as mental ills through a combination of tangible and intangible media:

> Theophrastus writes in his Treatise of Enthusiasm, that Musick cures many Passions and Diseases both of the Mind and Body.... Baptista Porta ... says, that Madness is to be cur'd by the Harmony of a Pipe made of Hellebore; because the Juice of that Plant is held good for the same Purpose: and the Sciatica, by a musical Instrument made of Popular; because of the Virtue of the Oil, that is extracted from that Tree, in mitigating those Kinds of Pains.[61]

The Anatomy of Melancholy also marks that diseases could be "either procured by Musick or mitigated," and speaks of music's particular power either to intensify melancholy and love mania or to revive the languishing soul.[62]

The association of music (and chanted words or curses) with therapy or the induction of disease is an old one, and Keats must have read Lucretius and Burton well. The poet invokes music and the power of rhythmic words both to vex and soothe, as local therapeutic instruments and as organic pharmaceutical enchantments: "O that I had Orpheus lute—and was able to cha[r]m away all your Griefs and Cares—" he says to Bailey in 1817;[63] Peona leads Endymion "like some midnight spirit nurse," her tears are balm and her words are medicine, "Her eloquence did breathe away the curse" (I, 412–13); in Circe's bower, the "curst magician's" "tears, and smiles, and honey-words" and the "dew of her rich speech" weave a "net" of "thralldom" (III, 555, 426–29) for Glaucus, and Endymion pleads with her "—tease me not / With syren words" (II, 954–55).

If "All lovely tales that we have heard or read" are "An endless fountain of immortal drink / Pouring unto us from the heaven's brink" (*End.*, I, 22–24), this proves to be literally true in at least two of Keats's poems where the pharmaceutical substance or enchantment turns out to be a tangible book or scroll of rhyming words. Hum, the magician in the *The Jealousies*, takes from his "bright casket of pure gold" a "legend-leaved book" and gives it to Elfinan to use as a love-philtre: "Take this same book,—it will not bite you, sire; ... Though it's a pretty weight, it will not tire, / But rather on your journey keep you warm"; this "potent charm" will warm, invigorate, and make euphoric the fairy king even as it sedates and drives mortal "Bertha to a fainting fit" (510–22). A true and selfless physician where Elfinan is not, and bearing not so much a love potion as a true potion for life and sense, Endymion also administers a scroll of prophecy to the dead lovers and the aged Glaucus. To renew and invigorate all at Glaucus's behest, he takes the scrolls' "minced leaves" in "pieces small as snow" and, "with quick hand, the charm applied." Perfumed sound, "Delicious symphonies, like airy flowers, / Budded, and swell'd, and full blown," greet Endymion's magical therapy; like the wine-imbued music in the earlier scene of the awakening of Adonis, when "down swell'd an air / Odorous and enlivening" like the vaporous "nectar'd clouds" of "delicious wine," so now the "two deliverers" taste "a pure wine" "from fairy-press ooz'd out," an intangible synaesthetic potion that is delicious, perfumed and musical, "the richest overflow / Of joy that ever pour'd from heaven (III, 746, 768–790, 801–6, II, 510–14).

There are fewer clear distinctions than would first seem, and more connections than one could suspect, between Apollo's laurel and Apollo's pestilence—between quills and plague-arrows, the reedy syrinx and the pipy hemlock, tinctured syrops and melting airs, solutions sweet and pungent charms, poisoned pens and perfumed fires, sounding odors and siren words.

Chapter 12

Specific Pharmaka

Friar Lawrence tells us of the great and powerful grace that lies in herbs, plants, and stones; Keats, especially in *Endymion* and the early poetry, shows himself to be poet and "sage of mickle lore" because he is a priest of the "world's herbal" (*Otho*, III, ii, 123) who combines both a priestly knowledge of mythological pharmaceuticals with a nineteenth-century homeopathic belief in specific medicines; one who prescribes not only the mythical dittamy, grains of paradise, and cassia but also calomel, antimony and the "droop-headed flowers" of ipecacuanha. Linnaeus said that herbal plants were "medical jewels" gracing the countryside that few eyes saw and fewer minds understood.[1] When Keats evokes plants from "The range of flower'd Elysium" and the listening Earth, we can be certain that he does so with full medical comprehension. The herbs are invoked not just for their conventional poetic beauty, euphony, and mythological significance but for their specific pharmaceutical power, their botanical "net whose thralldom" (*End.*, III, 427–28) extends beyond poetic sound and mythic appearance over the body, the senses, and the mind.

"Some of the most active and powerful drugs are preparations from our common plants," Salisbury's *Botanist's Companion* warned in 1816, in pharmaceutical echo of the Romantic (and particularly Keatsian) sense of the immense potential for good or evil within the everyday and the commonplace. Salisbury's comments in his manual summarize what must have been more expansive injunctions in his spring 1816 course on medical botany at Guy's Hospital on the vital requirement that the physician's knowledge of botanical pharmacy be complete; that this knowledge extend beyond the textbooks on the materia medica used in the classrooms, and beyond the prescriptive staff pharmacopoeia used in the hospital wards, to a practical knowledge of *all* current and traditional botanical substances. "A knowlege of botany to the Physician is highly essential as a branch of his profession," Salisbury told his students; they were to remember that "although the Materia Medica of the present day does not contain that stock of indigenous vegetables which were formerly prescribed" the physician nevertheless could not "be held excused for his want of a scientific knowledge of such [plant items] as are poisonous" or medicinally useful; the physician was supposed to supplement his knowledge of pharmacy as best he could during the years of his practice since "the plants of every country and climate afforded medicine sufficient for the maladies thereof" and his knowledge of these "is a duty the public has a right to demand of him."[2]

In his course on pathology and therapeutics at Guy's, James Curry gave parallel instructions: students were to know the materia medica by their several names as "adopted by the Colleges of London, Edinburgh, and Dublin," and "if the article be a vegetable, its *Natural Order*, with a view to shew how far there is a connection between the *botanical character*, and the *medical virtue* of plants. 3dly, the Natural History of the Article;—the country, soil, and situation producing it; the modes by which it is obtained;—and the processes it undergoes before it is brought hither."[3] Practical physic and surgery of the early nineteenth century thus invoked and recommended the equally practical knowledge of the botanists in the field, and the ancient doctrine of herbal signatures was incorporated by Romantic medicine into its practical theory for the reading of pathological signs and the prescribing of homeopathic therapy. Keats's knowledge of the world's herbal, given his age's dictate to know and cure fully, would have to be thorough. His sources for botanical agents and pharmaceutical influences would have to include not only the instruction of Curry, Salisbury, and Cooper, nor just the botany texts like Thornton's *New Family Herbal* or his popular *Science of Botany* that were used for instruction at the London hospitals, but general and traditional sources like Culpeper's *Herbal* (revised in 1800 by Dr. Sibley), and ongoing almanacs and herbs manuals like that being compiled by the pharmacist (and brother-in-law to Clarke) John Towers.[4]

The priest-physician at the start of *Endymion* carries, along with his milk-white vase of "mingled wine," "a basket full / Of all sweet herbs that searching eye could cull," wild thyme, valley-lillies, and cresses (I, 155–60). Calidore's bower is dressed with "dock leaves," "spiral foxgloves," "wreaths of ivy," "the wild cat's eyes," and "the drooping flowers / Of whitest cassia" ("Calidore: A Fragment," 49–50, 95–96). In "I stood tip-toe" "clumps of woodbine" take "the soft wind / Upon their summer thrones" (36). Old Meg makes garlands of "woodbine fresh" ("Old Meg She was a gypsy," 17). "To George Felton Mathew" seeks a "flowery spot" overgrown with "the dark-leav'd laburnum's drooping clusters" and the "drooping buds" of cassia (37, 41–44). All these plants were medicines from English folklore recognized in the official pharmacopoeias of the early nineteenth century: dock-leaves, laburnum, and and cat's eyes were used as soothing poultices; thyme and cresses pacified stomach ailments; foxglove, ivy, and lilies of the valley were sources for stimulating pharmaceutical substances; and an infusion of cassia or woodbine, Keats's favorite flower, was prescribed to coat and cure ulcers of the mouth and stomach.[5]

The visual and poetic brilliance of Apollo's golden charms (in a poem like "God of the golden bow") and Porphyro's "baskets bright / Of wreathed silver" (272–73) must be checked by our knowledge of the poet's knowledge that muriate of gold was used in the treatment of syphilitic afflictions and cancerous ulcers and that nitrate of silver was used as a tonic for epilepsy and as an scouring escharotic for sloughing ulcers and warts.[6] Again, when the poet calls for "The leaves of willow and of adder's tongue" for Lamia's "aching forehead" (II, 223–24), we must know that he invokes in these two plants not just the traditional emblems of sorrow and grief but the real therapeutical soothing of the sedative juice in the adder's tongue fern and the acetyl in willow bark. Lamia's aching head, we may presume, is at least partly induced by the metaphorical circle of ditamy that Apollonius draws around her. Ditamy or dittany was famous for its medicinal properties: the Homeric Greeks knew it for its ability to expel weapons from wounds, and Aristotle supposedly told Alexander the Great that a circle described on the floor with dittany juice would kill a poisonous snake or a venomous maiden.[7] Over the years, ditamy retained its place in the folk pharmacopoeia for a variety of purposes: both white and bastard ditamy grow wild in Britain,[8] and in Keats's time the plant was used both as an antidote for animal venom and as a remedy for plague. But dittany was also sacred to the moon goddess, Diana—and we recall that just before Endymion has his mesmeric vision of his fair enchantress, there blossoms before him "a flowery spell" not unlike the one Lamia as poison damsel casts for Lycius, "a magic bed / Of sacred ditamy, and poppies red" (I, 554–57).

On Apollo's healthful isle of Delos in *Hyperion* grow olives, poplars, beeches, hazels, and palms (III, 24–27), and in *Isabella* we are told of how "She withers, like a palm / Cut by an Indian for its juicy balm" (446–48). The palm, giving life with its juicy balm, dies, much as Isabella's basil, an aromatic tonic "more balmy than its peers / Of basil-tufts in Florence" is fed by her balmlike tears and draws "Nurture besides, and life, from human fears" and "From the fast mouldering head" at its roots (428–30). The metaphor of a substance giving life through death, or death through its vivifying potency, reminds us that Keats never forgot the uncertain and facile composition of mythical and tangible *pharmaka*: odiferous pharmaceutical substances in his poetry, like Isabella's basil, that "jewel, safety casketed," come forth "and in perfumed leaflets spread" intimations of life and death (431–32); they transform and intertwine through their ductile nature the meanings of life and death.

Flowery spots in the poetry are undermined by the teaching of James Curry on the dangers of sleeping amid too many flowers;[9] the creeping plants that form these inspirational bowers portend of the common assumption of English folk medicine that most flowering vines were poisonous. The poet of *The Fall of Hyperion* sees "an arbour with a drooping roof / Of trellis vines, and bells, and larger blooms, / like floral censers" (I, 26–28)—dispensing pungent albeit unspecified potions through the air. The bower of Adonis in *Endymion* is a more specific conveyor of pharmaceutical charm; even as it represents the traditional springtime of life and love, it bears sacred blossoms of sorrow like myrtle and lilies and nourishes ductile creepers like "little bindweed" carrying botanical substances of life or death through their vines "of glossy sprout:" tonic "ivy-mesh, / Shading its [poisonous] Ethiop berries," soothing "wood-bine, / Of velvet leaves and bugle-blooms divine," the stimulating medicinal poison "Convolvulus in streaked vases flush," and the acrid poison clematis (traveler's joy) or "virgin's bower, trailing airily" (II, 412–17).[10] So near to death grows life; all remedies bear poisons: like Adonis's vigorously creeping vines or binding weeds—"All tendrils green, of every bloom and hue, / Together intertwin'd and trammel'd" (410–11). Poisons color, bind, convey, suffocate, smooth, and invigorate life.

Hellebore and digitalis according to the materia medica of Cullen, Murray, Monro, and Duncan were frequently prescribed narcotic medicines; as narcotics they were also, as Orfila documented in 1814 and as the poet certainly knew, established poisons. Medical botany courses at Guy's taught by Thornton and Salisbury instructed of their use as emetics, in small doses because of their violent purging powers.[11] The two drugs deserve mention here for their initial power to stimulate the heart and pulse of cardiac patients, madmen, lovers, and poets. In the poem to Mary Frogley, her "dark hair that extends / Into many graceful bends" is compared to the creeping "leaves of hellebore" that "Turn to whence they spring before" (14–16). Like laurel, hellebore was a sacred herb in Greek mythology: Helicon was famous for its incantations as well as its medicinal herbs, especially for the nine-leaved black hellebore, which, like digitalis, has a stimulative effect on the heart, and could either cause or cure insanity. Hippocratic medicine, according to Duncan in the *Encyclopaedia Britannica* of 1810, established the phrase "*to have need of hellebore*" as a euphemism for being "out of one's senses."[12] Lemprière mentions this mythical vine, the town of Anticyra, "famous for the ellebore," and the association of this town and its produce with Neptune.[13] Decorative hellebore vines, the Christmas flower in both its black and white varieties, are a class of plants frequently grown in English gardens (including, of course, the Chelsea Physic Garden). Robert Burton describes the syrup of hellebore as a cure for black choler and love melancholy; William Battie's *Treatise on Madness* (1758) notes hellebore's power as an antimonial vomit and "anti-maniacal" drug,[14] as does Robert Thornton's *New Family Herbal* (1810); and Orfila discusses it as an acrid poison, like convolvulus, that induces intoxication, palpitations, inflammation, vertigo, voicelessness, lethargy, and cold swoon.[15] Babington and Curry of Guy's Hospital recommended hellebore, as well as nightshade and wolfs-bane, as recorded cures for insanity.[16] Both traditions find conflicting, uneasy place in the stirring yet "soothing medicine" Neptune administers for the unrequited moon madness of the fledgling poet Endymion in Keats's poem. The digitalis in "O Solitude's" "fox-glove bell" and in the "spiral foxgloves" of Calidore's bowers (which Keats also mentions in his *Physiological Note Book*)[17]

is, as all early-nineteenth-century physicians would know, a bitter, acrimonious, and nauseating herbacious potion like hellebore, a "most valuable and
safe medicine in small doses," for it "restores strength and the life force," and
"a very dangerous poison" in large doses, for it induces anxiety, sleeplessness,
convulsions, vertigo, and fatal coma.[18] During his botanical excursions with
medical students from the London hospitals, William Salisbury would warn
not only of the drug's potency but of the plant's innocuous appearance:
"Medical practitioners should make themselves perfectly acquainted with this
plant, as the leaves are the only part used," and these "not being readily
discriminated when separated from the flowers" occasion severe illness when
mistaken for lesser herbs.[19]

The priest-physician of Book I of *Endymion* bears a vase of "mingled wine"
and dispenses health and life from a basket "full of all sweet herbs." But Circe,
the undeniably false physician of Book III, bears "a branch of mistletoe" as
parasitic and poisonous caduceus, and "from a basket emptied to the rout /
Clusters of grapes, the which they raven'd quick / And roar'd for more" (III,
510–512). Her fatal *pharmakon*, which Keats describes elsewhere as a "sooty
oil" (521), is unassimilable poison: it does not balm, it tranforms; not food but
parasite, it does not nourish, it vacuously stimulates; it fosters not evolution
but degradation to bestiality; yet, as a "charm" (518) of unspecified malignancy, it is nonetheless also a specifically poisonous "black dull-gurgling
phial" (515). Circe's Tartarean forest full of Upas or poison trees reminds us
that when Keats chose to do so, he had no trouble recognizing—and making
clear the distinction—between poisonous and medicinal substances.

In the poet's work we find mention of specific toxic substances from both the
mineral and animal kingdoms. Among the mineral poisons in the poetry one
finds listed nitre and nitrous acid (*The Jealousies*, 294, 657–58), phosophorus
(*Lamia*, I, 152),[20] brass, and other poisonous metals: "Instead of sweets" Saturn's (or Hyperion's, in *The Fall of Hyperion*) "ample palate took / Savours of
poisonous brass and metal sick" (*Hyp.*, I, 188–89; *Fall of Hyp.*, II, 33–34); and in
his last letter to Fanny Brawne in August 1820, Keats remarks, "The last two
years taste like brass upon my Palate." The metallic taste and ulcerated mouth
Keats describes is common to mercury poisoning, but it is also an initial sign of
poisoning by another escharotic, lead; late symptoms of lead poisoning are
headaches, cramps of the legs, rheumatism in the extremities, and most pertinent, a "palsied state of muscles of the arms and hands, taking away all power of
grasping any thing, and even of lifting the hand to the mouth. . . ."[21] We recognize these symptoms in the rheumy, listless "pain of feebleness" of the Titans
and in Saturn's "palsied tongue," "aspen-malady," and "old right hand [lying]
nerveless, listless, dead" (*Fall of Hyp.*, I, 429; *Hyp.*, I, 93, 94, 18); we also perceive
the tragic signs of these symptoms as they are conveyed by the bright melancholy and feeble malaise of the dying consumptive.

The cold "Night-swollen mushrooms," lilies of the valley, and "berried holly"
of *Endymion* (I, 215, 157; IV, 205), the narcissus of "I stood tip-toe" (164, 180),

the periwinkle or baleful blue Italian "flower of death" of "Dear Reynolds" (101), the "ardent marigolds" of the young poet ("I stood tip-toe," 48), and the "faded marigolds" of the melancholy and lovelorn Endymion (II, 397)[22] are all examples of poisonous flowers and plants in Keats's poetry. The specifically chosen botanical poisons of the "Ode on Melancholy" warrant close attention, for they compound both technical knowledge and metaphorical truth in their fraught potion for recognizing the signs of false and true melancholy.

> No no, go not to Lethe, neither twist
>   Wolf's-bane, tight-rooted, for its poisonous wine;
> Nor suffer thy pale forehead to be kiss'd
>   By nightshade, ruby grape of Proserpine;
> Make not your rosary of yew-berries,

but when the true "melancholy fit shall fall," the poet tells us, "Then glut thy sorrow on a morning rose, / Or on the rainbow of the salt sand-wave, / Or on the wealth of globed peonies" (1–5; 11–17). In a letter that explains the philosophical *pharmakon* of the "Ode on Melancholy," Keats writes: "Circumstances are like Clouds continually gathering and bursting—While we are laughing the seed of some trouble is put into the wide arable land of events—while we are laughing it sprouts is [it] grows and suddenly bears a poison fruit which we must pluck—."[23] Keats may have known enough of medicine and the nature of life not to believe in poison trees, but he did believe in poison fruits or flowers—both literal and metaphorical—and in their compelling attraction and potency. Wolfsbane, nightshade, yew berries, and the globed peony are all poison fruit; they are nerve poisons, narcotico-acrids that act on the nervous system and brain and have the power at once to irritate to intensity and to stupify. They are not sensitive plants so much as fatally sensitizing potions.

Wolfsbane, also known as monkshood, blue rocket, and aconite, is a poisonous plant commonly found in mountainous countryside. It resembles the garden horseradish and the mandrake, the plant with the shrieking humanoid root that Burton proposed as a cure for insomnia.[24] Mythology has flowering wolfsbane growing at the entrance to the infernal underworld, for, when Cerberus's saliva fell to the ground, the "witch-flower" aconite sprang forth;[25] the root of this plant, its most poisonous part, meanwhile recalls for us the "roots of relish sweet" that the chthonian belle dame sans merci feeds Keats's swooning knight. Aconitine, an alkaloid extracted from "tight-rooted" wolfsbane (*aconitum napellus*), is, according to Orfila, the most swift and deadly of known vegetable poisons, with one-sixteenth of a grain proving fatal to humans. Wolfsbane's "poisonous wine" causes a tingling sensitivity and then numbness of the parts of the body to which it is applied, even as it preserves the intensity of the intelligence until moments before death. Aconitine was Van Helmont's drug of choice to prove that his soul resided in his chest. It is important to remember that the specific effects of aconitine are all directed at the cerebro-nervous system: it causes anxiety, fear of suffocation, intoxication, agitation bordering on frenzy, madness, idiocy from destruction of brain functions, and general mental derangement.[26]

"But off, Despondence! miserable bane!" Keats says in "Sleep and Poetry" (281) to the subject of the present ode. Banes destroy life; in a letter of 1819 Keats vows, because of the false love letters sent to the dying Tom Keats by Wells, that he will be opium or ratsbane to Wells's vanity. The original draft of "Melancholy" started to invoke "henbane," not wolfsbane: henbane or *hyoscyamus niger* is a simple narcotic producing physical and mental senselessness; it was a commonly used anodyne and inexpensive substitute for opium in the early nineteenth century. That Keats chose to invoke the complex nerve poison wolfsbane over the simple debilitative henbane tells us much of the kinds of sensations and poetic inducements that the "Ode" comes to reject.[27]

On 25 June 1816, Alexander Marcet of Guy's Hospital read the paper "On the Medicinal Properties of Stramonium" to the Medico-Chirurgical Society of London. He noted the use of this new medicine by "Dr. Storck of Vienna" and the "modern German practitioners" for cases of asthma, rheumatism, the plague, palsy, epilepsy, delirium, hydrophobia, and mania. He then discussed his own use of the drug on certain terminal cancer cases and, in particular, on some breast-cancer patients of Astley Cooper in the research ward at Guy's. He concluded by marking that the drug's greatest efficacy and "most promising property" lay in its power of "allaying some of the most obstinate and severe kinds of pain," especially that extreme and various pain of chronic disease or incurable cancer, "more effectually than any other narcotic medicine."[28] *Datura stramonium*, the thorn apple, jimson's weed, devil's trumpet, stinkweed, or horn of plenty, belongs to the toxic *Solanacaea* family of plants; other *solanum* are the bittersweet or woody nightshade common to English thickets and the deadly nightshade or *atropa belladonna* of the "Ode on Melancholy." The potent agent of all these plants is the alkaloid atropine; present in all the parts of these plants, including the nectar and odorous resin, it is found in greatest quantity in deadly nightshade, especially in this plant's black and "ruby" seeds.

Belladonna was used as a cosmetic by Italian court ladies during the Renaissance as a symbol of death that served to blacken the eyes during mourning and as a means to beauty that dilated the eyes and made the face appear pale and bewitching. John Locke prescribed the leaves of *solanum dulcamera* as a poultice for breast cancers and as a healing tea for consumptive ulcers of the lungs.[29] Hahnemann prescribed *atropa belladonna* during the scarlet fever epidemic in Konigslutter in 1799, and his research with the drug, though it did not cure the fever, did lead to his doctrine of infinitesimal doses.[30] In 1816 Salisbury documented the use of belladonna, in eighteenth-century medicine and in contemporary practice at Guy's Hospital, for dropsies, ulcerations, asthma, convulsions, cataracts, and cataract surgery; he specifically marked the heavy internal use of belladonna in the research ward as a desperate remedy for terminal breast cancer and unremitting mania or melancholy; an unmistakable sign of the drug's presence in the body in large dosage, he said, was "a remarkable kind of staring, [which] exhibited a very affecting scene."[31] Orfila classified deadly nightshade among the most severe narcotico-acrids for its ability to derange rapidly both the senses and the cerebro-nervous system. Wolfsbane and nightshade grow side by side in the homeopathic bed of the Chelsea Physic Garden as related nerve poisons. Like aconite, atropine manifests itself with the following symptoms: intense thirst, paleness, tremors, palpitations, glittering and dilated pupils, severe and unremitting agitation, convulsions, exhilarating intoxication, vertigo, "gay delirium," incoherence of speech, vacant countenance, "a sort of madness and fury," terror, and "horrible imaginings," followed by blindness, loss of senses, movements, memory, and perception, and death; even on those rare occasions where the atropine is removed from the system, the blindness endures.[32]

Suffer not "thy pale forehead to be kiss'd / By nightshade, ruby grape of Proserpine," Keats warns us. In the symptoms of the belladonna, or bittersweet, or thorn apple, we see echoes of the bewitching effects la belle dame sans merci has on the knight at arms—his pale face, febrile, anguished intensity, and *her* wild eyes, which become his own when he is abandoned; and of the "starv'd lips" "With horrid warning gaped wide" of the "pale kings, and princes," and "Pale warriors" that form the characters of his visions (37–42). We are reminded, also, of Thomas Lovell Beddoes's Amala, that "lovely-faced murderess, / With eyes as dark and poisonous as nightshade";[33] of the botanist E.T.A. Hoffmann's *Datura Fastuoso* or gorgeous thorn-apple that grows in glittering beauty through strange potion in an extranatural garden of poison flowers and tells enchantingly of love and death;[34] and of Hawthorne's Rappaccini's daughter, "nourished with poisons from her birth upward, until her whole nature was so imbued with them, that she herself had become the deadliest poison in existence. Poison was her element of life. With that rich perfume of her breath, she blasted the very air. Her love would have been poison!"[35] Most of all, from among the many daughters of Milton's Eve, we remember the alluring and fatal potency of Glaucus's Circe with her glittering eyes and hissing tongue and serpentine Lamia with her "bitter-sweet" mouth (I, 59). Like la belle dame sans merci in her poem, and like the *belladonna*, Keats's Circe and Lamia blind with the kiss of nightshade: they tempt to love and death, to glittering beauty at the price of total deprivation, to exhilarating intensity at the cost of hideous death. The scarlet berries of deadly nightshade find parallel, at least for Keats, in Proserpine's pomegranate that bears either rosy seeds of life or ruby grapes of death; what they represent as botanical potions, bewitching personages, and mythological complexes find unifying place in Proserpine herself, who is goddess of springtime and fruitful union but also wife of Pluto and prevailing presence over the icy lake of Avernus and the fatal waters of Lethe.

The small red berries of the yew tree are easily mistaken for the scarlet berries of belladonna and, hence, must also find parallel in the ruby grapes of Proserpine; their melancholic potion must further compound itself with the knowledge that, for the early nineteenth century, the atropine from deadly nightshade was the best stimulating antidote for prussic acid, the rapid and paralyzing poison in yew berries. Salisbury reminded his students of the botanical folk truth that yew foilage was highly palatable and poisonous to cattle.[36] Wordsworth speculated in 1816 that yew branches were not poisonous "while united by a living spirit to their native tree" and became toxic only upon "being dissevered."[37] In fact, not just the berries of the yew but the leaves, bark, and aromatic water distilled from these, Orfila and Brodie tell us, contain prussic acid or bitter almond, a poison that is absorbed through the senses or nerves to paralyze and kill instantaneously without any visible deterioration of the physical functions or mental powers.[38] But laurel, as we know, also owns as its active agent the almond-scented poison prussic acid. Thus, when Keats warns us to "Make not your rosary of yew-berries" in the "Ode," he invokes not just the religious melancholy symbolized by the dark and sorrowful yew trees of English churchyards, nor just the deadly albeit winning yew bows remembered in Wordsworth's poem "Yew Trees" (1803), but the dark underside of golden Apollo's fragrant laurel wreaths and almond vales.

Fragrance and devotional (or poetic) chant combine with literal potion to strengthen metaphorical truth; proven poison combines with mythical ambiguity to intensify poetic complexity. If the self-indulgent melancholy that Endymion cultivates while rustling through vales where "dark yew trees" grew is false, divisive, and fatal, another unifying poetic melancholy is promised with the devotional blessing "Let fall a sprig of yew-tree in his path" (IV, 673; I, 732). And, when under the healing influence of Peona, the fledging poet Endymion promises to "poll / The fair-grown yew tree, for a chosen bow" (I, 482), it does not finally matter whether this bow is to make Apollo's music or cast his plague-arrows for both bring forth unbidden a true melancholy that heals. "Let my bower be of yew" (30) prays the simple jingle of 1818, "Welcome joy, and welcome sorrow," carrying at once both the familiar Keatsian paradox of joyous sorrow and the poet's profound belief in intense, stressed acquiescence.

In "the wealth of globed peonies," paradigm of the stationed intensity and captured fullness of the Keatsian moment of ripeness, reside, held in perfect balance, all the literal and paradoxic significations of poison and melancholy that the "Ode" would convey. The peony or globeflower, over ten varieties of which flourish in the north corner of the Chelsea Physic Garden and find place in Salisbury's *Botanist's Companion*, belongs to the same family of poisonous plants, Jussieu's *Ranunculaea*, as wolfsbane; in appearance, taste, and smell, its root closely resembles that of the black hellebore; its flower, meanwhile, resembles that of the water-spearwort or *ranunculus flamula*, source for a common antidote to plant poisons.[39] Along with the yew and the laurel, the peony bears legendary connections with poetry, with the healing hymn and the stirring paean. In addition to the familiar Keatsian image of passing life at its fullest and evanescent beauty at its ripest, the ode's "globed peonies" bear intimations of wolfsbane's mythical connection with the underworld and its pharmaceutical power to numb fatally the senses and preserve the intensity of the mind; it bears also intimations of black hellebore's mythical grove at the foot of Mount Helicon and its chemical power to induce fantasies and provoke madness and of the Phrygian's hellebore-pipe harmony that healed lunacy. Unlike wolfsbane, nightshade, and yew berries, whose symptoms tell us much about the kinds of sensations that the "Ode on Melancholy" comes to reject, the peony is the only poison invoked in the ode that serves for Keats as a medium and representation of true melancholy. It is a symptom of melancholy like the other poisons, but in its ambiguous multiplicity it is also a prescription or sign of the way to poetic truth. The place of the peony in English folk medicine complements Keats's poetic use of the plant: the plant was governed by the Sun-god of Druidic medicine and, as such, prevailed over harmful melancholia and nervous disease; male peony root was prescribed for epilepsy and the hysteria that sometimes followed childbirth; peony seeds were administered to combat nightmares and melancholic dreams.[40] In its multiple prescriptive role, Keats's peony fully manifests its source in Paeon, epithet of Apollo as god of healing in late Greek tradition, and finds embodiment in Endymion's patient and (long) suffering "midnight spirit nurse," Peona (I, 413).

"There is a very life in our despair, / Vitality of poison,—a quick root / Which feeds these deadly branches," and life suits "Itself to Sorrow's most detested fruit," Byron says in Childe Harold (III, 34). The peony plant, with its swollen, poisonous flowers and reedy stems, transforms itself into the true and living image of poetic melancholy much as, in Greek tradition, Paeon turned paean and healing turned hymn. So also, fair Syrinx turns ductile reed, and Pan's lovesick melancholy is transmuted into music that issues forth from this reed to soothe his poisoned mind. In Endymion, Pan sits "through whole solemn hours" thinking of "how melancholy loth" he "wast to lose fair Syrinx" and harkening to

> The dreary melody of bedded reeds—
> In desolate places, where dank moisture breeds
> The pipy hemlock to strange overgrowth.
> (I, 238–43)

Syrinx and the "pipy hemlock" are both "bedded reeds," and their hollow forms inspire music to ease spiritual desolation; the peony, representing the ripeness of life even as it bears death, is also a reedy plant, and malignant black hellebore reeds produce music to cure melancholy.

Keats's lines further portend not only of the mysterious link between music and poison and the indeterminate and ductile nature they share (a connection that he derived most directly from Virgil's second Eclogue, "I have a pipe formed of seven uneven hemlock-stalks, a gift Damoetas once gave me"[41]), but of the naturalists' sense of the interconnection between poisonous matter and monstrous or festering growth. The hemlock of the "Ode to a Nightingale" is, despite its philosophical pedigree, a common English weed; a malevolent harbinger of spring in the Chelsea Physic Garden, it grows in rank abandon at the water's edge of stagnant ditches, offal pits, and runoff streams from slaughterhouses and refuse heaps.[42] We are to expect poison from standing water Blake warns us in *The Marriage of Heaven and Hell*. Early-nineteenth-century naturalists saw that the dank and desolate places like the malarial Pontine Marshes that might inspire dreary melodies in lovelorn poets were precisely the places where poisonous weeds like fetid hellebore and rank hemlock grew, where venomous snakes abided, and where morbid poisons festered and gave form (if not symbol) to cancers and parasites. Apollo's "misty pestilence" strikes Hyperion "as from a scummy marsh" of Satanic indeterminacy (I, 257–58), we recall, and Hermes finds Lamia the "palpitating snake" luxuriating unhappily amid "The taller grasses and full-flowering weed" (I, 44–45). Life turns excessive monstrous growth, ripeness turns to rot and stagnation, beauty proves hollow, and art shows its first source in the lush and poisonous forms of life.

The attempt to foster "the droop-headed flowers all" in melancholy's physic garden is fraught with danger, for the melancholy, too often, is false, and the garden becomes an arbor of poisonous weeds—a "haggard scene" not unlike Circe's tartarean thicket in *Endymion*: a remote forest of dark, upturned roots cast amid "rushes Stygian" that bears monstrous shapes "serpenting / Shewing tooth, tusk, and venom-bag, and sting" (III, 496–506). Weeds flourish in such a hellish garden, and the "Ode's" nightshade, henbane, and wolfsbane were all, as Keats well knew, common weeds. Alexander Marcet's description of the nightshade family shows them to be tubular plants similar to hemlock, commonly found "in dunghills and among rubbish"; henbane is also found in compost heaps and "uncultivated places," according to the *Encylopaedia Britannica* of 1810; and Orfila notes that wolfsbane "grows in sheltered and moist places" in mountains and deep forests.[43] "I hold those base weeds with tight hand," Ethelbert says in *Otho*, "Waiting but for your sign to pull them up / By the dark roots, and leave her palpable, / To all men's sight, a lady innocent" (III, ii, 135–39). Whether "Lethe's" weeds of false melancholy can be pulled up by their dark and parasitic roots to reveal "Veil'd Melancholy" in her "sovran shrine" is a question answered only through poison's medium of transforming indirection. Parasitic weeds hide but they also conduct: "Pipes will I fashion of the syrinx flag, / That thou mayst always know whither I roam" (*End.*, IV, 686–87) Melancholy promises the poet, with the same guarantee as does Endymion to his beloved. We must recognize, know, and follow the properties of that which we would shun. The "forest branches and the trodden weed" with which the Grecian urn is "overwrought" (42–43) become thus the dark and melancholic inner side of the urn's known pure but hollow form. And in Hyperion's mournful dream of premonition, the mortally-poisoned Titans are invoked, in dark image of their uncreative state, as "lank-eared Phantoms of black-weeded pools" (I, 230)—at once monstrous growth and putrefying rotting vegetation, hollow vesicles of their former selves, sedimented, cloudy trophies of melancholy. Their silence is fit transmutation of their case: it is "The dreary music of bedded reeds" long hollowed out and long dead. The poet as physician must bear sad but strenuous witness to the quietude of their "haggard scene," removed and too late, with neither the healing aid of Peona nor the pipy music of Syrinx.

Chapter 13

Antidotes

> She dwells with Beauty—Beauty that must die;
> And Joy, whose hand is ever at his lips
> Bidding adieu; and aching Pleasure nigh,
> Turning to poison while the bee-mouth sips.
> (21–24)

True melancholy is the antidote to false melancholy; it is also an antidote to being "too happy in thine happiness," as the poet of the "Ode to a Nightingale" discovers (6). It is an intensity to dull the ache of Pleasure or an intensity more acute than the ecstasy of Joy; it is a bitterness whose taste counters the cloying sweetness of Joy's grape, or else a honey more sharp because its complex sweetness cuts the sickening simplicity of other honeys. A true antidote, it distinguishes its own variegated substance through the revelation and neutralization of other more simple compounds.

When King Mithradates of Pontus (131–63 B.C.) sought to immunize himself against all poisons, he did so by drinking the blood of ducks that had been fed upon toxic principles; a magician who dabbled in pharmaceutical concoctions, Mithradates sought to devise a universal antidote or *alexipharmakon* and so lent his name in legend to all such potions or *mithridatium*. The other personage connected with the notion of a universal panacea or wondrous polyvalent drug was the Greek medical advisor to Nero, Andromachus, who is credited with inventing a complex *theriacum* that was of special avail against the poison of venomous beasts or *theria*.[1] Belief in the possibility of a sovereign prescription, a compound that served at once as an antidote to all poisons and remedy for all diseases, prevailed through the Middle Ages, when polypharmacy was at its height, and up until the late eighteenth century. Galen's opium compound, mithridate, was probably the most enduring among the many substances of dubious properties that succeeded one another as the reigning prophylactic in the European pharmacopoeia. The

Kendal Black Drop, another opium compound, achieved notoriety as an all-purpose prescription (and mention in Coleridge's *Notebooks*) during the early nineteenth century.[2]

William Heberden's *Essay on Mithidatium and Theriaca* (1745) did much to discredit such concoctions and the overall superstition that an *alexipharmakon* could exist, although the search for such a potion continued through the eighteenth century. During the years of Keats's medical apprenticeship, belief in a sovereign remedy gave way to the verity that certain potent substances could function as antidotes to other specific pharmacological substances. Peruvian bark was a known antidote for antimony or tartar emetica, mercury or corrosive sublimate was an accepted antidote for lead poisoning, as foxglove or digitalis was for wolfsbane or aconite, belladonna or atropine for laurel or prussic acid, and opium or morphine for belladonna. By 1842 the notion of antidotes whether specific or general was abandoned; no longer speaking of "the administration of poisons" to counteract poisons,[3] Christison speaks in terms of chemical neutralizers and constitutional stimulants.[4] But even as anatomical observation disclosed the variety of diseases and implied a like variety of cures, interest in a miraculous antidote to all deviations from health was kept alive by reports from the Americas on the multipurpose therapeutic properties of exotic vegetable and animal substances. August St. Hilaire, in the *Edinburgh Philosophical Journal* (1825), lists among "proven" antidotes to plant poisons the seeds of the leguminous *Mucunaguaçu, Cebera Ahovai* and *Thevetia*, "the gall of a toad," manihoe worms that feed on the poisonous juice of the manihoe plant, and, most curious of all, "the leaves of certain sensitive plants" like the *Herba casta* and the Rubiaceae species.[5] The Royal Institution's *Quarterly Journal* meanwhile, in 1820, had published an account complete with case studies of how the fruit of the *feuilla cordefolia* had been proved to be "a powerful antidote against vegetable poisons," especially those of "rhus toxicodendron, hemlock and nux vomica."[6] Reports such as these made common cause with English and European folklore on antidotes—as in the case of a memoir in Nicolson's *Journal* in 1805 on recent confirmation of an old folk remedy, venomous spiders' webs, as an internal medicine superior to bark for fevers, as a salve for wounds, and as an antidotal balm for the poisonous bites of insects and snakes.[7]

Notions of the antidotal or miraculous substance that functioned against poison, disease, or death, derive ultimately from the mythical nectar and ambrosia that, at once, sustained life, prevented death, and granted immortality to the gods. Nectar derives from the Greek noun for death (*Nek*) and the Greek verb (*tar*) to overcome. Lemprière has the following entry for ambrosia:

> The food of the gods was called *ambrosia*, and their drink *nectar*. The word signifies immortal. It had the power of giving immortality to all those who eat it. *It was sweeter than honey, and of a most odiferous smell.* . . . . *It had the power of healing wounds*, and therefore, Apollo, in Homer's Iliad, saves Sarpedon's body from putrefaction, by rubbing it

with ambrosia; and Venus also heals the wounds of her son, in Virgil's Aeneid, with it. *The gods used generally to perfume their hair with ambrosia*, as Juno when she adorned herself to captivate Jupiter, and Venus when she appears to Aeneas.[8]

The sweet substance, "sweeter than honey" and endowed with powers of healing, preventing death, perfuming, and seducing (as love-philtre), finds further substance in the Greek *theriaka*, the antidote to the poison of venomous beasts (*theria*) and universal prophylactic against pestilential disease, which is the etymological and pharmaceutical source for the English "treacle." All perfumed sweetness and magical potency of treacle, ambrosia, and nectar find lowest common denominator in honey and the folk belief (still current among country physicians in the early nineteenth century) in the medicinal powers of honey as anodyne, balm, antidote, and vivifying agent.

"The sweetest honey / Is loathsome in his own deliciousness / And in the taste confounds the appetite," Friar Lawrence says to Romeo in warning that "violent delights have violent ends / And in their triumph die, like fire and powder, / Which as they kiss consume."[9] Christopher Ricks is correct in noting that Keats evokes honey and its attributes not just for its consumptive sweetness, nor even for its sticky potential to clog, but to repudiate at once two conflicting systems, a gross hedonism that through excess and satiation "coarsens its own appreciation of physical sensation," and a "sour puritanism which repudiates the delights of physical sensation on the grounds that after all even honey palls and satiates. . . . Keats's evocations of honey recognize both the inherent precariousness of such delight and . . . the inherent uncertainty of our response to it. . . ."[10] "Sweet" and "sweetness" consume over four columns in the *Concordance* to Keats's poetry; the word *honey* by itself and in hyphenated form occurs twenty times in the poetry, the adjectival *honied* ten times. *Endymion* has a weakness for nectar: in Neptune's underworld paradise "Nectar ran / In courteous fountains to all cups outreach'd," and the loveless Endymion is rescued repeatedly "from the drear abyss / Of death" by "a breathless honey-feel of bliss" (III, 925–26; I, 903–5). Where the concept of sweetness or honey occurs in the mature poetry, it is not only distant from the benign and gummy joys of Endymion's most childish moments, it is also a yet more complex evocation than Ricks implies. True to its mythic, seductive, and medical origins, the sweetness of Keatsian honey belongs with the ambiguous and far from benign potion of the consuming and consumptive *pharmakon/alexipharmakon* itself.

In a note to explain his phrase "Untasted honey" in *The Temple of Nature* (II, 302), Erasmus Darwin suggests that because the "anthers and stigmas of flowers are probably nourished by the honey, which is secreted by the honey-gland called by Linneus the nectary; and possess greater sensibility or animation than other parts of the plant," butterflies and bees "by living upon honey probably acquire a higher degree of animation, and thus seem to resemble the anthers of flowers. . . ."[11] Darwin's remarkable speculation on how bees could be sensible (sensitive) like flower stamen, and more animated than

other life forms because they fed exclusively on honey, is a small reverbera-
tion of two important concerns of contemporary science: whether certain
"sensitive" plants bridged the gap between vegetable and animal kingdoms,
and between irritability and sensibility, and whether we indeed become what
we consume.

The life of bees, and especially their social instinct, was a popular subject
for speculation among intellectuals of the time.[12] The specific source for
Darwin's darwinian musings on the animation of bees and men was an article,
"Poisonous and Injurious Honey of North America," by Benjamin Smith Barton published at the turn of the century.[13] The article was printed in a number
of literary and natural philosophy journals in England and North America over
the next decade, and it fueled the debate on the nature and reciprocity of
vegetable and animal poisons. Toxicologists knew that honey and sugar increased the effects of the toxic principle in vegetable poisons found in wolfsbane, traveler's joy, and the peony or globeflower.[14] Physicians and naturalists
of the early nineteenth century now found it proved to their dismay that
hardly pure sustenance or harmless salve, honey was a complex substance
that could on occasion convey virulent toxicity; the source for this toxicity
appeared to be at once the poisonous plants that produced it as well as the
venomous insects that gleaned it. (The speculative implications of Barton's
research for contemporary poetry are legion and extend well beyond Keats.
Coleridge's Christabel, for example, serves Geraldine a "wine of virtuous powers" made, by her mother, "of wild flowers" [188–89]; we are left to question
whether it is Geraldine's lips that render the wine toxic, whether the wine's
sweetness intensifies Geraldine's toxicity, or whether the wine is a "Solution
sweet" like Porphyro's love-philtre in The Eve of St. Agnes, a homemade brew
less virtuous and more ambiguous than Christabel can ever say.)

"Honey will always partake," Barton informed his readers, "of the smell, the
taste, and the general properties, of the flowers from which it is obtained."[15]
The flowers from which bees and wasps collected their "pernicious honey"
included several readily recognizable to English readers: the wild honey-
suckle, thorn apple and other nightshade, dwarf laurel and ivy, the various
mountain laurel, hemlock, and wolfsbane.[16] Symptoms of honey poisoning
usually mirror the toxic effects of the plants from which it is collected: one of
Barton's examples is the plentiful and bittersweet honey of thorn apple or
datura stramonium, to which bees are particularly partial ("Bees quaff it"), and
which induces all the symptoms of nightshade poisoning.[17] Barton's plants,
all well-established vegetable poisons, are also and specifically the poison
flowers that produce richest juice in Keats's poetry (Isabella, 104). And if bees
"know there is richest juice in poison-flowers" such as these, we must also
remember that "poison-flour" was a common name at this time for subli-
mated arsenic trioxide, the chemists' deadly flour of arsenic.

Barton's article renewed the folk belief that those bees that produced poisonous honey also poisoned themselves with this honey, "some of the dis-

eases of these little insects may arise from this source," and he cited research on elm honey, which not only poisoned the bees sipping it but infected whole flocks and hives and poisoned storehouses of benign honey.[18] He raised, thus, questions not only of the nature of poison but also of the nature of bees and of reciprocal infection.

The next two decades of physicians and naturalists attempted to answer these questions and succeeded only in furthering the indistinctions. Astley Cooper's lecture on poisons at Guy's Hospital grouped wasps, hornets, vipers, and mad dogs in one category as creatures whose bite transferred infection, and he spoke of the venom of each in the same terms.[19] St. Hilaire found Barton's theory of bees poisoning themselves improbable because venomous insects must undoubtedly carry their own immunity or antidote to venom: "This honey, in fact, has been sucked by the bees; it has resided in their intestines; they have only collected it, by returning a thousand and a thousand times to the same flower; and if it could prove as hurtful to them as to man, it is impossible to conceive that they would have stored it up in their cells."[20] Bees could not poison themselves, but they could alternately nourish and poison other creatures with their honey. To Barton's claims that different hives of the same bees in the same tree could provide honeys of benign and pernicious properties,[21] St. Hilaire added that the honey in the same hive could be innocent or malignant and that the honey in a given bee could be tainted or impregnated with pharmaceutical power by the insect's resting on a particular flower.[22] (We might wonder here whether it is the digitalis that "Startles the wild bee from the fox-glove bell" in "O Solitude" [8], whether the picture of pretty animation finds literal truth in the pharmaceutical power to animate that was known to reside in the essence of foxgloves.) Moreover, contrary to the folk belief that only red honey was poisonous, Barton and St. Hilaire found that honey came in white, gray, yellow, red, and brown varieties, yet neither taste nor odor nor color distinguished the poisonous variety.[23]

Hence, contrary to Pope's conceit of the "nice bee" whose sense "so subtly true / From the pois'nous herbs extracts the healing dew" (Essay on Man, I, 219–20), the oblivious "little almsmen of spring-bowers" do not know the properties of the richest juice they extract. Recognition of venom or poison thus belongs not with the bees who are immune from the needs of distinction but with the naturalist, the beekeeper, the pathologist—and, perhaps, the poet. A bitter aftertaste according to St. Hilaire,[24] a recognition after the fact, or after the infection, is the only distinguishing mark of malignancy in literal honeys. So also may be the case with metaphorical honeys, for Lycius in Lamia tastes, too late, the "bitter-sweet" of Lamia's "woman's mouth" (I, 59–60, 149). And the stationing moment of the "Ode on Melancholy"—"Turning to poison while the bee-mouth sips" (24)—can contract and expand at once to the physiological concerns with the source, medium, and reciprocity of a poison, and to the poetic, metaphysical concern with the human psyche's power to recognize and reciprocally transmute pleasure and pain.

"Honey from out the gnarled hive I'll bring, / And apples, wan with sweetness," Endymion promises his Indian Maid; he will plant the sides of the rill she loves "with dew-sweet eglantine, / And honeysuckles full of clear bee-wine," and thereby, as poet, "entice" the crystal rill "to trace / Love's silver name upon the meadow's face" (IV, 682–83, 697–700). An early sonnet of 1815 invokes the sacred nectar of "Hybla's honied roses / When steep'd in dew rich to intoxication"; its poet resolves to "taste that dew" gathered, if necessary, by "spells, and incantations" "when the moon her pallid face discloses" ("Had I a man's fair form," 10–14). An intoxicating sweetness of "clear bee-wine"—or "honey dew," as Kubla Khan discovered—charms forth magical scenes, faces, and words. An inebriation exceeding that induced by spirits, a delirium fostered on gay dreams ("a breathless honey-feel of bliss," End., I, 903), and an excess of joyful and sorrowful emotions are the first symptoms of poisoning by honey. Subsequent symptoms are far less equivocal. Barton witnessed honeys like that gathered from the dwarf laurel producing vertigo, "ferocious" delirium, convulsions, profuse perspiration, foaming, intense internal pain, palsy, and occasionally death. St. Hilaire's own symptoms, after swallowing two tablespoons of lecheguana wasp honey (which appeared, he says, no different from common bee honey) were what Elfinan would call "the torture of the wasp" (The Jealousies, 198) and a far cry from the "honied indolence" of the "Ode on Indolence" (37): the toxic "milk of paradise" produced numbing debility, hallucination, black misting of the vision, a hyperactive imagination, and "violent combat" in the mind.[25]

Such violent delights have violent ends. When the poet of The Fall of Hyperion consumes a feast of fruits "Sweet smelling, whose pure kinds" he could not know, and drinks a mysterious "transparent juice," we are told that the sweet fruits were first "By angel tasted, or our Mother Eve" and that the juice had been "Sipp'd by the wander'd bee" (I, 32–34, 43–44). These substances prove to be, upon consumption and in their aftertaste, "a domineering potion." We cannot tell where, or when, the potion received its potency. Did bee and angel, or Mother Eve, imprint the otherwise pure substances and impart influences to them? Did they taint or turn to poison as they sipped otherwise benign substances? Or did they act as catalysts in bringing forth a latent potency in the potion? Or was it the human apprehension or consumption that revealed, or perhaps even created for itself, the domineering potency? Most of all, to what extent is the sweetness of this barely tangible potion connected with Lamia's "weïrd syrops" (I, 107) and the "lucent syrops" of the love-philtre that Porphyro brings forth for his unconscious bride?

In "I stood tip-toe" the poet wishes for "three words of honey" that he might tell the wonders of Cynthia's bridal night (209–10). In the story of Endymion and Cynthia, Circe, the false physician who breathes "ambrosia," weaves a "net [of] thralldom" "With tears, and smiles and honey-words" for Glaucus; this barely tangible but fiercely entrapping potion is brewed from the "dew of her rich speech" (III, 454, 426–29). Words and honey, as *pharmaka*, partake of the same properties; both serve duty in the concoction of the possessing love-philtre whose ambiguous powers depend as much upon the intentions of the lover as upon the condition of the beloved. The love-philtre carries always the potential danger of violent knowledge: in this regard it is similar perhaps to what the poet of *The Fall of Hyperion* comes to know and definitely akin to what the lovers of *Lamia* know.

Offerings of honey and tongues were made to Hermes in his role as god of eloquence, according to Lemprière,[26] and in Keats's poem the nymph, in response to Hermes' eloquent and voracious love, "like new flowers at morning song of bees, / Bloom'd, and gave up her honey to the lees" (*Lamia* I, 142–43). Hermes, though perhaps more beelike than eloquent in his importunate insistence, is neither angel tasting nor bee sipping. His kiss taints and bleaches: the nymph, "like a moon in wane, / Faded before him" (136–37), and his love, even if it is divine, is at once parasitic and predatory. Lamia, Hermes' less divine accomplice, speaks though "her throat was serpent" words that come like Circe's "as through bubbling honey, for Love's sake" (I, 64–65); and her potion for her beloved, "dew so sweet and virulent" (I, 149), taints Lycius, bleaches her own self to "a deadly white" (II, 276), and produces all the apprehending violence of a dream turned nightmare. With Lamia, as with Hermes, as they kiss they consume; in the poem of their amours, sweet seduction and honeyed love turn violent delight.

Chapter 14

The Ambiguity of Snakes

The pharmacopoeia of Keats's poetry is compounded everywhere by the fluid presence and subtle, essential ambiguity of snakes. Beddoes's protagonist in "Death's Jest-Book" likens the action of thoughts born of spoken words in transforming a countenance to the imperceptible dissolution of "sugar melting in a glass of poison";[1] and Shelley's Jupiter in *Prometheus Unbound* recalls both Hamlet's yearning for self-slaughter and Sabellus's liquid fate upon being bitten by a seps when he feels dissolved "Like him whom the Numidian seps did thaw / Into a dew with poison."[2] A reciprocity prevails between all poisons: "Night-shade with the woodbine kissing; / Serpents in red roses hissing; / Cleopatra, regal drest, / With the aspics at her breast"—these lines from "Welcome joy, and welcome sorrow" (14–17) carry both the natural philosopher's awareness that a transforming power is the attribute shared by all toxicities, as well as the familiar Keatsian paradox of joy and sorrow symbolized by the *pharmakon* itself. Poisons, whether vegetable or animal, melt, dissolve, and transform primary essences; nowhere is this characteristic mark of toxicity better exemplified than in the seemingly mysterious way in which the simple bite of a venomous creature (bee or snake) transforms completely the physiological composition of a complex and larger body. For Circe, for Scylla, for la belle dame sans merci, and most of all for Lamia as we shall see in this chapter, Keats drew at once on the traditions of classical medical mythology, on the research of toxicologists and naturalists of his time, and on the fascination of the mesmerists and early psychologists with the reputed hypnotic power of snakes.

Spence, Lemprière, and Tooke, Keats's primary sources for Greek medical myth, observe that the snake is celebrated for its practical knowledge of medicinal herbs as well as for its wisdom, judgment, prudence, and foresight; for its power of diagnosis and prophecy, and for its ability to transform tangible elements and intangible thoughts. Serpents are the common attribute of all the primitive deities that preside over healing: the serpent Sachan was a healing god to the Babylonians; the Phoenician god of health, Esmus, was represented by a snake; in Genesis, the serpent is the lord of the mysteries, and Moses makes a bronze serpent to heal the people; and in ancient Greece, where the coupling of snakes was a forbidden sight,[3] the Greek deities connected with healing and therapeutic wisdom, Apollo, Aesculapius, Hygeia-Minerva, and Hermes, were all endowed with snake symbols. Apollo Medicus is always represented with snake symbols in Greek art; he is shown sometimes killing the fierce and malignant Python and at other times nurturing benign and quiet snakes. Lemprière notes that the snakes fed at Apollo's temples were credited with the power of prophecy and knowledge of futurity, and Spence marks that all the deities who share Apollo's power of healing "almost always have a serpent by them." Aesculapius is always depicted with two snakes, one wreathed about his staff and the other supporting his hand with its head; serpents were "more particularly sacred" to Aesculapius, "not only as the ancient physicians used them in their prescriptions; but because they were the symbols of prudence and foresight, so necessary in the medical profession."[4] Aesculapius appeared to the plague-stricken populace of Rome in the shape of a serpent, nd the god usually appeared in the guise of a snake in the dreams of incubating patients at his temples; the prescriptive mithridatum cut in bronze in the temple of Aesculapius at Epidaurus, moreover, had the flesh of vipers as its basic compound.[5] Hygeia and Minerva were names for the same deity, according to Lemprière; Hygeia-Minerva, in her role as goddess of health and the wisdom of dreams,[6] is often shown as a veiled figure holding a serpent in one hand with a cup in the other out of which the serpent drinks. More elaborate representations of Hygeia-Minerva show her, like Apollo, surrounded by snakes of benign and ferocious aspect.

Hermes-Mercury, the god of magic, barter, eloquence, philosophy (as the Egyptian bird-god Thoth-Mercury), and deceit, and prototype of the false physician, carries a winged wand entwined by two serpents as "the emblem of his power" given to him by Apollo in exchange for the lyre that he had stolen. Hermes wields this caduceus as a true pharmakon, a quicksilver potion to weave spells and dreams, to lull Chiône to sleep, to conduct the souls of the dead to the infernal regions, to raise dead persons to life, and, in Keats's Lamia, to transform beings. An accomplice most subtle to the serpent Lamia, Hermes swears by his "serpent rod" to change Lamia's "gordion shape" to "a woman's" form: "with languid arm, / Delicate" he puts "to proof the lythe Caducean charm" (I, 89, 132–33) and so acts as mercurial catalyst to the many transformations of the poem itself.

In May 1819, after the publication of both his first volume of poetry and Endymion and just after he had composed the "Ode on Melancholy," Keats considered signing up on an Indiaman as a ship's surgeon. His decision was inspired largely by the need to support himself and escape London, but other less immediate intellectual interests also played a part. The work of the ships' doctors and Anglo-Indian surgeons were an important research feature of early-nineteenth-century medicine.[7] Their medical adventures in India paralleled those of Humboldt in South America and made fascinating reading for Romantic intellectuals (including James Curry of Guy's, who had spent eight months in Bengal doing research). Their reports of tropical diseases, moreover, expanded the classifications of current European nosologies, rendered far more complex notions on the multiplicity of disease, and undermined all functioning theories of disease in contemporary use. Their firsthand accounts of snakes and snakebite, like Patrick Russell's four-volume *Account of Indian Serpents* (1796–1809), did much to encourage research on snake venom and fueled popular and medical interest in the mesmeric power of animals.

Astley Cooper, Everard Home, and John Williams were among the many British medical practitioners of the period who published research on vipers and other poisonous snakes; Orfila and Christison devoted long sections in their treatises to the effects of snake venom.[8] A letter by J. Hector St. John in 1782, which was widely reprinted until as late as 1827, told about a pair of bewitched boots that had been bitten by a rattlesnake without their wearer's knowledge or apparent wounding, which subsequently killed the wearer as well as his son and a villager who thereafter became possessors of the boots.[9] Preposterous stories such as these did much to increase both the popular fascination with snakes and the researchers' overall interest in the nature of poisonous reptiles. Everard Home read to the Royal Society in 1810 on rattle-snake venom and in 1812 on the neck and rib motion of snakes, and Thomas Smith, in 1818, crediting both Everard Home and the journal stories of the traveling naturalists, gave the society an evolutionary account of the development of hollow or poisonous fangs in serpents.[10]

Early-nineteenth-century research on snake poison is distinguished by its pervasive mystification over the nature and composition of venom; Orfila's definitive account of viper poison, for example, defines by negatives:

> It is neither acid nor alkaline, for it does not redden the tincture of the croton tinctorium, nor does it turn the syrup of violets green. It is neither acrid nor burning, and only leaves on the tongue an impression analogous to that of the fresh fat of animals: it has a slight smell, similar to that of the fat of the viper, but it is much less nauseous; with the acids it produces no effervescence; if mixed with water, it thickens and turns it of a slight white colour; but if merely put into a bason of water, it sinks to the bottom. It does not burn when exposed to the flame of a candle, or on red hot coals. When fresh, it is rather viscous; and when dry, it sticks like pitch. It appears to be of the nature of gum.[11]

The nature and function of snake venom could not be assayed. It was a substance so mysterious that it defied all tests and undermined all theories of disease; it was clear only as a testament to the inchoate state of chemistry at this time. Snake venom could be known only by the symptoms it produced (which included all the varieties of mental and bodily disease, from intoxication and delirium to local pain and internal disorders), and by what Everard Home called "the intensity of the poison."[12] For Christison, snake poison was an animal acrid related to acridulous vegetable poisons, and he included it in the same category as cantharides, venomous fish, the "sweltered venom" of toads (like Albert's "brace of toads" in *Otho*), and decayed animal matter.[13] For Orfila, who marked both the varying and contingent intensities of the poison, and its tendency to affect only warm-blooded animals, snake venom coagulated the blood, destroyed irritability and in general acted upon the body and the mind by "carrying a putrefying principle into the fluids";[14] it was, thus, like "the cankering venom, that had riven |Endymion's| fainting recollections" (I, 396–97), an unspecifically virulent ductile element that cleaved, decomposed, and violently disrupted a prior harmony of elements in the organism. Eau de luce, the Tanjore pill, Humboldt's Guaco plant juice, Dr. James' Powder, the Kendal Black Drop, brandy, porter, madeira, and other fine old wines, laudanum, arsenite of potash, sulphuric ether, ammonia, and volatile alkali[15] were among the many dubious antidotes to snake bite, and their conflicting ineffectiveness led researchers like Home to conclude that the recovery from "poisonous bite" is not dependent upon medicines.[16]

Iäpetus discovers the limits of viper poison in *Hyperion* and strangles a serpent "because the creature could not spit / Its poison in the eyes of conquering Jove" (II, 46–48). The power of venomous snakes was confined to warm-blooded mortals, but within this context, as the early nineteenth century discovered, their potency was unlimited and legion. "The eyes are lively and sparkling; its look is audacious, especially when irritated. The tongue is gray, and bifurcated; and, when animated, the animal moves it with impetuosity, so that it appears like a burning dart."[17] That Orfila's treatise on tangible poisons should concern itself with the viper's sparkling eyes and their ability to communicate irritation and willfulness, and with the viper's excessively animated tongue and its resemblance to apostolic fire tells us much about the early nineteenth century's fear that there existed an intangible component to venomous power, that poison did not always operate through visible media, and that venomous elements could subtly penetrate and possess both the mortal body and the immortal mind.

Through the intensity of their eyes, the rapidity of their movements, and the singularity of their sounds, no less than through the tangible poison in their mouths, snakes owned, according to a Romantic age that had yet to chart the physical implications of fear and stress, a "fascinating faculty" that could at once possess and, through its fascination, destroy. We are reminded of Geraldine's extraordinary powers as a false physician in Coleridge's *Christabel* and must ponder that poem's snakelike potential for medical subterfuge. Indeed, the fascination of snakes was of limitless import not only to the physiologists who were studying the nature of poison in the pharmacy of disease but to the evolutionists who were classifying natural instincts and to the physicians and philosophers of mind (and lovers and poets) who were pondering the phenomena of animal magnetism.

Black snakes, rattlers, and other well-known serpents were commonly believed to have the power of fascinating or charming other animals. J. S. Blumenbach devoted a section in his *Über die natürlichen Verschiedenheiten* to the mesmeric power of snakes and other creatures, and in 1798 he added his authority to the debate on the subject by proposing that the "whole charm" of the rattlesnake's hypnotic power was due to three causes: its intense stare, the singular mesmeric noise of its rattles, and a mephitic "stupefying vapour" emitted from its body.[18] Toads, hawks, owls, cats, and tigers were all credited with the magical power to hypnotize and render motionless, but serpents, according to contemporary naturalists, "Beyond all other animals" possessed "most eminently this occult power."[19] Naturalists like John Toplis who favored the notion of the occult power of snakes told stories of their particular influence on human beings: of persons becoming transfixed by a snake's stare with "all power of moving ... taken from them" until the snake's eye was distracted, and of persons who found themselves unable to remove their gaze from an approaching snake, and even inclined to lean toward it, and who became listless and "very sick" for days after the "enchantment."[20] Other naturalists, like M. de la Cépède and William Barton, ascribed the fascinating power of snakes not to any extrasensory source but to a fetid breath or mephitic vapor exuded by the snake; this odor could be smelled by sensitive animals like horses from great distances, and at close range it could afflict small creatures like birds "with a kind of asphxy."[21]

The "two vipers" in *Otho the Great*, "from whose jaws / A deadly breath went forth to taint and blast" (III, ii, 151–53), pay token recognition to the theory of serpentine mephitism, and Lorenzo's courteous greeting to the two brothers' "serpents' whine" in *Isabella* (189–90) pays passing homage to another common belief that snakes could charm and destroy through either a high-pitched whine or a terrifying rattle.[22] The fantastic phenomenon of birds that became paralyzed and fell or flew from branches into the waiting jaws of serpents became a focal point for all Romantic naturalists concerned with this subject since it accommodated at once theories about the serpent's bewitching eyes, its fetid vapors, and its mesmerizing sounds. Efforts to refute fanciful theories such as these gave rise to even more unusual albeit naturalistic attributions. The more pragmatic naturalists sought to explain the phenomenon simply as the reaction of a weakened bird that had been bitten and poisoned by the serpent weeks or days prior to its fall. Others, like Everard Home, focused on the singular head and neck motions of snakes and the way in which these motions evolved to facilitate their magnetic energy.[23] The influential Benjamin Smith Barton carried naturalistic explanation further and saw the phenomenon as the result not of any psychic power or mephitic substance in the snake but of parental instinct in the bird: birds fell prey to serpents during the hatching season only because, in an expression of supreme self-sacrifice, the parent birds acted as suicidal decoys for their young.[24] All this bears relevance at one ironic remove to the scene in *Lamia* where the serpent, after her transformation, stands straight "on a sloping green of mossy tread" by the edge of a forest "About a young bird's flutter from a wood" (I, 179–82), waiting for a young bird like Lycius to fall—victim of his failing wings (or heart) or her fascinating eyes and honey sounds; or, perhaps, as recipient of the misplaced parental instincts of an immortal spirit for a mortal bird.

Serpentine enchanters with fascinating eyes weave through the earlier poems of Keats in anticipation of Lamia. Mary Frogley has a "honied voice" and is "an enchantress" who the poet hopes will "never spill / Blood of those whose eyes can kill" ("Hadst thou liv'd in days of old," 66–68); the medusan-locked la belle dame sans merci holds the knight in thrall with her "wild wild eyes" and "roots of relish sweet" (31, 25); Porphyro, prefiguring Lamia's ambiguous role as both enchanter and victim, steals as serpent into "this paradise" of Madeline's chamber only to become "entranced" while gazing "upon her empty dress" (*Eve*, 244–46). Circe, the "Cruel enchantress" of *Endymion*, whose fire "like the eye of gordian snake, / Bewitch'd" (III, 413, 494–95), anticipates "Circean"-headed Lamia with her "brighter eyes and slow amenity" (I, 293) most closely in all her serpentine and ductile indeterminacies. Bearing mythological connections with Hermes, Circe also possesses a knowledge of venomous herbs and magical incantations like the mythological snakes.[25] Moreover, she bears not only the tangible transforming potencies of a "black dull-gurgling phial" (III, 515) but also, like Lamia, the power to sting the mortal psyche and poison its dreams. Glaucus's cry in *Endymion* when he is deprived at once of Circe's presence and his "o'er-sweetened" dreams, "Stung / And poisoned was my spirit" (III, 601–2), articulates the echoing shriek Lycius gives at the end of *Lamia* when his potent and ever-replenished "bewildering cup" turns sudden hollow emptiness.

Can the elemental composition of Lamia be known, assayed, and held constant? At her simplest, she is a "palpitating snake" who hides "cirque-couchant" amid the poisonous and reedy "taller grasses and full-flowering weed" in a "dusky brake" akin to Circe's Avernian and reed-choked "thorny brake" (I, 44–46; *End.*, III, 493). At her most complex, she is, in alliance with Hermes the Lethean magician, a giver of dreams. Lamia laments to Hermes that life as a snake is a deathly state: "When from this wreathed tomb shall I awake!" (I, 38). Her piteous lament is suspect: in mythology the snake is associated not only with wisdom and prophecy but also and specifically, in the myth of Prometheus (which Keats would have learned from Bacon or Erasmus Darwin, if not directly from his several mythological readers), with renovated youth.[26] Darwin's note on the Portland Vase tells of how the manes or lemures of the dead are received by a beautiful female who plays with a serpent, symbol of immortal life from "its annually renewing its external skin."[27] Whatever the constrictions of her "serpent prison-house" (I, 203), or

ever-changeable skin, Lamia is nevertheless an immortal snake with a composite origin in the divine and the beastly that far escapes the confines of her
many skins.

The original Lamia was a beautiful mortal woman loved by Jupiter whom
Juno rendered deformed and whose children were destroyed so that she
became insane and was driven to swallow the children of others. *Lamiae*, Keats
read in Lemprière, were monsters of Africa who had "the face and breast of a
woman, and the rest of the body like that of a serpent." Their hissings were
"pleasing and agreeable," and they "allured strangers to come to them, that
they might devour them." Other terms for the *Lamiae*, according to Lemprière,
were *Lemures* or manes, and *Larvae*: *Lemures* were insane spirits of the dead who
terrified the good, haunted the impious, and, in the guise of beautiful but
witchlike women, enticed young children only to devour them; *Larvae* were
wicked spirits or apparitions that issued forth from graves at night wearing
frightful and deforming masks, or *larva*, that paralyzed with terror all who
glimpsed them. As witch-spirits, Lamiae took upon themselves the making of
philtres, according to Burton, which they used "*to force men and women to love and
hate whom they will,* [and] to cause tempests, disease, etc."[28] Keats's Lamia
shows herself, at least genealogically, to be a fitting accomplice to the deceiving and bartering "star of Lethe," Hermes. She has many skins and manifold
masks.

> Then, once again, the charmed God began
> An oath, and through the serpents ears it ran
> Warm, tremulous, devout, psalterian.
> Ravish'd, she lifted her Circean head.
>   (I, 112–5)

The fascination is clearly mutual: if Lamia as a snake fascinated the charmed
and winged god, then Hermes' oath, a potent charm, runs warm and impassioned as a life force through the cold-blooded snake's invisible ears to ravish
her. A taking-of-possession of each other follows mutual hypnosis. The neither "devout" nor "psalterian" nor "tremulous" language that seals the dubious pact between the two creatures well suits their indiscriminate natures
and certain knowledge of each other:

> "Thou smooth-lipp'd serpent, surely high inspired!
> Thou beauteous wreath, with melancholy eyes,
> Possess whatever bliss thou canst devise,
> Telling me only where my nymph is fled,—
> Where she doth breathe!" "Bright planet, thou hast said,"
> Return'd the snake, "but seal with oaths, fair God!"
> "I swear," said Hermes, "by my serpent rod,
> And by thine eyes, and by thy starry crown!"

> Light flew his earnest words, among the blossoms blown.
> Then thus again the brilliance feminine:
>   (I, 83–92)

Exaggerated courtesy, a beguiling sophistry, and a flattery that masks a mutual recognition of one another's deceiving modes mark this negotiation and exchange of oaths. These are no Hippocratic oaths but vows to lend suspect medicines for secret ends.

Hermes praises the serpent's smooth lips that drip honied words and mask venomous fangs; he invokes the menacing beauty of her tightly coiled body and the poisonous melancholy of her eyes; and his prescription, "Possess whatever bliss thou canst devise," counsels selfishness and sophistic manipulation, medicines suited to the snake's condition and to the masquerading physician who prescribes them. Lamia's response to the mercurial god— " 'Bright planet, thou has said,'/ Return'd the snake, 'but seal with oaths,' fair God!' "—mimics the tones of the Enemy of Mankind and manifests a Miltonic distrust of gods. The light-footed and even lighter-worded Hermes swears obligingly by the serpent's mesmerizing eyes and by her magician's "starry crown." The poet, meanwhile, by describing the phosphorescent serpent as a "brilliance feminine," reminds us of the kind of flashy, selfish, devising knowledge that Hermes and Lamia share: it is mercurial, planetary, inconstant, delusive, disingenuous like Hermes' "earnest words," sophistic like Thoth-Mercury the patron of rhetoric, and self-reflecting like the spontaneous release of phosphorus in putrefaction. Like dubious magicians, Hermes and Lamia glow in the dark. Theirs are *ignis fatuum*, foolish fires of forbidden knowledge and love.

In mirror image of his winged "lythe Caducean charm," the god of magicians, tricksters, thieves, and sophists in *Lamia* bears physical attributes of snake and bird. As swift as "a bright Phoebean dart," Hermes strikes for the Cretan isle where Lamia and the nymph hide (I, 78–79); he is "dove-footed" and hovers Satanic "on his pinions" "Like a stoop'd falcon ere he takes his prey," but he is also able to glide snakelike "silently / Round bush and tree, soft-brushing, in his speed, / The taller grasses" (I, 42–44, 66–67).[29] In the ambivalent world of *Lamia*, if immortal cold-blooded snakes can turn mortal women for warm "Love's sake" and still preserve their serpentine powers, immortal deities can also turn mortal predators (bird or snake) and simulate mortal love with "celestial heat" for the sake of cold- blooded possession. All this takes place, of course, through false medicine, amid "pervading brilliance and perfume" and to "the strains / Of powerful instruments" and "nectarous cheer" (II, 174, 204–7). Music hath strange charm, especially the borrowed (or stolen) ductile music of Hermes, who, we remember, stole Apollo's lyre so that he might barter for a caduceus from Apollo in exchange for the lyre. Keats invokes the "ravishments" of "Hermes' pipe" when it was used to hypnotize and lull the hundred-eyed Argus to sleep. (*End.*, II, 875–77), and he describes how Lamia, as a mortal woman, swivels her regal white neck in an unmistakable and singular snakelike motion (I, 244–45), a visualized yearning call to Lycius. The young sophist-to-be, victim of the multiple charm of her eyes, motions, and sounds, looks back "Orpheus-like at an Eurydice:"

> For so delicious were the words she sung,
> It seem'd he had lov'd them a whole summer long:
> And soon his eyes had drunk her beauty up,
> Leaving no drop in the bewildering cup,
>   (I, 247–53)

Clearly "One, whose voice was venomed melody" (*Epipsychidion*, 256), Lamia with her serpentive eyes and hollow throat makes music that turns delicious albeit bewildering love potion in much the same magical, quicksilver way that the snake-entwined wand of light-fingered Hermes turns reed instrument for the making of musical sleeping charms for an Argus, warm-blooded love-philtres for a "swoon'd serpent" (I, 132) like Lamia, or dream potions for the thirsting throat and mind of a hopelessly hypnotized apprentice-sophist like Lycius.

Like that full-flowering weed the hydra-plant, which grows amid festering waters of monstrous plant growth and pestilential poisons, snakes multiply and breed forth in the ambiguously fertile and often preternaturally strange world of lush beauty and extravagant excess that is *Lamia*. The serpentine qualities of Hermes and Lamia are exceeded in their preternaturalism only by those snakelike and predatory qualities of Lycius, the boy-victim, and Apollonius, the rational sophist. In them, the ambiguity of snakes finds its expression as the facile (in Apollonius) and deceiving (in Apollonius and Lycius) sophistry of snakes.

Lycius, wishing to fill his heart "With deeper crimson, and a double smart," ponders with feverous love and sophistic guile how he can turn union into full bondage so as to "entangle, trammel up and snare," "and labyrinth," Lamia's soul in his (II, 50–54). When Lamia demurs at the revelation of such a wedding, Lycius "thereat was stung, / Perverse, with stronger fancy," and his coiled "mitigated fury" is "like / Apollo's presence when in act to strike / The serpent" (II, 69–70, 78–80). But if Lamia plays Python briefly to Lycius's righteous Apollonian fury, it is soon discovered that the "stronger fancy" with which Lycius is stung has its origins in his own psyche and pride of possession as a lover. Lycius stings himself with the supernal denouément of a wedding feast to which his beloved tutor, who has nurtured him (and specifically his psyche and mind), Thoth-like, as a young bird, comes literally to hypnotize and metaphorically feed upon, or at least sting, melt, and remove the bloom from, Lycius's blushing bride. Lycius's stinging remedy is his own self-deceit. The serpent's skin that he has assumed as his marriage robe will be a winding sheet coiled tightly about his soon-to-be-breathless body.

As a sophist, Apollonius is both a respected tutor of ancient Greek philosophy and rhetoric and a perverse thinker skilled in deceit and the art of hollow reasoning. This latter role bears kinship to that of the false physician, for Apollonius's rhetoric can doctor minds and is a charm that can alternately pierce and trammel vulnerable psyches. His "patient thought" is empowered thus with the primary potencies of the bird and snake symbols of the god of rhetoric and philosophy, Thoth-Mercury: it sees keenly and, like the poison of the seps and other venomous serpents, it is able "to thaw, / And solve and melt" the "tender-person'd Lamia . . . into a shade" (II, 161–62, 238). The sophist arrives at the wedding ceremony with all the transforming, subversive malignancy of a morbid poison or a beastly venom to "infest / With an unbidden presence the bright throng" (II, 166–67). More than Lamia, Apollonius manifests the fascinating power possessed by certain beasts and persons to transfer through the rays of their eyes "certain spiritual vapours" that "infect the other party"—as described in *The Anatomy of Melancholy*; Burton's examples of this infecting glance are, pertinently, the royal basilisk "that kills [from] afar off by sight" and Philostratus's Ephesian, who was "of so pernicious an eye, he poisoned all he looked steadily on."[30] Thus Apollonius fixes his knowing eyes "without a twinkle or stir / Full on the alarmed beauty of the bride," and "his lashless eyelids stretch / Around his demon eyes" (II, 246–47, 288–89).

Whether these are the eyes of a fascinating snake or a hypnotizing magician, a predatory bird or a sucking parasite, whether they possess or keenly see, their glance "Like a sharp spear, went through her utterly, / Keen, cruel, perceant, stinging" and Lycius's "sweet bride withers at their potency," as the grass once withered when she foamed forth (II, 290, 300–301). More predatory a creature than either Hermes or Lamia, for his prey is beauty, Apollonius casts "Some hungry spell that loveliness absorbs" (II, 259). Lamia is a victim of the sophist's guile that, like that magical art of Hermes, the patron of deceiving philosophy, sees sharply and knows as kindred the sinuous mode of snakes. When at Apollonius's infecting bidding Lamia breaths "death breath," her fate is at once and self-reflectively her retribution and her reward, the fetid and mephitic breath of a serpent and the exotic but often rank miasma of a too-fertile and undifferentiated marsh. Apollonius's remedy is her disease.

In this murky poem of too many snakes, Lamia is at once both more but also far less of a snake. Once freed from her "serpent prison-house," she cannot be held constant to any one form, source, mask, or element. She associates freely with her manifold natures and multiple origins, and, like her poem, is as changeful and unpredictable as a waking dream or a nightmare. "So rainbow-sided" and "touch'd with miseries" of unknown hue is Lamia that to Hermes' keen wisdom she seems to be "some penanced lady elf, / Some demon's mistress, or the demon's self" (I, 54–56). Mortals like Lycius have more trouble distinguishing her variegated features and many more potential forms of her from which they must choose. She is "a gordion shape of dazzling hue" (I, 47), like the Scitalis in *The Bestiary*[31] able to transfix and capture by the beautiful splendor of her dappled markings. She is a malevolent sister of Glaucus's sweet Scylla, part snake where the other is part fish.[32] She is a fair cousin of Milton's serpent, whose form, with its crested head, carbuncle eyes, and "burnisht Neck of verdant Gold" was both "pleasing" and "lovely."[33] She is a crested basilisk, relative to the fabulous reptile of Greek mythology that was hatched by a serpent from a cock's egg, whose hissing terrified and whose breath and look were fatal, and she wears the sign of the magician "Upon her crest . . . a wannish fire / Sprinkled with stars, like Ariadne's tiara" (I, 57–58). She is jeweled like a medieval therapeutic charm of pearls and precious stones, "Vermillion-spotted, golden, green, and blue" (I, 48). She is an ever-transmuting chemical experiment whose reaction, as it de-etherealizes from divine substance to mortal flesh, turns her multicolored skin "A deep volcanian yellow" that made "gloom of all her frecklings, streaks and bars, / Eclips'd her crescents, and lick'd up her stars "(I, 155–60). The "dew so sweet and virulent" that she spews forth during this hardly cold-blooded chemical reaction defies, nevertheless, like literal snake venom, all the tests of chemistry and all attempts to assay it: "it does not burn"[34] like Hermes' divine fire nor does it freeze the philosophic liquid in Lycius's veins. Her "smooth-lipp'd" "woman's mouth with all its pearls complete" (I, 83, 60) foams forth like the Pythia or Pythonissa who deliver the oracles at Apollo's temple in prophetic frenzy (described for Keats in Potter's *Antiquities*);[35] then depending upon whether her prophecy is intended for a Hermes or a Lycius, "her elfin blood in madness" runs or else foams "sweet greeting" to already "ravish'd ears" (I, 147, 268–69). She is an iridescent, electric gymnotus eel[36] "full of silver moons, that, as she breathed, / Dissolv'd, or brighter shone, "(I, 51–52); her glowing phosphorescence is at once a sign of the presence of subtle life and a symptom of the putrefaction of animal bodies in swamps and graveyards. Her ability to shock with pleasure or "double smart" parallels the late-eighteenth-century notion of electricity as a potent conveyor of medical substances and finds perverse truth in the physician John Walsh's belief that the electric eel or torpedo was an "animate phial," like the Leyden jar, able to transmit similar curative powers.[37] If Milton's serpent was "the subtlest Beast of all the Field"[38] because it possessed the attributes and intelligence of all the other animals in Paradise, then Keats's Lamia, "Striped like a zebra, freckled like a pard, / Eyed like a peacock, and all crimson barr'd" (I, 49–50), dappled in beauty and varioloid in effect, splendidly patterned and malignantly pocked, tinctured and tincturing, possesses all the powers, physical and psychical, of her many natures and her multicolored plenitudinous potencies. She is, in effect, all skin—or all ductile and infecting hollow form.

Lamia's first sighting of her victim is on the eve of the "Adonian feast" when " 'gainst a column [Lycius] leant thoughtfully / At Venus' temple porch, 'mid baskets heap'd / Of amorous herbs and flowers, newly reap'd" (I, 316–20). Had Lycius plucked lush and pungent fennel, which is the favorite food of serpents,[39] from out the baskets of amorous herbs, he may have satisfied the designing serpent and so preserved his own dream of the truth of sophistry's designs. Had he seized some sacred dittany from the sacrificial herbs intended for Venus and inscribed a charmed circle about him with its juice,[40] he might have trapped and killed a poisonous snake, or, better, saved himself from the venom of a poison damsel. Certainly, in at least one of her numerous roles, Lamia wears over her porous skin the weeds of the poison girl. Her lineage in this regard would include the poisonous maiden inoculated with snake venom who was given as a gift to Alexander the Great[41] and Rappacini's deadly daughter who was nurtured on poisonous plants and miasma. It would include, also, the poison girls used in medieval times for destroying enemies through infections with the deadly pox. Closer to home, and in reverse tradition, it would include the virginal poison girls or boys of the eighteenth and early nineteenth century in Europe, who were employed for therapeutic purposes during epidemics of venereal disease either as a cure for syphilis or as protection against its infection.[42] As poison girl, Lamia could be both the source of deadly infection and a pure innocent possessed and made victim of the intricate and infecting sophistic designs of Lycius and Apollonius.

Lamia's equivocating form questions which state, that of a serpent or that of a woman, is the more complicated one. Sources for this puzzling ambiguity between women and snakes in Western tradition are as multiple as the serpent's skins. "Heva" means "snake." Adam, in *Paradise Lost*, addresses Eve after his loss of paradise as "Thou serpent"; Samson, also, finds Dalila "a manifest Serpent," and to her "fair enchanted cup, and warbling charms" responds, "So much of Adder's wisdom I have learn't / To fence my ear against thy sorceries."[43] More pertinent to Lamia is the story of the Medusa. Keats would have read in Lemprière that Medusa was the only one of the three Gorgons who was "subject to mortality." Loved by Neptune for her beautiful locks and seduced by him in the temple of Minerva, she was punished by Minerva for violating the temple's sanctity. Her hair was turned into serpents, and, when Perseus captured her and cut off her head for the aegis of his patron, Minerva, the blood from the severed head gave rise to the serpents of Africa. A variant to the myth, which Lemprière notes, has Medusa and her sisters born with snakes on their heads instead of hair, yellow wings, brazen hands, impenetrable scaly bodies, and mesmerizing eyes that "had the power of killing or turning to stones."[44] With her "bright wreath of serpent-tresses crown'd, / Severe in beauty, young MEDUSA" frowns upon a grim but "dazzled field" of fire and destruction in *The Botanic Garden*: "Erewhile subdued, round WISDOM's Aegis roll'd / Hiss'd the dreadful snakes, and flamed in burnish'd gold." In a note to these lines, Darwin marks that while the face of the Greek Medusa on Minerva's shield represents "rage or pain," the Egyptian Medusa symbolizes the veiled goddess of wisdom herself, with "snaky hair, and a beautiful countenance, which appears intensely thinking; and was supposed to represent divine wisdom."[45] A dazzling distortion of pain and an intense countenance, and a form and face that represent wisdom come together in Darwin's connection of Minerva and the Medusa. We are reminded not simply of Lamia but of her connections to the veiled, snake-wrapped and cup-bearing figure of Hygeia and, most significantly, to the severe and frightening veiled beauty of Moneta in *The Fall of Hyperion*, whose origins must be found in Minerva-Hygeia's role as the goddess of wisdom and the prophecy of dreams.

"The principle of the imagination resembles the emblem of the serpent, by which the ancients typified wisdom and the universe, with undulating folds, for ever varying and for ever flowing into itself, —circular, and without beginning or end," Hazlitt said in 1820.[46] The intensely intelligent Lamia deals most of all with the furthest or subconscious realms of the imagination. Her guise as an incubus or masked, lemure-like manes belongs ultimately with her imaginative power to incubate or induce dreams. She creates forms that melt, she veils substance and renders it unseen, and for immortals like Hermes, she makes the fleeting dreams that mortals know turn real and endure. We are witness to this power in the serpent's own description of the dream of invisibility she has created for Hermes' nymph;

> Free as the air, invisibly, she strays
> About these thornless wilds; her pleasant days
> She tastes unseen; unseen her nimble feet
> Leave traces in the grass and flowers sweet;
> From weary tendrils, and bow'd branches green,
> She plucks the fruit unseen, she bathes unseen:
> And by my power is her beauty veil'd
> To keep it unaffronted, unassail'd
> By the love-glances of unlovely eyes,
> Of Satyrs, Fauns, and blear'd Silenus' sighs.
> Pale grew her immortality, for woe
> Of all these lovers, and she grieved so
> I took compassion on her, bade her steep
> Her hair in weïrd syrops, that would keep
> Her loveliness invisible, yet free
> To wander as she loves, in liberty.
>   (I, 94–109)

Lamia's compassion, like the dream that she creates for the nymph out of this compassion and then abruptly terminates out of self-interest for (Hermes') love's sake, is suspect medicine. She makes "loveliness invisible," and by her power is the nymph's "beauty veil'd" in a manner reminiscent of the "hungry spell which loveliness absorbs" cast by Apollonius when he preys on beauty. In her "weïrd syrops"-induced dream, the nymph "tastes unseen," "bathes unseen," "plucks the fruit unseen" from possibly poisonous vines, and her unseen nimble feet leave traces but no footprints (like serpentine Lamia) upon the grass. The nymph strays about invisibly in what she believes to be "thornless wilds" but that we know from the poem *Endymion* to be a thorny and dusky brake, a thicket of weeds and bracken. The purpose of this dream is to keep the nymph "unaffronted, unassail'd / By the love-glances of unlovely eyes"—of satyrs, fauns, and Silenus but not those possessing eyes of a fascinating serpent and, at the serpent's behest, a mesmerizing god. The nymph's immortality grows pale from the woe of "unlovely eyes," but the strange syrup of Lamia's compassionate venom turns this paleness into Newtonian colorlessness: invisibility.

Lamia's dream-making power is a mixed blessing, the nymph discovers; it assumes as many guises as the serpent herself. At times, Lamia induces dreams in herself: "And sometimes into cities she would send / Her dream, with feast and rioting to blend" (I, 213–14); as such, revealing the abilities of both hypnotizer and ventriloquist, Lamia projects herself into other times and other actions. On other occasions, Lamia induces pleasurable dreams of sight, not invisibility, at once in others and herself: "She breath'd upon his eyes, and swift was seen / Of both the guarded nymph near-smiling on the green" (I, 124–25). Whether her breath be the creating ether of an immortal, or the miasmic vapor and mephitic breath of a serpent, Hermes' dream nonetheless proves to be real, enduring, and unalloyed. Hermes' eyes find their mark, the nymph melts into visibility through Lamia's power, and homeless love turns union.

More complex, bearing the fragrance of vision and the odor of mortality, is the dream Lamia induces in Lycius. To incubate this dream, the many-colored Lamia bears a tinctured cup to her victim in sinister echo of the snake-entwined cup Hygeia-Minerva bears to her patient or aspiring prophet. The enchanting words she sings to summon forth the ensuing dream come "as through bubbling honey," but the throat from which they come "was serpent" (I, 64–65), and the honey could be the toxic variety. Lycius, pale dreamer that he is, functions through his senses without any power of discrimination; "so delicious" is the draught from Lamia's "bewildering cup" that "soon his eyes had drunk her beauty up, / Leaving no drop" (I, 250–53). He consumes and absorbs loveliness, like his sophistic tutor, Apollonius, and like his deceitful lover, Lamia. But, unlike his two masters, Lycius cannot distinguish what he consumes. He cannot tell whether the cup he drinks from bears a rainbow substance sweet and virulent or a white ether pure and tasteless—or, if the cup is all hollow and bewildering form, a conduit to invisibility that in the mortal world, as the conclusion of the poem proves, is white nothingness and a winding sheet.

In *Otho the Great* Ludolph says of the villainess, Auranthe, "Even as the worm doth feed upon the nut, / So she, a scorpion, preys upon my brain" (V, v, 158–59). His metaphor invokes both the legend of the intense and growing pain of the scorpion's sting and the early-nineteenth-century toxicologists' belief that the scorpion's venomous bite produced mania and terminal lunacy.[47] Lamia, as serpent or scorpion turned dream-maker, stings, preys upon, vexes, infects, colors, dissolves, consumes, whitens, and venoms all of Lycius's days to a final nothingness that includes both Lycius and his dream, her lover, and herself. "For pity do not melt," Lycius cries (I, 271) at the start of his dream and her dream-making. But of course he and she must melt, and the poem unwinds to whiteness both the tinctured dream and the variegated hollowness of its serpentine creator.

We cannot determine whether Lamia is a ghost or ghostly reality, a mortal woman or an immortal snake, a masked incubus or a perverted Hygeia figure who incubates diseases of the imagination, a venom that infects Lycius's body or a dissolving dream that is all in his mind. We can sense that all of the dreams that Lamia induces, in Hermes, the nymph, herself, and Lycius, are dreams of union, sinuous and entwining dreams that challenge distinction and separation. She exhibits in this unifying and undifferentiating task the dark underside of the healing mesmerizer or animal magnetism, a perverted form of negative capability where possessive, consumptive creation is attained through a purportedly compassionate projection of the self outward and into other beings. Lamia's poison melts by making visible, and dissolves by making invisible both substance and the intangible traces of her cure. Like Circe's potions, and the herbs with which Lamia decks her palace on her wedding day, her venom, once turned amorous, turns bewildering, melting poison. Her bewildering cup is thus a true love-philtre: it unifies, according to the intents of the giver, and unification becomes dissolution. Divisive and vexing morbidity turns lovely phantasmagoric fusion with Lamia's art; her infection then remedies evanescent beauty to extinction.

Chapter 15

Morbid Fevers

In the still and moony hour
  Of that calm entwining sleep,
From the utmost tombs of earth
The vision-land of death and birth,
    Came a black, malignant power,
    A spectre of the desert deep:
And it is Plague, the spotted fiend, the drunkard of the tomb;
Upon her mildewed temples the thunderbolts of doom,
And blight-buds of hell's red fire, like gory wounds in bloom,
    Are twisted for a wreath;
And there's a chalice in her hand, whence bloody flashes gleam,
While struggling snakes with arrowy tongues twist o'er it for a stream,
And its liquor is of Phlegethon, and Aetna's wrathful stream,
    And icy dews of death.

Like a rapid dream she came,
  And vanished like the flame
    Of a burning ship at sea,
But to his shrinking lips she pressed
    The cup of boiling misery.[1]

In this poem of 1823 called "The Romance of the Lily," T. L. Beddoes evokes plague as a literal and metaphorical "spotted fiend" of "black, malignant power." She is a spectre bearing a snake-infested chalice of boiling misery; the "blight-buds" on her forehead and her "mildewed temples" show her to be an inhabitant of deserts and dank marshes; most of all, she is a dark and misty vision "From the utmost tombs of earth." Beddoes's vision of an infecting and consuming malignancy without distinction or boundary does more than remind us of enchantresses like Lamia and *Endymion's* Circe; when we recall that Beddoes was a doctor like his father, Thomas Beddoes, the images of this poem that he calls a "romance" evoke every idea current in the early nineteenth century on the subject of malignant pharmacies or morbid poisons or (as we now call them) infectious diseases.

"The morbid poisons," according to Joseph Adams, "are those which convey a diseased action from one animal to another of the same, or of a different species." Such "diseased action" could be brought about "by vapour, contact, or wound," or bite, or by some other more subtle medium of influence.[2] To the physicians and pathologists of Keats's time, morbid poisons were the secretions of animals in healthy and diseased states and the vapors of dungeons, marshes, slaughterhouses, and cemeteries. There was little difference between what resulted when one was bitten by a venomous snake or a rabid dog, between the vapors of morbid decaying matter and those emanating from infectious animal bodies. Morbid poisons produced similar symptoms to those induced by animal and insect venoms: William Babington did experiments with hydrophobic dogs at Guy's Hospital, and sought by inoculating other animals with the saliva of these dogs to reveal the occasion and infective nature of madness; Everard Home showed by dissection how snakebite produced the same changes in the brain as did acute diseases like meningitis.[3] Both malevolencies attacked organs and systems with the same whimsical diversity and, as Astley Cooper marked, the stages in the progress of disease were often no different from the patterns of a given poison's effects.[4] Nowhere is the early-nineteenth-century's confusion between tangible venoms and the notion of contagion more apparent than in Orfila's resolution to the Institute of France that his next project, for which his work on poisons best prepared him, would be a study of how "the fluids of living animals, undergo alterations and become poisonous" and diseased.[5]

Hahnemann's doctrine of *similia similibus* and infinitesimal dosage proved to have multiple applications for contemporary theorists of disease and contagion. A miasma produced a fever; cinchona also produced a fever. So also did the sting of a venomous snake or insect, the touch of an electric eel, the vapors of hospitals and carrion grounds, the odor of a cat, the effluvia of mutton,[6] and the bite of a rabid animal. The influence of these morbid poisons depended upon the constitution of the victim, and slow poisoning could result, as Coleridge and Astley Cooper among others noted, as much from minute doses of mercury or arsenic as from the much-delayed effects of dogbite or "marsh miasmata."[7] Indeed, the disease that most concerned Thomas Beddoes the elder, hydrophobia, became a catchall for the *similia similibus* thinking on contagions and poisons. The occasion of hydrophobia combined notions of venomous bite with notions of mediumistic contagion; it produced physical as well as mental symptoms; its incubation period was thought to vary between a few hours and several years; and it supported the well-subscribed theory that disease was largely due to nervous or psychical weakness.[8] Its purported cures, in consequence of its multiple symptomatics, included virtually every substance in the pharmacopoeia: of especial worth was Virginia snakeroot, which cured rattlesnake bite and mad-dog bite,[9] hydro-carbonic gas, which Coleridge recommended as an experimental drug,[10] and ground *scutellaria lateriflora* or laurel powder, which was commonly used to control the symptoms of mental instability.[11] To the theories and cures subsuming hydrophobia, Orfila's *Toxicology* added psychosomosis: the Frenchman cites cases where hydrophobia resulted spontaneously, without contact, from the look of a rabid animal—and one instance where a young woman died of hydrophobia after being severely frightened while she was washing linen under a dark bridge.[12]

Venomous volcanic exhalations that escaped from the depths of the earth caused epidemic fevers according to Seneca and Roman medicine. Cadmus, in Book III of Ovid's *Metamorphoses*, does battle with a horrible serpent, and its stygian breath makes the air tainted or noisome—*"vitiatas inficit auras"*; the great plague of Book VII begins with a "murk" that hides the sun and four months of "hot south wind, and deadly airs" during which "serpents came crawling" to taint the streams with poison; at the plague's height, bodies lie rotting and the air is defiled by "One smell of death"—*"vitiantur odoribus aurae."*[13] In 1793 the senior Beddoes defined a vitiated air as an atmosphere turned to fixed air, or carbon dioxide. In its earlier usage, *vitiate* or *vitiated* meant "depraved, infected, spoiled," or tainted with *"vitium or vice."*[14] To this tendency to connect noxious odor with malicious intent belongs, also, the ancient belief that from sick persons and malevolent personages (such as sorcerers and enchantresses) alike emanated harmful odors that produced disease.[15]

To these notions and contemporary research on poisons, contagion, and harmful influences belongs the theory commonly held during the Romantic period that the "noxious powers" of morbid poisons that produce fever are derived from "human effluvia, generated commonly in the confined miserable huts of penury and wretchedness," in the "the putrid atmosphere of marshes," and in the "the damp unventilated cells of imprisonment." "Animals exposed to [any of] this malignant vapour, feel it absorbed into the system" and are then affected with its attendant symptoms.[16] Babington and Curry taught their students at Guy's Hospital that the "effluvia of marshes (called *marsh miasmata*") was "the most common cause of intermitting and remitting fever"; Curry's specific example of the "states of air" and "certain winds" that excite fever was "the east wind in England"[17]—a companion air to the "sickening east wind" that finds pestilential place in The Fall of Hyperion (I, 97). Keats shows himself well acquainted with these and other current notions on contagious vapors and harmful airs. Isabella in The Pot of Basil ask her brothers, "What dungeon climes / Could keep" Lorenzo off so long (259–60). The poet prescribes the clean and moving air of "a dry, gravelly, barren, elevated country" to the ailing Taylor:

> You should no[t] have delay'd so long in fleet Street; leading an inactive life as you did was breathing poison: you will find the country air do more for you than you expect. But it must be proper country air; you must choose a spot. What sort of

place is Retford? You should live in a dry, gravelly, barren, elevated country open to the currents of air, and such a place as is generally furnnish'd with the finest springs—The neighborhood of a rich inclosed fulsome manured arrable Land especially in a valley and almost as bad on a flat, would be almost as bad as the smoke of fleetstreet.

An earlier letter finds the poet evoking Spenser's potent enchantress Acrasia (from whom Lamia and Circe derive some of their powers) for the proper image of the occasional psychosomatic origins of such harmful airs: "—Such a quelling Power have these thoughts over me, that I fancy the very Air of a deteriorating quality—I fancy the flowers, all precocious, have an Acrasian spell about them—I feel able to beat off the devonshire waves like soap froth—"[18] The breathing of poison in nature's air bears contagion to the body, but, sometimes, the mind exudes its own maleficent malaria upon the wholesome natural environs. The "proper country air" was prescribed by poets and physicians of the early nineteenth century; the age's philosophers of mind, meanwhile, cautioned repeatedly against the tainting odors of the febrile mind, and the Acrasian spells of a "rich inclosed fulsome" fancy, or a diseased imagination.

Contagion springs from the metaphorical mix of Erasmus Darwin's *Botanic Garden* as a "drowsy FOG" that slumbers on "the sedge-wove bog," creeps with "webbed feet o'er midnight meadows," and "flings his hairy limbs on stagnant deeps."[19] Coleridge and Keats were justifiably nauseated by such vapors issuing from Darwin's imagination. The Romantic physician in Darwin glosses these lines in a note with the reductive declaration, "All contagious miasmata originate either from animal bodies, as those of the small pox, or from putrid morasses";[20] the mixed contagion of his poetic metaphors highlights nevertheless his age's mystification over the nature of infectious influence. If the noxious odor of putrifying vegetable and animal substances, volcanic exhalations, and the vitiated air of enclosed spaces were recognized malaria and a veritable pharmacy of disease, the principle through which these morbid poisons produced infection was a mystery. The Mitchillian theory of fever and contagion invoked chemistry to say that oxide of septon or nitrous gas, released during putrefaction and volcanic eruptions, was the principle of contagion.[21] Other theories, marking that nitrous acid was often prescribed as a cure or antidote *against* infection, sought for the principle of infection elsewhere, for example, in a "subtle secretion from the blood itself"[22] or in the weakness of a given constitution at a specific time. Coleridge, who probably visited the Pontine Marshes in 1806, classified contagious diseases in two categories: "Those which spring from organized living beings, and from the life in them, and which enter, as it were, into the life of those in whom they reproduce themselves"; and those "which spring from dead organized, or unorganized matter, and which may be comprehended under the wide term *malaria.*"[23] The former were diseases requiring immediate contact with the infecting agent; the latter were diseases that, invisibly, were "supposed to stain, corrupt, or *infect* the air...."[24]

With both categories of contagion, as Hunterian medicine diagnosed first, predisposition and the individual constitution were vital factors. Astley Cooper taught that with morbid poison, "its effects depend upon the state of the constitution at the time the poison is introduced" and that "its action is modified by the peculiar condition of the patient."[25] Coleridge described how one "may have passed a stagnant pond a hundred times without injury: [yet if] you happen to pass it again, in low spirits and chilled, precisely at the moment of the explosion of the gas: the malaria strikes...."[26] Babington and Curry speculated in their course on the practice of medicine at Guy's that "perhaps the particular *electric* state of the atmosphere, as connected with Galvanic influence, may have considerable power in occasioning healthy or morbid effects from atmosphere."[27] The metaphorical and metaphysical implications of theories such as these, however inaccurate to a later century, are profound. Ludolph's thought in *Otho the Great* on "the discoloured poisons of a fen, / Which he who breathes feels warning of his death" (II, i, 22–23), partakes of these theories. Its notions directly underlie the poet's statements in the 1819 letter to Taylor[28] on temperament, disposition, and healthful and malarial atmospheres. Pestilential winds and miasmatic vapors, according to Keats and his generation of Romantic physicians, wreak havoc upon the constitution of those predisposed to their infecting influence: the excessively enervated man of power, the obsessively indolent poet or man of genius "who is not sensitively alive," and the unnaturally energized or overwrought and wasted consumptive lover.

Climate conspires with constitution and the state of the infected psyche, according to Romantic medicine. The Romantic poet Keats is "convinced there is as harmful Air to be breath'd in the country as in Town,"[29] but "After dark vapours" of infection, the physician in him knows, "comes a day / Born of the gentle south, and clears away / From the sick heavens all unseemly stains" of poison and miasma (1–4). Like the "poison-wind" that ravages through Canto IV of Darwin's *Botanic Garden*,[30] the early-nineteenth-century atmosphere bore, according to its doctors, pestilential "tainted air" of "suffocative breath" and "poisoned javelin"; it also bore, according to its poets and *Naturphilosphen*, breezes of regenerative energy like Shelley's West Wind, and the subtly soothing, disinfecting essence that winds through Coleridge's Aeolian Harp. On Latmos, the Keatsian poet finds not pestilential winds but breezes "ethereal, and pure" that "crept through half closed lattices to cure / The languid sick; it cool'd their fever'd sleep, / And soothed them into slumbers full and deep" ("I stood tip-toe," 221–24). These cool airs cure "The languid sick," be they febrile youths, wasted consumptives, too-indolent poets, or melancholic lovers. They also serve as antidotes to contagion, and the airs of lovesick Pan's syrinx pipe can be summoned to "Breathe round our farms, / To keep off mildews, and all weather harms" (*End.*, I, 283–84).

The smoke from the "lofty sacrificial fire" in *The Fall of Hyperion*, meanwhile, signals vision, the cure of a blind dreamer and his regeneration as a poet, a metaphysical change akin to mid-May's aerial transformation when "the sickening east wind / Shifts suddenly to the south" bringing "the small warm rain" that disinfects, removing odors and stains, and "Melts out the frozen incense from all flowers," be they pregnant with essences medicinal or poetic (I, 96–103). Keats's repeated evocation of malarial winds of "misty pestilence," and health-giving, wholesome, and inspirational airs, becomes far from random. These winds are hardly such "Whose language is . . . a barren noise" (*Fall of Hyp.*, II, 4–5). They posit by diffused indirection those notions from Romantic medicine on the subject of beneficial and malevolent airs that Keats would have to know. They exemplify directly one way in which the confused and various medical theories of the poet's time can be assimilated and transformed as *pharmaka* for the "simple" complexities of compounded poetic truth.

Chapter 16

Feverous Love

Isolde, the prudent Queen, *was brewing in a vial a love-drink so subtly devised and prepared, and endowed with such powers,* that with whomever any man drank it he had to love her above all things, whether he wished it or no, and she love him alone. They would share one death and one life, *one sorrow and one joy.*

. . . .

We all desire our amorous fancies and wish to keep company with Love. No, Love is not such as we make her for one another in the spurious way we do! We do not look facts in the face: *we sow seeds of deadly nightshade* and wish it to bear lilies and roses! Believe me, this is impossible. We can only garner what has been put into the ground, and accept what the seed bears us. We must mow and reap as we have sown. *We cultivate Love with guile and deceit and with minds as bitter as gall, and we then seek joy of body and soul in her!* But, instead, *she bears only pain and evil and poison-berries and weeds,* just as her soil was sown. And when this *yields bitter sorrow, festers in our hearts and there destroys us,* we accuse Love of the crime and say she is to blame whose fault it never was.

"Ah, Tristan and Isolde, this draught will be your death!" Brangane cries when she learns that they have consumed Queen Isolde's love potion. "It is in God's hands!" responds Tristan, giving voice to the ambiguity of his own narrative, "Whether it be life or death, it has poisoned me most sweetly!"[1] The versatile and frequently disguised Tristan is a musician who speaks diverse languages and tells many fictions. He is poisoned twice through a festering sword wound in the thigh and once by the sharp tongue of the serpent of Anferginan. The dragon's tongue, which robs him of his senses until he is cured by Queen Isolde, also enables him, as the agent of King Mark, to win the young Isolde. From the scene where he first arrives in Ireland as a musician dying in hideous, rank, and putrid form, we know that Tristan makes sweetest and most enchanted music when he is most poisoned. Queen Isolde, whose powers the young Isolde inherits, combines a knowledge of medicine and secret pharmacy with the power of interpreting dreams and fortelling the future. The love

203

drink that she brews thus bears all meaning within its potion as a fateful and infecting *venin* or philtre of Venus: intended to make her daughter love and be loved by a man she has never seen and ought to hate (Mark), it succeeds too well in making her love the musician who is her father's killer and whom she thinks she hates; its sweet sustenance nurtures their love and consummates the festering doom first begun by her father's poisoned sword.

In the opulent palace of Mark, Tristan and Isolde's love is nourished by deceit. In the "wasteland" that is the Lover's Cave, the two lovers need take no food and nourish themselves merely by gazing at one another; they are consumed by one another and, consuming, are sustained. The story of their romance is intended to provide for us a like, and likely ambiguous, *pharmakon*:

> *This is bread to all noble hearts. With this their death lives on. We read their life, we read their death, and to us it is sweet as bread. Their life, their death are our bread. Thus lives their life, thus lives their death. Thus they live still and yet are dead, and their death is the bread of the living.*[2]

Love's frenzy, as a stroke of fate, malevolently infecting poison and purifying force in romance tradition, is further intensified in Tristan as a sustaining yet consumptive potion: the bread of life and death. The nightshade and poison berries that Tristan sows with his enchanting music, and garners with his guile, serve also as sacramental food. To this notion of love as a sacramental and sacrificial complex that consumes as it is consumed, albeit at some ironic distance, belongs Keats's sentiment that

> Love in a hut, with water and a crust,
> Is—Love, forgive us!—cinders, ashes, dust;
> Love in a palace is perhaps at last
> More grievous torment than a hermit's fast.
> (*Lamia*, II, 1–4).

"He that never had sorrow of love never had joy of it either," warns Gottfried von Strassburg of the divided nature of commitment to sacramental love. And, when the passionately sensitized consumptive poet writes to Fanny Brawne, "My Creed is Love and you are its only tenet," his medical condition serves at once as reason and metaphor to the energized ambiguity of such an intense, self-sacrificing commitment to a love that bears in equal potion benediction and torment.[3]

The "God of warm pulses, and dishevell'd hair, / And panting bosoms" in Keats is also a potion of "sweetest essence." He is a "Bright-winged Child" whose pinions fan away "All death-shadows" and cast out "glooms that overcast / Our spirits"; but he is also an "unseen light in darkness," an "eclipser / Of light," and a "delicious poisoner" whose "venom'd goblet" we "quaff until / We fill" (*End.*, III, 978–89). Isabella in her poem sings a fair ditty "of delicious love and honey'd dart" (78), and, when Love in *Endymion* sheds from his pinions "a nectarous dew" (III, 892), we may presume that it is of the same substance as that which Keats invokes when he writes to Fanny: "Would I could take a sweet poison from your lips to send me out of it."[4] The cynical eye of *The Jealousies* meanwhile discovers that "grains of paradise" or *Amorum Meleguetta*, the medieval medicine and sweetmeat tincture, is a "sly douceur" and, like poisonous "nitre pure / Goes off like lightning" (294–300) and burns the wings of lover, butterfly, and Cupid himself. In the love letters, we recall, Fanny Brawne is Keats's "sweet Physician" and "the only medicine" that can mitigate the "weight and tightness" of his chest, but she is also the sweet substance that will bring death upon possession or absorption.

Cupid's bright arrows pierce and infect with influence in a manner akin to those dark arrows of Apollo; his darkness brings light much as Apollo's misty pestilence serves to reveal mock lyrists and cure real poets in *The Fall of Hyperion*. His potion as a "delicious poisoner" is kindred in complexity and ambiguity to the potent substance of the first *pharmakeus*:[5] far from being a self-consuming artifact,[6] it bears close resemblance in tincture, sound, and influence to what Coleridge defined as the partly assimilable poisonous medicine, the magical, unstable element that had the potential to be either cankering poison or transforming beneficence and whose power depended upon the constitution of the subject and the potency of its occasion.

The ambiguous nature of the love-philtre, coming full circle in Keats and in tradition, finds place in the dual nature of mythical Eros. As Keats would have read in Spence, love is often represented in Greek art by two Cupids "by the name of Eros and Anteros:" "One of these chief Cupids was looked on as the cause of love; and the other, as the cause of its ceasing. . . ." Keats's "winged boy," "warm Love," and "Bright-winged Child" is also Eros-Anteros, and it is in this role that he is the consort of Psyche: "a Cupid fondling or burning a butterfly, is just the same with [the Greek artists] as a Cupid caressing or tormenting the goddess *Psyche*, or the soul."[7]

> Deep let her drink of that dark, bitter spring,
> Which flows so near thy bright and crystal tide;
> Deep let her heart thy sharpest arrow sting,
> Its temper'd barb in that black poison dyed.

From Circe's curse of the guileless goddess in Mary Tighe's *Psyche*, which was a source for both the "Ode to Psyche" and the Circe-Scylla episode in *Endymion*, we can apprehend as Keats did the dark underside of Psyche's passion.[8] Medicine, mythology, and romance tradition served Keats well on the passionate contraries in that delicious poisoner and patron of warm pulses and disheveled hair. The poet in Keats no less than the physician or consumptive patient could see no contradiction in presenting love as grievous torment or soothing balm, as morbid pest or life-giving charm, as infecting or naturally germane. In the fever and the flush of love, as we shall see, Keats's love-verses could diagnose alternately, depending on the constitution of the subject or the potency of its occasion, symptoms of disease and signs of health. Cupid's cure bears everywhere the Keatsian potential to become love's disease.

"Can Love be Cured by Remedies of Plant Origin?" was the title of François Bossier de Sauvages's thesis for his degree in medicine received in 1726.[9] De Sauvages was better known to later medical generations for his monumental classification of diseases (*Nosologia Methodica*, 1763) and for his contribution to medical semiotics by serving as the primary inspiration for Landré-Beauvais's distinction between symptom and sign. His thesis on the vegetable cures for love is significant to us because it highlights the essential confusion made by the European medical profession from the middle of the eighteenth century up through Keats's time between afflictions of the heart and diseases of the chest, between love and tubercular consumption.

Consumption, which maintained its literal meaning through the seventeenth and eighteenth centuries, was an eating up of the flesh, a melting, a wasting, or a hollowing-out of the human subject. *Phthisis*, the Greek word for consumption, was a symptom common to several patterns of disease, and Richard Morton's *Phthisiologia: or a Treatise of Consumptions* (1685), the first extensive study of the subject "wherein the difference, nature, causes, signs and cures of all sorts of consumptions are explained," proposed that there were many kinds of consumption, all with the same, related, baffling symptoms.[10] Laënnec's *Traité de l'auscultation médiate* (1819) was key in distinguishing tuberculosis from the unqualified catchall termed "phthisis." But it was William Cullen who first focused on the pulmonary form of consumption, which he attributed to an "acrimony" in the blood; this acrimony, like most escharotic poisons, invisibly (at first) inflamed, irritated, corroded, melted, and wasted the lungs and chest.[11] For Cullen, the feverous "hectic flush" was synonymous with tubercular consumption, and living proofs of this littered the clinical wards for incurables at Guy's Hospital during the eighteenth and early nineteenth centuries. Babington and Curry taught the primary tubercular symptoms to be a hectic fever, cough, and a marked "puriform expectoration" as clear sign of the eating up from within.[12] Thus, for the generation of physicians who were influenced by Cullen, among whom Keats's teachers numbered, the wasting agitated consumptive and distracted overintense lover were juxtaposed as common victims of a poison in the blood—theirs was a debilitating passion or a diseased nervous energy. Keats expresses this duality of physical and nervous disease when he describes his symptoms in the fall of 1820: "My Chest is in so nervous a State, that any thing extra such as speaking to an unaccostomed Person or writing a Note half suffocates me. This Journey to Italy wakes me at daylight every morning and haunts me horribly." "Every thing I have in my trunks that reminds me of her [Fanny] goes through me like a spear. The silk lining she put in my travelling cap scalds my head. My imagination is horribly vivid about her—I see her—I hear her."[13]

The symbolic, as well as medical, implications of this kind of conceptualizing on love and disease during the Romantic period were profound. As Foucault notes, "In the nineteenth century, a man, in becoming tubercular, in the fever that hastens things and betrays them, fulfills his incommunicable secret. That is why chest diseases are of exactly the same nature as diseases of love: they are the Passion, a life to which death gives a face that cannot be exchanged."[14] Moreover, for an age that defined both life and disease in terms of energy, the sign of tubercular consumption was Janus-faced: it manifested itself in the paradoxical symptoms of impassioned frenetic intensity or oversensitivity (energy recklessly expended) and debilitative weakness or failure of will (energy used up). Phosphorus was prescribed alike for wasting consumption of the lungs and "to restore and revive young persons exhausted by excesses" because it "appears to give a certain degree of activity to life"[15]— through, presumably, its immediate and visible glowing or inflaming effects. To the early nineteenth century especially, which saw in the strong emotionalism and purported hyperactive sexuality of the tubercular patient proof of an interconnection between passion and consumption, there could be no clear distinction between the warm glow of the lover and the hectic flush of the consumptive. Too often, the one was a sign to the other's symptom: passion used up and could be used up, like energy, for, as Keats says in *Endymion*,

> 'Tis the pest
> Of love, that fairest joys give most unrest;
> That things of delicate and tenderest worth
> Are swallow'd all, and made a seared dearth,
> By one consuming flame. . . .
> (II, 366–69)

The pest of love turns desire into ravenous betrayal, its feverish passion can be the pattern of diseased energy, and its intense delicacy and imaginative sensitivity could mask a monstrous ravening consumption.

With Keats's generation, inevitably the medical signs were reversed and tuberculosis was seen as a symptomatic variant of the affliction of love, be this love fulfilled and expended, or denied and therefore intensified to escharotic, corrosive acrimony. "My dear Brown, I should have had her when I was in health, and I should have remained well," the terminally consumptive poet diagnoses sadly in 1820 of how his fevered love might have been expended and thereby prevented from becoming a monstrous consuming energy. But he also speculates on the paradox of a love that exceeds consumption or expenditure. "If I had any chance of recovery [from consumption], this passion would kill me."[16] Separated from Fanny Brawne and in Italy to die, the poet's condition gave all signs of what a physician of the early nineteenth century would recognize as the symptoms of diseased energy or love morbidly transformed by its own excess intensities. Thomas Mann in *The Magic Mountain* proposes that all symptoms of disease are merely disguised manifestations of the power of love, for all "disease is only love transformed." Blake, of course, had already warned of heaven and hell, of how "He who desires but acts not, breeds pestilence." The intensely dying patient in Keats, during those last weeks in Rome, saw no energized ambiguity in his consuming fervor (of endeavor) as the poet of *The Fall of Hyperion* once did. He saw in his feverous state only the waste of a devotional love transformed and an artistic endeavor deformed by its own fervor into the medical symptoms and signs he had once learned and subsequently learned to fear.

Febrile images recur throughout Keats's poetry, from the feverish fit in which Hildebrand curses Porphyro's house (*Eve*, 100–102), to the "forehead hot and flush'd" of the inspired aspiring poet ("Lines on Seeing a Lock of Milton's Hair") to the consumptive fever of the lover in the late poems. G. E. Stahl first recalled the etymology of fever from the word *februare*, to expel ritually something that was mysterious and indefinable. Robert Thomas's definition of fever on the first page in his popular handbook, *The Modern Practice of Physic* (1816), is typical of Romantic medicine's confusion over the phenomenon:

> It has no symptom invariably attendant on it, which can point out its real nature or essence. The pulse . . . may be small, weak, slow, contracted, and unequal; or it may be strong, quick, full and regular; hard or soft, according as the fever is at the commencement, increase, height, or in the remission and termination; or as the genus and nature of the fever may chance to differ. So, also, the heat may be equally diffused, or confined to particular parts: sometimes the external parts are cold, with a sense of internal heat; at others, there is general heat or cold over the body; and sometimes the heat is not greater than what is natural.

(When Babington and Curry's published outlines of their course on the practice of medicine at Guy's, they devoted over fifty-six pages to the various natures of fever; the *Encyclopaedia Britannica* in 1810, also, allocated fifty-two pages in its entry "Medicine" to febrile disease.) Fever was an unspecified "determination of the blood" for Romantic medicine, and consumption of the chest was an exemplary febrile disease of which the first sign was a rapid pulse.

A rapid pulse, the influential eighteenth-century physician Hermann Boerhaave (1668–1738) said, was the only recognizable pathognomonic sign of a fever. Boerhaave employed the Baconian method in his attempt to form a reliable definition of fever: he collected many instances of fever and salvaged three factors common to all fevers: shivering, heat, and a quick pulse. But although this triad was present in all fevers, Boerhaave found that only the rapid pulse was present *continuously* as a pathognomonic sign through all phases of the fever. Hence, as Boerhaave taught the next generation of clinicians, a fever consists in a rapid pulse; physicians of the eighteenth and early nineteenth centuries could thus diagnose a fever to be present by the quality of the pulse alone.[17] The first page of notes that Keats made of Cooper's lectures bears all marks of this clinical instruction: the poet notes the importance of the pulse in reading signs of energy or debility, of how in fever there is "a determination of Blood to the Head" and away from the chest, and of the appropriate treatments for a "diminished" or "quick unhealthy irritable pulse."[18]

Axioms in philosophy, of course, were not axioms for the poet until they were proved upon the pulses. Keats's poetry, as we have seen, repeatedly invokes life and its loss or gain through images of pulse, artery, and blood. Glaucus sees Endymion, and his blood "no longer cold" gives "mighty pulses" and "Grew a new heart" (III, 304–6); in *The Fall of Hyperion* the debilitating cold strikes for the poet's carotid arteries "to put cold grasp / Upon those streams that pulse beside the throat" (I, 124–25). Often, especially in the early poetry, Keats deliberately allies the signs of love's energy with the symptoms of fever's illness:

> Within my breast there lives a choking flame—
> O let me cool it the zephyr-boughs among!
> A homeward fever parches up my tongue—
> O let me slake it at the running springs!
> Upon my ear a noisy nothing rings—
> O let me once more hear the linnet's note!
> Before mine eyes thick films and shadows float—
> O let me 'noint them with the heaven's light!
> Dost thou now lave thy feet and ankles white?
> O think how sweet to me the freshening sluice!
> Dost thou now please thy thirst with berry-juice?
> O think how this dry palate would rejoice!
> If in soft slumber thou dost hear my voice,
> O think how I should love a bed of flowers!—
>   (*End.*, II, 317–32)

The lover's burning chest, parched tongue, dry palate, ringing ears, and rheumy, filmed eyes are all symptoms of his fevered condition. Their treatment, a cold bath, berry juice, and slumber in a bed of flowers are as likely a cure as the poet's spavined couplets can hope to accomplish. The heart is, as tradition and *The Eve of St. Agnes* mark, "Love's fev'rous citadel" (84), and the alliance of love's energy and sickness's fever is intensified to deliberate fusion in the third stanza of the "Ode on a Grecian Urn." There, satiated "breathing human passion" leaves in the wake of its consumption "A burning forehead, and a parching tongue" (28–30), even as its opposite, "For ever panting" immortal love, endures as a permanent debility of unsatiation, an agape inedibility of cold continuity and hollow form. The stanza's lines on mortal and immortal love, taken from an underlying theme in Burton's *Anatomy of Melancholy*, point to the familiar binary nature of Love, of soothing Eros and tormenting Anteros.[19] This dichotomy Keats seeks to heal through the imaginative fusion of the symptoms of love and fever (which he had learned from medicine), so that they stand at once as signs of health and of disease, of life and of its deprivation.

The primary sign to be recognized in diagnosing pulmonary phthisis (which Cullen had named "the hectic fever") was its hectic quality; this hectic nature manifests itself in periodic febrile fits and a warm, moist, "malar flush."[20] But a warm blush is love's proper hue Milton tells us; it distinguishes the lover be he mortal or immortal, soothed or tormented, no less than does his hectic pulse. When Adam asks the angel Michael how the heavenly spirits express their love, the angel responds "with a smile that glow'd / Celestial rosy red, Love's proper hue. . . ."[21] So also does the mortal lover in *Endymion* wish that his beloved's cheek would "mantle rosy-warm / With the tinge of love," so that the blush might "soothe [his] madness" (IV, 311–14). The immortal Hermes, meanwhile, burns with a tormented "celestial heat" from winged heels to ears and blushes "from a whiteness, as the lily clear . . . into roses" (*Lamia*, I, 22–25).

> Flush every thing that hath a vermeil hue,
> Let the rose glow intense and warm the air,
> And let the clouds of even and of morn
> Float in voluptuous fleeces o'er the hills;
> Let the red wine within the goblet boil,
> Cold as a bubbling well; let faint-lipp'd shells,
> On sands, or in great deeps, vermillion turn
> Through all their labyrinths; and let the maid
> Blush keenly, as with some warm kiss surpris'd.
>   (*Hyp.*, III, 14–22)

Thus Keats relates the hectic nature of the maid surprised by some warm kiss to the vermeil flush of natural things at Hyperion's rising, from the intense response of the rose to the passive voluptuousness of clouds. The psychology of blushing in living organisms that "vermillion turn / Through all their labyrinths" is important to a number of Keatsian subjects, as Christopher Ricks has demonstrated; the focus here is on the physiology of blushing and its significance to the signs of life and disease. In the physiological response of warm color evoked by Hyperion's appearance, Keats pays homage both to the traditional notion of Hunterian medicine that the blood was the vital principle and to the common belief of contemporary science that the blood, as the only secretion separated from all other, had to be at once a stimulant, a nourishment for generating heat, and a key to the presence of health.[22]

The manifested living quality of the blood, the "Blush [of] joyous blood though every lineament" (*Otho*, I, i, 28), could thus be read by Romantic medicine as a clue to health or disease. Byron's Manfred sees in the spirit of Astarte "no living hue, / But a strange hectic—like the unnatural red / Which Autumn plants upon the perish'd leaf" (II, iv, 99–101). Astley Cooper, who had learned Hunter's theory of the blood well, taught his students that inflammation could be "healthy or unhealthy:" in an injured but otherwise healthy constitution it acted as "a vis medicatrix naturae" or "restorative principle," but when it arose "without any obvious cause" it was "*an evil* without any corresponding advantage," "an unhealthy kind" that arose "from an *irritable* constitution, and from the *enfeebled* state of the affected part."[23] To the verse above on the dawning health or restorative vitality in nature at Hyperion's appearance must therefore be juxtaposed the unhealthy inflammation of Hyperion's palace upon receiving the premonition of his fellow Titans' enfeebled state: the Sun-god's abode

> Glar'd a blood-red through all its thousand courts,
> Arches, and domes, and fiery galleries;
> And all its curtains of Aurorian clouds
> Flush'd angerly. . . .
> (I, 179–84)

Thus also does Lycius, in *Lamia*, learn of the unnatural inflamation of his stricken lover from the touch of her hand: " 'Twas icy, and the cold ran through his veins; / Then sudden it grew hot, and all the pains / Of an unnatural heat shot to his heart" (II, 251–53). When Lycius's love reveals itself as self-consumption "in self despite, / Against his better self," his passion turns unhealthy inflammation and takes on "a hue / Fierce and sanguineous as 'twas possible" to expose the "dark veins" of the disease that will infect and waste both Lycius and Lamia (II, 72–77). Closer yet to the poet alone in Rome is the quiet image in "To Autumn" of Apollo touching "with rosy hue" the soft-dying day.

> O what can ail thee, knight at arms,
>   So haggard and so woe-begone?
> The squirrel's granary is full,
>   And the harvest's done.
>
> I see a lily on thy brow
>   With anguish moist and fever dew,
> And on thy cheeks a fading rose
>   Fast withereth too.
>   (5–12)

Keats's White Goddess, according to Robert Graves, was the pale enchantress la belle dame sans merci; she was the poet's emblem of the destructive aspect of love, of frustrated creative endeavor, and of death by consumption. Graves based his theory on the biographical context and symptomatic language of the poem itself. The poem, enclosed in the journal letter to George and Georgiana Keats, was composed at a time when the poet knew of his intense passion for Fanny and read in his own symptoms of inflamed intensity, "anguish moist and fever dew" (induced initially by the exhaustive cold of the Scottish walking tour), the signs of his own consumption. Nor could the poet have failed to read the signs correctly and know his fate, Graves says, because barely six months before "he had seen the lily on Tom's brow, the hectic rose on his cheek, his starved lips a-gape in horrid warning, and had closed his wild wild eyes with coins, not kisses."[24] As Fanny Brawne represented life and love to Keats, so also did his passion for her, which both masked and manifested itself by the symptoms of consumption, represent a wasting death that would preempt and leave agape love and life for the poet.

The glittering radiance of Keats's belle dame sans merci, like that of Graves's White Goddess, impels and repels, her sinister beauty attracts and mocks. Since it is her bright potion that wastes her victims and turns them "death-pale," the poet correctly transfers the lily on her brow to the fevered brows of her victims, the "Pale warriors" and "pale kings, and princes too" (37–38). Other pale enchantresses in Keats's poetry evoke such whitening, corrosive, melting effects with the intensity of their love-philtres: bright Cynthia greets Endymion and "sooth'd her light / Against his pallid face" until he feels "the charm / To breathlessness" (III, 104–6); Lycius is "sick to lose / The amorous promise" of Lamia's sweet albeit Acrasian potion, and at the threat of its withdrawal, swoons, "murmuring of love, and pale with pain" (I, 287–88); in the melancholy storm of Keats's blanched dream of Dante's Francesca, both the young temptress and her dreaming victim mirror the blood-draining, wasting intensity of unresolved passion: "Pale were the sweet lips I saw, / Pale were the lips I kiss'd, and fair the form / I floated with" (12–14). Tinctured union turns white dissolution and ethereal love proves wasting *venin*; it transforms its flushed, warm-pulsed victims into airy, disembodied, colorless, hollow forms—lovers fit only for a Grecian urn.

Infectious love can be felicitous and exemplary to life and health. With typical Keatsian but also pharmacological reciprocity, the poem *Isabella; or, the Pot of Basil* bears illness as its dominant metaphor[25] even as its subject, or essence, is love. This malady of love remedies itself, and, like Brunonian excitability and its reciprocal cures, it is a standard of health whereby the deprivation of love is revealed as the true illness:

> They could not in the self-same mansion dwell
> Without some stir of heart, some malady;
> They could not sit at meals but feel how well
> It soothed each to be the other by;
>   (3–6)

When apart but in the same mansion, Isabella and Lorenzo feel the presence of some recurrent malady; together, briefly, they feel the cure of "how well / It soothed each to be the other by." Afflicted "with sick longing," they spend "A whole long month of May in this sad plight" (23–24). The recurring deprivation of love through separation turns "their cheeks paler by the break of June" (26) and their bodies conspire to worsen the disease; Lorenzo finds that "the ruddy tide" of his heart "Fever'd his high conceit of such a bride," it "Stifled his voice, and puls'd resolve away" (43–46). Unable to speak their cure (a declaration of love), the lovers languish

> Until sweet Isabella's untouch'd cheek
>   Fell sick within the rose's just domain,
> Fell thin as a young mother's, who doth seek
>   By every lull to cool her infant's pain:
> "How ill she is," said he, "I may not speak,
>   And yet I will, and tell my love all plain."
>   (33–38)

As Lorenzo does here, the lovers tell their love all plain by reading therapeutically in each other's faces the signs of each other's symptoms:

> If Isabel's quick eye had not been wed
>   To every symbol on his forehead high;
> She saw it waxing very pale and dead,
>   And straight all flush'd;
>   (51–54)

Lorenzo's face, "flush with love" that is requited, is a standard of health for all and especially his beloved to see; it is a direct contrast to the "sick and wan" faces of Isabella's unlovable brothers (213–15). Isabella, while Lorenzo is alive, is "wed / To every symbol on his forehead high" and reads there, with the keenness of a physician's or a lover's eye, the health of his love and the imminent paleness of his end. Lorenzo, once dead, reads his beloved's face with an eye turned keenly, hungrily, morbid:

> "Though I forget the taste of earthly bliss,
>   That paleness warms my grave, as though I had
> A Seraph chosen from the bright abyss
>   To be my spouse: thy paleness makes me glad;
> Thy beauty grows upon me, and I feel
> A greater love through all my essence steal."
>   (315–320)

Lorenzo's spirit sees in Isabella's face the pale symptoms of their mutual and final deprivation; it reads there the signs of their dying love. In death, Lorenzo also infects and wastes with his festering deprivation. His fate recalls that of Tristan, deprived of Isolde's love and therefore victim of a wasting and excoriating leprosy in symbol of his self-consuming, insatiable, driving passion.[26] Isabella's paleness warms her lover's loveless grave and makes him glad. As she fades, her beauty grows upon Lorenzo, and he thrives like a hungry, eczematic parasite upon her slowly waning life. His leprous deathliness is responsible for the increasing whiteness of her features, and he gains strength and joy from viewing her developing resemblance to "A Seraph chosen from the bright abyss."

Like Apollonius the sophist and the predatory keen-eyed enchantresses Lamia and la belle dame, the dead Lorenzo owns "some hungry spell which loveliness absorbs." The love potion turns malignant according to the malevolent intention of the giver, but also according to the unwholesome albeit loving or constitutional disposition of the lover. Alive, lovers feed wholesomely and self-sufficiently upon their love; separated by death, their food turns poison and the one consumes the other. "What feverous hectic flame / Burns in thee, child?" the nurse asks Isabella just after her malignant vision of her wasting lover (348–49), as Lorenzo's withering infection becomes her obsessive disease. The deprivation of love, a true disease, thus steals the blooming symptoms of love and health that it might mask its true signs and masquerade, briefly, as a greater love and a more intense life.

This is Isabella's paradoxical pot of basil. Royal basil, the fragrant, pungent, sweet herb whose botanical name is *basilicum*, was considered an all-purpose medicine in English folklore. Basilicum ointment was a royal remedy believed to be of specific use as an antidote to the crested basilisk's venom, and the Old French *basile* and modern French *basilic* are applied without differentiation to both the serpent and the plant.[27] The pathological spontaneously anatomizes, for "Disease is an autopsy in the darkness of the body"; it is dissection alive.[28] Isabella's forest dissection of her lover's corpse, which is occasioned by her disease of deprived or pathological love, brings about a kind of union for the separated lovers and a kind of life for their disease of deprivation. From "the wormy circumstance" within the pot, bound in a sinuous scarf perfumed with the "odorous ooze" of a "cold serpent pipe" (410–12) and nurtured by tears of loss, springs a preternatural basil plant:

> And so she ever fed it with thin tears,
>   Whence thick, and green, and beautiful it grew,
> So that it smelt more balmy than its peers
>   Of basil-tufts in Florence; for it drew
> Nurture besides, and life, from human fears,
>   From the fast mouldering head there shut from view:
> So that the jewel, safely casketed,
> Came forth, and in perfumed leafits spread.
>   (425–32)

Isabella lives for this plant, and her love for Lorenzo draws soothing nutriment from its "balmy" leaves; the plant, in turn, draws nourishment from her tears, and the basil flourishes weedlike with more than natural vigor, "as by magic touch," or potion fed (459). The more she droops toward her deathly lover, the more the basil in parasitic reversal grows lush, tall, and looming; like Lorenzo's spirit, it consumes her life. Beneath the plant's health lies Isabella's disease, the substantial residue of a healing, salubrious love turned virulent infection. No less an emblem than Pan's syrinx, with which he makes sweet music of his love turned poison, Isabella's pot of basil, a bright urn for her tears and her lover's remains, over which she sings melancholic ditties, breeds sweet corruption. It is a hollow medium of conveyance, a medicine or *pharmakon* born of a poisoned love, an antidote for life deprived of love, richest juice borne by a ductile poison flower to nurture an already poisoned damsel, a love-philtre that elicits nurturing tears because of the debilitated disposition of its recipient, an unnatural energy masquerading as the energy of life, a Janus-faced symbol of disease and remedy, of living and dying: an urn for life.

When Isabella's brothers question what to them is a monstrous growth in a plant and a mysterious withering of their sister, they discover, as *The Second Book of Kings* warns of the pottage made of wild gourds, that "*there is* death in the pot."[29] Lorenzo's severed head, a mute testimony to the murder of love wrapped in a perfumed scarf, a deathly gourd of food for Isabella's deprived love, is morbid and infecting. "The thing was vile with green and livid spot" (475), and its tinctures bear death. It is, indeed, a strangely appropriate nutriment for a poisoned love and a morbid remedy for an already diseased life. Like the corpses in Shelley's *Revolt of Islam* that turn a drinking well into "A caldron of green mist made visible / At sunrise" and spreads virulent plague throughout the golden city (X, 21), the ductile "perfumed leafits" of Isabella's soothing and medicinal green plant spread infection symbolically and literally. They do so because their roots draw sustenance from the green and morbid putrefaction of what was once a human lover and energy from the red "feverous hectic flame" and thin tears of what was once a healthy love. They are the emblem or sign of love as consumption, of love hollowed out. But " 'Twas love; cold,—dead indeed, but not dethroned" (400), and Isabella cannot see the transformation of her love wrought through its deprivation by her brothers and through the consumptive generation of nature. She sees green leaves where her brothers see green mold, her vision is her potion, a remedy for love lost. Isabella's hollowed pot of sweet basil, her passion's flower, is a blooming, consuming, festering symptom of her murdered love read as a fragrant and enduring sign of her green memory. Through the royal basil and the crested basilisk of her love, the poem and its readers "taste the music of that vision pale" (392).

PART IV

ORGANIC PERFECTION

I *always somehow associate Chatterton with autumn.*

Keats, Letters, 2: 167

> Yet let me tell my sorrow, let me tell
> Of what I heard, and how it made me weep,
> And know that we had parted from all hope.
>> (*Hyp.*, II, 259–61)

The speaker seeking audience in these lines is Clymene, daughter to Oceanus and the youngest of the newly displaced Titans. She wishes to tell of how she came to comprehend her replacement by Apollo and why the Titans must accept their succession and displacement by beings more perfect. Clymene speaks as an artist, "with hectic lips, and eyes up-looking mild," and her metaphor is the creation of music:

> I stood upon a shore, a pleasant shore,
> Where a sweet clime was breathed from a land
> Of fragrance, quietness, and trees, and flowers.
> Full of calm joy it was, as I of grief;
> Too full of joy and soft delicious warmth;
> So that I felt a movement in my heart
> To chide, and to reproach that solitude
> With songs of misery, music of our woes;
> And sat me down, and took a mouthed shell
> And murmur'd into it, and made melody—
> O melody no more! For while I sang,
> And with poor skill let pass into the breeze
> The dull shell's echo, from a bowery strand
> Just opposite, an island of the sea,
> There came enchantment with the shifting wind,
> That did both drown and keep alive my ears.
> I threw my shell away upon the sand,
> And a wave fill'd it, as my sense was fill'd
> With that new blissful golden melody.
>> (II, 262–80)

Clymene seeks with "songs of misery" to counteract the "sweet clime" that breathes "Too full of joy" from a land of fragrance and quietness. Her music of the Titans' woes, far from reproaching the clime's "calm joy," or replacing it with sounds of sorrow, signals more and greater music—"There came enchantment with the shifting wind"—that drowns the original timid song even as it preserves and stirs the musician. The

artistic challenge from "a bowery strand, / Just opposite" proves insurmountable and far too strong for the goddess's "poor skill." Her sad
melody, wrought through the "dull shell's echo," is undone and overcome by a music more perfect, the healing art of the newly formed
artist, Apollo. Dull echoes and the feeble stir "Of strings in hollow
shells" are superseded by Delphic harps and the "soft warble from the
Dorian flute" (I, 131; III, 10–12). Defeated and charmed at once by
artistry more consummate than her own and by instruments more true,
Clymene casts her shell back where she had found it. The shell's fate at
water's edge proves image and echo of her own: "I threw my shell away
upon the sand, / And a wave fill'd it, as my sense was fill'd / With that
new blissful golden melody."

When the sea-god Glaucus meets Endymion in the briny underworld
of Book III of *Endymion*, he, too, carries a seashell, which he hands to the
young artist moments before Endymion works his miracle of reanimation for the dead lovers: "Here is a shell; 'tis pearly blank to me, / Nor
mark'd with any sign or charactery— / Canst thou read aught?" (III, 761–
63). The dispossessed and wrinkled Glaucus cannot read the cyphers of
his world. The shells of his environment are blank reflectors; without
echo or sound they are, like his overwrought cloak, nothing but meaning-
less images of natural chaos. Glaucus needs Endymion to tell their
story: to return meaning to them, to fill them up again somehow. Unlike
Glaucus, the daughter of Oceanus knows her music as a naturalist and
an artist, and she reads in her skeletal instrument the very pattern of
natural law. Clymene's "mouthed shell," a fossil picked from the ebbing
tide and then returned to it, speaks volubly through its hollowness of
life, not of the empty stasis of perfection (as does the Grecian urn) but of
the ever-replenished progress of perfection: an ever "new [and] blissful
golden melody," an endless supersession of note and form, a vital evolution of species that drowns the old even as it keeps alive the new:

> A living death was in each gush of sounds,
> Each family of rapturous hurried notes,
> That fell, one after one, yet all at once,
> Like pearl beads dropping sudden from their string:
> And then another, then another strain,
> Each like a dove leaving its olive perch,
> With music wing'd instead of silent plumes,
> To hover round my head, and make me sick
> Of joy and grief at once.
>   (II, 281–89)

The music of Apollo's medicine makes the melancholy Titans sick of joy and grief at once; its perfumed enchantment stirs the numbed life within them even as it purges their disease of mortality and intensifies their immortal pain. No static art of marble petrification, Apollo's music neither stations, to use Keats's term, nor can be stationed. Each family of rapturous notes comes forth successively yet seemingly all at once like new species in nature's history. Images from two very different creation stories, that of Noah's doves after the flood as described in Genesis and that of the lowly mollusk's attempt to make beauty of its pain as described by the naturalists, support this vision of the natural evolution of music. Apollo's music can drown and keep alive existing forms simultaneously because its "rapturous hurried notes" falling "one after one" embody the ever-replenishing "living death" of the natural law of supersession articulated by Clymene's father. "We fall by course of Nature's law, not force," Oceanus has just said, speaking with the voice of "far-foamed sands" and tides of what he knows to be "eternal truth." As his "giant-race" once found their forms to be "compact and beautiful," of "purer life" than Heaven and Earth and the most perfect of living species, so now on the Titans' heels "a fresh perfection treads" and they "perforce, must be content to stoop" (II, 181–87, 199–212, 179).

Like Clymene's shell, the Titans are fossils. They are resonant skeletal remains of an earlier history and generation; once perfect, they are echoing proof of what the early nineteenth century had discovered to be the ever-perfectibility of the forms of life through the gradual extinction of generations. Fossils, not just those of still-extant creatures collected by the naturalists and exhibited in the British Museum and in John Hunter's collection but the exotic and giant fossils of extinct forms recently discovered by the paleontologists, were of extraordinary importance to the Romantic theorists of life. These fossils were tangible proof of a principle of continuing perfection in nature, of the fulfillment or completion of certain life forms that were subsequently sacrificed and rendered obsolete in the interest of future yet unrealized perfections. Before the nineteenth century, the concept of continuity in the theories of life—from Aristotle to Leibnitz—did not signify any sort of transformation of the species but merely the reproductive continuation of fixed and immutable species: "Only with the nineteenth-century did the concepts of the reproductive continuity of life and of the intergradations between species become fused in the idea of evolution. . . . And the search for intermediate forms was to shift from a belief in their present existence ... to a search for missing links among the fossil relics of past life."[1] Biological change and the proof of extinct forms, furthermore, wrought a linguistic change in the meaning of the word *perfection*. For the early-nineteenth-century thinkers, perfection was not static achievement but something inextricably linked with their age's newfound sense of biological and perceptual evolution.

No Romantic thinker, however distant in subject from the naturalist's discovery of peculiar yet recognizable fossils of extinct life forms, could be unmoved by the conceptual implications of these strange bones. Byron marked the importance of Cuvier's giant fossils to his thinking on creation in *Cain*, and we know how these influenced his opinion of Milton's creation story in *Paradise Lost*. Keats, meanwhile, showed early recognition of the significance of these discoveries and the revelation of such "secrets" in nature's history. "A cold leaden awe" strikes the poet Endymion when he views upon the ocean floor "skeletons of man, / Of beast, behemoth, and leviathan, / And elephant, and eagle, and huge jaw / Of nameless monster" (III, 133–36). H. W. Piper has speculated that these lines reveal a direct acquaintance with the fossilized carvings discovered in limestone at Guadeloupe in 1805, findings that attracted considerable notice, for they were anticipated by Cuvier in his *Mémoires sur les epèces d'éléphants vivants et fossiles* (1800).[2] Endymion, certainly, can tell the histories of his world: he reads its bones and he hears the "music of our woes" echoing through its variegated shells. In the description of these mammoth skeletons as "sculptures rude / In ponderous stone, developing the mood / Of ancient Nox," we are to recognize the distinct bearing that they have upon the dispossessed Titans of the later Hyperion poems; we are to recognize also the "knowledge enormous" that these Titans bear when they find themselves no longer perfect.

As a circular and convoluted vessel alternately filled and emptied by living substance and as a fossil of a former life and a current home for smaller (and perhaps newer) living sea forms, Clymene's shell is the visual image of the new concept of "fresh perfection" or evolutionary development within otherwise perfected species that was beginning to dominate contemporary conceptualizations on life. "Thus, then, Life itself is not a *thing*—a self-subsistent *hypostasis*—but an *act* and *process*," Coleridge remarked in summary of what natural history (and metaphysics) had proved of life.[3] Life was the evolution of life, a process that could include nature's past organic completions within the framework of future "fresh perfections." A principle of perfection existed in nature that was itself evolutionary. The very perfections of underlying substance and attribute that were accomplished through this principle of perfection necessarily precluded all notions of stasis, excess, or fulsome and final completion. Perfection and process were not mutually exclusive but dynamic polarities allied in the interest of perpetual, superseding novelty. A vision not of ageless forms but of the pied beauty of nature and of the endless potential of this beauty thus overwhelmed and replaced earlier visions of changeless and perfected repetition. Evolution in nature had proved itself Romantic. It was an art or a process born (and sustained) of itself.

"All life is from the sea; the whole sea is alive. Love arose out of sea-foam." Oken among German natural philosophers of the early nineteenth century had first charted a physiophilosophy of life based upon life's generation in primitive seas. Erasmus Darwin among English doctors of the Romantic age sought, also, to explain the very temple of nature through the patterned origin of microscopic life in primeval oceans.[4] Buffon, the evolutionist best known to Keats, had proposed in 1749 that mountains, marbled rocks, and other Titanic geological formations were all formed of seashells and created during a cataclysmic and revolutionary occasion (the deluge) when "all the shell-fish were raised from the bottom of the sea, and transported over the earth." In the variety of petrified seashells found everywhere on earth, whose prior life was mute testimony that there were "neither mountains, marble, nor rocks, nor clays, nor matters of any kind" antecedent to them, Buffon read the history of nature's past and the prophecy of life's future forms.[5] Early-nineteenth-century science now found creation, teeming and recreating truly and verifiably, at water's edge. The iconography of Romantic art, meanwhile, had placed the seashell—that natural object that nevertheless suggested by its echoing power not the objective world but the recreated one born of the poet's self—as its symbol of artistic creativity. The instrumental music created by Clymene and Apollo through seashells and fluted husks of life forms upon the bowery strands of Hyperion's story evolves in ever-perfectible organic multiplicity. The music's common theme—and form—is Romantic evolution.

Chapter 17

Glaucus's Cloak

In the weft of Glaucus's blue mantle, in *Endymion*, every ocean form, quick-sand, whirlpool, storm, calm, and deserted shore find emblem and appointed place. Likewise, every living shape "That skims, or dives, or sleeps, 'twixt cape and cape" finds detail and correspondent pattern in the heavy warp of the cloak. These sea forms of gigantic whale or minute fish show their anatomy—to even "the very hardest gazer's" eye of physiologist, artist, or naturalist—to be perfect. They have no need for improvement; indeed notions of progress or development would be alien to their self-sufficiency:

> And, ample as the largest winding-sheet,
> A cloak of blue wrapp'd up his aged bones,
> O'erwrought with symbols by the deepest groans
> Of ambitious magic: every ocean-form
> Was woven in with black distinctness; storm,
> And calm, and whispering, and hideous roar,
> Quicksand and whirlpool, and deserted shore
> Was emblem'd in the woof; with every shape
> That skims, or dives, or sleeps, 'twixt cape and cape.
> The gulphing whale was like a dot in the spell,
> Yet look upon it, and 'twould size and swell
> To its huge self; and the minutest fish
> Would pass the very hardest gazer's wish
> And shew his little eye's anatomy.
> (*End.*, III, 196–209)

This picture of teeming perfection with its echoes of the real and imagined sea creatures in Buffon's portrait of primeval life[1] belongs as much to nature as to art. For what the comparative anatomists of the Romantic age saw in nature were precisely these "symbols . . . Of ambitious magic" that are wrought by spell upon the cloak of the god of the sea. Their existential verity was established moreover as much through observation as through the exercise of imagination. The gulping whale upon the cloak of many species, a mere "dot in the spell" of its design, can under intense scrutiny "size and swell / To its huge self." So, also, could the forms, fossils, and fragments of the living world, through the creative vision of the evolutionists, swell and flesh into the shapes of things past and those to come. Early-nineteenth-century science thus used not just reason and observation but the same bright speculative power to unveil the mysteries of nature as did the creative artist in his reflections of these mysteries. Their "retrospective prophecy," to borrow T. H. Huxley's phrase, was of the very same order as the imaginative vision of the Romantic artist. The "deepest groans / Of ambitious magic" could be for Romantic evolutionists a natural "music of our woes," "songs of misery" at once creative and necessary.

Glaucus's magical yet natural cloak is a cypher of life parallel to Clymene's shell and the songs of misery it unwinds. Woven into its rich texture "with black distinctness" is the pattern of "living death" that perpetuates this life. The dual functions of the garment coexist: the cloak bears the vital power of supersession as the mantle laid upon the new poet, Endymion, but it also serves as "the largest winding sheet" in nature for the wrapping of Glaucus's aged bones. Like the Grecian urn, the cloak maintains the designs of life upon its surface even as it contains mortality; unlike the urn, it does so as a natural object. Mirrored upon the cloak of the sea, and perfected in every detail of its design, the Romantic evolutionists read, thus, the terrible beauty of life's organic perfections.

The concept of evolution began as a sense of unrolling something primordially complete and eventually came to imply something being unrolled, completed, perfected. This change matched the transference from belief in a supernatural, simultaneous creation of fixed and immutable life forms to belief in the progressive mutation and development of the species.[2] The idea of evolution was conceptualized by the Greeks in both its forms: Heraclitus's aphorism, *Panta rhei*—"everything flows"—was perhaps the clearest expression of the sense of development in evolution; Lucretius's notion "that SEEDS have SEEDS," wherein a variety of self-sufficient and completed embryos of perfect animals endlessly reproduced to constitute the various species, summarized best the sense of a one-time, simultaneous creation of all life forms.[3]

Evolutionary theory in Europe through the middle of the eighteenth century was dominated by the conservative belief in a supernatural and instantaneous creation of all the life forms. According to this theory of preformation, a primordial blueprint of life ensured that the variety of created species always existed, and their reproduction without mutation was the mere substantiation of this blueprint. Embryos, themselves an expression of preexisting forms, contained in rudimentary form all the parts of the mature organism, and the only development possible was that from immature to mature forms. Buffon, in the second half of the eighteenth century, proposed first the notion of neutral life matter and the consequent development and limitation in animal formation: all creatures, he said, "are in themselves equally perfect, the animal, according to our mode of perception, is the most complete, and man the most perfect animal."[4] The turn of the century thus saw the replacement of the theory of preformation in evolution with a more verifiable and contingent theory of the evolutionary development and perfection of the species. Advances in biological thinking brought a new and larger sense of the word *development* as it applied to natural existence: life was not so much a fully created entity unrolled in time as it was an evolving complex, a natural process that was to be unfolded fully and completed over time. Early-nineteenth-century evolutionary speculation proposed, for the first time, that a general natural process—a natural history—existed over and above specific natural processes.[5] "Nature herself came to be seen as a process in time and the individual phenomena at any moment, instead of being fixed and parallel shapes repeated and repeated since creation's day, were cross-sections of their own development and metamorphosis. They could be truly grasped only by looking before and after."[6] The progressive mutation or perfection of the species occurred, according to the evolutionists of the early nineteenth century, through small-scale gradual change, termed "phyletic gradualism" or "synthetic evolution" by twentieth-century science, or through sudden change by mysterious and revolutionary speciation events that punctuated the equilibrium of nature.

Romantic thinkers by and large favored the latter version of radical evolutionary change wrought by sudden and energetic upheaval within existing and seemingly sufficient (or perfect) patterns. They posited a history of radical bursts of progress among the life forms, occasioned by unspecified environmental or internal challenge, that punctuated enduring periods of natural quiescence and perfect reproduction. Because of these strange (or at least unidentified) events, natural history was dramatized by episodes of rapid advancement and change among the species. These episodes interrupted briefly the condition of relative stasis and inaction that otherwise characterized the complacency of nature.

The "punctuated equilibrium" of nature, a term from twentieth-century evolutionary science, is a concept one might well identify with Keats. It is exemplified in *Hyperion*, as we shall see in this part, in the complacent Titans' rude awakening from their long dream of power to the sudden and acute consciousness of other and more perfect, but as yet unidentified and therefore mysterious, knowledge and beauty. Hyperion's world changes because it has been perfect too long and because an as-yet-unspecified energy or intensity for greater accomplishment challenges this very perfection to its own transformation and undoing. Romantic evolution brought change because perfection episodically and from some internal necessity required fresh perfections. Although Charles Darwin's version of synthetic evolution (the gradual and progressive transformation of old species through the steady accumulation of small-scale genetic novelties as influenced by natural selection) has dominated conceptualizations on the life forms since the late nineteenth century, recent years have seen renewed interest in the possibility of sudden and mysterious episodic change in nature and consciousness like that portrayed in *Hyperion*.[7] This concept was of course first proposed by such diverse Romantic evolutionists as Lamarck, Cuvier, Erasmus Darwin, Schelling, Oken, and Herder.

When Lucretius speculated about "what Sort of SEEDS" might have formed the human race, and queried, "Can violent Laughter scrue their little Face? / Or can they drop their briny Tears apace?"[8] he performed the familiar speculative leap that has always linked even the most physiological of theories of evolution with those broader philosophic issues of feeling, consciousness, and the imagination. What the evolutionists of all ages and especially those of the Romantic age see upon the cloak of the sea is a Keatsian version of the material sublime: a Lamian vision of horror and loveliness, the mighty whale and minute fish at play, but also the shark at savage prey. They read "the first page" of life's mysteries "Upon a lampit rock of green sea weed / Among the breakers," but they also see through the "wide sea's" cloak of many species to the place "where every maw / The greater on the less feeds evermore" ("Dear Reynolds," 87–95, 103).

The questions that we are led to ask at the end of the verse-epistle to Reynolds concerning the poet's dark vision of the sea adapt themselves to the shifted patterns that the evolutionists of the period saw upon the face of nature. Was their vision of the species on Glaucus's coat the product of Newtonian reason and mechanistic observation? Were these species seen to form real skeletons upon an ocean floor? Or were they "sculptures rude" in an imaginary sea? Were these embroidered figures "symbol divine, / Manifestations of that beauteous life / Diffus'd unseen throughout eternal space" (*Hyp.*, I, 316–18)? Was the evolutionists' speculative picture of what lies beneath the cloak of the sea—of former species and forms to come, and of the means of their survival or extinction—the simplest productions of what Dougald Stewart called the creative imagination? Or worse, as Keats queries in his verse-epistle, were these shrouded pictures the diseased extensions of this imagination, creatures of a mortal fancy "brought / Beyond its proper bound" and a limited imagination "Lost in a sort of purgatory blind" (78–80)?

No less than its poets, the natural historians of the Romantic age found themselves cursed and blessed at once with double vision; they witnessed the dark visitations of Hyperion's foreboding dreams of change as well as the bright future of progress that Apollo feels in pain but cannot yet see. They saw the shadowed complacency of nature's perfection *and* the scarlet promise of future perfections—all in seemingly ever-replenished variety. With the help of the same artistic imagination, they, too, saw too far.

One evolutionist of Keats's period, William Lawrence, found in his vision of ambiguous perfecting variety in nature's species the pattern and promise of social perfection in man:

> This resemblance [within a species] must not be understood in a rigorous sense; for every being has its individual characters, of size, figure, colour, proportions. In this sense, the character of variety is stamped on all of Nature's works. She has made it a fundamental law, that no two of her productions shall be exactly alike; and this law is invariably observed through the whole creation. Each tree, each flower, each leaf, exemplifies it; every animal has its individual character; each human being has something distinguishing . . . in mental as well as corporeal physiognomy. This variety is the source of every thing beautiful and interesting in the external world—the foundation of the whole moral fabric of the universe.[9]

The character of variety in nature, for Lawrence and other radical intellectuals in 1817, patterned the very goals of personal liberty and political enlightenment that they proposed for the perfection of human society. Perfection was relative, actual as well as potential, and a fundamental law in all of nature's creations; a biological and social fact. The perfecting of the lower species by Nature implied a like perfecting in the community and consciousness of what the evolutionists and scientists called "the most perfect of animals," man.[10]

In his *Consolations in Travel; or Last Days of a Philosopher* published posthumously in 1830, Humphry Davy made whimsical note of a peculiar creature that had fascinated the scientists and philosophers of his time. Called the *Proteus Anguinus*, the creature had been the subject of lively speculation in the years following 1801 when a paper by the Viennese physician Charles Schreibers discussing the animal's place in evolutionary history and describing firsthand observations of it alive and in dissection was read to the Royal Society by Sir Joseph Banks.[11] The *Proteus Anguinus* became an enduring scientific curiosity because it was a paradox of living form and seemed in all respects to be a living fossil. It was amphibious but lived and breathed in mountainous regions; it had eyes but seemed to be blind; and cast eons before from some subterranean sea into a small land-bound lake in the Carniola region of Germany, it survived untouched by natural or unnatural change in self-sufficiency (or perhaps perfection) with an odd assortment of parts gleaned from different species or perhaps owned by an otherwise extinct "mixed" species.

Schreibers's paper and attached drawings portrayed a four-limbed eel-like creature with a long-finned tail, a duck-bill mouth, forearms with three residual fingers, hind legs with two-toed feet, large and apparently sightless eye sockets, able to breath without nostrils, able to move like a fish, and able to emit a loud serpentine hiss that belied its small eight-to-eleven-inch size. This "singular and ambiguous animal" that could not survive long or be cultivated outside its environment, Schreibers found comparable to Linnaeus's siren and the South American salamander; all three were anomalies of creation, deliberately nonspecific of the characteristics of given species and, because of this, of great evolutionary import.[12] Natural historians of the Romantic period could not decide whether this strange medusa of the unexplored mountains and subterranean caverns of Germany was a fully and perfectly developed creature that had achieved the zenith of the life power, or whether it was the larva or first form of a yet to be evolved species. Linnaeus had been unable to decide whether the *Proteus Anguinus* was a perfect or imperfect animal and gave it no place in his evolutionary design. Laurenti, in 1768, called it "a perfect animal"; J. Herman, in 1783, and T. G. Schneider, in 1799, said it was an imperfect animal; Schreibers, unable to decide whether the creature was the larva of some unknown species or an already perfected creation, cites Baron Zois, who observed a live *Proteus Anguinus* in 1799 and declared it to be "an animal in a perfect state, and sui generis."[13] The *Proteus Anguinus* had either proved its allocated perfection within a given albeit unknown species or it had transcended the limitations of known species to a new and uncharted perfection of being.

The ambiguity of *Proteus Anguinus* made it a natural symbol and synonym among natural philosophers for what they called "the most perfect of animals." William Lawrence's socially perfected humankind, seen from the correct side of the microscope, became the *Proteus Anguinus*. For, surely, man was such a creature, too: perfect within a limited species, aspiring to greater self-development through a seemingly unnatural mixture, and threatened at once by the complacency of nature and the change of natural environment. Both existences were perfect, limited, random products of chance and predestined victims of perfection. Byron's whimsical summation on the life of man, and on his place in natural creation, could be read as a response to the evolutionary myths surrounding the protean creature: "What a strange thing is the propagation of life!—A bubble of Seed which may be spilt in a whore's lap—or in the Orgasm of a voluptuous dream—might (for aught we know) have formed a Caesar or a Buonaparte—"; "The lapse of ages *changes* all things—time—language—the earth—the bounds of the sea—the stars of the sky, and every thing 'about, around and underneath' man, *except man himself*, who has always been, and always will be, an unlucky rascal. The infinite variety of lives conduct but to death, and the infinity of wishes lead but to disappointment. All the discoveries which have yet been made have multiplied little but existence."[14] Natural chance governs the reproduction of talent and seeming perfection in the human species. Nevertheless, amid the evolution and erosion in nature, man endures without apparent change or chance at perfection, indifferent like the *Proteus Anguinus* to the evolutionary shiftings "about, around, and underneath" him. As Keats said, the life of man is like a great mountain: immovable and seemingly untouched by time but, because subject to the laws of nature for its existence and perception, always vulnerable at some future evolutionary moment to radical upheaval in the interests of greater, or fresh, perfection.

The most perfect of creatures was not perfect precisely because, as the Romantic natural philosophers correctly sensed, perfection had to include the possibility of change and novelty within biological and perceptual stasis as these might be occasioned by unknown future stimuli. The DNA molecule of twentieth-century science, like the *Proteus Anguinus* of Humphry Davy's generation, embodies within its formula both the concept of a perfected or finished cell of life and the concept of a living entity patiently awaiting development because of the same innate contingency for accidental mutation or episodic development that it owns in common with larger natural phenomena. Lewis Thomas qualifies his assertion that "the greatest single achievement of nature to date was surely the invention of the molecule of DNA" with a whimsical caveat concerning both DNA and the nature of scientific conceptualization:

> We have evolved as scientists, to be sure, and so we know a lot about DNA, but if our kind of mind had been confronted with the problem of designing a similar replicating molecule, starting from scratch, we'd never have succeeded. We would have made one fatal mistake: our molecule would have been perfect. . . . The capacity to blunder slightly is the real marvel of DNA. Without this special attribute, we would still be anaerobic bacteria and there would be no music. Viewed individually, one by one, each of the mutations that have brought us along represents a random, totally spontaneous accident, but it is no accident at all that mutations occur; the molecule of DNA was ordained from the beginning to make small mistakes.[15]

Keats and his generation of Romantic physicians would have understood this capacity in physical nature and consciousness to evade consistently the stasis of perfection—and to blunder accidentally yet inexorably into and upon strange and wonderful, and occasionally terrifying, creations.

Chapter 18

English Evolution

Keats's letters manifest an informed knowledge of all the basic concepts on evolution available to his generation from theorists in England and Europe; this knowledge extends from the simplest notions of the biological regeneration of parts to the more sophisticated systems of embryonic formation and social development, and it even ranges to *Naturphilosophie*'s absorbing vision of the progress of human consciousness. The long missive of April 1819 to the George Keatses considers the prospects for human happiness and comes to doubt that the sustained or singular exertion of physical or intellectual exertion can create such perfection on earth:

> But in truth I do not at all believe in this sort of perfectibility—the nature of the world will not admit of it—the inhabitants of the world will correspond to itself—Let the fish philosophize the ice away from the Rivers in winter time and they shall be at continual play in the tepid delight of summer. Look at the Poles and at the sands of Africa, Whirlpools and volcanoes—Let men exterminate them and I will say that they may arrive at earthly Happiness—The point at which Man may arrive is as far as the paralel state in inanimate nature and no further—For instance suppose a rose to have sensation, it blooms on a beautiful morning it enjoys itself—but there comes a cold wind, a hot sun—it can not escape it, it cannot destroy its annoyances—they are as native to the world as itself: no more can man be happy in spite, the world[ly] elements will prey upon his nature—[1]

Nature's species are bound to their parallel state in inanimate nature, their talents and environments bind and are bounded by one another, happiness or the degree of perfection is fully limited by an innate imperfectibility necessary to natural progress.

"Our bodies every seven years are completely fresh-materialed—seven years ago it was not this hand that clench'd itself against Hammond—We are like the relic garments of a Saint: the same and not the same: for the careful Monks patch it and patch it: till there's not a thread of the original garment

231

left, and still they show it for St. Anthony's shirt." The September 1819 letter to
the George Keatses thus begins with the straightforward Hunterian theory of
the regeneration of parts but shifts quickly, in response to an earlier comment
on the changing human personality, to the poet's version of contemporary
notions on the thought processes and evolution of mind:

> From the time you left me, our friends say I have altered completely—am not the
> same person . . . —I dare say you have altered also—every man does. . . . This is the
> reason why men who had been bosom friends, on being separated for any number
> of years, afterwards meet coldly, neither of them knowing why—The fact is they are
> both altered—Men who live together have a silent moulding and influencing power
> over each other—They interassimilate.[2]

Changes in friends and interpersonal relationships find their metaphor in
biological necessity and their source in the fresh perfections of human consciousness. Influence, injury, and sometimes even the smallest of causes can
occasion great alterations in physiology or thought; and when the poet remarks in the same letter that he is "convinced however that apparently small
causes make great alterations," he is expressing his parallel belief not just in
the punctuated equilibrium of nature but in the progressive enlightenment of
human communities:

> All civiled countries become gradually more enlighten'd and there should be a
> continual change for the better. Look at this Country at present and remember it
> when it was even though[t] impious to doubt the justice of a trial by Combat—
> From that time there has been a gradual change—Three great changes have been in
> progress—First for the better, next for the worse, and a third time for the better
> once more.[3]

The gradual episodic advance of civilization patterns itself upon the like
advance of intelligence in the species as predicted by the evolutionists: the
poet thinks "Wordsworth is deeper than Milton," but he also believes this
manifestation of superior intelligence is partly owed to the passage of natural
(biological) time and "has depended more upon the general and gregarious
advance of intellect, than individual greatness of Mind—."[4] The evolution of
organic species, the progress of human society, the intuitions of consciousness, and the overall advance of mind are all subject, for Keats, to the same
Lamarckian law of Romantic evolution: fresh perfection though the episodic
alterations that must punctuate, and alternately hinder and advance, the
complacent stasis of fulfillment in nature.

> We fall by course of Nature's law, not force
> Of thunder, or of Jove. Great Saturn, thou
> Hast sifted well the atom-universe;
> But for this reason, that thou art the King,

> And only blind from sheer supremacy,
> One avenue was shaded from thine eyes,
> Through which I wandered to eternal truth.
> And first, as thou wast not the first of powers,
> So art thou not the last; it cannot be:
> Thou art not the beginning nor the end.
>   (*Hyp.*, II, 181–90)

Unlike Saturn who is blind from sheer supremacy, and unlike his counterpart in *Endymion*, Glaucus, who cannot read the natural signs of his briny world, Oceanus sees the pain and necessity of evolutionary truth. The sea-god's explanation to his fellow Titans of why they, "all calm" and at "the top of sovereignty," are therein "fated" to be excelled, gives articulation to his daughter Clymene's music and its Apollonian answer. It verbalizes, as we will see in the next two chapters of this part, all of the major physiological and metaphysical theories of evolution available to prevailing Romantic science. The long speech by Oceanus in *Hyperion* also sets the pattern, as we will see in subsequent chapters of this part, for Keats's evolving justification of mortal pain as the necessary catalyst for poetic creativity and spiritual development in a Romantic age.

Survey of Keats's poetry from the perspective of Oceanus's speech shows, furthermore, that the evolution of organic life is a persistent subject and nascent metaphor for poetic creativity. "I stood tip-toe" calls the living transactions between stream and bowery green "an interchange of favours" (85) to evoke concepts of the interdependence of species and of the formation of life through the interplay of opposing forces. Organic and perceptual life "interassimilate" as the letter above marked, and the poem *Endymion* presents Adonis, "safe in the privacy / Of this still region all his winter-sleep" but "rear'd / Each summer time to life" (II, 477–80), as the embodiment of the cyclic schedule by which this interassimilation occurs. Cyclical and interdependent life encompasses "the birth, life, death / Of unseen flowers in heavy peacefulness" (*End.*, I, 233–34), of species, and of natural forces. By the rules of evolutionary life, nothing dies: "the stars their antient courses keep, / Clouds still with shadowy moisture haunt the earth, / Still suck their fill of light from sun and moon, / Still buds the tree, and still the sea-shores murmur. / There is no death in all the universe" (*Fall of Hyp.*, I, 419–23). By the ravening formula of this same life everything dies: the greater upon the lesser feed evermore according to the verse-epistle to Reynolds, and in the mortal world of the "Ode to a Nightingale" hungry generations tread one another down. Oceanus and his poet have much to explain in less than one hundred lines of poetry.

William Lawrence in 1817 took issue with superstitious English naturalists who argued that fossil elephant bones had to belong to some extant species because "Providence maintains and continues every created species" and Divine assurance to Noah guaranteed "that no race of animals will any more cease." He offered his own study of physiology, zoology, and the natural history of man as "the fullest evidence that many species and genera of animals have been annihilated" in the interest of greater organic perfection in nature.[5] The concept of annihilation of certain species in nature was known to Keats; he, like Lawrence, invoked it to protest a similar kind of sanctimony: "Parsons will always keep up their Character, but as it is said there are some animals, the Ancients knew, which we do not; let us hope our posterity will miss the black badger with tri-cornered hat."[6] The gradual extinction of the purportedly less perfect species did not trouble Romantic intellectuals in the same way it did Tennyson and other Victorians perhaps because it was seen as a concept tied inextricably to a parallel notion of evolving perfection in nature and consciousness. Unlike the ages that preceded and followed, Romantic evolution theory focused by design and inclination upon potential development (including self-development) as the primary implication of structure.

J. F. Blumenbach, whose work on comparative anatomy was translated into English by William Lawrence in 1807 and could be found in the Physical Society library at Guy's during Keats's time at the hospital, argued conclusively that humans were one species, thereby changing the focus of evolutionary inquiry from a study of pigmentation (which had dominated theories of evolution at least since Kant) to a study of structure. His concept of *Bildungstrieb*, formulated in 1789, was a decisive attempt to establish development as the primary purpose of all organic structure. Blumenbach said that all living organisms "from man down to maggots, and from the cedar to common mould or mucor," owned an inherent "effort or tendency which, while life continues, is active and operative; in the first instance to attain the definite form of the species, then to preserve it entire, and, when it is infringed upon, so far as this is possible, to restore it."[7] *Bildungstrieb* was an innate impulse in all living creatures toward self-development and—within the existential contingencies of the given species—self-perfection. Distinct from the universal properties and peculiar qualities of organized bodies, it was the physiological equivalent, and perhaps the pattern, of what Romantic theorists of society or mind called "aspiration." Blumenbach's *Bildungstrieb* found quick passage into evolutionary theorizing of the decade following its formulation. Variations upon the concept can be traced in the thinking on spiritual progress of the German natural philosophers, in Lamarck's notion of appetence, in the delineations on structure of French and English mechanists like St. Hilaire and Lawrence, in the clinical lessons born of comparative anatomy taught by Astley Cooper, and in the vitalistic medicine of Hunterians like Abernethy and Joseph Henry Green.

When Astley Cooper was made professor of comparative anatomy to the Royal College of Surgeons in 1813, the appointment was a formal example of the increasing tendency of Romantic medicine to link human physiology and the treatment of human life with the study of comparative anatomy. Guy's Hospital during this time had its own teaching Museum of Comparative Anatomy adjacent to its operating theatre,[8] and Cooper brought to his lectures on surgery and human anatomy pertinent information from the best that was known of zoology and natural history; he also referred his students to the remarkable collection of bones and specimens in the Hunterian Museum. His teachings regularly included discussion of the classification of animals, the physiological similarities of organ or limb among certain mammals, the skeletal distinction befitting the habits of each species, the importance of the development of teeth to the ascending scale of animal life, and all other adaptations among animal species that were relevant to the economy and health of man.[9]

The importance of comparative anatomy to medicine was presupposed by all medical professors of Keats's time. Cooper was merely following the example of his surgeon-teacher, John Hunter, who, according to Joseph Henry Green, had given the seal of approval to this linkage "by including the human anatomy in that science of *Comparative* or *Universal Anatomy*, which commences with the first rudest forms of organic individuation" and concludes with the most perfect of all animals, humankind.[10] Hunter, of course, had drawn on contemporary observations of animal anatomy for his influential theorizing on the life of blood. The practice of mid-eighteenth-century science to judge the relative superiority of living beings and to key their gradation on the animal scale according to their ability to generate heat or electricity[11] was subsumed by Hunter's formulations on the evolution of circulatory systems. The place of a creature within the overall economy of nature, the strength of this impulse to self-development, and the perfectability of its species were all proportionate to the structural sophistication of the creature's heart and circulatory system.

The influence of Hunter's treatise on the blood upon the English physicians who succeeded him, and specifically upon the vocabulary of their own formulations on life and evolution, was pervasive. The human circulatory system became the measure by which animal systems were classified and differentiated in the scale of being: "The circulation in the vessels of the more imperfect animals, in which a great artery supplies the place of a heart, is of a very different nature from that of the more perfect animals."[12] The more perfect beings had better hearts. But the circulatory system of the blood in man, because it was common to so many forms of being, was also the means whereby, "under the influence of the same appetites" and impulses to self-perfection, human kind was able to "receive new matter . . . [and] perfect or animalize it. . . ."[13] The perfection of self could define and place a being within a given species; or it could be the means for showing the being's distinction from its purported species. Evolution alternately animalized or perfected new matter, and organic perfection, episodically, proved itself incomplete.

> In earth, sea, air, around, below, above,
> Life's subtle woof in Nature's loom is wove;

> Points glued to points a living line extends,
> Touch'd by some goad approach the bending ends;
> Rings join to rings, and irritated tubes
> Clasp with young lips the nutrient globes or cubes;
> And urged by appetencies new select,
> Imbibe, retain, digest, secrete, eject.
> In branching cones the living web expands,
> Lymphatic ducts, and convoluted glands;
> Aortal tubes propel the nascent blood,
> And lengthening veins absorb the refluent flood;
> Leaves, lungs, and gills, the vital ether breathe
> On earth's green surface, or in the waves beneath.[14]

Thus Erasmus Darwin explained in blushing excess the origin of human society within the temple of nature. He placed all species within the pattern of this origin and speculated, correctly, that the evolution of life on earth began not at the traditional date of 4004 B.C. but "perhaps millions of ages before the commencement of the history of mankind. . . ." For Darwin, the physiological evidence of human evolution was borne witness in the structure of every species, living or extinct. Indeed, the very pattern was set in the evolution of the first "living filament" that emerged endued "with the power of acquiring new parts attended with new propensities, directed by irritations, sensations, volitions, and associations; and thus possessing the faculty of continuing to improve by its own inherent activity, and of delivering down those improvements by generation to its own posterity, world without end."[15] Furthermore, the evidence of comparative anatomy charted not just the inevitable physical emergence of man but also the evolution of humankind's emotional and perceptual life:

> Next the long nerves unite their silver train,
> And young SENSATION permeates the brain;
> Through each new sense the keen emotions dart,
> Flush the young cheek, and swell the throbbing heart.
> From pain and pleasure quick VOLITIONS rise,
> Lift the strong arm, or point the inquiring eyes;
> With Reason's light bewilder'd Man direct,
> And right and wrong with balance nice detect.
> Last in thick swarms ASSOCIATIONS spring,
> Thoughts join to thoughts, to motions motions cling;
> Whence in long trains of catenation flow
> Imagined joy, and voluntary woe.[16]

Darwin was neither a poet nor a metaphysician, but his speculative powers as an evolutionist were keen and imaginative, and he was more often correct than later generations of scientists would acknowledge.[17] He had correctly proposed the origin of life in primeval waters, the long duration between the formation of first life and the emergence of human life, the heretical truth that evolution proceeded "by its own inherent activity" and without divine intervention. He had declared, moreover, that the primary influences occasioning the transformation of species were the "three great objects of desire," lust, hunger, and security, and in the courting contest of birds that were armed with spurs he found proof of a truth applicable to all of living nature, namely, "that the strongest and most active animal should propagate the species, which should thence become improved."[18] These laws of organic nature far from excepting the human species found their fullest expression in it. English intellectuals of the early nineteenth century could not ignore Erasmus Darwin's revolutionary and often terrifying science of life.

"When we consider all these changes of animal form, and innumerable others, which may be collected from the books of natural history; we cannot but be convinced, that the fetus or embryon is formed by the apposition of new parts, and not by the distention of a primordial nest of germes, included one within another, like the cups of a conjurer."[19] Natural history in his time proved beyond doubt to Darwin that there were no primordially perfected forms, no animalcules or homunculi, but indistinguishable and structureless living filaments that developed and evolved into adulthood according to the laws of their particular species. Embryogenesis followed the laws of evolution, and all embryos were the microcosmic expressions of natural history and the oceanic origin of life: even "quadrupeds and mankind in their embryon state are aquatic animals; and thus may be said to resemble gnats and frogs."[20] Malformed fetuses and monstrous births were therefore a vital aspect of embryology because, as accidents or lacunae in the process of organic perfection, they revealed by default the mysterious pattern of evolutionary life.

The importance of these peculiar creations to the study of man was not lost on early-nineteenth-century thinkers. They were often the starting point for research on the nature of vitality, as well as the basis for speculations on the evolutionary laws of organic life and the development of consciousness in the most perfect of species. When Richard Saumarez wrote his philosophical treatise on the principle of life in 1799, he felt compelled to include contemporary knowledge of embryology in his speculations and to invoke specifically the research on the sexual reproduction of mammals and fish of John Haighton, lecturer in midwifery at Guy's Hospital.[21] Haighton's lectures on midwifery in 1816–1817, in turn, were devoted not so much to maternal care as to discussion of unusual births and fetal malformations; they included numerous case histories of congenital disease in infants and the gynecological implication of "monstrous" formation in miscarried embryos.[22] Astley Cooper's well-known research on the human reproductive organs,[23] meanwhile, was his own particular contribution to contemporary interest in embryology, fetal malformation, genetic evolution, and the influence of disease upon these subjects.

Endymion's fantasies of embryonic forms in an underseas womb and "new-minted" lovers, the aborted infruition of the Grecian urn's lovers, the fascinating recreations of Lamia, the signs of new birth in nature observed by the almost-poet of "I stood tip-toe," the abortive transformation of la belle dame's knight, the rebirth and initiation of Apollo to his new domain in *The Fall of Hyperion* are all expressions (perhaps at some whimsical remove) of the preoccupation of Romantic medicine with signs of organic formation in nature, formations that scientists believed could reveal the vital dynamics of life and perhaps prophecy the future of being. Joseph Henry Green's Coleridgean vision of the vital dynamics of the universe marked both the literal and the conceptual potential of contemporary knowledge of embryonic evolution: "The changing form of the embryo bears the impress of its transitional and incomplete character, while it ever preserves the promise and prophecy of the being into which it is to be finally evolved." If John Hunter's research on the blood was the first step toward disclosing the nature of vitality, his research on inherited fetal malformations was to demonstrate to Green first the connection between a knowledge of embryology and the comprehension of the law of life, a connection that enabled the decades following Hunter to define evolution as life's self-revealing process of organic perfection:

> And it did not escape Hunter, as a consequence of the same law, that Congenital Defects, hitherto comprehended under the vague designation of monstrosity, are to be explained by the development of the embryo being interrupted and arrested at some early stage of its regular evolution, and that the defective form, which is the result, is analogous to the form and structure of an inferior class. And thus if in the human embryo these defective forms constitute a series of transient epochs, which are repetitious of the types, that denote the grades of the ascending scale of animated being, in like manner all the lower forms in relation to the highest may be regarded as abortions, by anticipation[,] of nature's mature work, the human frame.[24]

Malformed or defective human embryos were not proof of malfeasant visitations by dark spirits but rather propitious freaks of nature, "accidents" wherein intermittently otherwise inscrutable patterns of being were exposed. For Green and other Romantic physicians of his generation, there were no monsters in nature, only (in retrospective vision) abortive interruptions in the process of perfection. These interruptions epiphanized through their distinctions or malformations the energy engendered beneath the surface of complacent nature. Everything that lived was holy and revelatory of the law of organic and perceptual evolution.

The specimens of Hunter's museum, a catalogue of which could be found in the Physical Society Library at Guy's during Keats's time, illustrated Hunter's "apprehension of life as a law," according to Green. "It is in this Museum," Green exhorts his peers in the Royal College of Surgeons, that one finds "the pledge and proof of John Hunter's pre-eminent and original merit, that of having first presented the facts of comparative anatomy in and as a connected scheme of graduated development" so as to furnish "the grounds of a new science, the science of Comparative or Universal Physiology" wherein "every part of the organized creation [could] give intelligibility to every other part. . . ."[25] The museum's purpose, read by Green, was

> to exhibit every order of living beings, from the 'rudimental chaos of life' to the *Mammalia*, as so many embryonic states of an Organism, to which nature from the beginning had tended; to exhibit nature as labouring in birth with man, and her living products as so many significant types of the great process, which she is ever tending to complete in the evolution of the organic realm. And in recognizing by the light of this idea man as the ultimate aim and consummation of nature, we shall see in each stage of the ascending scale, with evidence increasing directly as the ascent, at once the opposition and harmony of two great tendencies;—on the one hand that of nature to integrate all into one comprehensive whole, and consequently retaining each part;—and on the other hand, the tendency to integration in the parts, or that by which each more and more secures the privilege of being in, from, and for itself, as the anticipated type of its final achievement in the Individuality of man.[26]

Through the occasion of Hunter's museum, Green interpreted evolutionary life as what he called the vital dynamism of "comparative perfection" in nature. Evolution in Green's Romantic age was not simply a concept of progress, as it was in later decades of the nineteenth century; it was dynamic, episodic, often simultaneous, and received first pattern from the image of biological growth. The comparative anatomical perfections of organisms in nature served the final evolution of man; the perfecting of humankind and human consciousness, meanwhile, wrought to completion and full intelligibility natural design. Between the lines of Green we read Coleridge. Through Green, we intuit *Naturphilosophie*'s sweeping theory of universal life above and behind the motley collection of embalmed freaks, skeletons, skulls, and shells once gathered by the primary English surgeon known to the Romantic age; the old bones and briny creatures of the Hunterian Museum were John Hunter's consciously Romantic and humanly intuitive contribution to the divine history of human consciousness.

Chapter 19

European Evolution

Abraham Trembley's discovery in 1740 of that monstrous freak of nature, the underwater polyp, inspired extraordinary speculations among scientists on the nature of life and led to speculative research during the rest of the century on the creature's strange evolution and reproductive advantage.[1] Trembley's polyp was a plant-structured organism of the *Obelia* genus and, like the freshwater hydra and anemone and the ocean-borne medusa, it exhibited attributes that were both animal and botanical. This peculiar zooid propagated itself through ovum as well as budding shoots; it could even multiply itself from vermiform segments when it was cut into pieces. Polyps and medusae like that other peculiarity of nature, the sensitive plant, and like Davy's hypothesis, the *Proteus Anguinus*, undermine conventional distinctions between plant and zoophyte; they disrupt the presupposed distinctions between the categories in nature. Henry Baker, Martin Folkes, Réaumur, Jussieu, and Maupertuis were among the many scientific thinkers who first responded to Trembley's discovery with fascination and speculative abandon. The nature of materialism and of animality, the attributes of vitality, the secrets of generation, the freak advantages of polygeneration, the nature of the soul and its place of residence, the question of whether animal souls were divisable— these were some issues that were inspired to new variations by the polyp's existence. They were also subjects that established the parameters for the study of evolution during the nineteenth century.

Buffon took Trembley's polyp as decisive proof of his notion that nature was composed of organic molecules and that organisms from the least to the most highly evolved of creatures were composed of the same living molecular entities. "The animals and plants which are capable of multiplying and reproducing by means of all their parts are organized bodies composed of other similar organic bodies, whose original constituent parts are similarly organic, whose accumulated mass is discernible to the eye, but the original parts of which we are able to perceive only through reasoning and analogy," Buffon said in 1749, in volume 2 of his *Histoire Naturelle*. "This leads us to believe," he added, "that there is in nature an infinity of organic particles, actually existing and living, and whose substance is the same as that of organized beings. . . ."[2] For Buffon, the all-nourishing living matter, distributed universally throughout nature, was a composite of living atoms or molecules endued with the peculiar properties of their particular source in animate nature. His theory of pangenesis followed accordingly:

> Reproduction takes place only through the same matter's becoming superabundant in the body of the animal or plant. Each part of the body then sends off (*renvoie*) the organic molecules which it can not admit. Each of these particles is absolutely analogous to the part by which it is thrown off, since it was destined for the nourishment of that part. Then, when all the molecules sent off by all the parts of the body unite, they necessarily form a small body similar to the first, since each molecule is similar to the part from which it comes. It is in this way that reproduction takes place in all species. . . . There are, therefore, no preexisting germs, no germs contained within one another *ad infinitum*; but there is an organic matter, always active, always ready to be shaped and assimilated and to produce beings similar to those which receive it. Animal or vegetable species, therefore, can never, of themselves, disappear (*s'épuiser*).[3]

Although Lamarck and the generation of evolutionists that followed Buffon were to disprove his notion of the survival of all species, his concept of organic evolution and of the species as real entities endured to influence all subsequent evolutionary formations. Buffon's doctrine of the unity of organic molecules in nature and of the capability of these particles nevertheless to carry hereditary specificity in the event of reproductive occasion allowed both for the uniform replication of organs, organisms, and species and for the parallel and future mutation of the life forms upon demand of environmental or other necessity. Although these molecules bore the potential of hereditary specificity, they changed only in response to necessity: they were first and foremost the nutritional substance of all living existence, "an organic matter"—passive, receptive, and "always ready to be assimilated and to produce beings similar to those who receive it." Buffon's molecules adapted to the nutritional demands of their particular creatures, replicated themselves in reproduction and changed as the creatures changed.[4] "Though nature appears always the same," he said in his supplement of 1778, "she passes nevertheless through a constant movement of successive variations, of sensible alterations; she lends herself to new combinations, to mutations of matter and form, so that today she is quite different from what she was at the beginning or even at later periods."[5] Thus Diderot in *D'Alembert's Dream* (1769) could evoke Buffon and anticipate his comment in the supplement to see the known universe as breeding ground for a second generation of totally different and unforeseeable beings nourished by the same, original molecular substance; thus also could he imagine human polyps, born of human molecular matter and modeled upon Trembley's polyp, inhabiting Jupiter and Saturn. "Our bodies on the contrary, and all other objects have many forms, each of which is compounded, divisible, variable, and perishable; and has a relation to different organs; through which we perceive them. Our bodies, and matter in general, therefore, have neither permanent, real, nor general properties, by which we can attain a certain knowledge of them," Buffon said.[6] The very sameness of organic mo-lecularity ensured its capability for endless and multiple variations; Buffonian nature could be "the same and not the same" and ever "fresh materialed" like the patched relic garment of a saint described above by Keats.

Keats read Buffon in Barr's 1792 edition in the spring of 1818 while nursing Tom through the first onset of his illness and while composing his verse-epistle to Reynolds. A. D. Atkinson has traced the poet's comments on the finitude of water and intellect and the consequences of Milton's gormandizing brain (in the 24 March 1818 letter to Rice) and his mention of Kamchatka, "sea and travel" (in the 25 March 1818 epistle to Reynolds) to Keats's parallel reading of Robertson's *History of America* (1777) and Buffon's *Natural History* (1749–1804).[7] Certainly we identify at first glance the evolutionary musings that underlie the poet's closing vision in the verse-epistle when the narrator sees "too distinct into the core / Of an eternal fierce destruction," "where every maw / The greater on the less feeds evermore," "The shark at savage prey—the hawk at pounce, / The gentle robin, like a pard or ounce, / Ravening a worm" (93–103). So also do we recognize the source in Romantic evolutionary thought, if not in Buffon specifically, of Keats's comparison of Wordsworth and Milton in a letter five weeks later (on 3 May 1818, also to Reynolds): in continuation of his speculations on the size of Milton's gormandizing brain, he proposes that Wordsworth's revelation in "Tintern Abbey" of greater intel-lectual depth than Milton depends "more upon the general and gregarious advance of intellect, than individual greatness of Mind."[8] What we have to recognize is the coincidence in the spring of 1818 of Keats's reading in evolu-tion and the sudden revelation of his poetic talent in the verse-epistle to Reynolds. What we have to absorb into our comprehension of Keats's poetry are the marked connections between the poet's musings on physical and intellectual evolution during 1818 and his parallel formulations on poetic purpose, passivity of mind, and the receptive poetic character.

A letter to Haydon on 8 April 1818 uses the familiar Lamarckian term from Romantic evolution for creative recomposition in nature as a metaphor for the perception of beauty: it speaks of "the innumerable compositions and decompositions which take place between the intellect and its thousand materials before it arrives at that trembling delicate and snail-horn perception of Beauty—."[9] The 3 May 1818 letter comparing Milton's and Wordsworth's respective evolutions of mind in biological time is also the "Mansion of Life" letter[10] wherein Keats articulates his sense of the poet's humanitarian task, first advanced in the verse-epistle written five weeks before, by expressing his full belief that the poet's primary concern is with a world "full of Misery and Heartbreak, Pain, Sickness and oppression. . . ." In late December of 1817, Keats had begun to formulate his thoughts on negative capability and the necessity of passive receptivity to the creation of intensity in art.[11] The poet's comments on the subject continued and evolved through the spring and summer of 1818. A 19 February letter to Reynolds stresses the importance of unmotivated absorption in the passing evolution of life and resolves, "Let us open our leaves like a flower and be passive and receptive—budding patiently under the eye of Apollo and taking hints from every noble insect that favors us with a visit. . . ."[12] A 27 October letter to Woodhouse culminates the defining of negative capability with a description of the "Poetical character" as something distinct from "the wordsworthian or egotistical sublime," a creative receptivity able through imaginative selflessness to lose its individual distinction (or selfish specificity) in the substance and feelings of the living object it would nourish and re-create in poetry: "A Poet is the most unpoetical of any thing in existence; because he has no Identity—he is continually in for—and filling some other Body." Keats further notes of his own "Poetical" character: "Not one word I ever utter can be taken for granted as an opinion growing out of my identical nature. . . . When I am in a room with People . . . then not myself goes home to myself: but the identity of every one in the room begins to press upon me that, I am in a very little time annihilated—not only among Men; it would be the same in a Nursery of children. . . ."[13]

The poetic character described by Keats assimilates all selves of individuality into its own selflessness and, in the process, is itself assimilated by these. His own musings on natural evolution and the formation of species during the spring and summer of 1818 (and not just the familiar influence of Hazlitt documented by Bromwich and others since Bate) were what encouraged Keats first to reject the subjective or egotistical distinctions between individuals of the species and to seek, instead, the parallels, connections, and shared purposes born of deep instinctual commonality—a common substance, or substrata—among the life forms; to see, as he says in a letter of March 1819 to the George Keatses, the bright eagerness of living purpose uniting fieldmouse, stoat, hawk, and man.[14] Nor would it be farfetched to assume that Keats found in the neutral capability for either hereditary specificity in reproduction or self-annihilation in other-nutrition of the Buffonian molecule and in the ever-adaptable, unified incentive to life and life change of the "animate matter" formed of these molecules—"always active, always ready to be shaped and assimilated and to produce beings similar to those which [first] receive it"—support for his own conception of the poet's contra-Wordsworthian, contra-egotistical, receptive, neutral capability in creation.

Lamarck found the pattern of evolution not in the eternal animation of molecular matter, as did his mentor, Buffon, but in the pervasive tendency to decomposition of natural substance. Physical nature for Lamarck tended only to decomposition; there was no chemical fixity in the universe, and the chemical pattern of composition and decomposition applied alike to organic and inorganic matter, in physiology as in geology. Life evolved through an eternal dynamism of decomposition and recomposition. In his *Recherches sur l'organisation des corps vivants* (1802), Lamarck described life processes as a composite movement of growth and aging (or decay) with growth seen as the increase in mass resulting from the youthful retention of needed materials from the environment and aging seen as the progressive hardening of the given organism's initial pliancy through its lifelong efforts at ingestion and digestion of the environment. "The mechanism of evolution" was, as Lamarck saw it, "perfectly analogous to the mechanism of erosion. Eventually, the organism silts up and dies."[15] Within the Lamarckian mechanism of evolution, the animal series were not a chain or ladder so much as a moving staircase or escalation of being: nature constantly creates life at the bottom and life fluids are ever at work complicating and perfecting structures; "there is a perpetual circulation of organic matter up the moving staircase of existence, and of its lifeless residue spilling as chemical husks back down the other side...."[16] Every evolutionary action had its reaction, every animation in nature necessitated a deanimation elsewhere in nature; decomposition followed evolutionary advance and, in its eternal escalation of being from finite matter, animate life left behind echoing reminders of past composition, inanimate but lifelike husks and shells of former being.

Only life could act, according to Lamarck; as the Brunonian physicians also said, life and activity (including latent activity) were one. In the dialogue of Lamarckian evolution articulated in his *Philosophie zoologique* of 1809, nature is a plastic force forever producing living entities of all variety from the most rudimentary of forms, the protozoa, to the most advanced of beings, man. An action of progressive differentiation and perfection of organization marks the occasion of distinct species and preserves the organic forms as a visible sequence. This sequence of living forms would be a perfect and enduring continuum but for two influences: the innate tendency to complication or perfection of the living forms themselves, and the obtrusive, inert, "dead hand" of inorganic matter in the environment that occasions discontinuities in the organic drive to perfection of living nature. The discontinuities or roadblocks forced into the active sequence of life by the presence of inorganic substances of former life thus manifest themselves as gaps or ghostly pauses in the tangible, sequential forms of life. The inorganic environment does not act on life; rather, its ever-decomposing substance provides the occasion for the actions or reactions of life: "Changes in the environment lead to changes in needs; changes in needs produce changes in behavior; changes in behavior become new habits which may lead to alterations in particular organs and ultimately in general organization;" and the inanimate environment proves to be "a shifting set of circumstances and opportunities to which the [living] organism responds creatively, not precisely as an expression of its will ... but as an expression of its whole nature as a living thing."[17]

Lamarck's extended research on invertebrates, the seven-volume *Histoire naturelle des animaux sans vertèbres*, was published between 1815 and 1822 and included a volume of plates of fossil shells. The 1815 preface to the first volume summarized Lamarck's four laws of evolution and contained a clear articulation of what can be identified as the particularly Romantic aspect of Lamarckian evolution: the concept of the creative response of the organism to environmental interruption, a response that produces either new organs and thereby new species to punctuate and rapidly escalate an otherwise tranquil equilibrium of nature, or, when a given species was unsuccessful in its creative response to environmental necessity, a disruption of the continuum of living forms that is permanently recorded as a missing space or lacuna in the sequence of beings. Appetency or longing, an impulse to change, governs the evolution of new organs or parts in living creatures according to the second law of Lamarck: "The production of a new organ in an animal body results from the supervention of a new want (*besoin*) continuing to make itself felt, and a new movement which this want gives birth to and encourages."[18] Species evolved because their individual members, driven by a *sentiment intérieur* (inner feeling), changed to meet the demands of the environment; this change, which subsequently became hereditary, occurred because of creatural yearning, a biological impulse, an existential need to respond to environmental challenge, perhaps even an inner will or striving that expressed the whole nature or being of the living creature.

The impetus for evolution thus came from within, and from life. In the dynamic interaction between organic life and lifeless matter, the living organism had the monopoly on chemical creativity. Lamarck asserted the primacy of life over inorganic nature and the primacy of a species' individual aspiration to evolve over both the tendency to decomposition and the pattern of enduring consistency or immutable perfection in animate existence. Thus formulated by Lamarck, the very idea of evolution became Romantic. The passage between Lamarck and *Naturphilosophie* is inescapable. Indeed, the Faustian aspiration of German Romantic thought found its first parallel—and perhaps its lowest common denominator—in the biological impulse to evolve conceived by Lamarckian evolution.

Long before Goethe addressed the perfectibilities and tendencies to error of the human form divine in *Faust*, he advanced his version of creatural evolution. He proposed that every living being was a complex of independent elements referable to one model or primordial "idea," and that individuality was merely a metamorphic variation of an original yet timeless interindividual pattern. The *Urpflanze* or *Modell* of Goethe was conceived as a prototype that was complex and all-inclusive; unlike Buffon's molecule, which was posited as the simplest unit of nature's construction, and unlike Robinet's monad, which was portrayed as a sophisticated elemental form generative of all beings (to which it bore some contextual connection), Goethe's prototype was a universal form that manifests itself only in a multiplicity of individual modulations.[19] The Goethean prototype of living existence was static, like an intellectual principle, but its realizations or modulations in the world were disparate and diverse. Hence, perfection for Goethe was variable and always vulnerable to supersession: it resided temporarily in that individual modulation that attained the fullest realization of the model and manifested the most recent (in biological time) and therefore most complex embodiment of the prototype. The *Urpflanze* was, thus, the best expression and the last link in any proposed or real chain of being:

> If it is possible to arrange all the realizations of the prototype in matter in a scale of perfection, then it must be permissible to conceive of each one as the prototype of all those which are inferior to it. The most perfect link is the prototype of the chain of being. Man is the prototype of the animal kingdom and God of the entire creation. All the animals are variations of man, and all existents are representative variations of God. This is a Romantic elaboration of the central idea in Goethe's natural philosophy.[20]

In the evolutionary thinking of Goethe and *Naturphilosophen* like Oken, Herder and Schelling (copies of Schelling's and Herder's works could be found in the Physical Society Library at Guy's in 1816), present life tells the pattern of former life, and prototypes appear at the hypothetical end—not the beginning—of creation. The prototype becomes the last in an endless series of self-realizing aspirations. Evolution faces forward but the meaning of life is known by retrospection, and the definition of perfection must be eternally postponed, amended upwards, and itself perfected.

Naturphilosophie conceived of nature as a continuing process of organic self-evolution. Schelling, in particular, conceived of the world as one organism animated by an intelligence or spiritual principle for development (*Weltseele*); he subordinated the mechanical to the vital and saw nature and mind as polar directions of one activity or absolute advanced by an uninterrupted succession of stages that were marked by ascent and revealed through limitation in a series of points of arrest.[21] According to Schelling's reading of the natural evolution of nature and mind, the processes of nature from the inorganic to the most complex of the organic are stages in the self-realization of nature (*Von der Weltseele*, 1798); the processes of perception were likewise stages in the self-realization of mind, and because nature and mind were one activity, mind was at once product and culmination of nature as well as symbol of the *Weltseele*; and because everything in existence partakes of one organization or activity, the inorganic and perceptual worlds show the same formative activity in various parallel degrees or potencies (*Erster Entwurf eines Systems der Naturphilosophie*, 1799). As the species marked the stages or points of arrest in the advance of nature, so also did the conceptual activities from the rational and theoretical to the imaginative and aesthetic mark the stages in the perceptual evolution of mind.

Schelling's evolutionary principle displayed a yearning for fruition or perfection remarkably kindred to what Lamarck described as the appetence or creative will to live and evolve of the individual organism. In 1809, Schelling writes:

> It can readily be seen that in *the tension of longing necessary to bring things completely to birth* the innermost nexus of the forces can only be released in a graded evolution, and *at every stage in the division of forces there is developed out of nature a new being whose soul must be all the more perfect the more differentiatedly it contains what was left undifferentiated in the others.* It is the task of a complete philosophy of nature to show how each successive process more closely approaches the essence of nature, until in the highest division of forces the innermost center is disclosed.[22]

In the *Naturphilosophie* of Schelling, nature (and mind) bring forth new perfections born of the very aspirations or creative wills-to-evolve of the less-perfect creations that have preceded them. In this "graded evolution," each higher stage appears to undermine and to negate the preceding species or life form to which it owes its evolutionary impetus and existence; in actuality, it is a fulfillment of the appetence, aspiration, or latent tendency to advance beyond itself of the prior organism or perceptual entity.

From the perspective of biological or historical time, evolution implied the replacement and negation of species and life forms; from the retrospective perspective (or prophecy) of a universal philosophy of nature like that espoused by Goethe, Schelling, and other *Naturphilosophen*, evolution was the fulfillment of a prior generation's aspirations and ideas. "Every combination of force and form is neither stability nor retrogression, but progress. Take off the outer shell and there is no death in Nature. Every disturbance marks the transfer to a higher type," Herder had said, before Schelling, of the remarkable law of perfectibility or fresh perfection encompassed by the worldview of *Naturphilosophie*.[23] We are to know the future by the prophecy or retrospective vision of the past. "There is no death in all the universe, / No smell of death—" Saturn's lament in *The Fall of Hyperion* (I, 423–24) is a mortal and limited perspective, born of his race's impending end, of this retrospective vision of deathlessness and illimitation in nature. Keats's very real story of the fall of the mythical Titans, we shall see shortly, can encompass both perspectives.

Oken was the most important *Naturphilosophe* to follow Schelling and perhaps the most perceptive of the German evolutionists. Oken was a pantheist in the German tradition (though he developed his philosophical system independent of Schelling) as well as a practical physiologist who did important work in anatomy and comparative zoology. His importance to English Romanticism through his influence on Coleridge, Erasmus Darwin, and Faraday (and indirectly through his influence on Oersted) is incalculable. His primary place in Romantic medicine is ensured by his anticipation of modern cell doctrine in his theory of infusoria, his recognition of the true nature of protozoa, and

his correct conception (shared with Goethe) of the skull as fused vertebrae.[24]
Among his contemporaries Oken was recognized most for his construction of
a biology of the species that reflected the actions of the mind. Oken proposed
that the entire animal kingdom represented the several senses whereby man
perceived nature and that the animal classes were nothing other than graded
representations of the human sense organs.

Oken first outlined his novel evolutionary theory in his treatise *Gundriss der
Naturphilosophie* in 1802. There were five classes of animals, each corresponding
to a particular sense: the Dermatozoa or invertebrate class (worms), in which
the skin or sense of touch predominated; the Glossozoa or piscean category
(fish), in which the tongue, or sense of taste and glossial manipulation, was
highly developed; the Rhinozoa or amphibian class (reptiles), in which nasal
passages open to the air and the area of the brain necessary to a developed
sense of smell appear for the first time; the Otozoa or bird category, in which
the organ of hearing becomes independent and external and a correspondent
hollow space appears within the skull; and the Ophthalmozoa or mammal
class, in which a keen sense of sight developed by an advanced brain predomi-
nates over the other four already perfected senses. The living species of
nature were recompositions in five classes of man's disintegrated five senses,
the same five senses whereby the composite and perfected mind of man
perceived nature. For Oken and *Naturphilosophie* no less than for the mechanistic physiologists of the Romantic era, man was the end product of nature and
the most perfect of the animals: "Man is the summit, the crown of nature's
development, and must comprehend everything that has preceded him, even
as the fruit includes within itself all the earlier developed parts of the plant. In
a word, Man must represent the whole world in miniature."[25]

Evolution faced forward and developed in time, for Oken as for Schelling
and Goethe, but its meaning unfolded retroactively and was known retrospec-
tively because the process embodied past spiritual aspirations and priorly
conceived ideas. This was necessarily so because "the spiritual is antecedent
to nature" and, therefore, any philosophy of nature must "commence from the
spirit." In his expansive *Lehrbuch der Naturphilosophie* (1809–1811), Oken sought
to delineate just how this evolutionary process of mind and nature, in all its
precedents, corollaries, sequels, and retrospection worked:

[As] the whole of the Animal Kingdom, e.g., is none other than the representation
of the several activities or organs of Man; naught else than man disintegrated. In
like manner nature is none other than the representation of the individual activities
of the spirit. As, therefore, Zoology can be termed the Science of the Conversion of
Man into the Animal Kingdom, so may Physio-philosophy be called the Science of
the Conversion of Spirit into Nature.[26]

The animal species anticipated severally the perceptual perfections of man
because the parallel aspirations and ideas of the universal mind animating

both preceded them; "conversion" of man into animal kingdom or spirit into nature is nothing other than retroactive recognition, the perception of what was already present in the spiritual past as it finds embodiment within the given existence. Perfection in organic nature, as in conceptual creation, carries within it the seed or idea of its own supersession and the aspiration of its own doom.

In Oceanus's voice of wind and tides in *Hyperion* all of the dominant conceptions of Romantic evolution find peculiar harmony:

> Mark well!
> As Heaven and Earth are fairer, fairer far
> Than Chaos and blank Darkness, though once chiefs;
> And as we show beyond that Heaven and Earth
> In form and shape compact and beautiful,
> In will, in action free, companionship,
> And thousand other signs of purer life;
> So on our heels a fresh perfection treads,
> A power more strong in beauty, born of us
> And fated to excel us, as we pass
> In glory that old Darkness: nor are we
> Thereby more conquer'd, than by us the rule
> Of shapeless Chaos. Say, doth the dull soil
> Quarrel with the proud forests it hath fed,
> And feedeth still, more comely than itself?
> Can it deny the chiefdom of green groves?
> Or shall the tree be envious of the dove
> Because it cooeth, and hath snowy wings
> To wander wherewithal and find its joys?
> We are such forest-trees, and our fair boughs
> Have bred forth, not pale solitary doves,
> But eagles golden-feather'd, who do tower
> Above us in their beauty, and must reign
> In right thereof; for 'tis the eternal law
> That first in beauty should be first in might:
> Yea, by that law, another race may drive
> Our conquerers to mourn as we do now.
>   (II, 205–31)

Heaven and Earth are fairer far than Chaos and blank Darkness in conformity with the escalation of being proposed by Lamarck and Schelling; they are compact in form and shape in a manner similar to the Goethean prototype that embodies all prior perfection in its current form. Lamarck said that life acts and advances itself through the organism's will or appetence for greater complexity; Goethe spoke of the refinements of the prototype or spirit through innate aspiration; and Schelling addressed the tension of longing necessary for fruition and greater differentiation and perfection in natural or

conceptual life. So, also, Heaven and Earth in Oceanus's counsel find themselves "In will, in action free," and display a "thousand other signs of purer
life." The "fresh perfection" of evolutionary law defined variously but consistently by historians of life from Buffon to Oken finds equal consistency in the
poet's equation of "fresh perfection" with a "power more strong in beauty." "We
fall by course of Nature's law, not force," Oceanus has said earlier (II, 181), and
he now describes the power of the beauty that is to replace them because it is
more perfect. It is "born of us," he says, as an innate aspiration or longing that
is "fated to excel us" once it is embodied, much "as we pass / In glory that old
Darkness." The visible and tangible recomposition of life matter through need
and appetence defined by Lamarck accordions, through the conceptions of
Oceanus, into Schelling's vision of transcendent light (or beauty) surpassing
darkness.[27]

Only a fixed perspective sees what Lamarck called the dead hand of matter
where there is life, negation where there is fulfillment, and conquest where
there is evolution or fresh perfection. "Say, doth the dull soil / Quarrel with the
proud forests it hath fed, / And feedeth still, more comely than itself? . . . / Or
shall the tree be envious of the dove / Because it cooth, and hath snowy
wings . . . ?" Oceanus asks. His rhetoric of accomplished supersession assumes the concept of inevitability common to all prevailing evolutionary
thought. The ability of the Buffonian molecule to renounce specificity in the
interests of future life, to nurture other and different organisms while renounc-
ing its own hereditary possibilities, finds place in Oceanus's metaphor of the
"dull soil" feeding proud forests that in turn nurture winged creatures; the
self-sacrificial purpose of this nonspecific "dull soil" harbors, meanwhile, the
very lack of fixity in nature posited by Lamarck as well as the escalation of
being upon the nutritional husks or past perfections of organic matter proposed by him and the *Naturphilosophen*. The manifest continuity of life precludes the apparent negation of organic matter. Yearning, aspiration, and the
anticipation of their fulfillment likewise precludes the resentment of specific
creatural forms.

Oceanus's final assertion, "We are such forest-trees, and our fair boughs /
Have bred forth, not pale solitary doves, / But eagles golden-feather'd, who do
tower / Above us in their beauty" (224–27), is a poetic encapsulation of just
how the fixed biological and historical perspective of death, negation, replacement, and conquest in nature becomes, through the shifting retrospective
vision advanced by Schelling, fulfillment, fresh perfection, and transcendent
beauty wherein the forms and ideas of an earlier generation are made flesh.
Oceanus's "sad truth" of what has occurred is nothing other than nature's
evolutionary "eternal law" for future life. The Titans were not conquered; they
preempted themselves. They bore the aspiration or idea of their own supersession, and their innate beauty—or their ability to conceive of greater beauty—
fulfilled the perfections of their forms in other forms. There is no death in
nature, as Herder said, only the promise (or perception) of greater beauty.

Chapter 20

Evolution of Mind

It is the eternal law "That first in beauty should be first in might," Oceanus says in *Hyperion* (II, 229). But what is beauty? The sea-god's conjunction of the concept of comparative perfection in the species common to Romantic evolutionary thought with a more diffuse but no less comparative concept of aesthetic ascendancy avoids a fixed definition of beauty; it nevertheless carries important and specific reverberations for the meaning of power and perception in Keats. To the equation of fresh perfection with "a power more strong in beauty" in *Hyperion* belongs, as we shall see, a larger Keatsian equation of intensity and "fairness"—in life as in art. According to Oceanus's speech, perfection is nothing other than the present embodiment of beauty, and his adjectives for greater perfection ("fairer far," "purer," "more comely") propose an ideal of surpassing fairness or life power that is itself necessarily most vulnerable to being surpassed: "by that law, another race may drive / Our conquerors to mourn as we do now" (II, 230–31). The familiar laws of Romantic evolution theory serve thus to articulate an escalatory yet equivocal aesthetic theory based in mythology but also, for Oceanus and his peers, upon current perception. By this mythic theory, the evolution of life is prescribed by beauty and by, specifically, the subjective perception of beauty. Life evolves according to a law of beauty, the perception of which ensures the fulfillment of life. Life is comparative because beauty is comparative, an indefinable and changing entity whose occasional comprehension by perfected life forms ensures the formation of future and more perfect forms. Because of their advanced and revolutionary perception of greater perfection or beauty than their own, the perfected forms fulfill their type and occasion the obsolescence of their kind. Oceanus and Clymene, lest we forget, are the two Titans who perceive beauty in *Hyperion*, and it is in their apprehension of this partly alien beauty as greater than their own that they fulfill their innate personal aspirations to greater life expression and, at once, know their race's doom.

251

> Have ye beheld the young God of the Seas,
> My disposessor? Have ye seen his face?
> Have ye beheld his chariot, foam'd along
> By noble winged creatures he hath made?
> I saw him on the calmed waters scud,
> With such a glow of beauty in his eyes,
> That it enforc'd me to bid sad farewell
> To all my empire. . . .
>   (Hyp., II, 232–39)

Oceanus *sees* the young god of the seas and reads in the characters of his face his own dispossession; he comprehends the "glow of beauty" in his supplanter's eyes and communicates the consequent message of power, "might," to the shut-up senses and stifled ears of his fellow Titans (II, 175). In parallel perceptual recognition, Clymene *hears* the beauty of an invisible Apollo: "enchantment with the shifting wind," a "new blissful golden melody" that hovers round her head and overwhelms her senses to make her sick "Of joy nd grief at once." Once she has heard Apollo, Clymene is unable to stop hearing his music despite her voluntary or willful attempts at "stopping up" her "frantic ears." She is pursued by a voice "sweeter than all tune" crying Apollo's name, an Apollo she lacks the power to see but can hear too well until she is forced to comprehend the "living death" prophesied in the new melody. She must then translate the melody's intense message into the dull terms acceptable to the other, less-attuned Titans: "I fled, it follow'd me, and cried 'Apollo!' / O Father, and O Brethren, had ye felt / Those pains of mine" (II, 276–95). Until we suffer we cannot know, Keats said. These two Titans know the power of beauty.

Through Oceanus's and Clymene's perceptual powers of sight and sound—his vision of the young sea-god's glorious form and her audition of young Apollo's golden sound—they receive the message of beauty, might, and replacement. Oken had described for his Romantic generation a biology of species that reflected the actions of the mind and embodied the perceptions of the senses: in it, man was the summit of evolutionary achievement and able to comprehend through the appropriation of prior sensory developments all that preceded him, but, because all natural and conceptual creation "proceeded from the spirit," man was also the last and least of future conceptual perfections. As sea-borne deities who own a more heightened attunement to beauty than does the rest of their race, Oceanus and Clymene occupy a position among the Titans similar to Oken's exemplary man among the natural species. Theirs is a sensory and cognitive appropriation of new beauty, a sudden advance in perception. This act of perception involves sensory apprehension, a power to recognize beauty that exceeds that of the other Titans and a yearning comprehension of beauty that is at once familiar and strange. They know and feel kinship with the beauty they perceive, even as they imaginatively sense it to be alien and beyond their own capacity for life intensity. Their recognition of the new beauty partakes of its manifestation or fulfillment and at the immediate cognitive level occasions it. Apollo's power of beauty, his "might," derives partly from Clymene's sensory perception and innate recognition of it, and her acknowledgment of her own fulfillment and displacement through it is equivalent to Oceanus's suddenly "enforce'd" farewell to his kingdom as occasioned by his vision of the young sea-god's face. But both Titans' full apprehension of the new beauty involves an imaginative perception of difference or otherness born of their very kinship and yearning knowledge of it. Both perceive a beauty that they know they cannot achieve or perfect.

As the Romantic evolutionists sought out the similarities or kinships between creatural forms in order to differentiate the species, assign levels of life perfection, and name the stages in the escalation of beings, as they invoked sensory or perceptual development as proof of the distinctions and advances of the life species, so also do Oceanus and Clymene compare what they see and hear of the new order of gods with their own accomplished perfection: they enlist their perfected senses to comprehend yet greater sensitivity or life power; they feel kinship with the new beauty born of them but perceive ultimate difference and overweening supersession by greater sensory and perceptual might. Their fulfillment is their apprehension, a fearful understanding of power and pain. Oken and the *Naturphilosophen* maintained that all perceptual acts advance and supplant simultaneously. The perceptual evolution of the two sea-borne divinities of *Hyperion*, Oceanus and Clymene, culminates in a painfully communicable, fatal truth, at once balm and piercing *pharmakon*. They know and feel fully an intensity of knowledge that the other Titans must know without feeling fully.

> This gradation and evolution of animated matter is not simple and uniform; nature is ever rich, fertile, and varied in act and product:—and we might perhaps venture to symbolize the system of the animal creation as some monarch of the forest, whose roots, firmly planted in a vivifying soil, spread beyond our ken; whose trunk, proudly erected, points its summit to a region of purer light, and whose wide-spreading branches, twigs, sprays, and leaflets, infinitely diversified, manifest the energy of the life within. In the great march of nature nothing is left behind, and every former step contains the promise and prophecy of that which is to follow, even as the oak exists potentially in the acorn; and if nature seems at any part to recede, it is only as it were to gather strength for a higher and more determined ascent.[1]

To explain "the system of animal creation" in his Hunterian Oration before the Royal College of Surgeons in 1840, Joseph Henry Green, the former demonstrator of anatomy from Guy's during Keats's tenure there, invokes Oceanus's image of the forest tree that arises from dull albeit vivifying soil to bear creatures of light. The metaphor is a familiar one, common to the rhetoric of organic growth in Romantic thinkers from Blake to Erasmus Darwin, but its use by Green and by the poet of *Hyperion* is significant because it is specifically

evolutionist in its invocation and deliberately evocative of both the physiological and the transcendental theories of evolution known to Romantic thought.
Oceanus's "eagles golden-feather'd," offspring of "proud forests," are creatures
as real as those depicted in their special form by Buffon and Lamarck as well
as imaginative creations of perception; his speech to the displaced Titans is
as much a pragmatic statement on the inevitable laws of nature as it is an
elaborate metaphysical construct on the necessary evolution of mind and
imagination in the perception of beauty. Green, also, describes the pattern of
animal creation as gleaned from his practical knowledge of anatomy, physiology, and natural history, but his concept of evolution borrows from Schelling's
metaphysical notion that "all birth is a birth out of darkness into light" and
beyond that from Van Helmont's abstract theory of creation as material and
immaterial light[2] to posit a larger pattern of perceptual evolution.

Oceanus's eagles belong to the "region of purer light" invoked by Green;
Green's delineation of "the great march of nature," wherein "nothing is left
behind, and every former step contains the promise and prophecy of that
which is to follow," likewise presumes an evolution of mind prior to the
physiological evolution in nature known to his audience of physicians and
surgeons. Nature gathers strength (or sense) for a higher and more determined ascent parallel to the stages of development in perceptual evolution or
the imaginative intuition of beauty; for Green, as for the wiser Titans of
Hyperion, the evolutionary concept of comparative or progressive perfection
applies alike to matter and mind, and the perceptions of both admit of no
perfected completion.

"Whence that completed form of all completeness? / Whence came that
high perfection of all sweetness?" Endymion asks of the moon (I, 606–7), a
question that his poet knows cannot be answered. As Oceanus's speech in
Hyperion and the practical knowledge of the Romantic evolutionists attest,
there is no "high perfection" or "completeness" in nature, only progressive
"fresh perfection," the vital dynamic born of the "energy of life" described by
Green. Prichard's summary in 1829 of what his generation of physicians knew
of the evolution of life spoke of the perfection of living forms as limited at
once by time and by the challenge of surpassing novelty:

> To exist in successive generations, which, one after another, rise, flourish, and
> decay; . . . to assume a particular form; *to subsist in perfection for a definite space of time;*
> and then, after giving origin to new germs or rudiments . . . to fall at length a prey to
> the dissolving powers of the external elements, are properties common to all
> organized beings; *common alike to the lords of the creation, and to the pot-herbs and legumes*
> which contribute to their daily food.[3]

The same limitations applied, the *Naturphilosophen* had said, to the development of creatural nervous systems and the advance of mind in man. Coleridge, as early as 1817 (as we discussed in Part II), saw the living species as

progressive degrees or "intensities" of life power, with each fresh albeit limited perfection representing "some intenser form of reality;" "the degrees or
intensities of Life" in the overall ascent of creative power (which Coleridge,
following Schelling, called "potences") consisted in "the progressive realization" of the *tendency to individuation*" of life and, hence, greater individuation in
the life form was to be equated with greater intensity, beauty, or realization of
the "true Idea of Life."[4] The transcendental physiology orated in J. H. Green's
Hunterian Lecture of 1840 was a translation into the language of contemporary science of Coleridge's ideas on the evolution of life and perception; it
occurs by way of Green's own rereading through the lens of medical physiology of Coleridge's German inspirations, Schelling, Herder and Oken.

Irritability and sensibility, for the Romantic physiologists as for Green, were
evolutionary signposts of the degree of life energy or intensity in the given
organism; as the rudimentary expressions of the presence of a nervous system
and brain, they were also proof for Green's transcendental physiology of the
necessary evolution of perception. The presence of a nervous system and brain
is clear signal of "an inward and central unity" in the creature, according to
Green, and the full "evolution of life into sensibility" occurs "when the power of
sensibility becomes central and predominant;" in mammals, "the superordina-
tion of the Sensibility is ultimately accomplished."[5] But feeling implies knowledge of and sensitivity to self in Green's vital dynamics: "If the aim of animated
being be the achievement of sensibility, and of the subordination of the inferior powers thereto, by which the animal exists from itself, in itself, and,
though imperfectly, for itself, in order to the full presentation of this ultimate
end, nature must not only feel, she must know her own being; that is, mind
must be superadded to life."[6] Sensibility is the self-reflection of life: "In other
words, in the functions of sensibility, it exists for itself as life; but the self-
existence still remains as an alien and inexplicable thing, unless it shall exist
for itself likewise reflectively, not as life merely, but as mind. The self-reflection
must itself be reflected."[7] Coleridge's metaphysical equation of the degree of
intensity in life power with the potency of individuality of life expression
becomes, in the physiological vision of the physician Green, an inspired equation of living sensibility and perceptual sensitivity. Physical self-realization
becomes sensory-cum-mental self-knowledge. Both are expressions—in degrees of sensitivity—of perceptual vision.

Speaking as a physiologist to others concerned with the natural history of
life, Green saw nothing unexpected in advising the members of the Royal
College of Surgeons in 1840 that they should conduct their research knowing
that "the object of the history of nature" was to be "preface and portion of the
history of man;" that their very "knowledge of nature" must be seen "as a
branch of self-knowledge and outwardly realized history of our own consciousness and conscious being."[8] The study of nature leads not simply to the study
of man but, more accurately, to the study of mind and consciousness. As
Oceanus in *Hyperion* once equated living "might" with the perception of beauty

and the intuitive ability to self-reflect and know otherness, Green now defines life power in terms of mind and perceptual will as the originator of distinctions in the sensitivities or intensities of life: "It is then in the human mind that we seek the ground and origin of the assumption of power, cause, efficiency; and this ground we readily trace in the mind as that ultimate fact of the consciousness, which we call Will, as the power essentially of origination;" furthermore, "it cannot be denied that, in attributing powers to outward nature, and in ascribing its changes to these as causes, the human mind silently transfers its own constitution to the outward, and assumes that the subjective ground of nature is in kind one with man's inward being."[9] The subjective philosophy of Coleridge and the *Naturphilosophen* thus becomes Green's objective truth, a cumulative medical and artistic vision, a practical philosophic message fit for the ears of the physicians and surgeons of 1840.

Evolution for Keats, whether it be of life forms or their nervous systems or human minds or the perception of beauty by scientist or artist, is always comparative and progressive and always bound by laws of finitude. The 19 March section of the long epistle to the George Keatses begins with a comparison of instinct in man and hawk:

> The greater part of Men make their way with the same instinctiveness, the same unwandering eye from their purposes, the same animal eagerness as the Hawk—The Hawk wants a Mate, so does the Man—look at them both they set about it and procure on[e] in the same manner—They want both a nest and they both set about one in the same manner—they get their food in the same manner—The noble animal Man for his amusement smokes his pipe—the Hawk balances about the Clouds—that is the only difference of their leisures.

Instinct and the same animal eagerness and commonality of life purpose connect hawk and man in Keats's natural history. The existential similarity between humans and very real hawks leads Keats to speculate on the marked change and progress of intellect between species real and imaginary, between animals, mankind, and "superior beings"—eagles golden feathered or creatures of purer light:

> May there not be superior beings amused with any graceful, though instinctive attitude my mind m[a]y fall into, as I am entertained with the alertness of a Stoat or the anxiety of a Deer? Though a quarrel in the streets is a thing to be hated, the energies displayed in it are fine; the commonest Man shows a grace in his quarrel—By a superior being our reasoning[s] may take the same tone—though erroneous they may be fine—This is the very thing in which consists poetry; and if so it is not so fine a thing as philosophy—For the same reason that an eagle is not so fine a thing as a truth—[10]

In the characteristic reasoning of Romantic evolution, the very likeness between creatures highlights their difference and reveals the pattern of ascending being. The instinct of man and hawk is the same, but the many forms of grace revealed by stoat, deer, eagle, "commonest" man, and superior being, while related as expressions of advancing sensibility in the "grand march of intellect," serve nevertheless to heighten distinction, individuality, particularity, and a specific perfection of perceptual being. Where the evolutionary speculation of Alexander Pope's angels may have seen linkage in natural creation and shown a Newton where we show an ape, Romantic evolutionists and poets like Keats read in the kinships of related nature the promise of greater complexity and individuality, fresh perfection, and finer beauty. Life is the tendency to individuation, as Coleridge said, and greater individuality shows a higher intensity or concentration of life energy. The energy is the same but differences, between species or within species—like those distinguishing Oceanus and Clymene from the other Titans in *Hyperion*—point the path of perceptual advance and an escalation in the perception of beauty.

An eagle may not be so fine a thing as a truth, nor poetry so fine a thing as philosophy; nevertheless, in Romantic evolution, eagles can be real and conceptual creations simultaneously. In Keats's version of this evolution, moreover, the truths of philosophy are to be proved upon the pulses or mortal realizations of beauty, through the retrospective prophecy and healing vision of the poet. The Keatsian aspiration, declared as early as 1816 in "Sleep and Poetry," is to "do the deed / That my own soul has to itself decreed," namely, to develop a paradoxical poetic vision, a bird's-eye view from within, that can "pass the countries that I see / In long perspective" and yet simultaneously "and continually / Taste their pure fountains" (97–101). Poetic evolution, like the transcendental evolution proposed by Schelling and others after him, faces forward in long perspective and comprehends its own self-generated design in retrospection; its message is immediate existential truth. It begins passage in the realm "Of Flora, and old Pan," reading there "A lovely tale of human life;" it passes "on, and on" through to Apollo's vales of "almond blossoms and rich cinnamon," that region of sense and intensity explored at length in the "Ode on Melancholy." These seemingly unmixed joys of sensibility and sight are then passed by, transcended "for a nobler life" where the poet finds fit vision in "the agonies, the strife / Of human hearts" (101–25). This vision of the human heart comprehends or encompasses both the metaphysical "Shapes of delight, of mystery, and fear" and a physical "sense of real things" come "doubly strong" in its perception of beauty (138, 157).

"We have all of us one human heart." The recollection of Wordsworth's line from "The Old Cumberland Beggar" in the March 1819 letter cited earlier supported and encouraged Keats's musings on the evolutionary relation of perceptual powers in creatures from stoats to humans to imaginative "superior being." Musings on Wordsworth's greater anxiety for humanity and what this means in terms of poetic achievement "—whether or no he has an extended vision or a circumscribed grandeur—whether he is an eagle in his nest, or on the wing—" in an 1818 letter prompt a speculative disquisition on

the evolution of individual human perception and conclude that Wordsworth's greater humanity represents a poetic *and* perceptual advance in the
development of genius.

> Well, I compare human life to a large Mansion of Many Apartments, two of which I
> can only describe, the doors of the rest being as yet shut upon me—The first we step
> into we call the infant or thoughtless Chamber, in which we remain as long as we do
> not think—We remain there a long while, and notwithstanding the doors of the
> second Chamber remain wide open, showing a bright appearance, we care not to
> hasten to it; but are at length imperceptibly impelled by the awakening of the
> thinking principle—within us—we no soon[er] get into the second Chamber, which I
> shall call the Chamber of Maiden-Thought, than we become intoxicated with the
> light and the atmosphere, we see nothing but pleasant wonders, and think of
> delaying there for ever in delight: However among the effects this breathing is father
> of is that tremendous one of sharpening one's vision into the heart and nature of
> Man—of convincing ones nerves that the World is full of Misery and Heartbreak,
> Pain, Sickness and oppression—whereby this Chamber of Maiden Thought be-
> comes gradually darken'd and at the same time on all sides of it many doors are set
> open—but all dark—all leading to dark passages—We see not the ballance of good
> and evil. We are in a Mist—*We* are now in that state—We feel the "burden of the
> Mystery," To this point was Wordsworth come, as far as I can conceive when he wrote
> "Tintern Abbey" and it seems to me that his Genius is explorative of those dark
> Passages. Now if we live, and go on thinking, we too shall explore them.[11]

Since C. D. Thorpe's able discussion of this letter,[12] critics have found in it
ample evidence for Keats's philosophy and the formation of his aesthetic
theory. For our purposes, what cannot be forgotten is the sequence between
Keats's reading of Buffon and the formulations here on the evolution of
perception and, specifically, poetic perception. Keats sees the development of
human life in terms of mind and intellectual advancement; he sees the absorbing awareness of misery, heartbreak, pain, and sickness as an expression of
advanced nervous sympathy and vocational conviction in poet or physician;
he sees Wordsworth's exploration of the dark passages of the mind and his
attempt to medicine the mind through poetry as testaments to the further
perfection of human genius in a prescient and humane Romantic age.

The poet of Tintern Abbey is deeper than all previous poets, including
Milton and the poet-physician of *Endymion*, because of his intuitive concern
with the unexplored regions of the psyche—or heart: "He is a Genius and
superior [to] us, in so far as he can, more than we, make discoveries, and shed
a light on them." Wordsworth's intellectual superiority over Milton depended
less upon "individual greatness of Mind" and "more upon the general and
gregarious advance of intellect" proposed by the evolutionists of the time. But
it is also true that Milton's philosophy "may be tolerably understood by one
not much advanced in years" because the poet of *Paradise Lost* "did not think
into the human heart, as Wordsworth has done." Gifted with the "extended

vision" of an eagle, Wordsworth is saved from any other parallel with a bird of prey by his concern for humanity. Wordsworth's special ability to "see into the life of things," manifest in "Tintern Abbey" according to Keats, is a unique advance of mind in his time: it proved "there is really a grand march of intellect—, It proves that a mighty providence subdues the mightiest Minds to the service of the time being, whether it be in human Knowledge or Religion."[13] Wordsworth's "extended vision" was an individual achievement for him personally but it is also, as poetry, an extraordinary occasion of creative reaching—what Lamarck may have called a novel speciation event punctuating an equilibrium of natural truth, or what Schelling might have called a sudden point of light appearing to arrest and to transcend current consciousness and extend yet further a providential escalation of perceptual being. Wordsworth's special humanity advanced the consciousness of his species. Or more simply in the words of Keats: Wordsworth's intuition into the human heart became, once placed in service to the time being and received into the world as poetry or perfected form, both his and not his, like the patched relics and garments of a saint. Wordsworth indeed "martyrs himself to the human heart,"[14] and his evolutionary act of self-sacrifice for the fresh perceptions of future generations ensures, at least for the time being, that a poem can be as fine and perfected a thing as a truth.

From the evidence of the letters we know that Keats read the works of Milton in tandem with those of Buffon during the spring of 1818: the comments on water and matter constituting the habitable globe in the 24 March letter to Rice, which have been traced by Atkinson to specific sections in Buffon, begins with mention of Milton's cumulative contribution to the world and concludes with speculations on the size of Milton's brain and its consequences; a 27 April letter to Reynolds, which directly precedes the 3 May evolution-of-mind-inspired "Mansion of Life" letter discussed above, notes that the poet has lately feasted "upon Milton."[15] It is hardly unexpected, therefore, that Keats should couch his formulations on the evolutionary advance of consciousness and the development of the aesthetic sense of a poet in terms of the comparative poetic achievements of Wordsworth and Milton. This interlacing of evolutionary concepts from contemporary physical science and *Naturphilosophie* with thoughts on the perception of beauty and the evolution of a poet reiterates our understanding that the idea of evolution pervades the subjects addressed by *Hyperion* and *The Fall of Hyperion* and carries important ramifications for any discussion of the successes and failures of both poems. It underlies, as we shall see, Keats's rejection of Milton and his formulation of an aesthetic theory for himself that in contradistinction to Milton's mode of perceiving beauty incorporates evolutionary notions of finitude and self-sacrifice and rejects predatory "might":

Very good—but my dear fellow I must let you know that as there is ever the same quantity of matter constituting this habitable globe—as the ocean notwithstanding the enormous changes and revolutions taking place in some or other of its demesnes—notwithstanding Waterspouts whirlpools and mighty Rivers emptying themselves into it, it still is made up of the same bulk—nor ever varies the number of its Atoms—And as a certain bulk of Water was instituted at the Creation—so very likely a certain portion of intellect was spun forth into the thin Air for the Brains of Man to prey upon it—You will see my drift without any necessary parenthesis. That which is contained in the Pacific and lie in the hollow of the Caspian—that which was in Miltons head could not find Room in Charles the seconds—he like a Moon attracted Intellect to its flow—it has not ebbed yet—but has left the shore pebble all bare—I mean all Bucks Authors of Hengist and Castlereaghs of the present day—who without Milton's gormandizing might have been all wise Men—[16]

A finite quantity of matter and a certain bulk of water, as Buffon said, were instituted at creation; life evolved and developed, as Lamarck said, through the composition and decomposition of these finite substances. Intellect developed, according to the *Naturphilosophen*, according to the same conceptual patterns as physical evolution. Keats assumes all this and proposes a like finitude of matter and mind, even as he rejects the transcendental evolutionists' idealistic vision of unexhaustible creative perfection. Only a certain portion of intellectual energy was spun forth for the brains of men to prey upon. Because of Milton's extraordinary perceptual needs, because of his conceptual "appetences," because of his continuing and absorbing ability to draw intellectual nutriment to the perfection and apprehension of his creative endeavors, he "left the shore pebble all bare" and depleted the very life energy of future creative minds. Milton's gormandizing brain fed too deeply upon a finite source for its creative perfections. Keats began his evolutionary-aesthetic musings with the question "Did Milton do more good or ha[r]m to the world?" His answer would be that Milton thwarted the potential perfections of his own and future generations. Milton's accomplishments, however perfect, depleted and undermined other existences because they were necessarily predatory and expressions of intellectual "might." They were the immediate occasion of Charles II's moderate stupidity, they led to a rash of bad dramatists in the next century, and were probably a causative reason for the Castlereaghs of Keats's time.

If Keats's evolutionary deductions vis-à-vis the size of Milton's brain seem remarkably presumptive, we counter with the knowledge that Keats did come to believe that it was *Paradise Lost* as a perfected form, an intellectual version of Lamarckian "dead matter," that blocked the living vision of the poet of *The Fall of Hyperion*. We know that Milton's genius proved a harmful influence upon Keats's perceptual aspirations, and we have the young poet's own explanation in September 1819 of how the Miltonic influence could prevail as a dominating and predatory genius upon his imagination:

> The Paradise lost though so fine in itself is a curruption of our Language—it should be kept as it is unique—a curiosity, a beautiful and grand Curiosity. The most remarkable Production of the world—A northern dialect accommodating itself to

greek and latin inversions and intonations. The purest english I think—or what ought to be the purest—is Chatterton's—The Language had existed long enough to be entirely uncorrupted of Chaucer's gallicisms and still the old words are used—Chatterton's language is entirely northern—I prefer the native music of it to Milton's cut by feet I have but lately stood on my guard against Milton. Life to him would be death to me. Miltonic verse cannot be written but it [in] the vein of art—I wish to devote myself to another sensation—.[17]

The most remarkable production of the world is just that: an accomplished, finished production, a fossilized existence of a former mode of aesthetic being. Keats rejects the example of this existence as a representation of perceptual history foreign to contemporary modes of aesthetic perception and chooses instead the "native music" of his evolutionary contemporaries, Chatterton and Wordsworth. The very means by which Milton achieved the aesthetic perfection of *Paradise Lost* are the reason that he cannot be a good example for Romantic imaginations: "Milton in every instance pursues his imagination to the utmost—he is 'sagacious of his Quarry,' he sees Beauty on the wing, pounces upon it and gorges it to the producing his essential verse."[18] The predatory pursuit of beauty by the imagination, which was the mode of perception that Milton used to finest effect to seize and fix, or "station" his poetic quarry, was an expression of aesthetic might and a reflection of the evolutionary level of Miltonic perception. Milton's gormandizing brain and undermining influence upon future generations of artists paralleled the original gorging of beauty in *Paradise Lost* to produce "essential verse"; as Milton's imagination preyed on living beauty there, so also has the powerful rhetoric of his verse preyed upon the perceptual substance of artists ever since; his kind of genius has thus occasioned and then ensured the sacrifice of generations.

The predatory instinct in art becomes the dominant characteristic of that art according to Keats's evolutionary aesthetics. Hence, the writing of Miltonic verse in a Romantic age is a deathly harking back to an earlier and less humanitarian mode of existence, to a survivalist seizure of beauty: "Life to him would be death to me," an artful revival of a once valid and living predatory means of comprehending beauty. Instead, Keats would devote himself "to another sensation:" he would advocate for himself and his generation of poets a passive receptivity to beauty, "another" more advanced evolutionary mode of perception that shuns the consumptive appropriation of beauty and forswears preemptive "might" for negative capability and sacrificial retrospective prophecy. By it, as we shall see from an examination of the predicaments of the Titans and Apollo in the Hyperion poems, the Titans peremptory beauty of power as a depleting force in a finite environment must be supplanted by Apollo's receptive and self-depleting sensitivity to beauty.

H. W. Piper has proposed that Keats "learned to see beauty as the purpose of a developing universe" from the "cold philosophy of his medical school"—

specifically, from a paper on natural selection according to "beauty" by W. C. Wells, a physician to St. Thomas's Hospital during Keats's tenure at Guy's.[19] In his paper published in 1818, which was discussed before the Physical Society of Guy's Hospital prior to being read before the Royal Society in 1813, Wells invoked the idea of natural selection that had been suggested earlier by Buffon, Herder, Lamarck, and Erasmus Darwin and tied it to the notion of physical beauty. Given what he saw to be a pattern in human history wherein darker races were successively enslaved by lighter-skinned races, Wells supposed a link between appearance and the potential for civilization in man, between outward deformity of form and inward or intellectual limitation:

> Lastly: it appears probable from the reliques of ancient art, that the early inhabitants of Egypt were of the negro race. If then the negroes of Africa were ever to be civilized, their woolly hair and deformed features would, perhaps, in a long series of years, like those of the Egyptians, be changed. On the other hand, their present external appearance may possibly be regarded not only as a sign, but as a cause of their degraded condition, by preventing in some unknown way the proper development of their faculties; for the African negroes have in all ages been slaves; and the negroes in the eastern seas are in no instance, I believe, masters of their handsomer neighbours. . . .[20]

Beauty appropriates from lesser beauty much as life consumes lesser life in the evolutionary struggle for survival, and superior beauty becomes the sign of superior physical organization and, most of all, superior intelligence or perceptual ability. Wells's presumptive premise for his equation of life power, beauty, and civilized "might" was, of course, the European notion of what constituted physical beauty; Blumenbach and William Lawrence among others before Wells had proposed as much in their natural histories of man, and the phrenologists had presumed as much in their gradations of human skulls by race and origin.

Keats almost certainly derived the ideas of Oceanus's declared natural law in *Hyperion*, "That first in beauty should be first in might," from contemporary evolutionists and men like Wells. It would be a mistake to deduce from this that Keats is merely expressing a version of natural selection in his poem, or, worse, that he is invoking a specific Western concept of what constitutes the beautiful to support his aesthetic theory. Keats's notion of beauty is at once more diffuse and more specifically evolutionary in the perceptual sense than any prevailing opinion on the subject he might have encountered. Beauty in Keats is indeed tied to life power, as it is with evolutionists like Wells, Lawrence, and Blumenbach. But by life power (as we saw in Part II) the poet means not "might" in the predatory sense of being able to appropriate other (lesser) life forms for self-survival but, rather, life intensity or an acute vulnerability to external forces and, therefore, extinction. In this regard, beauty for Keats may well be a perceptual sensitivity or receptivity to beauty. Clymene's and Oceanus's ability to sense a new and different beauty in the new order, we recall, proved them to be more perceptually advanced than their fellow Titans in *Hyperion* even as they are judged to be weak and docile, at once "over-wise" and "over-foolish" (II, 309–10). They knew with pain the new beauty and it rendered them passive; their ability to imagine or feel without possessing the life intensity of Apollo and the young god of the sea, furthermore, occasioned the ascendancy of the new breed of gods.

From this context Apollo's purported greater beauty, especially from the evidence of Book III of *Hyperion* as we shall see, could well be his higher ability to perceive beauty in the life forms about him; to see through apparent deformity and beyond "eternal fierce destruction;" to comprehend the beauty of life not through an appropriation into the self of external feeling matter but through a negative capability for feeling sympathy without an imposition or a loss of the self; to perform a gigantic imaginative act of self-sacrifice "portion'd to a giant nerve." All this becomes more plausible when we realize that the perception of beauty described in *The Fall of Hyperion*, as it is embodied in the intense and brooding sensitivity of Apollo's poet, is synonymous with the full apprehension of pain. Pain is a prerequisite for the ascent of life into "some intenser form of reality." It requires as such an evolution of imagination parallel to the necessary ascension of mortal pain.

Chapter 21

The Freaks of Imagination

The creative perceptions of an immortal imagination, according to the *Natur-philosophen*, engender the mortal realizations of beauty in nature. Vision of these natural beauties by a creative mind, according to the Keats of 1818, will engender an evolution of imagination and comprehensive advance in parallel stages of perceptual intensity. The would-be poet's projected tour of the North of England will be "a sort of Prologue to the Life I intend to pursue:" "I will clamber through the Clouds and exist. I will get such an accumulation of stupendous recollections that as I walk through the suburbs of London I may not see them—I will stand upon Mount Blanc and remember this coming Summer when I intend to straddle ben Lomond—with my Soul!" Stupendous recollections and perceptual anticipations of these memories will nurture the imaginative evolution of the poet and foster his future artistic creations. Keats acknowledges, furthermore, the multiple advances and false starts involved in every creative gesture: "I have ever been too sensible of the labyrinthian path to eminence in Art (judging from Poetry) ever to think I understood the emphasis of Painting," he says to Haydon in the same letter of April 1818. "The innumerable compositions and decompositions which take place between the intellect and its thousand materials before it arrives at that trembling delicate and snail-horn perception of Beauty—I know not your many havens of intenseness—nor ever can know them—."[1] The language of physical evolution and biological chemistry can thus chart the labyrinthine path to eminence in art taken by the creative imagination; it can delineate the innumerable perceptual actions that take place between the intellect and its materials, highlight the interstices and false starts between these actions, and mark the many havens of intenseness (or pain) reached and surpassed in the attainment of a particular "trembling delicate and snail-horn perception of Beauty."

False starts in the mortal realization of beauty, in nature as in mind, consti-tute important signposts in the evolutionary advance of each. They are the natural imperfections that reveal best the aspirations of biological and artistic perfectioning. An earlier chapter of this part has noted the importance of the embryologists' study of fetal malformations to the early-nineteenth-century's theorizing on vitality and evolution. The subject here is the imaginative implications of deformity and monstrosity—as much for the imagination itself as for the creations engendered through it—in the aesthetic evolution proposed by Keats.

To the retrospective vision of the Romantic evolutionists, malformed embryos revealed, by default, signs of the mysterious pattern of evolutionary life. A corollary issue for the philosophers of mind and speculative physiologists of the period was the question of the mind's influence through the agencies of emotion or imagination upon embryonic formation. The eighteenth century, largely because of Maupertuis's study of pygmies, giants, albinos, polydactyls, and other "monstrous" mutants, saw the beginnings of a scientific interest in the various causes of mutations and birth defects. An important section of Maupertuis's *Vénus Physique* (1745) was devoted to the possible effects of maternal imagination upon the fetus. Molecules of matter were endowed with intelligence, desire, aversion, and memory in primitive form, according to Maupertuis, and hence made possible a principle of sympathy within the organism. Because of the extensive connection between fetus and mother, a violent commotion in the humors or blood of the latter could affect the whole process of development in the former; emotions of fear, or high anxiety, or horrific imaginative sympathy—of, say, the mother's witnessing of executions or torture—could retard growth or occasion gross deformation of the infant.[2] Buffon (Keats's first source for evolutionary thought) considered Maupertuis to be one who had "reasoned better than all those who have written before him on this subject" of generation, and he described the *Vénus Physique* as a treatise that "although very short, assembles more philosophical ideas than there are alltold in several great volumes on generation. . . ."[3] Buffon addressed the issue of maternal imagination and the fetus in his long chapter in *Histoire Naturelle* on human generation and embryonic development; he agreed with Maupertuis and his followers that violent emotional or imaginative agitation of the mother could result in deformity or death of the fetus and used the newest embryological data to illustrate how maternal affliction of the senses or mind could affect uterine harmony and traumatize fetal formation into monstrous growth or deformation.[4]

"*If a woman* (saith Lemnius) *at the time of her conception, think of another man present or absent, the child will be like him,*" Burton proposed in his discussion of the effects of the unhealthy imagination upon conception in *The Anatomy of Melancholy.*[5] Burton's proposal, however ironic, was a theory that Goethe gave fictional form in *Die Walverwandtschaften* (*Elective Affinities;* 1809) and that Erasmus Darwin gave scientific credit in *Zoonomia.* To a Romantic age that found creative source and perhaps belief in what Keats called the sanctity of the imagination and the holiness of the heart's affections, speculations such as this on the charged effect of the imagination upon physical and perceptual creations were imminently verifiable.

Benjamin Bablot's publication in 1788 of his *Dissertation sur le pouvoir de l'imagination des femmes enceintes* marked the beginning of a renewed interest in the subject during the Romantic age. Bablot defended seventeenth-century notions like those of Burton of the direct influence of the imagination upon the fetus and invoked Mesmer's theory of hypnotic influence to support his arguments that a disturbed maternal imagination could produce disease and deformity in the fetus as well as its mother. In example of how a mother's imagination might reflect upon fetal formation, Bablot "compared the mother to a painter and the fetus to a canvas." The agency of spirits or nerve fluid played "the role of the painter's brush. As the imagination of the painter produces a picture on the canvas, so the imagination of the mother can sketch on the fetus the features of different external objects that she had thought about."[6] The mother's imagination served thus as a kind of camera lucida; what she saw of terror or sublimity at a distance could be reproduced upon the immediate blank features of her child. Bablot's fanciful connection between real objects envisioned by a mother and the parallel shape of birthmarks painted on her child were easily refuted by an invocation of Buffon and Maupertuis on the subject, but the issues raised by his treatise on the overall connection between parental imagination and procreation endured for a generation of Romantic scientists and metaphysicians. When Erasmus Darwin drafted his chapter on generation in *Zoonomia*, he felt compelled to theorize on the effects of the paternal imagination during conception upon fetal formation. The male imagination could impress Hartleian "vibrations" upon the embryo, and the father's ideas during intercourse could imprint their visual impressions upon the sex and features of his offspring: "Hence I conclude, that the act of generation cannot exist without being accompanied with ideas, and that a man must have at that time either a general idea of his own male form, or of the form of his male organs; or an idea of the female form, or of her organs; and that this marks the sex, and the peculiar resemblance of the child to either parent."[7]

By the terms of Romantic conception, the offspring of procreative yearning embodied aspiration in its physical *and* imaginative form. We are fully what our parents conceive or, in the case of Erasmus Darwin, what our fathers think. Goethe's painterly portrait of the elective affinities that operate in human relationships (*Die Walverwandtshaften* was itself a concept borrowed from contemporary chemistry) invoked the paternal and maternal imaginations for the creation of its climactic, composite product. The child of a loveless but legal union between Charlotte and Eduard, conceived during a moment of intense and passionate yearning for absent individuals they secretly love, is born bearing the features of the lovers for whom they aspire; born to Charlotte and Eduard, the child is the conceptual progeny of Ottolie and the Captain. The conceptions of the mind can thus powerfully overwhelm, to form or deform, the productions of the body. The jars filled with freak embryos and monstrous births in the Hunterian Museum and on the walls of operating theatres of London hospitals like Guy's and St. Thomas's testify to the widespread interest in fetal malformations during the early nineteenth century; almost certainly, they provided fuel for contemporary speculations among metaphysicians on the imaginative occasion of these deformities. John Haighton's inclusion of a discourse on freak births in his 1817 lectures on midwifery to the students of Guy's Hospital, and his notation that fetal deformities seemed to originate with the very beginnings of the embryo and were perhaps occasioned at conception,[8] are specific testimony to the immediate medical import of the issues raised by the Romantic age's speculative connection of imaginative and physical creation.

The peculiar creations of nature, those freaks of form or surface that disrupted the uniformity of species, were emblems of nature's capacity to blunder, its capacity to evade the stasis of perfection. Read by the evolutionists of the Romantic age as signposts to the possibility of fresh perfection and deformed aspirations to the ideal of future generations, they were at once the pattern and the manifestation of the evolution of imaginative mind. The issues of conceptual deformity find specific aesthetic possibility in the circumstances of Keats's poetry from *Endymion* to *Lamia*. For example, in Book I of his story Endymion blushes for the "freaks of melancholy" (I. 962) that simultaneously manifest the aspirations and betray the false starts in the evolution of his poetic psyche. His failures at imaginative vision and his abortive attempts at self-conception become thus the shadowy points that delineate his real journey to poetic realization. The poem *Lamia* presents another and quite different variation on the evolutionary consequences of imaginative misperception. We customarily treat Lamia as an evolutionary freak because of her ambiguous place between species, and we usually ascribe her imaginative origin to the fanciful albeit deformed creatures, the lamiae, described by Burton in *The Anatomy of Melancholy*. But Keats's *Lamia* illustrates the pattern and consequences of evolutionary malformation in many more ways than Burton's story would suggest. Beyond her female form and her preexistence as an immortal serpent, Lamia exists in the present of the poem's world as an imaginative deformity born of the misconceptions of Lycius and Apollonius. She is, first, a product of Lycius's adolescent imagination, a beautiful fantasy improperly but powerfully conceived by the partly evolved conceptual apparatus of a young philosopher trained only in sophistry. When she is conceived by the sophist Apollonius at the end of the poem, she fares no better and finds shape as an evanescent serpent, a multicolored ugliness or legendary fantasy that does not deserve to exist in a world of cold philosophy. Seen through Newtonian whiteness and a blinded imagination, Lamia is what Apollonius and Lycius *think* and what their feeble imaginations envision. They cannot imagine her as she can (or would) imagine herself. Lamia's attempts at self-fashioning throughout the poem fail because they must depend upon the imaginative skills of creatures outside (and perhaps below) her own creatural aspiration. Her many forms are evolutionary shortcuts that reveal the freakish consequences of creation born of conflicting conceptual aspirations and seen without the appropriate conceptual skills and retrospective vision of Romantic evolutionist or artist. As a conception of Keats, Lamia is clearly and deliberately flawed: she is a creature of imagination "brought beyond its proper bound."

An earlier poem, "The Eve of St. Mark," presents a more startling vision of evolutionary consequence and imaginative defection. The creatures graven on the "warm angled winter screen" of Bertha's fire in "The Eve of St. Mark" could be taken from a natural history picture book: "doves of Siam, / Lima mice, / And legless birds of paradise, / Macaw, and tender av'davat, / And silken-furred Angora cat" (77–82). But in the firelight of an overheated and immature imagination they are "many monsters," conceptual portents that would "fill / The room with wildest forms and shades" (78, 84–85). Furthermore, and in example of how the fanciful conception of the mind can overwhelm all other creation, they seem to mirror the "golden broideries" of the "curious volume" Bertha has been reading, where "the stars of heaven, and angels' wings, / Martyrs in a fiery blaze, / Azure saints mid silver rays, / Aaron's breastplate, and the seven / Candlesticks" of St. John are all jumbled together in freakish juxtaposition in the single creature or imaginative creation that is the legend of St. Mark. The "Cherubim and golden mice" of St. Mark's legend, and the "Lima mice / And legless birds of paradise" of Bertha's fire screen (30–38, 79–80) are parallel artistic visions, fanciful imaginative constructs of seemingly impossible creations that are nevertheless true to the evolutionary condition of the imagination of the "poor cheated soul" who finds herself "taken captive" and "dazed with saintly imageries" (25–27, 56, 69) on the eve of St. Mark. The ghostly deformities envisioned by Bertha's imagination imprint a monstrous frightfulness on the already fanciful creations peopling St. Mark's legend; they also make true and larger than life the decorative creatures borrowed from natural history that the artisan has pictured imaginatively upon the fire screen. Bertha, hysterical and overwrought, is what she beholds upon the page and screen, and her imagination bears the evolutionary imprint of its own deceptive origins.

The unfinished fragment of Hyperion, itself cast as an epic of power and development in life, is perhaps the most sustained poetic expression by Keats on the evolutionary consequences of imaginative misconception. The Titans were a breed of giants in legend. Keats marks their monstrous stature and connections to the extinct fossils "Of beast, behemoth, and leviathan" that inhabit Endymion's "monstrous sea" when he describes these evolutionary fragments "Of nameless monster" to be "of Saturn's vintage." (III, 129–36; 69). But the "mammoth-brood" that peoples the desolate terrain of Hyperion like prehistoric stone monuments in "dismal cirque . . . upon a forlorn moor" (I, 164; II, 35) is also a company of shadows and ghostly forms. Hyperion addresses his fellow Titans as "O dreams of day and night! / O monstrous forms! O effigies of pain!" (I, 228). They are monstrous fantastical forms and shadowy manifestations of real pain and, as such, both substantial and imaginative creations of unknown origin. As "dreams of day and night" and "Phantoms pale ... thrice horrible and cold" (I, 255–56), they bear distinct connection to the shadows and giant eagle's wings that seem to inhabit the peripheries of Hyperion's palace and darken his vision (I, 183–85); meanwhile, these "shady visions" (I, 244) that Hyperion believes he sees, are a gigantic version of the self-engendered shadows Bertha imagines in "The Eve of St. Mark" and as such are symptomatic of the disturbed imagination and its potential for creative malformation. The Titans are simultaneously monstrous substance and horrific apparition. Hyperion both conceives and misconceives his fellow brood in his dream-invocation of them. Their species' predicament in the poem is an evolutionary lesson in the formation of the real and the imaginary.

In *Vital Dynamics*, Joseph Henry Green proposed a principle of devolution as a necessary component to his doctrine of progressive perfection in the natural and conceptual forms. He speculated whether the promise of evolutionary ascent was reserved for only a few of a given species while the rest remained frozen in their condition until they came to serve by comparison as examples of the overall species' degradation in time:

[V]ariety of type, instead of being measured, as in all the orders of animals hitherto, by evidences of ascension in the scale of life, admits the application of a canon of progressive perfection only to a small number of the *mammalia*; while the rest must be contemplated as a degradation, or, to use the language of crystallography, as decrements from the human, assuming the human form as the ideal type of the whole class. In short, in all those classes or *genera* of the *mammalia* which would remain, and which could not without derangement of the universal *organismus* be lost, even when men, and men in the full prerogatives of humanity, shall exist in all the climes of the earth, and shall every where have civilized and humanized nature—in these, I say, the former scale of gradual ascent will still be demonstrable; but the rest can be considered only as mutilated and imperfect copies by an anticipation of the human, to be measured, not so much by what is possessed in each, as by what is wanted, and by the necessary influence and modifying effect of the latter on the former,—even as in the human being, that which would have been perseverance and fortitude, if a proportionate power of comparative judgment had been added, by the mere absence of this gift degenerates into brute and dogged obstinacy.[9]

A species or genera can contain principles of ascent and descent within itself: certain advanced qualities in some members of a species can highlight an implicit (and perhaps impending) devolution in the species as a whole. The absence of these special attributes in the majority of the species, meanwhile, reveals them to be imperfect anticipations or deformed expressions of the species as an ideal whole. The pattern holds true with regard to the spiritual or conceptual composition of a species or class: perseverance or fortitude in certain humans can degenerate into brute and dogged obstinacy in other humans, and the mere absence of comparative judgment in those who otherwise operate "in the full prerogatives of humanity" can highlight the point of their conceptual descent to brute comprehension and reveal them to be "decrements from the human."

Keats's mammoth but shadowy breed of Titans in *Hyperion* constitutes an imaginative version of this notion of apparent formation and inherent deformation within a species. Saturn and Hyperion are the leaders of the Titans; they exemplify, as such, the ideal of their physical and spiritual type. Oceanus and Clymene, on the one hand, and Enceladus, on the other, provide us with the comparative perspective on the Titans' fixed condition. In the unusual perceptual qualities possessed by Oceanus and Clymene, in their freak power to perceive alien beauty and acknowledge change, we see what it is that the Titans lack for their survival in a freshly perfected world. In the brute obstinacy and dogged immobility of Enceladus, degenerate attributes that are hardly apparent in leaders like Saturn and Hyperion, we comprehend the current deformity of the mammoth breed and the reason that they must become extinct.

Enceladus forms one of a group of Titans who are "the brawniest in assault": "Coeus, and Gyges, and Briareüs, / Typhon, and Dolor, and Porphyrion." Unlike Thea, Saturn, Hyperion, Oceanus, and Clymene, who are able to wander through the desolate regions of their world, these brawny Titans are fully immobilized, "pent in regions of laborious breath; / Dungeoned in opaque element, to keep / Their clenched teeth still clench'd, and all their limbs / Lock'd up like veins of metal, cramped and screw'd"; they are "Without a motion" and can feel nothing but dull, brute pain (II, 18–27). Among the Titans "chained in torture" and denied the freedom to wander, Enceladus is distinguished as more perfect by his power of partial motion and by his ability to speak and express emotion. We find "Shadow'd Euceladus" "on a crag's uneasy shelve, / Upon his elbow rais'd, all prostrate else" (II, 64–66), and he is the first among his group to see Saturn and shout, "Titans, behold your God!" (II, 110). Clearly, "huge Enceladus" represents his group of immobilized Titans and will speak for their perspective (II, 304). The change wrought in Enceladus's emotions "once tame and mild / As grazing ox unworried in the meads; / Now tiger-passion'd, lion-thoughted, wroth" (II, 66–69) may be appropriate to the occasion, but it is nonetheless fully symptomatic of the large-scale disturbance in the evolution of this species. Because Enceladus is passionate and wrathful where he was once properly tame and mild as befit his external form, his mental imbalance and overwrought condition manifest the devolution of his stricken tribe. His emotional disturbance, furthermore, reveals through its deforming influence on his perceptual powers the sad and imminent extinction of his race. His rousing speech to the Titans is an epiphany of their residual power, a brief manifestation of life energy that serves to illuminate the pathos of their fate:

> Speak! roar! shout! yell! ye sleepy Titans all.
> Do ye forget the blows, the buffets vile?
> Are ye not smitten by a youngling arm?
> Dost thou forget, sham Monarch of the Waves,
> Thy scalding in the seas? What, have I rous'd
> Your spleens with so few simple words as these?
> O joy! for now I see ye are not lost:
> O joy! for now I see a thousand eyes
> Wide glaring for revenge!'—
>
> . . . .
>
> "Now ye are flames, I'll tell you how to burn,
> And purge the ether of our enemies;
> How to feed fierce the crooked stings of fire,
> And singe away the swollen clouds of Jove,
> Stifling that puny essence in its tent.
> O let him feel the evil he hath done;
> For though I scorn Oceanus's lore,
> Much pain have I for more than loss of realms:
> The days of peace and slumberous calm are fled;
> Those days, all innocent of scathing war,
> When all the fair Existences of heaven
> Came open-eyed to guess what we would speak:—
> That was before our brows were taught to frown,
> Before our lips knew else but solemn sounds;
> That was before we knew the wingèd thing,
> Victory, might be lost, or might be won.
>   (Hyp., II, 316–42)

Enceladus speaks for the extinct creature. Only Keats, in an age most concerned with the fresh perfections of life, would seek to imagine and embody the experience of generic extinction. Enceladus's words of action do not match his energy of life: his "ponderous syllables, like sullen waves / In the half-glutted hollows of reef-rocks" (II, 305–6) come forth from a fulfilled and therefore dying creature; they are glutted with the futility and desperation appropriate to their speaker's doomed race. Enceladus's counsel of action and the use of limited power parallels the counsel of revenge of Moloch, "the strongest and the fiercest spirit" in Milton's Hell. Unlike Moloch, Enceladus seeks not so much the revenge born of limited might as an impossible regeneration of life—victory, lost or won—through a power less vital than that which has replaced it. The Titans cannot "purge the ether" of their "enemies," nor can they stifle the "puny essence" of new life in its tent because ether and essence are indestructible; most of all, they cannot make of their newly achieved mortality a future immortality. Enceladus has grossly misconceived the condition of his brethren; he, not Clymene or Oceanus, is "over-wise" and "over-foolish."

An imaginative proposition for salvation conceived by an ox that has been forced to think like a lion or tiger must bear all the marks of its bastard pedigree. Enceladus's speech stands as a conceptual freak and bears only the evolutionary significance of its deformity. It is false counsel because it is based on a misconception of former might as life. Enceladus counsels the use of limited and fast-waning power when he and his fellows have known only unlimited power: "days of peace and slumberous calm ... all innocent of scathing war," "When all the fair Existences of heaven / Came open-eyed to guess what we would speak." Since that time, "before our brows were taught to frown, / Before our lips knew else but solemn sounds," the Titans have experienced the consequence of finitude: imminent extinction. The finitude of life and mind, and of the poem's present, cannot regenerate a prior, perceived infinitude. The story of Hyperion and his giant breed, correctly conceived and imagined, must be about the fall of Hyperion. When Enceladus sees Saturn and declares, "Titans, behold your God!" at the start of the great debate in *Hyperion*, he is already wrong. His newly revealed deformity of form has anticipated a more serious malformation of perception. Saturn is no longer the Titans' god, and the infinite power or might that they believe they have has already passed elsewhere and shown itself to be finite.

Chapter 22

Saturn's Query of Force

"Who had power / To make me desolate? whence came the strength? / How was it nurtur'd to such bursting forth . . . ?" Saturn asks (*Hyp.*, I, 102–4). He speaks as leader of the fallen Titans and first among the newly extinct creatures, and his question bears all the incomprehension of his physical and perceptual circumstance. Saturn cannot conceive how even as almighty "Fate seem'd strangled in [his] nervous grasp" (105), power, elsewhere and seemingly nurtured in secret, rendered him and his tribe desolate. He presumes that this power is located in a specific entity, that it was robbed from him, and that it is therefore recoverable by him:

> Saturn must be King.
> Yes, there must be a golden victory;
> There must be Gods thrown down, and trumpets blown
> Of triumph calm, and hymns of festival
> Upon the gold clouds metropolitan,
> Voices of soft proclaim, and silver stir
> Of strings in hollow shells;

Most of all, "there shall be / Beautiful things made new, for the surprise / Of the sky-children" (I, 125–33). So certain is Saturn in the fixity of his perception that the power that has replaced him is the same as that force he once owned that he resolves to give command even before this "lost" power is recovered. What he has just imagined of "golden victory" and a recovered heaven must and will "Be of ripe progress" (I, 124–26).

But, as we know, Saturn speaks with the feverish fancy and false energy of waning unrecoverable power. The signal passion of his speech reveals the symptoms of his disease: "passion lifted him upon his feet, / And made his hands to struggle in the air, / His Druid locks to shake and ooze with sweat, / His eyes to fever out, his voice to cease" (I, 135–38). The powerless Saturn cannot see that he and his fellows are "Scarce images of life," frenzied wills driven by disease but without the impetus of life force, "lank-eared Phantoms" devolved from divine (ideal) form to multiple, emotional shadows of "the mortal world beneath," monstrous forms of inaction and pain (II, 33; I, 334, 228–30)—fossils literal and metaphorical. Racked by the shakings of intense fever, with nervous grasp, "faded eyes," and dulled senses, unable to hear "Thea's sobbing deep" (I, 90, 139), and barely able to speak, his physical symptoms confirm what we already suspect about his flagging mental powers and consequent perceptual deformities. Saturn cannot conceive new beauty, nor can he perceive a beauty or power (Apollo's) that is not his own. Heaven and earth do not know Saturn "thus afflicted, for a God" (I, 56); the Titans are no longer "sky-children" but fissured geological faults of their prior forms; their only music is not hymns and trumpets of victory but the painful lament "Of strings in hollow shells" of former being.

When Saturn proclaims "there shall be / Beautiful things made new, for the surprise / Of the sky-children," he reveals the deforming and deluding extent of his misperceptions. Saturn cannot make the beautiful things of former existence and the past perfections of his own race anew nor can he make new beauty of extinct form. The possibility of fresh perfection or another order of power (beauty) is simply out of the question—Saturn's question—and beyond his cognition. His querulous reiteration of his question at the end of his speech to Thea, and after his physical symptoms have been catalogued, bears all the signs of a once-coherent but now distraught and disintegrating mind: "But cannot I create? / Cannot I form? Cannot I fashion forth / Another world, another universe, / To overbear and crumble this to nought?" (I, 141–44). Matter cannot be crumbled to nought and the Lamarckian "dead hand" of inanimate substance cannot create; it can only interfere, feebly, with future creation. The newly extinct Saturn cannot overbear with former might. The sleeping giant's question echoes thus without need of answer in the "barren void" of his environment (I, 119): as we have already been told, "no force could wake him from his place" of emptiness and stasis (I, 22). The passing fevers of Saturn's brain, his imagination's forced vision of "ripe progress" as the repossession of heaven and the impossible return of extinct being, are nothing but diagnostic signs yet to be read of a newly revealed illness or imperfection of physical and conceptual being.

David Hume in 1739 conceived of *"efficacy, agency, power, force, energy, necessity, connection* and *productive quality"* as "all nearly synonymous."[1] This perspective, allied with the eighteenth-century belief that all forces were identical and therefore indestructible and recoverable,[2] may well underlie Saturn's problem of perception. He mistakes the agency of nature's law, evolutionary necessity, for "Fate" accidentally strangled in his nervous grasp; he confuses the debilitating energy of his agitated will with productive force; he connects the haunted desires of his fallen race with a vision of universal efficacy; he presumes overt force and latent might to be synonymous. Most of all he trusts—

with the naivete of a child or an undeveloped creature—that the "sharp lightning" and simple thunder of his art (I, 59–62) is identical with the subtle efficacy, connection, and nurturing quality of Apollo's new beauty and "untremendous might" (II, 155).

Old Saturn conceives with the ancient idea and fixed perspective of "hoary majesty" (I, 59) and thereby betrays, to borrow a metaphor from *The Fall of Hyperion* (I, 70), the faultures within his monumental race. He presumes that power, like matter, is indestructible and therefore recoverable; that perfection was fixed and completed in the Titans; that their fall is but a temporary contamination, not a fault in being, of their perfect order. Because the Titans can comprehend only one law of might and peremptory power as a solitary force in the universe, they will never understand the Romantic evolutionary concept of fresh perfection—why they must "cower beneath what, in comparison, / Is untremendous might" (II, 154–55) and why they must be succeeded by what seems to be a "puny essence" and an "infant thunderer" (II, 331; I, 249). Saturn is indeed their leader in incomprehension when he misunderstands current power as former might and misreads the "strange thunders" from Apollo's "potency of song" ("Sleep and Poetry," 231). Misunderstanding power, he inevitably proposes to misuse power like the "poets Polyphemes" in "Sleep and Poetry" whose "themes / Are ugly clubs . . . / Disturbing the grand sea" of life (231–35). His ill-conceived proposal of brute power reveals his full kinship with the obstinate energy and sullen force of Enceladus and the other "bruised" Titans who lie immobile "vast and edgeways; like a dismal cirque / Of Druid stones, upon a forlorn moor" (II, 34–35). Physically less brutish than they, Saturn is perceptually more deformed. Correct in conceiving of himself and his fellow "gods" as immortal matter, his perception of this matter as single and indistinguishable eternal power nevertheless reveals them all to be "decrepit things" devolving into brute mortal matter.

Physiologists of the Romantic period measured the quantity of vitality in a given organism according to the degree of sensitivity it displayed toward external stimuli. Romantic evolutionists measured the quality of life force and escalation of being among the species according to the developed intensity of their senses and the degree of perceivable individuality or distinctions of self within a given species. Imperfections in the senses, whether genetic or wrought by disease, were a mark of lesser vitality and of evolutionary fault. Saturn's dulled and disintegrating senses revealed one by one in the course of the poem, mark his compounding perceptual degenerations. We are told early in the epic that Saturn's right hand is nerveless, that in his "icy trance" he is indifferent to the sound of Thea's sobbing and hardly able to speak, and that his "realmless eyes were closed" (I, 19). In Book II, Oceanus, with an advanced perceptual vision unusual to his kind, diagnoses for us the real condition of Saturn's sensory might: "thou art the King . . . [and] blind from sheer supremacy, / One avenue was shaded from thine eyes, / Through which I wandered to eternal truth" (II, 184–87). Romantic evolutionists like Oken proposed sight to be the highest of the five senses and a mark of advanced creatural perfection. But, among the Titans, Saturn is most blind and, like King Lear, his lack of physical vision proceeds from a prior debility of perceptual vision; unable to see the growing limitations of his senses, Saturn will never see "eternal truth" and the new beauties of fresh perfection. Ripeness is all in Lear's as in Saturn's realmless world. Lamarckian evolution proposed that large numbers of minute and invisible adaptations during periods of evolutionary stasis burst forth into visibility at moments of major revolutionary change among the species and served as retrospective heralds to the seemingly sudden escalation of being.[3] Saturn's query, "How was it nurtur'd to such bursting forth?" manifests the extent of his failure of vision. Blind Saturn can have no inkling of what is to come. He sees neither intrinsic limitation, nor ripeness, nor extrinsic change. Hardly a "fore-seeing God" like the Apollo Keats describes in a letter of 1818,[4] Saturn hardly knows himself "thus afflicted, for a God." The peremptory beauty of power of the Titans was a depleting force in the universe, Keats would say, apropos the genius of Milton; in the sightlessness of their king, we see that it has come to consume itself. We are to read the Titans' sudden manifestation of mortal emotion as yet another sign of the devolution from godly being to lesser, and perhaps human, form. Coelus beholds his sons acting "most unlike Gods:" once "Unruffled, like high Gods, ye liv'd and ruled: / [but] Now I behold in you fear, hope, and wrath; / Actions of rage and passion; even as / I see them, on the mortal world beneath, / In men who die" (I, 328–35). Saturn's face, meanwhile, reflects the Titans' emotional turmoil: "direst strife;—the supreme God / At war with all the frailty of grief, / Of rage, of fear, anxiety, revenge, / Remorse, spleen, hope, but most of all despair.... for Fate / Had pour'd a mortal oil upon his head, / A disanointing poison..." (II, 91–98).

The Titans mirror and mimic human emotions, but their fate could be at once much worse and far less specific than the mortality they reflect yet cannot comprehend. The supreme sign of their fate, again, can be found in Saturn. Unable to recognize his own physical appearance—"tell me if this feeble shape / Is Saturn's; tell me if thou hear'st the voice / Of Saturn; tell me if this wrinkling brow, . . . / Peers like the front of Saturn" (I, 98–102)—the Titan leader passes on to a more profound unrecognition:

> I am gone
> Away from my own bosom; I have left
> My strong identity, my real self,
> Somewhere between the throne and where I sit
> Here on this spot of earth.
> (I, 112–16)

Romantic evolution proposed a principle of individuation among the higher species, and it saw in the distinctions and varieties of individual selves the mark of ascent or higher being. But Saturn finds he has no self and, worse, that the emotions he feels are fleeting reflections of a lower mortal being that undermine his quest for fixity and permanence as a god. His acknowledged absense of a self is a void real and felt; it precludes sympathy with life forms other than his own and preempts benign acts of love or the divine version of Keatsian negative capability. Saturn is without "godlike exercise," without "influence benign," and he is denied "all those acts which Deity supreme / Doth ease its heart of love in" (I, 107–12). "Smother'd up, / And buried" (106) by neutral and indestructible matter, "this spot of earth," with which he foolishly identified his power as a god, Saturn's fate is at once indeterminate among other beings and self-destructively determinate among the Titan species.

Indeed, given that they are unable to find distinctive or enduring selves and equally unable to project outward in sympathy or appropriation to other species of being, the void that is the Titans' power must turn, and finally collapse, upon itself. To force and vex the powers of life, according to the Brunonian theory of Romantic physiology, was the physical equivalent of psychological despair and suicide. The Titans' myth of "sad feud . . . and rebellion / Of son against his sire" (I, 321–22) becomes, as it is told by Keats in *Hyperion*, a yet more involuted expression of self-debilitation. "Thy thunder, conscious of the new command, / Rumbles reluctant o'er our fallen house," Thea tells Saturn; "thy sharp lightning in unpractised hands / Scorches and burns our once serene domain" (I, 60–63). The "new command" and "unpractised hands" belong among the newly fallen Titans and not their purported foes, among those giants like Enceladus who would act against nature and either speed or reverse natural process—as the sonnet "On Fame" says:

> It is as if the rose should pluck herself,
>   Or the ripe plum finger its misty bloom,
> As if the Naiad, like a meddling elf,
>   Should darken her pure grot with muddy gloom.
>   (5–8)

Like the suicides in Dante's Wood of Sorrow, the self-violation among the Titans is engendered by a despair born of a gross misapprehension of the self. It recalls the bleak emptiness of the elephant's prayer of reversal to Circe, the false physician of *Endymion*: "Only I pray, as fairest boon, to die, / Or be deliver'd from this cumbrous flesh, . . . / And merely given to the cold bleak air" (III, 550–54). It connects more directly however with the projected suicides of inadequacy of two of Keats's dreamers who cannot grow up: Lycius, who empties "his limbs of life" once his arms are "empty of delight" (*Lamia*, II, 307–8), and Endymion, who resolves "My kingdom's at its death, and just it is / That I should die with it" (IV, 940–41). Suicide is not an assertion of self, nor yet is it an assertion of that which is not yet found or permanently lost. New to their role as *fallen* Titans, creatures of immortal substance who are on the road to extinction and partly conscious of this fact, the Titans can neither die nor continue in power. Powerless to live as they would, they are also powerless to die as they wish.

No wonder Hyperion, the last Titan in power who has yet to fall, the only "one of the whole mammoth-brood [who] still kept / His sovereignty, and rule, and majesty" (I, 164–65), has bad dreams. Hyperion knows that despite his power as Sun-god he cannot make the dawn burst forth early:

> Fain would he have commanded, fain took throne
> And bid the day begin, if but for change.
> He might not: No, though a primeval God:
> The sacred seasons might not be disturb'd.
> Therefore the operations of the dawn
> Stay'd in their birth, even as here 'tis told.
> (I, 290–95)

Indeed, arrested in the dark moment before dawn (and forever in the poem of his name), Hyperion sits still, "still snuff'd the incense, teeming up . . . yet unsecure," waiting alone with his visions of premonition and half-knowledge: "For as among us mortals omens drear / Fright and perplex, so also shuddered he" (I, 167–70). Not "prophesyings of the midnight lamp," nor death knells, nor "gloom-bird's hated screech," nor the dog's howl, "But horrors, portion'd to a giant nerve" transfix Hyperion. He sees or thinks he sees in his agitation "eagle's wings, / Unseen before by Gods or wondering men" that darken his palace of light; he hears or thinks he hears "neighing steeds . . . / Not heard before by Gods or wondering men" that challenge the silent melody of his domain (I, 171–85). The final horror is that the dark visions and frightful sounds assail Hyperion *at home*: "into my centre of repose, / The shady visions come to domineer, / Insult, and blind, and stifle up my pomp" (I, 243–45). The distraught and frenzied Titan has already displayed all the physical signs of nervous torment;[5] the shady visions that now come to blind and stifle him are without doubt the symptomatic nightmares of his psychic disease.

Just what Hyperion sees in his sick dream of a moment before dawn is described in his words in some fifty-odd lines of poetry after we have first been told that the unfallen Titan has been sensing "omens drear." In the "great main cupola" of his "own golden region" of the West, upon an empty and echoing "mirrored level" (I, 221, 224, 257), Hyperion's dreams take dark form and shadowy substance:

> O dreams of day and night!
> O monstrous forms! O effigies of pain!
> O spectres busy in a cold, cold gloom!
> O lank-eared Phantoms of black-weeded pools!
> Why do I know ye? Why have I seen ye?
> (I, 227–31)

"Why / Is my eternal essence thus distraught / To see and to behold these horrors new?" Hyperion asks, in corollary to Saturn's query of power. In response, "A mist arose, as from a scummy marsh" from the empty, mirrored level; this sympathetic ectoplasm signals further psychic disturbance, and the Sun-god feels a parallel agony, "Like a lithe serpent," creep through his Titan bulk (I, 232–33, 257–63).

Hyperion's as-yet-unfallen power, the purported answer to Saturn's question, is the power to dream in this wise. "Phantoms pale . . . thrice horrible and cold" and the aching, gradual agony induced "From over-strained might" (I, 255–56, 263)—these are the sights and sensations from his nightmare that blind Hyperion and deform his waking vision. The Sun-god would wish to see the "blissful light," "crystalline pavillions, and pure fanes" of his "lucent empire," but he is unable to see "The blaze, the splendor, and the symmetry" of harmonious perfection; blinded by the shadows of his mind, he sees nothing "but darkness, death and darkness" (I, 237–42). This is Hyperion's sick dream of premonition of the Titans' fall to extinction. The immortal giants have already fallen from "power," we know, but the vision Hyperion has here is of what will become of them *after* they have fallen from life. Like the "dreaming thing" castigated by the goddess Moneta (in *The Fall of Hyperion*), Hyperion is a fever of himself, but in his diseased dream (and because he is the sole possessor of residual power among the Titans), he sees truly of the Titans' imminent condition. Where the rest of the "mammoth-brood" see themselves as fallen but Titans still, with the ability to either restore fixed perfection or destroy themselves and their giant molds, Hyperion sees them for what they will be shortly: lank-eared phantoms of black-weeded pools, spectres in cold gloom rising from a leveled mirror of the void, hollow effigies or monstrous forms of prior pain—or, hulks deformed by the passage of time, behemoth shells of former life, giant fossils left standing in stagnant water.[6] Hyperion's nightmares, seen with the retrospective vision of the Romantic evolutionist and read with the semiotic premonitions of the Romantic physician, present the clearest portrait of the final collapse of Titanic power upon itself. As the repository of residual power sickened most by the plague of perceptual reversal, Hyperion is self-consumptive and able only to generate overwrought, sickly dreams born of his mind's despair.

Hyperion's light, from off the leveled mirror of his waking dream, reveals first the dark places of his mind and then the dark places of the fallen Titans' new location:

> In pale and silver silence they remain'd,
> Till suddenly a splendour, like the morn,
> Pervaded all the beetling gloomy steeps,
> All the sad spaces of oblivion,
> And every gulf, and every chasm old,
> And every height, and every sullen depth,

> Voiceless, or hoarse with loud tormented streams:
> And all the everlasting cataracts,
> And all the headlong torrents far and near,
> Mantled before in darkness and huge shade,
> Now saw the light and made it terrible.
> It was Hyperion:—a granite peak
> His bright feet touch'd, and there he stay'd to view
> The misery his brilliance had betray'd
> To the most hateful seeing of itself.
>   (II, 356–70)

This bleak and terrifying region of silence, beetling gloomy steeps, sad spaces of gulf and chasm, voiceless heights, sullen depths, everlasting cataracts, headlong torrents, and loud tormented streams presents itself as a psychological landscape of the Titans' psychic state even as it endures as a real and substantial residence for their physical bulks. We are reminded of other psychological landscapes described by Keats: of the "sombre place" Endymion happens upon after the bower of Adonis, where he finds "ten thousand jutting shapes, / Half seen through deepest gloom, and griesly gapes, / Blackening on every side" and feels a consequent "change / Working within him into something dreary,—/ Vexed like a morning eagle, lost, and weary, / And purblind amid foggy, midnight wolds " (II, 628–36); or of the forest Ludolph visits in *Otho the Great* with its "thick oppressive shade," "dull boughs" and "oven of dark thickets" that presage "a suffocating death,—/ A gnawing—silent—deadly, quiet death!" (V, i, 19–23). But, where Endymion and Ludolph's places of psychic distress are passing moods, the Titans' place is permanently real as befits their immortal substance; as such, it nonetheless reflects their communal perception or mind at the very end of its tether.

Hyperion's light, at once diagnostic and reflective of his own state, lights up this Titanic residence that is otherwise "lorn of light" "To the most hateful seeing of itself" (I, 118; II, 370). In this region and contrary to what the Titans have thought so far, Hyperion is no Sun-god but merely, we are told, "*like* the morn" (II, 357). His reflected and reflecting light recalls that "other light" described in *Endymion* as "quick and sharp enough to blight / The Olympian eagle's vision" but nevertheless "dark, / Dark as the parentage of chaos" (II, 909–12). Prior to Hyperion's appearance the Titans' abode had been "a den where no insulting light / Could glimmer on their tears; where their own groans / They felt, but heard not," a "shady sadness of a vale / Far sunken from the healthy breath of morn, / Far from the fiery noon, and eve's one star" (II, 5–7; I, 1–3). Before Hyperion's insulting light came among the mammoth brood, furthermore, they had no requirement either to acknowledge fully their condition to themselves or to be conscious of one another's pain. They did not hear one another's groans because "thunderous waterfalls and torrents hoarse" deafened them as much to themselves as to others (II, 8); the darkness of their semicomatose state, "Dungeon'd in opaque element," permitted them to remain "uncertain where" the crags and "rugged stone" of their immortal material ("a constant bulk") began or ended (II, 23, 9–16); individual and transfixing pain, meanwhile, had isolated and contained them within their own miseries—"Each one kept shroud, nor to his neighbour gave / Or word, or look, or action of despair" (II, 39–40). The nightmarish light of Hyperion's consciousness changes all this: what was once

> Mantled before in darkness and huge shade,
> Now saw the light and made it terrible.
> It was Hyperion:—a granite peak
> His bright feet touch'd. . . .
>			(II, 365–68)

Hyperion's gift to his fellow Titans—born of his anxious self and its waning power—is a gift of cruel light; cruel, and not merely insulting because it originates from one of them and therefore cannot be denied as alien power. Hyperion's sudden recognition of the Titans' condition, his terrible light that they cannot ignore, born as it is of what he fears he will become, is a perception that fixes the giant race as fossils in a lifeless substance; the best image for this cognition is, indeed, a granite peak. The material sublime of Hyperion's preceding nightmare becomes thus the Buffonian "constant bulk" of the Titans' physique, and his premonitions become the promontories and chasms of their self-mirroring environment. Revealed by the terrible light reflected from the nightmare of one of their own kind who "still holds power," and forced into a kind of surrogate consciousness of themselves, they are "betray'd" and deformed yet further because Hyperion recognizes them to be the composite substance, at once real and imaginary, of his worst dreams. His consciousness among them, at its most stressed and distorted and "in thousand hugest phantasies," indeed makes "a fit roofing to this nest of woe" (II, 13–14).

Hyperion does not imagine the Titans' pain so much as reflect it in huge and fanciful form. He knows only his own pain and, hugely self-absorbed, cannot possess a sympathetic imagination of pain in others; neither a priest nor a physician of their desolation (Fall of Hyp., I, 227), he can only impose his present psychic pain upon the Titans' physical condition as he apprehends it through his dreams; he then appropriates their pain made visible by his conscious "light" into the shadows of his future imagined and anticipated pain. The brilliance of Hyperion's misery betrays the Titans' misery into the "dull shade" of a worse dream (Lamia, II, 104–5), which is to be the worst nightmare yet born of their fixed perceptual place.

> Damp awe assail'd me; for there 'gan to boom
> A sound of moan, an agony of sound,

> Sepulchral from the distance all around.
> Then came a conquering earth-thunder, and rumbled
> That fierce complain to silence: while I stumbled
> Down a precipitous path, as if impell'd.
> I came to a dark valley.—Groanings swell'd
> Poisonous about my ears. . . .
>   (*End.*, III, 483–91)

This description of a sick ward filled with the sounds and postures of pain, where Circe practices false medicine as a potent goddess of "pains resistless," could serve as well to describe "the precincts" of the "nest of pain," the Titans' new environment, which Thea is able to encircle in her widespread "trembling arms" (II, 90). Earlier chapters of this book have discussed Romantic medicine's notion of fixed or vitiated air and its theories of noxious contagion as contexts for Keats's conception of places like these as regions of sterility and ill health that are at once empty of life and containers for the shadowy contaminations of former life. Keats's visualization of the Titans' last residence as a vast sickroom, moreover, is a familiar subject among his readers.[7] The Titans are indeed "sick" but what interests here is the nature of their "immortal sickness" or, since their environment reflects their afflictions, what constitutes the pain "and sorrow of the place" where the giants lie immobilized and without hope of cure (I, 90). What interests further is the perceptual transition from an evocation of the concept of venomous exhalations of stagnant matter (a theory of physical disease) to the fully visualized poetic image of a mist from a scummy marsh summoned by the medium of Hyperion's diseased dream. In a poem describing the American landscape as a nightmare vision of nature gone wrong because it is the "Dungeoner of [his] friends," Keats conceives of a "monstrous region, whose dull rivers pour / Even from their sordid urns unto the shore," a place without dryads and gods:

> Unown'd [even] of any weedy-haired gods;
> Whose winds, all zephyrless, hold scourging rods,
> Iced in the great lakes, to afflict mankind;
> Whose rank-grown forests, frosted, black, and blind,
> Would fright a Dryad; whose harsh herbaged meads
> Make lean and lank the starv'd ox while he feeds;
> There flowers have no scent, birds no sweet song,
> And great unerring Nature once seems wrong.
>   ("What can I do to drive away," 30–43)

Out of the poet's deprivation springs a horrific image of a place that enervates and reverses the powers of life without presenting the recognizable signs of specific affliction. So also do the Titans feel deprivation and debilitation without knowledge of specific affliction. Theirs is "the pain of feebleness," as we are told in *The Fall of Hyperion* (I, 429); they feel pain unending but without intensity and giant sorrow without knowledge or consciousness. They feel pain but they cannot read, apprehend, or diagnose it. Their environment is themselves turned inside out, a vacuous dungeon or sordid urn like those described above, where the imperfections or mistakes of nature are buried. It is a place constructed, nevertheless and simultaneously, by their fading minds to contain them as they contain it in their "nervous grasp" and widespread or crucified "trembling arms." Very simply, like the knight of la belle dame sans merci, the Titans do not know except with fragmentary knowledge what it is that ails them. Their immortal sickness that kills not is without sign or semiotic import; it is a hoarse and debilitating vacuity that mirrors itself without end.

Discovered by Hyperion's nightmare light to be without beauty and without power, the Titans, finally, present a picture of dreadfulness *without* sublimity.[8] They are still immortal, but no longer "divine" they must endure as hulks or shells of their former living selves. Hell is indeed emptiness for the extinct Titans; they and their abode portray jointly the otherwise indescribable underside or hollowed inside—a place without life but also without art—of the Grecian urn as conceived in Keats's ode. They cannot see outside their petrified urn and, within it, they know only the distorted echoes of their former divine perceptions; here, without the form and perfection of the Grecian urn, they reflect the unsublime horror of lifelessness without art. Like the disembodied Lycius at the end of *Lamia* and the visionary chastised by Moneta in *The Fall of Hyperion*, they are dreamers vexed to hollowness after the dream has ended.

"My power, which to me is still a curse, / Shall be to thee a wonder," the "Sole priestess of [the Titans'] desolation" says to the physician-poet of *The Fall of Hyperion* (I, 243–44, 227). The retrospective vision and distancing perspective of *The Fall of Hyperion* (which is also the evolutionist "wonder" of the Romantic physician noted earlier) serves as a comprehensive pendant to Keats's portrait of the Titans in *Hyperion*. The earlier poem reads as an inquiry into the nature of mortality and the Titans' peculiar brand of lifeless immortality; the later poem provides a revelatory display of the "sad sign[s] of ruin" and fall in a code "humanized" to a mortal poet's senses (*Hyp.*, I, 336; *Fall of Hyp.*, II, 1–6). In the first *Hyperion*, despite the many mirrors in his environment, Saturn can neither recognize his own face nor find his features as he remembers them in what he sees of its image. In the second, framed poem of *The Fall of Hyperion*, Moneta reveals to the "dull mortal eyes" of her poet that "this old image here, / Whose carved features wrinkled as he fell, / Is Saturn's" (I, 224–25). Mortality in Keats is consciousness of one's disease and ever-imminent death. Moneta and her poet see Saturn's wrinkles and age, but because the awareness of aging and death is an expression of advanced creatural consciousness, we presume that Saturn does not see what he has become in their eyes. In *Hyperion*, Thea wonders if she should disturb Saturn's "slumbrous solitude" and awaken the sleeping god from his "icy trance" (I, 69–

71); in *The Fall of Hyperion*, Moneta knows that Saturn cannot be awakened to consciousness of either a new order or his own race's extinction. When Saturn notes that there is "No smell of death" in his universe and vows "—there shall be death—" (*Fall of Hyp.*, I, 424), he simply does not know of what he speaks. He and the other Titans act mortal in *Hyperion* and show sad sign of ruin, but they remain immortal substance and hence without consciousness of death or their own deathly symptoms. Foolishly confident of their immortality and fully mistaking its consistency, they imagine themselves as continuing possessors of youthful "godlike exercise:" they hold fast and with stubborn insistence, but for an occasional bad dream, to an image of peremptory power as if it is real. The brawny bodies of a leviathan breed as presented in *Hyperion* thus stand revealed in *The Fall of Hyperion* as mostly face—Saturn's "wrinkling" face, Thea's physiognomy with "listening fear in her regard," Moneta's wan face "bright blanch'd / By an immortal sickness"—and little else (II, 336, 257–58; I, 88, 338). As their memories of prior-owned physical power fade, the Titans become in ironic reversal embodiments of the shell of consciousness, skulls or empty containers of the mind with markings or wrinkles on their surfaces. There is "No stir of life" in "the shrouded vale" of the giants' last residence, no consciousness except that reflected on Moneta's face and borne witness to by the poet's perception as he remembers and reconstructs it from the "antichamber of [his] dream" (I, 310, 465–68). Saturn's face in *The Fall of Hyperion* bears a hieroglyphic pattern, nature's wrinkles, signifying the state of his present consciousness.

The fall to extinction, as a fall from eternity or simultaneity into time, can be perceived as gradual or sudden depending upon the perspective of the creature who feels or sees the descent. Extinct creatures, the naturalists of the Romantic age said, survive as shadows or traces of memory in the features of the newly perfected beings. Keats knew from Hesiod's *Theogony* that the world of the gods was not above natural law; he knew from the natural philosophy of his time that "every thing belonging to the earth" had to submit "to certain and immutable laws of destruction" and that the great agent of chemical decay was "the principle of change" and therefore "a principle of life."[9] When the poet of *The Fall of Hyperion* scrutinizes the Titans in their dark hollow of a vale, he recognizes Saturn's pain to be a dulling "pain of feebleness," diagnoses the change that has turned Saturn from "a God into a shaking palsy," and marks the Titan's progressive earthly decay: "he feebly ceas'd, / With such a poor and sickly sounding pause, / Methought I heard some old man of the earth / Bewailing earthly loss" (I, 429, 426, 438–41). The Titans belong to the earth no less than do "the hollows of time-eaten oaks" and, given their immortal place in legend and in the poet's mortal consciousness, they endure "deathwards progressing / To no death" (I, 408, 260–61). They endure in a "deadening ether that still charms / Their marble being" (*End.*, II, 209–10), ever less themselves and seemingly more and more "the faulture of decrepit things" or "nature's rocks toil'd hard in waves and winds" (I, 69–70). Theirs is indeed the "posthumous existence" Keats feared so much, a waiting for a death that does not come because they cannot conceive of it, just as they cannot conceive of process and fresh perfection. They survive thus as fading memories of their former selves that simultaneously fade and are reorganized as the memories of nature by the discerning mortal consciousness of poet, physician, and natural philosopher.

Chapter 23

Apollo's Power of Life: Sympathetic Genius

Apollo, the "fore-seeing God" of poetry and medicine in legend, who is to replace the Titans' peremptory force in *Hyperion* with the "untremendous might" of "a youngling arm," asks a very different question to Saturn's query of force. He asks not the aggressive "Who had power?" but "Where is power?"

> Whose hand, whose essence, what divinity
> Makes this alarum in the elements,
> While I here idle listen on the shores
> In fearless yet in aching ignorance?
> (*Hyp.*, III, 103–7)

The passive and receptive young god does not assume power or perfection as Saturn did; he does not seek predatory might or the conquest of other life: it is not his pestilential or appropriating energy that precipitates the "alarum in the elements" leading to the downfall of Hyperion's mammoth breed, nor does his physician's hand inflict the "dull pain" that the Titans feel as they fall. Rather, the young creator of music and future beauty in the universe sits "idle," his perception at once attuned to and apprehensive of knowledge, and listens "In fearless yet in aching ignorance." Apollo's imminent supremacy in the universe of the poem, we have already been told by Oceanus and Clymene, is a power more strong—or more intense—in beauty. But intensity, as the Romantic evolutionists believed and as Keats insisted as early as 1817, was the measure of life, sense, mind, and art. Apollo's fresh beauty must therefore constitute a greater physical and conceptual vitality than what it supplants; it must bear a sharper sensitivity to external stimuli, a deeper sense of internal sympathy, a greater vulnerability to pain, a more subtle power of perception, and, most of all, a heightened and healing receptivity to the beauty and pain of other life forms. "That which is creative must create itself," Keats said in 1818, when speaking of the genius of poetry:[1] not even Apollo on the threshold of supremacy in *Hyperion* can recognize immediately the nature of his own power as it is diffused through the universe. He waits for knowledge without any of the Titans' "irritability of imperfection" (to borrow John Hunter's phrase) to seize and know alien existence; he seems content with half-knowledge as if this is a deliberate perceptual stance and, unlike Saturn, does not query or reach irritably after fact and reason. The new god's poetic genius or physic is a receptive intensity and his "power" in this (as we shall discuss in this chapter) is a self-evolutionary and sympathetic, visionary but also depleting, finite process.

I wish you knew all that I think about Genius and the Heart— . . . I must say of one thing that has pressed upon me lately and encreased my Humility and capability of submission and that is this truth—Men of Genius are great as certain ethereal Chemicals operating on the Mass of neutral intellect—by [but] they have not any individuality, any determined Character. I would call the top and head of those who have a proper self Men of Power—[to Bailey, 1817]

[In a disquisition with Dilke on various subjects] several things dovetailed in my mind, & at once it struck me, what quality went to form a Man of Achievement especially in Literature & which Shakespeare posessed so enormously—I mean *Negative Capability*, that is when man is capable of being in uncertainties, Mysteries, doubts, without any irritable reaching after fact & reason—Coleridge, for instance, would let go by a fine isolated verisimilitude caught from the Penetralium of mystery, from being incapable of remaining content with half knowledge. This pursued through Volumes would perhaps take us no further than this, that with a great poet the sense of Beauty overcomes every other consideration, or rather obliterates all consideration. [to Tom and George Keats, 1817]

If then he [the Shakespearean artist, the Keatsian "Man of Achievement"] has no self, and if I am a Poet, where is the Wonder that I should say I would [write] no more? Might I not at that very instant [have] been cogitating on the Characters of saturn and Ops? It is a wretched thing to confess; but is a very fact that not one word I ever utter can be taken for granted as an opinion growing out of my identical nature—how can it, when I have no nature? When I am in a room with People if I ever am free from speculating on creations of my own brain, then not myself goes home to myself: but the identity of every one in the room begins to press upon me that, I am in a very little time anhilated—not only among Men; it would be the same in a Nursery of children: I know not whether I make myself wholly understood. . . . [to Woodhouse, 1818][2]

In *Hyperion*, Apollo's genius-in-waiting is not Saturn's priorly owned power; his selflessness is not to be mistaken for the Titans' predatory force; his fine ability to comprehend beauty in other life forms does not preempt his identity as poet of neutral genius and god of healing. Keats's 1817–1818 comments on poetic genius and negative capability, cited above, clearly inform and direct the conception of Apollo in the early poems and *Hyperion*. The evolution of Apollo as poetic deity and god of new beauty in Book III of *Hyperion*, meanwhile, presages the portrait of the development of finite consciousness in the poet-character in *The Fall of Hyperion* and continues the Keatsian formulation of aesthetic perfection. *Hyperion's* Apollo and the mortal poet portrayed in *The Fall of Hyperion* must serve in tandem in any discussion of the evolution of artistic consciousness in Keats.

The term "negative capability," used by Keats to describe the person of genius or achievement in art or science, derives meaning first from the concepts of contemporary electrochemistry. "Negative," as it is used to describe something "characterized by the absence, instead of the presence, of distinguishing features; devoid of, or lacking in, distinctly positive attributes," was a term "in very common use in the nineteenth century."[3] Derived conceptually from Voltaic medicine's use of positive agents and negative receptors, and advanced by the electrochemical theories of scientists like Priestley, the idea of a negative or latent power, a power to receive action that was passive but otherwise equal in its receptivity to the agency of a presupposed and singular positive force, became a commonplace of Romantic thought. Coleridge could speak of a law of polarity as the law of life and conceive of positive and negative agencies together constituting life; Brunonian medicine could invoke pharmaceuticals as positive incitants of failing force or negative absorbents of excess energy; Hutton and Cuvier could speak of the negative agency of geological formation in the development of creature and climate; and Fuseli could speak of the visual capacity of "negative colour" in his lectures on painting. Romantic power could be twofold, and negative capability could exist as a real entity and fraught concept in science as in art.

John Locke, in his *Essay Concerning Human Understanding*, connected the "idea of power" with the notion of change, alteration, and relation: "Power thus considered is twofold, viz. as able to make, or able to receive any change. The one may be called *active*, and the other *passive* power."[4] Locke's conception of power as two-fold, as "the idea of a power in any agent to do or forebear any particular action, according to the determination or thought of the mind," presumed volition; it concerned itself not with "original power" but with the "idea of power," and saw thinking—as the power to *freely* receive ideas or thoughts from the operation of any and all external substances—to be preeminently a passive power or receptive capacity.[5] The controversy generated by Locke's distinction between active and passive power, and by his characterization of the will as equally powerful or free in overt action, as when suspended in deliberate forbearance, continued through the eighteenth century to influence (often in ways that Locke would have eschewed) formulations on the mind and the imagination as well as on the body drawn by the philosophers and physiologists of the late eighteenth and early nineteenth centuries.

When Thomas Reid published his "commonsensical" *Essays on the Powers of the*

Human Mind near the turn of the century, he described himself as opposed to both the Humean notion of power as singular and indistinguishable force and the Lockean concept of power as twofold. Nevertheless, because his three-volume work was cast as a summary of the philosophies of mind of his time, Reid could not dissipate the widely current concept of passive power from his own thought: "Power is not an object of any one of our external senses, nor even an object of consciousness ... it is not seen, nor heard, nor touched, nor tasted, nor smelt," and, hence, "Power is one thing; its exertion is another thing." In the process of describing consciousness as a speculative power rather than an active power, Reid proposed further that "power lies behind the scene" and beyond consciousness as latent, prior to and distinct from any exertion or action of the mind.[6] Galvanists of the late eighteenth century had presumed power to be passive until provoked, and electromagnetists and chemists of the early nineteenth century borrowed from the galvanists when they formulated their ideas on latent or negative poles of energy. Romantic medicine also, especially in its English and Brunonian guise, posited a passive property or vital capacity in living bodies that was power quite distinct from muscular action and nervous force, an unexerted energy or latent and corollary "principle in the body of receiving impressions;" Brunonian physicians of Keats's time, in particular, would "speak of the *vital capacity* in the *passive* voice, as only susceptible of being acted upon."[7] Thus, when Romantic philosophers of mind, like Reid, spoke in Lockean terms of a passive power in human consciousness that was parallel to the power of human action, they allied themselves conceptually with the physical scientists of their period. Both shared the same speculative belief, and perhaps the same sources for this belief, that power might be twofold: not just active and overt force but, alternately, passive, receptive, negative, and vitally capable energy.

It has been customary among Romantic scholars to trace Keats's conception of the negative capability of the artist to the example of Hazlitt. In his essays "On the Human Imagination" and "On the Principles of Human Action," Hazlitt described the imagination as naturally unselfish and outgoing, and essentially "disinterested;" in an 1817 essay on posthumous fame, he described the particular selflessness or self-negation of Shakespeare's genius:

He was almost entirely a man of genius ... in him this faculty bore sway over every other ... he revelled in the world of observation and of fancy.... He seemed scarcely to have an individual existence of his own, but to borrow that of others at will, and to pass successively through 'every variety of untried being,'—to be now *Hamlet*, now *Othello*, now *Lear*, now *Falstaff*, now *Ariel*. In the mingled interests and feelings belonging to this wide range of imaginary reality, in the tumult and rapid transitions of this waking dream, the author could not easily find time to think of himself, nor wish to embody that personal identity in idle reputation after death, of which he was so little tenacious while living.[8]

The peculiar or egotistical identity of Hazlitt's Shakespeare, or Keats's Shake-spearean poet, is obliterated in the multiple identities that he observes through his "sense of Beauty" and, therein, assumes. Keats's description of the negative capability of the man of achievement and of the press of identi-ties upon his poetic nature in the letters cited above echo Hazlitt's terms and continue his age's formulations on passive imaginative force:

> As to the poetical Character itself, (I mean that sort of which, if I am any thing, I am a Member; that sort distinguished from the wordsworthian or egotistical sublime; which is a thing per se and stands alone) it is not itself—it has no self—it is every thing and nothing—It has no character—it enjoys light and shade; it lives in gusto, be it foul or fair, high or low, rich or poor, mean or elevated—It has as much delight in conceiving an Iago as an Imogen. What shocks the virtuous philosop[h]er, de-lights the camelion Poet. It does no harm from its relish of the dark side of things any more than from its taste for the bright one; because they both end in specula-tion. A Poet is the most unpoetical of any thing in existence; because he has no Identity—he is continually in for—and filling some other Body—The Sun, the Moon, the Sea and Men and Women who are creatures of impulse are poetical and have about them an unchangeable attribute—the poet has none; no identity—he is certainly the most unpoetical of all God's creatures.[9]

To have "no character" in the perception of other life and no "identical nature" during the comprehension of alien beauty is not, in Keats's mind, to be empty of life or perceiving consciousness. When Keats describes the negative capa-bility of the poetic self that he would aspire to, and it is a perceiving self quite distinct from the Wordsworthian "egotistical sublime" and the Miltonic preda-tory appropriation of beauty, he conceived of this artistic self's power as an adaptive receptivity or sympathetic force born of the artist's vital ability to imagine other life fully and comprehensively.

There are, to put it simply, two kinds of hollowness in Keats: the hollowness of Grecian urns and hemlock stalks discussed earlier, and the intensely vital capacity—or receptivity—of the Keatsian artist described above. The former variety contains without response and draws energy into its fixed and lifeless self; the latter receives and responds by rendering up its limiting "identical" self and expanding its living consciousness of other life. The receptive power of the artist (described in the letters, embodied in the evolving consciousness of Apollo in *Hyperion* and the poet in *The Fall of Hyperion*, and revealed in the poems of Keats's maturity) neither frets after knowledge nor seeks irritably after facts and conviction; it is content to receive and to forget itself in its sympathetic absorption of the passing world. Let us not "go hurrying about and collecting honey-bee like, buzzing here and there impatiently from a knowledge of what is to be arrived at: but let us open our leaves like a flower and be passive and receptive—budding patiently under the eyes of Apollo and taking hints from every noble insect that favors us with a visit—sap will be given us for Meat and dew for drink," Keats said, early in 1818, in description of his developing "sense of Idleness" and belief in the creative potential of the indolent or suspended consciousness.[10]

> O fret not after knowledge—I have none,
> And yet my song comes native with the warmth;
> O fret not after knowledge—I have none,
> And yet the evening listens. He who saddens
> At thought of idleness cannot be idle,
> And he's awake who thinks himself asleep.
> ("O thou whose face hath felt the winter's wind," 9–14)

What the thrush says to the poet's evolving consciousness here, and what the fledgling poet himself said in 1817 on the distinction between men of power and men of (Shakespearean) genius, finds clarification in a statement on the "Disposition of Dilke," written in September 1819 while Keats was composing *The Fall of Hyperion*. Dilke, a man of politics and power, "thinks of nothing but 'Political Justice,' " "cannot feel he has a personal identity unless he has made up his Mind about every thing," and, "preresolved" on all subjects, "will never come at a truth as long as he lives; because he is always trying at it." Instead, Keats advises, "The only means of strengthening one's intellect is to make up one's mind about nothing—to let the mind be a thoroughfare for all thoughts. Not a select party."[11]

Keats's developing concept of negative capability in the artist may seem directly reminiscent of the contemplative genius evoked by Wordsworth in "Expostulation and Reply" and described at length by Hazlitt in his "On Living to One's Self:" "He sees enough in the universe to interest him without putting himself forward to try what he can do to fix the eyes of the universe upon him. . . . He reads the clouds, he looks at the stars. . . . [But] All this while he is taken up with other things, forgetting himself."[12] The vital capacity of the Keatsian poetic genius is nevertheless distinct from the "wise passiveness" of Wordsworth's philosopher and Hazlitt's man "who lives wisely to himself," "looks at the busy world through the loop-holes of retreat," and "not troubled by their passions," takes "an interest . . . in the affairs of men [that is] calm, contemplative, passive [and] distant. . . ."[13] In Keats, negative capability or passive receptivity in the artist involves *immediate* nervous sympathy with other creatural forms; it requires an alert and attentive consciousness and a deliberate forgetting of the "identical nature" of the self in the imaginative vision of the living object's predicament. Passive imaginative force in Keats presumes commitment—to that which is outside the self. We recall that Apollo, in *Hyperion*, as a new god on the threshold of power and at a time when he should feel "most happy" at his imminent reign and fresh perfection of beauty, feels sadness, frustration, melancholy, and nonspecific pain:

> I strive to search whereof I am so sad,
> Until a melancholy numbs my limbs;

> And then upon the grass I sit, and moan,
> Like one who once had wings.—O why should I
> Feel curs'd and thwarted, when the liegeless air
> Yields to my step aspirant? Why should I
> Spurn the green turf as hateful to my feet?
> Goddess benign, point forth some unknown thing:
> Are there not other regions than this isle?
>   (*Hyp.*, III, 88–96)

The new-formed poetic deity is reluctant of his power and unwilling to assume new dominion. Hardly "distant" and able to "live wisely to himself," still in a condition of "half-knowledge," he is nevertheless fully caught up in "the tummult and rapid transitions" of the Titans' horrific "waking dream" of replacement and fresh perfection. He is involved before he comprehends the event. Because of his negative capability for feeling as others feel, Apollo is able to intuit what he does not know of the Titans' condition and this feeling takes precedent over his "step aspirant" and purported "identical nature." Apollo feels with immediacy and commitment, without philosophic distance and the mediation of "a retreat," what the Titans feel of passion and pain. Nor does this preclude his feelings of novelty and higher (more intense) power or beauty as poetic deity. Apollo's might does not neutralize the Titans' pain, nor does he project himself into the giants' condition with an empathy that neutralizes his consciousness of himself as their replacement.[14] Rather, his is a sympathetic imaginative response that comprehends the Titans' misery and absorbs it without joy into the feeling of new supremacy. The poetic deity's newly evolved consciousness commits him to a full and passionate imagination of the Titans' pain; his ascendancy and their pain are both heightened simultaneously in him as a single complex of divine perception: he feels both immediately and, thus, feels as a god feels. This is Apollo's conscious sympathy, his negative capability, his vital capacity for life and the reading of life.

All of the aesthetic concepts that Keats uses in his description of Apollo's nature and the poet's vital capacity, terms that we commonly trace to literary influences like Hazlitt—sympathy, intensity, the acute and internalized response to contrast and pain—find corollary place and perhaps first source in Romantic medicine's reading of life. We know that Romantic physicians and surgeons from John Brown to Astley Cooper spoke of the real sympathy between parts, the irritating power of diseased tissue upon remote organs, and the profound influence of the diseased mind upon the body's health. Cooper taught his students that

> *there exist between all parts intimate relations*, corresponding with each other and carrying on a *reciprocal interconnection of action.* . . . Thus, *impressions not only produce effects on the part to which they are directly applied; but, in consequence of the freedom of nervous communication, remote parts of the body are becoming affected by them*, and many of its natural functions are supported by *sympathetic communication.*

John Hunter had spoken of inflammation as an increased action of life power or "that power which a part naturally possesses," and he saw in "healthy inflammations" of the body a manifest and attendant "increase in power."[15] Hunter's influential theory of the living body as a "Constitution" or "system of interdependent parts" and "balanced forces," furthermore, saw "the powers constituting the life of an animated body" as existing "in various degrees of intensity and of relative subordination in different individuals" according to these creatures' vital resistance to death or their capacity for the stimulus of life.[16] Coleridge, as Part II notes, borrowed concepts from the physiologists of his time when he framed his theory of the evolution of life species and consciousness: the true "Idea of Life" was a power or *"tendency to individuation"* that subsisted in all existences "and the degrees or intensities" of this tendency formed the species whose life ascendancy was to be measured by "the degrees, both of intensity and extension" reflected in their vital capacity and manifest by their organic complexity.[17] Finally, when Barclay summarized the tenets of Romantic physiology for Keats's generation in 1810, he declared that the degree of intensity or vital capacity in an organism marked its relative perfection and place in the evolutionary advance of existence: "It is a general rule, that the stronger the affinity between life and an organized being, the more imperfect is the animal; hence the zoophites, whose whole organization consists in a mouth, a stomach, and a gut, have a life exceedingly tenacious, and difficult to be destroyed."[18] Polyps, frogs, and mollusks, according to Barclay and other Romantic physicians, had a high affinity for life because of their simple organization, their energy was not easily dispersed when they were cut up precisely because of their physical simplicity or low intensity of life. Like the worm of Keats's "God of the golden bow," they are "too low-creeping for death" as we know it (11). More perfect creatures, those with more sophisticated physical organizations and more intense and subtle perceptual powers (and for Keats these would include the race of Apollo in *Hyperion* and the burdened and receptive poet in *The Fall of Hyperion*) were more vulnerable to destruction precisely because of their extended, intense, and stressed vital capacity for the stimulus of (other) life.

Keats said that "the excellence of every Art is its intensity," its capability for "making all disagreeables evaporate, from [because of] their being in close relationship with Beauty & Truth." The poet's description of artistic intensity occurs in the same letter of 1817, just prior to his definition of negative capability in the artist. The occasion for both statements was a visit to see Benjamin West's "Death on a Pale Horse". Keats found the painting to be fair, given West's age and conceptual immaturity, but he criticized it for having "nothing to be intense upon; no woman one feels mad to kiss; no face swelling into reality," and cited instead the example of Shakespeare's genius: "Examine King Lear & you will find this exemplified throughout; but in this picture we have unpleasantness without any momentous depth of speculation excited, in which to bury its repulsiveness—."[19] Romantic scholars assume, correctly, that Keats's comments here follow Hazlitt's criticism of the flat theatrics of West's painting and his praise of the profound intensity of passion in *King Lear*.[20] It would be shortsighted to presume, however, given the prevalence of the concept of intensity in Romantic medicine and the poet's (and, no doubt, Hazlitt's) knowledge of its centrality to contemporary theories of life and evolution, that Keats's inspiration for his formulations on artistic intensity was simply literary. The concept of intensity permutated late Romantic thought in its scientific, literary, and aesthetic guises. In Keats at least, the intensity of life and the intensity of art were not so very different conceptually as well as in fact from each other: both connoted a receptive power to contain and respond to the forces of existence, both manifest energy by degrees and in profound variation, both excited or inspired a depth of speculation in creation. Keatsian intensity, in art and in artist, in life and in creativity, must necessarily be read in the full context of the knowledge of its age.

In notes on the psychology of feeling, Schiller evoked ideas parallel to Keats's sense of intense art's power to inspire more intense emotion and imaginative speculation and to make all disagreeables vanish into its own intensity of feeling: every true feeling "immediately affects a further feeling of the same kind and thus grows," Schiller said. "The greater and more complex it becomes, the more kindred feelings it arouses in all parts of the thought organ until it eventually dominates absolutely and occupies the whole expanse of the soul. Accordingly every feeling is self-generating; [and] any given state of our emotional faculty contains the beginning of a subsequent, similar state of greater intensity."[21] Intensity stimulates and promotes further intensity according to Schiller, Keats, and other Romantic literary physicians; the false intensity of an overstimulated imagination, a mood or vision without comprehension, or the heightening contrast of feeling (like West's representation of "Death") is sterile as much in physiological as in aesthetic terms.

In his treatise on the contrasting texture and sympathetic tissue of organs, Bichât, the foremost scientist among the French physiologists of the Romantic period, found himself speaking of beauty and truth, pain and pleasure, creativity and its comprehension in terms that Keats would have recognized and understood:

> The action of the mind in each several sentiment of pain or pleasure, which has been the effect of a sensation, consists in a comparison between this sensation, and that by which it has been preceded, a comparison, which is not the result of reflection, but the involuntary effect of the first impression of the object. Now, the greater the difference between the actual and the past impression, the livelier will be the sentiment.... The consequence is, that in proportion as the same sensations are repeated, the less impression do they make upon us, because the comparison between the present and the past become less sensible. Pain then and pleasure naturally tend to their own annihilation. The art of prolonging our enjoyments,

consists in varying their causes. Indeed were I to regard the laws of our material organization only, I might almost say, that constancy is but one of the happy dreams of the poet, and that the sex to which we at present bend, would possess but a very weak hold upon our attentions were their charms too uniform; I might almost assert that were every female cast in the same mould, such mould would be the tomb of love.[22]

Bichât's comments on the importance of contrast in the psychology of feeling continue Schiller's thought on the passage from intensity to intensity. The French physiologist's unexpected statements on the perception of beauty and the interrelated sensations of pleasure and pain in human psychology, placed at the start of his textbook on the nature of organic tissues, sounds surprisingly like Keats on the nature of intensity and the evolutionary perception of sensation as expressed both in the 1817 passage cited above[23] and in the later poems. The sensation of pleasure or pain parallels the mind's sentiment (feeling) of pleasure or pain; their true reflection (in mind or in art) promotes and incites further and more intense reflections; the truth (or beauty) of each can be measured only by the contrast in intensity reflected by each. Because intensity of feeling precludes repulsiveness or disagreeable contrast, the singular, artful, or excessive expression of either pain or pleasure occasions its annihilation. We are reminded of the passage from intensity to intensity, in its most positive situation, in *Endymion*: "there are / Richer entanglements, enthrallments far / More self-destroying, leading, by degrees, / To the chief intensity: the crown of these / Is made of love and friendship, and sits high / Upon the forehead of humanity" (I, 798–803). At the other extreme, we are reminded of the singular intensity of mood at the end of the verse-epistle to Reynolds that is occasioned by an imagination "brought / Beyond its proper bound" where the increasing and self-generated intensity of the dark mood exhausts itself into a nonfeeling or vision of blank nothingness. Most of all, we are reminded of the numbing poisons of the "Ode on Melancholy," their tendency to make pain and pleasure neutralize, not intensify, each other and their power to make the "disagreeables" of each sensation increase falsely instead of evaporate into the intensity of true "feeling" or "passion." Romantic medicine measured life's quickness and advance according to the organism's degree of sensitivity and equivalent vulnerability to destruction. The intensity of art, for Keats, is also to be conceived as it is in physical life in terms of degrees of sensitivity, receptive capacity, and perceptual responsiveness to sensations given and received. Keats read life and measured its art as a student of Romantic medicine; he was consistently, as Arthur Henry Hallam reminded us in 1831, a poet of sensation.

"Gorge the honey of life," Keats advises his friend Reynolds in September 1818, "I conjure you to think at Present of nothing but pleasure...." This advice, seeming to parallel the mood of intense physical pleasure of the early poetry, comes in fact at a time when the poet is most unhappy, "drinking bitters" at the thought of his brother's impending death, living "in a continual fever" of abstract images born of his frustrated art, and feeling such sympathy with the suffering Tom that, as Keats writes, "His identity presses upon me so all day that I am obliged to go out...."[24] The more abstracted poems of Keats's maturity, meanwhile, recur to images of intense physical pain: Princess Bellanaine in the satiric ballad *The Jealousies* casts a glance so potent and intensely real toward Coralline that the nurse flinches as if her heart was in "an hour-long pinch, / Or a sharp needle [was] run into her back an inch" (VIII, 69–72); the child's fantasy "Song of Four Fairies" has Dusketha sport with the Salamander and promise the "Sprite of Fire" that at its "supreme desire" she will "Touch the very pulse of fire / With my bare unlidded eyes" (80–86); in the magical *Eve of St. Agnes*, Angela's real high anxiety produces "agues in her brain" even as Madeline's self-imposed ritual of silence occasions the suffocating pain of a heart stifled and a throat swollen to bursting (189, 204–7).[25] As a serpent, Lamia knows the dull intensity of suffocating pain when her ranging spirit is enclosed in a narrow "prison-house;"[26] as a woman, she feels the sharp intensity of "scarlet pain" in her transformation; as an immortal spirit, meanwhile, she reminds Lycius that finer spirits have—as do the more advanced or perfected beings of Romantic evolution—greater appetites and multiple, complicated senses to satisfy: "What taste of purer air hast thou to soothe / My essence? What serener palaces, / Where I may all my many senses please, / And by mysterious sleights a hundred thirsts appease?" (*Lamia*, I, 154, 282–85). "Rarified" spirits like Lamia, conceived in Keats's imagination as intensities of being through the sympathetic negative capability of an intense art, possess *more*, not fewer, senses. Theirs is a complicated physiology of sensation and a sophisticated psychology of feeling.

Intellectual focus on the issue of sensation and the use of sensations as a measurement of life and mind began with Locke and with the mid-eighteenth-century research on the varying sensitivity of plant and animal life. Botanists of the Enlightenment had proposed first that "the idea of life naturally implies some degree of perceptivity" and, as we saw in Part II, they used the example of sensitive plants like the mimosa to prove that life was intensity, that the advance of life from plant to animal could be charted by the increase of sensitivity in the forms of existence, and that the repeated stimulation of this sensitive intensity or life power in the organism could result in the temporary (in the lower forms) or permanent (in the higher forms) exhaustion of the living creature.[27] When Romantic physiologists, evolutionists, philosophers of mind, and theorists of artistic imagination invoked the concepts of intensity and receptive sensitivity, they paid unconscious homage, whatever their immediate sources for these ideas, to those botanical researchers of the preceding century and their strange speculations on the perceptual powers—green thoughts?—of vegetables.

Goethe, for example, saw nothing unusual in conceiving of the poet's morphology in terms of a living plant-organism or comparing aesthetic consciousness and the morphology of a flower. His comments on poetic genius and the evolution of a passive creative imagination initially preceded his scientific research on *The Metamorphosis of Plants* (1790), and he advanced their formulation in light of the ideas engendered by his study of plants:

> Nobody has a right to prescribe to the gifted individual the areas in which he should be active. The mind from its center shoots out its radii toward the periphery; as soon as it comes up against something it comes to rest there and sends out fresh lines of experiment from the center. |1807|

> I was possessed of the developing, growing, unfolding method, and absolutely not of the method that sets things side by side and orders and arranges them. |1794|

> I let objects produce their effects on me, in all patience and quietness, then I observe these effects and take pains with myself to give them back or reproduce them, true and undistorted. This is the whole secret of what people are pleased to call genius. |1812|

> The very greatest genius would not get very far if it had to bring forth everything out of itself. What is genius if it is not the capacity to make use of everything that it meets with? |1832|[28]

Similar to Goethe's conceptions are Keats's on the poetical character, the negative capability of the chameleon poet, and his declared antipathy to the fixed and made-up mind and to "consequitive reasoning" as well as his description of the intense receptivity of Apollo's genius in *Hyperion* and his own resolve to "open our leaves like a flower and be passive and receptive—budding patiently . . . and taking hints from every noble insect that favours us with a visit—." These formulations, so remarkably parallel, on the evolution of artistic perception point not to simple influence but, rather, stand as a larger testament to the intellectual currency of Keats's thoughts and their complex and inextricable genealogy in the science and art of his age.

"In the calm grandeur of a sober line / We see the waving of the mountain pine," Keats said ("I stood tip-toe," 127–28), in elliptic description of the identical generative energy animating natural entity and poetic consciousness. As the scientific-literary genius of the Romantic era, Goethe had conceived of artistic creativity as a living activity kindred to the life force, and had described the poet's genius as if it were the archetype of the living plant-organism. His outline of the behavioral morphology of poetic genius seemed to be an outline of life itself: he treated the plant as "the epitome of all becoming" and saw the poet's manifested creative consciousness mirrored in the epiphany of the flower. Plants were to be studied, according to Goethe, in the full cycle of living, from seed to flower, death and more seed, for "as the glory and the climax comes the end, the orgasm of the flower, dying into being. . . ."[29] When we see Apollo become an artist at the end of *Hyperion* and so "Die into life," and when we know that his "living death" comprehends with self-debilitating intensity both the glad supremacy of beauty in his new race's being and the intense pain of the fallen Titans, we are forced to recognize further that Keats was fully conversant with the intellectual traditions of his age and a true contributor to Romantic theories on the evolution of consciousness and artistic genius.

Chapter 24

The Imagination of Life

When Novalis described poetry as generation and resolved to call a collection of his thoughts on art *Blütenstaub*[1] or "pollen," he expressed a belief common among Romantic poets and artists: that the creative consciousness is life generating and reflects the patterns of organic creation in its imagination of life and life forms. The Romantic concept of the generative power of poetry nevertheless holds a particularly poignant place in any understanding of Keats's conception of art and, especially, his own art. Intense art for Keats, whether that of the immortal Apollo in *Hyperion* and the early poems or that of the mortal poet of *The Fall of Hyperion* and the later poetry, debilitates and exhausts itself in its creations.[2] It is unable to cast a "cold eye" on life and death, in W. B. Yeats's phrase, and, bound by its passionate identifications with life in all its fresh perfections and deathly dissolutions, necessarily shares in the finitude of the life force as first conceived by the Romantic evolutionists. Apollo's superiority of beauty over the Titans in *Hyperion* constitutes a Coleridgean manifestation of "an intenser form of reality" in an ever-evolving consciousness; it is a revelatory instance of aesthetic accomplishment, but it is also a passing and therefore unrecoverable perceptual moment. The epiphany of Apollo's "fresh perfection" presupposes, like Goethe's flower, a parallel enervation or consumption of the perceiving artistic self. The high intensity of the god's imaginative conception of other life—what Keats would consider to be both his legendary duty to heal and sympathize and his poetic and evolutionary duty to replenish and re-create in endless succession out of himself—exhausts his own and ultimately finite life power. In the intensity of Keatsian art, be it that of the divine Apollo or that of a burdened mortal poet, the familiar evolutionary pattern is reversed in final consequence: grosser (unconscious) created life feeds upon finer (conscious) creating life, and life is indeed "nourished by its proper pith." In the imagination of life, the later physical pattern consumes the prior perceptual aspiration. Thinking exhausts, and intense or creative thinking exhausts the most, much as Bernard Mandeville and other physicians of the late seventeenth century had first proposed:

> [I]f witty Men and Blockheads spend the same Time in Thinking, the first must in all likelyhood waste the most Spirits: Nay, it is unreasonable to suppose, that the slow and heavy Thinking of a drowsy thick-sculled Fellow, should require as much Agility and Workmanship of the Spirits, as the quick and sprightly Thoughts of a clear-headed, ingenious Man; and to me it seems highly probable that there is no more Action, or greater Labour perform'd in the Brain of the first, when he is broad awake as he can be, than there is in that of the latter, when he is half asleep.[3]

The quickness, "Agility," and thin-skulled negative capability of a perceiving artistic mind can "waste" the very "Spirits" of an "ingenious Man" and use up its own advanced quota (by the laws of Romantic evolution) of life energy. Not just in the Hyperion poems and the "Ode on a Grecian Urn" but in other poems, from the sonnet "When I have fears that I may cease to be" to the ode "To Autumn," Keats recurs to the idea that the sympathetic capability of his intense art necessarily depletes its own living substance and that the creative consciousness necessarily exhausts its being. "A teeming brain," for Keats, "becomes a ripe field; the act of writing is the reaping of that field; to have written all the poems one has been born to write is to have gleaned the full harvest from that teeming brain"; but, as Vendler notes further, the fear named in the sonnet endures through the later poems as a felt anxiety that "a high pile of books will leave a field entirely bare, the last gleanings gone, the teeming brain empty and stripped."[4] This unnamed fear was to become for Keats an acknowledged poetic truth born of the practical facts of physical and perceptual evolution as he had learned these from the scientists and physicians of his era.

What does the consciousness of a poet such as Keats's figure of Apollo envision of the perfections and dissolutions of life? And how does the healing sage of Keats's world read imaginatively in the living hieroglyphics of his subject? More simply yet, what and how does Keats's Apollo see? The "fore-seeing" god of poetry, medicine, music, and pestilence, just after he has asked his question of power's residence and just before his own ordeal of pain, finds that he can read the signs of Mnemosyne's mute face:

> Mute thou remainest—mute! yet I can read
> A wondrous lesson in thy silent face:
> Knowledge enormous makes a God of me.
> Names, deeds, grey legends, dire events, rebellions,
> Majesties, sovran voices, agonies,
> Creations and destroyings, all at once
> Pour into the wide hollows of my brain,
> And deify me. . . .
> (Hyp., III, 111–18)

The mortal poet of *The Fall of Hyperion*, just after his ordeal of tyrannic potion and suffocating cold and just before he is forced to bear witness to the Titans' pain, finds that he, too, like Apollo in the earlier fragment, can read the visionary signs etched behind Moneta's wan and "deathwards progressing" visage:

> Whereon there grew
> A power within me of enormous ken,
> To see as a God sees, and take the depth
> Of things as nimbly as the outward eye
> Can size and shape pervade.
> (I, 302–6)

This knowledge read by Apollo and the mortal poet is the knowledge as prophetic vision discussed in Part III, a comprehending potion of imaginative insight and sympathetic recognition born of sorrow and pain. Two early comments by Keats suggest this kind of intuitive knowledge or internal sight. In 1817 the poet allowed that "the simple imaginative Mind may have its rewards in the repeti[ti]on of its own silent Working coming continually on the spirit with a fine suddenness . . . [so that you would think] even then [that] you were mounted on the Wings of Imagination so high," but he discounted these simple and self-interested joys for the philosophic vision of "a complex Mind—one that is imaginative and at the same time careful of its fruits—who would exist partly on sensation partly on thought." A letter of 1818 rejected unequivocally all self-centered, unsubstantiated imaginative play—"any Man may like the Spider spin from his own inwards his own airy Citadel"—for the philosophic insight of maturity that does not "dispute or assert but whispers results . . . and thus by every germ of Spirit sucking the Sap from the mould ethereal every human might become great. . . ."[5] The concept of a visionary mind careful of its fruits, alert to the life around it yet patient to the receipt of knowledge, was soon absorbed into the poet's definition of negative capability. Coleridge's definition of intuitive knowledge (from Plotinus) seems to describe at one level the kind of patiently won imaginative power that Keats commends:

> It is not lawful to enquire from whence it sprang, as if it were a thing subject to place and motion . . . it either appears to us or it does not appear. So that we ought not to pursue it with a view of detecting its secret source, but to watch in quiet till it suddenly shines upon us; preparing ourselves for the blessed spectacle as the eye waits patiently for the rising sun.[6]

Another definition by Coleridge in the *Biographia Literaria* of what he calls "the philosophic imagination" anticipates even more closely the healing and insightful kind of knowledge that Keats came to believe essential to the art of the physician-poet of his time.

> They and they only can acquire the philosophic imagination, the sacred power of self-intuition, who within themselves can interpret and understand the symbol, that the wings of the air-sylph are forming within the skin of the caterpillar; those only, who feel in their own spirits the same instinct, which impels the chrysalis of the horned fly to leave room in its involucrum for antennae yet to come.[7]

Coleridge's vision of the philosophic imagination and what the poetic psyche sees incorporates his reading of Fichte, who in 1800 had also conceived of philosophy in terms of an evolving "air-sylph:" as "the power that shall first set free the imprisoned Psyche and unfold her wings, so that, hovering for a moment above her former self, she may cast a glance on her abandoned slough, and then soar upwards thenceforward to live and move in higher spheres."[8] But the sources for Coleridge's symbol of the poetic psyche are not simply Fichte, German idealism, and, perhaps, Apuleius's myth of Psyche. His conception of the forming air-sylph necessarily incorporates knowledge from the theories of physiologists like Alexander von Humboldt and evolutionists like Erasmus Darwin, for whom the butterfly and the caterpillar were at once patent metaphors and tangible verities in the science of life and organic development.

Contemporary medical treatises on human insight and animal instinct also must find place in Coleridge's and other Romantic writers' conceptions of the evolution of poetic intuition and the philosophic imagination. Speculations on the nature of intuition and the interconnection of instinct and insight abounded during the early nineteenth century. Given wide currency among laymen by the popular journals, these speculations were fueled by the research of the evolutionists and given serious credibility in treatises by philosophers and scientists. For example, when the brain physiologist Charles Bell published his *Idea of a New Anatomy of the Brain* in 1811, he proposed that the "operations of the mind are confined not by the limited nature of things created, but by the limited number of our organs of sense" and went on to speculate on the consequences of a sixth sense: "What would be the effect on our minds, even constituted as they now are, with a superadded organ of sense ... [given that] once brought into activity, the organs can be put in exercise by the mind and be made to minister to the memory and imagination, and all the faculties of the soul."[9] Keats, no less than Coleridge and his peers, also incorporates his age's philosophic and scientific fascination with the possibilities of intuition and instinctive insight into his definition of poetic perception. Medical semiotics of the early nineteenth century required the physician to read the signs beneath the skin of diseased creation. Romantic natural history, meanwhile, instructed the evolutionist to interpret the hieroglyphics of the fossil world and anticipate with sixth sense the past completions and fresh perfections of a living world. When Keats proposes that he would exchange identities with any living creature and feel as it feels (be, for example, "a Sparrow ... take a part in its existence and pick about the Gravel"[10]), or describes in poems like the Hyperion fragments his own mortal vision as a poet, he displays the full knowledge and ability of his scientific and literary generation to read life. The visionary or philosophic sight of the Romantic artist and the imaginative intuition of the Romantic physician become, through the "fore-seeing" figure of Keats's Apollo, the same power of life.

Apollo's evolutionary art in *Hyperion*, his very foresight or prophetic vision as the poet describes it, takes the depth and finitude of all things. He sees with a practical and sympathetic intensity born both of his legendary purpose as the god of poetry and medicine and of his particular location in Keats's perception of the poet as healing creator in a diseased and always dying world. Apollo has the ability to see both the wings of the air-sylph forming within the skin of the caterpillar and the wrinkles on immortal Saturn's "carved features" forming as he falls to extinction. "Creations and destroyings" pour into the wide hollows of Apollo's brain simultaneously, and he is able to see at once the fresh perfections of his new kingdom and the "abandoned slough" of former Titanic self. He envisions crystallizations as yet unrealized in organic and perceptual life even as he witnesses the hollowed shells and statuary petrifications of matter and mind. He feels joy and sorrow simultaneously, pleasure at new creation and new music and pain more intense than the Titans' pain of loss.

Apollo's hollowed-out, aching consciousness of life matches the brooding intensity of the poet who must "feel the giant agony of the world" and the negative capability of the Keatsian physician who must "seek no wonder but the human face" (*Fall of Hyp.*, I, 157, 163). Youthful consciousness brings to the Keatsian poet imaginative powers to see "the small / Breath of new buds unfolding," to read "the tender greening / Of April meadows," and to "breathe away ... all scummy slime / From off a crystal pool" of life until he sees his "own image from the bottom peep" ("Sleep and Poetry," 168–71; *End.*, III, 330–32). The sympathetic vision of maturity, meanwhile, ensures a depletion of this poetic self in the envisioning of other selves, and a consequent, consuming nightmare of the dissolution of life's physical and perceptual perfections. The poet of *The Fall of Hyperion*, we must remember, sees something far more debilitating than the "destroyings" that Apollo intimates in his vision of natural fall and Titanic self-violation. Mortal where Apollo is not, able to see with foresight but nevertheless denied the positive vision of butterfly wings forming within the caterpillar's living skin, the chilled and already enervated poet is given retrospective sight of "high tragedy" as it is reenacted in "the dark secret chambers" of Moneta's skull. He sees not new life forming but its conscious passage, an "electral changing misery" that is neither life nor death but the continual pain of dissolving consciousness (I, 243–82). He is then commanded to recreate in mortal terms and out of his finite consciousness what he has seen of this immortal "deathward" progression.

> Who hath not loiter'd in a green church-yard,
>   And let his spirit, like a demon-mole,
> Work through the clayey soil and gravel hard,
>   To see scull, coffin'd bones, and funeral stole;
> Pitying each form that hungry Death hath marr'd
> And filling it once more with human soul?

This description of what the imagination can conceive of death and recreate of former life "is holiday to what [is] felt" (*Isabella*, 353–59) by the poet of *The Fall of Hyperion* during his vision of "enormous ken,"[11] for he sees not the death or destruction of physical existence but the final extinction of conscious being. He sees not merely the gristly matter of operating theatre or morgue, nor just the horrific panorama of nature red in tooth and claw, but, far worse, the terrifying spectre of the goddess of memory as a "blank splendor," a visage "visionless entire" (I, 267–69). Behind and within the boundaries of Moneta's skull are the fragmented memories of creativity of a former immortal species that is now a "wither'd race" (I, 288). The mortal poet must read and imagine these hieroglyphics of prior creativity before they fade and even as they fade into lifeless matter and become the void of a skull without consciousness. His imaginative vision of the immortal Titans' pain of extinction, born as it is of a most mortal negative capability, requires the foresight of an intuitive philosopher, the retrospective prophecy of a Romantic evolutionist, and the ability to feel pain "Without stay or prop" (I, 388) of a Keatsian poet. The "wonders" of Titanic dissolution, as in the sonnet on seeing the Elgin Marbles, induce "a most dizzy pain" in the poet "That mingles Grecian grandeur with the rude / Wasting of old time"(11–13). The creation of a mortal poetry that heals "immortal sickness" presupposes the felt imagination of pain: " 'tis nearly pain / To be conscious of such a coronet" in poetry ("On Receiving a Laurel," 7–8); it requires, furthermore, a suffering more intense than that capable by the life to which it bears witness. Hence, Keats, by the fall of 1818, is fully resolved that he "will assay to reach as high a summit in Poetry as the nerve bestowed upon me will suffer."[12]

In Keats's unfinished story of *Hyperion*, both the Titans and the replacement race of Apollo suffer great pain. Their pains are nevertheless quite distinct in kind and in intensity. The Titans feel the "cruel pain" of extinction, a pain that is at once a physically numbing "pain of feebleness" of life completed and the dulling awareness of a dissolving consciousness that can know no more creation. They feel intensely but without intensity and must therefore be advised by Oceanus to receive this pain as a neutralizing balm called truth (I, 44, 429; II, 202, 243). Far different is the pain Apollo knows in his triumph of fresh perfection:

> Soon wild commotions shook him, and made flush
> All the immortal fairness of his limbs;
> Most like the struggle at the gate of death;
> Or liker still to one who should take leave
> Of pale immortal death, and with a pang
> As hot as death's is chill, with fierce convulse
> Die into life: so young Apollo anguish'd.
>   (Hyp., III, 124–30)

Young Apollo listens "in aching ignorance" for the impending sound of "dire events" and "rebellions" in his promised domain; he hears the inescapable "murmurous noise of waves" and the "sovran voices" of change in the universe until "bright tears / Went trickling down the golden bow he held," and he knows the simultaneous agonies of "Creations and destroyings" that are wrought by his "new blissful golden melody" (III, 114–20, 38–43; II, 279–89). Pain is the prerequisite of Apollo's supremacy, and the particular intensity of this pain is the mark of his novel or newly evolved imaginative power. The god of music and poetry in Keats's universe feels intensely and with intensity the pain of new life; his pain of sharp pangs and "fierce convulse" verifies new creation in himself and his race even as it stimulates to dull pain the fading life of past perfections in the Titans. The music of his anguish confirms the truth of his creativity.

Romantic physiologists and philosophers of mind alike saw pain as a requisite for the ascent of life into some higher form of existence. The evolution of the butterfly presupposed the pain of the chrysalis, sentient beings felt pain commensurate with the pleasure of advanced organic and sensory complexity, and the terms of conscious being allied the levels of consciousness (of self and of other life) with the degrees of pain that might be felt or intuited. Physiologists of the Romantic period spoke of the sensations of pain and pleasure as a dual sensory complex that could be known to the conscious mind only as a self-generating contrast of intensities. Bichât, in particular, was to compare the lack of sentience in minimal organic life to the human mind in a state of indifference: "It is evident that the domain of absolute pleasure or pain, is much less extensive than that of these feelings when relative. The very words agreeable, or painful, imply a comparison made between the impression received by the senses, and the state of mind on which it is received."[13] The mind in a state of indifference or indolence, when "Pain [has] no sting, and pleasure's wreath no flower" ("Indolence," 18), shows itself to be without consciousness of intensity—therefore, of lesser life.

When Lamia presents herself as "Not one hour old, yet of sciential brain / To unperplex bliss from its neighbour pain," she proposes to do what no Romantic physician or philosopher believed possible. When she sets out to "Define" the "pettish limits" of pleasure and pain "and estrange / Their points of contact, and swift counterchange," the too-skillful serpent reveals herself to be not a physician but, rather, a magician; through the "specious chaos" of her "sure art" she creates dreams out of "ambiguous atoms" in consciousness (*Lamia*, I, 191–16). Romantic healers, whether scientific or artistic, could not "unperplex" the sensations of conscious being; nor could they "estrange" the points of contact of pain and pleasure in the human mind; nor yet could they deny the "swift counterchange" of these sensations in the imagination of beauty.

Hence, everywhere in Keats's poetry, pleasure and pain form one complex intensity of feeling, as Romantic medicine decreed they must, and pleasure is known, increasingly, through the conscious imagining of pain. "A butterfly, with golden wings broad parted, / Nestling a rose" in "Sleep and Poetry" seems "convuls'd as though it smarted / With over pleasure," and the epiphany of its sensory existence is displayed through an image of sharp pain (343–45). Pan, in "I stood tip-toe," knows the fate of his Syrinx through an image of painful sound, "a lovely sighing of the wind," "a half heard strain, / Full of sweet desolation—balmy pain" (159–62). Secular "Music's golden tongue" insinuates itself into the shrinking ear of the Beadsman in *The Eve of St. Agnes* as an unwanted sensation of painful delight and, caught between the pains of expiation and pleasure despite himself, the aged ascetic finds himself "Flatter'd to tears" (20–21). The poet experiences the beauty of Cassandra as a burning heart and, because of this, knows "only pains, / They were my pleasures" ("Nature withheld Cassandra," 10–14). Even the bliss of love in *Endymion* finds repeated image not merely as a conventional "Sweet paining" but as a heartache physical and sharp until we wonder, "is grief contain'd / In the very deeps of pleasure . . . ?" and anticipate therein the intense stressed substance of the "Ode on Melancholy" (*End.*, II, 856, 773, 823–24).

Images of pain, "branched thoughts, new grown with pleasant pain," and evocations of pleasure as it is imagined through the known experiences of pain, multiply in the poems of Keats's maturity in the very pattern of "the wreath'd trellis of a working brain" that is used to dress the "rosy sanctuary" of the feeling soul in the "Ode to Psyche" (52, 59–60). The poet found himself ever less free from "the trammels of pain" and ever more conscious that, while pleasure might be "oft a visitant" to less conscious existence, "pain / Clings cruelly to us, like the gnawing sloth / On the deer's tender haunches" ("On Receiving a Curious Shell," 24; *End.*, I, 906–8). His awareness that he could not "shut his eyes" to the pains of the world, like the young Endymion, combined with his physician's knowledge that "Imagination gave a dizzier pain" in retrospection to each initial experience of pain; his knowledge in creative maturity that "All is cold beauty" in the world unless it is experienced in the intensity of its existence combined, simultaneously, with an intense awareness that for the poet of negative capability "pain is never done" (*End.*, III, 1008–9; "On Visiting the Tomb of Burns," 8). The rapt visualizations of pain in the great odes, the Hyperion poems, and the last lyrics are all products of this complex awareness of the multiple counters of pain in consciousness, and of the constitutive role of pain in human perception. "Until we are sick, we understand not," the poet said in 1818, and he went on to observe that we can know only what we imagine fully, that pain was knowledge and "Sorrow is Wisdom."[14] More that his medical and literary peers, Keats knew that his poetic task as a physician who would heal the sorrows of mankind was to read pain in all its forms and, with an intuitive imagination of the pain of all the life forms and through the intensity of his art, to make the disagreeables of its variety vanish.

Hazlitt characterized the imaginative power of the Romantic physician or anatomist as an ability to overcome "the sense of pain and repugnance, which is the only feeling that the sight of a dead and mangled body presents to ordinary men" and to become absorbed instead by "an entire new set of ideas" on the nature of life.[15] In his intuitive reading of the diseased body's pain, the Romantic physician put aside the disagreeables of initial sensation to focus on a perceptive imagination of the creature before him and the consequence of its pain for past and future existence. Artists, for Hazlitt, like their medical counterparts, "see beauty where others see nothing of the sort, in wrinkles, deformity, and old age. They see it . . . in the dark shadows . . . as well as in the splendid colours . . . in an angel's or a butterfly's wings. They see with different eyes from the multitude. But true genius," Hazlitt adds, especially that visionary genius of the scientist and artist of the Romantic era, "though it has new sources of pleasure opened to it, does not lose its sympathy with humanity." "However painful may be the objects with which the Anatomist's knowledge is connected, he feels that his knowledge is pleasure," Wordsworth also said, in his preface to *Lyrical Ballads* (1802), when he noted that all sympathy with pain is "produced and carried on" through "subtle combinations with pleasure."[16] Hazlitt's formulations on "true genius" closely anticipate Keats's definition of the intuitive genius of the physician-poet. Moreover, when Hazlitt speaks in 1822 of the "sympathy [that] is indispensible to truth of expression" and notes that "to sympathise with passion, a greater fund of sensibility is demanded in proportion to the strength or tenderness of the passion,"[17] he could be echoing Keats's earlier ideas on the debilitative effects of the artist's identification with other life and on the Romantic poet's necessary sympathetic imagination of pain.

Whether pain can be imagined is the opening question of Elaine Scarry's *The Body in Pain: The Making and Unmaking of the World* (1985), as she connects the story of physical pain with the "expansive nature of human *sentience*" and speculates that "the story of *expressing* physical pain eventually opens into the wider frame of *invention*." A chapter on the "relation between physical pain and imagining" carries the analogy further to propose that pain might well be the imagination's natural state:

> The only state that is as anomalous as pain is the imagination. While pain is a state remarkable for being wholly without objects, the imagination is remarkable for

being the only state that is wholly its objects. . . . Physical pain, then, is an intentional state without an intentional object; imagining is an intentional object without an experienceable intentional state. Thus, it may be that in some peculiar way it is appropriate to think of pain as the imagination's intentional state, and to identify the imagination as pain's intentional object.[18]

Pain and the imagination, for Scarry, "are each other's missing intentional counterpart" and "together provide a framing identity of man-as-creator. . . ."[19] Just this equivocation of pain and imagination as counterparts or near-analogous states occurs in Keats's tendency to envision pleasure through images of pain, in his conception of Apollo's artistry or life power in *Hyperion* as a higher sensitivity to pain, and in his overall belief that the imagination of pain in other life is essential to creative, healing vision in the poet.

The imagination of pain, the ability to intuit and to read correctly from within the signs of illness as if they were one's own disease was a necessity for the Romantic physician. More than an issue or philosophic question, it underlay the very tenets of medical semiotics and its theory of the comprehension of disease. Given Keats's resolve to describe the poet's task through the lens of the physician, his need to imagine pain was at once extensive and acute. With the other thinkers of his generation, he believed that although all of nature could feel pain, the consciousness of pain was singular to the human imagination. As Scarry says, the "naturally existing external world" is

wholly ignorant of the "hurtability" of human beings. Immune, inanimate, inhuman, it indifferently manifests itself in the thunderbolt and hailstorm, rabid bat, smallpox microbe, and ice crystal. The human imagination reconceives the external world, divesting it of its immunity and irresponsibility not by literally putting it in pain or making it animate but by, quite *literally*, "*making it*" *as knowledgeable about human pain as if it were itself animate and in pain.*[20]

The natural world's ignorance of human pain becomes, in Keats's physician-poet, a willed resolve to use the advanced form of conscious being given him by "Nature's law" to re-create other life as if it were his own, to imagine the pain of other existence through the knowledge of human pain, and to reconstruct the "feeling" of the leafless tree and frozen brook in "drear nighted December" as if these creations were endowed with human sentience and memory.

> In drear nighted December,
>   Too happy, happy tree,
> Thy branches ne'er remember
>   Their green felicity—
> The north cannot undo them
> With a sleety whistle through them,
> Nor frozen thawings glue them
>   From budding at the prime.

> In drear nighted December,
>   Too happy, happy brook,
> Thy bubblings ne'er remember
>   Apollo's summer look;
> But with a sweet forgetting,
> They stay their crystal fretting,
> Never, never petting
>   About the frozen time.
>   (1–16)

The poet remembers "green felicity" for a tree that cannot, and so feels in retrospect the "sleety whistle" and freezing glue of the north wind as it passes through the tree's re-created "green felicity;" he gives memory of "summer's look" and happy "bubblings" to a brook now frozen into stilled insentience, and so gives a human awareness of "frozen time" to a brook that would perhaps prefer, were it endowed with memory and the human consciousness of pain, the much more tolerable "sweet forgetting" of its prior existence. "The feel of not to feel it" (21) becomes, thus, a particularly human experience of consciousness imagining itself as an insentient and unconscious void. The poet feels what the brook and tree cannot feel of their wintry tragedy, but, because of his imagination, he feels this nothingness as a human being—more intensely and with "dizzier pain." "I shriek'd; and the sharp anguish of my shriek / Stung my own ears," Keats says of the self-consciousness of human pain (*Fall of Hyp.*, I, 126–27). We understand now why the poet in *The Fall of Hyperion*, when forced to bear the "load" of the extinct Titans' "eternal quietude / Ponderous upon [his] senses," feels pain more intense than that immortal pain known by the Titans in their frozen, petrified, or less conscious, state (I, 388–92). We understand, further, why the poet's recreation of this vision that even the goddess of memory will forget in time, from out of his "own weak mortality," is a mark of a higher consciousness and a more intense albeit more vulnerable power of life.

The "great end" of poetry, Keats said, was "that it should be a friend / To sooth the cares, and lift the thoughts of man" ("Sleep and Poetry," 245–47). The task in sustaining the visions that the poet would re-create as medicine for the pains of humankind, Keats knew from the start, was not easy:

> The visions are all fled–the car is fled
> Into the light of heaven, and in their stead
> A sense of real things comes doubly strong,
> And, like a muddy stream, would bear along
> My soul to nothingness: but I will strive
> Against all doubtings, and will keep alive
> The thought of that same chariot, and the strange
> Journey it went.
>   ("Sleep and Poetry," 155–62)

The difficulties of poetic vision—the poet's evolutionary task—furthermore, presupposed debilitation and self-sacrifice. To the definition of "sensibility" in contemporary evolution theory as "the living thing exists for itself" or "life self-reflected, as already existing for itself"[21] was to be contrasted poetic sensibility or the self-effacing negative capability of the poet who lived and felt for others and envisioned the pain of others. In Romantic evolution, organic life sacrificed itself for the fresh perfections of new or other life: "Broad leaved fig trees . . . foredoom / Their ripen'd fruitage; yellow girted bees / Their golden honeycombs . . . / The chuckling linnet its five young unborn / . . . low creeping strawberries / Their summer coolness; pent up butterflies / Their freckled wings; yea, the fresh budding year / All its completions" (End., I, 252–60). Even among a given species, "hungry generations," as in the "Ode to a Nightingale" (62), tread one another down in the inexorable escalation of particular being. But in his story of the ascension of beauty in the *Hyperion* poems, where Apollo's self-effacement and vulnerability replaces the Titans' egotistical might, Keats offered an alternate and generous *poet's* vision of evolution. Thinkers of the revolutionary period absorbed current ideas of evolution even as their egalitarian senses were repelled by the implications of superiority and voracious replacement among species and races inherent in these ideas.[22] To the Romantic yearning for an alternate, benign vision of the evolution of life and consciousness to contrast Erasmus Darwin's picture of "one great Slaughter-house the warring world"[23] belongs Keats's conception of the poet as a self-sacrificing physician able to comprehend and assume the pain of others. To the contemporary evolutionists' portrayal of nature as a battleground of survival, to the poet's own horrific vision embodying this picture of nature of the shark at savage prey, the hawk at pounce, and the gentle robin ravening a worm ("Dear Reynolds," 103–5), Keats posited the creature who willingly renders up its existence for others: "the rose [that] leaves herself upon the briar, / For winds to kiss and grateful bees to feed" ("On Fame," 9–10), or the poet who "martyrs himself to the human heart" and makes human suffering "the main region of his song."[24]

The poet's belief in the human potential for generosity was fundamental and willed: " 'We have all one human heart'—there is an ellectric fire in human nature tending to purify—so that among these human creature[s] there is continually some birth of new heroism—."[25] Self-sacrifice or the deliberate exposure of the self's vulnerability is an evolutionary fact of human nature for Keats, one that is related to the human consciousness of pain in other living creatures. Hence, in Keats's poetic universe, there is a continual birth of new heroism and fresh perfecting of perceptual sympathy in the evolution of humankind and human kindness. The necessary consumption of life by life is countered by the negative capability possible to human perception. Recurring images of prolonged suffering from Glaucus to Moneta telescope thus, according to the laws of a benign or heroic evolution, into the figure of the poet who suffers as a physician: an Apollo (in *Hyperion*) who triumphs because of, not in spite of, his vulnerability and generosity of spirit, a mortal poet (in The Fall of Hyperion) who has a greater and more enduring consciousness of pain than the immortal creatures he envisions precisely because of his debilitated mortality.

Inner vision, "To see as a God sees, and take the depth / Of things," wreaks outer deprivation, as we have seen, and the perfection of an art like that of the first Apollo's healing music necessitates a willed "living death" in "each gush of sounds" (Fall of Hyp., I, 304–5; Hyp., II, 281). "How many bards gild the lapses of time!" becomes an exclamation real and true to this deliberately heroic law of evolution delineated by Keats: the poet's task is a task of willful self-sacrifice, the use of the physical and perceptual self to decorate the lapses and lacunae of time and being and render coherent an ever-perfecting world of discrete suffering. Keats makes his figure of the poet interchangeable with the meaning, and the fragility, of life. Music from his poet's lyre, like that first music made by the god of healing upon a once-living tortoise's hollow and variegated shell, must be listened to by "the whole universe" "in pain and pleasure." "The birth / Of such new tuneful wonder" and the parallel ascension of suffering in the poet (Hyp., III, 65–67), what Keats sees as an ever-expanding mortal consciousness of pain, as in the principle of fresh perfection of Romantic evolution, is never done.

Chapter 25

Reading Life

Keats's last and perhaps most perfect ode, "To Autumn," provides the pattern and the sign to the poet's final, diagnostic reading of life.

> Season of mists and mellow fruitfulness,
>   Close bosom-friend of the maturing sun;
> Conspiring with him how to load and bless
>   With fruit the vines that round the thatch-eves run;
> To bend with apples the moss'd cottage-trees,
>   And fill all fruit with ripeness to the core;
>   To swell the gourd, and plump the hazel shells
>   With a sweet kernel; to set budding more,
> And still more, later flowers for the bees,
> Until they think warm days will never cease,
>   For summer has o'er brimm'd their clammy cells.
>   (1–11)

The ripened life of autumn's harvest is a compound potion of tangible substance and intangible illusion. The poet would have us read between the rows of "gold autumn's whole kingdoms of corn" ("Apollo to the Graces," 6) and ponder whether the picture of autumn's harvest represents a process of abundancy and maturation, as it should, or whether it is an illusory excess summoned in the face of finitude. Autumn's brief bounty is clearly suspect from the start. The season of mellow fruitfulness and distinct substantial creation is also a season of disorienting mists that chill the body, confuse the senses, blur the lines of physical existence, and provoke the anxieties of rational consciousness. The inductive warmth of autumn makes it an unlikely—and perhaps too close—"bosom-friend" of the maturing and therefore wintry sun. Sun and season together conspire for mutual benefit (much as Hermes and Lamia did in *Lamia*): they seduce with pain and pleasure, loading and blessing vine, tree, and blossoming plant until nature fruits and flowers simultaneously as an unearthly paradise removed from mortal time. Autumn's activity to "swell the gourd, and plump the hazel shells" is a pressure, an ambivalent physical sensation reminiscent of, as Ricks describes it, "the pressure of sleep and of opiate";[1] its overweening need to "fill all fruit with ripeness to the core" prompts the realization meanwhile that at the core physical life disintegrates first. In the never-never land of *Endymion*'s sea palace, a parallel superabundance prevailed:

> Nectar ran
> In courteous fountains to all cups outreach'd;
> And plunder'd vines, teeming exhaustless, pleach'd
> New growth about each shell and pendant lyre.
> (III, 925–28)

But there the fantasy was real, at least for the dead lovers who are "reanimated" from their icy tombs at the stroke of a dreaming poet's wand. Here, in the seasonal world of Keats's maturity, nothing teems exhaustless and the bees and flowers are autumn's fools. We are to read in autumn's ability to mimic and outdo the summer in fostering life, in its ability to set flowers "budding more, / And still more" and to make the bees "think warm days will never cease," a cruel and illusory excess of life. The "hurry and alarm / When the bee-hive casts its swarm" upon hearing "the autumn breezes sing" of winter ("Fancy," 63–66) presages the "frozen time" of drear-nighted December: sleety thawings will glue the flower buds, summer's overbrimming honey will congeal around the larvae, and some juveniles will not grow wings and instead rot at the core of the hive.

Life is *too* much in late autumn, and a harvest is always ambiguous. We are reminded of the premature harvest forced forth to honor Pan in Book I of *Endymion* when the fig trees foredoom their fruit, the yellow bees surrender the sweetness and larvae of their "golden honeycombs," the overexcited butterflies give up their "freckled wings," and the chuckling linnet abandons "its five young unborn / To sing" for the indifferent Pan; the forced growth of this scene finds further, unnatural parallel in a subsequent harvest scene when nature is overripe: "deepest shades" turn "deepest dungeons," "heaths and sunny glades" fill with "pestilential light," "taintless rills" seem "sooty, and o'er-spread with upturned gills / Of dying fish," and the "vermeil rose" is overblown "In frightful scarlet" with "its thorns out-grown / Like spiked aloe" (I, 252–59, 692–98). Premature and too-late harvests in the early poetry anticipate yet another vision of ripeness where the harvest turns out to be only an anticipated harvest born of the fears of a "teeming brain:" the poet's vision of "high piled books, in charactry" holding "like rich garners the full-ripen'd grain" of his aspirations, all harvest shadows dissipated by "the magic hand of chance" and preempted by the premonitions of real death ("When I have fears," 1–8). This autumnal harvest of poetic achievement seen as horrific unfulfillment by a young and dying poet, in turn, reminds us of the "feast of summer fruits" that the poet of *The Fall of Hyperion* tastes and knows on closer inspection to be not an immortal cornucopia but picnic leavings abandoned by the gods—the "refuse of a meal" (I, 28–38). These harvests foreshadow and foredoom autumn's leavings in an ode that is no ode and, certainly, no picnic.

Within autumn's seasonal illusion of life as abundance and fruitful excess, as pictured in stanza I of "To Autumn," can be found mute promise of autumn's minimal life, a shallow bounty of gnats, crickets, and twittering swallows summoned briefly to life and or activity by the sad music of stanza 3. Autumn's harvest beauty, a process or procession of sacrifice like that graven on the Grecian urn of Keats's other ode to life, is dependent upon the experience of transience. It is a passing pleasure felt through the pain or knowledge of what follows after the illusion of boundless or eternal life fades.

> Who hath not seen thee oft amid thy store?
>   Sometimes whoever seeks abroad may find
> Thee sitting careless on a granary floor,
>   Thy hair soft-lifted by the winnowing wind;
> Or on a half-reap'd furrow sound asleep,
>   Drows'd with the fume of poppies, while thy hook
>   Spares the next swath and all its twined flowers:
> And sometimes like a gleaner thou dost keep
>   Steady thy laden head across a brook;
>   Or by a cyder-press, with patient look,
>   Thou watchest the last oozings hours by hours.
>   (12–22)

This neutral, winnowed out, sexless, and barely alive figure of Autumn is a distant cousin of Humboldt's Genius of Rhodes. Stilled to conserve its minimal energy where the Genius was once the taut container of maximum vitality, Keats's Autumn does not actively prevent putrefaction so much as futilely trust that passive inaction will allow it to escape the onset of death. Shored up amid its stores, the figure represents the lull or void after living action has ceased: it is asleep after the grain has been gathered and the field furrowed, it is a gleaner without function, and a "silent watcher" not of new worlds and pacific oceans but, rather, one that broods with "patient look" and eyes dulled "with the fume of poppies" on the "last oozings" of the cider press. Perhaps this figure of residual life, like those flowers spared by the sickle, will escape the harvest of winter. Perhaps also, as the young bees think, "warm days will never cease." Keats the physician knows the consequence of life better.

If the ambiguous figure of Autumn reminds us in its stillness of the carved revelers of the Grecian urn and the petrified Titans in their eternal quietude of extinction, it is nevertheless without the beauty of an art object or the natural wonder of behemoth fossils. What chills most about its lassitude is that the symptom reflects less energy—and pain—than do these figures. The figure neither conceives of autumn's bounty nor anticipates "the feel of not to feel it" that will follow shortly, as the poet knows, in drear-nighted December. It is not a symbol of benignity despite its soft hair and merciful sickle, nor is it a horrific symptom of malignant, voracious death. Stilled in time, the figure simply does not know time and so stands as a sign for residual existence without consciousness that the poet reads through his own horror of mortality. Autumn, as Keats personifies it, is quite distinct from other figures of old age in the poetry: from Glaucus who must "wither, droop, and pine" for one thousand years, from Moneta whose pale visage will always be "deathwards progressing," even from Angela the old beldame "weak in body and in soul" who dies "palsy-twitch'd, with meagre face deform" in *The Eve of St. Agnes* (90, 375–76). Autumn's distinction from these is its neutral torpidity, a specific albeit erroneous concept from Romantic physiology that recognized a third state in physical organization, "*a state of neutrality intermediate between that of life and death,* a state into which certain animals are plunged in consequence of the stoppage of respiration." Because animals did not breathe in this state and could purportedly "survive" for centuries, it was considered to be a condition quite separate from the dormancy of seeds or the "suspended animation" of animals "benumbed by winter."[2] The notion of being suspended or preserved in a state of neutral torpidity that was neither life nor death nor any state between these, however physically improbable, was nevertheless imaginatively real to the dissociation from life and vacuity of consciousness that Keats wished to portray in his personification. The Autumn of Keats's poem is an entity that is unheroically indifferent to life and death; its unfulfillment and suspension from process signals the obverse of fruition. Neither a person nor a tangible existential verity, by escaping harvest and the consequence of ripeness the figure eludes—and is so denied—the breath of life. Because of all this, the figure represents, at its best, a poet's memory of a harvest that never happened because the seeming growth portrayed by life was too meager an illusion to sustain an ode of bounty.

"Life must be undergone, and I certainly derive a consolation from the thought of writing one or two more Poems before it ceases—."[3] We are to read the concept of organic ripeness in "To Autumn" in the context of the poet's premonition of his own limited harvest and premature end. The lines from Book XI of *Paradise Lost* that Keats underlined in his copy of Milton give poignant emphasis to the fate of a poet harshly plucked before he was "for death mature" and to his inability to conceive of ripeness except in ambiguous terms:

> So may'st thou live, till like ripe Fruit thou drop
> Into thy Mother's lap; or be with ease
> Gather'd, not harshly pluckt, for death mature.[4]

Cognizant of the finitude of life as a physician and able to rationalize the poetic truth of *King Lear*, "Men must endure / Their going hence even as their coming hither, / Ripeness is all,"[5] Keats nevertheless saw autumn's harvest as a fiction of maturity and bounty that masked a real indifference to life and pain. His protest, cast in the sober colors of three stanzas to "Autumn," remains the protest of life of the debilitated "King of the butterflies" in *Endymion*: "I did wed / Myself to things of light from infancy; / And thus to be cast out, thus lorn to die, / Is sure enough to make a mortal man / Grow impious" (IV, 952, 957–61). "I fear I am too prudent for a dying kind of Lover," Keats wrote to Fanny Brawne during the last months of his life; too prudent to deny the truth of what he knew of life's cycle, he was also too conscious of the shortcuts life took to maintain the illusion of universal fruition in nature at autumn: "There is a great difference between going off in warm blood like Romeo, and making one's exit like a frog in a frost."[6]

Seasonal nature was indeed "one great slaughterhouse," the Romantic physician knew. With its confusion of the seasons and deceitful promise of endless completions, autumnal process could be a Romantic poet's nightmare of the seasons turned inside out.

> Last night I looked into a dream; 'twas drawn
> On the black midnight of a velvet sleep,
> And set in woeful thoughts; and there I saw
> A thin, pale Cupid, with bare, ragged wings
> Like skeletons of leaves, in autumn left,
> That sift the frosty air. One hand was shut,
> And in its little hold of ivory
> Fastened a May-morn zephyr, frozen straight,
> Made deadly with a hornet's rugged sting,
> Gilt with the influence of an adverse star.
> Such was his weapon, and he traced with it,
> Upon the waters of my thoughts, these words:
> 'I am the death of flowers, and nightingales,
> And small–lipped babes, that give their souls to summer
> To make a perfumed day with: I shall come,
> A death no larger than a sigh to thee,
> Upon a sunset hour.'[7]

Beddoes's physician's vision of a skeletal Cupid as grim reaper of autumn, born without innocence and able to kill with the breath of spring, presents the same nightmare sight of the telescoping of seasons that Keats sees in his vision of autumn's purported "mellow fruitfulness."

Spring and summer can not only masquerade as each other and assume the fictions of each other, as they do in Beddoes's dream; too often for Keats they can be conceived only in the worst terms of each other:

> Summer's joys are spoilt by use,
> And the enjoying of the spring
> Fades as does its blossoming;
> Autumn's red-lipp'd fruitage too,
> Blushing through the mist and dew,
> Cloys with tasting. . . .
>   ("Fancy," 10–15)

Summer anticipates the cloying taste of autumn, and autumn the fading blossoms of spring. The "wholesome drench of April rains" in "The Eve of St. Mark" recollects the prior winter in its "chilly sunset," "unmatur'd green vallies cold," "thorny bloomless hedge," and "daisies on the aguish hills" (4–12). At the tomb of Robert Burns, in mute mockery of the frenzy of human creativity, the "short-lived, paly summer is but won / From winter's ague, for one hour's gleam" (5–6). The seasons fold into one another thus, and winter can play at being autumn in order to harvest the premature growth of a chilly spring.

As Keats reveals in his last "ode," the simultaneity of flower, fruit, and death in the autumn of his young mind can undermine both the sequential promise of external nature's seasons and the consequence of continual "new heroism" in the evolving conception of human kindness.

> Where are the songs of spring? Ay, where are they?
>   Think not of them, thou hast thy music too,—
> While barred clouds bloom the soft-dying day,
>   And touch the stubble-plains with rosy hue;
> Then in a wailful choir the small gnats mourn
>   Among the river sallows, borne aloft
>   Or sinking as the light wind lives or dies;
> And full-grown lambs loud bleat from hilly bourn;
>   Hedge-crickets sing; and now with treble soft
>   The red-breast whistles from a garden-croft;
>   And gathering swallows twitter in the skies.
>   (23–33)

In the last stanza that he will write to the occasion of autumn, Keats conceives of its ripe event in terms of minimal existence, abandonment, boundary, and the final pause before the cessation of the life cycle. The songs of autumn are the sounds of distress and departure: the occasional "wailful choir" of small gnats who might not survive the sunset, the intermittent "loud bleat" from grown "lambs" ready for shearing shed or slaughterhouse, and the persistent, ominous "twitter" of swallows gathering to leave. The images of life in the last stanza of "To Autumn" mirror the portrait in the *Aeneid*, of the souls of the dead on the river banks in the underworld, an understandable link since we know that Keats translated Virgil during the early years of his apprenticeship to the surgeon Hammond. Davenport has noted two similes used by Virgil to describe the throng that are of particular interest to Keats's message of autumn:

> They are, first, 'as many as the leaves that fall *in the first cold Autumn*' and, second, 'as many as the *birds that gather* (glomerantur) *when the cold year drives them across the sea.*' Birds gathering for migration have links, in fact, with both the decay of autumn and with the dead generations of mankind. The wailful choir of gnats may also be linked with Virgil's account of the souls who must stay on the hither bank and for a hundred years 'wander' and 'float hovering' (volitant) about 'these shores' until they are permitted to return to the still and fenny waters (stagna) that they yearn for (exoptata).[8]

Birds, gnats, poets, and friends—"they all vanish like Swallows in October."[9] For his gathering birds of passage, Keats had a more immediate source than Virgil, for journals and societies functioning between 1812 and 1826 reveal considerable general interest in England in the instincts of migratory birds and the interpretive consequence of these instincts for human intelligence and behavior. The nesting habits of swallows in particular generated a variety of papers on the birds' flight schedules and intimations of the season, their abandonment of unfledged nestlings at first frost, their return at spring to board up those nests containing dead baby birds, and of the blind necessity of their instinct to bury the mistakes or imperfections of a prior season: one report of 1818 told of returning swallows that found a sparrow and her young living in an old nest and promptly buried them with spring "building materials" in a remarkable display of blind instinct and indifference to life that was not their own.[10] A chill and indifferent spring follows, as in the poem "Fancy" and the sonnet at Burns's tomb, the agues of winter and the premature creations of autumn; and nature has but small and enclosing space for those living mistakes exposed by the passage of seasons.

The poet of "To Autumn," abandoned by the swallows and unable, like Milton, to pounce upon "Beauty on the wing" for the production of "essential verse," is left at twilight with the present moment of consciousness, defined by Thomas Brown as "a *bright point,—ever moving,* and yet, as it were, ever *fixed,—*which divides the *darkness of the future* from the *twilight of the past.*"[11] The produce of autumn is indeed for Keats just such a moment bound by the present and rescued briefly from the twilight of past springs and the darkness of future winters. Nothing positive links the "stationing" of the process of autumn in three stanzas here with those flushed and "tip-toe" Keatsian moments of globed peonies and brimming capacity that we connect with his best poetry. "To Autumn" attempts to put in the best possible light of poetic consciousness that bounded moment "One minute before death" in nature that Keats recognized as a physician and was to know shortly as a patient; it captures the moment of ebbing sensation when "a palsied chill" seizes "those streams that pulse beside the throat," the cold grows "stifling, suffocating, at the heart," and gnat, fledgling, frog, and poet alike strive "hard to escape / The numbness" (*Fall of Hyp.*, 122–32). By the end of his impossible ode to autumn, Keats has read through the fruition of process and the abundance of fresh perfection, in nature and in mind, to a stilled, dark point of incompletion and recession.

Life, for Keats, is the ebbing of life. What the physician saw in the clinic for the terminally ill—a specific exhaustion of mortal life that could not be stopped by any medicine and a general wanton display of the ebbing of finite energy in mankind—was the very same thing that the poet envisioned in nature at large. Both kinds of healers read life through the advanced perceptual lenses of their various disciplines, and their readings of life's "leavings" proved to be identical: life was the sight and the sign of its painful depletion. In a Romantic age that had made life the primary subject of inquiry and generated numerous and conflicting testimonials on the nature of life,[12] Keats's portrait of life in autumn stands at the point of consensus on the subject among the physiologists and philosophers of his time. All would acknowledge that life, invisible until the moment of "first flush," could only be known at ebb, and all would agree that the life force revealed itself in the physical world of creatures through the debilitating albeit generative windings down of its own finite energies.

> Stop and consider! life is but a day;
> A fragile dew-drop on its perilous way
> From a tree's summit; a poor Indian's sleep
> While his boat hastens to the monstrous steep
> Of Montmorenci. Why so sad a moan?
> Life is the rose's hope while yet unblown;
> The reading of an ever-changing tale;
> The light uplifting of a maiden's veil;
> A pigeon tumbling in clear summer air;
> A laughing school-boy, without grief or care,
> Riding the springy branches of an elm.
> ("Sleep and Poetry," 85–95)

The ability to conceive of life's brevity with positive image dissipated quickly in Keats. From nearly the start of his poetic career and then with increasing frequency in maturity, Keats found himself reading the "ever-changing tale" of life in the "Language pronounc'd" by *The Fall of Hyperion*, and he invariably saw life's creations through that poem's image of running sand in an hourglass: "The sands of thy short life are spent this hour / And no hand in the universe can turn / Thy hourglass..." (I, 107, 114–17). The revived dead lovers of *Endymion* pour down the stairs of Neptune's hall "as easily / As hour-glass sand" and their swift passage of descent, as "fast, as you might see / Swallows obeying the south summer's call," reminds us of the perilously fragile condition of their reanimation (III, 814–16). The imperceptible creep of sand when "Time's sea hath been five years at its slow ebb" reiterates for us the mind's ability to distort time with "sweet remembering" and "eclipse" the swift ebbing of mortal existence in a poet (1–14). The poet's "Castle-builder" is shown us in the moment when he finds among the fragments of his fantasy "A skull upon a mat of roses" and "An hour glass on the turn, amid the trails / Of passion-flower" (42–5). Even the poet's attempt to capture spring gladness and "the feel of May" "After dark vapours have oppressed our plains" finds expression in a language of ebbing passage that ties together the images of "a sleeping infant's breath—/ The gradual sand that through an hour glass runs—/ A woodland rivulet—a poet's death" (6, 9–14).

   "When one subtracts from life infancy (which is vegetation),—sleep, eating, and swilling—buttoning and unbuttoning—how much remains of downright existence? The summer of a doormouse."[13] Byron's forthright estimate of the actual time of life summarizes his age's sense of the inexorable passage and dilution of existential time; his "doormouse" is also an evolutionary cousin of the field mouse whose ebbing existence Keats would measure and know through the limitless negative capability of a finite poet. To the young poet "Still scooping up the water with [his] fingers, / In which a trembling diamond never lingers," minutes are always "flying swiftly," "time is fleeting, and no dream arises" without the picture of life at fluid ebb ("To Charles Cowden Clarke," 19–20; "On Receiving a Laurel," 1, 9). The description of tides and of the moon's depleting force by Buffon and the Romantic evolutionists influenced not just the poet's language in his estimate of Milton's oceanic intellect[14] but, clearly, his overall conception of life, whether physical or perceptual, as the ebbing of a limited and fragile energy. Endymion's enervated request for healing from his sister, Peona, "help to stem the ebbing sea / Of weary life" (I, 709) becomes, for the physician-poet of Keats's maturity, a real choice to be made in the drab face of life's finitude: "I must choose between despair & Energy—I choose the latter—though the world has taken on a quakerish look with me, which I once thought impossible—."[15] "Every thing is spoilt by use" the poem "Fancy" warns, just after its description of the telescoping of seasons (68), and "I stood tip-toe" provides graphic image of the careless waste in finite life: "fair clusters" of "spreading blue bells" are "rudely torn / From their fresh beds, and scattered thoughtlessly / By infant hands, [then] left on the path to die" (43–46). Yet, even without use, natural life expends itself with a wantonness and waste that highlights the downward passage of mortal existence. The "droop-headed" peony, despite its symbolic role in the legend of healing and its physical image in Keats's poetry of life at the flush, blooms and sheds its petals at once during the summer solstice; "Fast fading violets cover'd up in leaves" fade nevertheless before nightfall; "the hot sun count[s] / His dewy rosary on the eglantine;" and wan primroses are "gather'd at midnight / By chilly finger'd spring" ("Melancholy," 13–17; "Nightingale," 47; Isabella, 187–88; End., IV, 970–71). Blossoms "hang by a melting spell / And fall they must" until "the bare heath of life presents no bloom" ("Ah! woe is me!" 13–14; "To Hope," 4). Thus, not just in Melancholy's garden of sorrow but everywhere in Keats's poetry of life, images of "sweet life leaving" ("Ah! woe is me!" 17) multiply in a pitiful harvest of existence.

The winnowed and deliberately minimal figure of Autumn in the final ode is merely the poet's last, least embodiment of the ebbing of life. More poignant in retrospect are the depletions of springtime, those numerous human images of youthful life at quick ebb and youthful consciousness in sudden passage that pattern the poetry from start to finish: of "sweet Isabel" falling "By gradual decay from beauty" in the space of a few weeks; of Madeline abandoned "to fade and pine" in a sudden winter storm; of Endymion witnessing a "dread waterspout" come to "wipe [his] life away like a vast sponge of fate;" of Leander seen in a "horrid dream" quickly "Sinking away to his young spirit's night," with a series of bubbles from the ocean floor as the only reminders of his heroic consciousness; of Chatterton seen in a recurring personal nightmare, his "majestic" voice "Melted in dying murmurs" even as it begins, and his poetic consciousness experiencing night and day simultaneously as an adjacent, present and only time of creativity (*Isabella*, 256; *Eve*, 329; *End.*, III, 346–49; "On a Leander," 7–14; "Oh Chatterton," 6–7). Life ebbs too soon for the fledglings of autumn; in creation they, especially, find that all too quickly "The day is gone, and all its sweets are gone"

> Faded the flower and all its budded charms,
>   Faded the sight of beauty from my eyes,
> Faded the shape of beauty from my arms,
>   Faded the voice, warmth, whiteness, paradise—

all vanish "unseasonably at shut of eve, / When the dusk holiday" begins to weave its "woof of darkness" (5–12).

An enormous gulf separates the first affirmation of limitless creation, "The poetry of earth is never dead," from the modest backwash of that affirmation, a late and limited acknowledgment that "The poetry of earth is ceasing never;" yet, for Keats, the sad recognition of the distinction requires but fourteen lines of verse ("The Grasshopper and Cricket," 1–14). In the poet's world of rapid maturity and premature fruition, autumn follows spring directly without summer and often without succession. Too often in this world of speeded-up time, spring reveals itself to be a simultaneous autumn and, for the one who knows that the creations of life are always at ebb, the cricket's autumnal chorus proves no substitute for the grasshopper's song foolishly spent. Little time and less than an image separate the fragility of a sleeping infant's breath in spring from a poet's death in autumn for, in Keats's physician's vision of the ebb of life, June "breathes out life for butterflies" of all species for sun and frost to harvest ("To Some Ladies Who Saw Me Crown'd," 11). For a Romantic poet who has numbered too often the fading moments preceding the last flush of life in creatural forms and who has seen that "the bare heath of life" can all too easily and quickly "present no bloom," the sacred task to see existence in the spent wings of an air-sylph, read fresh perfection in the pains of extinction, and portray life in the bleak meagerness of "a few strips of green on a cold hill" in Burns's country ensures immediate and irrecoverable debility of the poetic self. Ebbing life feeds on other ebbing life, and bleak Brunonian exhaustion can result from the stress of overwrought intensity; the intense art of Romantic medicine feeds rapidly upon the finite life intensity or negative capability of its poet until, as Moneta declares in *The Fall of Hyperion* (I, 241), "The sacrifice is done...."

Notes

INTRODUCTION

1. Lester S. King's *The Medical World of the Eighteenth Century* (1958; reprint, New York: Robert E. Krieger, 1971), Philip Ritterbush's *Overtures to Biology: The Speculations of Eighteenth-Century Naturalists* (New Haven: Yale University Press, 1964), and Daniel M. Fox and Gilbert J. Gall's *Photographing Medicine: Images and Power in Britain and America Since* 1840 (Westport, Conn.: Greenwood Press, 1988) are fine examples of these established historical parameters in the history of science. Literary critics have continued the scientific historian's paradigm, for they usually trace the literary interest in science to the importance of Charles Darwin's theory of evolution and the Victorian concern with industrial progress. Two admirable books of recent years serve as good examples: Peter Morton's *The Vital Science: Biology and the Literary Imagination, 1860–1900* (London: Allen & Unwin, 1984), and George Levine's *Darwin and the Novelists: Patterns of Science in Victorian Fiction* (Cambridge: Harvard University Press, 1988).

2. "From Newton to Darwin the preference of romantic thinkers for the sciences of life is as striking as the predilection of rationalistic thinkers for the physical sciences. So it was that Voltaire popularized physics and Rousseau botany. So it was that Paley referred a moral philosophy to astronomy and Bernardin de Saint-Pierre to natural history. It is no accident that the *Jardin des Plantes* was the one scientific institution to flourish in the radical democratic phase of the French Revolution, which struck down all the others." C. C. Gillispie, "Lamarck and Darwin," in *Forerunners of Darwin: 1745–1859*, ed. Bentley Glass, Owsei Temkin, and William L. Straus, Jr. (Baltimore: Johns Hopkins University Press, 1959), p. 277. See also Thomas S. Kuhn's *The Structure of Scientific Revolutions* (Chicago: University of Chicago Press, 1962).

3. The *Dictionary of the History of Science*, ed. W. F. Bynum, E. J. Browne, and Roy Porter (Princeton: Princeton University Press, 1981), locates the revival of microscopical studies that occurred during the early nineteenth century in the German states, and proposes it as an inevitable outgrowth of the concern with development, history, and form of *Naturphilosophie* (p.60). The research on microscope lenses by scientists like Coddington, Brewster, and Wollaston, and the discoveries of microscopist-botanists like Robert Brown suggest that microscopical studies were at least as extensive in pragmatic Britain.

4. Humphry Davy, *Consolations in Travel, or The Last Days of a Philosopher*, in *The Collected Works of Sir Humphry Davy*, ed. John Davy, 9 vols. (London: Smith, Elder, 1840), 9:245; *The Prelude*, XIII, 234–35, in *William Wordsworth: Selected Poems and Prefaces*, ed. Jack Stillinger (Boston: Houghton Mifflin, 1965), p. 353. Edward Profitt has noted the extent to which Romantic art and poetry is "imbued with a sense of fidelity to things observed," and remarks that Wordsworth's stated goal in the preface of 1802—"at all times . . . to look steadily at . . . [the] subject"—is a "model of scientific procedure." "Science and Romanticism," *Georgia Review* 34 (1980):56–57.

5. *The Letters of John Keats, 1814–1821*, ed. Hyder E. Rollins, 2 vols. (Cambridge: Harvard University Press, 1958), 2:81; 1:179. These volumes will be cited hereafter as *Letters*.

6. Othmar Keel, "The Politics of Health," in *William Hunter and the Eighteenth-Century Medical World*, ed. W. F. Bynum and Roy Porter (Cambridge: Cambridge University Press, 1985), pp. 225–36. Keel cites convincingly and at length from Joseph Frank's 1804 journal of his medical tour of England and A. Flajani's 1807 book compiling his firsthand comparison of European and British clinical instruction.

7. I am indebted to Keats scholars Aileen Ward, Robert Gittings, Stuart Sperry, and Donald Goellnicht, who have walked the wards of Guy's with Keats before me, as well as to Keel (cited above) and the *Report of the Commissioners Concerning Charities in England*, 1840 (London: W. Clowes & Sons, 1840), for the comparative status and routine of teaching and practice at Guy's Hospital. The report is cited hereafter as *Charity Commission Report*.

8. See Andrew Baster, "The Library of Guy's Hospital Physical Society, 1775–1825," Parts I–III, *Guy's Hospital Gazette* 98 (1984): 32–36, 75–78, 115–18. Guy's Hospital preceded St. Thomas's Hospital and their sister hospitals in the formal organization and cataloguing of its medical library.

9. *Transactions of the Physical Society, Guy's Hospital* (MS, Wills Library, 1813–1820). Cited hereafter as *Transactions*.

10. John Gregory, *Lectures on the Duties and Qualifications of a Physician*, ed. and rev. by James Gregory (1805; reprint, Philadelphia: M. Carey & Son, 1817), p. 16; B. C. Brodie, *An Introductory Discourse on the Duties and Conduct of Medical Students and Practitioners* (London: Longman, 1843), p.26. Gregory's treatise was frequently reprinted during the late eighteenth century and early nineteenth century; it was supplanted to some degree by Thomas Percival's widely prescribed textbook, *Medical Ethics; or a Code of Institutes and Precepts Adapted to the Professional Conduct of Physicians and Surgeons* (Manchester: J. Johnson, 1803), and often supplemented with monographs like Brodie's.

11. "The Poetical Works of William Wordsworth," *North British Review* 13 (August 1850): 494–95 (attributed to David Masson by the *Wellesley Index to Victorian Periodicals*).

12. I am particularly indebted to Donald Goellnicht's *The Poet-Physician: Keats and Medical Science* (Pittsburgh: University of Pittsburgh Press, 1984) for its original research on the biographical specifics of Keats's medical years, and I gladly assume here his achievement in ensuring that all Keatsians acknowledge the relevance of medicine to the early Keats. *Romantic Medicine and John Keats* is not a discipline-specific study of the scientific resonances and conjectured medical sources of discrete ideas or images in Keats, as Goellnicht's volume is (the pioneering aspect of his task precluded broad discussion of issues and sustained treatment of the poems); nor does my book propose the medical perspective to be merely one aspect of lesser reward or "an additional way of interpreting [Keats's] work" (p. 7), as he does.

13. Helen Vendler's connective reading of the odes in *The Odes of John Keats* (Cambridge: Harvard University Press, 1983) is a thoroughly engaging reading; her description of Keats's image-transformations (p. 10) is helpful to my point on the poet's syncretic use of medical images and concepts in his mature poetry.

14. See Ben Ross Schneider, Jr.'s *Wordsworth's Cambridge Education* (Cambridge: Cambridge University Press, 1957).

15. Susan Wolfson's *The Questioning Presence* (Ithaca: Cornell University Press, 1986), on the interrogative mode connecting Wordsworth and Keats is a wholesome advance on this tradition, for it preserves the individuality of the two poets.

16. *The Poems of John Keats*, ed. Jack Stillinger (Cambridge: Harvard University Press, 1978), *The Fall of Hyperion*, I, 189–90. All future references to the poems will use this edition and appear in parentheses in the text. I use short titles throughout; the poems *Endymion*, *Hyperion*, and *The Fall of Hyperion* are abbreviated as *End.*, *Hyp.*, and *Fall of Hyp.*

17. *The Opposing Self* (New York: Viking Press, 1955), pp. 7, 49 (reprint of "The Poet as Hero: Keats in His Letters," 1951).

18. Jeffrey Meyer's recent *Disease and the Novel, 1880–1960* (London: Macmillan, 1985) is a case in point. Iain McGilchrist's review of the book reiterates this fallacy: "The absence of English novels of disease may reflect the absence of disease as a component of English Romanticism. . . . That disease [a European neurasthenia, from Nietzsche to the French decadents], which raged so near, seems never to have arrived in England, and the great figures, both poets and novelists, of English Romanticism seem either too innocent or too ironic to be victims of it." TLS, 13 December 1985, p. 1415.

PART I

1. Lemprière's work was first published in 1788, Tooke's in 1698, and Spence's in 1747; all three, in multiple editions, were readily available during the Romantic period. The poet's other sources for Greek and Latin mythology included Edward Baldwin's *Pantheon* (1806), Chapman's Homer, Cooke's Hesiod, Sandy's Ovid, Booth's Diodorus Siculus, and Ronsard's A *Michel de l'hospital*; see Claude Lee Finney, *The Evolution of Keats's Poetry*, 2 vols. (Cambridge: Harvard University Press, 1936), 2:494–95. Ian Jack, *Keats and the Mirror of Art* (Oxford: Oxford University Press, 1967), pp. 176–90, discusses the special place Apollo had in the evolution of Keats's personal mythology.

2. J. Lemprière, "Apollo," in his *Bibliotheca Classica, or, A Classical Dictionary* (London: T. Cadell & W. Davis, 1820), p. 76; Andrew Tooke, *The Pantheon* (London: C. Elliot, 1783), p. 31; J. Spence, *Polymetis* (London: R. J. Dodsley, 1755), on the Greek artists' Apollo, pp. 90ff.. Lemprière (pp. 76–77) and Tooke (pp. 29–30) also describe the various iconography of plant, animal, and instrument attributed to Apollo. Keats owned a copy of Lemprière in the 1806 edition; he had access to the 1755 edition of Spence and the 1781 edition of Tooke. I deliberately confine my citations to these three sources so as to limit the permutations of the myth to those elements Keats would have known for certain. The Lempière volume will be cited hereafter as *Classical Dictionary*.

3. See Lemprière, "Aesculapius" and "Chiron," *Classical Dictionary*, pp. 23–24, 179; Tooke, *Pantheon*, pp. 314–16.

4. See Homer, *Odyssey*, 4:230–33, on physicians as the race of Paeon; see also Lemprière, "Paeon," *Classical Dictionary*, p. 535. Keats's coinage of Peona, as the name for the "midnight spirit-nurse" of *Endymion*, is undoubtedly derived from these references and from the common folk remedy purportedly used first by Apollo, the peony root.

5. See Goellnicht, *Poet-Physician*, pp. 163–4; Robert Gittings, "John Keats, Physician and Poet," *Journal of the American Medical Association* 224 (1973): 51–55, and "This Living Hand," *Medical History* 16 (1972): 10; Walter H. Evert, *Aesthetic and Myth in the Poetry of Keats* (Princeton: Princeton University Press, 1965), pp. 95–96.

6. Lemprière, "Apollo," *Classical Dictionary*, p. 76; Tooke, *Pantheon*, p. 38; Spence, *Polymetis*, pp. 97–98. Spence describes not just Apollo but "the Medicean group of figures."

7. See Tooke on Apollo-Phoebus, *Pantheon*, p. 38.

8. Spence, *Polymetis*, pp. 84–86; Tooke, *Pantheon*, pp. 36, 41. It is entirely appropriate to the tradition that blind Homer, in Keats's first "Ode to Apollo," should be described with a soul that "looks out through renovated eyes" (11–12).

9. Tooke, *Pantheon*, p. 32. Lemprière, "Mercurius," *Classical Dictionary*, p. 459, proposes Mercury as the inventor of the lyre: "He was not the inventor of the lyre, as some have imagined, but Mercury gave it him, and received as a reward the famous caduceus. . . ." Spence, *Polymetics*, p. 107, says Horace first described Hermes' invention of the lyre.

10. It is ironic that the American Medical Association has chosen as its emblem not Aesculapius's reliable staff but Hermes' suspect and winged caduceus.

Chapter 1

1. Charles Cowden Clarke and Mary Cowden Clark, *Recollections of Writers* (London: Sampson, Low, Marston, Searle, & Rivington, 1878), pp. 129–30. On Keats's deliberate choice of medicine, see Aileen Ward, *John Keats: The Making of a Poet*, rev. ed. (New York: Farrar, Straus & Giroux, 1986), p. 59, and Bernard Blackstone, *The Consecrated Urn: An Interpretation of Keats in Terms of Growth and Form* (London: Longman, 1959), pp. xii–xiii.

2. *Letters*, 2:70.

3. *Letters*, 2:112–13; see also 2:114: "I have my choice of three things—or at least two—South America or Surgeon to an I[n]diaman—which last I think will be my fate."

4. *Letters*, 2:298. See also Charles Brown, on Keats's fears of practicing surgery as they reflect an anxiety for life not, as commonly presumed, a distaste for seeing gore and blood: "My last operation . . . was the opening of a man's temporal artery. I did it with the utmost nicety; but reflecting on what passed through my mind at the time, my dexterity seemed a miracle. . . ." *Life of John Keats* (1841), reprinted in *The Keats Circle*, ed. Hyder E. Rollins, 2d ed., 2 vols. (Cambridge: Harvard University Press, 1965), 2:56. Keats may have resolved that he did not have the steady hand to be a good surgeon, but he did not give up on medicine and pharmacy, and we know from Severn that on board the ship to Italy he acted as doctor to the other dying consumptives.

5. *Letters*, 2:115.

6. *Letters*, 1:276–77. This is also the letter in which Keats says he is glad he kept his medical books and will review them from time to time.

7. See Goellnicht, *Poet-Physician*, pp. 12–47, for a full description of the specifics of Keats's training and the history of the Apothecaries Act; on p. 45 Goellnicht concludes that Keats completed the twelve-month dressership even though he had already decided to try his hand at poetry in the fall of 1816, and his first volume of poetry was to be published on 3 March 1817.

8. "Medical School of St. Thomas's and Guy's," *London Medical and Physical Journal* 34 (1815): 259; Goellnicht, *Poet-Physician*, reproduces this and the register page showing the courses for which Keats received credit from the Society of Apothecaries (pp. 23–24); he notes (pp. 31–32) that it is not clear whether Keats took a separate course in materia medica in addition to Salisbury's one in medical botany.

9. A report in the *London Medical Repository* 6 (1816): 341–42 describes the broad areas of the examination; p. 345 lists Keats as one of those who passed it. The *Encyclopaedia Britannica* entry is based on the *London Pharmacopoeia* or *Pharmacopoeia Officinalis Britannica*, according to the entry's author, Andrew Duncan, Jr., Stuart Sperry has demonstrated that Keats's knowledge of pharmacy and chemical botany may well have extended beyond what was required by Apothecaries' Hall and what he learned from Salisbury, Curry, and Cholmeley because of his association with John Towers, a well-known dispensing chemist and botanist; see Sperry, "Isabella Jane Towers, John Towers, and Keats," *Keats-Shelley Journal* 28 (1979): 35–38.

10. Thomas Percival, *Medical Ethics* (Manchester: J. Johnson, 1803), reprinted in Chauncey D. Leake, *Percival's Medical Ethics* (Baltimore: William & Wilkins, 1927), pp. 113, 116–17. Percival was the editor of the influential *Memoirs of the Literary and Philosophical Society of Manchester*. Aileen Ward, in her discussion of medical ranks, notes that at the beginning of Victoria's reign there were fewer than three hundred licensed physicians in Britain as opposed to the burgeoning numbers of surgeons and surgeon-apothecaries. *John Keats*, pp. 23–24. It is important to remember that well before 1815 the surgeon-apothecaries of England described themselves as "General Practitio-

ners" of medicine. *Medicine in* 1815 (London: Wellcome Historical Medical Library, 1965), Item 13, p. 19.

11. Astley Cooper, *Lectures on the Principles and Practice of Surgery, as Delivered in the Theatre of St. Thomas' Hospital*, 2d ed. (London: F. C. Wesley, 1830), p. 4. Because Cooper did not publish his own lectures, the edition by his apprentice and Keats's roommate, Frederick Tyrrell (which appeared first in the mid-1820s, with an American edition in 1839), and this one are the fullest and the most reliable amid a jumble of student notes, outlines, and pirated versions of the lectures; see Russell C. Brock, *The Life and Works of Astley Cooper* (London: E. & S. Livingston, 1952), p. 108.

12. This is a directly transcribed catalogue from *Anatomical and Physiological Note Book*, ed. Maurice Buxton Forman (London: Oxford University Press, 1934).

13. A. Flajani, *Saggio filosofico intorno agli stabilimenti scientifici in Europa apartenenti alla medicina* (1807), as cited and translated by Othmar Keel, "The Politics of Health," in *William Hunter and the Eighteenth-century Medical World*, ed. W. F. Bynum and Roy Porter (Cambridge: Cambridge University Press, 1985), p. 234. (Flajani's journal of his tour was translated into French by L. Odier in 1811.) Keel uses Flajani's study, Joseph Frank's 1804–1805 journal of his tour of English and Scottish medical schools, and Auguste Gauthier's *Discours préliminaire sur l'histoire des cliniques* (1824) to document his assertion that modern clinical instruction began in England long before the establishment of the French clinic in 1794.

14. C. Newman describes how medical schools in England, unlike those chartered on the Continent, invariably started as small practical clinics in the local infirmaries and city hospitals before they became institutionalized as universities. "The Hospital as a Teaching Centre," in *The Evolution of Hospitals in Britain*, ed. F.N.L. Poynter (London: Pitman, 1964), p. 200. Maureen McNeil, *Under the Banner of Science: Erasmus Darwin and His Age* (Manchester: Manchester University Press, 1987), p. 131, notes that full-scale clinical teaching began in Edinburgh in 1748, at the Royal Infirmary, which was specifically built for practical instruction. Toby Gelfand proposes that London "emerged as the world centre for clinical learning during the second half of the eighteenth century" and that British medical teachers eclipsed "their neighbors across the channel" because of the private-enterprise nature of hospital teaching in England; he notes, significantly, that London surgical publications were double the number of Paris publications during the period. "Hospital Teaching as Private Enterprise in Hunterian London," in *William Hunter and the Eighteenth-century Medical World*, ed. Bynum and Porter, pp. 129, 138–39.

15. Keel cites Vicq d'Azyr in "Politics of Health," p. 224; see also Matthew Ramsey, *Professional and Popular Medicine in France, 1770–1830* (Cambridge: Cambridge University Press, 1988), for the larger social implications of the origin of medical practice in France.

16. Keel, "Politics of Health," citing Flajani, p. 226; on pp. 229–30 Keel notes from a surgeon's letter of 1793 that the combination of the two hospitals into one school gave pupils at either hospital the opportunity of attending upward of seven hundred patients. Some of these case histories and the admission records of patients at Guy's and St. Thomas's during Keats's residency there can be found in the Greater London Record Office.

17. H. C. Cameron, *Mr. Guy's Hospital, 1726–1948* (London: Longman, 1954), p. 95, also chaps. 1–3; see also Brock, *Life and Works of Astley Cooper*, p. 4.

18. The revised will issued by the governors of the hospital in 1732 is quoted by R. M. Wingert, *Historical Notes on the Borough and the Borough Hospitals* (London: Ash, 1913), p. 88. The original will of 1725 also had a special provision, the first of its kind in England, for incurable lunatics; the "Lunatick Ward" established under this provision was reserved for female patients after 1797. A resolution by the hospital governors in 1783 required the hospital physicians and surgeons to attend these patients and make regular reports on their condition. See Cameron, *Mr. Guy's*

Hospital, 71–72; Samuel Wilks and G. T. Bettany, A *Biographical History of Guy's Hospital* (London: Warden, Lock, Bowden, 1892), p. 95. Keats would have attended this ward as a dresser, see Goellnicht, *Poet-Physician*, pp. 166–67.

19. For the serious diseases and injuries commonly seen and treated in the Guy's wards during Keats's tenure at the hospital, see *Clinical Cases and Lectures taken by Joshua Waddington at Guy's Hospital, between Dec. 1st, 1816, and May 1st, 1817* (MS, Wills Library); for the unusual and desperate cases, see Astley Cooper, *Notes on Cases*, 1816–1818, 2 vols. (MS, Library of the Royal College of Surgeons).

20. For the selection and duties of the dresser, see *Charity Commission Report*, p. 684; Ward, *John Keats*, pp. 49–50, 54–55 (she speculates that it was Astley Cooper who recommended Keats to the post); Goellnicht, *Poet-Physician*, pp. 37–41.

21. Astley Cooper's words on Lucas, Jr., quoted by Bransby Blake Cooper, *The Life of Sir Astley Cooper*, 2 vols. (London: John W. Parker, 1843), 1:302.

22. See *Transactions*. Gregory Johnson was secretary to the society from 1790 to 1825. For a survey of scientific societies of the period, see James E. McClellan, *Science Reorganized: Scientific Societies in the Eighteenth Century* (New York: Columbia University Press, 1985).

23. Andrew Baster, "The Library of Guy's Hospital Physical Society, 1775–1825, Part 1," *Guy's Hospital Gazette* 98 (February 1984): 32–36; "Part 3" (April 1984): 117.

24. The minutes of the society meetings in the *Transactions* express this faith in Curry; see also Baster, "The Library of Guy's Hospital Physical Society, Part 2" (March 1984): 77–78; "Part 3" (April 1984): 117. It is interesting that Curry, who is usually slighted by Keats's medical biographers as an ill-educated country doctor who prescribed calomel too frequently—see William Hale-White, *Keats as Doctor and Patient* (London: Oxford University Press, 1938), p. 27, and Goellnicht, *Poet-Physician*, p. 31—should be one who can be documented as well read. When Curry's personal library was catalogued and sold by Sotheby's after his death in 1820, it fetched the tidy sum of 2000 pounds.

25. My list is taken from the manuscript of the shelflist, *A Numerical Catalogue of Books in the Library of the Physical Society, Guy's Hospital*, dated 1817, in Wills Library at Guy's. Although additions were made to this list in 1829 (in a different hand), I have verified my list of books actually on the shelves against records of books purchased in the minutes of the society, and against the 1823 printed catalogue (with hand corrections), both of which are in Wills Library. William Babington and James Curry's *Outlines of a Course of Lectures on the Practice of Medicine* (London: T. Bensley, 1802–1806) cites most of the medical and scientific authors in my list, giving credence to my point that Keats's teachers read widely and were well educated.

26. John Gregory, *Lectures on the Duties and Qualifications of a Physician* (1805; reprint, Philadelphia: M. Carey & Son, 1817), pp. 51–52.

27. See Ivan Waddington's discussions in *The Medical Profession in the Industrial Revolution* (Dublin: Gill & Macmillan, 1985), especially pp. 9–17, 23–24, 46–47, of how the apothecaries of early-nineteenth-century England were "the most efficient part of the profession," and of how they undermined the newly established professional divisions with their comprehensive knowledge and skills so as to truly deserve by 1820 their professional description "General Practitioners of Medicine." See also James Wardrope on how "the same fundamental knowledge" insured that "the healing art is one," and of the need to keep the intellectual roads between surgeon, physician, and apothecary open, in "Surgery," *Encyclopaedia Britannica* (1810), 20:25. McNeil, *Under the Banner of Science*, pp. 131–33, also describes how intellectual need and the hospital training programs for general practitioners broke down the professional divisions within medicine.

28. Astley Cooper, *Surgical Lectures*, taken by William Compson (MS, Wills Library, 1817–1818), p.

7; Alexander Marcet, An Essay on the Chemical History and Medical Treatment of Calculous Disorders (London: Longman, 1817), pp. xiii–xiv.

29. For Cooper's instruction under Gregory, see Bransby Blake Cooper, The Life of Sir Astley Cooper, 2 vols. (London: John W. Parker, 1843), 1:158–60. Andrew Duncan's "Medicine," in the Encyclopaedia Britannica of 1810 runs from p. 187 to p. 486 and is based on Gregory's Conspectus Medicinae Theoretica (1782), the best summary of prevailing theoretical medicine; we can deduce that the instruction Cooper received from Gregory was thorough and not just in practical surgery.

30. The British Library owns Banks's personal, inscribed copy of Curry's Observations on Apparent Death from Drowning (London: E. Cox, 1815); Curry mentions his Bengal trip in his "History of a Case of Remitting Ophthalmia and Its Successful Treatment by Opium" (London: G. Woodfall, 1812). For information on ties between Banks and members of the Royal Society, see H. B. Carter's Sir Joseph Banks: 1743–1820 (London: British Museum, 1988); for a general history of the society, see Henry Lyons, The Royal Society (New York: Greenwood Press, 1968), and Dorothy Stimson, Scientists and Amateurs: A History of the Royal Society (New York: Henry Schuman, 1948).

31. See H. J. Jackson, "Coleridge's Collaborator, Joseph Henry Green," Studies in Romanticism 21 (1982): 161–68. For Tieck's circle, see Roger Paulin, Ludwig Tieck: A Literary Biography (Oxford: Oxford University Press, 1985).

32. The document is dated 21 March, 1821; Medicine in 1815, Item 15, p. 6. For an account of the operation, see Cooper, Life of Sir Astley Cooper, 2:226–30.

33. The influence of Hunter and Brown should not be underestimated. In The Friend, Coleridge called Hunter "the profoundest, . . . physiological philosopher of the latter half of the preceding century," and it is verifiably true that Hunter's genius dominated Romantic medicine and medical philosophy in England and France during the period. George R. Potter cites from The Friend in "Coleridge and the Idea of Evolution," PMLA 40 (1925): 384. See also L. S. Jacyna, "Images of John Hunter in the Nineteenth Century," History of Science 21 (1983): 87ff.; and Lester S. King on the parallel and preemptive genius of Hunter and Bichât, and their shared debt to Morgagni, in The Medical World of the Eighteenth Century, (1958; reprint, New York: Robert E. Krieger, 1971), p. 296. Brown is widely acknowledged by the Naturphilosophen, especially Schelling, who based part of his philosophy on the Brunonian paradigm; for Virchow's estimate of Brown, see W. R. Trotter, "John Brown and the Nonspecific Component of Human Sickness," Perspectives in Biology and Medicine 21 (1978): 259–60. McNeil has addressed Darwin's importance to British medicine and located him within the school of Brown (Under the Banner of Science, p. 149), and Desmond King-Hele has amply demonstrated Darwin's influence on Romantic medicine and poetry in Doctor of Revolution: The Life and Genius of Erasmus Darwin (London: Faber, 1977) and Erasmus Darwin and the Romantic Poets (New York: St. Martin's Press, 1986).

34. In 1815, Spurzheim was lecturing to large groups in London. The way in which German ideas entered English Romantic thought and artistic circles, through the translations and reviews of German literature and philosophy by William Taylor and Henry Crabb Robinson, has been traced by F. W. Stokoe, German Influence in the English Romantic Period, 1788–1818 (Cambridge: Cambridge University Press, 1926), see especially pp. 50–53. The German influence on English physicians and scientists (and vice versa) has not been well tracked; we do know that men like Beddoes, Erasmus Darwin, and Davy were well acquainted with Naturphilosophie and German literature in general. Public enthusiasm for the German dramatist Kotzebue was at its height in England in 1799, when there were over twenty-seven extant translations (ibid., 48–49); Keats mentions Kotzebue in Letters, 2:85, 194, and we know that Kotzebue's son was a scientist who explored the Pacific in 1825.

35. Trotter marks the influence of Brown on Broussais's clinical practice in "John Brown and the

Nonspecific Component of Human Sickness," pp. 259–60. Cuvier, who attended Caroline University near Stuttgart, was to become one of the founders of *Naturphilosophie*; Geoffroy St. Hilaire, who collaborated with Cuvier at the Museum d'Histoire Naturelle and was a colleague of Lamarck at the Jardin des Plantes (where Alexander von Humboldt was a frequent visitor), publicly acknowledged the importance of Schelling and the Germans to his philosophy of nature. See C. C. Gillispie, *The Edge of Objectivity* (Princeton: Princeton University Press, 1960), p. 268. Furthermore, Robert Darnton's study of *mesmérisme* and *magnétisme animal* in *Mesmerism and the End of the Eighteenth Century in France* (Cambridge: Harvard University Press, 1968) would suggest that mesmerism and electromagnetic therapy may have returned, by way of its popularity among the German *Naturphilosophen*, to haunt medical practice in the French clinics after the Revolution. John Livingston Lowes discusses Coleridge's continuing fascination with mesmerism and animal magnetism in *The Road to Xanadu*, rev. ed. (Boston: Houghton Mifflin, 1964), p. 231. The subject, partly because of Faraday's work, was taken seriously by English physicians like J. H. Green, who we know discussed mesmerism with Coleridge on several occasions. See also William Gregory on Faraday's "para-magnetism," which he describes as "Ferro-magnetism," in *Letters to a Candid Inquirer on Animal Magnetism* (Philadelphia: Blanchard & Lea, 1851), p. 73.

36. F.W.J. Schelling, *On University Studies*, trans. E. S. Morgan (Athens: Ohio University Press, 1966), p. 135; William Lawrence, from a lecture of 1817, in *Lectures on Physiology, Zoology, and the Natural History of Man* (London: J. Callow, 1819), pp. 49–50; J. H. Green, *An Address Delivered in King's College, London* (London: B. Fellowes, 1832), p. 30. Green means "science" with an upper-case "S," in the Coleridgean sense of universal knowledge.

Chapter 2

1. Andrew Duncan, Jr., "Medicine," in *Encyclopaedia Britannica* (1810), especially 13:187–98 on the Hippocratic example.

2. From *Precepts*, cited in W.H.S. Jones's discussion, "Greek Medical Etiquette," *Proceedings of the Royal Society of Medicine* 16 (1923): 12, 16; also A. Castiglioni, A *History of Medicine*, trans. E. B. Krumbhaar (New York: Knopf, 1947), pp. 157–58. In the four Hippocratic tracts, *Oath, Decorum, Precepts,* and *Law,* "appeal was made to the artistic instinct," Jones says (p. 12).

3. *Friedrich Schiller: Medicine, Psychology and Literature*, ed. Kenneth Dewhurst and Nigel Reeves (Berkeley: University of California Press, 1978), pp. 254–55; Novalis, cited by Elizabeth Sewell, *The Orphic Voice: Poetry and Natural History* (New Haven: Yale University Press, 1960), pp. 201–2. See also my discussion of Goethe on poetry and the living organism in Part IV.

4. William Lawrence, *Lectures on Physiology, Zoology, and the Natural History of Man* (London: J. Callow, 1819), p. 13; J. Hunter, *Treatise on the Blood, The Works of John Hunter*, ed. James F. Palmer, 4 vols. (London: Longman , 1835), 3:6–7; J. H. Green, *Vital Dynamics: The Hunterian Oration Before the Royal College of Surgeons*, 14 February 1840 (London: William Pickering, 1840), pp. 4–5; Brodie, *Discourse on the Duties and Conduct of Medical Students and Practitioners* (London: Longman, 1843), p. 32. Brodie's examples are Shakespeare, Bacon, Addison, and Johnson.

5. Astley Cooper, *Surgical Lectures*, 2 vols. (MS, Wills Library, 1817–1818), 1:1–3; Alexander Marcet, *Some Remarks on Clinical Lectures, Being the Substance of an Introductory Lecture Delivered at Guy's Hospital* (London: Woodfall, 1818), pp. 18–19.

6. Michel Foucault, *The Birth of the Clinic*, trans. Sheridan Smith (New York: Random House, 1973), p. 32; Foucault makes an interesting point on the secularization of the priest's role into the humanitarian practice of medicine.

7. In his introduction to the exhibition catalogue *Medicine in 1815* (London: Wellcome Historical Medical Museum, 1965), p. 1.

8. Percival's *Medical Ethics* (Manchester: J. Johnson, 1803; reprinted in Chauncey D. Leake, *Percival's Medical Ethics* [Baltimore: William & Wilkins, 1927]), was commissioned as a "scheme of professional conduct" by the trustees of the Manchester Infirmary in 1791, but in its revisions, to which Erasmus Darwin and William Heberden contributed, it became the familiar and popular (at least until 1847) book on ethics of British and U.S. medicine. John Gregory's *Lectures on the Duties and Qualifications of a Physician* (1772, 1805; reprint, Philadelphia: M. Carey & Son, 1817) was revised and enlarged by his brother James in 1805 to become almost as popular a textbook as Percival's. James Gregory's public battle over medical ethics with the Edinburgh College of Physicians is an example of how charged and far-reaching the issue was; see the college's face-saving *Narrative of the Conduct of Dr. James Gregory, toward the Royal College of Physicians of Edinburgh* (Edinburgh: Peter Hill, 1809). Brodie's philosophic *Discourse* was first delivered as a lecture to St. George's Hospital in 1843. James Wallace's *Letters on the Study and Practice of Medicine and Surgery* (Glasgow: Richard Griffin, 1828) was frequently used as the basis for instruction in ethics in the regimental hospitals. Anthony Carlisle's four-lecture pamphlet in *15 Museum Lectures* (MS, Royal College of Surgeons, 1818) and Abraham Banks's *Medical Etiquette* (London, 1839) are examples of the handbooks on conduct in circulation in London. See also Maureen McNeil's discussion of how the increasingly "individualistic approach to medical practice and professional identity" in England led to an increase of interest in medical ethics as the century proceeded, *Under the Banner of Science* (Manchester: University of Manchester Press, 1987), pp. 133–34.

9. Gregory, *Duties*, pp. 16–18; Wallace, *Letters*, pp. 36–37; Brodie, *Discourse*, pp. 18–19. For the list of "related" disciplines, see Gregory, *Duties*, p. 9, Brodie, *Discourse*, p. 26.

10. Wallace, *Letters*, pp. 17–18; Brodie, *Discourse*, pp. 7–8, 16–17; Gregory, *Duties*, p. 21. The "commitment" of the medical practitioner to his practice as compared with the "wanton exuberance" of the poet is a recurring subject in ethics treatises of the late eighteenth century; see John Millar, *A Discourse on the Duty of Physicians* (London: J. Johnson, 1776).

11. Gregory, *Duties*, pp. 12–13, 22–23 (Shakespeare is Gregory's example of a person with humanity); Carlisle, *15 Museum Lectures*, II, III; John Abernethy, *Introductory Lectures . . . Delivered Before the Royal College of Surgeons* (London: Longman, 1815), p. 5; Brodie, *Discourse*, pp. 12–13, 22–23; Banks, *Medical Etiquette*, p. 93.

12. Percival, *Medical Ethics*, p. 71; Gregory, *Duties*, pp. 25, 48–49; Cooper, summarized in *Outlines of the Lectures on Surgery* (London: G. Woodfall, 1822), Lecture I, in full in *Lectures on the Principles and Practice of Surgery*, 2d ed. (London: F.C. Wesley, 1830), pp. 2–3. See also *The Lectures of Sir Astley Cooper*, ed. Frederick Tyrrell (Philadelphia: Haswell, Barrington, & Haswell, 1839), p. 21. Wallace's advice to parents and guardians is in his *Letters*, p. 26.

13. Gregory, *Duties*, pp. 26–27; Percival, *Medical Ethics*, pp. 73–75, 87–88; Duncan, "Medicine," p. 412 (this entry in the *Encyclopaedia Britannica*, 1810, has a whole section on "moral treatment" of the insane).

14. See Wallace, *Letters*, p. 20; Brodie, *Discourse*, pp. 20–21.

15. See Lawrence on the prior century's "more modern but equally deplorable condition, of servile submission to the dogmas of schools and sects, or subjections to doctrines, parties, or authorities." *Lectures on Physiology, Zoology, and the Natural History of Man*, p. 50.

16. See Duncan's manifesto on the medicine of the new era, and his condemnation of the barbaric connection of magic and religion, "Medicine," p. 187. All the contemporary ethics texts reiterate the distinction between the new, verifiable, and antidogmatic medicine and prior centuries' mix of magic, false theory, and exclusive knowledge. See Percival on *nostrums, Medical Ethics*, p. 104. The connections between medicine and magic are old: see Northrop Frye's discussion of the Greek *pharmakeus* (druggist) and *pharmakos* (magician) in *The Anatomy of Criticism* (1957; reprint, New York: Antheneum, 1970), pp. 41–48, 148–49; Jacques Derrida, "Plato's Pharmacy," in *Dissemination*,

trans. Barbara Johnson (Chicago: University of Chicago Press, 1981), p. 130; Lewis Thomas, *The Youngest Science* (New York: Viking Press 1983), pp. 52–53, on the connections between the Old English *laece* (meaning "doctor," from the root meaning for "leech") and the early Germanic *lekjaz* (meaning "enchanter" or "speaker of magic words").

17. Lemprière, "Mercurius," *Classical Dictionary*, pp. 458–59; Joseph Spence, *Polymetis* (London: R. & J. Dodsley, 1755; reprint, London: J. Johnson, 1802), pp. 106–8; Andrew Tooke, *The Pantheon* (London: C. Elliot, 1783), pp. 52–53. Among other proofs of Hermes-Mercury's "thievish propensity" Lemprière notes: the god stole Admetus's cattle and "the quiver and arrows of the divine shepherd [Apollo], and he encreased his fame by robbing Neptune of his trident, Venus of her girdle, Mars of his sword, Jupiter of his sceptre, and Vulcan of many of his mechanical instruments" (p. 459). In his discussion of the variety of Hermes' magic in *Hermes the Thief: The Evolution of a Myth* (Madison: University of Wisconsin Press, 1947), Norman O. Brown describes the Greek "cursing tablets" and connects these with Hermes' reputation as "the whisperer" or "spellbinder" and patron of secret oaths, recipes, runes, and rhymes (pp. 12–15). Jacques Derrida, in "Plato's Pharmacy," *Dissemination*, p. 88, also uses the tradition of Thoth (the Egyptian Hermes) and its association with rhetoric to address the ambiguity of the word. Keats would have known of the associations of Thoth from his reading (*The Keats Circle*, ed. Hyder E. Rollins, 2d ed., 2 vols. [Cambridge: Harvard University Press, 1965], 2:254) of Edward Davies's *Celtic Researches* (London: J. Booth, 1804), pp. 109–12.

18. Douglas Bush, "Notes on Keats's Reading," PMLA 50 (1935): 785–806, proposed Marlowe's *Hero and Leander* and Ovid as sources for Hermes in *Lamia*; the multiple associations of Hermes noticeable in my gloss here would suggest Keats had a much fuller knowledge of the myth's variations. It would be easy to see Hermes and other figures of the false physician in Keats's poetry as the poet's contribution to the long tradition of medicial satire. In truth, Keats's purpose in these figures is more profound than mocking: they define by contrast the character of the true physician. Not even the satiric ballad, *The Jealousies* (which in my opinion has little to do with any of the physical sciences) can be shown to partake of the conventions of medical satire; the fact that it is a satire written by a doctor is not enough.

19. *Letters*, 1:387, 267, 293, 271.

20. Readers of Keats often exaggerate the "conflict" between poetry and medicine, poetic aspiration and humanitarian duty, in *Endymion*. See Clement Notcutt's preface to *Endymion* / A *Poetic Romance* (London: Oxford University Press, 1927), pp. xviiiff.; Wolf Hirst, *John Keats* (Boston: Twayne, 1983), p. 21. *Endymion* is better read through the roles of its many physicians from Circe through Endymion and the ways in which these personae factor in Keats's definition of poetic purpose and the Hazlitt-inspired ethic "to apply not the touch [sting] of the scorpion but the touch of the Torpedo to youthful hopes" (*Letters*, 2:72). See Donald C. Goellnicht's discussion, *The Poet-Physician* (Pittsburgh: University of Pittsburgh Press, 1984), p. 187, on how Endymion as "shepherd-poet-physician" represents the culmination of earlier verse models of the physician.

21. Brodie, *Discourse*, pp. 22–23 (my italics). Brodie says best what was common advice in all the ethics books of the period. The relevance of the passage to the "Ode on Indolence" is obvious.

22. *Letters*, 1:271.

Chapter 3

1. Robert Burton, *The Anatomy of Melancholy*, ed. A. R. Shilleto, 3 vols. (1893; reprint, London: G. Bell, 1913), 2:21. Trilling's point, that Romantic poets "thought that poetry depended upon a condition of positive health in the poet, a more than usual well-being," supports this idea; see "The Poet as Hero: Keats in His Letters," in *The Opposing Self* (New York: Viking Press, 1955), p. 7.

2. I am indebted to Stuart M. Sperry's reading of the poem, *Keats the Poet* (Princeton: Princeton University Press, 1970), pp. 117–31. Claude's painting portrays the scene of Psyche's abandonment by Cupid.

3. *Letters*, 1:287.

4. M. H. Abrams's words on a characteristic shared by Romantic poets, *The Mirror and the Lamp* (New York: Oxford University Press, 1953), p. 55.

5. Arnold's example is the "Ode on a Grecian Urn." See *Essays in Criticism / Second Series* (London: Macmillan, 1891), p. 113; *On the Study of Celtic Literature and On Translating Homer* (London: Macmillan, 1902), p. 125.

6. Friedrich von Schlegel, *The Philosophy of Life, and Philosophy of Language*, trans. A.J.W. Morrison (London: Henry G. Bohn, 1847), pp. 75–76.

7. Michel Foucault quoting Bichât in *Anatomie générale*, *The Birth of the Clinic*, trans. Sheridan Smith (New York: Random House, 1973), p. 146; also pp. 126, 195.

8. Andrew Bell, "Anatomy," in *Encyclopaedia Britannica* (1810), 2:175, 181; Astley Cooper and Henry Cline, Jr., *Anatomical Lectures* (MS, Royal College of Surgeons, 1812), p. 1; Bransby Blake Cooper, *The Life of Sir Astley Cooper*, 2 vols. (London: John W. Parker, 1843), 2:53; Astley Cooper, *Lectures on the Principles and Practice of Surgery*, 2d ed. (London: F. C. Wesley, 1830), p. 2; Joseph Henry Green, *The Dissector's Manual* (London: For the author, 1820), pp. xlvi–xlvii, and *Outlines of a Course of Dissections* (London: For the author, 1815), pp. 1, 3, 7. See also John Abernethy, *The Hunterian Oration for the Year 1819* (London: Longman, 1819), p. 34, and William Lawrence's *Lectures on Physiology, Zoology, and the Natural History of Man* (London: J. Callow, 1819), pp. 54–55, on the importance of dissection and the anatomist's sight.

9. See Foucault, *Birth of the Clinic*, p. xii; I cite Foucault here but prefer Friedrich Schlegel's prior and larger delineation of the Romantic physician's "penetrating glance."

10. *The Autobiography and Memoirs of Benjamin Robert Haydon*, ed. Thomas Taylor (London: Davies, 1926), p. 235; Benjamin Robert Haydon, *Lectures on Painting and Design*, 2 vols. (London: Longman, 1844–1846), 2:28, 219–20.

11. *The Complete Works of William Hazlitt*, ed. P. P. Howe, 21 vols. (London: J. M. Dent, 1930–1934), 18:147 (my italics); 4:73, 75. In the latter essay Hazlitt declared Hogarth's pictures to be "works of science" and "plates of natural history." I am indebted to David Bromwich for pointing out the significance of the last passage to Keats, and for his reminder of the frequency with which Hazlitt paired artistic and scientific vision, *Hazlitt: The Mind of a Critic* (New York: Oxford University Press, 1983), pp. 220–21; see also pp. 363–67.

12. *Letters*, 1:192. Keats met Hazlitt in 1818, attended his lectures that year, and borrowed manuscript copies of those he had not heard from Reynolds. The influence (and intellectual association, according to Bromwich, *Hazlitt*, p. 362) of Hazlitt on Keats has been well documented by scholars like Clarence Thorpe, Walter Jackson Bate, and Claude Lee Finney. See Finney, *The Evolution of Keats's Poetry*, 2 vols. (Cambridge: Harvard University Press, 1936), 1:238.

13. In his 1802 revision of the "Preface to *Lyrical Ballads*," *Selected Poems and Prefaces*, ed. Jack Stillinger (Boston: Houghton Mifflin, 1965), p. 455: "Whenever we sympathize with pain, it will be found that the sympathy is produced and carried on by subtle combinations with pleasure.... The Man of science, the Chemist and the Mathematician, whatever difficulties and disgusts they may have had to struggle with, know and feel this. However painful may be the objects with which the Anatomist's knowledge is connected, he feels that his knowledge is pleasure; and where he has no pleasure he has no knowledge."

14. Constable, quoted by Russell Noyes in *Wordsworth and the Art of Landscape* (Bloomington: Indiana University Press, 1968), p. 251.

15. Wollaston was elected interim president of the Royal Society when Joseph Banks died; he

saw himself as a rival not only of Davy but of Faraday. For his contributions to optics, see his "A Method of Examining Refracture and Dispersive Powers, by Prismatic Reflection," *Philosophical Transactions* 92 (1802): 365–80; "On a Periscopic Camera Obscura and Microscope," *Philosophical Transactions* 102 (1812): 370–77; "Description of a Single-Lens Micrometre," *Philosophical Transactions* 103 (1813): 119–22.

16. William Hyde Wollaston, "Description of the Camera Lucida," *Journal of Natural Philosophy, Chemistry, and the Arts* 17 (1807): 1–5, and *Philosophical Magazine* 27 (1807): 343–47. Camera lucidas were sold at Newman's medical supplies store in Soho. Athanasius Kircher's invention of the Aeolian lyre and camera obscura (mentioned by Abrams in *The Mirror and the Lamp*, p. 61) is another example of the meeting of Romantic science and art in a single inventor.

17. Hazlitt, *Works*, vols. (London: J. M. Dent, 1930–1934), 4:74; the entry on Lister in *Encyclopaedia Britannica* (1910), 16:778; "Charles Brown's *Walks in the North*," in *Letters*, 1:432. Brown mentions their seeing "a circulating library, a fossil museum, an exhibition of Mr. Green's drawings, and a camera obscura [sic]"; since he adds that the scene was in miniature and laments the loss of "magnitude," we can be certain it was a camera lucida.

18. See "Symptom," in *Dictionary of the History of Science*, p. 408; Lester S. King's translation of Landré-Beauvais, *Séméiotique, ou trâite des signes des maladies* (Paris: Brosson, 1813), p. 3, in *Medical Thinking: A Historical Preface* (Princeton: Princeton University Press, 1982), p. 79. See also Foucault, *Birth of the Clinic*, p. 94: "Between sign and symptom there is a decisive difference . . . the sign is the symptom itself, but in its original truth." English physicians like George Wallis anticipated Landré-Beauvais's theory of signs when they emphasized the need to isolate distinguishing first symptoms in diseases that otherwise "seem to have a near affinity" once they progressed, *The Art of Preventing Disease Through Rational Principles* (London: Robinson, 1796), pp. 276–77.

19. "Diagnosis," in *Dictionary of the History of Science*, p. 99.

20. *Birth of the Clinic*, p. 122.

21. *Dictionary of the History of Science*, p. 99, which goes on to say that the invention of endoscopes, ophthalomoscopes, and specula later in the century were all part of Romantic medicine's attempt to visualize pathology in the living; Astley Cooper, *Lectures on Anatomy and the Principle Operations of Surgery*, taken by Joshua Waddington, 2 vols. (MS, Wills Library, 1816), 1:1.

22. William Babington and James Curry, *Outlines . . . Practice of Medicine* (London: T. Bensley, 1802–1806), p. 1; James Curry, *Heads of a Course of Lectures on Pathology, Therapeutics, and Materia Medica* (London: T. Bensley, 1804), p. 5. See also William Babington, *Lectures on Therapeutics* (MS, Wills Library, 1796), p. 3, on indicative signs: "Symptoms are the *Principium indicans*. The Rules or principles by which we are directed to the cure of Disease is the *Indicatio*. The Remedies or Means employed to affect the Cure are the *Indicata*."

23. Keats's 1820 medical verdict on himself is taken from two letters, six months apart, *Letters*, 2:252, 321.

24. In the *Regimen*, I, xii; Andrew Duncan, Jr., "Medicine," in *Encyclopaedia Britannica* (1810), 13:190. The Greek and Egyptian practice of predicting the future by examining the viscera of animals, and the herbalists reading of the "doctrine of signatures" in plants would seem to be corruptions of an earlier Hippocratic example in the reading of real signs.

25. *The Collected Works of Sir Humphry Davy*, ed. John Davy, 9 vols. (London: Smith, Elder, 1840), 8:308, 317.

26. Wordsworth, "Preface to *Lyrical Ballads*" (1802), *Selected Poems and Prefaces*, ed. Stillinger, p. 456.

27. From the "Intimations Ode," 186, 200, in *Selected Poems and Prefaces*, ed. Stillinger, pp. 190–91. The term "naturalistic imagination" belongs to Stillinger.

Chapter 4

1. *Letters*, 1:295, 301; 2:238.

2. *Buffon's Natural History*, 10 vols. (London: J. S. Barr, 1792), 4:64–65 (my italics).

3. See Graeme Tytler, *Physiology in the European Novel* (Princeton: Princeton University Press, 1982). Charles Bell's *Essays on the Anatomy of Expression* (London: Longman, 1806), includes some remarkable illustrative drawings.

4. Kenneth Dewhurst and Nigel Reeves, eds., *Schiller: Medicine, Psychology and Literature* (Berkeley: University of California Press, 1978), p. 279.

5. Alexander Gode-von Aesch's translation of the older Schlegel in *Natural Science in German Romanticism* (New York: Columbia University Press, 1941), p. 223. His discussion of the *Natur-philosophen's* connection of physiognomics and the origin of language is fascinating: "This conception of language . . . [is] but one aspect of the more general notion that everything is sign and symbol, that the whole world has 'merely indicatory or physiognomic significance.' The whole world should be interpreted as a gigantic system of hieroglyphics, as the *language* of God or the *book* of nature" (p. 219).

6. Helen Vendler has suggested that lessons in morbid anatomy lie behind details of Moneta's face; *The Odes of Keats* (Cambridge: Harvard University Press, 1983), p. 214. More interesting yet is the practical description of the signs of the face of death, which they called "the Hippocratic face," found in textbooks and encyclopedias of the period: "When a patient (says he [i.e., Hippocrates]) has his nose sharp, his eyes sunk, his temples hollow, his ears cold and contracted, the skin of his forehead tense and dry, and the colour of his face tending to a pale-green, or lead colour, one may pronounce for certain that death is very near at hand. . . . This observation has been confirmed by succeeding physicians, who have, from him, denominated it the *Hippocratic face.*" Andrew Duncan, "Medicine," in *Encyclopaedia Britannica* (1810), 13:190. For a discussion of Keats's sources in Greek art for the face of pain, see Ann Mellor's "Keats's Face of Moneta: Source and Meaning," *Keats-Shelley Journal* 25 (1976): 65–80.

7. Elaine Scarry, *The Body in Pain: The Making and Unmaking of the World* (New York: Oxford University Press, 1985), pp. 4–7.

8. *Letters*, 2:102–3; cf. 1:279 on sickness and knowledge. See also Michael E. Holstein's discussion in "Keats: The Poet-Healer and the Problem of Pain," *Keats-Shelley Journal* 36 (1987): 32–49.

9. See James Gregory's *Conspectus Medicinae Theoretica* (1782) as adapted to contemporary practice in Duncan, "Medicine," p. 212.

10. Paul de Man, "The Negative Road" (1966), in *John Keats*, ed. Harold Bloom (New York: Chelsea House, 1985), p. 33.

11. James Russell Lowell, "Lowell on Keats," in *Keats: The Critical Heritage*, ed. G. M. Matthews (New York: Barnes & Noble, 1971), p. 360.

PART II

1. Alexander von Humboldt, "Die Lebenskraft oder der Rhodische Genius," *Die Hören* 1, no. 5 (1795): 90–96; reprinted in *Gesammelte Werke*, 6 vols. (Stuttgart: J. G. Cottaschen, 1844), 6:303–7.

2. Alexander von Humboldt's accounts of his scientific expeditions to South America and Mexico between 1799 and 1804 were translated into English in 1814. Coleridge met the Humboldt brothers in Rome in 1805; Astley Cooper met the younger Humboldt in 1792 during his visit to the Continent. The frequency with which both brothers' names recur in contemporary scientific

journals and textbooks, as well as the records of their lectures and collaboration with English physiologists like Cooper, attests to their renown in England.

3. "Psyche," *Classical Dictionary*, p. 645. See also Joseph Spence, "a Cupid fondling or burning a butterfly is just the same with them as a Cupid caressing or tormenting the goddess Psyche, or the soul," *Polymetis* (London: R. & J. Dodsley, 1755; reprint, London: J. Johnson, 1802), pp. 69–71.

4. Friedrich von Schiller, "Philosophy of Physiology" (1779) in *Friedrich Schiller: Medicine, Psychology and Literature*, ed. Kenneth Dewhurst and Nigel Reeves (Berkeley: University of California Press, 1978), pp. 152–55.

5. S. T. Coleridge, *Inquiring Spirit*, ed. Kathleen Coburn (Toronto: University of Toronto Press, 1979), p. 259; "Appendix C to *Aids to Reflection*," in *The Complete Works of Samuel Taylor Coleridge*, ed. W.G.T. Shedd, 7 vols. (New York: Harper, 1863), 1:387, 391–92.

6. Until well into the century, biology and physiology were virtually synonymous expressions. Treviranus's use of the term was followed, also in 1802, by Lamarck's, to denote a more narrow and mechanistic discipline: "Biology: this is one of the three divisions of terrestrial physics; it includes all which pertains to living bodies and particularly to their organization, their developmental processes, the structural complexity resulting from prolonged action of vital movements, the tendency to create special organs and to isolate them by focusing activity in a center, and so on." William Coleman's translation of Treviranus and Lamarck in *Biology in the Nineteenth Century: Problems of Form, Function, and Transformation* (New York: Wiley, 1971), pp. 1–2. See also Hans Driesch, *The History and Theory of Vitalism*, trans. C. K. Ogden (London: Macmillan, 1914), p. 101.

7. Michel Foucault, *The Order of Things*, trans. A. M. Sheridan Smith (London: Tavistock, 1970), chap. 5. See also Jacques Roger's discussion of Foucault, "The Living World," in *The Ferment of Knowledge: Studies in the Historiography of Eighteenth-century Science*, ed. G. S. Rousseau and Roy Porter (London: Cambridge University Press, 1980), p. 258.

8. William Lawrence, *An Introduction to Comparative Anatomy and Physiology: Being the Two Introductory Lectures Delivered at the Royal College of Surgeons on the 21st and 25th of March, 1816* (London: Callow, 1816), p. 35.

9. Marcet's research on the chemistry of the Dead Sea and the Jordan River began in 1807; Bailey's essays, written in 1818, are mentioned in *The Keats Circle*, ed. Hyder E. Rollins, 2d ed., 2 vols. (Cambridge: Harvard University Press, 1965), 1:26.

10. See L. Pierce Williams, *Michael Faraday* (New York: Basic Books, 1964), p. 63.

11. Trevore H. Levere argues convincingly, from evidence in the letters and notebooks and from circumstances surrounding the 1816 date of the Jacksonian Prize of the Royal College (for which Coleridge wrote the *Essay on Scrofula*, to which this is an offshoot), for the 1817 completion date of the *Theory of Life*. He also marks the strong presence of Coleridge's ideas on life in Green's lectures to the college in 1824, and in Green's Hunterian Oration before the college, "Vital Dynamics," in 1840. See *Poetry Realized in Nature: Samuel Taylor Coleridge and Early Nineteenth-century Science* (New York: Cambridge University Press, 1981), pp. 43–44. J. H. Haeger, "Coleridge's 'By Blow': The Composition and Date of *Theory of Life*," *Modern Philology* 74 (1976): 20–41, proposes a completion date of 1819, and possibly as late as 1823, for the *Theory of Life*; he sees Abernethy's 1819 Hunterian Oration as the stimulus for the essay and speculates that it may have been ghostwritten for James Gillman to give as a Hunterian Oration lecture.

12. Levere, *Poetry Realized in Nature*, p. 44.

13. In a letter to George and Georgiana, Keats recounted that the dominant topics of Coleridge's monologue were metaphysics, sensations, dreams, and consciousness. *Letters*, 2: 88–89.

14. Shelley, "On Life," in *Shelley's Poetry and Prose*, ed. Donald H. Reiman and Sharon B. Powers (New York: Norton, 1977), pp. 475–76. M. H. Abrams has noted how life is the "ground-concept" for all Romantic thought: "Life is itself the highest good, the residence and measure of other goods,

and the generator of the controlling categories of Romantic thought." *Natural Supernaturalism: Tradition and Revolution in Romantic Literature* (New York: Norton, 1971), p. 431.

15. Robert E. Schofield, quoting William Heberden in a posthumously published 1802 essay (in Robert T. Gunther, *Early Science in Cambridge* [Oxford: For the author, 1937], p. 284), *Mechanism and Materialism: British Natural Philosophy in An Age of Reason* (Princeton: Princeton University Press, 1970), p. 191.

16. Friedrich von Schlegel, *The Philosophy of Life*, trans. A.J.W. Morrison (London: Henry G. Bohn, 1847), p. 76. Foucault and others since have made much of this "illuminating gaze" of the first clinicians for the birth of modern medicine; see *Birth of the Clinic*, pp. xiiff., 107–23.

Chapter 5

1. Friedrich von Schlegel, *Philosophy of Life*, trans. A.J.W. Morrison (London: Henry G. Bohn, 1847), pp. 4, 74, 525.

2. "The possibility of a living matter is unthinkable; the concept contains a contradiction for lifelessness, inertia, is the essential characteristic of matter," Kant said in his *Metaphysical Principles of Science*, see translation and discussion by Hans Driesch, *History and Theory of Vitalism*, trans. C. K. Ogden (London: Macmillan, 1914), pp. 75–76, 100.

3. In 1798 J. C. De La Mettrie described for the English intellectuals how Kant's two forces, termed the attractive and repulsive (which La Mettrie traced to Newton), proved a source for other notions of forces, like the caloric force, the luminous force, the electric force, the magnetic force, the galvanic force, even the *vita propria* and *nisus formativus* or plastic force of Blumenbach; "On the System of Forces," *Philosophical Magazine* 2 (1798): 277–78.

4. Treviranus, as quoted by Leonard R. Wheeler, *Vitalism: Its History and Validity* (London: H. F. & G. Witherby, 1939), pp. 56–57.

5. F. W. J. Schelling, *On University Studies*, trans. E. S. Morgan (Athens: Ohio University Press, 1966), p. 136; see also Driesch, *History and Theory of Vitalism*, pp. 93–94.

6. See Trevor H. Levere's discussion of Coleridge's (and J.H. Green's) understanding of Schelling, *Poetry Realized in Nature* (New York: Cambridge University Press, 1981), pp. 67–68.

7. Hans Christian Oersted, *The Soul in Nature, with Supplementary Contributions*, trans. Leonora and Joanna B. Horner (1852; reprint, London: Dawsons, 1966), p. 18.

8. Lorenz Oken was a biologist and philosopher, a professor of medicine at Jena and an editor of the literary periodical *Isis*; at Basle, he was a professor of medicine and philosophy. See his *Elements of Physiophilosophy*, trans. Alfred Tulk (London: Ray Society, 1847), pp. 1–2; Oken's first formulation on "Physio-philosophy" appeared in his *Grundriss der Naturphilosophie, der Theorie der Sinne, und der darauf gegründeten Classification der Thiere* (1802).

9. *Wordsworth: Poetical Works*, ed. Thomas Hutchinson, rev. Ernest de Selincourt (London: Oxford University Press, 1904), *The Excursion*, IX, 1–9. Coleridge's proposal of a presence in nature that is "At once the Soul of each, and God of all," an indwelling soul that informs all the material universe and constitutes all modes of consciousness, occurs also in his "Religious Musings" and in "The Destiny of Nations." See M. H. Abrams's discussion in "Coleridge's 'A Light in Sound': Science, Metascience, and Poetic Imagination," in *The Correspondent Breeze: Essays on English Romanticism* (New York: Norton, 1984).

10. Schiller, "Philosophy of Physiology," in *Friedrich Schiller: Medicine, Psychology and Literature*, ed. Kenneth Dewhurst and Nigel Reeves (Berkeley: University of California Press, 1978), p. 154.

11. John Barclay, "Physiology," in *Encyclopaedia Britannica* (1810), 16:446.

12. Alexander Gode-von Aesch, citing Hufeland, in *Natural Science in German Romanticism* (New York: Columbia University Press, 1941), p. 199.

13. Girtanner, "Memoires sur l'Irritabilité, Considerée comme le Principe de Vie dans la Nature Organisée" (1790) and *Essay on the Kantian Principle* (1796) as discussed by Everett Mendelsohn, *Heat and Life: The Development of the Theory of Animal Heat* (Cambridge: Harvard University Press, 1964), pp. 169–70; and Gode-von Aesch, *Natural Science in German Romanticism*, pp. 195–96.

14. The latest of Humboldt's accounts on the life force in eels appeared in England in 1820; see note 29 below.

15. In his *Florae Fribergensis, or Aphorisms on the Chemical Physiology of Plants* (1793), quoted by Philip Ritterbush in *Overtures to Biology* (New Haven: Yale University Press, 1964), p. 189; see also Humboldt's "On the Chemical Process of Vitality," *Journal of Natural Philosophy, Chemistry, and the Arts* 1 (1797): 359–64.

16. *Al. von Humboldt und Aimé Bonpland's Reise* (1807); the frontispiece is reproduced by Ritterbush in his *Overtures to Biology*. Goethe returned the accolade by mentioning Alexander von Humboldt in Ottolie's diary in *Die Walverwandtschaften* (1830), translated by R. J. Hollingdale as *Elective Affinities* (Harmondsworth, U.K.: Penguin, 1971), p. 215. It should be noted here that Alexander von Humboldt did not consider himself a *Naturphilosophe* but an empiricist: he praised the speculative philosophy, joined the *Naturphilosophen* in their search for an essential unity in nature, and believed *Naturphilosophie* and empiricism need not be hostile to one another. See H.A.M. Snelders, "Romanticism and Naturphilosophie and the Inorganic Natural Sciences, 1797–1840," *Studies in Romanticism* 9 (1970): 193. Schelling's declaration on Brown is from his "On the Study of Medicine and the Theory of Organic Nature" (1802), in *On University Studies*, p. 135.

17. John Brown, *The Elements of Medicine*, translated by the author, revised and corrected with a biographical preface by Thomas Beddoes, 2 vols. (London: J. Johnson, 1795), 1:266. Brown's theory found wide currency in England and Europe, and an even wider applicability to other established theories. See, for example, William Alexander's use of it the "Effects of Opium on the Living System," *Memoirs of the Literary and Philosophical Society of Manchester* 6 (1805): 3–4. See also Fielding H. Garrison, *An Introduction to the History of Medicine* (Philadelphia and London: W. B. Saunders, 1929), pp. 409ff. on Broussais's and La Mettrie's use of Brunonian theory.

18. Robert Kinglake, "On the Nature and Properties of Vital Power," *Medical and Physical Journal* 2 (1799): 130–31, 126–28; his earlier *Dissertation on the Physiological Origins of the Vital Power* (1794) addresses the diversity of nature and quality that animal excitability can take in various organs.

19. J. Thompson, citing Cullen, in *An Account of the Life, Lectures and Writings of William Cullen*, M.D., 2 vols. (Edinburgh: Blackwood, 1859), 1:317. Cullen founded the Glasgow medical school in 1744; though he made no truly original contribution to medical science, his influence on the practice of medicine in England (and on pupils like John Brown) was enormous. See Garrison, *History of Medicine*, p. 358.

20. *De partibus corporis humani sensibilibus et irritabilibus* (1752) set up the theory of irritability. Schofield calls Haller the greatest of the Germanic influences on mid-century British physiology; *Mechanism and Materialism*, pp. 201–2. The English version of the theory appeared in 1755. The entry "Irritability" in the current *Encyclopaedia Britannica* (1810), vol. 11, focuses on the sensation of pain and provides a useful sense of Haller's theory during Keats's time.

21. Johann Friedrich Gmelin, *Irritabilitatem Vegetabilium* (1768), identified six hundred flowers with irritable anthers and forty plants with irritable leaves; see Ritterbush, *Overtures to Biology*, pp. 147–48.

22. Benjamin Stillingfleet, "A Discourse on the Irritability of Some Flowers," *Literary Life and Selected Works of Benjamin Stillingfleet* (London: Longman, 1811), pp. 210, 214–15.

23. See Kinglake, "On the Nature and Properties of Vital Power," pp. 128–29, on the diversity of forms and expressions that excitability can take.

24. The German translation of Galvani appeared in 1793. See the entry "Galvanism" in the *Encyclopaedia Britannica* (1810), 9:331–445, which emphasizes the parallel between observable

physical electricity and this "animal" variety. Volta, of course, soon proved that there was only one type of electricity; in 1843 du Bois-Reymond proved that the electric power and nerve force were identical, and the advent of biochemistry revealed the common electromagnetic origin of electrical and chemical energy. See F. Kraüpl Taylor, *The Concept of Illness, Disease and Morbus* (London: Cambridge University Press, 1979), pp. 98–99.

25. Mary Shelley's "Introduction to *Frankenstein, or the Modern Prometheus*" (1818), written in 1831 for the third edition. Reprinted in *The Norton Anthology of English Literature*, ed. M. H. Abrams et al., 2 vols. (New York: Norton, 1979), 2:886.

26. See Robert Darnton's *Mesmerism and the End of the Enlightenment in France* (Cambridge: Harvard University Press, 1968).

27. Samuel Taylor Coleridge, *Inquiring Spirit*, rev. ed., ed. Kathleen Coburn (Toronto: University of Toronto Press, 1979), p. 47. See also p. 50, where Coleridge declares animal magnetism and electricity to be manifestations of the same power.

28. See "Extract of a Letter from Mr. Humboldt to Mr. Blumenbach, Containing new Experiments on the Irritation Caused by the Metals with Respect to Their Different Impressions on the Organs of Animals," *Journal of Natural Philosophy, Chemistry, and the Arts* 1 (1797): 256–60. This account was almost certainly seen by Coleridge and others. Barclay's entry "Physiology" in *Encyclopaedia Britannica* (1810), 16:478, lists the principles that Humboldt found necessary to excite irritability, and notes that Humboldt considered the electric force or galvanic fluid as "the source of nervous power" in the universe.

29. Alexander von Humboldt, "Account of the Electric Eels, and of the Method of Catching Them in South America by Means of Wild Horses," abridged from his *Personal Narrative*, in *Edinburgh Philosophical Journal* 2 (1820): 244–45. The first full translation of Humboldt's account of his adventures with the botanist Bonpland in South America (1799–1804) appeared in England in 1814; the Guy's Physical Society Library acquired copies of the original and the translation in 1815.

30. Ibid., 246–47.

31. See the late edition with annotations of *The Works of John Brown*, ed. W. C. Brown, 3 vols. (London: Johnson & Symonds, 1804), 2:188. Barclay, "Physiology," p. 466, also notes the centrality to Brown's system of the notion of life as a forced state.

32. See Michel Serres's discussion in "Turner Translates Carnot," *Hermes: Literature, Science, Philosophy*, ed. Josué V. Harari and David Bell (Baltimore: Johns Hopkins University Press, 1982), p. 56.

Chapter 6

1. Lucretius, *Of the Nature of Things*, trans. Thomas Creech, 2 vols. (London: T. Warner & J. Walthoe, 1722), vol. 1, Bk. II, 64–65, 72–80.

2. John Henry Wegenblass, "Keats and Lucretius," *Modern Language Review* 32 (1937): 539; Erasmus Darwin, *The Temple of Nature; or, the Origin of Society: A Poem, with Philosophical Notes* (London: J. Johnson, 1803), II, 41–44.

3. Friedrich von Schlegel, *The Philosophy of Life*, trans. A.J.W. Morrison (London: Henry G. Bohn, 1847), pp. 121–22.

4. Darwin, *Temple of Nature*, IV, 383–88; I, 247–50; see also Additional Note I.

5. Lucretius, *Nature of Things*, vol. 1, Bk. I, 319–21. Democritus of Abdera (460–360 B.C.) was actually the first to propose invisible living atomies in the body and the soul, whose movements were the cause of life and mental activity (Fielding H. Garrison, *An Introduction to the History of Medicine* [Philadelphia and London: W. B. Saunders, 1929], p. 90). For the debunking of the doctrine of spontaneous generation by Spallanzani, Vallesneri and others, see Arturo Castiglioni,

A *History of Medicine*, trans. E. B. Krumbhaar (New York: Knopf, 1947), p. 612, and Bentley Glass, "The Idea of Biological Species," in *Forerunners of Darwin: 1745–1859*, ed. Glass et al. (Baltimore: Johns Hopkins University Press, 1959), p. 42.

6. Lorenz Oken, in *Die Zeugung* (1805), in *Elements of Physiophilosophy*, trans. Alfred Tulk (London: Ray Society, 1847), pp. 180–87. It is fortunate that Oken was only an indirect source for Keats—the temptation to view the Indian Maid in *Endymion* from the perspective of the doctrine of *Ur-Schleim*, and to add to this Rick's whimsical perspective of "slippery blesses" in Keats, would otherwise be too great to resist.

7. Darwin, *Temple of Nature*, I, 295–302, 333–34; Bernard Blackstone, *The Consecrated Urn* (London: Longman, 1959), pp. 156ff. (Blackstone quotes from a footnote on p. 43 of Taylor's translation of four Dialogues.)

8. Lavoisier and his associates, Macquer and Sage, analyzed the waters of the Dead Sea in 1778. Alexander Marcet, "An Analysis of the Waters of the Dead Sea and the River Jordan," *Philosophical Transactions* 97 (1807): 296–314, especially 296–99.

9. Ibid., pp. 313–14; see also Garrison, *History of Medicine*, p. 66, on the medicinal legends of the River Jordan.

10. See Erasmus Darwin's note on Beauchamp and Volney's account of the volcanic country where the River Jordan begins, *The Botanic Garden; A Poem, in Two Parts* (London: J. Johnson, 1791), Part One, IV, 294n.

11. William Babington, Alexander Marcet, and William Allen, *A Syllabus of a Course of Chemical Lectures Read at Guy's Hospital* (London: W. Phillips, 1816), pp. 9–10.

12. See Everett Mendelsohn's discussion of Lavoisier and Priestley, *Heat and Life* (Cambridge: Harvard University Press, 1964), p. 134. Priestley and chemists of his time imagined a principle to exist in all combustible bodies called philogiston. Darwin's *Botanic Garden*, Part One, IV, 39–46, provides a colorful summary of the vital properties of Priestley's and Lavoisier's "pure air." "Whence in bright floods the VITAL AIR expands, / . . . Fills the fine lungs of all that *breathe* or *bud*, / Warms the new heart, and dyes the gushing blood; / With Life's first spark inspires the organic frame, / And, as it wastes, renews the subtile flame." For a definition of "fixed air," see William Nicolson, *The First Principles of Chemistry* (London: Robinson, 1792), pp. 183–84.

13. *The Collected Works of Sir Humphry Davy*, ed. John Davy, 9 vols. (London: Smith, Elder, 1840), 8:333.

14. *Letters*, 2:156–57; cf. Robert Burton, *The Anatomy of Melancholy*, ed. A. R. Shilleto, 3 vols. (1893; reprint, London: G. Bell & Sons, 1913), 2:73–74. This letter to Taylor, written in 1819, follows Keats's reading of Burton in an 1813 edition.

15. *Botanic Garden*, Part One, IV, 64–67; 290–93; Byron's concept of unhealthy air borne within the prison at Chillon parallels this idea.

16. Table Talk, 7 April 1832, in *Specimens of the Table-Talk of Samuel Taylor Coleridge*, ed. H. N. Coleridge (London: John Murray, 1851), p. 169; Beatrice, in Shelley's *The Cenci* finds a real and psychological "clinging, black, contaminating mist" about her that dissolves her flesh "to a pollution" and poisons "the subtle, pure, and inmost spirit of life!" (III, i, 14–23; this and other citations of the poetry in the text are from Donald H. Reiman and Sharon B. Powers, eds., *Shelley's Poetry and Prose* [New York: Norton, 1977]).

17. Babington et al., *Syllabus of a Course of Chemical Lectures*, pp. 13–14. See also Robert Thornton, "A Remarkable Case of Internal Pain in the Heel, and an Incipient Mortification, Cured by the Inhalation of Vital Air," *Philosophical Magazine* 3 (1799): pp. 213–15; also James Curry, *Observations on Apparent Death from Drowning* (London: E. Cox, 1815), p. 17. Thornton was lecturer in medical botany at Guy's before Salisbury, and physician to the General Dispensary in pneumatic medicine.

18. Marie Boas, "The Establishment of Mechanical Philosophy," in *Osiris: Studies of the History and*

Philosophy of Science and on the History of Learning and Culture 10 (1952): 509 (quoting from Newton's *Opticks*, Query 9 and Query 10).

19. Van Helmont's use of the concept of light to explain life and soul was complex and influential upon later generations. Lester S. King provides a good description of its conceptual importance in *The Philosophy of Medicine* (Cambridge: Harvard University Press, 1978), pp. 127–29. Mendelsohn (*Heat and Life*, p. 40) notes that Van Helmont's theory was a distinct advance for living chemistry in that it rejected the notion of innate animal heat in favor of a specific cause.

20. Lionel Trilling, classroom lecture, Columbia University, spring 1974; Stuart M. Sperry, *Keats the Poet* (Princeton: Princeton University Press, 1970), p. 302. Contemporary notions of the volcanic origins of the earth typified by the passage in *The Botanic Garden* (Part One, II, 13–16) provide a curious angle on this volcanian transformation of Lamia.

21. Babington et al., *Syllabus of a Course of Chemical Lectures*, pp. 8–9.

22. *Botanic Garden*, Part One, I, 193–204. John Livingston Lowes, of course, has amply demonstrated in *The Road to Xanadu*, rev. ed. (Boston: Houghton Mifflin, 1964) the source for the shiny creatures in the Mariner's rotting sea in Coleridge's readings on luminescent life and phosphorescence in James Cook's account of voyages in the Pacific Ocean, Father Bourze's letter in the *Philosophical Transactions* on the "Luminous Appearances in the Wakes of Ships," and Priestley's chapter in the *Opticks* on "Lights from Putrescent Substances." Sailors called the substance found floating on the oceans, a mix of marine life and putrifying matter, "Corpusance."

23. See *Botanic Garden*, Part One, Additional Note IX to I, 192 (on luminous insects) and Additional Note X to I, 237 (on phosphorus); also see I, 182, and note on Beccari's shells.

24. Nathaniel Hulme, "Experiments and Observations on the Light which is Spontaneously Emitted, with Some Degree of Permanency, from Various Bodies," *Philosophical Transactions* 9 (1800): 161–87; and "A Continuation of the Experiments and Observations on the Light which is Spontaneously Emitted from Various Bodies; with Some Experiments and Observations on Solar Light, when imbibed by *Canton's* Phosphorus," *Philosophical Transactions* 92 (1802): 403–26. By 1802 Hulme's research had begun to suggest a difference between the spontaneous light of living creatures and the phosphorus of decaying matter in that oxygen had an effect on the latter but not on the former (p. 406).

25. "Luminosity produced by Compression, Friction, and Animal Bodies," *Edinburgh Philosophical Journal* 4 (1820–1821): 216–19.

26. See, for example, Darwin's Additional Note X to *Botanic Garden*, I, 237, where he cannot tell if phosphoric light is a product of life or deathliness. The medicinal use of phosphorus as a vivifying agent at this time, "to give a certain degree of activity to the life" of consumptive patients, and "to restore and revive young persons exhausted by excesses," only furthered the scientific paradox. See Alphonsus Leroi, "Extract of Experiments and Observations on the Use of Phosphorus Administered Internally," *Philosophical Magazine* 2 (1798): 290–93.

27. All meanings for the verb *to dissolve* are taken from the *Oxford English Dictionary*.

28. As in George Ernst Stahl's notion that the essence of life lay in its preservation from corruption, living and nonliving differed fundamentally in that the former was exempt from corruption, and the latter necessarily dissolved. See John Barclay, "Physiology," in *Encyclopaedia Britannica* (1810), 16:457.

29. Byron, *Don Juan*, ed. Leslie A. Marchand (Boston: Houghton Mifflin, 1958), Canto IX, 16.

30. Thomas Mann, *The Magic Mountain*, trans. H. T. Lowe-Porter (New York: Knopf, 1946), p. 495.

31. In "Why did I laugh tonight?", 9. For Hunter, death was not merely the absence of life or the vacuous remnant of life's cessation, but an active positive phenomenon of living which triggered the cessation of life. See his discussion in *The Works of John Hunter*, ed. James F. Palmer, 4 vols. (London: Longman, 1835), 3:114ff.

32. Michel Foucault, *The Birth of the Clinic*, trans. A. M. Sheridan Smith (New York: Random House, 1973), pp. 140–41.

33. See William Empson's discussion in *Seven Types of Ambiguity* (New York: New Directions, 1947), p. 272. The doctor in Keats would not fail to be fascinated by the curious interconnection of life, death, and the symbol of this interconnection in human passion—seen in the lines of another poet-doctor, T. L. Beddoes: "When Melveric's heart's heart, his new-wed wife, / Upon the bed whereon she bore these sons, / Died, as a blossom does whose inmost fruit / Tears it in twain, and in its stead remains / A bitter poison-berry . . ." ("Death's Jest-Book; or The Fool's Tragedy," III, iii), in *The Poetical Works of Thomas Lovell Beddoes*, ed. Edmund Gosse 2 vols. (London: J. M. Dent, 1890), 2:60.

34. See John Alderson, *An Essay on Apparitions*, rev. ed. (London: Longman, 1823), pp. 35–36; the essay was first published in 1810 in the *Edinburgh Medical and Chirurgical Journal*.

Chapter 7

1. John Hunter, *Treatise on the Blood*, in *The Works of John Hunter*, ed. James F. Palmer, 4 vols. (London: Longman, 1835), 3:34. John Keats, *Anatomical and Physiological Note Book*, ed. Maurice Buxton Forman (London: Oxford University Press, 1934), Fourth Page, p. 5. Astley Cooper and Henry Cline, Jr., *Anatomical Lectures Delivered at St. Thomas's Hospital*, 2 vols. (MS, Royal College of Surgeons, 1812, 1814), is useful in verifying the extent of Hunter's influence on contemporary teachings on the blood, veins, arteries (lectures 2, 3, 4), and on the nature of coagulation.

2. *Treatise on the Blood*, *Works*, 3:111.

3. Ibid., 33–34; see also 78–90; also Cooper and Cline, *Anatomical Lectures*, 2:7–9, on coagulation. The five living powers Hunter ascribed to the blood were widely summarized in textbooks of the early nineteenth century; John Barclay, "Physiology," *Encyclopaedia Britannica* (1810), 16:465, recites these powers of the blood according to Hunter, as does J. C. Prichard's A *Review of the Doctrine of a Vital Principle* (London: Sherwood, 1829), p. 131.

4. Hunter, *Works*, 1:227, defines what he means by the "stimulus of death:" "Whenever death takes place it excites an action in every part that is muscular: they contract, and this is the action of death."

5. Prichard, *Review of the Doctrine of a Vital Principle*, p. 19, referring to Hunter, *Works*, 4:20.

6. Hunter, *Works*, 1:219. See Philip C. Ritterbush, *Overtures to Biology* (New Haven: Yale University Press, 1964), p. 188.

7. *Treatise on the Blood*, *Works*, 3:33–34; p. 89, specifically notes the characteristic "unsettled state, having no communication with the brain," and being "independent of the nerves," of the blood.

8. A fact noted by contemporary scientists like John Ferriar, "Observations Concerning the Vital Principle," *Memoirs of the Literary and Philosophical Society of Manchester* 3 (1790): 227–28.

9. J. and C. Bell, *The Anatomy and Physiology of the Human Body*, 7th ed., 2 vols. (London: Longman, 1829), 1:3.

10. "Blood," in *Encyclopaedia Britannica* (1810), 3:747; the entry continues:

After it is allowed that the blood contains the vital principle, it becomes another question not very easily solved, Whence is this vital principle derived?—For this we can only discover two sources; namely, the chyle or aliment from which the blood is prepared, and respiration. The latter hath been commonly held as the principle source of the vital principle; and, for a long time, it was generally thought that there was a kind of vivifying spirit in the air, which being absorbed by the blood at each inspiration, communicated to that fluid the quality necessary for preserving animal life. As a proof of this it was urged, that life cannot be supported without respiration, and that air which hath been often breathed ceases to be capable of supporting life; because when once it has been totally deprived of its vivifying spirit, it can communicate none to the blood in any subsequent respirations.—This doctrine, however, hath been denied, and generally thought to be exploded by modern discoveries.

11. See John Ferriar, "Observations Concerning the Vital Principle," *Memoirs of the Literary and Philosophical Society of Manchester* 3 (1790): 222: "Mr. Hunter attributes to the blood, a power of forming and renewing parts, by its proper efforts, apparently carried, in some cases, almost to a degree of rationality."

12. E. W. Goodall has identified this dewy ooze with the serum from clotting blood, in "Some Examples of the Knowledge of Medicine Exhibited in the Poems of Keats," *Guy's Hospital Gazette* 40 (1936): 239. Donald C. Goellnicht believes a closer source for these lines is the vapor released by warm, standing blood before it separates, as described by Blumenbach in *Institutions of Physiology*: "While still warm, it emits a vapour which has of late been denominated an animal gas.... This, if collected, forms drops resembling dew, of a *watery* nature"; *The Poet-Physician* (Pittsburgh: University of Pittsburgh Press, 1984), p. 188. The view of blood as a living fluid under the lens of a microscope was probably all that Keats needed for this image. See the entry "Blood," in William T. Brande's *Dictionary of Science, Literature and Art* (New York: Harper, 1846): "When viewed under the microscope it appears to consist of very minute *red globules* or spheroids floating in a colourless fluid." Also, *Quincy's ... Medical Dictionary* (1817), in its entry "Blood" (p. 118), notes how "the microscope discovers that the blood contains a great number of round globules, which are seen floating about in a yellowish fluid, the serum."

13. See entry in *Quincy's ... Medical Dictionary* on warm- and cold-blooded animals; also Thomas Young, "The Croonian Lecture. On the Function of the Heart and Arteries," *Philosophical Transactions* 99 (1809): 28. Anthony Carlisle's well-known research on how the multiplicity of veins in lemurs and sloths functioned, provides a curious angle upon Lamia's unusual genesis from cold-blooded snake and bloodless, ghostly lemure; see his "Account of a Peculiarity in the Distributation of Arteries sent to the Limbs of Slow-moving Animals; Together with Some Other Facts," *Philosophical Transactions* 90 (1800): 98–108. This research, in turn, gave new vigor to the Aristotelian notion of innate heat (of the heart) as the source of life and all its powers from nutrition and movement to sensation and thought.

14. See Young's discussion of "the powers" of circulation, and of the early nineteenth century's belief that the throbbing action of the heart was the source of arterial action and other such signs of life, "On the Function of the Heart and Arteries," pp. 21–22. See also A.P.W. Philip's "On the Sources and Nature of the Powers on which the Circulation of the Blood Depends," *Philosophical Transactions* 121 (1831): 489–96. The empurpled verse describing Apollo's life-giving power to make the stars "silvery splendour pant with bliss" (*Hyp.*, III, 100–3) would suggest a hematological source for its metaphor.

15. See note 7 above.

16. Hunter also proposed that, after the blood, the stomach was a seat of life and more essential than the brain. (See C. H. Wilkinson, *Elements of Galvanism, in Theory and Practice; with a Comprehensive View of Its History, from the First Experiments of Galvani to the Present Time*, 2 vols. [London: John Murray, 1804], 1:175.) The Promethean importance of the stomach (or liver) would have appealed to those Romantic thinkers who found convincing Milton's theory of ingestion, being, and sinning in *Paradise Lost*. A Keatsian variation on this scientific and poetic tangle would be: "The flower must drink the nature of the soil / Before it can put forth its blossoming" ("Spenser, a jealous honorer of thine," 11–12).

17. Bacon, the sculptor of the façade of Guy's Hospital, undoubtedly saw the wooden boss of pelican and brood at Southwark Cathedral before he arranged his composition of figures pertinent to the art of healing. Keats, too, would have seen the boss on the roof of the original chapel at Southwark, which was destroyed by fire in 1831. The boss of the pelican and her brood was salvaged, and is now mounted on the wall of the new wing of the cathedral. R. M. Wingert's description of the façade, *Historical Notes on the Borough and the Borough Hospitals*, p. 92, includes a description of the bird as " 'the kind of life-rendering pelican' " whose young are "'repasted with her blood.' " He gives no source for his quotations, nor does he invoke either Renaissance iconography or the tangible inspiration at the Cathedral.

Chapter 8

1. John Hunter, "On the Vital Principle" (1786), in *The Works of John Hunter*, ed. James F. Palmer, 4 vols. (London: Longman, 1835), 1:221–23.

2. John Keats, *Anatomical and Physiological Note Book*, ed. Maurice Buxton Forman (London: Oxford University Press, 1934), Tenth Page, p. 58.

3. Ibid., Ninth Page, pp. 56–57.

4. Astley Cooper, *The Lectures of Sir Astley Cooper*, 5th U.S. ed., ed. Frederick Tyrrell (Philadelphia: Haswell, Barrington, & Haswell, 1839), p. 6. Cooper's words are from an evening course on surgery that Keats probably took, according to Donald C. Goellnicht, *The Poet-Physician* (Pittsburgh: Pittsburgh University Press, 1984), p. 27. The rest of the lecture, on aging, recalls the description of Glaucus's rapid progress from youth to old age in *Endymion*: "My fever'd parchings up, my scathing dread / Met palsy half way: soon these limbs became / Gaunt, wither'd, sapless, feeble, cramp'd, and lame" (III, 636–38).

5. William Babington and James Curry, *Outlines . . . Practice of Medicine* (London: T. Bensley, 1802–1806), pp. 25, 33.

6. Ibid., p. 33; John Haighton, "On Life," in *Lectures on the Physiology of the Human Body. Delivered at Guy's Hospital* (MS, Wills Library, 1796), p. 7.

7. William Lawrence, *Lectures on Physiology, Zoology, and the Natural History of Man* (London: J. Callow, 1819), pp. 6–7.

8. Ibid., pp. 12, 52, 66, 70–71n.

9. Ibid., pp. 66, 81.

10. Ibid., pp. 52, 96. Lawrence's opinions had considerable impact upon religious debate of the time. Robert Ryan, *Keats: The Religious Sense* (Princeton: Princeton University Press, 1976), explores that subject as it relates to Keats.

11. William Lawrence, "Life," in *The Cyclopaedia; or, Universal Dictionary of Arts, Sciences, and Literature*," ed. Abraham Rees, 39 vols. (London: Longman, 1819), vol. 20. Consciousness as the ghost in the machine is Gilbert Ryle's famous phrase for Romantic mechanism; see Hans Eichner, "The Rise of Modern Science and the Genesis of Romanticism," PMLA 97 (1982), 11–12.

12. Xavier Bichât, *Recherches physiologiques sur la vie et la mort* (1800), translated as *Physiological Researches on Life and Death* by F. Gold (Bristol: Longman, 1816), pp. 10–11. Bichât believed there was a basic conflict between the vital forces of animal life and those of physics and chemistry; his *propriétés vitales* were similar to—and no more metaphysical than—gravity, electricity, and other physical forces. See John Barclay's discussion and citation of Cuvier in "Physiology," in *Encyclopaedia Britannica* (1810), 16:465.

13. Aram Vartanian, quoting La Mettrie, in "Trembley's Polyp, La Mettrie, and Eighteenth-Century French Materialism," *Journal of the History of Ideas* 11 (1950): 271–72.

14. Cabanis later recanted his mechanism, sought psychosomatic connections between the

moral and physical natures, and saw life as something superadded to matter in the manner of Stahl, Hunter, and Abernethy; see Leonard Richmond Wheeler in *Vitalism: Its History and Validity* (London: H. F. & G. Witherby, 1939), p. 32.

15. In his *Theory of Life*, which took first form as early as 1816 and was essentially complete by 1817 as a specific response to the Abernethy-Lawrence debate. See M. H. Abrams, "Coleridge and the Romantic Vision of the World," in *The Correspondent Breeze* (New York: Norton, 1984), pp. 205–12.

16. See Everett Mendelsohn's discussion of the invasion of biology, even as it was being formed as a science, by physics and chemistry, *Heat and Life* (Cambridge: Harvard University Press, 1964), pp. 5, 91.

17. See Robert E. Schofield, *Mechanism and Materialism* (Princeton: Princeton University Press, 1970), p. 277.

18. What the mechanists did, of course, was to confuse the distinction between "organism," which belonged to Romantic and vitalistic philosophy, with "organization," a confusion criticized first by the anatomist John Barclay, in *An Inquiry into the Opinions, Ancient and Modern, Concerning Life and Organization* (Edinburgh: Bell & Bradfute, 1822), p. 340. See Owsei Temkin's discussion of the coincidence of biological and social uses of the term, "Basic Science, Medicine, and the Romantic Era," *Bulletin of the History of Medicine* 37 (1963): 118. See also Jacques Roger's discussion of the subject in "The Living World," in *The Ferment of Knowledge*, ed. G. S. Rousseau and Roy Porter (London: Cambridge University Press, 1980), pp. 270–71: "Was this enough to give birth to the concept of 'organization,' which was to become so important at the beginning of the nineteenth century? It is true that the word appears at that time, and that a mechanical interpretation of a living organism should lead to the idea of a necessary correlation of its parts."

19. *The Keats Circle*, ed. Hyder E. Rollins, 2d ed., 2 vols. (Cambridge: Harvard University Press, 1965), 2:185–86.

20. See Ryan, *Keats: The Religious Sense*, pp. 59–60; George Macilwain's *Memoirs of John Abernethy* (London: Hatcherd, 1856), p. 198, notes attendance at Abernethy's lectures of students from the Borough hospitals. Palmer, in his "Life of John Hunter" (*Works*, 1:147), notes that the Hunterian Orations at the museum were established in 1813 by Baillie and Home, and that in addition to members of the college, "senior pupils attending the London hospitals are by courtesy allowed to be present."

21. Bransby Blake Cooper, *The Life of Sir Astley Cooper*, 2 vols. (London: John W. Parker, 1843), 1:95, 249ff.

22. Temkin's article "Basic Science, Medicine, and the Romantic Era" provides the best historical survey of the Abernethy-Lawrence quarrel, and of the continuation of the debate after Lawrence left the fray.

23. Lawrence, "Life."

24. John Abernethy, *Physiological Lectures, Exhibiting a General View of Mr. Hunter's Physiology, and of his Researches in Comparative Anatomy; Delivered Before the Royal College of Surgeons in the Year 1817*, 2d ed. (London: Longman, 1822), pp. 333ff.

25. John Hunter, "Observations and Experiments on the Vegetable Economy," *Essays* (1861), 1:341, cited by Philip C. Ritterbush, *Overtures to Biology* (New Haven: Yale University Press, 1964), p. 188; also *Works*, 1: 214, 217, 221.

26. John Abernethy, *Introductory Lectures* (London: Longman, 1815), pp. 78–79.

27. John Abernethy, *The Hunterian Oration, for the Year 1819* (London: Longman, 1819), p. 29, and "Postscript," pp. 59–60n. The reference to Milton's brain was from a contemporary article ridiculing mechanistic doctrine; the question of how great art was produced if the brain was nothing more than a productive organ like the liver or stomach brought speculations of all colors—

Keats's own ponderings on the size of Milton's brain and the finite nature of intellect (*Letters*, 1:255), must belong to the mechanistic theories that engendered such speculations. See also Abernethy, *Introductory Lectures*, pp. 19, 26–27, 32–33, 57.

28. See Abernethy, *Introductory Lectures*, pp. 35, 40–43.

29. On ibid., p. 41 Abernethy actually invokes the image of a "universal chemist" residing in all living bodies.

30. Erasmus Darwin, *Zoonomia; or the Laws of Organic Life. In Three Parts*, ed. Samuel L. Mitchell, 2 vols. (1802; reprint, Philadelphia: Edward Earle, 1818), 1:20–22, 393, 80; see also Erasmus Darwin, *The Temple of Nature* (London: J. Johnson, 1803), p. 13.

31. Prichard, *Review of the Doctrine of a Vital Principle*, pp. 10, 116, 141–42.

32. H. W. Piper, in *The Active Universe* (London: University of London / Athalone Press, 1962), p. 115, says that the belief "that inanimate objects were in a literal sense alive came nearest to establishing itself as scientific orthodoxy during Wordsworth's most active poetic life;" he cites Cabanis's saying in 1802, "Today we are sufficiently informed about fundamentals to regard as chimerical that distinction which Buffon tried to establish between living and dead matter or between organic and inorganic particles" (in *Rapports du Physique et du Moral de l'homme* [1802], 2:362). Such a view would have been impossible to maintain in 1817, given the advance of mechanistic ways of thinking among Keats's generation.

33. See Shelley, "On Life" in *Shelley's Poetry and Prose*, ed. Donald H. Reiman and Sharon B. Powers (New York: Norton, 1977), pp. 476–78: "It is infinitely improbable that the cause of mind, that is, of existence, is similar to mind. It is said that mind produces motion and it might as well have been said that motion produces mind" (p. 478). "Whatever may be his true and final destination, there is a spirit within him [man] at enmity with nothingness and dissolution (change and extinction). This is the character of all life and being.—Each is at once the centre and the circumference; the point to which all things are referred, and the line in which all things are contained.—Such contemplations as these materialism and the popular philosophy of mind and matter, alike forbid; they are consistent only with the intellectual system" (p. 476).

Chapter 9

1. See "Of the Electric Property of the Torpedo" (1773), "On the Vital Principle"(1786) and "Account of the *Gymnotus Electicus*" (1775), in *The Works of John Hunter*, ed. James F. Palmer, 4 vols. (London: Longman, 1835), 1:221ff., 223ff.; 4:212, 398–400, 414.

2. John Hunter, "Experiments on Animals and Vegetables, with Respect to the Power of Producing Heat," *Philosophical Transactions* 45 (1775): 457, 452–54, *Works*, 4:131–55; and "On the Vital Principle" (1786), *Works*, 1:221–22.

3. Erasmus Darwin, *The Temple of Nature* (London: J. Johnson, 1803), I, 227–46.

4. Erasmus Darwin, *Zoonomia*, ed. Samuel L. Mitchell, 2 vols. (1802; reprint, Philadelphia: Edward Earle, 1818), 1:44–46 (on iron particles and animal muscles), 393–428 (on embryos).

5. Darwin, *Temple of Nature*, Note to II, 47; Additional Notes I and VI. Bernard Blackstone, in *The Consecrated Urn* (London: Longman, 1959), says Darwin's scientific poetry was the "best introduction to Keats;" he also notes that *Endymion's* pattern is built upon ideas of growth and rebirth.

6. *Collected Letters of Samuel Taylor Coleridge*, ed. E. L. Griggs, 4 vols. (Oxford: Oxford University Press, 1959), 4:807.

7. *Inquiring Spirit*, ed. Kathleen Coburn, rev ed. (Toronto: University of Toronto Press, 1979), pp. 258–59 (from *The Friend*). Contemporary "Grand Theory" physics, which posits four forces in the universe (electromagnetism, gravity, the weak force, and the strong force) appear to echo aspects of Coleridge's thinking here.

8. The task of tracing Coleridge's sources for the "law of polarity" must be left to other scholars. Among recent works, Trevor H. Levere's *Poetry Realized in Nature* (New York: Cambridge University Press, 1981) provides the best summary of the issues and influences on the subject. Raimonda Modiano, in *Coleridge and the Concept of Nature* (Tallahassee: Florida State University Press, 1985), pp. 138–86, writes an important chapter on Coleridge and the *Naturphilosophen*; Thomas McFarland, in *Romanticism and the Forms of Ruins* (Princeton: Princeton University Press, 1981), has a chapter called "Coleridge's Doctrine of Polarity and its European Contexts."

9. Otherwise known as "Appendix C to *Aids to Reflection*," conceived and written between 1816 and 1817, according to Levere, see note 11, Part II.

10. *Theory of Life*, in *The Complete Works of Samuel Taylor Coleridge*, ed. W.G.T. Shedd, 7 vols. (New York: Harper, 1863), 1:374–75, 378, 386, 387, 391, 388.

11. M. H. Abrams, "Coleridge's 'A Light in Sound'," in *The Correspondent Breeze* (New York: Norton, 1984), pp. 171, 175; see also Owen Barfield's discussion in *What Coleridge Thought* (Middletown, Conn.: Wesleyan University Press, 1971), pp. 141ff. Thomas McFarland, *Coleridge and the Pantheist Tradition* (Oxford: Oxford University Press, 1969), sees *Theory of Life* as an attempt to formulate a system of nature that is *not* pantheistic (p. 324).

12. Raymond Williams, in *Keywords: A Vocabulary of Culture and Society* (New York: Oxford University Press, 1976), notes the synonymity of "organic" and "mechanical" before the nineteenth century, and specifically credits Coleridge (and his reading of the German natural philosophers) for his early perception of the distinction (p. 190).

13. *Table Talk*, 23 May 1830, in *Specimens of the Table Talk of Samuel Taylor Coleridge*, ed. H. N. Coleridge (London: John Murray, 1851), pp. 80–81.

Chapter 10

1. Erasmus Darwin's "Additional Note XXII—Portland Vase" (to *The Botanic Garden* [London: J. Johnson, 1803], Part One, II, 321), is full of torches, butterflies, and positioned and lassitudal figures reminiscent of Humboldt's myth.

2. According to Robert Gittings, *John Keats: The Living Year* (Cambridge: Harvard University Press, 1954), p. 26, the sonnet was drafted eight months before the ode.

3. Schiller, "Philosophy of Physiology," in *Friedrich Schiller: Medicine, Psychology and Literature*, ed. Kenneth Dewhurst and Nigel Reeves (Berkeley: University of California Press, 1978), pp. 152–53.

4. Bernard Blackstone invokes lines from *Endymion* (III, 229–33) to support his claim that the Grecian urn is a funerary vessel that reconciles all contraries of life and death, and the elemental forces of earth, air, fire and water in its form (*The Consecrated Urn* [London: Longman, 1959], p. 331):

> Aye, 'bove the withering of old-lipp'd Fate
> A thousand Powers keep religious state,
> In water, fiery realm, and airy bourne;
> And, silent as a consecrated urn,
> Hold sphery sessions for a season due.

See also David Bromwich's discussion of Hazlitt's sense of the Elgin Marbles as "instances of power" and cold self-sufficiency—and Keats's parallel perceptions in his sonnet on the Marbles and in the ode (*Hazlitt: The Mind of a Critic* [New York: Oxford University Press, 1983], p. 391).

5. The *Oxford English Dictionary* specifically cites line 42 of the "Ode on a Grecian Urn" for these

meanings, and notes that the modern sense, "Elaborated to excess; over-laboured," was not used until 1939. I am indebted to John Barnard's annotation to this line, *John Keats: The Complete Poems*, 2d ed. (Harmondsworth, U.K.: Penguin, 1973), p. 651.

6. Joseph Spence, *Polymetis* (London: R. & J. Dodsley, 1755; reprint, London: J. Johnson, 1802), pp. 69–71.

7. As Walter Jackson Bate, *John Keats* (New York: Oxford University Press, 1966), p. 514, and critics since have noted.

8. William Hazlitt, "On the Elgin Marbles," in *The Complete Works of William Hazlitt*, ed. P. P. Howe, 21 vols. (London: J. M. Dent, 1930–1934), 18:145–47.

9. Adalbert von Chamisso, "The Crucifixion," trans. A. I. du P. Coleman, in *The German Classics*, ed. Frank Thilley, 20 vols. (New York: German Publication Society, 1913), 1:320–400.

10. Helen Vendler, *The Odes of John Keats* (Cambridge: Harvard University Press, 1983), p. 128; Bromwich's discussion of power and the Elgin Marbles and of Hazlitt's distinctions between the cold and disassociated art of painting and the expressive sympathy and process-borne art of poetry (in *Hazlitt: The Mind of a Critic*, pp. 391–92), as these relate to Keats's sonnet and ode, is more relevant to the subject at hand.

11. Blackstone, *Consecrated Urn*, p. xiii.

12. See Norman O. Brown, *Hermes the Thief* (Madison: University of Wisconsin Press, 1947), p. 57.

13. In *Phytologia*; see Elizabeth Sewell's discussion in *The Orphic Voice* (New Haven: Yale University Press, 1960), p. 209.

14. Gittings has noted the importance of Burton's *Anatomy of Melancholy* to the main themes and philosophy of the "Ode on a Grecian Urn," *Living Year*, pp. 136–37. Karen Swann's article on *Christabel* and hysteria reminds one of the importance Burton's *The Anatomy of Melancholy*, ed. A. R. Shilleto, 3 vols. (1893; reprint, London: G. Bell & Sons, 1913) placed on the hysterics' symptomatic inability to communicate their troubles: "And yet will not, cannot again tell how, where, or what offends them" (1:416); " 'Christabel': The Wandering Mother and the Enigma of Form," *Studies in Romanticism* 23 (1984), 536.

15. John Bayley, "Keats and Reality," in *Proceedings of the British Academy* (London: Oxford University Press, 1962), pp. 92–93.

16. See Stuart M. Sperry, *Keats the Poet* (Princeton: Princeton University Press, 1970), pp. 117–31. Mary Visick, " 'Tease Us Out of Thought': Keats's *Epistle to Reynolds* and the Odes," *Keats-Shelley Journal* 15 (1966): 87–98, discusses the importance to the epistle of the two paintings by Claude Lorrain.

PART III

1. *Letters*, 1:125.

2. Lionel Trilling, "The Poet as Hero: Keats in His Letters," in *The Opposing Self* (New York: Viking Press, 1955), p. 49.

3. See the definition of aetiology under "Medicine" in the 7th edition of the *Encyclopaedia Britannica* (1842), 14:522, which begins with the meaning of the root verb "to blanch," "whiten," or "purify" before going on to an ambiguous definition of aetiology as a doctrine of morbific causes or "the various powers that are capable of exercising an injurious influence on the human economy. . . ."

4. Samuel Taylor Coleridge, marginal note to Southey's *Life of Wesley* (2 vols., 1820), 1:239; from the manuscript in the Berg Collection, New York Public Library, cited by Carl Woodring in his

forthcoming edition of the *Table Talk* (2 vols., 1990; 1:374n.), vol. 14 of *The Collected Works of Samuel Taylor Coleridge* (general editor, Kathleen Coburn), 17 vols. (Princeton: Princeton University Press, 1969–).

5. Hahnemann first published these ideas in a 1796 paper, and then expanded them in his *Organon* (1810); see Thomas Lindsley Bradford, *Life and Letters of Dr. Samuel Hahnemann* (Philadelphia: Boericke & Tafel, 1895), p. 50.

6. Michel Foucault, *The Birth of the Clinic*, trans. A. M. Sheridan Smith (New York: Random House, 1973), pp. 131, xii.

7. *Letters*, 1:196; *The Keats Circle*, ed. Hyder E. Rollins, 2d ed., 2 vols. (Cambridge: Harvard University Press, 1965), 2:73ff.

8. *Letters*, 1:245.

9. F. W., J. Schelling, "On the Study of Medicine and Organic Nature," in *On University Studies*, trans. E. S. Morgan (Athens: Ohio University Press, 1966), pp. 138–39; 140.

10. Schiller, "On the Animal and Spiritual Nature of Man," in *Friedrich Schiller: Medicine, Psychology and Literature*, ed. Kenneth Dewhurst and Nigel Reeves (Berkeley: University of California Press, 1978), p. 283.

11. Friedrich von Schlegel, *Philosophy of Life*, trans. A.J.W. Morrison (London: Henry G. Bohn, 1847), p. 123.

12. Xavier Bichât, in his introduction to *Anatomie générale appliquée à la physiologie et à médicine* (1801).

13. On Cullen and the widespread influence of Brunonianism through the nineteenth century, see F. Kraüpl Taylor, *The Concept of Illness* (London: Cambridge University Press, 1979), p. 98; William Alexander, "Effects of Opium on the Living System," *Memoirs of the Literary and Philosophical Society of Manchester* 6 (1805): 1–97.

14. For John Birch (1774–1815) and his electric therapy, see Philip C. Ritterbush, *Overtures to Biology* (New Haven: Yale University Press, 1964), p. 47.

15. Joseph Henry Green, *Vital Dynamics* (London: William Pickering, 1840), p. 45.

16. Joseph Adams, *Observations on Morbid Poisons, Phagedaena, and Cancer* (London: J. Johnson, 1795), p. 54; see also Green, *Vital Dynamics*, pp. 80–81, on individual constitutions.

17. John Abernethy, *Introductory Lecture for the Year 1815* (London: Longman, 1815), pp. 116–17; *The Hunterian Oration for the Year 1819*, (London: Longman, 1819), pp. 29ff.

18. "Disease," in *Quincy's . . . Medical Dictionary*; Andrew Duncan, Jr., "Medicine," in *Encyclopaedia Britannica* (1810), 13:208.

19. William Babington and James Curry, *Outlines . . . Practice of Medicine* (London: T. Bensley, 1802–1806), p. 1.

20. Coleridge, in his note to a review of a paper by Thomas Beddoes on "slow" hydrophobia appearing twelve years after the dog bite, in *Collected Works*, vol. 2, *Watchman*, ed. Lewis Patton (1970), p. 275n.

21. *Letters*, 1:171; James Curry taught the students at Guy's to use mercury for all hepatic complaints and venereal disease; see his 1809 monograph on the subject.

22. H. C. Cameron, *Mr. Guy's Hospital* (London: Longman, 1954), pp. 145–65; Alexander Marcet, "On the Medical Properties of Stramonium," *Medico-Chirurgical Transactions* 7 (1819): 546–75; on hemlock as a poultice for cancers, see Everard Home, *Observations on Cancer* (London: Bulmer & Nicol, 1805) p. 154, Robert John Thornton, *A New Family Herbal* (London: Richard Phillips, 1810), pp. 317–22, and "Materia Medica," in *Encyclopaedia Britannica* (1810), 13:755; for Astley Cooper's final conclusions on the subject, see his *The Anatomy and Diseases of the Breast* (Philadelphia: Lea & Blanchard, 1845).

23. Home, *Observations on Cancer*, especially pp. 149–53.

24. Novalis, in a fragment entry for his encyclopedic project; Susan Sontag's translation, in *Illness as Metaphor* (New York: Farrar, Straus & Giroux, 1978), p. 14.

25. F. W. J. Schelling, *Of Human Freedom* ("Philosophical Inquiries into the Nature of Human Freedom," 1809), trans. James Gutmann (Chicago: Open Court, 1936), pp. 41–42.

26. Everard Home, "Introduction," *Observations on Cancer*, p. vi.

27. *Letters*, 1:292.

Chapter 11

1. See Lloyd G. Stevenson, *The Meaning of Poison* (Lawrence: University of Kansas Press, 1959), pp. 2–3.

2. John Hunter was a witness for the defense in the famous Bath trial of John Donnellan for the murder of Theodosius Boughton; the murder weapon was cherry laurel extract. Robert Christison says in 1842 that extract of laurel (prussic acid) "is now almost as familiar as opium among poisons, [and] rivals them all in subtilty and rapidity of action. . . . One grain, or about four drops has repeatedly proved fatal to man within three quarters of an hour;" "Poison," in *Encyclopaedia Britannica* (1842), 16:177. M. J. B. Orfila's *A General System of Toxicology, or a Treatise on Poisons, Found in the Mineral, Vegetable and Animal Kingdoms, Considered in their Relations with Physiology, Pathology, and Medical Jurisprudence*, trans. Joseph G. Nancrede (Philadelphia: M. Carey & Sons, 1817), pp. 262–63, documented the sources and symptoms of laurel/prussic acid poisoning, and had cited earlier seventeenth- and eighteenth-century experiments with the poison by Bohn, Bucholz, Roloff, and Gehler; on bitter almond, see ibid., pp. 225–40, and B. C. Brodie, "Experiments and Observations on the Different Modes in Which Death is Produced by Certain Vegetable Poisons," *Philosophical Transactions* 101 (1811): 183–85. Burton's prescription of laurel is in *The Anatomy of Melancholy*, ed. A. R. Shilleto, 3 vols. (1893; reprint, London: G. Bell & Sons, 1913), 2:261.

3. William Salisbury, *The Botanist's Companion*, 2 vols. (London: Longman, 1816), 2:135–36. Keats's most direct source for his knowledge of laurel poisoning would have been Salisbury, who succeeded Robert John Thornton as lecturer in medical botany at Guy's Hospital in 1814. Salisbury described the laurel family of plants and other sources for prussic acid, like almond and peach pits, in detail; he warned against the use of bitter almond as a culinary flavor, mentioned the traditional and external use of "Daphne Mezerum" for "obstinate ulcers and ill-conditioned sores," and told of the dangerous myth that laurel was a cure for syphilis; his description of the burning mouth, epileptic symptoms, and rapid death induced by prussic acid in all its guises of plant and potion finds parallel in Orfila's *Toxicology*, cited above (*Botanist's Companion*, 2:35, 54–55, 135–136; see also Robert John Thornton, *New Family Herbal* [London: Richard Phillips, 1810], pp. 486–92). Robert Thomas's popular handbook of medicine, *The Modern Practice of Physic* (London: Longman, 1816), pp. 426–36, summarizes the general knowledge of poisons among the English populace during Keats's time. Keats's knowledge of Apollo's Pythia and "*the prophetic Plant*" has been traced by Douglas Bush and others to the poet's reading of John Potter's *Archaeologia Graeca: Antiquities of Greece* (London, 1775). Given Keats's request of Reynolds in 1817—"Borrow a Botanical Dictionary—turn to the words Laurel and Prunus [and] show the explanation to your sisters and Mrs. Dilk. . . ." (*Letters*, 1:133)—it would seem that the poet's knowledge of poisonous laurel was thorough and well supplemented by contemporary medical botany.

4. Jacques Derrida, in his assay of Plato's pharmacy in the *Phaedrus*, in *Dissemination*, trans. Barbara Johnson (Chicago: University of Chicago Press, 1981), pp. 62–171, discovered this compounding duality in 1968; Marjorie Levinson, *Keats's Life of Allegory: The Origins of A Style* (London: Blackwell, 1988), p. 214, finds a crossing of the Derridian *pharmakon* and supplement in the "full draught" of *The Fall of Hyperion*.

5. "Poison," in *Encyclopaedia Britannica* (1911), 21:893.

6. Stevenson, *Meaning of Poison*, p. 4.

7. Owsei Temkin, "The Concept of Infection," in *Ferment of Knowledge*, ed. G. S. Rousseau and Roy Porter (London: Cambridge University Press, 1980), p. 125; see also his "An Historical Analysis of the Concept of Infection," in *Studies in Intellectual History* (Baltimore: Johns Hopkins University Press, 1953), pp. 123–27.

8. See *Report of the Commissioners Concerning Charities in England* (London: W. Cloves & Sons, 1840), p. 753.

9. See Donald C. Goellnicht on Keats's attendance, possibly in the spring of 1816, of Salisbury's course, *The Poet-Physician* (Pittsburgh: University of Pittsburgh Press, 1984), p. 32.

10. Richmond Lattimore's translation, *The Odyssey of Homer* (New York: Harper, 1965), Book IV, 226–30 (Robert Fitzgerald translates this as "herbs of all kinds, maleficent and healthful," *Homer: The Odyssey* [New York: Doubleday, 1961], p. 72); *Romeo and Juliet*, act 2, sc. 3, lines 25–26.

11. *Romeo and Juliet*, act 2, sc. 3, lines 15–16.

12. "The *Protagoras* classes the *pharmaka* among the things that can be both good (*agatha*) and painful (*aniara*)," Derrida, *Dissemination*, p. 99.

13. The library (of the Physical Society) of Guy's Hospital acquired a copy of Orfila in translation in 1815. Even before the English translation appeared, Orfila's work was reviewed in periodicals like the *Medico-Chirurgical Journal and Review* (1 [1816]: 413–35); the U.S. edition appeared in 1817. Thomas Houlston's *Observations on Poisons; and on the Use of Mercury in the Cure of Obstinate Dysenteries* (London: R. Baldwin, 1784), a short study of mercury, mineral poisons, and canine madness, was perhaps the only English study of the period to precede Orfila's definitive work.

14. See Robert Christison, *Treatise on Poisons* (1829) reprinted by J. T. Ducatel as *Manual of Practical Toxicology* (Baltimore: William and Joseph Neal, 1833); also his entry, "Poison," *Encyclopaedia Britannica* (1842), 16:174–83.

15. Humboldt's *curare* came from the bark of a South American plant called *verjuco di mavacure* (See Christison, *Treatise*, p. 287); see August de St. Hilaire, "Account of the Poisonous Plants of the Southern Parts of Brazil," *Edinburgh Philosophical Journal* 14 (1825–1826): 264.

16. N. P. Foersch's account was published in two articles in *The London Magazine*, in 1783–1784; Erasmus Darwin reprints these articles in his "Additional Notes" to *The Botanic Garden* (London: J. Johnson, 1791), Part Two, III, 238, pp. 188–94.

17. See John Livingston Lowes, *The Road to Xanadu*, rev. ed. (Boston: Houghton Mifflin, 1964), p. 18.

18. Orfila, *Toxicology*, p. 310. Darwin's verse is curious for its mixing of vegetable and animal metaphors in its description of the tree's venom:

> Fierce in dread silence on the blasted heath
> Fell UPAS sits, the HYDRA-TREE of death.
> Lo! From one root, the envenom'd soil below,
> A thousand vegetative serpents grow;
> In shining rays the scaly monster spreads
> O'er ten square leagues his far-diverging heads;
> Or in one trunk entwists his tangled form,
> Looks o'er the clouds, and hisses in the storm.
> (*The Botanic Garden*, Part Two, III, 237–44)

19. Orfila makes specific reference to working with Astley Cooper and Alexander Marcet on poison cases; *Toxicology*, pp. 246–47, 249.

20. In Astley Cooper's *Outlines* this lecture on poisons is number 36; for the full version of the

lecture, see his *Lectures on the Principles and Practice of Surgery*, 2d ed. (London: F. C. Wesley, 1830), pp. 439–59.

21. Orfila observed Brodie's experiments in London; he cites Brodie on the effects of poisons like foxglove, prussic acid, and snake venom in his *Toxicology*. See Benjamin C. Brodie, "Experiments and Observations on . . . Certain Vegetable Poisons" (1811), and "Further Experiments and Observations on the Action of Poisons on the Animal System," *Philosophical Transactions* 102 (1812): 205–27. James Curry cites Brodie's papers above in his book on drowning and the ingestion of poisons, *Observations on Apparent Death from Drowning* (London: J. M'Creery, 1809), p. 160.

22. Orfila, *Toxicology*, p. 1; *Quincy's . . . Medical Dictionary* (1817), p. 641; Christison, "Poison," 174; Cooper, *Lectures* (1830), pp. 439–40.

23. *Quincy's . . . Medical Dictionary* (1817), p. 641.

24. *Table Talk*, 25 May 1832, in *Specimens of the Table Talk of Samuel Taylor Coleridge*, ed. H. N. Coleridge (London: John Murray, 1851), p. 177.

25. William Babington, *Lectures on the Materia Medica* (MS, Wills Library, 1796), p. 1.

26. *Table Talk*, 13 May 1833, in *Specimens of the Table Talk*, pp. 242–43. Coleridge's definition of medicine as partly assimilated substance would stand at an angle to Stanley Fish's metaphor of medicine as a self-consuming artifact—as something consumed in the working of its own best effects, and something that consumes the subject through its purging power. *Self-Consuming Artifacts* (Berkeley: University of California Press, 1972), p. 3.

27. Andrew Duncan, Jr., *The Edinburgh New Dispensatory* (Edinburgh, 1803), p. 1 (based on Cullen's and Lewis's *Materia Medicas*).

28. Thomas Percival, "A Physical Inquiry into the Powers and Operations of Medicines," *Memoirs of the Literary and Philosophical Society of Manchester* 3 (1790): 197–98.

29. "Materia Medica and Pharmacy," in *Encyclopaedia Britannica* (1810), 13:707; based on the 1803 *Edinburgh New Dispensatory*, this entry was probably written by Andrew Duncan, Jr.

30. Christison, "Poison," pp. 182–83. Astley Cooper, in his discussion of the new drug iodine as "a very active poison," articulates the same point that Christison makes of poisons and medicines in general; see *Lectures* (1830), pp. 454–55.

31. Percival, "Operations of Medicines," p. 203.

32. Orfila, *Toxicology*, pp. 6–11, 26, 201–203, 205, 235, 244, 284, 360.

33. Cooper, *Lectures* (1830), p. 440. Christison's *Treatise* collapses Orfila's six classes into four: irritants that produce inflammation and destruction, narcotics that produce disorder of the nervous system, narcotico-acids that produce inflammation and narcotism simultaneously, and morbid secretions that reproduce disease; by 1842, with the development of the notion of the transmission of disease, Christison is able to say that the class of morbid poisons is no longer part of the toxicological system and belongs, instead, among the natural diseases. See his *Treatise*, pp. 37, 203–4; "Poison," 178.

34. William Cullen, *A Treatise on the Materia Medica* (1789), in J. Thompson, ed., *An Account of the Life, Lectures and Writings of William Cullen*, 2 vols. (Edinburgh: Blackwood, 1859), 2:131, 217.

35. Erasmus Darwin, "Articles of the Materia Medica," Appendage to *Zoonomia*, ed. Samuel L. Mitchell, 2 vols. (1802; reprint, Philadelphia: Edward Earle, 1818), 1:30–31, 80.

36. John Murray, *Elements of Materia Medica and Pharmacy*, 2 vols. (Edinburgh, 1804), 1:95. Murray was lecturer in chemistry and materia medica at Edinburgh and Göttingen.

37. John Keats, *Anatomical and Physiological Note Book*, ed. Maurice Buxton Forman (London: Oxford University Press, 1934), First Page, p. 9.

38. Murray, cited in Duncan's entry, "Materia Medica," *Encyclopaedia Britannica* (1810), 13:707, which itself divides medicines into sixteen "stimulant" categories: emetics, expectorants, diaphoretics, diuretics, cathartics, errhines, sialagogues, emollients, refrigerants, astringents, tonics,

stimulants, antispasmodics, narcotics, anthelmintics, and chemical remedies. This should be contrasted with Erasmus Darwin's seven categories in his "Materia Medica," Appendage to *Zoonomia*, 1:3.

39. Brodie, "Experiments and Observations," p. 178; Cooper, "On Poisons," *Lectures* (1830), p. 440. Brodie's research, for example, showed alcohol and bitter almond to act on the brain, upas antiar to act on the heart, emetic tartar and corrosive sublimate to act on the brain and heart at once.

40. Christison, *Treatise*, p. 22, "Poison," 175; Orfila, *Toxicology*, p. 238; see also Darwin, on arsenic, "Materia Medica," Appendage to *Zoonomia*, 1:55.

41. Percival, "Operations of Medicines," pp. 198–99.

42. Duncan, "Materia Medica," 704.

43. Keats, *Anatomical and Physiological Note Book*, Fifth Page and Thirteenth Page, pp. 49, 64.

44. Percival, "Operation of Medicines," pp. 202–3.

45. Cooper, *Lectures* (1830), pp. 458–59.

46. *Table Talk*, 13 May 1833, in *Specimens of the Table Talk*, p. 243. Christison's concluding remarks in his entry, "Poison," pp. 182–83, highlight the series of inexplicables concerning the action of poisons and how little is known, even in 1842, of the functions of poisons and drugs.

47. John Abernethy, "Anatomy Lecture II" (1817) cited in George Macilwain, *Memoirs of John Abernethy* (London: Hatchard, 1856), p. 199.

48. Janice Sinson, *John Keats and "The Anatomy of Melancholy"* (London: Keats-Shelley Memorial Association, 1971), p. 22, from the 1893 *Anatomy of Melancholy* edition by Shilleto, 2:246. Sinson says that Keats first read Burton in April 1819, in the 1813 London edition (p. 14). We are reminded of Coleridge on drugs and national character in *Table Talk*.

49. N. L. Vauquelin, "Analysis of Deadly Nightshade, Atropa Belladonna," *Journal of Natural Philosophy, Chemistry, and the Arts* 31 (1812): 352.

50. See Jack Stillinger, in his notes to *The Poems of John Keats* (Cambridge: Harvard University Press, 1978), pp. 265–70; Christopher Ricks, *Keats and Embarrassment* (Oxford: Oxford University Press, 1974), p. 129.

51. See Alethea Hayter, *Opium and the Romantic Imagination* (Berkeley: University of California Press, 1968), p. 19, and Salisbury, *Botanist's Companion*, 2:119, 124.

52. Norman O. Brown quoting Plutarch, *Hermes the Thief* (Madison: University of Wisconsin Press, 1947), p. 57.

53. Lucretius, *Of the Nature of Things*, trans. Thomas Creech, 6th ed., 2 vols. (London: T. Warner & J. Walthoe, 1722), I, Bk. I, 944–57.

54. Walter Scott's *Letters on Demonology and Witchcraft* (1830), for example, refers to a pharmacologist as "A user of pharmaceutical enchantments."

55. Thomas Percival, *Medical Ethics* (Manchester: J. Johnson, 1803); reprinted in Chauncey D. Leake, *Percival's Medical Ethics* (Baltimore: William and Wilkins, 1927), p. 104; Abraham Banks, *Medical Etiquette* (London, 1839), p. 11.

56. Derrida, *Dissemination*, p. 132n.

57. See Fielding H. Garrison, *An Introduction to the History of Medicine* (Philadelphia and London: W. B. Saunders, 1929), p. 82; William Godwin, *The Pantheon* (London: Thomas Hodgkins, 1806), p. 61.

58. Sinson, *John Keats and "The Anatomy of the Melancholy,"* p. 25; Burton, *Anatomy*, 2:288.

59. "To Perfume," in *The Poetical Works of Thomas Lovell Beddoes*, ed. Edmund Gosse, 2 vols. (London: J. M. Dent, 1890), 2:245.

60. See note to these lines in *John Keats: The Complete Poems*, ed. John Barnard, 2d ed. (Harmondsworth, U.K.: Penguin, 1977), p. 567.

61. "The Pipe with PHRYGIAN Airs disturbs their Souls," Lucretius, *Of the Nature of Things*, I, Bk. II, 585. See Thomas Creech's note to this line, 1:142–43.

62. Burton, *Anatomy*, 2:132–37. For the traditional associations in Greek legend, see E. Ashworth Underwood, "Apollo and Terpsichore: Music and the Healing Art," *Bulletin of the History of Medicine* 21 (1947): 639–73.

63. *Letters*, 1:182.

Chapter 12

1. It is significant that the revised edition of Nicholas Culpeper, *The English Physician Enlarged with Three Hundred and Ninety-Six Medicines Made from English Herbs*, ed. E. Sibley (London: J. Satcherd, 1800; reprint, Manchester: S. Russell, 1807, 1813), uses Linnaeus's famous remark as its epigram; Astley Cooper taught that "Tartrite of antimony and ipecacuanha both produce vomiting," *Lectures on the Principles and Practice of Surgery*, 2d ed. (London: F. C. Wesley, 1830), p. 457. Keats, of course, prescribed "a strong dose" of simplex, an emetic, for the "degenerated race" of contemporary poets who were "Pulvis Ipecac" (*Letters*, 1:241).

2. William Salisbury, *The Botanist's Companion*, 2 vols. (London: Longman, 1816), 1:1–2.

3. James Curry, *Heads of a Course of Lectures on Pathology* (London: T. Bensley, 1804), p. 23.

4. Robert John Thornton, *A New Family Herbal* (London: Richard Phillips, 1810); Culpeper, *The English Physician*; John Towers, *The Domestic Gardener's Manual* (1830), whose possible influence on Keats is discussed by Stuart Sperry in "Isabella Jane Towers, John Towers, and Keats," *Keats-Shelley Journal* 27 (1978): 35–58. Thornton preceded William Salisbury as lecturer in medical botany at Guy's Hospital; his *New Family Herbal* was popular and much reprinted, with the first edition appearing as a handsomely illustrated folio edition.

5. For the use of woodbine, see Joseph Adams, *Observations on Morbid Poisons* (London: J. Johnson, 1795), p. 82. My reconstruction in the following section of what Keats may have known of specific drugs relies on Cullen's *Materia Medica* (1789), John Murray's *Apparatus Medicaminum or Elements of Materia Medica and Pharmacy* (Edinburgh, 1804, 1810), Donald Monro's *Medical and Pharmaceutical Chemistry*, E. Darwin's "Materia Medica" in *Zoonomia*, ed. Samuel L. Mitchell, ed., 2 vols. (1802; reprint, Philadelphia: Edward Earle, 1818); *The Edinburgh New Dispensatory* (1803); and *Encyclopaedia Britannica* (1810), as well as the works of Salisbury, Thornton, Culpeper, Orfila, and Christison.

6. On the medicinal use of gold, see A. S. Duportal and Thomas Pellitier, "On Some Preparations of Gold Lately Employed Medicinally," *Journal of Natural Philosophy, Chemistry, and the Arts* 32 (1812): 179–85; on the medicinal use of silver, see Andrew Duncan, Jr., "Materia Medica," in *Encyclopaedia Britannica* (1810), 13:702. Burton discussed the use of precious stones and metals in the cure of melancholy and Keats marked these passages; of the therapy of precious stones Keats had the following marginal comment: "This list of precious stones and their virtues is very curious.... Precious stones are certainly a remedy against melancholy: a valuable diamond would effectively cure mine." Janice Sinson, *John Keats and "The Anatomy of Melancholy"* (London: Keats-Shelley Memorial Association, 1971), p. 21.

7. Lloyd G. Stevenson, *The Meaning of Poison* (Lawrence: University of Kansas Press, 1959), pp. 18–19.

8. See *John Keats: The Complete Poems*, ed. John Barnard, 2d ed. (Harmondsworth, U.K.: Penguin, 1977), p. 566.

9. James Curry, *Observations on Apparent Death from Drowning* (London: E. Cox, 1815), Appendix on Poisons, p. 181.

10. John Barnard, "Keats's Tactile Vision: 'Ode to Psyche,'" *Keats-Shelley Memorial Bulletin* 33 (1982): 15, notes how "English" this bower is—all the plants are distinctly and intentionally native to the English countryside; see Salisbury, *Botanist's Companion*, 2:83, on bindweed, convolvulus, clematis, and virgin's bower.

11. See Thornton, *New Family Herbal*, pp. 554–55, and Salisbury, *Botanist's Companion*, 2:59, 75, on black and white hellebore.

12. Andrew Duncan, Jr., "Medicine," in *Encyclopaedia Britannica* (1810), 13:195.

13. See Graves, *The White Goddess*, rev. ed. (New York: Farrar, Straus & Giroux, 1966), p. 386; J. Lemprière, "Anticyra," *Classical Dictionary*, p. 64.

14. William Battie, *A Treatise on Madness* (London: J. Whiston & B. White, 1758), p. 2; Robert Burton, *The Anatomy of Melancholy*, ed. A. R. Shilleto, 3 vols. (1893; reprint, London: G. Bell & Sons, 1913), 3:223.

15. M.J.B. Orfila, *A General System of Toxicology*, trans. Joseph G. Nancrede (Philadelphia: M. Carey & Son, 1817), pp. 6–7; 205–208; also Robert Christison, *Treatise on Poisons* (1829; reprinted as *Manual of Practical Toxicology* [Baltimore: William & Joseph Neal, 1833]), pp. 270–274. Salisbury, *Botanist's Companion*, 2:59, 75, notes the acrimonious taste and ensuing effects of hellebore.

16. William Babington and James Curry, *Outlines . . . Practice of Medicine* (London: T. Bensley, 1802–1806), pp. 206–7; see also Culpeper, *The English Physician*, pp. 153–54.

17. Keats, *Anatomical and Physiological Note Book*, ed. Maurice Buxton Forman (London: Oxford University Press, 1934), First Page, p. 9; Salisbury, *Botanist's Companion*, 2:55–56, and Thornton, *New Family Herbal*, pp. 590–607, describe the properties and use of foxglove in Keats's time. Culpeper, *The English Physician*, pp. 134–35, marks the folk fondness for foxglove as a herb of Venus of a "gentle cleansing nature" and "friendly to nature."

18. Orfila, *Toxicology*, pp. 293–98; Christison, "Poison," p. 178. Orfila quotes extensively from "the well-known treatise on foxglove (*digitalis pupurea*) of Mr. Sanders."

19. See his *Botanist's Companion*, 2:56–57.

20. On nitre and nitrates, and poisonous metals, see Christison, *Treatise*, pp. 86–89, 132–62; on phosphor and phosphorus, see ibid., p. 60; also Thomas Houlston, *Observations on Poisons* (London: R. Baldwin, 1784), pp. 25–30, and Curry, *Observations on Apparent Death from Drowning* (Appendix, pp. 160ff.), on escharotics, cantharides, arsenic, corrosive sublimate, emetic tartar, poisonous mushrooms, and so on.

21. Henry Clutterbuck, "On the Cure of . . . Poison of Lead," *Philosophical Magazine* 6 (1800): 120–21; Orfila, Christison and Erasmus Darwin also speak of lead poisoning (see especially Darwin, *Zoonomia*, 2:110–11). W. Hale-White in *Keats as Doctor and Patient* (London: Oxford University Press, 1938), p. 89, notes the symptoms of mercury poisoning in Keats's passages quoted in the text and comments that mercury poisoning was common at that time since it was frequently prescribed medicine. Keats took mercury himself, so he would know the symptoms; see *Letters*, 1:171.

22. In his *Toxicology*, Orfila discusses sixteen kinds of poisonous mushrooms, which he categorized among the animal venoms; see also Christison, "Poison," 178. On narcissus poisoning, see Orfila, *Toxicology*, p. 224. On lily-of-the-valley and marigold poisoning, see Orfila, *Toxicology*, pp. 6–7, 166, 167.

23. *Letters*, 2:79; Leon Waldoff's discussion of Freud's "Mourning and Melancholy" in *Keats and the Silent Work of Imagination* (Urbana: University of Illinois Press, 1985), especially pp. 22–23, is an important perspective on the kind of melancholy Keats refers to in his ode. For the poet's own distinction between "Imaginary grievances" and "real woes," see *Letters*, II, 290–91.

24. Burton, *Anatomy*, 2:290–91.

25. Graves, *The White Goddess*, p. 53.

26. Sources for the effects of aconitine or wolfsbane poisoning are Orfila, *Toxicology*, pp. 218–21, and cases, p. 289; Salisbury, *Botanist's Companion*, 2:44, 136–37; Benjamin C. Brodie, "Further Experiments and Observations on the Actions of Poisons on the Animal System," *Philosophical Transactions* 102 (1812): 186; Thornton, *New Family Herbal*, pp. 549–51. See also "Poison," in *Encyclopaedia Britannica* (1911), 21:895. Walter A. Wells, *A Doctor's Life of Keats* (New York: Vantage Press,

1959), p. 61, notes that aconitine, in infinitesimal doses, was a common medicine of Keats's day. Van Helmont's use of aconitine to locate his soul is discussed at length by Thomas Arnold, *Observations on the Nature, Kinds, Causes and Prevention of Insanity*, 2 vols. (London: Richard Phillips, 1806), 1:149–54.

27. "Whenever an anodyne is wanted, and opium disagrees, this herb, and the preparations from it, may be prescribed"; Duncan, "Materia Medica," p. 750. Other sources for henbane or *hyosciamus niger* poisoning are Salisbury, *Botanist's Companion*, 2:60; Thornton, *New Family Herbal*, pp. 181–85; Orfila, *Toxicology*, pp. 255–56; Christison, *Treatise*, pp. 221–22; the first source adds that smoke and extract of seeds of henbane is "an excellent remedy in toothach."

28. Alexander Marcet, "On the Medicinal Properties of Stramonium," *Medico-Chirurgical Transactions* 7 (1819): 546–75, especially 546, 548, 551. Marcet's *Hospital Practices* (MS, Royal College of Surgeons, 1804–1806) presents a variety of cases where stramonium was used for each of these diseases; his notes also mark its common use for any persistent and unremitting disease. See also Duncan, "Materia Medica," pp. 709, 751–52, for contemporary medicinal uses of *atropa belladonna*.

29. *Journal*, 14 October 1680 and 5 October 1688, in *John Locke* (1632–1704), *Physician and Philosopher: A Medical Biography; With an Edition of the Medical Notes in his Journals*, ed. Kenneth Dewhurst (London: Wellcome Historical Medical Library, 1963), pp. 195, 280; see also pp. 138, 143.

30. See Lester S. King, *The Medical World of the Eighteenth Century* (1958; reprint, New York: Robert E. Krieger, 1971), p. 170.

31. Salisbury, *Botanist's Companion*, 2:50–52, 55, 93, 139 (he cites from Cullen's and Murray's *Materia Medicas*).

32. For symptoms of *datura stramonium, solanum nigrum* (woody nightshade), and *atropa belladonna*, see Salisbury, *Botanist's Companion*, 2:51, 139; Thornton, *New Family Herbal*, pp. 176–80; Orfila, *Toxicology*, pp. 267–68, 285–89; Christison, "Poison," p. 177, and *Treatise*, pp. 222–24, 257; Duncan, "Materia Medica," p. 751; Brodie, "Experiments and Observations . . . ," p. 183, who sees *atropa belladonna* as an example of poison acting sympathetically without absorption; Marcet, "On Stramonium," pp. 550, 555–75; N. L. Vauquelin, "Analysis of Deadly Nightshade," *Journal of Natural Philosophy, Chemistry, and the Arts* 31 (1812): 356–57; and [Cecil] *Textbook of Medicine*, 15th ed. (New York: W. B. Saunders, 1979), p. 70. Duncan in the *Encyclopaedia Britannica* of 1810, and Marcet and Christison specifically mention the symptom of blindness. For the medical traditions of nightshade, see Culpeper, *The English Physician*, p. 205, and Peter V. Taberner, *Aphrodisiacs* (Philadelphia: University of Pennsylvania Press, 1979), pp. 115–16.

33. "Death's Jest-Book; or The Fool's Tragedy," act 2, sc. 3, in *The Poetical Works of Thomas Lovell Beddoes*, ed. Edmund Gosse, 2 vols. (London: J. M. Dent, 1890), 2:61.

34. E.T.A. Hoffmann (1776–1822) was a practicing botanist. He was influenced by Calderon, and in addition to his tales of enchantment wrote an opera, *Love and Jealousy*, that may have been based on Calderon's drama, *Poison and Antidote*. "Datura Fastuoso" is a story of love and death, the refusal of life, occult entrapment, lust, a mother fixation, youthful escapism, and dreams; its many themes operate around a gorgeous thorn apple growing through artful means in an unnatural garden of poisonous flowers; Count Fermino, a scientist-magician, conducts botanical experiments in this garden with the help of magical chemical potions that spur growth and enhance natural beauty and perfume in plants even as they prove fatal to humans; the count's sister plays a bewitching siren or an alluring but poisonous thorn apple to the youthful protagonist.

35. See Nathaniel Hawthorne, "Rappaccini's Daughter," in *Centenary Edition of the Works of Nathaniel Hawthorne*, ed. William Charvat et al. (Columbus: Ohio State University Press, 1974), 10: 117.

36. Salisbury, *Botanist's Companion*, 1:41. Wordsworth refers to this folk knowledge in his comments referred to in the next note.

37. "Letter to a Friend of Robert Burns," in *Literary Criticism of William Wordsworth*, ed. Paul M. Zall (Lincoln: University of Nebraska Press, 1966), p. 203.

38. Orfila, *Toxicology*, p. 269 (see also his entries on laurel and prussic acid); Brodie, "Experiments and Observations . . . ," p. 185; Christison, *Treatise*, p. 226. Christison, Brodie, and Orfila all speak of the power of this nerve poison, in all its chemical combinations, to paralyze and kill instantaneously all animals, without any apparent signs of absorption or alteration of the tissues; of its tendency to act through what they believe are all the "senses" since its application on the surface of the body is more effective than when it is introduced into any internal systems.

39. Christison's *Treatise* (p. 169) notes the similarity between the roots of black hellebore and the globeflower, and that the latter is often mistakenly prescribed for the former; pp. 165–66 notes the connection between the similarity of outward characteristics of plants—and their like effects on the animal system. For symptoms of Ranunculaea poisoning, see Orfila, *Toxicology*, pp. 229–30. Orfila remarks, p. 7, that of all the plants classified by Jussieu and Linnaeus and known to the early nineteenth century, only two bore names derived from the ancient deities of healing: the *vincetoxicum* or hairy Asclepias, and the peony. On the water-spearwort or *Ranunculus Flammula*, see Salisbury, *Botanist's Companion*, 2:91, 132.

40. See Culpeper, *The English Physician*, pp. 218–20; George Hartman, *The Family Physitian* (London: Richard Wellington, 1696), p. 33. Thornton's *New Family Herbal* (p. 544), notes that the maddoctor Willis prescribed peony root for epilepsy, and that Everard Home used the drug on two epileptic patients in Edinburgh with good results.

41. Virgil, Eclogue II, 37–38: *"est mihi disparibus septum compacta cicutis fistula, Damoetas dono mihi quam dedit olim . . . "* [Loeb ed.]; Miriam Allott notes this derivation in her edition, *The Poems of John Keats* (London: Longman, 1970), p. 130n.

42. Thornton, *New Family Herbal*, pp. 317–22.

43. Marcet, "On Stramonium," p. 547; Orfila, *Toxicology*, p. 218.

Chapter 13

1. See Arturo Castiglioni, *A History of Medicine*, trans. E. B. Krumbhaar (New York: Knopf, 1947), p. 383; Fielding H. Garrison, *An Introduction to the History of Medicine* (Philadelphia and London: W. B. Saunders, 1929), p. 104; J.H.G. Gratton and Charles Singer, *Anglo-Saxon Magic and Medicine* (London: Oxford University Press, 1952), p. 51.

2. See Molly Lefebure, *Samuel Taylor Coleridge: A Bondage of Opium* (New York: Stein & Day, 1974), p. 493.

3. Robert Christison, *Treatise on Poisons* (1829; reprinted by J. T. Ducatel as *Manual of Practical Toxicology* [Baltimore: William & Joseph Neal, 1833]), p. 25.

4. Robert Christison, "Poison," in *Encyclopedia Britannica* (1842), 16:175–76.

5. August St. Hilaire, "Account of the Poisonous Plants of Southern Parts of Brazil," *Edinburgh Philosophical Journal* 14 (1825–1826): 265. Geoffroy St. Hilaire, August's brother, was a colleague of Lamarck's at the Jardin des Plantes.

6. "Antidote for Vegetable Poisons," [The Royal Institution's] *Quarterly Journal for Science, Literature, and the Arts* 10 (1820–1821): 192; see also C. S. Parker, "Account of an Essential Oil," *Edinburgh Journal of Science* 1 (1824): 133–37.

7. C. L. Cadet, "A Memoir on the Web of Spiders," *Journal of Natural Philosophy, Chemistry, and the Arts* 11 (1805): 291. See also M. Amoreux, "Observation on Spiders, and Their Supposed Poison," *Philosophical Magazine* 6 (1800): 74–80, and N. M. Hentz, "Note Regarding the Spider Whose Web Is Employed in Medicine," *Edinburgh Philosophical Journal* 12 (1825): 184–85.

8. Lemprière, "Ambrosia," *Classical Dictionary*, p. 46 (my italics).

9. *Romeo and Juliet*, act 2, sc. 6, lines 9–13.

10. Christopher Ricks, *Keats and Embarrassment* (Oxford: Oxford University Press, 1974), p. 134.

11. Erasmus Darwin, *The Temple of Nature* (London: J. Johnson, 1791), II, notes to lines 268, 302, pp. 63, 66. Darwin lists among the plants from which bees gather injurious honey the rhododendron, azalea, datura stramonium, and futillaria or crown imperial. To glimpse the way in which naturalists of this time made connections between animal, vegetable and insect kingdoms, note that the futillary was also called "snake's head," and that frutillary was the name of a kind of butterfly. M. J. B. Orfila has a whole section on the venom of bees, wasps and honey in A *General System of Toxicology*, trans. Joseph G. Nancrede (Philadelphia: M. Carey & Son, 1817).

12. See, for example, "Observation on Bees" (1792), in *The Works of John Hunter*, ed. James F. Palmer, 4 vols. (London: Longman, 1835), 4:422–26.

13. Benjamin Smith Barton, "Some Account of the Poisonous and Injurious Honey of North America," *Philosophical Magazine* 12 (1801): 121–35; *Journal of Natural Philosophy, Chemistry, and the Arts* 5 (1803): 158–75. In *The Temple of Nature*, Darwin says he read Barton in the *American Transactions*.

14. See Christison, *Treatise*, p. 167, on the acrid poisoning agent of the *Ranunculaea* family: "The acrid principle in these plants is found to be increased by acids, sugar, honey and wine, and in fact is effectually destroyed only by water."

15. Barton, "Injurious Honey," p. 122.

16. Ibid., 127–28, 130–32; August de St. Hilaire, "Account of a Case of Poisoning, caused by the Honey of the Lecheguana Wasp," *Edinburgh Philosophical Journal* 14 (1825–1826): 91–100, speaks of the effects of honey gathered from wolfsbane (pp. 91–92). Note that Barton and St. Hilaire summarize past and contemporary accounts of other naturalists and voyagers in addition to providing their own firsthand experience.

17. Barton, "Injurious Honey," pp. 126, 132.

18. Ibid., p. 126.

19. Astley Cooper, *Lectures on the Principles and Practice of Surgery*, 2d ed. (London: F. C. Wesley, 1830), pp. 444–45.

20. St. Hilaire, "Account of the Poison Plants . . . of Brazil," pp. 269–70.

21. Barton, "Injurious Honey," pp. 123–25.

22. St. Hilaire, "Lecheguana Wasp," p. 92. Helen Vendler has placed the source of venom, with certainty, in Keats's bees; see *The Odes of John Keats* (Cambridge: Harvard University Press, 1983), pp. 177–78.

23. St. Hilaire, "Lecheguana Wasp," pp. 91, 92.

24. Ibid., pp. 92–94.

25. For symptoms, which they cite from reports and from firsthand observation, see Barton, "Injurious Honey," pp. 121–22, 127–28 (for dwarf-laurel honey symptoms); St. Hilaire, "Lecheguana Wasp," pp. 91–99 (his own experience, pp. 94–99).

26. Lemprière "Mercurius," in *Classical Dictionary*, p. 459.

Chapter 14

1. *The Poetical Works of Thomas Lovell Beddoes*, ed. Edmund Gosse, 2 vols. (London: J. M. Dent, 1890), 2:57.

2. *Prometheus Unbound*, III, i, 39–41; Sabellus's story is in Lucan's *Pharsalia*, IX, 762–88.

3. See Robert Graves, *The White Goddess* rev. ed. (New York: Farrar, Straus & Giroux, 1966), p. 248.

4. Lemprière, "Cassandra" and "Aesculapius," *Classical Dictionary*, pp. 159, 23–24; Joseph Spence, *Polymetis* (London: R. & J. Dodsley, 1755; reprint, London: J. Johnson, 1802), pp. 95, 132–33.

5. See Arturo Castiglioni, A *History of Medicine*, trans. E. B. Krumbhaar (New York: Knopf, 1947), p. 383.

6. Hygeia, according to Lemprière, is the daughter of Aesculapius and goddess of health, who received the name of Minerva from Pericles because of the healing wisdom she imparted to him in a dream. See *Classical Dictionary*, p. 554; also William Brande, "Hygeia," *Dictionary of Science, Literature and Art* (1846), and Spence, *Polymetis*, pp. 61–62.

7. See Fielding H. Garrison, *An Introduction to the History of Medicine* (Philadelphia and London: W. B. Saunders, 1929), p. 426. The Abbate Felice Fontana's treatise, *Ricerche fisiche sopra il veleno della vipera* (Lucca, 1767), was the starting point of modern investigation of serpent venoms; the work of two Anglo-Indian surgeons, Patrick Russell (1727–1805) and Sir Joseph Fayrer (1824–1909), hold high place thereafter; Fayrer's *Thanatophydia of India* (1872) classified all the venomous snakes of the tropics and became a classic of zoology.

8. Astley Cooper, *Lectures on the Principles and Practice of Surgery*, 2d ed. (London: F. C. Wesley, 1830), pp. 444–45; Everard Home, "The Case of a Man who Died in Consequence of the Bite of a Rattle-Snake; with an Account of the Effects Produced by the Poison," *Philosophical Transactions* 100 (1810): 75–88; John Williams, "On the Cures of Persons bitten by Snakes in India," *Philosophical Magazine* 4 (1799): 191–96; M.J.B. Orfila discusses rattlesnakes and six different tropical vipers and cites Everard Home in A *General System of Toxicology*, trans. Joseph G. Nancrede (Philadelphia: M. Carey & Son, 1817), pp. 64–78, 165–69; Robert Christison, *Treatise on Poisons* (1829; reprinted by J. T. Ducatel as *Manual of Practical Toxicology* [Baltimore: William & Joseph Neal, 1833]), pp. 183–93.

9. The serpent's fangs and poison sac were embedded in the boot leather. J. Hector St. John, "Letter of 1782," *Edinburgh Journal of Science* 7 (1827): 357–58.

10. Everard Home, "Observations Intended to Show that the Progressive Motion of Snakes is Partly Performed by the Means of Ribs," *Philosophical Transactions* 102 (1812): 163–68; Thomas Smith, "On the Structure of the Poisonous Fangs of Serpents," *Philosophical Transactions* 108 (1818): 471–76.

11. Orfila, *Toxicology*, p. 366.

12. Home, "Case of . . . a Bite of a Rattle-Snake," p. 86.

13. Christison, *Treatise*, p. 183. Albert, in *Otho the Great* (IV, i, 163–64) would "sooner crush and grind / A brace of toads" to produce, presumably, Shakespeare's "sweltered venom." The subject of toad sweat provides a curious angle on the issue of animal poisons: toad-venom, a yellow substance exuded from the skin of toads, was a folk-medicine and poultice in England and France, and Cuvier claimed it was not a poison; the effects of toad-venom on domestic animals that bit toads suggested otherwise, and renewed the question of *where* poison resided in venomous creatures. See J. Davy, "Observations On the Poison of the Common Toad," *Philosophical Transactions* 116 (1826): 127–28.

14. Orfila, *Toxicology*, pp. 366–68.

15. For antidotes to snake venom, see ibid., pp. 370–78, 397–98; Home, "Case of . . . a Bite of a Rattle-Snake," p. 87; John Williams "Cure of Persons Bitten by Snakes in India," pp. 191–96.

16. Home, "Case of . . . a Bite of a Rattle-Snake," p. 87.

17. Orfila, *Toxicology*, p. 365.

18. J. F. Blumenbach, "On the Fascinating Power of the Rattle-Snake, with Some Remarks on Dr. Barton's Memoir on the Subject," *Philosophical Magazine* 2 (1798): 251–52; see also Thomas Houlston, *Observations on Poisons* (London: R. Baldwin, 1784), pp. 13–24.

19. John Toplis, "On the Fascinating Power of Snakes," *Philosophical Magazine* 19 (1804): 379–81; Toplis refers much of his data to an article published by Colonel Ironside in vol. 14 of the *Philosophical Magazine*.

20. Toplis, quoting first-person accounts, "On the Fascinating Power of Snakes," p. 382.

21. De la Cépède's and William Barton's theories are recounted in Benjamin Smith Barton's "A Memoir Concerning the Fascinating Faculty which has been Ascribed to the Rattle-Snake and other American Serpents," reprinted in *Journal of Natural Philosophy, Chemistry, and the Arts* 7 (1804): 284–85; 8 (1804): 59–60.

22. See Benjamin Smith Barton, "Letter to Professor Zimmermann, on the Fascinating Faculty which has been Ascribed to the Rattle-Snake, and other American Serpents," *Philosophical Magazine* 15 (1803): 194.

23. Home, "Progressive Motion of Snakes," pp. 163–68.

24. Barton bases his theory of parental instinct and self-sacrifice on the purported facts that birds fall from trees into the jaws of snakes only during the hatching season and that only birds that nest in low bushes tend to fall; see "Memoir Concerning the Fascinating Faculty," pp. 108–15.

25. See Lemprière, "Circe" and "Scylla," *Classical Dictionary,* pp. 185–86, 698.

26. The serpent was supposed to have acquired immortality from the ass of Prometheus. Bacon tells the story in his *Works,* vol. 5, as cited and recounted by Erasmus Darwin in his Additional Note XXII [on the Portland Vase] to *The Botanic Garden* (London: J. Johnson, 1791), Part One, II, 321, pp. 55–56.

27. Ibid., pp. 55–56.

28. Lemprière, "*Lamiae,*" "*Lemures,*" and "*Larvae,*" *Classical Dictionary,* pp. 389–90, 394, 399; Robert Burton, *The Anatomy of Melancholy,* ed. A. R. Shilleto, 3 vols. (1983; reprint, London: G. Bell & Sons, 1913), 3:50–51.

29. Naturalists of this time were particularly intrigued by the way snakes moved. In his paper on the motion of snakes, Everard Home noted that the ribs of the snake's neck were of special significance to their peculiar motion, which he considered to be an evolutionary advancement, "a new species of progressive motion, and one widely different from those already known" and catalogued by natural philosophers ("Progressive Motion of Snakes," p. 164).

30. Burton, *Anatomy,* 3:97.

31. See *The Bestiary: A Book of Beasts,* trans. T. H. White (New York: 1960), p. 176: "Owing to the fact that it is a sluggish crawler and has not the power to overtake people by chasing them, it captures them as they stand stupified by its splendor."

32. John Beer has traced Coleridge's Geraldine to Andrew Tooke's Scylla, a figure of lust in *The Pantheon,* in *Coleridge the Visionary* (New York: Macmillan, 1959), pp. 200–201; see also pp. 74–75 on Leigh Hunt's and Coleridge's reading of Egyptian snake mythology in Tooke.

33. *Paradise Lost,* IX, 494–504.

34. See Stuart M. Sperry, *Keats the Poet* (Princeton: Princeton University Press, 1970), pp. 302–3; the burning test was a common form of chemical assaying. Orfila notes that snake venom "does not burn"—and so lacked heat-producing combustibility.

35. Potter's *Antiquities* (I, 324–26), cited in Miriam Allott, ed., *The Poems of John Keats* (London: Longman, 1970), notes, p. 671: "The person that delivered the oracles of the god [Apollo] was a woman, whom they called Pythia, Pythonissa, and Phoebas.... The Pythia ... was no sooner inspired but she began immediately to swell and foam at the mouth ... if the spirit was in a kind and gentle humour, her rage was not very violent; but if sullen and malignant, she was thrown into extreme fury."

36. See numerous articles on the Gymnotus eel and the phosphorescence of living creatures like fish, glowworms, eels, and stagnating matter in swamps and graveyards, in the *Philosophical Transactions* and other journals of the period.

37. Philip C. Ritterbush, *Overtures to Biology* (New Haven: Yale University Press, 1964), pp. 37–39, on the curative powers of gymnotic and torpedoes when placed in bathtubs with sick people, and

on John Walsh (1725–1795); on the earliest use of electrical therapy, see Henry Baker, "Letter . . . Medical Experiments of Electricity," *Philosophical Transactions* 45 (1748): 271–72.

38. *Paradise Lost*, IX, 86.

39. Ophelia gives this flower to the king in *Hamlet*, act 1, sc. 5, lines 36–40; see also *Paradise Lost*, IX, 581. "Fennel green" and sacred dittany grow in the pharmacopoeia of Endymion's festival, IV, 575. See also John Potter's description of the festival of Adonis in *Antiquities of Greece*, 2 vols. (London: 1755), I: 422. Asafoetida is the resinous extract of fennel, and its botanical properties are discussed by Robert John Thornton, A *New Family Herbal* (London: Richard Phillips, 1810), p. 285.

40. Lloyd G. Stevenson, *The Meaning of Poison* (Lawrence: University of Kansas Press, 1959), pp. 18–19.

41. Alexander's poison girl had been innoculated with snake venom in infancy and then nurtured on poisons; her secretions and breath were supposed to be deadly.

42. See N. M. Penzer, *Poison-Damsels and Other Essays in Folklore and Anthropology* (London: Charles J. Sawyer, 1952). See also Benjamin Lee Gordon, *The Romance of Medicine* (Philadelphia: F. A. Davis, 1945), p. 334, which traces the origin of this belief in the therapeutic powers of virginal adolescents to the first recognition of the true source for syphilis. The belief of the eighteenth and early nineteenth centuries in virginal adolescents' being able to provide protection from or cure of venereal disease no doubt had its source in popular misapplication of the principle underlying Jenner's use of cowpox for his smallpox vaccine.

43. *Samson Agonistes*, 934–37, 997–98.

44. Lemprière, "Medusa," *Classical Dictionary*, p. 449.

45. Darwin, *Botanic Garden*, Part One, I, 219–20; see also note to 218 ("Young Medusa frown'd"), p. 22.

46. *The Complete Works of William Hazlitt*, ed. P. P. Howe, 21 vols. (London: J. M. Dent, 1930–1934), 18:371.

47. See Orfila, *Toxicology*, p. 378. Scorpion bites "produce mania," bloodlessness, and fatal "numbness" (pp. 378–79).

Chapter 15

1. *The Poetical Works of Thomas Lovell Beddoes*, ed. Edmund Gosse, 2 vols. (London: J. M. Dent, 1890), 1: 13–14. See also René Girard on the literary presentation of the plague as a "process of indifferentiation," in *"To Double Business Bound": Essays on Literature, Mimesis, and Anthropology* (Baltimore: Johns Hopkins University Press, 1978), pp. 136–37.

2. Joseph Adams, *Observations on Morbid Poisons* (London: J. Johnson, 1795), pp. 47–48.

3. Samuel Wilks and G. T. Bettany, *Biographical History of Guy's Hospital* (London: Ward, Lock, Bowden, 1892), p. 191; Everard Home, "Case of . . . Bite of a Rattle-Snake," *Philosophical Transactions* 100 (1810): 83.

4. Astley Cooper, *Lectures on the Principles and Practice of Surgery*, 2d ed. (London: F. C. Wesley, 1830), p. 441; see also Robert Thomas, *Modern Practice of Physic* (London: Longman, 1816), pp. 220–28.

5. Orfila, as quoted by Vauquelin, Pinel, and Cuvier in the "Report of the Institute of France," reprinted in M.J.B. Orfila, A *General System of Toxicology*, trans. Joseph G. Nancrede (Philadelphia: M. Carey & Son, 1817), p. xlvii.

6. See John Abernethy, *Introductory Lectures* (London: Longman, 1815), p. 85.

7. See following note on Coleridge, and Keats's letter on the effect of mercury, 8 October 1817, to Bailey; also Cooper, *Lectures* (1830), p. 444.

8. See Coleridge on hydrophobia and slow poisoning, a response to an article on the subject by Thomas Beddoes, in *The Collected Works of Samuel Taylor Coleridge*, general editor, Kathleen Coburn, 17 vols. (Princeton: Princeton University Press, 1969–), vol. 2, *The Watchman*, ed. Lewis Patton (1970), pp. 274–75, 275n. Coleridge mentions Beddoes's starving weaver who went mad twelve years after being bitten by a dog, his sense of "lurking Poison," that "no Disease was ever yet cured, but merely suspended," and that inoculation functioned "like a Cathartic."

9. Lloyd G. Stevenson, *The Meaning of Poison* (Lawrence: University of Kansas Press, 1959), p. 20.

10. Coleridge, *Table Talk*, 23 May 1830, in *Specimens of the Table Talk of Samuel Taylor Coleridge*, ed. H. N. Coleridge (London: John Murray, 1851), pp. 80–82.

11. "Cure for the Hydrophobia," *Quarterly Journal for Science, Literature, and the Arts* 10 (1820–1821): 194; see also Thomas Houlston, *Observations on Poisons* (London: R. Baldwin, 1784), pp. 45–54.

12. Orfila's other sources on "spontaneous hydrophobia" are Doppert, Sauvages, Trecourt, Lecat, Koehler, Lavirotte, and Laurent; *Toxicology*, pp. 388–89.

13. See translation by Rolfe Humphries, *Ovid: Metamorphoses* (Bloomington: Indiana University Press, 1955), III, 76; VII, 500–567.

14. Stevenson, *Meaning of Poison*, p. 9.

15. Arturo Castiglioni, *A History of Medicine*, trans. E. B. Krumbhaar (New York: Knopf, 1947), p. 22; Alan Corbin has argued that an increased attention to smell marked French theories of disease (and class) between 1760 and 1880; *The Foul and the Fragrant: Odor and the French Social Imagination* (Cambridge: Harvard University Press, 1986).

16. Mr. Atkinson, "On the Use of Opium in Fever," *Medical and Physical Journal* 8 (1802): 50.

17. William Babington and James Curry, *Outlines . . . Practice of Medicine* (London: T. Bensley, 1802–1806), pp. 14, 50; James Curry, *Heads of a Course . . . Pathology* (London: T. Bensley, 1804), p. 11.

18. *Letters*, 2:155; 1:241–42.

19. Erasmus Darwin, *The Botanic Garden* (London: J. Johnson, 1791), Part One, IV, 81–86.

20. Note to line 82 (p. 168)—Darwin distinguishes between contagious miasmata from animal bodies and putrid morasses, and volcanic vapors.

21. See Alexander Tilloch, "A Short View of the Mitchillian Theory of Fever, and of Contagious Diseases," *Philosophical Magazine* 3 (1799): 177–88; see also American Correspondent on subject, ibid., 4 (1799): 35–43, 132–39. See further, *The Collecte Works of Sir Humphry Davy*, ed. John Davy, 9 vols. (London: Smith, Elder, 1840), 3:269.

22. See Tilloch, "Mitchillian Theory of Fever," p. 188; Dr. John Armstrong, "Lecture of 1821," *Lancet* 6 (1825): 194.

23. *Table Talk*, 7 April 1832, in *Specimens of the Table Talk*, p. 168. Coleridge annotated Sir John Pringle's *Observations on the Diseases of the Army* (1765), with a proposal to divide fevers into three kinds: hydroseptic, as in the Pontine Marshes; aeroseptic or chemico-atmospheric, as in typhus and plague; and zooseptic, as in smallpox. For this information, I am indebted to Carl Woodring and access to his manuscript of volume 14 in *The Collected Works of Samuel Taylor Coleridge*.

24. Coleridge, in a marginal note to an article in *Edinburgh Medical and Surgical Journal* 14 (1818): 468–69; *Collected Works*, vol. 13, *Marginalia*, ed. George Whalley, 2 vols. (1980–1984), 2:362.

25. Cooper, *Lectures* (1830), p. 442; the predisposition of certain constitutions to morbid influences was a familiar theme of Romantic medicine, see George Wallis, *The Art of Preventing Diseases and Restoring Health* (London: Robinson, 1796), p. 62.

26. *Table Talk*, 7 April 1832, in *Specimens of the Table Talk*, p. 168.

27. Babington and Curry, *Outlines . . . Practice of Medicine*, p. 14.

28. *Letters*, 2:156. H. E. Briggs says Keats's harangue on climate follows William Robertson's *History of America* (Dublin, 1777), *Works*, 1:343–45, and Hazlitt's "On Manner" in *The Round Table* (1817), *Works*, 1:111–24. See H. E. Briggs, "Keats, Robertson, and 'That Most Hateful Land,'" PMLA

59 (1944): 596–98. We might also recall Burton's digression on good and bad airs, and their influence on the cheery and melancholic temperaments, *The Anatomy of Melancholy,* ed. A. R. Shilleto, 3 vols. (1893; reprint, London: G. Bell & Sons, 1913), 2:74–75.

29. *Letters,* 2:157; Keats's comments recall Schlegel's comment cited above on the "chaotic struggle" in the atmosphere between healthy and harmful vapors.

30. *Botanic Garden,* Part One, IV, 63–71.

Chapter 16

1. Gottfried von Strassburg, *Tristan,* trans. A. T. Hatto (Harmondsworth, U.K.: Penguin, 1960), pp. 191–92, 202 (my italics), 195, 206.

2. Ibid., pp. 263, 44 (Prologue).

3. Ibid., p. 14 ("swem nie von liebe leit geschach, dem geschach ouch liep von liebe nie"); *Letters,* 2:224.

4. *Letters,* 2:133; see also 2:129, 264, on Fanny as a "sweet Physician" and the "only medicine" for the poet's consumption.

5. Jacques Derrida sees in Socrates/Eros the face of a *pharmakeus:*

Socrates in the dialogues of Plato often has the face of a *pharmakeus.* That is the name given by Diotima to Eros. But behind the portrait of Eros, one cannot fail to recognize the features of Socrates, as though Diotima, in looking at him, were proposing to Socrates the portrait of Socrates (*Symposium,* 203c, d, e). Eros, who is neither rich, nor beautiful, nor delicate, spends his life philosophizing (*philosophon dia pantos tou biou*); he is a fearsome sorcerer (*deinos goēs*), magician (pharmakeus), and sophist (*sophistēs*).

Dissemination, trans. Barbara Johnson (Chicago: University of Chicago Press, 1981), p. 117.

6. It is not possible to use the phrase "self-consuming artifacts" without reference to Stanley Fish's study of that title, which proposes that a text or the dialectician's art in a text is such an artifact, a medicine that consumes a reader in his response to its workings, and then consumes itself in the workings of its effects. Coleridge's definition of a medicine as a partly assimilated substance is more accurate. It applies effectively as a metaphor not only in my context but, I suggest, in Professor Fish's.

7. Joseph Spence, *Polymetis* (London: R. & J. Dodsley, 1755; reprint, London: J. Johnson, 1802), pp. 69–71; see also Lemprière, "Psyche," *Classical Dictionary,* p. 645.

8. Mary Tighe, *Psyche, or, The Legend of Love* (London: J. Carpenter, 1805), Bk. I, p. 15.

9. See Lester S. King, *The Medical World of the Eighteenth Century* (1958; reprint, New York: Robert E. Krieger, 1971), p. 205.

10. See Lester S. King, *Medical Thinking* (Princeton: Princeton University Press, 1982), pp. 16–18 (quoting Richard Morton, *Phthisologia: or a Treatise of Consumption,* 2d ed., [London: W. & J. Innys, 1720], extended title).

11. Cullen's "acrimony" was a catchall; he saw five distinct "diseases" that might give rise to the "hectic flush" of pulmonary phthisis: the coughing up of blood, abscess or empyema, catarrh, asthma, and tubercles. See King, *Medical Thinking,* pp. 27–29; also Robert Thomas, *Modern Practice of Physic* (London: Longman, 1816), pp. 260–73, for a summary of the disease current with Keats's training.

12. William Babington and James Curry, *Outlines . . . the Practice of Medicine* (London: T. Bensley, 1802–1806), pp. 101–2; see also Thomas Beddoes's essay on consumption in *Hygeia: or, Essays Moral and Medical,* 2 vols. (Bristol: R. Phillips, 1802), vol. 2, Essay Seventh, pp. 1–102.

13. *Letters,* 2:315, 351.

14. Michel Foucault, *The Birth of the Clinic,* trans. A. M. Sheridan Smith (New York: Random House, 1973), pp. 171–72. See also Kenneth Burke, "The Anaesthetic Revelation of Herone Liddell," *Kenyon Review* 19 (1957): 505–59, on the parallel use of the terms *consumption* and *nervousness* by Keats and others at that time, and of the active word, *fever,* as used to describe febrile energy and passionate love (pp. 547–49).

15. Alphonsus Leroi, "On the Use of Phosphorus . . . ," *Philosophical Magazine* 2 (1798): 290–91.

16. *Letters,* 2:351–52; see also Susan Sontag's discussion of passion and consumption, *Illness as Metaphor* (New York: Farrar, Straus & Giroux, 1978), pp. 20–22.

17. King, *Medical World of the Eighteenth Century,* p. 125. King calls Boerhaave "the most influential physician" of the eighteenth century.

18. Keats, *Anatomical and Physiological Note Book,* ed. Maurice Buxton Forman (London: Oxford University Press, 1934), First Page, p. 9: "Heat readily increases the Pulse—the warm bath will elevate the Pulse to 120. Cold on the contrary will diminish [and] soon reduce it. . . ."

19. Janice C. Sinson, *John Keats and "The Anatomy of Melancholy"* (London: Keats-Shelley Memorial Association, 1971), p. 26. Robert Burton further describes the disease of love as an "anguish of the mind," "a furious disease of the mind." *The Anatomy of Melancholy,* ed. A. R. Shilleto, 3 vols. (1893; reprint, London: G. Bell & Sons, 1913), 3:62–63.

20. King, *Medical Thinking,* pp. 26–27, quoting William Cullen, *First Lines of the Practice of Physic,* 4 vols. (London: T. Cadell, 1786), 2:359.

21. *Paradise Lost,* VIII, 614–21.

22. *Quincy's . . . Medical Dictionary* (1817), "The blood."

23. Astley Cooper, *Lectures on the Principles and Practice of Surgery,* 2d ed. (London: F. C. Wesley, 1830), p. 15; *The Lectures of Sir Astley Cooper,* ed. Frederick Tyrrell, 5th U.S. ed. (Philadelphia: Haswell, Barrington, & Haswell, 1839), pp. 23, 28 (my italics).

24. Robert Graves, *The White Goddess,* rev. ed. (New York: Farrar, Straus & Giroux, 1966), p. 431; also p. 427. Graves says the third constituent of the nightmare figure of la belle dame is the Spirit of Poetry, as represented in *Palmyrin of England* and the *Ballad of Thomas the Rhymer* (pp. 430–32)—she is the white enchantress or Death on a pale horse who grants poetic immortality to her victims.

25. Aileen Ward has noted how a "string of images of medicine and disease run through the poem like a dark vein through marble," in a new "direct confrontation with reality" born of Tom's illness and the memories revived in nursing him of Guy's hospital (*John Keats,* rev. ed. [New York: Farrar, Straus & Giroux, 1985], p. 174).

26. See Saul N. Brody's discussion of this episode in his *The Disease of the Soul: Leprosy in Medieval Literature* (Ithaca: Cornell University Press, 1974), pp. 179–86.

27. The Greek word for basil according to the *Oxford English Dictionary* means "royal," perhaps because basil was used "in some royal unguent, bath or medicine." The basilisk was a fabulous, malevolent serpent in Greek mythology whose hissing, breath, and look were believed to be fatally poisonous (in Pliny, and in a 1657 *Physician's Dictionary*). Whether or not Keats knew of the plant's serpentine legends, he would have read of the serpent from which the basil derives its name in Burton's *Anatomy,* 3:97, and in Pope's couplet, "The smiling Infant in his Hand shall take / The crested Basilisk and speckled Snake" (*Messiah,* 82). For the use of basil as a medicine, see Robert John Thornton, *New Family Herbal* (London: Richard Phillips, 1810), p. 587; as a folk antidote to poisons, see Nicholas Culpeper, *The English Physician,* ed. E. Sibley (London: J. Satcherd, 1800; reprint, Manchester: S. Russell, 1807, 1813), p. 34.

28. Foucault, *Birth of the Clinic,* p. 131.

29. 2 Kings 4:40 (King James version).

PART IV

1. Bentley Glass, "Idea of Biological Species," in *Forerunners of Darwin: 1745–1859*, ed. Glass et al. (Baltimore: Johns Hopkins University Press, 1959), p. 39.

2. H. W. Piper, *The Active Universe* (London: University of London / Athalone Press, 1962), pp. 187–89; Cuvier's paper "Skeleton of an Immense Species of Quadruped, Unknown until the Present, and found in Paraguay," first read in Paris in 1795, is a relevant connection here.

3. *The Complete Works of Samuel Taylor Coleridge*, ed. W.G.T. Shedd, 7 vols. (New York: Harper, 1863), vol. 1, *Theory of Life*, *p.* 416. *Hypostasis*, in medicine, meant an excess of blood in the organ or part: in metaphysics it referred to an underlying substance or attribute.

4. Leonard Richmond Wheeler, quoting Oken, in *Vitalism: Its History and Validity* (London: H. F. & G. Witherby, 1939), p. 55; Erasmus Darwin, *Temple of Nature* (London: J. Johnson, 1803), I, 295–302 and Additional Note VIII.

5. Georges Louis Leclerc Buffon, *Buffon's Natural History*, 10 vols. (London: J. S. Barr, 1792), 1:16–17. Buffon's entire description of the creation of Earth is framed in terms of fossilized shells and what these mean.

Chapter 17

1. See Georges Louis Leclerc Buffon, *Buffon's Natural History*, 10 vols. (London: J. S. Barr, 1792), 1:12–15.

2. Raymond Williams, *Keywords: A Vocabulary of Culture and Society* (New York: Oxford University Press, 1976), p. 103.

3. Fielding H. Garrison, *An Introduction to the History of Medicine* (Philadelphia and London: W. B. Saunders, 1929), p. 139; Lucretius, *Of the Nature of Things*, trans. Thomas Creech, 2 vols., 6th ed. (London: T. Warner & J. Walthoe, 1722), I, Bk. II, 934–46, 1034–39.

4. *Buffon's Natural History*, 2:256.

5. Williams, *Keywords*, pp. 103–4.

6. Owen Barfield, *Saving the Appearances: A Study in Idolatry* (New York: Harcourt, 1965), pp. 60–61.

7. The centenary of Charles Darwin's death in 1982 saw the consensus around the "synthetic" theory of evolution dissipate and brought renewed interest in Romantic notions of episodic (and revolutionary) change, according to Niles Eldredge and Ian Tattersall, *The Myth of Human Evolution* (New York: Columbia University Press, 1983). Stephen Jay Gould and Niles Eldredge announced in 1972 a theory of punctuated equilibrium that asserted evolution moved not with geological slowness but in abrupt fits and starts interspersed with long periods of no change in the species. See also Gould's argument in *The Mismeasure of Man* (New York: Norton, 1981).

8. "Can they decry / The greatest Secrets of Philosophy? / Discourse how Things are mix'd? Or comprehend / On what firm PRINCIPLES themselves depend?" Lucretius continues. *Of the Nature of Things*, I, Book II, 936–42.

9. William Lawrence, *Lectures on Physiology, Zoology, and the Natural History of Man* (London: J. Callow, 1819), pp. 82–83.

10. It is significant that the phrases "the *most perfect* of animals" and "the *most perfect* of higher animals," as synonyms for humankind, recur repeatedly in the *Philosophical Transactions* and other major scientific journals of the late eighteenth century and early nineteenth century. I would suggest that this is part of the developing sense of perfection as an evolving process, not a fixed and completed entity.

11. On 26 March 1801. C. Schreibers, "A Historical and Anatomical Description of a Doubtful

Amphibious Animal of Germany, Called, by Laurenti, *Proteus Anguinus*," *Philosophical Transactions* 91 (1801): 241–64.

12. See ibid., pp. 241–58; the paper includes plates of the whole and dissected creature, which resembles the human form in much the same way as does the mandrake root.

13. Ibid., pp. 243–45.

14. *Byron's Letters and Journals*, ed. Leslie A. Marchand, 12 vols. (Cambridge: Harvard University Press, 1973–1982), 9:47; 8:19–20.

15. Lewis Thomas, *The Medusa and the Snail: More Notes of a Biology Watcher* (New York: Viking Press, 1974), pp. 28–29.

Chapter 18

1. *Letters*, 2:101.

2. Ibid., p. 208.

3. Ibid., p. 193–94.

4. Ibid. 1:281.

5. William Lawrence, *Lectures on Physiology, Zoology, and the Natural History of Man* (London: J. Callow, 1819), p. 45.

6. *Letters*, 2:70; the letter goes on to propose an appendix to Buffon, with parsons and lawyers classified "in the same natural history of Monsters."

7. *Über den Bildungstrieb* (1789), from the translation by Elliotson as quoted by J. C. Prichard, *A Review of the Doctrine of a Vital Principle* (London: Sherwood, Gilbert & Piper, 1829), p. 215.

8. *Charity Commission Report*, p. 733.

9. Bransby Blake Cooper, *The Life of Sir Astley Cooper*, 2 vols. (London: John W. Parker, 1843), 2:186–87.

10. Joseph Henry Green, *An Address Delivered in King's College, London* (London: B. Fellowes, 1832), pp. 20–21.

11. See Philip C. Ritterbush, *Overtures to Biology* (New Haven: Yale University Press, 1964), pp. 33–34, whose example is Marmaduke Berdoe's *An Enquiry into the Influence of the Electric Fluid in the Structure and Formation of Animated Beings* (1771). Cf. John Hunter's "Experiments on Animals and Vegetables with Respect to the Power of Producing Heat," *Philosophical Transactions* 45 (1775): 457, 452–54.

12. Thomas Young, "On the Function of the Heart and Arteries," *Philosophical Transactions* 99 (1809): 20.

13. John and Charles Bell, *The Anatomy and Physiology of the Human Body*, 2 vols. (London: Longman, 1829), 1:2.

14. Erasmus Darwin *The Temple of Nature*, (London: J. Johnson, 1803), I, 251–264.

15. Erasmus Darwin, *Zoonomia*, ed. Samuel L. Mitchell, 2 vols. (1802; reprint, Philadelphia: Edward Earle, 1818), 1:397.

16. *Temple of Nature*, 1:269–80.

17. See Desmond King-Hele's estimate of Darwin's achievement, *Doctor of Revolution: The Life and Genius of Erasmus Darwin* (London: Faber & Faber, 1977), p. 245.

18. *Zoonomia*, 1:395–96.

19. Ibid., 1:395.

20. *The Temple of Nature*, Note to I, 295.

21. Richard Saumarez discusses Haighton's research in his "On Generation and the Principle of Life," *London Medical and Physical Journal* 2 (1799): 321.

22. See John Haighton, *Lectures on Midwifery and Disease of Women and Children. Delivered at the Theatre*,

Guy's Hospital, between the 1st of November, 1816, and the 1st of March, 1817, taken by Joshua Waddington (MS, Wills Library). We have no evidence that Keats took any midwifery courses at Guy's; nevertheless, the case histories in Haighton's lectures are quite representative of the kinds of patients that Keats would have seen and tended in the wards of the borough hospitals.

23. Published as *Observations on the Stricture and Diseases of the Testis* (Philadelphia: Lea & Blanchard, 1845), and *The Anatomy and Diseases of the Breast* (Philadelphia: Lea & Blanchard, 1845).

24. Green, *Vital Dynamics*, p. 40.

25. Ibid., p. 28.

26. Ibid., 37–39. See also pp. 59–60 on comparative perfection in nature: "The comparative perfection will consist in the emancipation and independence of the creature from the alien external powers, and its comparative superiority over them and power of commanding them, with the facility of adapting itself to the external relations in the greatest variety, and under the greatest change of these relations." Coleridge's use of the term "evolution" did not include an element of time.

Chapter 19

1. See Aram Vartanian, "Trembley's Polyp, La Mettrie, and Eighteenth-Century French Materialism," *Journal of the History of Ideas* 11 (1950): 259–60; Trembley's polyp replaced the traditional eighteenth-century metaphor, the swarm of bees, for the constitution of an organism formed of organisms; see Keats, "It has been an old Comparison for our urging on—the Bee hive." *Letters*, 1:232.

2. *Histoire Naturelle* (1749), 2:20–21, as translated by Vartanian in "Trembley's Polyp," pp. 280–81.

3. *Histoire Naturelle* (1749), 2:425, as translated by Lovejoy in his essay "Buffon," in *Forerunners of Darwin: 1765–1850*, ed. Bentley Glass et al. (Baltimore: Johns Hopkins University Press, 1959), p. 94; see also Buffon's description of generation in Georges Louis Leclerc Buffon, *Buffon's Natural History*, 10 vols. (London: J. S. Barr, 1792), 2:313–17.

4. See *Buffon's Natural History*, 2:318–19ff., on the molecules' power to nourish and replicate likeness.

5. *Histoire Naturelle*, Supplement 1778, 5:3, as translated by Lovejoy (note 3 above), p. 104.

6. *Buffon's Natural History*, 3:323.

7. A. D. Atkinson, "Keats and Kamchatka," *Notes and Queries* 196 (4 August 1951): 343–45. In volume 1 of *Histoire Naturelle*, Buffon summarizes the theories of the earth of William Whiston, Thomas Burnet, John Woodward, Leibnitz, Bourguet, and Scheutzer; Keats, therefore, would have been familiar with the basic ideas of evolution that had preceded Buffon's theories.

8. *Letters*, 1:281.

9. Ibid., p. 265.

10. C. D. Thorpe's term, in his discussion in *The Mind of John Keats* (New York: Russell & Russell, 1926), pp. 43–48.

11. *Letters*, 1:192–94.

12. *Letters*, 1:232.

13. Ibid., p. 387; David Bromwich has argued conclusively in his chapter on Keats (*Hazlitt: The Mind of a Critic* [New York: Oxford University Press, 1983], pp. 362–40) for Hazlitt's influence on (and kindred thinking with)—during 1818—Keats's formulations on aesthetics, intensity, negative capability, and Wordsworth's genius. I propose here that Romantic evolutionary thought had considerable influence on Keats's growth as a poet during this time—as perhaps it did on Hazlitt's growth as a critic also.

14. *Letters*, 1:80.

15. C. C. Gillispie, "The Foundation of Lamarck's Evolutionary Theory," *Archives internationales d'histoire des sciences* 9 (1956): 332; Gillispie's elegant discussion traces Lamarck's ideas on evolution back to 1776 and his treatise (*Hydrogéologie*) on the development of the earth.

16. C. C. Gillispie, "Lamarck and Darwin," in *Forerunners of Darwin*, ed. Glass et al., p. 271.

17. Gillispie, in his discussion of Lamarck's *Philosophie zoologique* (1809), in *Forerunners of Darwin*, ed. Glass et al., p. 270.

18. From the preface (1815), cited and discussed in the *Encyclopaedia Britannica* (1911) entry "Lamarck," 16:101. For a useful discussion of Lamarck's seminal role in the development of ideas on evolution, and of Cuvier's rivalry, see Pietro Corsi's *The Age of Lamarck: Evolutionary Theories in France, 1790–1830* (Berkeley: University of California Press, 1989). The intellectual associations among the French evolutionists, and between them and the German *Naturphilosophen*, are a fascinating and largely uncharted subject. For example, Cuvier, whose *Recherches sur les ossemens fossiles des quadrupèdes* (1812) and *Le règne animal* (1817) paralleled the appearance of Lamarck's famous history of invertebrates (1815–1822), collaborated with Geoffroy St. Hilaire (who was a close friend of Lamarck) and worked with him on the collection of thirteen thousand fossils at the Muséum d' Histoire Naturelle (Buffon's old Jardin du Roi, popularly called the Jardin des Plantes); St. Hilaire, who like Cuvier acknowledged the importance of German natural philosophy to his own ideas on nature, invited his friend Alexander von Humboldt to visit and use the fossil collection at the Muséum on several occasions; his *Philosophie Anatomique*, which appeared in 1818, was greatly admired by Goethe.

19. Goethe's ideas on evolution can be found in his *The Metamorphosis of Plants* (1790), *A Preliminary Sketch to a General Introduction to Comparative Anatomy* (1795), and *Formation and Transformation of Living Things* (1807). I am indebted to Alexander Gode-von Aesch's discussion of Goethe and Robinet in *Natural Science in German Romanticism* (New York: Columbia University Press, 1941), pp. 144–48; see also Charles Singer, *A Short History of Biology* (Oxford: Oxford University Press, 1931), pp. 216–17, for Goethe's contribution to biology and morphology (the study of the structure of living things, a term that Goethe invented).

20. Gode-von Aesch, *Natural Science in German Romanticism*, pp. 147–48.

21. For the nineteenth century's estimate of Schelling's contribution to the concept of evolution, see the entry "Evolution," *Encyclopaedia Britannica* (1911), 10:23–37.

22. F. W. J. Schelling, *Of Human Freedom*, trans. James Gutmann (Chicago: Open Court, 1936), p. 37 (my italics). One must not forget the influence of the ideas of *Naturphilosophie* and Schelling on evolutionists like Cuvier (who studied *Naturphilosophie* when he was at Caroline University near Stuttgart), and Erasmus Darwin. See Charles Coulston Gillispie, *Edge of Objectivity* (Princeton: Princeton University Press, 1960), p. 278, and Desmond King-Hele's discussion in *Doctor of Revolution* (London: Faber & Faber, 1977).

23. Johann Gottfried Herder (1744–1803), in his *Ideen Zur Philosophie der Geschichte der Menscheit* (1784–1791) cited in H. F. Osborn, *From the Greeks to Darwin: the Development of the Evolution Idea Through Twenty-Four Centuries* (New York: Scribner's Sons, 1929), p. 153. The Physical Society Library at Guy's Hospital owned a translation of Herder's book on the history of man during Keats's time there.

24. See Charles Singer, *A Short History of Biology*, pp. 217–18; also H. A. M. Snelders, "Romanticism and Naturphilosophie," *Studies in Romanticism* 9 (1970): 209–10.

25. Lorenz Oken, *Elements of Physiophilosophy* (from *Lehrbuch der Naturphilosophie*, 1809–1811), trans. Alfred Tulk (London: Ray Society, 1847), p. 2.

26. Ibid., pp. 2–3.

27. Tilottama Rajan, *Dark Interpreter: The Discourse of Romanticism* (Ithaca: Cornell University Press, 1980), has noted the similarity between the light and dark imagery of Schelling's formulations in

Of *Human Freedom* and Oceanus' words in II, 191–94, and ascribes this to "the prevalence of biological metaphors in the Romantic period" (p. 172).

Chapter 20

1. Joseph Henry Green, *Vital Dynamics* (London: William Pickering, 1840), pp. 109–10.

2. F. W. J. Schelling, *Of Human Freedom*, trans. James Gutmann (Chicago: Open Court, 1936), p. 35; Van Helmont on the luminosity on matter and light of mind, as discussed by Lester S. King, *The Philosophy of Medicine* (Cambridge: Harvard University Press, 1978), p. 128.

3. J. C. Prichard, A *Review of the Doctrine of a Vital Principle* (London: Sherwood, Gilbert & Piper, 1829), pp. 2–3 (my italics). An earlier version of this treatise was in the Physical Society Library at Guy's in 1816.

4. *The Complete Works of Samuel Taylor Coleridge*, ed. W.G.T. Shedd, 7 vols. (New York: Harper, 1863), vol. 1, *Theory of Life*, pp. 391ff.

5. Green, *Vital Dynamics*, pp. 36–37.

6. Ibid., p. 60; see also pp. 130–31.

7. Ibid., pp. 123–24.

8. Ibid., p. 43.

9. Ibid., pp. 52–53. Green's summation of natural and perceptual evolution almost certainly derives as much from the ideas expressed in Coleridge's *Theory of Life* as from those in the *Biographia Literaria* discussing the common substratum of body and spirit and the emergence of consciousness in the final "potence" or level of organization in life. See M. H. Abrams, "Coleridge's 'A Light in Sound,'" in *The Correspondent Breeze* (New York: Norton, 1984), pp. 173–74; also Leslie Pearce Williams, *Michael Faraday* (New York: Basic Books, 1964), p. 63.

10. *Letters*, 2:79–80.

11. Ibid., 1:280–81.

12. Clarence D. Thorpe, *The Mind of John Keats* (New York: Oxford University Press, 1926), pp. 43–48.

13. *Letters*, 1:281–82.

14. Ibid., pp. 278–79.

15. Ibid., p. 274.

16. Ibid., p. 255.

17. Ibid., 2:212.

18. Keats's "Notes on Milton's *Paradise Lost*," Book VII, 420–23, in *John Keats: The Complete Poems*, ed. John Barnard, 2d ed. (Harmondsworth, U.K., 1977), Appendix 4, p. 525. Keats's discussion of the "stationing" of Milton's art follows this remark.

19. H. W. Piper, "Keats and W. C. Wells," *Review of English Studies* 25 (1949), 158–59, and *The Active Universe* (London: University of London / Athalone Press, 1962), p. 193. Piper cites from Wells's paper, which was read before the Royal Society in 1813 but not published until 1818.

20. Wells, *Two Essays* (London, 1818), pp. 438–39, cited by Piper in his "Keats and W. C. Wells," p. 159.

Chapter 21

1. *Letters*, 1:264–65.

2. See Bentley Glass, "Maupertuis," in *Forerunners of Darwin 1745–1859*, ed. Glass et al. (Baltimore: Johns Hopkins University Press, 1959), pp. 75–6, and Lester S. King, *The Philosophy of Medicine* (Cambridge: Harvard University Press, 1978), pp. 172–73; also Aram Vartanian, "Trembley's Polyp,

La Mettrie, and Eighteenth-Century French Materialism," *Journal of the History of Ideas* 11 (1950): 281, on self-determination in the Maupertuan molecule. King points out that Maupertuis distinguished between emotions or imaginative incitements that could effect the formation of the fetus and the mother's random imagination of objects that could have no possible effect on the skin or facial features of the infant: "The fear a woman might experience at the sight of a tiger could cause the infant to perish entirely or have major deformities but not cause the child to be born brindled or with claws . . ." (p. 172).

3. Glass, quoting Buffon, in "Maupertuis," pp. 77–8.

4. Georges Louis Leclerc Buffon, *Buffon's Natural History*, 10 vols. (London: J. S. Barr, 1792), 3:1–316, especially 226–316, on the development of the fetus. Like Maupertuis, he denied earlier notions that naevi or superficial birthmarks were imprints of the mother's imagination of real objects.

5. Robert Burton, *The Anatomy of Melancholy*, ed. A. R. Shilleto, 3 vols. (1893; reprint, London: G. Bell & Sons, 1913), 1:293.

6. Lester S. King, *The Philosophy of Medicine* (Cambridge: Harvard University Press, 1978), p. 179. Bablot's ideas on the subject received continuing attention during the first decade of the nineteenth century; see, for example, the anonymous article, "Inquiry Whether Naevia Materna, with Which Children are Sometimes Born, Should be Attributed to the Imagination of the Mother," *Philosophical Magazine* 34 (1809): 347–49, which refers to several prior articles in the *Linnean Transactions*.

7. Erasmus Darwin, *Zoonomia*, ed. Samuel L. Mitchell, 2 vols. (1802; reprint, Philadelphia: Edward Earle, 1818), 1:412.

8. John Haighton, *Lectures on Midwifery* (MS, Wills Library, 1796), p. 212.

9. Joseph Henry Green, *Vital Dynamics* (London: William Pickering, 1840), pp. 129–30.

Chapter 22

1. G. S. Rousseau paraphrasing Hume, A *Treatise of Human Nature* (London: John Noon, 1739 [Bk. I, Pt. III, Sec. 14, pp. 155–72]), in G. S. Rousseau and Roy Porter, ed., *The Ferment of Knowledge* (London: Cambridge University Press, 1980), p. 31.

2. These notions were inherited by a generation of Romantic scientists and philosophers. See Leslie Pearce Williams's assumptions in his discussion of the concepts of power and being in Coleridge, in *Michael Faraday* (New York: Basic Books, 1964), pp. 64–65. When Tilottama Rajan declares that Keats makes Saturn and his race "not Greek Titans but Romantic Titans, symbolic of a ruined but recoverable perfection" (*Dark Interpreter* [Ithaca: Cornell University Press, 1980], pp. 156–57), she expresses the eighteenth-century conviction that forces are identical and perfection recoverable, and reveals precisely what is wrong with her discussion of evolution and the Hyperion poems. Perfection is not recoverable for Keats and his generation of scientists and poets; we know this because it is shown to be a misperception of Saturn.

3. In Romantic thinking these apocalyptic manifestations after long (apparent) quietude could be biological as well as political and spiritual events. Keats's poetry, of course, is full of these moments of sudden spiritual or perceptual advance, from the sonnet "Great spirits," to the ode "To Autumn."

4. *Letters*, 1:207.

5. Stuart M. Sperry, *Keats the Poet* (Princeton: Princeton University Press, 1970), p. 188.

6. Stillinger notes that the draft version of line 258, "as from a scummy marsh," used the adjective "stagnant." Jack Stillinger, ed. *The Poems of John Keats* (Cambridge: Harvard University Press, 1978), p. 337.

7. See Barry Gradman, *Metamorphosis in Keats*, (New York: New York University Press, 1980), p. 49.

8. See Marjorie Nicolson's discussion of the evolution of the Sublime as a " 'dreadful' Beauty" in *Mountain Gloom and Mountain Glory: The Development of the Aesthetics of the Infinite* (New York: Cornell University Press, 1959), especially pp. 324–25.

9. Claude Lee Finney, *The Evolution of Keats's Poetry*, 2 vols. (Cambridge: Harvard University Press, 1936), 2:505; *The Collected Works of Sir Humphry Davy*, ed. John Davy, 9 vols. (London: Smith, Elder, 1840), 9:259–60.

Chapter 23

1. *Letters*, 1:374.

2. Ibid., pp. 184, 193–94, 387. It seems certain, especially since Keats was defining his own poetic aspirations at this time in contradistinction to Wordsworth's ability, that the "Genius," "negative capability," or obliteration of the artist's "identity" during contemplation of other beauty or other life forms was a *real* entity, a latency of power and receptivity quite different from the "entire delusion" Wordsworth speaks of in the revised preface of 1802: "So that it will be the wish of the Poet to bring his feelings near to those of the persons whose feelings he describes, nay, for short spaces of time, perhaps, to let himself slip into an entire delusion, and even confound and identify his own feelings with theirs." *William Wordsworth: Selected Poems and Prefaces*, ed. Jack Stillinger (Boston: Houghton Mifflin, 1965), p. 453.

3. *Oxford English Dictionary*, "negative," 2:5.

4. John Locke, *An Essay Concerning Human Understanding*, ed. Alexander Campbell Frazer, 2 vols. (New York: Dover Publications, 1959), 1:309. "I confess power includes in it some kind of *relation*, (a relation to action or change.") Ibid., p. 310.

5. Ibid., p. 316 (Locke's example is the "idea of liberty"); see also discussion in 2:280ff. David Bromwich notes the influence of Locke's ideas on power on later philosophies of mind (see his *Hazlitt: The Mind of a Critic* [New York: Oxford University Press, 1983], pp. 33–34).

6. Thomas Reid, *Essays on the Powers of the Human Mind; to which are Prefixed an Essay on Quantity, and an Analysis of Aristotle's Logic*, 3 vols. (Edinburgh: Bell & Bradute, and F.C. & J. Rivington, 1819), 3:7–8, 12, 14–5. Reid's entire argument borrows the terms and organization of Locke; on 3:31, he describes his purported quarrel with Locke; on 3:6, he says power does not "admit of logical definition;" thereafter, his distinctions are Lockean.

7. William Alexander, "On the Effects of Opium on the Living System," *Memoirs of the Literary and Philosophical Society of Manchester* 6 (1805): 75; Mitchell's introduction to Darwin's *Zoonomia*, ed. Samuel L. Mitchell, 2 vols. (1802; reprint, Philadelphia: Edward Earle, 1818), 1:xxi–xxii. Alexander's essay on specific medicine, and Mitchell's survey of the idea of "power within" in Brunonian medical theory, express the range and currency of the concept of passive power in Romantic medicine. Had Benjamin Bailey's 1818 essay "What is Power?" survived, we might have been able to chart the specific sources in contemporary thought of the idea of passive power for Keats (see *The Keats Circle*, ed. Hyder E. Rollins, 2d ed., 2 vols. [Cambridge: Harvard University Press], 1:26, 42).

8. "On Posthumous Fame,—Whether Shakespeare Was Influenced by A Love of It?", *The Complete Works of William Hazlitt*, ed. P. P. Howe, 21 vols. (London: J. M. Dent, 1930–1934), 4:23. See discussions of Hazlitt and Keats by Finney, Bate, and Bromwich; the last is particularly perceptive on the depth of the connection between the two writers' thoughts on artistic genius:

What he [Keats] found most useful were Hazlitt's doubts about the predominance of the self in modern poetry: the egotistical, Hazlitt taught, was only one version of the sublime, and a limited one. The highest poetry makes us forget the identity of the poet in the many identities he assumes; thus Shakespeare had "only to think of any thing in order to become that thing, with all the circumstances belonging to it." He seems to us in dramatic works, as he passes from one character to another, "like the same soul successively animating different bodies." [Hazlitt: *The Mind of a Critic*, p. 374.]

9. *Letters*, 1:387.

10. *Letters*, 1:232; Keats's comments here are usually ascribed to Wordsworth's concept of "wise passiveness" in "Expostulation and Reply." There is a distinction of alert responsiveness in Keats's idea of artistic receptivity that goes beyond Wordsworth's notion and, finally, beyond Hazlitt's.

11. *Letters*, 2:213. It is significant that this statement comes in the same letter where he describes his choice of Chatterton over Milton, after his resolution to guard against the example of Milton's genius.

12. *Complete Works of William Hazlitt*, 8:91.

13. Ibid.

14. I am indebted to Bromwich's distinction between empathy in other writers and sympathy in Keats: "Empathy is the process by which the mind so projects itself into its object that a transfer of qualities seems to take place. Keats, on the other hand, was looking for a capability of so heightening the imagination's response to anything that the identities of both the mind and its object would grow more vivid *as what they are*" (Hazlitt: *The Mind of a Critic*, p. 375).

15. Astley Cooper, *The Lectures of Sir Astley Cooper*, ed. Frederick Tyrrell, 5th U.S. ed. (Philadelphia: Haswell, Barrington & Haswell, 1839), pp. 2–3 (my italics); *The Works of John Hunter*, ed. James F. Palmer, 4 vols. (London: Longman, 1835), 3:7–8. Palmer's gloss of this reads: "By '*power*' I apprehend, is here signified the resistance which is offered by living part to disorganization and death" (4:8n).

16. Joseph Henry Green, *Vital Dynamics* (London: William Pickering, 1840), pp. 81–2.

17. *The Complete Works of Samuel Taylor Coleridge*, ed. W.G.T. Shedd, 7 vols. (New York: Harper, 1863), vol. 1, *Theory of Life*, pp. 390–91.

18. John Barclay, "Physiology," in *Encyclopaedia Britannica* (1810), 16:465.

19. *Letters*, 1:192.

20. See *Complete Works of William Hazlitt*, 8:135–40, 4:257–72; also, the discussion by Claude Lee Finney, *The Evolution of Keats's Poetry*, 2 vols. (Cambridge: Harvard University Press, 1936), 1:244–45.

21. *Friedrich Schiller: Medicine, Psychology and Literature*, ed. Kenneth Dewhurst and Nigel Reeves (Berkeley: University of California Press, 1978), p. 282.

22. Xavier Bichât, *Physiological Researches on Life and Death*, trans. F. Gold (Bristol: Longman, 1816), pp. 49–50.

23. My remarks in this section assume a moderate consensus on what Keats means in his passage on intensity as summarized in glosses by Thorpe and Murry: "Here, in brief, seems to be Keats's theory as to the possibility of creating beauty out of the ugly and evil. Take any subject, however repulsive, and represent it in an art form with enough vigorous universal life-truth gleaming through to excite intense imaginative speculation and insight, and the unpleasantness vanishes" (Clarence D. Thorpe, *The Mind of John Keats* [New York: Oxford University Press, 1926], p. 137); "When the Truth which is apprehended in the form of Beauty is expressed in a work of art, there is generated an intensity which transmutes the elements of painfulness or ugliness in the thing represented. The work of art is 'intense,' and the man who truly experiences it also becomes 'intense' " (John Middleton Murry, *Keats*, rev. ed. [London: Jonathan Cape, 1955], p. 190).

24. *Letters*, 1:370, 369.

25. My examples here are but a few of the most painfully "sensational" images in Keats; R. H. Fogle and critics since have addressed the subject of sensation in Keats in detail and at length.

26. See Finney's discussion of Keats's annotations on Milton's serpent (Bk. IX, 179–91): "Whose spirit does not ache at the smothering and confinement—the unwilling stillness—the *waiting close*? Whose head is not dizzy at the possible speculations of Satan in the serpent prison? No passage of poetry can ever give a greater pain of suffocation" (*Evolution of Keats's Poetry*, 1:339).

27. Thomas Percival, "Speculations on the Perceptive Power of Vegetables," *Memoirs of the Literary and Philosophical Society of Manchester* 2 (1785): 115–6, 128. See also Victor Michelotti on the latent and compacted energy of seeds and the waning of sensitivity in the process of aging, "Experiments and Observations on the Vitality and Life of Germs," *Philosophical Magazine* 9 (1801): 240. Also D. J. Carradori, on the high degree of irritability of certain plants when they are in flower, "On the Irritability of the Sowthistle, and other Plants, with Farther Observations on the Irritability of Vegetables," *Journal of Natural Philosophy, Chemistry, and the Arts* 32 (1812): 138–43.

28. From *Über die neue Ausgabe de Goetheschen Werke* (1816), *Tag- und Jahresheften* (1807), *Ferneres in Bezug auf mein Velhältnis zu Schiller* (1812–1832), and the conversations with von Muller and Soret (1832), as translated by Elizabeth Sewell in *The Orphic Voice* (New Haven: Yale University Press, 1960), pp. 260–61.

29. Charles Coulston Gillispie, citing from the *Metamorphosis of Plants*, in *The Edge of Objectivity* (Princeton: Princeton University Press, 1960), p. 193; see also Sewell, *Orphic Voice*, p. 261.

Chapter 24

1. Elizabeth Sewell, quoting Novalis, *Schriften*, III, 290, in *The Orphic Voice* (New Haven: Yale University Press, 1960), p. 209.

2. Kenneth Muir's remark that the "new race" imagined by the poet of *Hyperion* is not "stronger" but "more sensitive and vulnerable," and Goellnicht's discussion of Keats's use of the consumptive "fever metaphor" to describe poetic creativity, are to my point here (Muir, "The Meaning of Hyperion," in his *John Keats: A Reassessment* [Liverpool: Liverpool University Press, 1969], p. 109; Donald C. Goellnicht, *The Poet-Physician* [Pittsburgh: University of Pittsburgh Press, 1984], p. 203).

3. Bernard Mandeville, A *Treatise of the Hypochondriack and Hysterick Diseases, in 3 Dialogues*, 3d ed. (London: J. Tonson, 1730), pp. 237–38.

4. Helen Vendler, *The Odes of Keats* (Cambridge: Harvard University Press, 1983), p. 234.

5. *Letters*, 1:185–86, 231–32.

6. Samuel Taylor Coleridge, in *The Collected Works of Samuel Taylor Coleridge*, gen. ed. Kathleen Coburn, 17 vols. (Princeton: Princeton University Press, 1969–), vol. 7, *Biographia Literaria; or, Biographical Sketches of My Life and Opinions*, ed. James Engell and W. J. Bate, 2 vols. (1983), 1:241.

7. Ibid., 1:241–2.

8. J. G. Fichte, *The Vocation of Man*, ed. Roderick M. Chisholm (New York: Bobbs-Merrill, 1956), p. 144. J. B. Beer discusses Coleridge's use of the myth of Psyche from Thomas Taylor's 1795 translation of Apuleius in the context of his passages on the evolution of the poetic psyche in *Biographia Literaria* (*Coleridge the Visionary* [New York: Macmillan-Collier, 1959], p. 138); Apuleius's myth of Psyche was a source for Keats also.

9. Sir Charles Bell, *Idea of a New Anatomy of the Brain* (1811; reprint, London: Dawsons, 1966), pp. 12–13.

10. *Letters*, 1:186.

11. For the physician Keats, physical death is not the ultimate horror or unimaginable terror that it was for Hazlitt; as with the physiologists of his time, death is a winding down of energy and a pending emptiness of life. See Hazlitt's discussion of West's "ruffian" Death, *The Complete Works of William Hazlitt*, ed. P. P. Howe, 21 vols. (London: J. M. Dent, 1930–1934), 18:137–38; also David

Bromwich, Hazlitt: The Mind of a Critic (New York: Oxford University Press, 1983), pp. 208–9. Real fear, in Keats, is reserved for the cessation of a once-creative consciousness.

12. Letters, 1:387.

13. Xavier Bichât, Physiological Researches on Life and Death, trans. F. Gold (Bristol: Longman, 1816), p. 48. See also pp. 47–49 on pain's tendency, like pleasure, to cloy, satiate, or neutralize itself.

14. Letters, 1:279. Julia Kristeva's conclusions on the constitutive role of suffering in human perception, in her discussion of Holbein's painting of the dead Christ and the nature of Dostoyevsky's melancholy in Soleil noir: Dépression et melancholie (Paris: Gallimard, 1987) is an important reiteration of this point.

15. "Of Imitation," in Complete Works of William Hazlitt, 4:73. It is interesting to speculate on the extent to which Hazlitt's formulation here derives from the idea common among contemporary physiologists that all sensations were initially disagreeable: "Every foreign body in contact for the first time, with a mucous membrane, is creative of a disagreeable sensation, which by repetition, is diminished, and at last becomes altogether imperceptible." Bichât, Physiological Researches, p. 48.

16. "Of Imitation," in Complete Works of William Hazlitt, 4:76; William Wordworth: Selected Poems and Prefaces, ed. Jack Stillinger (Boston: Houghton Mifflin, 1965), p. 455.

17. "On the Elgin Marbles," in Complete Works of William Hazlitt, 18:162.

18. Elaine Scarry, The Body in Pain (New York: Oxford University Press, 1985), pp. 22, 161–64.

19. Ibid., p. 169.

20. Ibid., pp. 288–89.

21. Joseph Henry Green, Vital Dynamics (London: William Pickering, 1840), p. 123.

22. Alexander von Humboldt's remarks challenging "superiority" of race are the best example of this paradox: "While we maintain the unity of the human species, we at the same time repel the depressing assumption of superior and inferior races of men. There are nations more susceptible of cultivation than others--but none in themselves nobler than others. All are in like degree designed for freedom." Cosmos (London: Henry G. Bohn, 1949), p. 368.

23. Erasmus Darwin, The Temple of Nature (London: J. Johnson, 1803), IV, 66.

24. Letters, 1:278–79; we should note that this is posed as a question, not as a description, of Wordsworth.

25. Ibid., p. 80.

Chapter 25

1. Christopher Ricks, Keats and Embarrassment (Oxford: Oxford University Press, 1974), pp. 208–9.

2. I refer to the Romantic scientists' fascination with creatures like the ageless Proteus Anguinus and "ancient" toads that could "reanimate" after being without respiration while preserved in underground caves; see Geoffroy St. Hilaire's discussion of a 150-year-old toad shown him by a Dr. Quenin in "Observations on Toads Found Alive at Great Depths in the Ground," Edinburgh Journal of Science 7 (1827): 358.

3. Letters, 1:293.

4. Paradise Lost, XI, 535–37.

5. King Lear, act 5, sc. 1, lines 9–11.

6. Letters, 2:281.

7. "A Dream," in The Poetical Works of Thomas Lovell Beddoes, ed. Edmund Gosse, 2 vols. (London: J. M. Dent, 1890), 2:264–5.

8. A. Davenport, "A Note on 'To Autumn,' " in John Keats: A Reassessment, ed. Kenneth Muir (Liverpool: Liverpool University Press, 1969), p. 99.

9. Letters, 1:154.

10. See John Gough, "Remarks on the Summer Birds of Passage, and on Migration in General," *Memoirs of the Literary and Philosophical Society of Manchester* 7 (1813): 453–65 (read 20 March 1812); Gavin Inglis, "On the Swallow," *Philosophical Magazine* 52 (1818): 272; 54 (1819): 321–24: recapitulated in John Blackwell's "On a Remarkable Fact in the Natural History of the Swallow-Tribe," *Memoirs of the Literary and Philosophical Society of Manchester* 10 (1831): 36–53.

11. Thomas Brown, *Lectures on the Philosophy of the Human Mind*, 4 vols. (Edinburgh: Longman, 1820), 2:366.

12. In 1822, two full years after the composition of "To Autumn," the physician John Barclay concluded that contemporary theories of life were as various as they were inconclusive, and that life's self-revelation through finitude was the only point of consensus among theorists:

> Without attempting to assign any particular cause, let us merely suppose that the cause of life is a subtle substance, of a quickly and powerfully mobile nature, that pervades everything. On this supposition, it may be not only the electric fluid, it may be the magnetic or the galvanic, it may be caloric, it may be the supposed ether of Newton, or it may be that incorporeal substance, that vegetative life, which Cudworth denominates the plastic nature. Yet take any or all of them separately or combined, and suppose the whole universally diffused. How is it explained?

An Inquiry into the Opinions, Ancient and Modern, Concerning Life and Organization (Edinburgh: Bell & Bradfute, 1822), pp. 490–91, cited in Philip C. Ritterbush, *Overtures to Biology* (New Haven: Yale University Press, 1964), p. 191.

13. *Byron's Letters and Journals*, ed. Leslie A. Marchand, 12 vols. (Cambridge: Harvard University Press, 1973–82), 3: 235.

14. See Georges Louis Leclerc Buffon, *Buffon's Natural History*, 10 vols. (London: J. S. Barr, 1792), 1:22–26.

15. *Letters*, 2:113.

REFERENCES

Abernethy, John. *The Hunterian Oration, for the Year* 1819. London: Longman, 1819.

———. *Introductory Lecture for the Year* 1815, *Exhibiting Some of Mr. Hunter's Opinions Respecting Diseases*. London: Longman, 1815.

———. *Introductory Lectures, Exhibiting Some of Mr. Hunter's Opinions Respecting Life and Diseases, Delivered Before the Royal College of Surgeons, London, in* 1814 *and* 1815. London: Longman, 1815.

———. *Physiological Lectures, Exhibiting a General View of Mr. Hunter's Physiology, and of his Researches in Comparative Anatomy; Delivered before the Royal College of Surgeons in the year* 1817. 2d ed. London: Longman, 1822.

Abrams, Meyer Howard. *The Correspondent Breeze: Essays on English Romanticism*. Foreword by Jack Stillinger. New York: Norton, 1984.

———. *The Mirror and the Lamp: Romantic Theory and the Critical Tradition*. New York: Oxford University Press, 1953.

———. *Natural Supernaturalism: Tradition and Revolution in Romantic Literature*. New York: Norton, 1971.

———. "Coleridge and the Romantic Vision of the World." In *The Correspondent Breeze*.

———. "Coleridge's 'A Light in Sound': Science, Metascience, and Poetic Imagination." In *The Correspondent Breeze*.

Ackerknecht, Erwin H. *Medicine at the Paris Hospital,* 1794–1848. Baltimore: Johns Hopkins University Press, 1967.

Adams, Joseph. *Observations on Morbid Poisons, Phagedaena, and Cancer: Containing a Comparative View of the Theories of Dr. Swediaur, John Hunter, Messrs. Foot, Moore, and Bell, On the Laws of the Venereal Virus*. London: J. Johnson, 1795.

Alexander, William. "An Essay, Physiological and Experimental, on the Effects of Opium on the Living System." *Memoirs of the Literary and Philosophical Society of Manchester* 6 (1805): 1–97.

Allott, Miriam, ed. *The Poems of John Keats*. London: Longman, 1970.

An American Correspondent. "Progress of Dr. Mitchill's Mind in Investigating the Cause of the Pestilential Distempers which Visit the Cities of America in Summer and Autumn. Being a Development of the Theory of Pestilential Fluids, as Published to the World in 1795, and the Succeeding Years." (Alexander Tilloch's) *Philosophical Magazine* 4 (1799): 35–43, 132–39.

Amoreaux, M. "Observations on Spiders, and Their Supposed Poison." (Alexander Tilloch's) *Philosophical Magazine* 6 (1800): 74–80.

"Anatomy." (Rees's) *Cyclopaedia* (1819), vol. 2.

"Anatomy." *Encyclopaedia Britannica* (1810), 2:174–278. By Andrew Bell.

Andrews, C. T. "Keats and Mercury." *Keats-Shelley Memorial Bulletin* 20 (1969): 37–43.

"Antidote for Vegetable Poisons." (The Royal Institution's) *Quarterly Journal for Science, Literature, and the Arts* 10 (1820–1821): 192–93.

"Apothecaries Bill." *London Medical and Physical Journal* 33 (1815): 423–24.

Arnold, Matthew. *Essays in Criticism / Second Series*. London and New York: Macmillan, 1891.

————. *On the Study of Celtic Literature and On Translating Homer*. London and New York: Macmillan, 1902.

Arnold, Thomas. *Observations on the Nature, Kinds, Causes and Prevention of Insanity*. 2 vols. London: Richard Phillips, 1806.

Atkinson, A. D. "Keats and Kamchatka." *Notes and Queries* 196 (4 August 1951): 340–46.

Atkinson, Mr. "On the Use of Opium in Fever." (T. Bradley and A.F.M. Willich's) *Medical and Physical Journal* 8 (1802): 50–53.

Babington, William. *Lectures on the Materia Medica, Delivered at Guy's Hospital*. MS, Wills Library, 1796.

Babington, William. *Lectures on Therapeutics, Delivered at Guy's Hospital*. MS, Wills Library, 1796.

Babington, William, and James Curry. *Outlines of a Course of Lectures on the Practice of Medicine as Delivered in the Medical School of Guy's Hospital*. London: T. Bensley, 1802–1806.

Babington, William, Alexander Marcet, and William Allen. *A Syllabus of a Course of Chemical Lectures Read at Guy's Hospital*. London: W. Phillips, 1816.

Babington, William, with James Perry (*sic*? Curry?). *Extracts from Lectures on the Practice of Medicine, Delivered at Guy's Hospital between January 1st and June 1st, 1817*. MS, Wills Library, 1817.

Baine, Rodney. *The Political Theory of Painting from Reynolds to Hazlitt*. New Haven: Yale University Press, 1986

Baker, Henry. "A Letter from Mr. Henry Baker F.R.S. to the President, Concerning Several Medical Experiments of Electricity." *Philosophical Transactions* 45 (1748): 270–75.

Banks, Abraham. *Medical Etiquette; or An Essay Upon the Laws and Regulations which Ought to Govern the Conduct of the Medical Profession in Their Relation to Each Other*. London, 1839.

Barclay, John. *An Inquiry into the Opinions, Ancient and Modern, Concerning Life and Organization*. Edinburgh: Bell & Bradfute, 1822.

————. "Physiology." *Encyclopaedia Britannica* (1810), 16:445–528.

Barfield, Owen. *Saving the Appearances: A Study in Idolatry*. New York: Harcourt, 1965.

————. *What Coleridge Thought*. Middletown, Conn.: Wesleyan University Press, 1971.

Barnard, John. *John Keats*. Cambridge: Cambridge University Press, 1987.

————. "Keats's Tactile Vision: 'Ode to Psyche.'" *Keats-Shelley Memorial Bulletin* 33 (1982): 1–24.

————, ed. *John Keats: The Complete Poems*. 2d ed. Harmondsworth, U.K.: Penguin, 1977.

Barton, Benjamin Smith. "Letter to Professor Zimmermann, on the Fascinating Faculty which has been Ascribed to the Rattle-Snake, and other American Serpents." (Alexander Tilloch's) *Philosophical Magazine* 15 (1803): 193–202; 295–300.

————. "A Memoir Concerning the Fascinating Faculty which has been Ascribed to the Rattle-Snake and other American Serpents." (William Nicolson's) *Journal of Natural Philosophy, Chemistry, and the Arts* 7 (1804): 271–85; 8 (1804): 58–62, 100–115.

————. "On the Supposed Fascinating Power of the Rattle-Snake, With a Remarkable Indian Tradition upon which it is Probable the Early European Settlers Founded their Popular Tales." (William Nicolson's) *Journal of Natural Philosophy, Chemistry, and the Arts* 13 (1806): 300–305.

———. "Some Account of the Poisonous and Injurious Honey of North America." (Alexander Tilloch's) *Philosophical Magazine* 12 (1801): 121–35. Also printed in (William Nicolson's) *Journal of Natural Philosophy, Chemistry, and the Arts* 5 (1803): 158–75.

Baster, Andrew. "The Library of Guy's Hospital Physical Society, 1775–1825, Part 1," *Guy's Hospital Gazette* 98 (February 1984): 32–36; "Part 2," 98 (March 1984): 75–78; "Part 3," 98 (April 1984): 115–18.

Bate, Walter Jackson. *John Keats*. New York: Oxford University Press, 1966.

———. *Negative Capability: The Intuitive Approach in Keats*. Cambridge: Harvard University Press, 1939.

Battie, William. *A Treatise on Madness*. London: J. Whiston & B. White, 1758.

Bayley, John. "Keats and Reality." In *Proceedings of the British Academy*, pp. 91–125. London: Oxford University Press, 1962.

Beddoes, Thomas. *Hygeia: Or Essays Moral and Medical, on the Causes Affecting the Personal State of our Middling and Affluent Classes*. 2 vols. Bristol: R. Phillips, 1802.

Beddoes, Thomas Lovell. *The Poetical Works of Thomas Lovell Beddoes*. Edited by Edmund Gosse. 2 vols. London: J. M. Dent, 1890.

Bedingfield, James. *A Compendium of Medical Practice*. London: Highley & Son, 1816. (His compendium of medical practice "for the past five years" as surgeon and apothecary to the Bristol Infirmary.)

Bell, Andrew. "Anatomy." *Encyclopaedia Britannica* (1810): 2:174–278.

Bell, Charles. *Essays on the Anatomy of Expression*. London: Longman, 1806.

———. *Idea of a New Anatomy of the Brain*. London: Dawsons, 1966. (Facsimile of 1811 edition.)

Bell, John, and Charles Bell. *The Anatomy and Physiology of the Human Body*. 7th ed. 2 vols. London: Longman, 1829.

Beer, J. B. *Coleridge the Visionary*. New York: Macmillan-Collier, 1959.

Bichât, Xavier. *Physiological Researches on Life and Death*. Translated by F. Gold. Bristol: Longman, 1816.

Bishop, W. J. *The Early History of Surgery*. London: Robert Hale, 1960.

Blackstone, Bernard. *The Consecrated Urn: An Interpretation of Keats in Terms of Growth and Form*. London: Longman, 1959.

Blackwell, John. "On a Remarkable Fact in the Natural History of the Swallow Tribe." *Memoirs of the Literary and Philosophical Society of Manchester* 10 (1831): 36–53. (Read 23 March 1826.)

"Blood." (Rees's) *Cyclopaedia* (1819), vol. 4.

"Blood." *Encyclopaedia Britannica* (1810), 3:742–51.

Blumenbach, Johann F. *Institutions of Physiology*. Translated from the Latin by John Elliotson. 3d ed. London: E. Cox, 1817.

———. *A Manual of Comparative Anatomy*. Translated from the German by William Lawrence. 2d ed., revised and augmented by W. Coulson. London: Simpkin, 1827.

———. "On the Fascinating Power of the Rattle-Snake, with some Remarks on Dr. Barton's Memoir on that Subject." (Alexander Tilloch's) *Philosophical Magazine* 2 (1798): 251–56.

Boas, George. *French Philosophies of the Romantic Period*. Baltimore: Johns Hopkins University Press, 1925.

Boas, Marie. "The Establishment of Mechanical Philosophy." *Osiris: Studies on the History and Philosophy of Science and on the History of Learning and Culture* 10 (1952): 412–541.

Boas, Marie, and Rupert Hall. "Newton's Mechanical Principles." *Journal of the History of Ideas* 20 (1959): 167–78.

Bonnycastle, John. *An Introduction to Astronomy.* 4th ed. London: J. Johnson, 1803.

Bose, Jagadis Chunder. *Researches on Irritability of Plants.* London: Longman, 1913.

Bradford, Thomas Lindsley. *The Life and Letters of Dr. Samuel Hahnemann.* Philadelphia: Boericke & Tafel, 1895.

Brande, W. T. "A Concise View of the Theory of Respiration." (William Nicolson's) *Journal of Natural Philosophy, Chemistry, and the Arts* 11 (1805): 79–86. (Brande was professor of chemistry and materia medica to the Apothecaries Company.)

———. "Chemistry." *Encyclopaedia Britannica* (1810), *Supplement* to 4th edition, 3 (1824), pp. 1–58.

———. "Dissertation Third: Progress of Chemical Philosophy." *Encyclopaedia Britannica* (1810), *Supplement* to 4th edition, 3 (1824), 1–79.

———. "A Sketch of the History of Alchymy." (The Royal Institution's) *Quarterly Journal of Science, Literature, and the Arts* 9 (1820): 225–39.

Brande, W. T., ed. *Dictionary of Science, Literature, and Art.* New York: Harper, 1846.

Briggs, H. E. "Keats, Robertson, and 'That Most Hateful Land,'" *PMLA* 59 (1944): 596–98.

Brock, Russell C. *John Keats and Joseph Severn: The Tragedy of the Last Illness.* London: Keats-Shelley Memorial Association, 1973.

———. *The Life and Work of Astley Cooper.* London: E. & S. Livingstone, 1952.

Brodie, Benjamin C. *An Introductory Discourse on the Duties and Conduct of Medical Students and Practitioners.* London: Longman, 1843. (To the Students of St. George's Hospital, 2 October 1843.)

———. "Experiments and Observations on the Different Modes in which Death is Produced by Certain Vegetable Poisons." *Philosophical Transactions* 101 (1811): 178–208.

———. "Further Experiments and Observations on the Actions of Poisons on the Animal System." *Philosophical Transactions* 102 (1812): 205–27.

Brody, Saul N. *The Disease of the Soul; Leprosy in Medieval Literature.* Ithaca: Cornell University Press, 1974.

Bromwich, David. *Hazlitt: The Mind of a Critic.* New York: Oxford University Press, 1983.

Brown, John. *The Elements of Medicine* [Elementa Medicinae Brunois, 1780]. Translated from the Latin by the author, revised and corrected with a biographical preface by Thomas Beddoes. 2 vols. London: J. Johnson, 1795.

———. *The Works of John Brown.* Edited by W. C. Brown. 3 vols. London: Johnson & Symonds, 1804.

Brown, Norman O. *Hermes the Thief: The Evoluation of a Myth.* Madison: University of Wisconsin Press, 1947.

Brown, Theodore M. "From Mechanism to Vitalism in Eighteenth-Century English Physiology." *Journal of the History of Biology* 7 (1974): 179–216.

Brown, Thomas. *Lectures on the Philosophy of the Human Mind.* 4 vols. Edinburgh: Longman, 1820.

Buck, Albert H. *The Dawn of Modern Medicine from the Earliest Part of the Eighteenth Century to about* 1860. New Haven: Yale University Press, 1920.

————. *The Growth of Medicine from the Earliest Times to About 1800.* New Haven: Yale University Press, 1917.

Buffon, Georges Louis Leclerc, Count of. *Buffon's Natural History, Containing a Theory of the Earth, A General History of Man, of the Brute Creation, and of Vegetables, Minerals, etc.* With notes by the translator. 10 vols. London: J. S. Barr, 1792.

Burke, Kenneth. "The Anaesthetic Revelation of Herone Liddell." *Kenyon Review* 19 (1957): 505–59.

Burton, Robert. *The Anatomy of Melancholy.* Edited by A. R. Shilleto. 3 vols. 1893; reprint, London: G. Bell & Sons, 1913.

Bush, Douglas. *Mythology and the Romantic Tradition in English Poetry.* New York: Norton, 1963.

————. *Science and English Poetry.* New York: Oxford University Press, 1950.

Bynum, W. F., and Roy Porter, eds. *William Hunter and the Eighteenth-century Medical World.* Cambridge: Cambridge University Press, 1985.

Byron, George Gordon. *Byron's Letters and Journals.* Edited by Leslie A. Marchand. 12 vols. Cambridge: Harvard University Press, 1973–1981.

————. *Don Juan.* Edited by Leslie A. Marchand. Boston: Houghton Mifflin, 1958.

Cadet, C. L. "A Memoir on the Web of Spiders." (William Nicolson's) *Journal of Natural Philosophy, Chemistry, and the Arts* 11 (1805): 290–94.

Caldwell, James Ralston. *John Keats' Fancy: The Effects on Keats of the Psychology of His Day.* Ithaca: Cornell University Press, 1945.

Cameron, H. C. *Mr. Guy's Hospital, 1726–1948.* London: Longman, 1954.

"Camera Lucida." *Encyclopaedia Britannica* (1810), 5:92; *Supplement* (1824), 2:587–89.

"Camera Lucida." *Encyclopaedia Britannica* (1842), 6:36–38.

"Camera Lucida" and "Camera Obscura." (Ree's) *Cyclopaedia* (1819), vol. 10.

Carlisle, Anthony. *15 Museum Lectures.* MS, Royal College of Surgeons, 1818.

————. "Account of a Peculiarity in the Distribution of the Arteries Sent to the Limbs of Slow-Moving Animals; Together with Some Other Similar Facts." *Philosophical Transactions* 90 (1800): 98–105.

Carradori, D. J. "On the Irritability of the Sowthistle, and other Plants, with Further Observations on the Irritability of Vegetables." (William Nicolson's) *Journal of Natural Philosophy, Chemistry, and the Arts* 32 (1812): 138–43.

Carter, H. B. *Sir Joseph Banks: 1743–1820.* London: British Museum, 1988.

Castiglioni, Arturo. *A History of Medicine.* Translated by E. B. Krumbhaar. New York: Knopf, 1947.

A Catalogue of Books in the Library of the Physical Society, Guy's Hospital. London, 1823. (With interleavings by hand of books missed in 1823 list, and books acquired since 1823; MS, Wills Library, 1850.)

Cavallo, Tiberius. *An Essay on the Theory and Practice of Medical Electricity.* London: For the author, 1780.

Chalke, H. D. "The Impact of Tuberculosis on History, Literature and Art." *Medical History* 6 (October 1962): 301–18.

Chamisso, Adalbert von. "The Castle of Boncourt," "The Lion's Bride," "Woman's Love and Life," "The Women of Weinsberg," "The Crucifix," "The Old Singer," "The Old Washerwoman," "The Wonderful History of Peter Schlemihl." In *The German Classics,* edited by Frank Thilley, 1:324–400. 20 vols. New York: German Publication Society, 1913.

Cholmeley, Henry James. *Outlines of a Course of Lectures on the Practice of Medicine Delivered in the Medical School of Guy's Hospital.* London: J. M'Creery, 1820.

Christison, Robert. *Treatise on Poisons* (1829). Reprinted by J. T. Ducatel as *Manual of Practical Toxicology*. Baltimore: William & Joseph Neal, 1833.

———. "Poison." *Encyclopaedia Britannica* (1842), 16:174–83.

"Circulation." (Rees's) *Cyclopaedia* (1819), vol. 10.

Clarke, Charles Cowden, and Mary Cowden Clark. *Recollections of Writers*. London: Sampson, Low, Marston, Searle, & Rivington, 1878.

Clarke, James F. *Autobiographical Recollections of the Medical Profession*. London: J. & A. Churchill, 1874.

Cline, Henry, Sr. *Extracts from His [William Cullen's] Lectures on Fevers*. Taken by Henry Cline. MS, Royal College of Surgeons, 1784.

———. *Lectures by Henry Cline, St. Thomas's Hospital, London*. 2 vols. Taken by William Newland. MS, Royal College of Surgeons, 1789.

———. *Notes on His Lectures on Surgery*. Taken by J. N. Shelley. MS, Royal College of Surgeons, 1804.

———. *Notes on Henry Cline's Lectures on Anatomy*, 2 vols. In hand of Henry Cline. MS, Royal College of Surgeons, 1790.

Cline, Henry, Jr., and Astley Cooper. *Notes of their Lectures on Anatomy*, 1814. 2 vols. In different hands. MS, Royal College of Surgeons, 1814.

Clutterbuck, Henry. "On the Cure of those Affections which Arise from the Poison of Lead." (Alexander Tilloch's) *Philosophical Magazine* 6 (1800): 119–22.

Coleman, William. *Biology in the Nineteenth Century: Problems of Form, Function, and Transformation*. New York: Wiley, 1971.

Coleridge, Samuel Taylor. *Biographia Literaria; or, Biographical Sketches of My Literary Life and Opinions*. Edited by James Engell and W. Jackson Bate. 2 vols. Princeton: Princeton University Press, 1983. Vol. 7 of *Collected Works*.

———. *The Collected Works of Samuel Taylor Coleridge*. General editor, Kathleen Coburn. 17 vols. Princeton: Princeton University Press, 1969–.

———. *The Complete Works of Samuel Taylor Coleridge*. Edited by W. G. T. Shedd. 7 vols. New York: Harper, 1863. Volume 1, *Aids to Reflection*, "Appendix C"—"Hints Towards the Formation of a More Comprehensive Theory of Life," pp. 373–416.

———. *Inquiring Spirit: A New Presentation of Coleridge from His Published and Unpublished Prose Writings*. Edited by Kathleen Coburn. Rev. ed. Toronto: University of Toronto Press, 1979.

———. *Marginalia*. Edited by George Whalley. 2 vols. Princeton: Princeton University Press, 1980–1984. Vol. 12 of *Collected Works*.

———. *Specimens of the Table Talk of Samuel Taylor Coleridge*. Edited by H. N. Coleridge. London: John Murray, 1851.

———. *Table Talk*. Edited by Carl Woodring. 2 vols. Princeton: Princeton University Press, 1990. Vol. 14 of *Collected Works*.

———. *The Watchman*. Edited by Lewis Patton. Princeton: Princeton University Press, 1970. Vol. 2 of *Collected Works*.

Cook, Albert, trans. *Homer: The Odyssey*. New York: Norton, 1967.

Cooke, Katharine. *Coleridge*. London: Routledge & Kegan Paul, 1979.

Cooper, Sir Astley. *The Anatomical and Surgical Treatment of Abdominal Hernia*. Philadelphia: Lea & Blanchard, 1844.

———. *The Anatomy and Diseases of the Breast. To Which are Added his Various Surgical Papers*. Philadelphia: Lea & Blanchard, 1845.

———. *The Anatomy of the Thymus Gland*. Philadelphia: Lea & Blanchard, 1845.

————. *The Lectures of Sir Astley Cooper, Bart., F.R.S., on the Principles and Practice of Surgery, with Additional Notes and Cases.* Edited by Frederick Tyrrell. 5th U.S. ed., from the last London ed. Philadelphia: Haswell, Barrington, & Haswell, 1839.

————. *Lectures on Anatomy and the Principal Operations of Surgery, Delivered at the Theatre, St. Thomas's Hospital, between January 1st and June 1st, 1816.* 2 vols. Taken by Joshua Waddington. MS, Wills Library, 1816.

————. *Lectures on the Principles and Practice of Surgery, as delivered in the Theatre of St. Thomas's Hospital.* 2d ed. London: F. C. Wesley, 1830.

————. *Lectures on the Principles and Practice of Surgery. Delivered at the Theatre, St. Thomas's Hospital, between 1st of October, 1815 and the 1st of June, 1816.* Taken by Joshua Waddington. MS, Wills Library, 1816.

————. *Mr. Astley Cooper's Lectures on Surgery as Delivered at St. Thomas's Hospital in 1814.* MS, Royal College of Surgeons, 1814.

————. *Notes on Cases, 1816–1818.* 2 vols. MS, Royal College of Surgeons, 1818.

————. *Observations on the Strictures and Diseases of the Testis.* Philadelphia: Lea & Blanchard, 1845.

————. *Outlines of the Lectures on Surgery, Delivered by Sir Astley Cooper, Bart., at St. Thomas's and Guy's Hospitals.* (Printed for the use of the students.) London: G. Woodfall, 1822.

————. *Surgical Lectures.* 2 vols. Taken by William Compson, 1 October 1817—1 January 1818. MS, Wills Library, 1817–1818.

————. "Observations on the Effects Which Take Place From the Destruction of the Membrana Tympani of the Ear." (Alexander Tilloch's) *Philosophical Magazine* 8 (1800): 359–65.

Cooper, Astley, and Henry Cline, Jr. *Anatomical Lectures Delivered at St. Thomas's Hospital by Mr. Cooper and Mr. Cline, Jr.* (1812). Taken by Thomas Egerton Bryant. MS, Royal College of Surgeons, 1812.

————. *Notes of Their Lectures on Anatomy* [at St. Thomas's Hospital]. 2 vols. In different hands. MS, Royal College of Surgeons, 1814.

Cooper, Astley, and Benjamin Travers. *Surgical Essays.* London: Cox, 1818.

Cooper, Bransby Blake. *The Life of Sir Astley Cooper, Bart., Interspersed with Sketches from his Notebooks of Distinguished Contemporary Characters.* 2 vols. London: John W. Parker, 1843.

Cooper, Lane. "The Power of the Eye in Coleridge." In *Studies in Language and Literature in Honor of James Morgan Hart*, edited by Clark S. Northrup et al. New York: Henry Holt, 1910.

Copeman, W. S. C. *The Worshipful Society of Apothecaries of London: A History, 1617–1967.* Oxford: Pergamon Press, 1967.

Corbin, Alan. *The Foul and the Fragrant: Odor and the French Social Imagination.* Cambridge: Harvard University Press, 1986.

Corsi, Pietro. *The Age of Lamarck: Evolutionary Theories in France, 1790–1830.* Berkeley: University of California Press, 1989.

Crighton, Alexander (physician to Westminster Hospital). *An Inquiry into the Nature and Origin of Mental Derangement. Comprehending a Concise System of the Physiology and Pathology of the Human Mind and a History of the Passions and their Effects.* 2 vols. London: T. Cadell, 1798.

Crombie, A. C. "Some Reflections on the History of Science and Its Conception of Nature." *Annals of Science* 6 (1948): 54–75.

Crook, Nora, and Derek Guiton. *Shelley's Venomed Melody*. Cambridge: Cambridge University Press, 1986.

Crookshank, F. G. "The Importance of a Theory of Signs and a Critique of Language in the Study of Medicine." In *The Meaning of Meaning*, edited by C. K. Ogden and I. A. Richards. London: Kegan Paul, 1946.

Cullen, William. *First Lines of the Practice of Physic*. 4 vols. London: T. Cadell, 1786.

Culpeper, Nicholas. *The English Physician Enlarged with Three Hundred and Ninety-Six Medicines Made from English Herbs*. Edited by E. Sibley. From the 4th ed. of 1651. London: J. Satcherd, 1800; reprint, Manchester: S. Russell, 1807, 1813.

"Cure for the Hydrophobia." (The Royal Institution's) *Quarterly Journal for Science, Literature, and the Arts* 10 (1820–1821): 194.

Currie, James. *Medical Reports on the Effects of Water, Cold and Warm, as a Remedy in Fever and Febrile Diseases*. London: T. Cadell & W. Davies, 1805.

Curry, James. *Examination of the Prejudices Commonly Entertained Against Mercury as Beneficially Applicable to most Hepatic Complaints, and to Various Other Forms of Disease, as well as to Syphilis*. London: J. M'Creery, 1809.

———. *Heads of a Course of Lectures on Pathology, Therapeutics, and Materia Medica; Delivered in the Medical School of Guy's Hospital*. London: T. Bensley, 1804.

———. *Lectures on Surgery by Alexander Monro, M.D. Transcribed from Notes of Lectures by Mr. Thorburn (1776), With Additions Delivered Between 1781–84*. 2 vols. MS, Royal College of Surgeons.

———. *Observations on Apparent Death from Drowning, Hanging, Suffocation by Noxious Vapours, Fainting-fits, Intoxication, Lightning, Exposure to Cold, etc . . . to Which is Added, the Treatment Proper in Cases of Poison*. London: E. Cox, 1815.

———. "History of a Case of Remitting Ophthalmia and its Successful Treatment by Opium." London: G. Woodfall, 1812; *Medico-Chirurgical Transactions* 3 (1816): 348–71.

Darnton, Robert. *Mesmerism and the End of the Enlightenment in France*. Cambridge: Harvard University Press, 1968.

Darwin, Erasmus. *The Botanic Garden; A Poem, in Two Parts*. London: J. Johnson, 1791.

———. *The Temple of Nature; or, The Origin of Society: A Poem, with Philosophical Notes*. London: J. Johnson, 1803.

———. *Zoonomia; or The Laws of Organic Life. In Three Parts*. (Part 3, "Articles of the Materia Medica," is an appendage to the first volume of most editions, with its own pagination.) Edited by Samuel L. Mitchell. 2 vols. 4th U.S. ed. 1802; reprint, Philadelphia: Edward Earle, 1818.

D'Avanzo, Mario L. *Keats's Metaphors for the Poetic Imagination*. Durham: Duke University Press, 1967.

Davenport, Arnold. "A Note on 'To Autumn.' " In *John Keats: A Reassessment*, edited by Kenneth Muir.

Davies, Edward. *Celtic Researches, on the Origin, Tradition and Language, of the Ancient Britons. . . .* London: J. Booth, 1804.

———. *The Mythology and Rites of the British Druids, Ascertained by National Documents. . . .* London: J. Booth, 1809.

Davies, R. T. "Keats and Hazlitt." *Keats-Shelley Memorial Bulletin* 8 (1957): 1–8.

Davy, Sir Humphry. *The Collected Works of Sir Humphry Davy, Bart*. Edited by John Davy. 9 vols. London: Smith, Elder, 1840.

Davy, John. "Observations on the Poison of the Common Toad." *Philosophical Transactions* 116 (1826): 127–31.

de Beer, Sir Gavin. "Jean-Jacques Rousseau: Botanist." *Annals of Science* 10 (September 1954): 189–223.

Delametherie (De la Mettrie, La Mettrie), J. C. "On the System of Forces." (Alexander Tilloch's) *Philosophical Magazine* 2 (1798): 277–82.

De Man, Paul. "The Negative Road" (1966). In *Modern Critical Views: John Keats*, edited by Harold Bloom, pp. 29–48. New York: Chelsea House, 1985.

Derrida, Jacques. "Plato's Pharmacy." In *Dissemination*, translated by Barbara Johnson. Chicago: University of Chicago Press, 1981.

Dewhurst, Kenneth. *John Locke (1632–1704), Physician and Philosopher: A Medical Biography; with an Edition of the Medical Notes in his Journals.* London: Wellcome Historical Medical Library, 1963.

Dewhurst, Kenneth, and Nigel Reeves, eds. *Friedrich Schiller: Medicine, Psychology and Literature* (with the first English edition of his complete medical and psychological writings). Berkeley: University of California Press, 1978.

Dictionary of the History of Science. Edited by W. F. Bynum, E. J. Browne, and Roy Porter. Princeton: Princeton University Press, 1981.

Dictionary of Science, Literature, and Art: Comprising the History, Description, and Scientific Principles of Every Branch of Human Knowledge; with the Derivation and Definition of All the Terms in General Use. Edited by W. T. Brande. New York: Harper, 1846.

Dictionary of Scientific Biography. Edited by Charles Coulston Gillispie. New York: Scribner's, 1970.

"Disease." (Rees's) *Cyclopaedia* (1819), vol. 11.

Driesch, Hans. *The History and Theory of Vitalism*. Translated by C. K. Ogden. London: Macmillan, 1914.

Doubleday, F. N. "John Keats and the Borough Hospitals." *Keats-Shelley Memorial Bulletin* 13 (1962): 13–17.

Dumeril, M. "Account of the Death of Mr. Drake by the Bite of a Rattlesnake." (David Brewster's) *Edinburgh Journal of Science* 7 (1827): 85–88.

Duncan, Andrew, Jr. *The Edinburgh New Dispensary*. Edinburgh, 1803.

———. (attributed or probable author). "Materia Medica and Pharmacy." *Encyclopaedia Britannica* (1810), 13:686–799.

———. "Medicine." *Encyclopaedia Britannica* (1810), 13:187–486.

Duportal, A. S. and Thomas Pelletier. "On the Preparation of Gold Lately Employed Medicinally." (William Nicolson's) *Journal of Natural Philosophy, Chemistry, and the Arts* 32 (1812): 179–185.

(David Brewster's) *Edinburgh Journal of Science*.

(Brewster and Jameson's) *Edinburgh Philosophical Journal*.

Eichner, Hans. "The Rise of Modern Science and the Genesis of Romanticism." PMLA 97 (1982): 8–30.

Elliot, G. R. "The Real Tragedy of Keats." PMLA 36 (1921): 315–31.

Elliot, John. *The Medical Pocket-Book*. 3d ed. London: J. Johnson, 1791.

Evans, B. Ifor. "Keats—The Man, Medicine and Poetry." *British Medical Journal* 3 (5 July 1969): 7–11.

Evert, Walter H. *Aesthetic and Myth in the Poetry of Keats*. Princeton: Princeton University Press, 1965.

Fass, Barbara. *La Belle Dame sans Merci and the Aesthetics of Romanticism.* Detroit: Wayne State University Press, 1974.

Ferguson, Oliver W. "Wharton and Keats: Two Views of Melancholy." *Keats-Shelley Journal* 18 (1969): 12–15.

Ferriar, John. "An Argument Against the *Doctrine of Materialism,* Addressed to *Thomas Cooper, Esq.*" *Memoirs of the Literary and Philosophical Society of Manchester* 4, Part I (1793): 20–44.

————. "Observations Concerning the *Vital Principle.*" *Memoirs of the Literary and Philosophical Society of Manchester* 3 (1790): 216–41.

Finney, Claude Lee. *The Evolution of Keats's Poetry.* 2 vols. Cambridge: Harvard University Press, 1936.

Fish, Stanley E. *Self-Consuming Artifacts: The Experience of Seventeenth-Century Literature.* Berkeley: University of California Press, 1972.

Fitzgerald, Robert, trans. *Homer: The Odyssey.* New York: Doubleday, 1961.

Fogle, Richard Harter. *The Imagery of Keats and Shelley: A Comparative Study.* Chapel Hill: University of North Carolina Press, 1949.

Ford, Newell F. *The Prefigurative Imagination of John Keats.* Stanford: Stanford University Press, 1951.

Foucault, Michel. *The Birth of the Clinic: An Archaeology of Medical Perception.* Translated by A. M. Sheridan Smith. New York: Random House, 1973.

————. *The Order of Things.* Translated by A. M. Sheridan Smith. London: Tavistock, 1970.

Fox, Daniel M., and Gilbert T. Gall. *Photographing Medicine: Images and Power in Britain and America Since 1840.* Westport, Conn.: Greenwood Press, 1988.

Frye, Northrop. *Anatomy of Criticism.* 1957; reprint, New York: Atheneum, 1970.

Fulton, John Farquhar. "Medicine in the Eighteenth Century." In his *Logan Clendening Lectures on the History and Philosophy of Medicine,* pp. 25–49. Lawrence: University of Kansas Press, 1950.

Fulton, John F., and Harvey Cushing, "A Bibliographical Study of the Galvani and Aldini Writings on Animal Electricity." *Annals of Science* 1 (1936): 239–68.

"Galvanism." *Encyclopaedia Britannica* (1810), 9:331–445.

"Galvanism." *Encyclopaedia Britannica.* 1824 Supplement to 4th, 5th, and 6th eds.

Garrison, Fielding H. *An Introduction to the History of Medicine.* Philadelphia and London: W. B. Saunders, 1929.

Gaull, Marilyn. "From Wordsworth to Darwin: 'On to the Fields of Praise.' " *Wordsworth Circle* 10 (Winter 1979): 33–48.

Gelfand, Toby. "Hospital Teaching as Private Enterprise in Hunterian London." In *William Hunter and the Eighteenth-century Medical World,* edited by W. F. Bynum and Roy Porter.

Gillispie, Charles Coulston. *The Edge of Objectivity: An Essay in the History of Scientific Ideas.* Princeton: Princeton University Press, 1960.

————. *Genesis and Geology.* Cambridge: Harvard University Press, 1951.

————. "The Foundation of Lamarck's Evolutionary Theory." *Archives internationales d'histoire des sciences* 9 (1956): 323–38.

————. "Lamarck and Darwin in the History of Science." In *Forerunners of Darwin: 1745–1859,* edited by Bentley Glass, Owsei Temkin, and William L. Straus, Jr.

Girard, René. "The Plague in Literature and Myth." In *"To Double Business Bound:" Essays on Literature, Mimesis, and Anthropology.* Baltimore: Johns Hopkins University Press, 1978.

Gittings, Robert. *John Keats.* London: Heinemann, 1968.

———. *John Keats: The Living Year, 21 September 1818 to 21 September 1819.* Cambridge: Harvard University Press, 1954.

———. "John Keats, Physician and Poet." *Journal of the American Medical Association* 224 (1973): 51–55.

———. "Keats and Chatterton." *Keats-Shelley Journal* 4 (1955): 47–54.

———. "Keats and Medicine." *Contemporary Review* 219 (1971): 138–42.

———. "This Living Hand." *Medical History* 16 (1972): 1–10.

Glass, Bentley. "Maupertuis, Pioneer of Genetics and Evolution" and "The Germination of the Idea of Biological Species." In *Forerunners of Darwin: 1745–1859*, edited by Bentley Glass, Owsei Temkin, and William L. Straus, Jr.

Glass, Bentley, Owsei Temkin, and William L. Straus, Jr., eds. *Forerunners of Darwin: 1745–1859.* Baltimore: Johns Hopkins University Press, 1959.

Godwin, William (Edward Baldwin). *The Pantheon: or Ancient History of the Gods of Greece and Rome.* London: Thomas Hodgkins, 1806.

Gode-von Aesch, Alexander. *Natural Science in German Romanticism.* New York: Columbia University Press, 1941.

Goellnicht, Donald C. *The Poet-Physician: Keats and Medical Science.* Pittsburgh: University of Pittsburgh Press, 1984.

Goethe, J. W. von. "*Versuch uber die Metamorphose der Pflangen zu Erklaren.*" Translated by Agnes Arber in "Goethe's Botany: *The Metamorphoses of Plants* (1790) and Tobler's *Ode to Nature.*" *Chronica Botanica* 10 (1946): 63–126.

Goldston, Iago. "Freud and Romantic Medicine." *Bulletin of the History of Medicine* 30 (1956): 489–507.

Gotshalk, D. W. *Art and the Social Order.* Chicago: University of Chicago Press, 1947.

Gough, John. "Remarks on the Summer Birds of Passage, and on Migration in General." *Memoirs of the Literary and Philosophical Society of Manchester* 7 (1813): 453–65.

Gould, Stephen Jay. *The Mismeasure of Man.* New York: Norton, 1981.

Gradman, Barry. *Metamorphosis in Keats.* New York: New York University Press, 1980.

Grattan, J.H.G., and Charles Singer. *Anglo-Saxon Magic and Medicine.* London: Oxford University Press, 1952.

Graves, Robert. *The White Goddess: A Historical Grammar of Poetic Myth.* Rev. ed. New York: Farrar, Straus & Giroux, 1966.

Green, Joseph Henry. *An Address Delivered in King's College, London, at the Commencement of the Medical Session, October 1, 1832.* London: B. Fellowes, 1832.

———. *The Dissector's Manual.* (Enlarged edition of *Outlines of a Course of Dissections*, printed for students of anatomy at St. Thomas's Hospital, 1815.) London: For the author, 1820.

———. *Outlines of a Course of Dissections.* London: For the author, 1815.

———. *Spiritual Philosophy: Founded on the Teachings of the Late Samuel Taylor Coleridge.* Edited by John Simon, with a memoir of the author's Life. London: Macmillan, 1865.

———. *Vital Dynamics: The Hunterian Oration Before the Royal College of Surgeons in London, 14 February 1840.* London: William Pickering, 1840.

Gregory, John. *Lectures on the Duties and Qualifications of a Physician.* Philadelphia: M. Carey & Son, 1817. (Reprint of *Lectures on the Duties and Qualifications of a Physician*, edited and corrected by James Gregory, Edinburgh, 1805.)

Gregory, William. *Letters to a Candid Inquirer on Animal Magnetism.* Philadelphia: Blanchard & Lea, 1851.

Guy's Hospital. *Pharmacopoeia in usum nosocomii a Thomas Guy, Armigero*, A.D. London, 1826. (Compiled by the staff to include all items from the British Pharmacopoeia.)

Guy's Hospital Reports. Edited by F. J. Stewart and Herbert French. London: J. A. Churchill, 1913.

Haeger, J. H. "Coleridge's 'By Blow': The Composition and Date of *Theory of Life*." *Modern Philology* 74 (1976): 20–41.

Hagelman, Charles W., Jr. "John Keats and the Medical Profession." Ph.D. diss., University of Texas, 1956.

———. "Keats's Medical Training and the Last Stanza of the 'Ode to Psyche.' " *Keats-Shelley Journal* 11 (1962): 73–82.

Haggard, Howard W. *Devils, Drugs, and Doctors: The Story of the Science of Healing from Medicine-Man to Doctor.* New York: Harper, 1929.

———. *Mystery, Magic, and Medicine: The Rise of Medicine from Superstition to Science.* New York: Doubleday, 1933.

Hahnemann, Samuel. *The Chronic Diseases, Their Peculiar Nature and Their Homeopathic Cure.* Translated by Louis H. Tafel. Philadelphia: Boericke & Tafel, 1904.

Haighton, John. *Lectures on Midwifery and Diseases of Women and Children. Delivered at the Theatre, Guy's Hospital, between the 1st of November, 1816, and the 1st of March, 1817.* Taken by Joshua Waddington. MS, Wills Library.

———. *Lectures on the Physiology of the Human Body. Delivered at Guy's Hospital.* MS, Wills Library, 1796.

Halevy, Elie. *The Growth of Philosophic Radicalism.* Translated by Mary Morris. Rev. ed. London: Faber & Faber, 1972.

Hale-White, Sir William. *Keats as Doctor and Patient.* London: Oxford University Press, 1938.

Hall, Alfred Rupert. *The Scientific Revolution, 1500–1800: The Formation of the Modern Scientific Attitude.* Boston: Beacon Press, 1966.

Haller, Albrecht von. *A Dissertation on the Sensible and Irritable Parts of Animals.* Introduction by Owsei Temkin. 1755; reprint, Baltimore: Johns Hopkins University Press, 1936.

Hamilton-Edwards, Gerald. "John Keats and the Hammonds." *Keats-Shelley Memorial Bulletin* 17 (1966): 31–36.

Hartman, Geoffrey. *Beyond Formalism: Literary Essays 1858–1970.* New Haven: Yale University Press, 1970.

Hartman, George. *The Family Physitian, or a Collection of Choice, Approv'd and Experienc'd Remedies, for the Cure of Almost all Diseases. . . .* London: Richard Wellington, 1696.

Hawthorne, Nathaniel. *The Centenary Edition of the Works of Nathaniel Hawthorne.* Edited by William Charvat, Roy Harvey Pierce, and Claude M. Simpson. Columbus: Ohio State University Press, 1970. Volume 10.

Haydon, Benjamin Robert. *The Autobiography and Memoirs of Benjamin Robert Haydon.* Edited by T. Taylor. London: Davies, 1926.

———. *Lectures on Painting and Design.* 2 vols. London: Longman, 1844–1846.

Hayter, Alethea. *Opium and the Romantic Imagination.* Berkeley: University of California Press, 1968.

Hazlitt, William. *The Complete Works of William Hazlitt.* Edited by P. P. Howe. 21 vols. London: J. M. Dent, 1930–1934.

"Health." (Rees's) *Cyclopaedia* (1819), vol. 17.

Henry, William. "On the Theories of the Excitement of Galvanic Electricity." *Memoirs of the Literary and Philosophical Society of Manchester* 7 (1813): 293–312.

Hentz, N. M. "Note Regarding the Spider Whose Web is Employed in Medicine." (Brewster and Jameson's) *Edinburgh Philosophical Journal* 12 (1825): 184–85.

Hilton, Nelson. "The Spectre of Darwin." *Blake: An Illustrated Quarterly* 15 (1981): 36–50.

Hoffmann, E.T.A. *The Serapion Brethren*. Translated by Alex Ewing. 2 vols. London: George Bell, 1886.

———. *The Tales of Hoffmann*. Translated by Michael Bullock. New York: Fredrich Ungar, 1963. ("Datura Fastuoso: The Georgeous Thorn-Apple," pp. 103–58).

Holloway, John. *The Charted Mirror*. London: Routledge & Kegan Paul, 1960.

Holstein, Michael E. "Keats: The Poet-Healer and the Problem of Pain." *Keats-Shelley Journal* 36 (1987): 32–49.

Home, Sir Everard. *The Hunterian Oration in Honour of Surgery, Instituted by the Executors of John Hunter, Delivered in the theatre of the College, Feb. 14, 1822*. MS, Royal College of Surgeons, 1822.

———. *Lectures on Comparative Anatomy*. London: G. W. Nicol, 1814–1928.

———. *Observations on Cancer, Connected with Histories of the Disease*. London: Bulmer, and G. & W. Nicol, 1805.

———. "The Case of a Man, who died in Consequence of the Bite of a Rattle-snake; with an Account of the Effects Produced by the Poison." *Philosophical Transactions* 100 (1810): 75–88.

———. "The Croonian Lecture. On the Changes the Blood Undergoes in the Act of Coagulation." *Philosophical Transactions* 108 (1818): 172–84 (read 20 November 1817).

———. "Observations Intended to Show that the Progressive Motion of Snakes is Partly Performed by Means of the Ribs." *Philosophical Transactions* 102 (1812): 163–68.

———. "Some Additions to the Croonian Lecture, on the Changes the Blood Undergoes in the Act of Coagulation." *Philosophical Transactions* 108 (1818): 185–98.

Hooper, Robert, ed. *Quincy's Lexicon-Medicum: A New Medical Dictionary; Containing an Explanation of the Terms in Anatomy, Physiology, Practice of Physic, Materia Medica, Chymistry, Pharmacy, Surgery, Midwifery, and the Various Branches of Natural Philosophy Connected with Medicine*. Philadelphia: R. Parker, M. Carey & Son, 1817.

Houlston, Thomas. *Observations on Poisons; and on the Use of Mercury in the Cure of Obstinate Dysenteries*. London: R. Baldwin, 1784.

Huber, Francois. *New Observations on the Natural History of Bees*. Edinburgh, 1806.

Huddleston, R. *A New Edition of Toland's History of the Druids*. Montrose: James Watt, 1814.

Hulme, Nathaniel. "A Continuation of the Experiments and Observations on the Light which is Spontaneously Emitted from Various Bodies; with some Experiments and Observations on Solar Light, when Imbibed by *Canton's* Phosphorus." *Philosophical Transactions* 92 (1802): 403–26.

———. "Experiments and Observations on the Light which is Spontaneously Emitted, with Some Degree of Permanency, from Various Bodies." *Philosophical Transactions* 90 (1800): 161–87.

Humboldt, Alexander von. *Cosmos*. Translated by E. C. Otté. 5 vols. London: Henry G. Bohn, 1949–1958.

———. "Account of the Electric Eels, and of the Method of Catching them in South America by Means of Wild Horses." (Brewster and Jameson's) *Edinburgh Philosophical Journal* 2 (1820): 242–49.

———. "Extract of a Letter from Mr. Humboldt to Mr. Blumenbach, Containing New Experiments on the Irritation Caused by the Metals with Respect to Their

Different Impressions on the Organs of Animals." (William Nicolson's) *Journal of Natural Philosophy, Chemistry, and the Arts* 1 (1797): 256–60.

———. "Die Lebenskraft oder der rhodische Genius." In *Gesammelte Werke*, 6:303–7. 6 vols. Stuttgart: J. G. Cottaschen, 1844. (Reprinted from *Die Hören* 1 (1795): 90–96.)

———. "On the Chemical Process of Vitality." (William Nicolson's) *Journal of Natural Philosophy, Chemistry, and the Arts* 1 (1797): 359–64.

Humphries, Rolfe, trans. *Ovid: Metamorphoses*. Bloomington: Indiana University Press, 1955.

Hunter, John. *The Works of John Hunter, F.R.S.* Edited by James F. Palmer. 4 vols. London: Longman, 1835–1837.

Hutton, James. *Dissertations on Different Subjects in Natural Philosophy*. Edinburgh and London: A. Strahan & T. Cadell, 1792.

"Irritability." *Encyclopaedia Britannica* (1810), vol. 11.

Inglis, Gavin. "On the Swallow." (Alexander Tilloch's) *Philosophical Magazine* 52 (1818): 271–82. "Some Further Remarks on the Swallow," 54 (1819): 321–24. (Letter written 29 August 1818; addition, November 1819.)

"Inquiry Whether Naevia Materna, with Which Children are Sometimes Born, Should Be Attributed to the Imagination of the Mother." (Alexander Tilloch's) *Philosophical Magazine* 34 (1809): 347–49.

Jack, Ian. *Keats and the Mirror of Art*. Oxford: Oxford University Press, 1967.

Jackson, H. J. "Coleridge's Collaborator, Joseph Henry Green." *Studies in Romanticism* 21 (1982): 161–79.

Jacyna, L. S. "Images of John Hunter in the Nineteenth Century." *History of Science* 21 (1983): 85–108.

James, D. G. *The Romantic Comedy*. London: Oxford University Press, 1948.

———. *Scepticism and Poetry: An Essay on the Poetic Imagination*. London: George Allen & Unwin, 1937; New York: Barnes and Noble, 1960.

Jarcko, Saul. "Auenbrugger, Laënnec, and John Keats." *Medical History* 5 (1961): 167–72.

Jones, John. *John Keats's Dreams of Truth*. New York: Barnes & Noble, 1969.

Jones, Leonides M. *The Life of John Hamilton Reynolds*. Hanover, N.H.: University Presses of New England, 1985.

Jones, W.H.S. "Greek Medical Etiquette." *Proceedings of the Royal Society of Medicine* 16 (17 January 1923): 11–17.

(William Nicolson's) *Journal of Natural Philosophy, Chemistry, and the Arts*.

Kames, Henry Home, Lord. *Elements of Criticism*. 6th ed. 2 vols. Edinburgh: John Bell & William Creech, 1785.

Keats, John. *Anatomical and Physiological Note Book*. Edited by Maurice Buxton Forman. London: Oxford University Press, 1934.

———. *The Letters of John Keats, 1814–1821*. Edited by Hyder Edward Rollins. 2 vols. Cambridge: Harvard University Press, 1958.

———. *The Poems of John Keats*. Edited by Jack Stillinger. Cambridge: Harvard University Press, 1978.

The Keats Circle: Letters and Papers and More Letters and Poems of the Keats Circle. 2d ed. Edited by Hyder E. Rollins. 2 vols. Cambridge: Harvard University Press, 1965.

Keegan, Hugh L. "Snakebite." In *Cecil Textbook of Medicine*, pp. 121–23. New York: Saunders, 1979.

Keel, Othmar. "The Politics of Health." In *William Hunter and the Eighteenth-century Medical World*, edited by W. F. Bynum and Roy Porter.

King, Lester S. *Medical Thinking: A Historical Preface.* Princeton: Princeton University Press, 1982.

——. *The Medical World of the Eighteenth Century.* 1958; reprint, New York: Robert E. Krieger, 1971.

——. *The Philosophy of Medicine: The Early Eighteenth Century.* Cambridge: Harvard University Press, 1978.

King-Hele, Desmond. *Doctor of Revolution: The Life and Genius of Erasmus Darwin.* London: Faber & Faber, 1977.

——. *Erasmus Darwin.* New York: Scribner's, 1963.

——. *Erasmus Darwin and the Romantic Poets.* New York: St. Martin's Press, 1986.

——. *The Essential Writings of Erasmus Darwin.* London: MacGibbon & Kee, 1968.

Kinglake, Robert. "On the Nature and Properties of Vital Power." *Medical and Physical Journal* 2 (1799): 127–31.

Kipperman, Mark. *Beyond Enchantment: German Idealism and English Romantic Poetry.* Philadelphia: University of Pennsylvania Press, 1986.

Knight, David M. "Chemistry, Physiology, and Materialism in the Romantic Period." *Durham University Journal* 64 (1972): 139–45.

——. "The Physical Sciences and the Romantic Movement." *History of Science* 9 (1970): 54–75.

——. "The Scientist as Sage." *Studies in Romanticism* 6 (1967): 65–88.

Kristeva, Julia. *Soleil noir: Dépression et melancholie.* Paris: Gallimard, 1987.

Kuhn, Thomas S. *The Structure of Scientific Revolutions.* Chicago: University of Chicago Press, 1962.

Larkey, Sanford V. "Magic and the Origin of Medicine." Unpublished abstract in the Ferdinand Hamburger, Jr., Archives, Johns Hopkins University. (Read to the History of Ideas Club, 11 January 1940.)

Lattimore, Richmond, trans. *The Odyssey of Homer.* New York: Harper, 1965.

Lawrence, William. *An Introduction to Comparative Anatomy and Physiology; Being the Two Introductory Lectures Delivered at the Royal College of Surgeons on the 21st and 25th of March, 1816.* London: J. Callow, 1816.

——. *Lectures on Physiology, Zoology, and the Natural History of Man, Delivered at the Royal College of Surgeons.* London: J. Callow, 1819; Benbow, 1822; James Smith, 1823. (Of courses taught in 1817.)

——. "Life." (Ree's) *Cyclopaedia* (1819), vol. 20.

Leake, Chauncey D. *Percival's Medical Ethics.* Baltimore: William & Wilkins, 1927.

Lefebure, Molly. *Samuel Taylor Coleridge: A Bondage of Opium.* New York: Stein & Day, 1974.

Lemprière, J. *Bibliotheca Classica, or, A Classical Dictionary; Containing a Copious Account of all the Proper Names Mentioned in Ancient Authors....* Corrected 11th ed. London: T. Cadell & W. Davies, 1820.

Leroi, Alphonsus. "Extract of Experiments and Observations on the Use of Phosphorus Administered Internally." (Alexander Tilloch's) *Philosophical Magazine* 2 (1798): 290–93.

Levere, Trevor H. *Poetry Realized in Nature: Samuel Taylor Coleridge and Early Nineteenth-Century Science.* New York: Cambridge University Press, 1981.

Levine, George. *Darwin and the Novelists: Patterns of Science in Victorian Fiction.* Cambridge: Harvard University Press, 1988.

Levinson, Marjorie. *Keats's Life of Allegory: The Origins of a Style.* Oxford: Blackwell, 1988.

Lewis, Thomas. *The Youngest Science: Notes of a Medicine-Watcher.* New York: Viking Press, 1983.

"List of Books by Guy's Men in the Wills Library, Guy's Hospital." *Guy's Hospital Reports* 67 (1913): 265–333.

Lloyd, G.E.R. *Early Greek Science: Thales to Aristotle.* New York: Norton, 1970.

Locke, John. *An Essay Concerning Human Understanding.* Edited by Alexander Campbell Frazer. 2 vols. New York: Dover Publications, 1959. (Facsimile of 1st ed.)

———. *Medical Notes in the Journals.* See Kenneth Dewhurst.

———. *Of the Conduct of the Understanding.* Edited by Francis W. Garforth. New York: Teachers College Press, Columbia University, 1966. (Reprint of 1st ed., 1706.)

Logan, James Venable. *The Poetry and Aesthetics of Erasmus Darwin.* Princeton: Princeton University Press, 1936.

The London Medical and Physical Journal. Vols. 33–54 (1815–1825).

The London Medical Journal (edited by Simmons). Vols. 9—11 (1788, 1789, 1790).

The London Medical Review and Magazine. Vol. 1 (March–August 1799); vol. 2 (September 1799–February 1800); vol. 3 (March–June 1800); vol. 4 (July–October 1800); vol. 5 (November 1800–February 1801); vol. 6 (March–July 1801); vol. 7 (August–December 1801).

Lovejoy, Arthur O. "Buffon and the Problem of Species." In *Forerunners of Darwin: 1745–1859,* edited by Bentley Glass, Owsei Temkin, and William L. Straus, Jr.

Lowell, Amy. *John Keats.* 2 vols. 1929; reprint, New York: Archon Books, 1969.

Lowes, John Livingston. *The Road to Xanadu: A Study in the Ways of the Imagination.* Rev. ed. Boston: Houghton Mifflin, 1964.

Lucretius, Titus Carus. *Of the Nature of Things.* Translated by Thomas Creech. 6th ed. 2 vols. London: T. Warner & J. Walthoe, 1722.

"Luminosity Produced by Compression, Friction and Animal Bodies." (Brewster and Jameson's) *Edinburgh Philosophical Journal* 4 (1820–1821): 216–19.

Lyons, Henry. *The Royal Society.* New York: Greenwood Press, 1968.

MacCulloch, J. "On Staffa." (Alexander Tilloch's) *Philosophical Magazine* 44 (1814): 445–51.

Macfie, Ronald Campbell. *The Romance of Medicine.* London: Cassell, 1907.

Macilwain, George. *Memoirs of John Abernethy, with a View of His Lectures, His Writings, and Character.* London: Hatchard, 1856.

MacKay, Charles. *Memoirs of Extraordinary Popular Delusions.* 2 vols. London: National Illustrated Library, 1852.

McGilchrist, Iain. "Review of Jeffrey Meyer's *Disease and the Novel, 1880–1960.*" TLS, 13 December 1985, p. 1415.

Mandelbaum, Maurice. "The Scientific Background of Evolutionary Theory in Biology." *Journal of the History of Ideas* 18 (1957): 342–62.

Mandeville, B. *A Treatise of the Hypochondriack & Hysterick Diseases, in 3 Dialogues.* 3d ed. London: J. Tonson, 1730.

Maniquis, Robert M. "The Puzzling Mimosa: Sensitivity and Plant Symbols in Romanticism." *Studies in Romanticism* 8 (1969): 129–55.

Marcet, Alexander. *A Case of Hydrophobia.* London: Woodfall, 1809.

———. *An Essay on the Chemical History and Medical Treatment of Calculous Disorders.* London: Longman, 1817.

———. *Hospital Practice and other Miscellaneous Cases and Practical Observations, 1804–1806.* MS, Royal College of Surgeons, 1804–1806.

———. *Some Remarks on Clinical Lectures, Being the Substance of an Introductory Lecture Delivered at Guy's Hospital. On the 27th of January, 1818.* London: Woodfall, 1818.

———. "Account of a Case in which Death was Preceded by a Dose of Arsenic and

Corrosive Sublimate, with Dissection" (1806). In *Hospital Practice and Other Miscellaneous Cases*. MS, Royal College of Surgeons, 1804–1806.

———. "An Analysis of the Waters of the Dead Sea and the River Jordan." *Philosophical Transactions* 97 (1807): 296–314.

———. "A Chemical Account of an Aluminous Chalybeate Spring in the Isle of Wight." (William Nicolson's) *Journal of Natural Philosophy, Chemistry, and the Arts* 32 (1812): 52–66, 85–100.

———. "On the Medicinal Properties of Stramonium; with Illustrative Cases." *Medico-Chirurgical Transactions* 7 (1819): 546–75.

Matthews, G. M., ed. *Keats: The Critical Heritage*. New York: Barnes & Noble, 1971.

McClellan, James E. *Science Reorganized: Scientific Societies in the Eighteenth Century*. New York: Columbia University Press, 1985.

McFarland, Thomas. *Coleridge and the Pantheist Tradition*. Oxford: Oxford University Press, 1969.

———. *Romanticism and the Forms of Ruin: Wordsworth, Coleridge and Modalities of Fragmentation*. Princeton: Princeton University Press, 1981.

McManners, John. *Death and the Enlightenment: Changing Attitudes to Death Among Christians and Unbelievers in Eighteenth-Century France*. New York: Oxford University Press, 1981.

McNeil, Maureen. *Under the Banner of Science: Erasmus Darwin and His Age*. Manchester: Manchester University Press, 1987.

The Medical and Physical Journal (London). Vols. 1–10 (1799–1803).

Medical Commentaries, Exhibiting a Concise View of the Latest and Most Important Discoveries in Medicine and Medical Philosophy (Edinburgh). Vols. 9–10 (1794–1795).

Medical Facts and Observations. Edited by Simmons (as a sequel to the *London Medical Journal*). London: vols. 1–7 (1791–1797).

"Medical School of St. Thomas's and Guy's." *London Medical and Physical Journal* 34 (1815): 259.

Medical Transactions, College of Physicians in London. Vols. 3–6 (1785–1815).

"Medicine." *Encyclopaedia Britannica* (1810), 13:187–486. By Andrew Duncan, Jr.

"Medicine." (Rees's) *Cyclopaedia* (1819), vol. 23.

"Medicine." *Encyclopaedia Britannica* (1842), 14:513–529. By William Thomson.

Medicine in 1815: An Exhibition to Commemorate the 150th Anniversary of the End of the Napoleonic Wars. Introduction by F.N.L. Poynter. London: Wellcome Historical Medical Museum, 1965.

The Medico-Chirurgical Journal and Review (London). Vols. 1–5 (1816–1818).

Medico-Chirurgical Transactions (Medical and Chirurgical Society of London). London: Longman, 1816, vols. 1–10.

Mellor, Anne K. "Keats's Face of Moneta: Source and Meaning." *Keats-Shelley Journal* 25 (1976): 65–80.

Memoirs of the Literary and Philosophical Society of Manchester. Edited by Thomas Percival. 1790–1830.

Mendelsohn, Everett. *Heat and Life: The Development of the Theory of Animal Heat*. Cambridge: Harvard University Press, 1964.

Merz, John Theodore. *A History of European Thought in the Nineteenth Century*. 4 vols. 1912; reprint, New York: Dover Publications, 1965.

Meyer, Jeffrey. *Disease and the Novel, 1880–1960*. London: Macmillan, 1985.

Michelotti, Victor. "Experiments and Observations on the Vitality and Life of Germs." (Alexander Tilloch's) *Philosophical Magazine* 9 (1801): 240–50.

Millar, John. A *Discourse on the Duty of Physicians Delivered at the Anniversary of the Medical Society, January 18, 1776*. London: J. Johnson, 1776.

Milton, John. *Complete Poems and Major Prose*. Edited by Merritt Y. Hughes. New York: Odyssey Press, 1957.

Modiano, Raimonda. *Coleridge and the Concept of Nature*. Tallahassee: Florida State University Press, 1985.

Monroe, John. *Remarks on Dr. Battie's Treatise on Madness*. London: John Clarke, 1758.

Moore, Cecil A. "The English Malady." In *Backgrounds of English Literature, 1700–1768*. Minneapolis: University of Minnesota Press, 1953.

Moorman, Lewis J. "John Keats, 1795–1821." *New England Journal of Medicine* 249 (July 1953): 26–28.

Morton, Peter. *The Vital Science: Biology and the Literary Imagination, 1860–1900*. London: Allen & Unwin, 1984.

"Mr. Salisbury's Botanical Excursions and Calendar of Flora, for May 1816." *London Medical and Physical Journal* 35 (1816): 516–17.

Muir, Kenneth. "The Meaning of 'Hyperion,' " in *John Keats: A Reassessment*.

————, ed. *John Keats: A Reassessment*. Liverpool: Liverpool University Press, 1969.

Mullen, Pierce C. "The Romantic as Scientist: Lorenz Oken." *Studies in Romanticism* 16 (1977): 381–99.

Murry, John Middleton. *Keats*. Rev. ed. London: Jonathan Cape, 1955.

————. *Keats and Shakespeare: A Study of Keats's Poetic Life from 1816 to 1820*. London: Oxford University Press, 1926.

Newman, C. "The Hospital as Teaching Center." In *The Evolution of Hospitals in Britain*, edited by F.N.L. Poynter.

Nicolson, Marjorie Hope. *Mountain Gloom and Mountain Glory: The Development of the Aesthetics of the Infinite*. Ithaca: Cornell University Press, 1959.

————. *Science and Imagination*. 1956; reprint, New York: Archon Books, 1976.

Nicolson, William. *The First Principles of Chemistry*. London: G.G.J. & J. Robinson, 1792.

Notcutt, H. Clement, ed. *Endymion/A Poetic Romance*. London: Oxford University Press, 1927.

A Numerical Catalogue of Books in the Library of the Physical Society, Guy's Hospital. MS, Wills Library, 1817. (With additions, 1829.)

Ober, William B. *Boswell's Clap and Other Essays: Medical Analyses of Literary Men's Afflictions*. Carbondale: Southern Illinois University Press, 1979.

Oersted, Hans Christian. *The Soul in Nature, with Supplementary Contributions*. Translated by Leonora and Joanna B. Horner. 1852; reprint, London: Dawsons, 1966.

Oken, Lorenz. *Elements of Physiophilosophy*. Translated by Alfred Tulk. London: Ray Society, 1847.

"On Mental Alienation" (from the *Dictionaire des Sciences Medicales*). *London Medical and Physical Journal* 39–40 (1818): 479–85.

"On the Poison of the Viper." (The Royal Institution's) *Quarterly Journal for Science, Literature, and the Arts* 10 (1820–1821): 193–94.

Orfila, M.J.B. *A General System of Toxicology: or, A Treatise on Poisons, found in the Mineral, Vegetable and Animal Kingdoms, Considered in their Relations with Physiology, Pathology, and Medical Jurisprudence*. Translated by Joseph G. Nancrede. Philadelphia: M. Carey & Son, 1817. (From the 1st London ed., 1815–1816; reviewed in *Medico-Chirurgical Journal and Review* 1 [1816]: 413–35.)

Osborn, Henry Fairfield. *From the Greeks to Darwin: The Development of the Evolution Idea Through Twenty-four Centuries.* New York: Scribner's, 1929.

Osler, Sir William. *The Evolution of Modern Medicine: A Series of Lectures Delivered at Yale University on the Silliman Foundation in April, 1913.* New Haven: Yale University Press, 1921.

Paget, Stephen. *John Hunter.* London: Unwin, 1897.

Paris, John Ayrton. *Pharmacologia; or, the History of Medical Substances, with a View to Establish the Art of Prescribing and of Composing Extemporaneous Formulae upon Fixed and Scientific Principles, in which the Intention of each Element is Designated by Key-Letters.* London: W. Phillips, 1820.

Park, J. R. "On the Periodic Suspension and Renewal of Function Observable in the Human Body." (The Royal Institution's) *Quarterly Journal of Science, Literature and the Arts* 6 (1820): 1–20.

Parker, C. S. "Account of an Essential Oil which Flows Spontaneously From a Tree in South America." (David Brewster's) *Edinburgh Journal of Science* 1 (1824): 133–37.

Paulin, Roger. *Ludwig Tieck: A Literary Biography.* Oxford: Oxford University Press, 1985.

Penzer, N. M. *Poison-Damsels and Other Essays in Folklore and Anthropology.* London: Charles J. Sawyer, 1952.

Percival, Thomas. *Medical Ethics; or A Code of Institutes and Precepts Adapted to the Professional Conduct of Physicians and Surgeons.* Manchester: J. Johnson, 1803. Reprinted in Chauncey D. Leake, *Percival's Medical Ethics.*

———. "A Physical Inquiry into the Powers and Operations of Medicines." *Memoirs of the Literary and Philosophical Society of Manchester* 3 (1790): 197–216.

———. "Speculations on the Perceptive Power of Vegetables." *Memoirs of the Literary and Philosophical Society of Manchester* 2 (1785): 114–30.

Peschel, Enid Rhodes, ed. *Medicine and Literature.* New York: Neale Watson Academic Publications, 1980.

"Pharmacia." (Rees's) *Cyclopaedia* (1819), vol. 27.

Pettit, Henry. "Scientific Correlatives of Keats' *Ode to Psyche*." *Studies in Philology* 40 (1943): 560–66.

Philip, A. P. Wilson. "On Stimulants and Sedatives." *London Medical and Physical Journal* 41–42 (1819): 142–45.

———. "On the Sources and Nature of the Powers on Which the Circulation of the Blood Depends." *Philosophical Transactions* 121 (1831): 489–96.

(Alexander Tilloch's) *Philosophical Magazine.*

Philosophical Transactions of the Royal Society of London.

The Physical Society, Guy's Hospital, Transactions. MS, Wills Library, 1813–1820.

"Physician." (Rees's) *Cyclopaedia* (1819), vol. 27.

"Physiology." *Encyclopaedia Britannica* (1810), 16:445–528. By John Barclay.

Piper, H. W. *The Active Universe: Pantheism and the Concept of Imagination in the English Romantic Poets.* London: University of London / Athalone Press, 1962.

———. "Keats and W. C. Wells." *Review of English Studies* 25 (1949): 158–59.

"Poison." (Rees's) *Cyclopaedia* (1819), vol. 28.

"Poison." *Encyclopaedia Britannica* (1842), 16:174–83. By Robert Christison.

"Poison." *Encyclopaedia Britannica* (1910–1911), 21:893–96.

Potter, George Reuben. "Coleridge and the Idea of Evolution." *PMLA* 40 (1925): 379–97.

Potter, John. *Archaeologia Graeca: Antiquities of Greece.* 2 vols. London: 1755.

Powell, Richard. "Some Cases, Illustrative of the Pathology of the Brain." *Medical Transactions, College of Physicians in London* 5 (1815): 198–256.

"Power." (Rees's) *Cyclopaedia* (1819), vol. 27.

Pownall, Governor. "On the Ether Suggested by Sir Isaac Newton, Compared with the Supposedly Newly Discovered Principle of Galvanism." (Alexander Tilloch's) *Philosophical Magazine* 18 (1804): 155–58.

Poynter, F.N.L. ed. *The Evolution of Hospitals in Britain.* London: Pitman, 1964.

Poynter, F.N.L. "Introduction." *Medicine in 1815,* pp. 1–4.

Prichard, J. C. A *Review of the Doctrine of a Vital Principle . . . with Observations on the Causes of Physical and Animal Life.* London: Sherwood, Gilbert, & Piper, 1829.

Priestley, F.E.L. "Newton and the Romantic Concept of Nature." *University of Toronto Quarterly* 17 (1948): 323–36.

Priestley, Joseph, ed. *Hartley's Theory of the Human Mind, on the Principle of the Association of Ideas; with Essays Relating to the Subject of It.* London: J. Johnson, 1775.

Profitt, Edward. "Science and Romanticism." *Georgia Review* 34 (1980): 55–80.

Purver, Margery. *The Royal Society: Concept and Creation.* Cambridge: M.I.T. Press, 1967.

(The Royal Institution's) *Quarterly Journal of Science, Literature and the Arts.*

Quincy's Lexicon-Medicum: A New Medical Dictionary. See Robert Hooper.

Raine, Kathleen. *Blake and the New Age.* London: Allen & Unwin, 1979.

Rajan, Tilottama. *Dark Interpreter: The Discourse of Romanticism.* Ithaca: Cornell University Press, 1980.

Ramsey, Matthew. *Professional and Popular Medicine in France, 1770–1830.* Cambridge: Cambridge University Press, 1988.

Reece, Richard. *The Medical Guide, for Use of the Clergy, Heads of Families, and Practitioners in Medicine and Surgery.* London: Longman, 1812.

Rees, Abraham, ed. *The Cyclopaedia; or, Universal Dictionary of Arts, Sciences, and Literature.* 39 vols. London: Longman, 1819.

Reid, Thomas. *Essays on the Powers of the Human Mind; to which are Prefixed an Essay on Quantity, and an Analysis of Aristotle's Logic.* 3 vols. Edinburgh: Bell & Bradute, and F. C. & J. Rivington, 1819.

———. *The Works of Thomas Reid, D.D., F.R.S.E.* Edited by G. N. Wright. 2 vols. London: Thomas Tegg, 1843.

Reiman, Donald H., and Sharon B. Powers, eds. *Shelley's Poetry and Prose.* New York: Norton, 1977.

"A Report from the Court of Examiners to the Court of Assistants of the Society of Apothecaries." *London Medical Repository* 6 (1816): 341–42.

Report of the Commissioners Concerning Charities in England, 1840. London: W. Cloves & Sons, 1840. "St. Thomas's Hospital," pp. 614–709; "Guy's Hospital," pp. 714–750. By Samuel Smith and Francis Offley Martin.

Reppert, Bertha. "Showy Hellebores Are a Standout in Early Spring." *New York Times,* 4 March 1984, sec. H, p. 31.

Ricks, Christopher. *Keats and Embarrassment.* Oxford: Oxford University Press, 1974.

Ritterbush, Philip C. *The Art of Organic Forms.* Washington, D.C.: Smithsonian Institution Press, 1968.

———. *Overtures to Biology: The Speculations of Eighteenth-Century Naturalists.* New Haven: Yale University Press, 1964.

Roger, Jacques. "The Living World." In *The Ferment of Knowledge,* edited by G. S. Rousseau and Roy Porter.

Rollins, Hyder Edward, ed. *The Keats Circle: Letters and Papers and More Letters and Poems of the Keats Circle*. 2d ed. 2 vols. Cambridge: Harvard University Press, 1965.

Royal College of Physicians of Edinburgh. *Narrative of the Conduct of Dr. James Gregory, toward the Royal College of Physicians of Edinburgh*. Drawn up and published by Order of the College. Edinburgh: Peter Hill, Manners & Miller, 1809.

Rousseau, G. S., and Roy Porter, eds. *The Ferment of Knowledge: Studies in the Historiography of Eighteenth-Century Science*. London: Cambridge University Press, 1980.

Russell, Patrick. "Observations on the Orifices found in Certain Poisonous Snakes, Situated Between the Nostril and the Eye. With some Remarks . . . by Everard Home." *Philosophical Transactions* 94 (1804): 70–77.

Ryan, Robert M. *Keats: The Religious Sense*. Princeton: Princeton University Press, 1976.

St. Hilaire, August de. "Account of a Case of Poisoning, Caused by the Honey of the Lecheguana Wasp." (Brewster and Jameson's) *Edinburgh Philosophical Journal* 14 (1825–1826): 91–100.

———. "Account of the Poison Plants of the Southern Parts of Brazil." (Brewster and Jameson's) *Edinburgh Philosophical Journal* 14 (1825–1826): 264–70.

St. Hilaire, Geoffroy. "Observations on Toads found Alive at Great Depths in the Ground." (David Brewster's) *Edinburgh Journal of Science* 7 (1827): 358.

St. John, J. Hector. "On the Poison of the Rattlesnake." (David Brewster's) *Edinburgh Journal of Science* 7 (1827): 357–58.

Salisbury, William. *The Botanist's Companion, or An Introduction to the Knowledge of Practical Botany*. . . . 2 vols. London: Longman, 1816.

———. "To the Editors." *London Medical and Physical Journal* 35 (1816): 430; 37 (1817): 425–26.

Saly, John. "Keats's Answer to Dante: *The Fall of Hyperion*." *Keats-Shelley Journal* 14 (1965): 65–78.

Saumarez, Richard. "On Generation, and the Principle of Life." *London Medical and Physical Journal* 2 (1799): 242–47, 321–26.

Scarry, Elaine. *The Body in Pain: The Making and Unmaking of the World*. New York: Oxford University Press, 1985.

Schaffer, William. "The History of the Treatment of Mental Disease." Unpublished abstract in the Ferdinand Hamburger, Jr., Archives, Johns Hopkins University. (Read to the History of Ideas Club, 14 March 1946.)

Schelling, Friedrich Wilhelm Joseph. *Of Human Freedom*. Translated by James Gutmann. Chicago: Open Court, 1936.

———. *On University Studies*. Translated by E. S. Morgan. Athens: Ohio University Press, 1966.

Schenk, H. G. *The Mind of the European Romantics: An Essay in Cultural History*. New York: Doubleday, 1969.

Schiller, Friedrich von. *Complete Medical and Psychological Writings*. In *Friedrich Schiller: Medicine, Psychology and Literature*, edited by Kenneth Dewhurst and Nigel Reeves.

Schlegel, Friedrich von. *The Philosophy of Life, and Philosophy of Language, in a Course of Lectures*. Translated by A.J.W. Morrison. London: Henry G. Bohn, 1847.

Schneider, Ben Ross, Jr. *Wordsworth's Cambridge Education*. Cambridge: Cambridge University Press, 1957.

Schofield, Robert E. *Mechanism and Materialism: British Natural Philosophy in an Age of Reason*. Princeton: Princeton University Press, 1970.

Schreibers, Charles. "A Historical and Anatomical Description of a Doubtful Amphibious Animal of Germany, Called, by Laurenti, *Proteus Anguinus.*" *Philosophical Transactions* 91 (1801): 241–64.

Serres, Michel. *Hermes: Literature, Science, Philosophy.* Edited by Josué V. Harari and David F. Bell. Baltimore: Johns Hopkins University Press, 1982.

Sewell, Elizabeth. *The Orphic Voice: Poetry and Natural History.* New Haven: Yale University Press, 1960.

———. "Keats' Imaginative Approach to Myth." In her *Undercurrents of Influence in English Romantic Poetry.* Cambridge: Harvard University Press, 1934.

Shelley, Percy Blysshe. *Shelley's Poetry and Prose.* Edited by Donald H. Reiman and Sharon B. Powers. New York: Norton, 1977.

Shorr, Philip. *Science and Superstition in the Eighteenth Century: A Study of the Treatment of Science in Two Encyclopedias of 1725–1750.* (Chamber's *Cyclopedia,* London 1728, Zedler's *Universal Lexicon,* Leipzig.) New York: Columbia University Press, 1932.

Shryock, Richard Harrison. *The Development of Modern Medicine.* New York: Knopf, 1947.

Siegfried, Robert, and Robert H. Dolt, Jr. *Humphry Davy on Geology: The 1805 Lectures for the General Audience.* Madison: University of Wisconsin Press, 1980.

Sikes, H. M. "The Poetic Theory and Practice of Keats: The Record of a Debt to Hazlitt." *Philological Quarterly* 38 (1959): 401–87.

Singer, Charles J. *Greek Biology and Greek Medicine.* London: Oxford University Press, 1922.

———. *A Short History of Biology.* London: Oxford University Press, 1931.

———. *A Short History of Medicine.* London: Oxford University Press, 1928.

Sinson, Janice C. *John Keats and "The Anatomy of Melancholy."* London: Keats-Shelley Memorial Association, 1971.

Smith, James Edward. "Some Observations on the Irritability of Vegetables." *Philosophical Transactions* 78 (1788): 158–65.

Smith, Thomas. "On the Structure of the Poisonous Fangs of Serpents." *Philosophical Transactions* 108 (1818): 471–76.

Snelders, H.A.M. "Romanticism and Naturphilosophie and the Inorganic Natural Sciences, 1797–1840." *Studies in Romanticism* 9 (1970): 193–215.

Sontag, Susan. *Illness as Metaphor.* New York: Farrar, Straus & Giroux, 1978.

South, John Flint. *Memorials of the Craft of Surgery in England.* Edited by Robert Gittings. 1886; reprint, London: Centaur Press, 1969.

Spence, Joseph. *Polymetis: or, An Enquiry Concerning the Agreement Between the Works of the Roman Poets, and the Remains of the Ancient Artists.* London: R. & J. Dodsley, 1755; reprint, London: J. Johnson, 1802.

Sperry, Stuart M. *Keats the Poet.* Princeton: Princeton University Press, 1970.

———. "Isabella Jane Towers, John Towers, and Keats." *Keats-Shelley Journal* 27 (1978): 35–58.

Stevenson, Lloyd G. *The Meaning of Poison.* Lawrence: University of Kansas Press, 1959.

Stillinger, Jack. *The Hoodwinking of Madeline and Other Essays on Keats's Poems.* Urbana: University of Illinois Press, 1971.

———. *The Texts of Keats's Poems.* Cambridge: Harvard University Press, 1974.

———. "Another Early Biographical Sketch of 'Young Keats.' " *English Language Notes* 18 (1981): 276–81.

———, ed. *The Poems of John Keats.* Cambridge: Harvard University Press, 1978.

———, ed. *William Wordsworth: Selected Poems and Prefaces.* Boston: Houghton Mifflin, 1965.

Stillingfleet, Benjamin. "A Discourse on the Irritability of Some Flowers." In *Literary Life and Selected Works of Benjamin Stillingfleet*. London: Longman, 1811.

Stimson, Dorothy. *Scientists and Amateurs: A History of the Royal Society*. New York: Henry Schuman, 1948.

Stocker, Richard, trans. *Pharmacopoeia Officinalis Britannica: Being a New and Corrected Translation of the Late Edition of the London Pharmacopoeia*. London: Cox, 1810.

Stockley, V. *German Literature as Known in England, 1750–1830*. London: Routledge, 1929.

Stokoe, F. W. *German Influence in the English Romantic Period, 1788–1818*. Cambridge: Cambridge University Press, 1926.

Strassburg, Gottfried von. *Tristan* (with fragments of the *Tristran* of Thomas). Translated and edited by A. T. Hatto. Harmondsworth, U.K.: Penguin, 1960.

"Surgery." *Encyclopoaedia Britannica* (1810), 20:24–112. By James Wardrope.

Swann, Karen. " 'Christabel': The Wandering Mother and the Enigma of Form." *Studies in Romanticism* 23 (1984): 533–553.

———. "Literary Gentlemen and Lovely Ladies: The Debate on the Character of *Christabel*." *English Literary History* 52 (1985): 397–418.

"Syllabus of Lectures During Winter, 1814, at St. Thomas' and Guy's Hospital." *London Medical and Physical Journal* 32 (1814): 258.

Taberner, Peter V. *Aphrodisiacs: The Science and the Myth*. Philadelphia: University of Pennsylvania Press, 1985.

Taylor, F. Kraüpl. *The Concept of Illness, Disease and Morbus*. London: Cambridge University Press, 1979.

Temkin, Owsei. "Basic Science, Medicine, and the Romantic Era." *Bulletin of the History of Medicine* 37 (1963): 97–129.

———. "The Concept of Infection." In *The Ferment of Knowledge*, edited by G. S. Rousseau and Roy Porter.

———. "An Historical Analysis of the Concept of Infection." In *Studies in Intellectual History*. Baltimore: Johns Hopkins University Press, 1953.

Textbook of Medicine (Cecil's). 15th ed. New York: W. B. Saunders, 1979.

Thomas, Keith Vivian. *Religion and the Decline of Magic*. New York: Scribner's, 1971.

Thomas, Lewis. *The Lives of a Cell: Notes of a Biology Watcher*. New York: Viking, 1974.

———. *The Medusa and the Snail: More Notes of a Biology Watcher*. New York: Viking, 1974.

Thomas, Robert. *The Modern Practice of Physic, Exhibiting the Character, Causes, Symptoms, Prognostics, Morbid Appearances, and Improved Methods of Treating the Diseases of all Climates*. London: Longman, 1816.

Thompson, J., ed. *An Account of the Life, Lectures and Writings of William Cullen*. 2 vols. Edinburgh: Blackwood, 1859.

Thomson, J. Arthur. *The Science of Life: An Outline of the History of Biology and its Recent Advances*. Chicago and New York: Herbert S. Stone, 1899.

Thomson, William. "Medicine." *Encyclopaedia Britannica* (1842).

———. "Pathology." *Encyclopaedia Britannica* (1842).

Thornton, Robert John. *A New Family Herbal: or Popular Account of the Nature and Properties of the Various Plants Used in Medicine, Diet, and the Arts*. London: Richard Phillips, 1810. (Addressed to Andrew Duncan; says his source is the *Edinburgh New Dispensatory*.)

———. "Correspondence with Mr. Arthur Aiken." (Alexander Tilloch's) *Philosophical Magazine* 19 (1804): 39–41, 144–218, 248–60, 360–63.

———. "A Remarkable Case of Internal Pain in the Heel, and an Incipient Mortifica-
    tion, cured by the Inhalation of Vital Air." (Alexander Tilloch's) *Philosophical
    Magazine*, 3 (1799): 213–15.
Thorpe, Clarence D. *The Mind of John Keats*. New York: Oxford University Press, 1926.
Tighe, Mary. *Psyche or, The Legend of Love*. London: J. Carpenter, 1805.
Tilloch, Alexander. "On the Nervous Power, and its Mode of Acting." (Alexander
    Tilloch's) *Philosophical Magazine* 15 (1803): 293–94.
———. "A Short View of the Mitchillian Theory of Fever, and of Contagious Diseases in
    General." (Alexander Tilloch's) *Philosophical Magazine* 3 (1799): 177–88.
Ting, Nai-Tung. "The Influence of Chatterton." *Keats-Shelley Journal* 5 (1956): 103–8.
Todd, Ruthven. *Tracks in the Snow: Studies in English Science and Art*. London: Gray Walls
    Press, 1946.
Tooke, Andrew. *The Pantheon*. London: C. Elliot, 1783.
Toplis, John. "On the Fascinating Power of Snakes." (Alexander Tilloch's) *Philosophical
    Magazine* 19 (1804): 379–84.
Towers, (George) John. *The Domestic Gardener's Manual; Being an Introduction to Gardening, on
    Philosophical Principles; to Which is Added, a Concise Naturalist's Kalindar, and English
    Botanist's Companion, or Catalogue of British Plants, in the Monthly Order of their Flower-
    ing*. London: Whittaker, Treacher, 1830 (Anonymously published "By a Horticul-
    tural Chemist.")
Transactions of the Physical Society, Guy's Hospital. MS, Wills Library, 1813–1820.
Trautmann, Joanne, ed. *Literature and Medicine: Topics, Titles and Notes*. Philadelphia: Soci-
    ety for Health and Human Values, 1975.
Trilling, Lionel. "The Poet as Hero: Keats in His Letters." In *The Opposing Self*. New York:
    Viking, 1955.
Trotter, W. R. "John Brown and the Nonspecific Component of Human Sickness." *Perspec-
    tives in Biology and Medicine* 21 (1978): 256–64.
Tuveson, Ernest Lee. *The Avatars of Thrice Great Hermes: An Approach to Romanticism*.
    Lewisburg: Bucknell University Press, 1982.
Tytler, Graeme. *Physiognomy in the European Novel*. Princeton: Princeton University Press,
    1982.
Underwood, E. Ashworth. "Apollo and Terpsichore: Music and the Healing Art." *Bulletin
    of the History of Medicine* 21 (1947): 639–73.
Utley, Francis Lee. "The Infernos of Lucretius and of Keats's *La Belle Dame Sans Merci*."
    English Literary History 25 (1958): 105–21.
Van't Hoff, Jacobus Henricus. *Imagination in Science*. Translated by Georg F. Springer. New
    York: Springer-Verlag, 1967.
Vartanian, Aram. "Trembley's Polyp, La Mettrie, and Eighteenth-Century French Materi-
    alism." *Journal of the History of Ideas* 11 (1950): 259–86.
Vauquelin, N. L. "Analysis of Deadly Nightshade, Atropa Belladonna." (William Nicol-
    son's) *Journal of Natural Philosophy, Chemistry, and the Arts* 31 (1812): 350–57.
Veatch, Robert M. *Death, Dying, and the Biological Revolution*. New Haven: Yale University
    Press, 1976.
Veith, Ilza. *Hysteria: The History of a Disease*. Chicago: University of Chicago Press, 1965.
Vendler, Helen. *The Odes of John Keats*. Cambridge: Harvard University Press, 1983.
Visick, Mary. " 'Tease Us Out of Thought': Keats's *Epistle to Reynolds* and the Odes." *Keats-
    Shelley Journal* 15 (1966): 87–98.

Waddington, Ivan. *The Medical Profession in the Industrial Revolution*. Dublin: Gill & Macmillan, 1985.

Waddington, Joshua. *Clinical Cases and Lectures taken by Joshua Waddington at Guy's Hospital, between December 1st, 1816, and May 1st, 1817*. MS, Wills Library, 1816–1817.

Wagner, Robert E. "Keats: 'Ode to Psyche' and the Second 'Hyperion.' " *Keats-Shelley Journal* 13 (1964): 29–41.

Waldoff, Leon. *Keats and the Silent Work of Imagination*. Urbana: University of Illinois Press, 1985.

Wallace, James. *Letters on the Study and Practice of Medicine and Surgery, and on Topics Connected with the Medical Profession*. Glasgow: Richard Griffin, 1828.

Wallis, George. *The Art of Preventing Diseases and Restoring Health, Founded on Rational Principles and Adapted to Persons of Every Capacity*. 2d ed. London: Robinson, 1796.

Ward, Aileen. *John Keats: The Making of a Poet*. Rev. ed. New York: Farrar, Straus & Giroux, 1986.

———. "Keats and Burton: A Reappraisal." *Philological Quarterly* 40 (1961): 535–52.

Ward, M. "Observations on the Effects of Opium Applied Externally." (T. Bradley and A. F. M. Willich's) *The Medical and Physical Journal* 6 (1801): 478–86.

———. "Observations on the Modus Operandi of Opium." (T. Bradley and A. F. M. Willich's) *Medical and Physical Journal* 7 (1802): 124–37, 497–506; 8 (1802): 325–48; 9 (1803): 335–48.

Wardrope, James. "Surgery." *Encyclopaedia Britannica* (1810), 20:24–112.

Wasserman, Earl R. *The Finer Tone: Keats' Major Poems*. Baltimore: Johns Hopkins University Press, 1953.

———. "The English Romantics: The Grounds of Knowledge." *Studies in Romanticism* 4 (1964): 17–34.

Weber, F. "Observations on the Effects of Opium on the Human Body." (T. Bradley and A.F.M. Willich's) *Medical and Physical Journal* 10 (1803): 435–43, 501–16.

Wegenblass, John Henry. "Keats and Lucretius." *Modern Language Review* 32 (1937): 537–52.

Wells, Walter A. *A Doctor's Life of John Keats*. New York: Vantage Press, 1959.

Wetterstrand, Otto Georg. *Hypnotism and its Application to Practical Medicine*. Translated by Henrik G. Petersen. New York: Putnam's Sons, 1897.

Wheeler, Leonard Richmond. *Vitalism: Its History and Validity*. London: H. F. & G. Witherby, 1939.

Whewell, William. *The Philosophy of the Inductive Sciences*. 2 vols. London: Frank Cass, 1967.

White, William A. *The Meaning of Disease*. Baltimore: Williams & Wilkins, 1926.

Wilkinson, C. H. *Elements of Galvanism, in Theory and Practice; with a Comprehensive View of its History, from the First Experiments of Galvani to the Present Time*. 2 vols. London: John Murray, 1804.

Wilks, Samuel, and G. T. Bettany. *A Biographical History of Guy's Hospital*. London: Ward, Lock, Bowden, 1892.

Willey, Basil. *The Eighteenth Century Background: Studies on the Ideas of Nature in the Thought of the Period*. New York: Columbia University Press, 1941.

Williams, John. "On the Cure of Persons Bitten by Snakes in India." (Alexander Tilloch's) *Philosophical Magazine* 4 (1799): 191–96.

Williams, Leslie Pearce. *Michael Faraday*. New York: Basic Books, 1964.

Williams, Raymond. *Keywords: A Vocabulary of Culture and Society*. New York: Oxford University Press, 1976.

Wingert, R. M. *Historical Notes on the Borough and the Borough Hospitals*. London: Ash, 1913.

Wolfson, Susan J. *The Questioning Presence: Wordsworth, Keats, and the Interrogative Mode in Romantic Poetry*. Ithaca: Cornell University Press, 1986.

Wollaston, William Hyde. "Description of a Single-lens Micrometer." *Philosophical Transactions* 103 (1813): 119–22.

———. "Description of the Camera Lucida." (William Nicolson's) *Journal of Natural Philosophy, Chemistry, and the Arts* 17 (1807): 1–5; (Alexander Tilloch's) *Philosophical Magazine* 27 (1807): 343–47.

———. "A Method of Examining Refractive and Dispersive Powers, by Prismatic Reflection." *Philosophical Transactions* 92 (1802): 365–80.

———. "On a Periscopic Camera Obscura and Microscope." *Philosophical Transactions* 102 (1812): 370–77.

———. "On Fairy-rings." *Philosophical Transactions* 97 (1807): 133–38.

Woodring, Carl. "On Looking into Keats's Voyages." *Keats-Shelley Journal* 14 (1965): 15–22.

Wordsworth, William. *Literary Criticism of William Wordsworth*. Edited by Paul M. Zall. Lincoln: University of Nebraska Press, 1966.

———. *William Wordsworth: Selected Poems and Prefaces*. Edited by Jack Stillinger. Boston: Houghton Mifflin, 1965.

———. *Wordsworth: Poetical Works*. Edited by Thomas Hutchinson, revised by Ernest de Selincourt. London: Oxford University Press, 1904.

Wycherley, H. Alan. "Keats: The Terminal Disease and Some Major Problems." *American Notes and Queries* 7 (1969): 118–19.

Yeats, Grant David. "History of a Case of Somnambulism." *Medical Transactions, College of Physicians in London* 5 (1815): 444–62.

Young, Thomas. "The Croonian Lecture. On the Functions of the Heart and Arteries." *Philosophical Transactions* 99 (1809): 1–31.

Index of Poems by Keats

Index of Proper Names

405

Index of Topics